JAMES MICHAEL

LISTON

A LIFE

JAMES MICHAEL
LISTON
A LIFE

NICHOLAS REID

VICTORIA UNIVERSITY PRESS

VICTORIA UNIVERSITY PRESS
Victoria University of Wellington
PO Box 600 Wellington

First published 2006

ISBN-13: 978 0 86473 536 2
ISBN-10: 0 86473 536 7

National Library of New Zealand Cataloguing-in-Publication Data

Reid, Nicholas, 1951-
James Michael Liston : a life / Nicholas Reid.
Includes bibliographical references and index.
ISBN 0-86473-536-7
1. Liston, James, 1881-1976. 2. Catholic Church—
New Zealand—Auckland—Bishops—Biography.
3. Bishops—New Zealand—Auckland—Biography.
I. Title.
282.932092—dc 22

Published with the generous assistance of
the Auckland Catholic Diocese

Printed by PrintLink, Wellington

CONTENTS

ILLUSTRATIONS

All photographs are copyright to the Auckland Catholic Diocesan Archives (ACDA), and used with permission.

PREFACE AND ACKNOWLEDGEMENTS

The figure was small and apparently frail, but the handshake was firm and the eyes clear.

'Well donnn-e! Well donnn-e!', he said, briefly gripping my hand as I passed across the stage at a Sacred Heart College prizegiving in 1969. The encounter lasted at most a few seconds and was, as far as I can remember, the only time I ever met James Michael Liston face to face. I was 17 and he, as I now realise, was 88 and about to go into retirement after nearly half a century as a bishop of Auckland.

Of course, it was the voice that made the biggest impression close up. It always did with schoolboys and with those adults who were not used to Auckland's Catholic sub-culture. James Michael Liston's voice swooped down sonorously at the end of phrases, which he would then draw out to extraordinary length. Spoken vowels became little arias. The voice was the butt of innumerable mimics. There was scarcely a Catholic schoolboy in the Auckland diocese who could not tell a joke with a punchline consisting of a swear word said in the distinctive Liston voice. In church circles, there were adult practical jokers, too.

On a rainy day, a priest-journalist on the diocesan newspaper *Zealandia* received a phone call in which the distinctive voice summoned him to bring some important files to Bishop's House. Balancing the bulky files on his head with one hand, gripping the handlebar with the other, the editor cycled through the rain the weary distance from St Patrick's Square to the episcopal residence in Ponsonby. The bishop greeted him with, 'Father, why have you brought me the-eeese?', and only then did the cyclist realise he had been the victim of a mischievous fellow-cleric.

Or again, a secretary in a diocesan office had three times been pestered by phone calls from her leg-pulling boyfriend doing the Liston voice. The phone rang a fourth time and the voice started again. 'For goodness sake stop it, Charlie', she protested. 'Old Black Joe could ring at any time.' In reply, the voice said, 'But it is Old Black Joe'. And indeed, this time it was.

Were these stories true or were they, like so many others, simply part of the imaginative folklore that Auckland Catholics developed around Liston? Like the story (demonstrably untrue) that Liston, as an instinctive Irish nationalist, always affixed upside-down to envelopes any stamps with the king's or queen's head on them, as a mark of disrespect for the British monarch? Late in his career, Liston had outlived most of his contemporaries and seemed to have been Bishop of Auckland forever. Religious broadcasting, and his frequent participation in civic ceremonies, had made him a familiar figure to the wider non-Catholic community too. There were a number of nicknames. Old Black Joe among a few Catholics, and Jimmy or Jimmy-the-Bishop to a wider group. Of course, nobody would have dared to use them in the presence of the archbishop himself.

The biographer of an eminent and long-lived public figure has to contend with at least some legend. In Liston's case, there is also the 'official' version of his life, which appeared in those brief public statements about himself which he sometimes made, and in occasional retrospective articles in the diocesan press which he controlled. While modifying the legend, this biography is not written in a spirit of iconoclasm. Nor, I hope, will it be confused with hagiography. It is a development of my doctoral thesis, *Churchman – a Study of James Michael Liston*, examined and accepted in 2004.

Many people deserve thanks for the interest, advice and support they gave me.

Special thanks are due to my thesis supervisors in the History Department of the University of Auckland. Associate-Professor Hugh Laracy was always available for consultation, was acute in pointing out any stylistic infelicities in drafts and was a mine of information on church lore. Associate-Professor Linda Bryder offered a different and very helpful perspective on church matters and encouraged me to clarify some points that had originally been expressed ambiguously. My thesis examiners, Dr David Hilliard and the late Dr Michael King, both offered cogent and constructive critiques.

I was assisted by the professionalism of many archivists and librarians. Fr Bruce Bolland and Marian Nee of the Auckland Catholic Diocesan Archives spent many months finding files for me and answering my queries. Additionally, Marian Nee helped search out the photographs. I received similarly efficient help from Sister de Porres of the Wellington Catholic Archdiocesan Archives; the staff of the Christchurch Diocesan Catholic Archives; Father John Harrison and Pauline Lee of the Dunedin Catholic Diocesan Archives; the curator of the Marist Archives, Wellington; Fr Damian McNeice and David Sheehy of the Dublin Archdiocesan Archives; Fr Peter Murphy of the Vatican's Australia and New Zealand desk;

Mgr Liam Bergin (rector) and Fr Albert McDonnell (vice-rector) of the Irish College, Rome; Cardinal Crezenzio Sepe and Guiseppe Laria of Propaganda Fide (Congregation for the Evangelisation of Peoples) and Collegio Urbano, Rome; Philip Doyle of Irish National Archives, Dublin; Mary Kelly, librarian of Holy Cross seminary, Ponsonby; Fr Tom O'Brien of the Missionary Society of St Joseph, Mill Hill, London; Norelle Scolay of Archives New Zealand; Iain Sharp of Auckland Public Library; the staff of the Auckland University Library microfilm room; and Claudia Orange and the staff of the Dictionary of New Zealand Biography.

Researching this biography necessitated considerable travel. I thank the following people for offering me hospitality and a bed when I was researching in archives outside Auckland: Francis, Vincent and Gemma Reid (England), Fr Matt Gaffney and the Rosminian priests (Dublin), the staff of the Irish College (Rome), Christopher and Bernardine Reid (Wellington), and the Christian Brothers (Christchurch and Dunedin).

I thank all those people (listed in the Bibliography) who agreed to be interviewed formally, or who answered more informal queries. At various times, helpful advice and opinions were offered by Judith Bassett, Peter Gibbons, the late Michael King, Judith Leydon, Basil Minihane, Peter Norris, Michael O'Meeghan, Russell Stone, Rory Sweetman, Ian Thompson and Kevin Walsh.

Bishop Patrick Dunn was generous in allowing me such prolonged and wide access to his diocesan archives. Bishop Dunn and Dame Sister Pauline Engel also undertook to read earlier drafts of some chapters and offered many valuable comments. It is important to note, however, that at no time was I directed in the matter of the judgements I made on the subject of this biography. I take personal responsibility for all opinions found here.

This biography could not have been written without the financial support of the Catholic diocese of Auckland and of a Top Achiever Doctoral Scholarship. I thank Bishop Dunn for the former, and the administrators of the Foundation for Research, Science and Technology for awarding me the latter. I also thank the History Department of the University of Auckland for enabling me to supplement my income by tutoring during three years of research.

Finally, I thank my wife Gabrielle and our children, whose positive attitudes offset the robust black dogs of my innate pessimism.

Nicholas Reid
February 2006

ABBREVIATIONS

AJHR	Appendix to the Journals of the House of Representatives
ANZ	Archives New Zealand
ACDA	Auckland Catholic Diocesan Archives
APL	Auckland Public Library
AS	*Auckland Star*
CCDA	Christchurch Catholic Diocesan Archives
CMG	Companion of the Order of St Michael and St George
CORSO	Council of Organisations for Relief Services Overseas
CWL	Catholic Women's League
DAA	Dublin (Catholic) Archdiocesan Archives
DCDA	Dunedin Catholic Diocesan Archives
DNZB	Dictionary of New Zealand Biography
HACBS	Hibernian Australasian Catholic Benefit Society
ICR	Irish College, Rome
MAW	Marist Archives, Wellington
MHAL	Mill Hill Archives, London
NZEF	New Zealand Expeditionary Force
NZH	*New Zealand Herald*
NZJH	*New Zealand Journal of History*
NZLJ	*New Zealand Law Journal*
ODT	*Otago Daily Times*
OP	Order of Preachers (Dominicans)
PPA	Protestant Political Association
SM	Society of Mary (Marists)
WCAA	Wellington Catholic Archdiocesan Archives

AFTER THE FUNERAL

1976

The Reputation of James Michael Liston

When James Michael Liston died at the age of 95 on 8 July 1976, he had been a Catholic priest for 72 years. Coadjutor-Bishop of Auckland from 1920 to 1929 and bishop in his own right from 1929 to 1970, he was the leader of New Zealand's most populous Catholic diocese for half a century. His own church had awarded him the personal title of Archbishop, but he had also received civic honours. The Yugoslav government made him a member of the Order of St Sava in 1936, for his promotion of the interests of New Zealand's Croat community. Two years later, France awarded him the Cross of a Chevalier of the Legion of Honour. In 1968, he was named CMG (Companion of the Order of St Michael and St George), and in 1970 the University of Auckland conferred an honorary LLD on him.

Throughout his career, his public life was regularly documented in both the church press and the mainstream press, while sheer longevity made him the subject of many people's memories, anecdotes and gossip. After his death, prompt judgements were made in numerous obituaries. For the daily newspapers, he was a formidable builder of community, unswerving in his Catholic loyalties but also a pioneer in ecumenical goodwill.[1] The two Catholic weeklies, Auckland's *Zealandia* and Dunedin's *New Zealand Tablet,* inevitably gave much more detail on Liston's ecclesiastical career. They also passed more nuanced judgements on his style of leadership, suggesting that he belonged to a past age of the church. The *Tablet* did, however, declare that Liston was 'in the judgement of this paper, the greatest single figure the Church in New Zealand has produced'.[2] In both secular and church newspapers, Liston was presented as diligent in his priestly duties, pious, hard-working, compassionate and accepting of members of all religions. The ecclesial controversies of the last decade of his episcopate were only briefly alluded to, while few mentioned earlier strife, such as his 1922 trial, and none enlarged on his youthful commitment to the cause of Irish independence. His involvement in early twentieth-century sectarianism was ignored except by implication, in the favourable comments on how ecumenical the response to his death was. Most conspicuously, there was no mention of his long and dogged political crusade against Communism. Obituarists were either ignorant of, or chose not to comment upon, the personal difficulties he had experienced as coadjutor to Bishop Henry William Cleary in the 1920s. Dying at the age of 95, Liston could be farewelled as a Grand Old Man.

In the years since Liston's death, brief references to him in some political biographies have confirmed his significance in national affairs, and hinted at his sympathies for the New Zealand Labour Party. Liston appears fleetingly in biographies of John A. Lee and of Michael Joseph Savage, both of whom he once regarded as personal friends.[3] He also features in Catholic institutional histories and works concerning movements in which he was involved.[4] Specific aspects of his career receive extended consideration in a few books. Peter Joseph Norris's history of Holy Cross College, Mosgiel, passes judgement on Liston's effectiveness as rector.[5] Michael Belgrave's history of Auckland's Mater Misericordiae Hospital gives considerable detail on Liston's guiding role.[6] Nicholas Reid's history of the Auckland Catholic diocesan press considers Liston's interventions and editorial policies.[7] Michael O'Meeghan's history of the archdiocese of Wellington makes negative comment on Liston's part in a dispute within the Catholic hierarchy in the early 1930s.[8] For most of these writers, Liston merits consideration simply because he is a part of Catholic history as student, rector or bishop.

It was six years after Liston's death that there appeared the first sustained critique of his episcopate, in Father Ernest Richard Simmons' diocesan history, *In Cruce Salus*. It is notable for its mixture of praise and reproof. Simmons gives Liston credit for encouraging lay movements, notes that his personal piety was always beyond question and says he was far more conciliatory than his predecessor, Bishop Cleary, in his comments on the nature of state schools.[9] Simmons does not take sides when he considers the matter of Liston's difficulties with Cleary, and records that Liston worked harmoniously with his auxiliary, Bishop Reginald John Delargey.

Despite the apparent conservatism of his later years, Liston was not, in Simmons' account, a reactionary. He was, 'apart from his monarchial style of ruling, a rather liberal bishop who did his best to keep up with the new ideas and tried loyally to put them into action'.

But this general endorsement is balanced by criticisms. Simmons admits these are partly shaped by the fact that he himself had been dismissed by Liston from his post as editor of *Zealandia*, and that for him it is difficult to write objectively.[10] He emphasises that Liston stayed on for too long as bishop, and was unable to adjust to either changes in society or the new post-conciliar plurality of the church.[11]

In his longest sustained characterisation of Liston, Simmons stresses his 'autocracy', theological inflexibility and unsubtle interpretation of the international political scene:

> ... he was implacably, and almost unreasonably, opposed to communism, to an extent which often led him to support unworthy and unchristian forces which were anti-communist.[12]

Twice Simmons finds it necessary to tell his readers that Liston was not naturally an intellectual.[13] A late vocation, Simmons was ordained priest in 1953.[14] He served under Liston's authority for 17 years, when the bishop was already in his seventies and eighties. His remarks seem the expressions of an intelligent priest-journalist sometimes exasperated by the attitudes of an admired, but elderly, superior.

A similar viewpoint is found in the varied writings of another Auckland diocesan priest. Felix Donnelly was eight years Simmons' junior, but was also ordained to the priesthood in 1953 and also served under Liston's authority for the last 17 years of Liston's episcopate. Despite his reputation for rejecting an older, more conservative church, however, Donnelly has some positive things to say about the elderly Liston. In his first published book, *Big Boys Don't Cry*, he notes the welcome moral support Liston gave him when he was the Auckland diocese's inspector of religious education.[15] However, he later claims that the Catholic church in Auckland suffered because Liston did not retire 'until his nineties'.[16] Donnelly provided a much more detailed interpretation of Liston in his autobiography, *One Priest's Life,* published in 1982. Again he states some positive things about Liston and mentions acts of personal kindness.[17] Yet his view of Liston is much darker than Simmons' one. He suggests that Liston applied unfair psychological pressures upon Catholic parents to make their sons (sometimes unsuitable for the role) enter the priesthood.[18] He calls Liston a 'law unto himself' when he ignored Rome's expectation that newly-ordained young priests not be sent to remote rural parishes.[19] He gives a serio-comic account of Liston making a visitation to Waihi parish, preaching an inappropriate sermon and privately criticising the congregation.[20] In the 1950s, says Donnelly,

> . . . younger priests were without redress; you had to simply survive without blotting your copybook by making complaints. Archbishop Liston had a memory longer than any elephant's and he never forgot or for that matter, forgave. [21]

At two points, Donnelly halts his narrative to assess Liston. In the first, he emphasises Liston's age, failing health and increasing bewilderment in a changing church, especially as he had not attended any of the sessions of the Second Vatican Council.[22] The second is notable for an attack upon Liston's personal pride:

> Outsiders saw him as a humble man, but he was not. He gave an impression of humility, but was one of the proudest men I have known. It was impossible for him to tolerate any questioning of his authority; as he saw it, his authority was akin to the divine right of kings. James Liston never forgot or forgave any challenge of his word. Once he made up his mind about something, which he said he did before the altar in prayer, he could not be changed. A priest who put his foot wrong by questioning Liston's authority was exiled from any closeness to him for life. Quite a number of priests spent much of their lives in frustrated anger at the rejection and most, alas, predeceased him. They seemed like stunted children who had failed to receive their father's approval. As a traveller around the diocese I found priests were almost obsessed by the Archbishop. He was clearly feared, and dominated many clerical lives. There was sadness within me at seeing some lives ruined because of Liston's lack of understanding; good and generous men grown bitter and cynical.[23]

Eight years later, Donnelly made Liston a minor character in his heavily didactic novel, *Father Forgive Them*, in which the hidebound old parish priest 'Monsignor O'Halloran' is transparently a hostile caricature of the deceased Remuera parish priest Monsignor John James Bradley.[24] Identified by his real name, James Michael Liston hovers on the fringes of the action only. Most references to him are wryly comic ones.[25]

Like Simmons, Donnelly drew on personal knowledge to present an image of Liston as an aged bishop who outstayed his best years.

Both men, as priests under Liston's authority, had enjoyed his favour and patronage, but had also been hurt by his criticisms and had endured his discipline. The same appears to have been true of an older diocesan priest, Thomas J. Ryder, who had been ordained in 1937 in Ireland. His tape-recorded reminiscences were published in 1999. They include an ambiguous description of Liston in the 1930s as 'extremely rigid but remarkably competent in getting the church off the ground'.[26] Elsewhere, Ryder claims that Liston was afraid of structural change that might have diminished his authority.[27] He expresses his annoyance that Liston overworked him when he emerged from hospital after a bout of tuberculosis, and is particularly irate that he was dismissed from his post as university chaplain.[28] With heavy irony he remarks, 'the Bishop had made up his mind, with the Holy Spirit to guide him, so he couldn't change'.[29] Later, Ryder says he was banished by Liston to Kawerau, after he had fallen out with Monsignor Bradley.[30] In Kawerau, he says, he revitalised parish liturgy in line with the innovations permitted by Vatican II, but 'the Archbishop never paid tribute to me for what I'd done in Kawerau because I'd gone there under a cloud, and with James Michael Liston there was no turning back'.[31]

Simmons, Donnelly and Ryder would probably all have agreed with the judgement of Michael King, in his brief sketch of the Catholic church in New Zealand, that 'Liston's growing conservatism and "creeping infallibility" imposed stress on his colleagues and [on] the priests of his diocese'.[32]

In a different context, King had already voiced the criticism that Liston, like so many of his generation, was monocultural and incapable of understanding the needs of Maori. King's biography of Whina Cooper reports a number of occasions when Liston collaborated with Cooper on projects that were important to her. Cooper claimed Liston was her personal friend. He had eased her path to remarriage within the church after she had been living in a *de facto* relationship.[33] He included her in a Catholic delegation to Wellington to present to government the Maori view on an educational issue.[34] He was delighted when she donated land for church use, and he supported her in her project to establish an urban centre for Maori in Auckland.[35] But, comments King,

> In general James Liston was not comfortable with Maori people, and he was not comfortable with them because he scarcely knew any, other than on a superficial basis. At best he regarded them as children who were sometimes innocent and devout and at other times devious and unreliable. At worst he saw them as people still

to be civilised, still prone to lapses in faith, heathenish beliefs and promiscuous behaviour. These unrealistic views were in part a consequence of his having left all evangelising among Maoris in his diocese to the Mill Hills.[36]

King states that Liston starved the Mill Hill Fathers of funds, forcing them to conduct their mission penuriously. Elsewhere he says that while Liston ordained to the priesthood Whina Cooper's kinsman Henare Tate, he also vetoed the idea of a special bursary for Maori seeking ordination.[37] King's misgivings appear to be borne out by a parochial history of Tauranga which gives details of Liston's stifling Mill Hill attempts to make liturgy more accessible to Maori congregations.[38]

Understandably, those who survive Liston recall him as an old bishop and are in a position to assess his whole career. But so far the only book-length study of any aspect of Liston's life centres on events from over half-a-century before his death, when he was comparatively new to Auckland. Rory Sweetman's *Bishop in the Dock* is a detailed account of Liston's prosecution for sedition in 1922.[39] It emerges as a case study in the sectarian feeling of an earlier New Zealand. There is considerable detail on the activities of the Protestant Political Association (PPA) and the Catholic Federation, competing ideologies of British imperialism and Irish nationalism, and the reactions of New Zealand's Catholic hierarchy and clergy to all these things. By the very nature of the book's subject, Liston is seen in the context of his Irish-Catholic heritage. Sweetman briefly revisited some of these issues when he contributed the entry on Liston to the *Dictionary of New Zealand Biography*. His summary of Liston's final years accords with the views of Simmons and Donnelly, Sweetman saying that Liston 'found it hard to relax his personal grip' when it came to controlling Auckland diocese in the 1960s.[40]

Liston's trial for sedition was notorious enough to find its way into general histories, but other accounts were little more than passing references.[41] Two popular histories of New Zealand make the sedition trial their sole mention of Liston.[42] Yet consideration of this dramatic episode suggests something else about Liston's posthumous reputation. It is a New Zealand reputation rather than an international one.

In Irish-Catholic migration, and in the personnel of the Catholic church, there has always been much exchange across the Tasman. It is difficult to write New Zealand church history without considering its Australasian context. It is curious that Liston has been ignored in

Australian works where one might expect to find him mentioned. An Irish-Australian prelate with whom Liston bears some comparison is Daniel Mannix of Melbourne. Like Liston, Mannix gained public notoriety at the time of the Irish struggle for independence. In 1922, Liston was tried for sedition. In 1920, Mannix was arrested at sea and prevented from entering Ireland by a nervous British government which feared that he would give moral support to Sinn Fein. But neither B.A. Santamaria, in his biography of Mannix, nor Patrick O'Farrell, in his account of the Irish in Australia, make comparisons with Liston when they come to this event in Mannix's life.[43] Similarly, while the biographer of Archbishop James Duhig of Brisbane considers how strongly Irish-Catholic feeling ran in Australia at the time, and how Duhig's conciliatory approach over British 'loyalty' contrasted with Mannix's more provocative stance, he does not make even an endnote of New Zealand's James Michael Liston.[44] Most extraordinarily, Jeff Kildea's full-length study of sectarianism in Australia between 1910 and 1925 touches on many issues that affected both Australian and New Zealand Catholics. It gives a full account of widely-reported confrontations between Australian Catholics and others, but finds no space to mention either Liston or the New Zealand situation.[45] A Catholic bishop being tried in a court of law may have been a momentous, or at least sensational, event in New Zealand, but it does not lift Liston's reputation beyond the national level.

And yet James Michael Liston *did* have a national reputation. The priest from Dunedin who became Bishop of Auckland was never metropolitan of the Catholic church in New Zealand. But his visibility was such that at last he was recognised informally as the church's patriarch. As such he was the local voice of a powerful international body. It was as a venerable high dignitary of that body that he was buried in 1976, when his own origins and background had almost been forgotten.

CHAPTER I

YOUNG LISTON

1881-1904

Parents, Ancestry and Irish Heritage

James Michael Liston was a New Zealander of Irish parentage. James Liston and Mary Sullivan were both natives of Ennis, County Clare, in the south-west of Ireland near the Shannon. In 1922, in a St Patrick's Day speech, their son gave what could be called the legendary version of his family's origins:

> Friends of Ireland, it is very fitting that I should be speaking to you this night, as my descent and the rank I hold in the church give me the right to speak. My parents were driven from the country in which they were born and in which they would have been content to live. Why were they driven out? Because their foreign masters did not want Irish men and women peopling their own land, but wanted to use it as a cattle ranch for the snobs of Empire. So my father and my little Irish mother and thousands of others had to go. They came to this country with the memory kept sacred of their privations and wrongs. They have left us the sacred traditions of their sorrow . . . [1]

This version of his parents' early life implies that they were driven out by English landlords, as part of the general tragedy of Irish dispossession in the nineteenth century. One can only assume that this was the tradition James Michael received from his parents. Later, cross-examined on this story after his speech led to a sedition charge, he elaborated:

> It is correct that both my parents came from Ireland, either in 1864 or 1865. I was referring to a long time past. They were born in 1847 and 1849 respectively – those being the famine years in Ireland. I admit that what was shown in the indictment down to 'snobs of Empire' is substantially correct. I was thinking of the eviction of my

own father and mother and three and three-quarter millions like themselves who were evicted! And I was recalling what evictions meant in Ireland – not people going from one house to another but being put out of their homes and their lands altogether.[2]

However much this version reflects Liston's family traditions, it does commit at least one factual error. According to their death certificates, James Liston and Mary Sullivan were born in 1844 and 1847 respectively.[3] Their obituaries in the *New Zealand Tablet* state that they were both born in Ennis, County Clare.[4] But the birth certificate of their son specifies that James was born in the parish of Kilraethas while Mary was born in the parish of Feikle.[5] It is a moot point whether they knew each other before they emigrated. The profession of the bishop's paternal grandfather (also called James) was given on his death certificate as 'farmer'. Mary's father, Martin Sullivan, was also described as a 'farmer', although in Ireland in the nineteenth century this designation did not necessarily mean landowner. It was often applied euphemistically to penniless tenants or farm labourers. Leaving Ireland 'either in 1864 or 1865', James tried his luck in Australia, first in Adelaide, then in Victoria, before settling on the West Coast of the South Island in 1867.[6] Details of Mary's migration are not known. It would appear that a considerable Liston family remained in Ireland. Basil Minihane, a Liston descendant, recalls that Listons intermarried with O'Tooles and continued to live in the vicinity of Ennis throughout the twentieth century.[7] In 1927, a Terence Liston of County Kerry, whose 'clannish' family had originated in County Limerick, wrote to Bishop Liston asking if they could possibly be related.[8]

It would also appear that at about the same time James was migrating to Australasia, other members of the extended Liston family were heading for the United States of America. In 1926, while visiting America, Bishop Liston made contact with Listons in both Chicago and San Francisco.[9] Again, in 1935, he 'found many relatives in Washington and more in Chicago – about fifty all told – including two priests'.[10] One was the Father Liston who drowned on North Atlantic convoy duty in the Second World War, while serving as a naval chaplain.[11] In old age, Archbishop Liston also became acquainted with a cousin, Joseph Liston of Gary, Indiana, whose parents had made the journey to Chicago from Limerick, which borders County Clare.[12] Upon his retirement, Sister Kieran Liston wrote from Rarotonga to congratulate him on his 'great achievements' in the name of 'all our Liston families' in America and

Ireland.[13] 'Chain migration' was a common phenomenon among the Irish 'who encouraged relatives and friends to follow them to the colonies'.[14] But James' sister Hannah appears to be the only member of his immediate family whom he encouraged to follow him to Australasia.[15] Years later, young James Michael was able to visit members of the extensive Liston family when he was a seminarian in Dublin. But he could not find any of his mother's Sullivan relatives and recalled, 'I do not remember [my mother] speaking of others who might be exiles, like herself'.[16]

Were the reasons for the migration of his parents as desperate as James Michael later suggested? New Zealand and Australia did not receive the 'Famine Irish'.[17] But the Famine could be seen as the beginning of a drastic and ongoing diminution in Ireland's population. The 1860s were still a time of mass migration. Over 800,000 Irish departed between 1861 and 1870.[18] Some of them were harried out by 'agrarian discontent and the rising tide of eviction' and others by an outbreak of cholera in 1866.[19] At journey's end in New Zealand, it is true that Irish arrivals were often perceived as having lower socio-economic status than British immigrants.[20] An 'endemic, if low temperature, xenophobia' has been detected in late nineteenth-century governments' attempts to limit Irish entry to New Zealand, not only because Irish were likely to be Catholics, but also because they were more likely to be unskilled and non-entrepreneurial.[21] None of this means that Liston's parents were necessarily refugees from cruel landlords. The generality of Irish immigrants to Australia and New Zealand in this period cannot be so readily categorised as victims. Like millions of other Europeans, many made a conscious decision to improve their chances by leaving an unpromising, but not desperate, situation.[22]

Those Irish who headed for Australia in the 1860s were generally more skilled than the 'Famine Irish' who had filled America's urban ghettos two decades earlier. They had a greater hand in opening up the country, especially in the gold-rush years.[23] One speculation is that Liston's parents may have left County Clare at a time when pasturage was overtaking traditional tillage farming, and hence opportunities for farm labourers were contracting as ploughing, planting and reaping were replaced by the munching of cattle.[24] Having noted all this, though, there is no doubt that belief in his parents' unwilling exile, inherited bitterness about this circumstance and resultant sympathy for the Irish nationalist cause were major factors in the formation of young James Michael Liston. His reference to 'a cattle ranch for the snobs of empire' suggests a strong family tradition of dispossession by wealthy, perhaps English, pastoralists.

On a more verifiable level, Liston's parents fitted into a general migratory trend. They arrived just before the Vogel era of migration that was to alter radically New Zealand's demographic composition.[25] They came by way of Australia, were unmarried and of rural background, as most Irish arrivals in New Zealand then were.[26] They were Catholic, like about three-quarters of incoming Irish.[27] They were from County Clare, which was equalled only by Kilkenny in the number of Irish it contributed to New Zealand's West Coast.[28] Additionally, County Clare was the most Catholic part of the Catholic mother-country, 97.8 per cent of its population being recorded as Catholic in 1861.[29]

A sense of Irish ethnicity was to be an important theme in Liston's early life, as was a sense of exile from ancestral roots. When he eventually left Dunedin diocese, he linked his own 'painful sacrifice of separation' with tributes to 'the generous faith of the Irish exiles who have made their home here and have built up the Church in this country'.[30] His own family's direct experience of Ireland ended little more than a decade before his birth. It was only in the 1880s that the New Zealand-born children of Irish immigrants began to outnumber their Irish-born parents. Catholicism being essential to Liston's conception of Irishness, it is also significant that the great majority of New Zealand's Catholic clergy in Liston's youth (such as Fr Michael Walsh, who baptised him) were still Irish-born.[31] Only in October 1884, when Liston was three years old, was the first New Zealand-born priest ordained.[32]

Throughout his life, Liston was to speak frequently of his Irish heritage, usually in terms that cast the pioneering Irish in heroic mould as hardy but pious children of the Faith. Such tributes, sentimental and idealised, were typical of those he voiced on many formal church occasions. In this, he was in a strong tradition of pious Irish Catholic national consciousness in New Zealand, perhaps typified by the eccentric Brother Egbert who constantly portrayed the Irish as a righteous nation wronged by the persecuting English.[33] As Bishop of Auckland, Liston's reverence for Irish Catholic pioneers was also seen in his concern to keep alive the memory of the earliest Irish Catholic resident in New Zealand, Thomas Poynton.[34] One part of Liston's story, though, is his gradual move from a youthful, fervent identification with Ireland's sufferings to a more universal conception of Catholicism and a greater readiness to identify with non-Irish, even non-Catholic, New Zealanders.[35]

James Liston and Mary Sullivan, the parents who passed on this fervent youthful sense of Irishness, made their separate ways to New Zealand. By 1868, James was a resident of Hokitika. He may well have been a witness to some of the disturbances there that year, between 'Fenian' and 'loyalist' miners, which have been somewhat fancifully interpreted as 'an Irish rebellion'.[36] How and when James and Mary met is unknown. Mary, too, appears to have reached New Zealand by way of Australia. Members of her family settled in Australia, and Sullivan descendants were still corresponding from Brisbane with Archbishop Liston late in his life.[37] James and Mary were married in Hokitika on 17 February 1874 by the French Marist Fr Aimé Martin.[38]

By this stage, James had already set up as an hotelier. His course from Victoria to the West Coast reminds us that where Irish miners went, Irish service industries (particularly hotels) followed. On his marriage certificate, he is identified as a 'brewer' and his bride is identified as a 'publican', probably meaning 'barmaid'.[39] The Listons' first three children were all born in Hokitika. Their eldest child died in infancy.[40] Their son John Patrick was born in 1877 and their daughter Mary Maud in 1879. Both were baptised by Fr Martin.[41] In 1879, James Liston moved with his family to manage a hotel in Palmerston in Otago, and by 1881 the family had settled in Dunedin. In the year of James Michael's birth, a standard advertisement for Liston senior's pub was placed in the *Tablet*. It read thus:

> LISTON'S ROBERT BURNS HOTEL – George Street North, Dunedin (Late of Hokitika and North-Western Hotel, Palmerston, Otago). First-Class Accommodation for Boarders and Travellers. One of Alcock's Prize Billiard Tables, also lovers of the game will find everything necessary to the sport. The cellars stocked with the best Ales and Liquors. A good table kept and terms moderate. J. LISTON, Proprietor.[42]

James Michael was born in Dunedin in 1881, and his younger sister Catherine Anne Josephine (generally known as Anne) arrived in 1883. Some official documents record that James Michael was born on 2 June 1881.[43] But throughout his life Liston celebrated his birthday on 9 June, the date given in most retrospective articles and biographical notices. Remarking on this discrepancy, one obituarist declared, 'he had a penchant for recording history as he judged best'.[44] Not that there was necessarily any conscious attempt to misrecord his birth date. It is at least possible that Liston himself simply misread the upper half of the numeral 2 written on his baptismal certificate, although it is equally possible that he was concerned to bring his birth date closer to the date of his baptism. He was baptised on 19 June 1881.

If there is a hint of uncertainty over *when* exactly Liston was born, there is also imprecision over *where* he was born. His birth certificate simply lists 'George Street, Dunedin' as his place of birth. Young James could well have been born in his father's Robert Burns Hotel, which was probably also the family home at that time. For the Irish Catholic community, there was no incongruity in hotels serving as places of religious worship, as well as family residences.[45] A pub was no inappropriate place for the birth of the future archbishop. The name 'James' was inherited from his father, but as one of his Sullivan cousins told him late in life, the middle name 'Michael' came from his mother's grandfather, Michael Sullivan of County Clare, who 'suffered dreadfully in the Famine'.[46]

Probably more significant for the adult James Michael himself was his baptism at St Joseph's. This was the beginning of his long association with what was soon to be the Catholic cathedral of Dunedin. St Joseph's in Rattray Street, begun as a simple wooden church by the Marist missioner Fr Delphin Moreau, had been blessed and opened in 1864.[47] To a plan of the architect Francis W. Petre, it was rebuilt as a more imposing cathedral under Bishop Patrick Moran in the early 1880s, and opened in February 1886, even though it lacked an intended spire.[48] Liston was to have a life-long sentimental attachment to this cathedral. Here he was baptised, received his first communion, was confirmed by Bishop Moran, served as an altar boy, according to one account 'received the call' to priesthood, was ordained by Bishop Verdon in 1904 and finally was consecrated as a bishop in 1920.[49] Frequently in his later career, he was to participate in functions that stressed the importance of this cathedral in his life, and its importance as a focal point for Dunedin's Catholic community.

To the end of his life, James Michael held his parents in the highest esteem. 'A gift from God for the children of a home and the neighbours, a saintly mother of charities and a greatly good, honourable father' was how he described them in one brief autobiographical note.[50] Elsewhere he claimed they were 'both of saintly quality'.[51] His view was endorsed by the Catholic hierarchy in 1919, when they were advising Rome on the desirability of raising Liston to the episcopate. The bishops characterised Liston's parents as 'Irish Catholics who led a saintly life, pillars of the church, setting a good example to everyone and . . . well known to the bishops'.[52] At the very least, it is clear that Mr and Mrs Liston were devout.

Above left: James Liston (1844-1901), descendant of West-of-Ireland peasants, immigrant, successful South Island publican and father of an archbishop.
Above right: Mary Liston, née Sullivan (1847-1902), the archbishop's mother as a young woman, showing the looks that she passed on to her son.
Left: Studio portrait of James Michael Liston (1881-1976), future archbishop, as a boy, early 1890s.

When he was retiring, Archbishop Liston made for his successor an inventory of the contents of Bishop's House, Ponsonby, including 'two silver candlesticks on altar: from our altar in Dunedin round which we gathered as children and with father and mother for rosary and evening prayer'.[53] The Listons had a wide circle of clerical and lay friends in Dunedin. Obituaries of both laid stress on their support for charities. Mary Liston was described as one whose –

> ... death will be sincerely mourned by a large number of people who had from time to time experienced her generosity, for she was ever ready to extend a helping hand to the necessitous, and her many private charities, performed so unostentatiously, will never be known, as she was one of those who liked to do good by stealth.[54]

James Liston senior became a member of the board of the *Tablet*. He appears also to have been an astute businessman, spending the 1880s and 1890s running a series of Dunedin pubs, the Robert Burns, the Douglas and the Criterion.[55] When he died in 1900, he willed everything to his wife.[56] She in turn, dying in 1902, left to her children (and to some charities) property worth the very respectable sum of £8516, 10 shillings and 7 pence, including eight sections of land and the balance of a mortgage owing to her on the Criterion Hotel.[57] In coming to New Zealand, the landless rural Listons had prospered as members of the Otago Catholic bourgeoisie.

This class was, however, a small one, just as the Catholic population of Dunedin was a minority. Only recently has the 'ethnic fractioning' of nineteenth century New Zealand Pakeha society received much attention from historians – the consciousness of New Zealand Scots as being distinctively Scots, English as being English, Irish as being Irish etc. It is possible to overstate this sensibility, as Patrick O'Farrell warns when he remarks that nineteenth-century Catholic Irish in New Zealand –

> ... adopted the general tone of the colony: they did not wish to be apart; there is in early New Zealand Irishry no celebration of itself, and even its later manifestations – such as Dan Davin's – are apologia rather than affirmations.[58]

In other words, New Zealand's Catholic Irish did not live in ghettos and on the whole functioned peaceably among their non-Irish fellow citizens. In 1890, an Irish Catholic, John Carroll, was even elected mayor of Dunedin. Nevertheless, it is clear that for Otago's Irish Catholics there was some sense of separateness, heightened by their being an ethnic and religious minority in what had begun as a Scots Presbyterian settlement. Erik Olssen remarks that the history of Otago is 'inexplicable' unless one takes into account the Presbyterian Free Church origins and hopes of the founders of Dunedin. He further notes that those Free Church founders resented the discovery of gold in Otago in the 1860s because, among other things, it brought in 'thousands of Catholic Irishmen (similar to those they had escaped by journeying into the wilderness)'.[59] In the year of Liston's birth, Presbyterians made up 42 percent of Otago's population while Catholics were just over 12 percent.[60] For the Catholic Irish, even in the early years of the twentieth century, a sense of not being part of the local civic establishment occasionally took the form of direct challenges to the cultural symbols of the Protestant majority. If, for example, non-Catholic settlers were insensitive enough to call an Otago town Cromwell, then the local Catholic church had to be called the Church of the Irish Martyrs lest anyone forget Cromwell's reputation with Irish Catholics.[61] More often, however, sectarian tensions in Liston's youth were confined to the hard words exchanged between the *Tablet* and various Protestant correspondents in the *Presbyterian Outlook* or the *Otago Daily Times*.

Dunedin Diocese and Its Leaders

The diocese in which Liston grew up not only represented a minority ethnic culture, but was new, large and chronically understaffed. Dunedin diocese was founded less than 12 years before Liston's birth.[62] It was geographically vast to anybody whose basis of comparison was a European diocese. In 1897, its bishop, Michael Verdon, described it as 'nearly as large as Ireland – larger than Leinster, Ulster, Munster and half of Connaught . . . but the Catholic population is very much scattered over a thinly populated country – we have about 21,000 Catholics'.[63] Comment on the vastness of antipodean dioceses has been a common trope for both historians and early observers.[64] However hackneyed such descriptions may sound, it remains true that Dunedin diocese, comprehending Otago, Southland and Stewart Island, was a sizeable pastoral care for a bishop, especially when roads were unsealed and transport slow.

The official tone of the diocese was articulated by its first bishop, Patrick Moran, who arrived to take up his appointment early in 1871 and died in 1895. For most of the 1870s, Moran dominated the Catholic church in New Zealand, taking additional charge of Wellington diocese for two years before Bishop Viard's successor was installed, and administering Auckland diocese in the four years between the departure of Bishop Croke and the arrival of Bishop

Steins. Ultramontane and shaped by the pontificate of Pius IX that had produced the *Syllabus of Errors* in 1864, Moran was suspicious of secular liberalism, saw Freemasonic conspiracy everywhere, and made the *Tablet* (which he founded in 1873 and personally edited for eight years) his mouthpiece on a range of controversial issues. Chief among these was the matter of education. Moran denounced the secular state system established in 1877 and campaigned for state assistance to Catholic schools. Over this issue he stood, unsuccessfully, for parliament in 1883. A successful administrator who diligently built up his diocese, Moran's outlook was based on the assumption that New Zealand Catholics were being assailed by the same anti-clerical forces then active in Europe. Hugh Laracy has remarked:

> Moran's inability to see the Catholic Church in New Zealand apart from that in Europe was clearly shown in his disgust with secular education, and in the overwrought way he represented it in the *Tablet*.[65]

Elsewhere, Laracy refers ironically to Moran's outlook as 'paranoid popery'.[66]

This man who was bishop of Dunedin for the first 14 years of Liston's life, who administered Liston's first communion and confirmation, was notably aggressive in pressing Catholic claims and in asserting a separate Catholic (and Irish) identity. In such respects, he was a typical product of Cardinal Paul Cullen's 'devotional revolution' in Ireland. Accordingly, he was 'not out of line with other Cullenites . . . he merely expressed himself more clearly and fought more often with his gloves off'.[67] There have been challenges to the accepted view that Cardinal Paul Cullen wrought a major change in the Irish practice of Catholicism between his arrival in Ireland as papal legate in 1850 and his death in 1878.[68] Nevertheless, the consensus remains that Cullen revivified and disciplined Irish Catholicism, giving it a confident, combative tone in its confrontations with the Anglo-Protestant Ascendancy. Charles Morris asserts that Cullen 'utterly transformed the Irish Church',[69] and that –

> . . . with more and better disciplined clergy, a shrinking and more bourgeois Catholic population, and newly won control over the educational system, Cullen was in a position to engineer a vast expansion of the Church's influence in Irish daily life.[70]

Some judgements on Cullen's achievement have been harsh, one biographer in effect accusing him of creating sectarian 'apartheid', planning a Catholic Ascendancy to replace the Protestant one, and hindering the development of a tolerant pluralist society in modern Ireland.[71] However, it is generally accepted that Cullen's influence was measurable in greatly increased attendance at church in Ireland; in the fostering of lay sodalities; and in what were later to be such characteristic Irish Catholic preoccupations as 'unquestioning acceptance of papal authority', the need to support charities and social work, the building-up of Catholic religious institutions and hospitals, opposition to secret societies and to violent revolutionism of any sort, even in Ireland's nationalist cause, and a more triumphalistic assertion of dogma.[72]

Cullen's world view and assumptions were very much those that Moran (who had been consecrated by him) applied in building up Dunedin. Indeed, as bishops of Irish origin assumed control of the Catholic church in Australia, and challenged the lingering French influence in New Zealand, Cullen's outlook became particularly relevant in these countries. A high number of Australasian bishops owed their appointments to him. Some of them were his relatives. They included his former secretary James Murray, who became Bishop of Maitland; his associates at the Irish College in Rome, James and Matthew Quinn, who became respectively bishops of Brisbane and Bathurst; and his nephew Cardinal Patrick Francis Moran of Sydney (no relation to the bishop of Dunedin).[73]

Not the least of Cullen's relatives was another nephew, Michael Verdon, who succeeded Patrick Moran as Bishop of Dunedin when Liston was not quite 15. Verdon had been dean and president of Holy Cross College, Clonliffe, Dublin (which his uncle had founded). From 1879 to 1886, he was vice-rector of the Irish College in Rome (of which his uncle had been rector and his cousin Moran vice-rector) and was then later president of St Patrick's College, Manly (which his cousin had founded).[74] James Michael Liston was to undertake his own priestly training in all three of these institutions. Michael Verdon was consecrated Bishop of Dunedin, by his cousin, in Sydney on Sunday 3 May 1896. He took over a diocese which had 39 churches and approximately 20,000 Catholics.

Verdon was a very different man from his predecessor, and it was not unusual for contrasts to be drawn between them. Unlike Moran, he was quiet and retiring in his demeanour, 'shy and deeply private by temperament' according to the historian of Manly college, and exercising 'a style of reclusive leadership' which came

Above: An image of the Dunedin Catholic Irish in their finery, 1899. Liston's parents are both visible among the guests at the wedding of T. Costello and Kitty Blaney at Blaney's Hotel.
Below left: Patrick Moran, Catholic bishop of Dunedin 1871-1895, fierce controversialist, founder of the *New Zealand Tablet* and chief purveyor of the Cullenite 'devotional revolution' to New Zealand.
Below right: Michael Verdon, Catholic bishop of Dunedin 1896-1918. His piety was a major influence on Liston, who kept this photograph of Verdon on his workdesk as daily inspiration.

to be thought of as necessary by subsequent rectors of the college.[75] The same writer calls him 'a delicate, painstaking, perfectionist type of person' who was more comfortable showing generosity to his inferiors (students, priests) than negotiating with his equals.[76] After Verdon's death in 1918, it became almost axiomatic for priests and Catholic journalists to apply the term 'saintly' to him. Verdon cultivated a particular sort of personal piety in which, for example, he could see permission to have the Blessed Sacrament 'reserved' in a convent chapel as a great 'consolation' for the resident nuns in their toilsome lives of teaching.[77] Yet for all their differences in temperament and style, Verdon's ecclesiology and assumptions were as much cast in the mould of his famous uncle as his Dunedin predecessor's had been.

Cardinal Cullen, who had at one stage recruited troops to defend the Papal States against encroaching Italian nationalism, insisted on complete loyalty to Rome, the pope and the magisterium.[78] He encouraged his priests to wear Roman clerical garb and to decorate their churches 'in the fashion of contemporaneous Roman basilicas'.[79] This entailed an 'Italianate Counter-Reformation' style.[80] These attitudes he passed on to later Irish hierarchs, such as Archbishop McQuaid of Dublin.[81] They were very much a part of the making of Michael Verdon.[82] Verdon's reverence for the Italian Catholic Reformation Saints, Philip Neri and Charles Borromeo, was part of his 'Romanita'.[83] So was his preference for having more talented seminarians sent to Rome for further training, and the very Roman decorations he arranged for New Zealand's national seminary.[84] While ordering Stations of the Cross for the seminary in 1906, Verdon wrote to the rector of the Irish College, 'I am sure that you feel very happy in Rome. After all there are very few places in the world where an ecclesiastic should feel so happy'.[85]

Liston was deeply influenced by Verdon, who encouraged his vocation, sponsored his studies and was his bishop for the first 14 years of his priesthood. Verdon's personality and principles, including his 'Romanita', were the subject of frequent eulogia by Liston.[86] In many respects, he regarded Verdon as 'the' bishop and his own ultimate role model. Throughout his career, as he many times affirmed, he kept a photograph of Verdon on his workdesk 'for guidance through reflection on his way, and for the seeking of his heavenly intercession'.[87]

Cullen. Moran. Verdon. Liston. No matter how much it might be modified by the New Zealand situation, the committed Irish Catholicism of Liston and his parents was ultimately enmeshed in

Cullen's 'revolution'. Brought by Liston's parents and their fellow immigrants, but also faithfully relayed by Bishops Moran and Verdon, this brand of Catholicism could be deeply implicated in Irish nationalism in some of its manifestations. But it was not an Irish national church in the way that Anglicanism was an English national church. Bishop Moran might lobby for an Irish hierarchy in New Zealand and fiercely resent the appointments of such conspicuously non-Irish bishops as Francis Redwood in Wellington, John Joseph Grimes in Christchurch and Edmund Luck in Auckland. Yet for Moran as for Liston and other devout Catholics, 'Romanita' qualified Irish nationalism. The True Faith was embodied in the Universal Church centred in Rome, not in an Irish national sect. If and when the claims of Rome and the claims of Ireland were in conflict, then the claims of Rome prevailed.[88]

If this was the general ideological sea young James Michael Liston swam in, it remains to ask how his priestly vocation was fostered, for not all sons of devout Irish immigrant parents chose to become priests.

Education, Seminaries and Priestly Formation

Liston's first formal schooling was at the Christian Brothers' School. The Irish order of teaching brothers had been invited to Dunedin by Bishop Moran in 1876, and had promptly established their first school in Rattray Street near St Joseph's.[89] John Patrick Liston was enrolled at the school at the age of eight in July 1885, and James Michael followed his older brother in January 1887, at the age of five-and-a-half. The school register notes that he was the school's 456th pupil since records began to be kept in 1885.[90] As a student, James Michael appears to have done well, winning the arithmetic prize in 1890 and the French prize in 1892.[91] An obituary article declared that 'a slim book in the seminary library at Mosgiel indicates his early proficiency in Latin', with apparent reference to exercises undertaken in his years of elementary schooling.[92] His earlier school days were important to him in another way, too. He was for a time in the same class as Michael James Hanrahan, who was four years his senior. Hanrahan, who in adulthood had thin ascetic features remarkably like Liston's own, was later to become New Zealand provincial of the Christian Brothers, with the religious name Brother Benignus. At about the same time that Liston began his priestly studies, Hanrahan (without his parents' knowledge) was spirited away to the Brothers' novitiate in Geelong, Australia, to begin his training.[93] This has been referred to as a 'kidnapping'.[94]

Much later, when he was Bishop of Auckland, Liston negotiated with his former classmate when he introduced the Christian Brothers into his diocese upon the foundation of St Peter's College in Epsom in 1939. As with the cathedral, so with the Christian Brothers' School, Liston was to feel a lifelong debt to it, often expressed on public occasions involving Christian Brothers' institutions.[95]

The Christian Brothers' School in Dunedin was later to enjoy a reputation as the nursery of bishops. It was the *alma mater* not only of Liston, but also of Cardinal Peter McKeefry and Bishop Hugh O'Neill.[96] No doubt all Catholic teaching institutions at that time encouraged vocations to the priesthood. Liston left no detailed account of the process by which he decided on the religious life, but there is some evidence that he was sensitive to the way his early decision was presented to the public. At the time of his sacerdotal diamond jubilee in 1964, an unsigned article in the *New Zealand Herald* declared –

> The habit of study began for Archbishop Liston at an early age. Before he was 12, his County Clare parents, who set themselves up in the hotel business in Dunedin, had decided on his vocation to the priesthood.[97]

The phrasing here suggests that James Michael himself had little to do with the decision. In 1970, however, near the time of Liston's resignation from his see, articles in the same newspaper gave quite a different impression. One said 'his own decision to be a priest was taken early'.[98] Another elaborated –

> It seems extraordinary – though not to him – that he made up his own mind at the tender age of 12 to devote his life to the Church. He was then an altar boy at the cathedral in Dunedin. Neither his mother nor his father, an Irish couple who held daily prayers in the private sitting room of their hotel, was responsible for his decision.[99]

This latter statement is so emphatic that it suggests Liston, in his interview with the journalist, had consciously corrected the earlier impression that he himself (with God) was not responsible for his own decision. Apart from his parents and his school, there was, however, another important influence. This was Fr Patrick Maguire Lynch, who had been ordained in 1882, the year after Liston's birth, and who was stationed at the cathedral where Liston attended and served mass.[100] Lynch was a personal friend of the Listons. He was sometimes erroneously described as 'the first New Zealander to be ordained'.[101] But he was born in Ireland and brought to New

Zealand at the age of ten. He arrived in Hokitika in 1869, shortly after James Liston senior settled there, and it is more than likely that the elder Liston would have come to know the Lynch family at that time. Father Lynch was cathedral administrator for a number of years and edited the *Tablet* for a period under Bishop Moran's direction. Some believed he would succeed Moran as bishop and Moran himself seemed to favour him. Lynch was *dignissimus* (most worthy) in the first *terna* voting after Moran's death.[102] But a group of senior clergy in the diocese, headed by Dean William Burke and Fr James O'Neill, lobbied vigorously against his appointment.[103] While Bishop Verdon was the spiritual mentor whom Liston was most ready to recall in later years, Father Lynch appears to have been the most immediate spiritual advisor of his boyhood.[104]

In February 1893, when he was not yet 12 years of age, Liston was sent by his parents, with the encouragement of Father Lynch, to live and study at St Patrick's College, Manly, near Sydney.[105] St Patrick's was then only five years old, having been opened on Cardinal Moran's initiative in 1888. It was still headed by its first president, Michael Verdon, with whom young Liston became acquainted over the next three years, before Verdon was called to be Bishop of Dunedin in April 1896. A 'junior seminary' of younger schoolboys was then integrated into the company of more mature seminarians. 'The mixing of the very young with the more mature . . . made it difficult to create a system of discipline that was better than juvenile.'[106] Liston was later sometimes reticent about Manly, as if it were a false start to his ecclesiastical career.[107] Nevertheless, as he began his secondary schooling there, he encountered people who were later to be important in his life – not only Verdon but also James Whyte, who was one of the professors and who succeeded Verdon as Bishop of Dunedin.[108] Matthew Brodie, later to be the first New Zealand-born Catholic bishop, was a student prefect.[109] Another New Zealander was Joseph Croke Darby. Both Brodie and Darby were, like Liston, the sons of publicans. Liston was enrolled in the grammar class in 1893, where he was 53rd in a seniority list of 55. He was in the humanity class in 1894 and the rhetoric class in 1895.[110]

Young students who entered Manly could expect to do all their priestly training there, but in many respects the most formative aspect of Manly upon Liston was the way he was abruptly withdrawn from the college after three-and-a-half years. In December 1896, when he returned home on holiday to Dunedin, his parents were appalled to discover that the 15-year-old was undernourished and in very poor health. Bishop Verdon wrote to Patrick Murphy, the man who had succeeded him as rector of Manly,

> My most promising subject James Liston will not be allowed to return to St Patrick's College. He was in very poor health indeed when he came home in December and his parents were greatly troubled by him. They brought him to the best doctor in Dunedin who forbade them to send him again to Manly. His parents will keep him at home for some months and then they will probably send him to Ireland to continue his studies.[111]

Most chroniclers of these events are aware that there was more to them than met the eye.[112] Possibly young Liston's medical condition really was as parlous as Verdon's letter stated. But even without this circumstance, Verdon was already dissatisfied with the Manly administration that had succeeded his own. Patrick Murphy, apparently on the authority of Cardinal Moran, had decided to economise on food and tighten up discipline at Manly, provoking a 'food crisis' and leading to a formal student protest presented by Matthew Brodie.[113] Verdon appears to have already been thinking of making alternative arrangements for the training of New Zealand priests (in four years he would found Holy Cross, Mosgiel). Meanwhile, it is hard to believe Liston's parents would 'probably send him to Ireland' without considerable encouragement from their bishop, especially as the seminary to which he was sent in Ireland was another which Verdon had once run.

Shortly after James Michael's 16th birthday, in June 1897, Bishop Verdon wrote to Archbishop William Walsh of Dublin, asking formal permission for Liston to study at Holy Cross seminary, Clonliffe, north Dublin.

> He is a very promising young fellow: he is pious, docile and talented. I speak from personal knowledge as he was under my care for three years in Manly College. He read Philosophy last year at Manly, though he was only 14 yrs. when he began. However he overworked himself and I did not send him back to Manly after Christmas Vacation. He is now quite strong. He is well able to pay his way, and I guarantee full payment of pension and extras due.[114]

As well as suggesting Liston's intellectual prowess, this letter is notable for attributing the boy's withdrawal from Manly to overwork rather than to ill health – and also for implying that it was Verdon, rather than Liston's parents, who chose not to send him back. There was a formal Dunedin farewell at which it was noted that 'young Mr Liston's health continues to give grave concern'.[115] Then James

Michael travelled to Ireland with Father Lynch, and made a short retreat with the monks of St Mellary Abbey.[116] He was enrolled in the BA class at Clonliffe on 11 September 1897. For most of the next three years, until July 1900, he was to pursue a general course in humanities, languages and philosophy.[117] As with some other places in his spiritual formation, Liston was to feel a lifelong attachment and obligation to the seminary at Clonliffe. In later years, he made it a habit to send the staff greetings every year at Christmas and on their college's feast day.[118] He also paid return visits there in 1935 and 1954. In November 1958, he contributed the following remarks on his student days to the college's centennial publication:

> The years have made me aware of my debt to Clonliffe for what it gave me of training and love for Ireland . . . I owe my years at Holy Cross College, Clonliffe, from September 1897 to July 1900, to the choice of my bishop, the Most Reverend Michael Verdon, Bishop of Dunedin, and one time president of Clonliffe. Being immature I learned slowly and had many lonely days at Clonliffe, but even then I understood somewhat, and later in ever-increasing measure, I saw how blessed I was in being a student there. So I keep in my mind clear pictures of the president, Canon Michael Walsh, the vice-president Father James Dunne, and the professors – Terence O'Donnell, Cornelius Ryan, John Waters, Michael Cronin and P.J. Walsh. I can recall their kindness and the skill of their training of us, their devotedness to duty and their personal holiness . . . little wonder that my memories are of a sensitive gratitude to them. I had the good fortune to be at Clonliffe with several who have since those far-off days enriched the Church and their native land: Monsignori Boylan and Shine; Monsignor Michael Curran and Canon Andrew Moriarty, with both of whom I was in Rome later. Here again friendship and the very thought of them have always been a spur to me.[119]

This is written in the courteous and polite language expected of a tribute in a church publication, and it may idealise young Liston's experience between the ages of 16 and 19. Nevertheless, the memory of 'many lonely days' rings true. In leaving Dunedin, Liston was farewelling his parents for the last time. They died before he returned to New Zealand late in 1903. It is tempting to see a sense of permanent separation (akin to his youthful sense of exile from the Irish homeland) influencing many of Liston's utterances in later life. When, for example, he wrote an appreciation of a recently-deceased Dunedin priest in 1916, he began with the desolate words,

Life is but a series of parting of friends. One by one they hurry past us, stretching out their hands in long farewell. We whisper goodbye to them – goodbye till we meet again in heaven – and as we turn once more to our unfinished tasks, try to win some comfort out of words.[120]

This is, in many respects, no more than the conventional Catholic piety that painted the world as a 'vale of tears' preceding the afterlife. Yet it would have special significance for one who never saw his parents after the age of 16, and was to spend most of his life separated from his three siblings.

For all that, the general impression of a studious, hard-working, withdrawn and lonely youth at Clonliffe has to be tempered by the fact that he was, in Ireland, able to spend holidays with his father's relatives (probably his aunts Honora, Mary Ellen, Nellie and Bridget) from whom he 'verified for himself all the old Irish national traditions of faith and fatherland'.[121] As the leading County Clare newspaper later recalled, he 'spent holidays at Ennis with the Aherne family who resided at Kilrush Road'.[122] He also holidayed with the Irish relatives of Dunedin clergy, the Coffeys and Foleys, at Ballinahinch.[123] He found none of his mother's relatives.[124] But he was sometimes in contact with his old mentor Father Lynch who had gone to Ireland for further training in the Redemptorist Order. Lynch reported visits from Liston in Ireland and England in 1898 and 1899, in the latter case when the student was being taken to Europe by Bishop Verdon. He noted Liston's 'marked success' at Clonliffe.[125]

As well as being able to do at least some socialising from Clonliffe, Liston proved himself enough of a New Zealander to develop one distinctly non-Irish pastime. To the more fervent Irish nationalists, cricket (along with rugby, soccer and hockey) was a 'foreign' or 'garrison' game associated with competitions played by the British Army in Ireland.[126] But, while paying for his required texts and 18-months' supply of porter, Liston also spent five shillings on a set of the *Book of Cricket*.[127] Cricket was to be a minor interest for the rest of his life. As Bishop of Auckland he sometimes enjoyed umpiring friendly matches between members of the clergy.[128] Likewise, he maintained a spectator interest in rugby, and even in old age could still recall the players who had been favourites in Dunedin in his childhood.[129]

No academic records survive from Liston's time at Clonliffe. But as a student he clearly did well enough to encourage Verdon to sponsor his further studies at the Irish College (Pontificio Collegio Irlandese) in Rome. Then situated on the Via Mazzarino, near the Bank of Italy and the church of St Agatha of the Goths, the Irish College was the third seminary that Liston had in common with its former vice-rector, Verdon.[130] It was also another seminary very much in the mould of its former rector, Paul Cullen. Rules for the entry of students stipulated that they had to be Irish, or at least have an Irish father; they had to be of sound constitution and have 'authentic commendations for piety and docility'; they had to have already been prepared in rhetoric and philosophy, and were required to sit an entrance examination in catechism and sacred history. They also had to be at least 17 years old. This was never an institution with a 'junior seminary' attached. While living at, and receiving some instruction in, the Irish College itself, seminarians took their lectures at the City College (Collegio Urbano) of Propaganda Fide. Therefore they also had to learn Italian pronunciation. Reading matter was strictly supervised. New entrants were told to bring 'a few more useful books: Holy Bible, Imitation of Christ, Manuale Clericorum, Horae Diurnae, English and other dictionaries, and Class-books. *Novels of all kinds are prohibited*'.[131] Summer holidays were taken under college supervision, at a villa the college maintained at Tivoli outside Rome, and incoming mail was censored.

Monsignor Michael Kelly had become rector in 1891 and was rector at the time of Liston's enrolment. Under his regime, students took two hours of lectures in the morning and two in the afternoon, Monday to Saturday, with Thursdays off. Within the college, oral and written examinations were administered by departments of philosophy and theology, and it was customary for students to take four years in their theology studies.[132] Inevitably, too, as one of 'several national colleges, generally for students of countries where post-Reformation governments did not allow the training of priests', the Irish College was a great encourager of 'Romanita', with 'a tradition of martyrdom and special fidelity' centring on the seventeenth-century martyr, Oliver Plunkett, whose portrait hung in the college's entrance hall.[133] Ultramontanism meant strong resentment of the new secular government of Italy, which had usurped control of the old Papal States after 1870.

Having travelled to Rome with Verdon, the 19-year-old Liston was enrolled at the college on 22 October 1900, being the college's 679th student since it had been re-established in 1826. The register shows that he was immediately placed in the second-year theology class, as he had already completed first-year theology studies at

Above: Liston (standing right rear) with his study group (*'camerata'*) at the Irish College in Rome, 1901.
Below left: Liston, aged 20, as a seminarian at the Irish College (Pontificio Collegio Irlandese) in Rome, 1901.
Below right: While in Italy, the seminarian Liston takes an excursion on horseback, c.1901.

Clonliffe. He was signed in on the same day as his contemporary from Clonliffe, Michael Curran.[134] Curran himself became vice-rector of the Irish College in 1919, and was rector from 1930 to 1939. He was to be important to Liston in the later 1920s, when Liston was in contention with Bishop Cleary and needed an informed friend in Rome.[135] Other student contemporaries included the Wexford-born James Joseph Kelly, the rector's nephew. Four years Liston's senior, Kelly was at the Irish College from October 1895 to May 1902, and was later to be the controversial editor of the *New Zealand Tablet*. Another contemporary was the Dubliner Timothy Hurley, who became a professor at Manly. Liston's own brief note on Pontificio Collegio Irlandese, written when he was in his nineties, emphasised his fond recollections of the rector Michael Kelly, of the vice-rector Edward Byrne (later Archbishop of Dublin) and of William Murphy, who replaced Kelly as rector in 1901. Kelly took Liston to the last reception of Pope Leo XIII in July 1901, and Liston was present when Kelly was consecrated in Rome as Coadjutor-Archbishop of Sydney in August 1901.[136]

Most retrospective articles and obituaries on Liston made a point of noting his academic brilliance. Such records as survive in Rome allow these claims and suggest he was a very sound doctoral student. In the Collegio Urbano examinations of 1900-01, Liston gained nearly top marks (9 out of 10) in theology, sacred theology and ecclesiastical history. In the examinations of 1901-02, he gained the highest possible marks (10 out of 10) in dogmatics, sacramental theology and moral theology. His marks were sound in archaeology (7 out of 10) and sacred scripture (8 out of 10). His only real failure was in Hebrew, for which he gained 5 out of 10 one semester, and 2 out of 10 the next.[137] This is surprising in that his facility with languages, and his ability in English, Latin, German, French and Italian, were points made in his favour when the New Zealand hierarchy was recommending him as coadjutor-bishop of Auckland.[138] Perhaps Hebrew, like Maori, was simply outside the European family of languages with which he was comfortable. Before his Roman studies were completed, Michael Verdon was already regarding Liston as potential academic staff for his newly-founded Mosgiel seminary. In May 1902, Verdon wrote to the rector saying he had 'professorships' for Liston and for Daniel Buckley, another student whom he was supporting in Rome.[139]

At the Irish College, Liston advanced through all the ecclesiastical grades that were then necessary preliminaries to ordination. He received the symbolic tonsure in May 1901, was admitted as 'ostiariatus et lectoratus' (porter and reader) in June 1902, exorcist and acolyte in February 1903, sub-deacon in March 1903 and finally deacon on 24 June 1903, before he left the college to journey back to New Zealand by way of Ireland and Australia.[140] There is no record of his having been affected by the outbreak of diphtheria among Irish College students in the last year of his residence.[141]

If Liston developed intellectually in his studies between the ages of 19 and 22, there were other experiences in Rome which enhanced both his 'Romanita' and his Irish loyalties. He was proud of the fact that he had unearthed a valuable volume that had belonged to the martyred Oliver Plunkett.[142] When Plunkett was eventually canonised, the 93-year-old Liston wrote to the Irish College saying that he was 'moved to tears' by reading Plunkett's story in *l'Osservatore Romano*. He reported, 'in 1902 I found as librarian for Cardinal Moran a small volume of St Thomas with the Blessed Oliver's signature. H[is] E[minence] told me where to find it!'[143] Possibly even more valued by him was the fact that, as he wrote, 'at the time of leaving Rome, I had the singular privilege of kneeling for his blessing, 16 September 1903, at the feet of the newly elected Pope Pius X'.[144] In 1935, as he later proudly told a party of schoolchildren, Liston offered mass at the tomb of this pope who had decreed that children could receive communion.[145] In May 1954, he was present at Pius X's canonisation. He called his meeting with the living pope, and his presence at the pope's canonisation, 'treasures of the soul'.[146] If Verdon was to remain 'the' bishop in Liston's mind, then in many respects Pius X was 'the' pope. It may well be that 'the first pope a person sees remains "the pope" for the rest of his life'.[147] But Pius X appears to have impressed Liston more than Leo XIII, whom he had seen two years previously.

The Making of Father Liston

Apart from the six months between Manly and Clonliffe, Liston had spent all the years from the age of 11-and-a-half away from home. How much did loyalty to, and nostalgia for, Clonliffe and the Irish College become Liston's substitutes for a lost family life? We can only speculate. The reality is that while Liston was on the other side of the world, he became an orphan. James Liston senior died on 5 August 1900 of cancer of the oesophagus. He was only 56 years old. Mary Liston died on 14 July 1902 after a long struggle with cancer of the bowel. She was only 55. Each was buried in Dunedin's Southern Cemetery after Bishop Verdon had said a requiem mass in the cathedral, James Gourley being the undertaker.[148] In Rome, it was the rector of the Irish College who personally brought James Michael news of his mother's death.[149] Liston returned to Dunedin late in 1903, over a year later. He paid to have a Station of the Cross in the South Dunedin basilica erected in his parents' memory.[150] In a letter to the rector of the Irish College he wrote,

> I have reached home at last and you can imagine how glad I was, even tho' homecoming has been robbed of its great pleasure. Tho' I miss dear Dad and Mother so much – indeed I never realized what their death meant till I got home – still it is grand to be here again with brother and sisters: all are well, except my elder sister who is very delicate. Of course they are all changed in many ways, except for their love for the returned exile. They do not see much change in me; except in so far as I have grown somewhat and have acquired a lovely brogue.[151]

There is the possibility that this sunny account disguised an impending family tragedy. In her probated will, Mary Liston left more property to James Michael than to her elder son John Patrick, and appointed James joint executor with Father James Coffey, who was later vicar-general of the diocese. James Michael was willed a sum of £600 (to be given on his ordination) over and above the otherwise equal division of the estate among the four siblings.[152] This could be read as no more than a pious Irish mother favouring her priest-son over her lay son, but it is also likely that by 1902 John was already well into the heavy drinking that was to kill him at the early age of 31 in 1909. James Michael destroyed all his purely personal correspondence on his retirement in 1970, and we do not have such letters as he would have received from New Zealand in his years as an overseas student. But it is at least feasible that news of his brother John's binges stimulated the publican's younger son 'at the time of his leaving Rome' to make 'a personal vow never to take drink'.[153] At least one earlier New Zealand Catholic bishop, Pompallier, had been accused by his enemies of being too fond of the bottle.[154] But Liston was unlike Pompallier and decided that altar wine would be the only alcohol to pass his lips.

Upon his return from Rome, the 22-year-old Liston, armed with a Doctorate of Divinity, was not quite old enough to be ordained. According to canon law, candidates for ordination had to have completed their 24th year and had to have passed the fourth year of their formal studies.[155] Liston met the latter criterion but not the former. A final annotation against his name in the Irish College register read, 'Imperitus per aetatem [sed] prominus ad prebyteratum ascendet' (Inexperienced in years [but] worthy to ascend to the priesthood).[156] Bishop Verdon had to seek a dispensation from Propaganda Fide to ordain his under-aged protégé.[157] In December 1903 and January 1904, Liston spent some time in retreat, and some time with family and Dunedin clergy. One priest whom he first came to know in this time was the Wexford-born Father Henry William Cleary, who had been editing the *Tablet* since he came to Dunedin from Australia in early 1898. Cleary's diary for January 1904 records him going on picnics and excursions to the Taieri Mouth with Dan Buckley, Father Coffey, Liston and Liston's two sisters Mary and Anne.[158]

On Sunday 31 January 1904, aged 22 and 8 months, James Michael Liston was ordained by Bishop Verdon in St Joseph's cathedral. He was only the seventh New Zealand-born Catholic priest. The *Tablet* noted that the cathedral was 'densely packed' for the 11 o'clock mass at which he was ordained, most of Dunedin's clergy being in attendance and the occasional sermon being preached by the Jesuit Fr J. Ryan.[159] Later Liston wrote to the Irish College rector that 'it was really the happiest day of my life – even tho' the absence of dear loved ones took away much of the pleasure. My brother and sisters were present and I know they were happy too'.[160]

The young priest had been made by his vocation and his aptitude in study, but also by his Irish heritage and the influence of his parents, of Bishop Verdon and of Father Lynch. He had acquired, in his first schooling and in three seminaries, a large network of clerical friends and associates who would be important to him in later life. Additionally, at both Clonliffe and the Irish College in Rome he had had reinforced a distinctively Irish piety and that characteristic identification with Roman culture and the interests of the pope that was known as 'Romanita'.

By 1904, James Michael Liston had spent nearly half his life in the all-male context of priestly training. He was about to spend the next 16 years in the same context.

CHAPTER II

FATHER LISTON

1904-20

Father Liston was ordained into a diocese that was still growing, but at a slower rate than it had been in the boom years of the late nineteenth century. Catholics made up 12.3 per cent of the population of Otago and Southland, and 11 per cent of the city of Dunedin itself.[1] The *relatio* which Bishop Verdon submitted to Rome in 1908 said there were 24,540 Catholics in the diocese, with 4,350 in Dunedin, 2,000 in South Dunedin and 2,050 in Invercargill. In the whole diocese at that time, there were 63 churches served by 36 priests.[2] There were also 19 Catholic schools with 1,690 pupils in 1896, when Verdon became bishop, and 29 schools with 2,632 pupils in 1918, the year of Verdon's death.[3] The diocese also contained a new seminary, Holy Cross College at Mosgiel, which was the particular care and pride of its founder and first rector, Bishop Verdon.

There had been other Catholic seminaries in New Zealand. Bishop Pompallier had maintained a short-lived one near Auckland.[4] There was a Marist seminary near Napier.[5] But before Holy Cross College was founded, there was no national seminary for secular priests. At a plenary council in Wellington in January 1899, Bishops Redwood, Grimes, Lenihan and Verdon agreed upon the establishment of such a seminary. Verdon, perhaps still motivated by dissatisfaction with the new management of Manly, volunteered to take responsibility for it.[6] Former dean and president of Holy Cross College in Clonliffe, former vice-rector of the Irish College in Rome and former rector of Manly, Verdon took a close interest in every aspect of the new college. He personally designed the college crest and chose the motto 'In Cruce Salus'.[7] In April 1899, he also paid £1,400 for the 11-acre site and the homestead that had belonged to a farming family called Burns, and he bought more land for expansion in April 1907.[8]

Named after Holy Cross in Clonliffe, the seminary was

appropriately opened on the feast of the Holy Cross, 3 May 1900. It had been Verdon's intention to staff it with Irish members of the Congregation of the Missions, commonly known as the Vincentians, but he had to make do with a staff of diocesan priests instead.[9] At first, Holy Cross was a financial burden to the diocese. It was paid for by students' fees, a diocesan seminary fund, and collections from the neighbouring parishes of Mosgiel and Allanton. In return, college staff had to serve these parishes and pay parish expenses. Building projects were sometimes underwritten by legacies, especially from wealthier diocesan priests. For all that, the college ran at a loss for its first five years. Bishops of other dioceses contributed as much as they saw fit. Despite his saintly demeanour, Verdon sometimes came close to complaining about the other bishops' minimal support, especially as the Marist bishops of Wellington and Christchurch were happy to see bright recruits go to their own establishment. 'The weight of supporting the seminary falls to me', he wrote to the rector of the Irish College in Rome.[10] Later he elaborated on this complaint, hinting that perhaps the rector could find some legacies in Ireland to help him out.[11] While he claimed to have paid off all outstanding debts by 1906, he still had to seek Propaganda's permission to take out a seven-year mortgage when he decided to add buildings in 1906-7.[12]

Like Manly, Mosgiel combined a minor with a major seminary. Its secondary school division was abolished only in 1932. It was a very small enterprise to begin with, having a total of eleven students on opening day, 18 students one year later and 25 by 1906.[13] Only three of the original intake were ordained, indicating that a significant number of boys came to Holy Cross in its early years without any clear vocation for the priesthood.

Nevertheless, the roll grew rapidly, and throughout Verdon's remaining episcopate, buildings and other amenities were added. In August 1900, Verdon blessed the foundations for the Italianate chapel, which was consecrated in 1901. In 1905, a brick building was constructed next to the original wooden one. A new wing was added in 1906-7, and in April of 1907 Verdon joined two more acres to the seminary property. By 1918, extensions were made to the chapel. At about the same time, four more acres, including the so-called Lagoon Paddock, were bought to expand the college's playing fields.

Verdon established the custom of holding in the seminary not only retreats for students, but also annual summer retreats for diocesan clergy. Jesuits led the first annual retreats, but soon Australian

Redemptorists took over. Some of them were distinguished preachers, the most notable being Patrick Clune (retreat-master 1906) who later became Archbishop of Perth. Clune returned to conduct a retreat in March 1909 for the first group of students to be ordained as subdeacons.

Verdon himself was rector with John Ryan as vice-rector, assisted by John's brother Michael Ryan and by Michael Headen. The Ryans had been recruited from All Hallows in Ireland. An early crisis in the institution's history came when Verdon dismissed John Ryan as vice-rector in 1901, without giving any reason, provoking unavailing student protests.[14] Only in July 1902 did Verdon appoint his next vice-rector, James Delaney. Meanwhile Michael Headen died of appendicitis, and Verdon himself had to take up his teaching duties for some months.[15] Verdon is usually described as the college's rector until 1910, but it is clear that in these early years most of the practical running of the college was done by the vice-rector. Verdon himself kept the college accounts until 1908, when he turned them over to Michael Ryan and James Liston.

Liston as Teacher at Mosgiel

This, then, was the new seminary to which Liston was assigned as soon as he was ordained. On 4 February 1904, the *Tablet* announced that Patrick O'Neill, who had been teaching at Holy Cross, was being transferred to Oamaru, while James Liston, 'who was ordained last Saturday', was going to Holy Cross. Also joining the staff was Daniel Buckley.[16] Some months previously, Verdon had already made clear his intentions for his two bright young Roman graduates. Before his ordination, Liston wrote to the rector of the Irish College,

> His Lordship is quite rapt [sic] up in the seminary and is making it a great success. He hopes to open next year with 25 students. It is a very charming spot: beautiful grounds and a fine house. He has lately added a lovely chapel – Roman basilica – and refectory etc. I believe I am to take up Philosophy and Mathematics. I feel sure my time there will be happy.[17]

Delaney, Liston, Buckley and Michael Ryan were to be joined (in 1907) by James Kavanagh from Australia.[18] This tiny staff was required to undertake a formidable teaching load. The student body was small, but staff had to prepare lessons covering the range from junior secondary school studies to advanced philosophy and theology. In 1904, a 'full seminary programme' was offered for the first time, and Verdon announced that henceforth all students could matriculate and take university courses while concurrently training for the priesthood. Liston was first assigned classes in philosophy, English, mathematics, plain chant and introductory scripture, while Buckley taught Latin and French and acted as dean.[19] By 1906, Liston was assigned (in a six-day teaching cycle) dogma, philosophy and higher mathematics for four days and sacred scripture for two days.[20]

In the period from 1904 to 1910, physical conditions at the seminary were Spartan and discipline firm. The buildings were bare, undecorated and unheated during the Otago winters. While students were allowed cold showers after games, they were permitted only one hot bath per week. Novel-reading was forbidden. Examinations were held twice yearly. Students could return home for the long summer holidays, but they stayed in college during the 12-day mid-winter holiday, and if they chose to take walks in nearby Mosgiel township, they were strictly forbidden to enter shops.[21] There were some outlets for students' physical energies. Cricket, one of Liston's favourite games, was encouraged by the staff and had a brief vogue, and there were rugged, vigorous hockey competitions.[22] Handball courts were built in 1902, with a regular handball competition and an annual sports day organised from 1904. The rougher game of rugby was not permitted in these early years, as there were strict prohibitions against students laying hands on one another. A debating club was set up in 1904, and students got up regular 'nigger minstrel shows', St Patrick's Day concerts (17 March), foundation day concerts (3 May) and concerts on Bishop Verdon's feast day (23 September).

It is to this early period of Liston's teaching career that there belongs an oft-quoted description written by one of his later colleagues, Edmund Lynch. Lynch placed Liston in a setting of physical privation:

> ... the classrooms, the corridors, the dormitories had an air of monastic bareness and austerity. The College was at the time somewhat below the limits of the material resources of colonial days. For this reason the men who pioneered Mosgiel College had to be physically tough and ready to make the best of available conditions, to accept life and labour in the raw. Nor was the climate then more favourable than it is to-day. All this would seem to provide enough ascetic exercises of self-denial and endurance for even a trappist. Yet Father Liston lived and worked in such conditions, and one observed that he did not ordinarily avail himself of what little bodily comforts the place provided, such as, for example, a fire during winter in his

room. The only concession he seemed willing to make to claims of comfortable living was to wrap himself in his Roman cloak while he sat in the middle of an uncarpeted, austerely furnished room and studied and prepared, often until midnight, lectures for classes (and what a round of classes!), for next day and for six days of the week. The observant eye might have seen near his bed an alarm clock with the hand set for 5:30 next morning. An Erasmus could not have successfully avoided austerities in those Spartan days of Mosgiel's beginnings. But here was a man that cheerfully made asceticism a deliberate part of his daily life.[23]

Lynch's description was written for a commemorative college publication when Liston was Bishop of Auckland. The language is both admiring and diplomatic. Yet it is tempting to find an element of irony here. Elsewhere in the article Lynch indulges in such grand hyperbole that he seems to be slyly suggesting a criticism of Liston's character. 'Will it be surprising', he asks, 'if we admit that it was no child's play to follow, to try to follow, the eager strides of this athlete of Christ?'[24] Is this an encoded way of telling us that Liston was more than a little fanatical in his duties?

Yet if we imagine only young Father Liston, wrapped in his Roman cloak in the small hours of a winter's night single-mindedly preparing lessons, we have to temper this image with an awareness of Liston's pastimes and cultivation of friends. In a sermon on Liston's sacerdotal golden jubilee, Bishop Joyce claimed that 'often in those early days, he rode long distances on horseback to far-flung Catholic communities to say his Mass in the depths of the Otago winter'.[25] This is picturesque and may even be true. But it is more likely that the young priest was riding his belt-driven French motorcycle, one of the first seen in Otago, 'which caused great excitement when it reached 25 miles an hour'.[26] A keen motorist even into his eighties, Liston was proud of this early acquisition and soon moved into driving his own car.[27] Far from being bound to his study and his books, Liston enjoyed travelling around New Zealand. In January 1905, he visited the North Island and called in on Matthew Brodie, who was at that time parish priest of Waihi.[28] In his holidays, he also took extensive motoring tours of the South Island. By 1918, James Coffey was reporting to Bishop Cleary, 'Fr Liston and I had a trip in a Ford car all around the South Island lately, West Coast, Nelson, Blenheim, Kaikoura and home'.[29] There were also Liston's trips to Dunedin to watch test matches.

Like other Mosgiel staff, Liston was regularly called on for diocesan priestly duties outside the seminary. He usually celebrated or preached at solemn high masses for St Patrick's Day, at the cathedral or the South Dunedin basilica.[30] With their training in liturgical music, staff and senior students of Holy Cross assisted the bishop in the solemn ceremonies of Holy Week. Liston was regularly among those who 'chanted' the Passion narrative on Good Friday at St Joseph's, or who preached on Holy Thursday or Easter Saturday (the Easter Sunday sermon in the cathedral was reserved for the bishop).[31] Holy Cross staff and other diocesan clergy also regularly attended, and provided music for, ceremonies of reception and profession for sisters at St Dominic's priory.[32] Liston and others were cantors at special requiem masses. Other special occasions that brought the Mosgiel staff into the city were high masses at the end of Forty Hours Devotions, and the feast day of St Joseph, patron of the cathedral. It was only after Liston was rector of Holy Cross, however, that he himself was frequently called upon to preach. He 'preached an impressive sermon on the Dignity of Priesthood' in 1911, preached the occasional sermon upon the visit of the Apostolic Delegate Cerretti in 1916, and preached when the new sanctuary and altar were blessed at the Church of the Immaculate Conception in 1918.[33] At the seminary, all staff participated in the annual picnic that Verdon held for the St Vincent de Paul orphans. Every January, about 60 orphans spent a day being entertained by Holy Cross staff and students. Later the bishops of Auckland (including Liston) made an orphans' picnic a fixture in their calendar.

A student caricature of Liston in his first year teaching at Mosgiel. Liston preserved this drawing among his papers.

Perhaps more important than this was Liston's part in administering the neighbouring parish. The Catholic parish of Mosgiel had been separated from the parish of Milton only when the seminary was established in 1900.[34] It included Outram, the Church of the Immaculate Conception in Mosgiel and the Church of the Sacred Heart in Allanton. Until the 1930s, the parish was looked after by seminary staff. Liston contributed to the pastoral care of the parish from his earliest days at Holy Cross to his last. The *Tablet* reported him presiding at farewell functions for parishioners in both 1906 and 1920 and (when he was rector of the college) giving permission for the college grounds to be used for a fund-raising parish fete.[35] Liston noted that he personally spent 'five delightful years on ministry' as parish priest of Mosgiel.[36] He was credited with starting the parish school there.[37] In later life, he continued corresponding with former parishioners, and was present at such functions as the golden jubilee of the Church of the Immaculate Conception in 1937.[38] As he was about to leave for Auckland in 1920, the *Tablet* spoke of the 'regret at his pending departure from amongst the people of the district, to whom he has greatly endeared himself'.[39] But in surviving records there is some confusion as to *when* exactly he was parish priest of Mosgiel, as opposed to being simply a member of Holy Cross's pastoral team. The brief parish history does not give specific dates for his personal pastoral care. At a farewell function from Mosgiel in 1920, a Mr A.F. Quelch implied that Liston was Mosgiel's parish priest as a very young priest, before he became rector of Holy Cross in 1910.[40] But the diocese's annual reports on parishes show that it was Liston who filed the reports on Mosgiel parish between 1910 and 1914, in his first years as college rector (after which point the reports were filed by Michael Scanlan and Cecil Morkane).[41] On balance, it seems more likely that Liston was the parish priest in the first years of his rectorship

In his six years as 'professor', the character of James Michael Liston was austere, certainly hard-working, keeping up with a very heavy load of preparation and teaching and additionally contributing to the care of neighbouring parishes, yet also cultivating a wide circle of friends among the clergy and indulging his interests in motoring and spectator sport. By January 1909, when the bishop returned from an extensive *ad limina*, Liston had clearly justified Verdon's academic plans for him.

But it was at this time that Liston suffered a personal tragedy. His brother John Patrick died on 2 February 1909, aged only 31.

Death notices in the *Tablet* are oddly reticent about John Liston's death, not even remarking that he was Father Liston's brother, and in later years James Michael said little about him.[42] The reason can be found in John Liston's death certificate, where the cause of death is given as 'acute alcoholism'.[43] To make matters worse, John Liston, a publican like his father, left behind a large young family. He had married Catherine Lynch in February 1903, and they had had a child almost every year until his death. His death certificate notes that he was the father of five daughters, ranging in age from five years to two weeks. His youngest daughter, Florence Agnes, was born on 21 January 1909. James Michael baptised his infant niece on 5 February 1909, a mere three days after his brother's death.[44] The widowed Catherine Liston, left with this large brood to raise, married the farmer John Boyle less that three years later.[45]

John's death left a profound mark on James Michael, who took his family relationships seriously despite being separated from his siblings for most of his young adulthood.[46] It was Henry William Cleary who said John's requiem mass, and apparently offered Liston many private words of comfort in his bereavement. Liston wrote –

> . . . just a line or two to say how deeply grateful I am for your many prayers and your exceeding great sympathy in my recent trouble. I cannot put into words the comfort you gave me on Wednesday; I can only say that I shall never forget your kindness.[47]

This was one of the more emotional ways in which Liston came to Cleary's attention, strengthening the bond between them and later making Cleary eager to have Liston as his coadjutor-bishop. More lastingly, Liston had his attitudes towards the abuse of alcohol confirmed. As a bishop, one of his most constant pastoral concerns was the welfare of alcoholic men. How much did he think of his brother when, in 1955, blessing the badges of members of the Pioneer Total Abstinence Association, he commended the association's promise 'to abstain from alcoholic drink in reparation to the Sacred Heart of Jesus for sins of excessive drinking'?[48] Or when, in 1967, he praised the work of the Auckland Alcoholism Trust Board?[49] Or when, in 1970, he gave to the *New Zealand Herald* an interview on the abuse of alcohol? 'He concedes', said the reporter, 'that alcohol, as a God-given gift, has its uses, but he insists that acceptance of the drinking of it as an ordinary thing in life is wrong.'[50] Strictly Thomist in its acceptance of the essential goodness of all creation, this statement still suggests a major concession on the part of a pious publican's son who was also an alcoholic's bereaved brother.

Rector of Mosgiel

On 12 December 1909, the first priests to graduate from Holy Cross were ordained – James McMenamin, Thomas Connolly, Leo Daly, Henry Woods, Cornelius Collins and Michael Scanlan, 'a day of joy too deep for words for the bishop', according to an account Liston wrote years later.[51] Verdon was now confident that the seminary had proven itself and that 'a supply of New Zealand-born clergy would be assured for the Church in this country'.[52] He decided to withdraw himself from direct administration of the college. Michael Ryan, the last of the college's original staff, resigned and prepared to return to Ireland. The time was right to put Liston in complete control.

Some sources assume that Verdon was rector until 1910.[53] Others use the term for Michael Ryan's three years of practical administration, 1907-10.[54] The reality appears to be that Verdon had gradually withdrawn from an active role as rector since 1907.[55] Whatever the terminology used for his predecessor, Liston's appointment as chief of the national seminary was an extraordinary vote of confidence by the bishop in a priest who was still only 28 years old. It is one indication that Verdon regarded Liston as a favourite and possible successor. Liston's appointment was interpreted by some as a new beginning for the college. James Coffey stated that Liston, as the first bishop's subordinate with full authority over Holy Cross, 'had had to create the traditions of the college'.[56] A later rector claimed that Liston 'had the greatest influence on the spirit of the seminary'.[57]

In the ten years that he was rector, Liston continued to work with a very small staff. In 1910, his first vice-rector was Daniel Buckley. The rest of the teaching staff consisted of James Kavanagh, the newly-ordained alumnus Michael Scanlan and Cecil John Morkane, who succeeded Liston as rector in 1920.

There were changes in staff during Liston's rectorship. Buckley left in 1912 to take up a position at the cathedral. James Kavanagh was away for all of 1912, returned for two years, then left permanently in 1915. He was succeeded by Edmund Lynch. Michael Scanlan fell ill in 1918, and for two years Daniel Vincent Silk, on loan from Auckland diocese, acted as his substitute. Silk was to be a parish priest to a venerable age in Auckland, under Liston's authority. In 1918, he was described as 'a good man, [who] spent a number of years in Propaganda and speaks Italian'.[58] In persuading Silk to take up his Mosgiel posting in 1918, Bishop Cleary wrote to him:

I believe that you would greatly enjoy the experience of temporary work down there, especially in association with so entirely lovable a man as Father Liston, the Rector of the College.[59]

At the same time Liston wrote to the Galway-born Silk, reassuring him that he would find the small staff of Mosgiel ethnically and socially congenial:

Collins you met in Auckland, Scanlan is one of our own, Lynch is a Waterford man, whilst Morkane and I were both fortunate enough to spend some of our student days in Rome.[60]

By 1920, the complete teaching staff under Liston consisted of Morkane, Lynch, Collins, Silk and Edwin Arthur Anderson, a convert from Anglicanism who had been ordained at Holy Cross in 1919, and in 1950 was still being described as 'the first and only convert to be ordained to the priesthood'.[61]

This small staff of five or six taught a full secondary school curriculum, ran courses in theology and philosophy, and prepared senior students for university examinations. Otago University exempted Holy Cross students from attendance at lectures, which meant that Holy Cross staff provided all their tuition, as well as running junior and post-primary, sub-matriculation and matriculation classes. In his final report as rector, Liston noted that Holy Cross took junior students through the matriculation course in three years (even though it was laid down in the university calendar as a four-year course). They taught theology as a four-year course, comprising moral theology, dogma, sacred scripture, church history, liturgy, preaching and scholastic philosophy. Those students who chose to do a three-year university degree chose their subjects from among mental science (logic and psychology), French, English, Latin, mathematics, economics, constitutional history and jurisprudence (but not ethics, history or philosophy, where courses set by the University of Otago – and possibly attitudes inculcated – would have been in conflict with courses in which Holy Cross specialised).[62] Small wonder that in a letter to Michael Curran, Liston said of this period of his career, 'I have certainly had a busy life – teaching, acting as bursar and dean and rector of a college took up 17 hours out of 24'.[63]

How effective was Liston as rector of Holy Cross College? More to the point, how well did he relate to staff and students? Was he unnecessarily disciplinarian or did he simply reflect the norms of Tridentine-style seminaries of that era? Surviving evidence has to be read with caution. Most appears in respectful church publications

Above: Teaching staff at Holy Cross College, Mosgiel, when Liston began there. Standing – Cecil Morkane and Daniel Buckley. Seated – P.J. O'Neill, James Delaney (deputy rector), D. O'Neill, Liston.
Below: Liston as rector of Holy Cross, Mosgiel, with his staff, early 1920.
Back row – Daniel Silk, Edmund Lynch, Cornelius Collins. Front row – Edwin Anderson, Liston, Cecil Morkane.

dating from Liston's lifetime. Comments are uniformly laudatory in such publications. Any criticisms (if they are such) are implied only, or are veiled in euphemism.

Typical of their laudatory tone was a speech made in Liston's presence in 1954, on the occasion of his sacerdotal golden jubilee. Students at Mosgiel, said the speaker, recognised Liston's –

> . . . fidelity to his duty, his constant appreciation of the high ideals of the Priesthood, his unwavering adherence to first principles. They also recall with gratitude his fatherly kindness in every student difficulty, his ready help in every troubled problem. The chilly corridors of the old Mosgiel were the warmer for his presence . . .[64]

A similar impression is offered in a sermon preached shortly after Liston's death by his former student, Francis Finlay. During the great influenza epidemic at the end of the First World War, Liston was said to have 'segregated the sick students and nursed them single-handed himself so that no one else would go in danger of infection'.[65] Though students formed a daily 'gargle parade' during this 1918 outbreak, it would appear that Mosgiel did not lose a single student to it. An enthusiastic judgement was made in the New Zealand hierarchy's reports to the apostolic delegate as they recommended Liston for the episcopate. He had occupied the role of rector for nine years, they said, 'with remarkable success from the spiritual and scholastic, as well as the financial, points of view' and had been a great success as the college's spiritual director.[66] The college's financial burdens were considerable during Liston's tenure. He was aware that not all the bishops supported the institution with equal enthusiasm.[67] Students were in residence for 46 of the 52 weeks of the year, yet the yearly pension was only £46. In effect, Liston had to feed and house students (and pay domestic staff) on the basis of £1 per student per week.[68] In his last report as rector, Liston was able to say, 'it has been a hard struggle to pay our way since the war, the cost of living having at least doubled', but that 'there is no debt whatsoever on College property'. He also opined,

> . . . unless I am much mistaken, there is an excellent spirit of discipline, earnestness, study [and] piety in the house. I have always found the boys very easy to handle: they take correction well.[69]

If all this sounds like conventional praise (and self-praise), there is good evidence that Liston implemented some humane reforms. From 1910, he allowed students to play rugby, 'the great safety valve', in jerseys and shorts. Up to that point, soutanes were required during sporting activities. Liston also permitted students to go into the city on the days before and after their main examinations, and from 1916 onwards permitted them to return home during their 12-day midwinter break (doubtless easing a little of the burden of providing their keep).[70] Liston also did his fair share of teaching at all levels 'from the humble "Who Made You" of the very juniors to the "De Trinitate" of the theologians'.[71] He appears to have impressed favourably at least some of the college's non-Catholic neighbours. Recalling her Mosgiel childhood, Vespa Miller remarked years later, 'to us, he was always "Father" Liston, the kindest, most loving, of all the many students and priests who walked down to those great gates'.[72]

The college had triumphs in its growing roll and impressive number of ordinands. It also had tragedies, like the death of the promising student Francis Yirrell (a convert from Anglicanism) from complications arising from an operation for goitre.[73] Liston made it his business to pick out those promising students who might benefit from extra priestly training in Rome, as he himself had. To Verdon's successor he recommended Hugh O'Neill as one such student, reminding him that he had earlier sent Leonard Buxton to Rome.[74] Liston further seems to have maintained the loyalty of the auxiliary staff. Dora, one of the cooks at Mosgiel, was later to be cook at St Benedict's, Liston's parish in Auckland.[75] Some of his acts of discipline seem perfectly reasonable. The student Gladstone W. Boyd wrote to Bishop Whyte in early 1921, just after Liston's departure for Auckland, begging to be taken back by Holy Cross. Liston had expelled him for his over-familiarity with a local woman. But as Boyd had already been expelled from the Marist seminary at Greenmeadows for similar behaviour, Liston appears to have shown considerable forbearance in taking him on as a student in the first place. Whyte refused to take Boyd back.[76]

Against this generally positive account of Liston's rectorship must be set the criticisms. Not all found Liston as 'entirely lovable' as Bishop Cleary did. Joe Martin, at Mosgiel from 1915, found Liston a 'cold' figure who enforced the rules against smoking rather too strictly, insisted that even the junior students had to be attired in collar, tie and soutane, and would not allow Martin to go home when his father became sick and his mother needed help in running a farm. Martin also told an anecdote suggesting Liston's rigidity of character:

> One night when I was pulling out my blankets to make my bed, I felt sure that a rat shot out and disappeared into the old fire place. Next

day I called John Rohan and we strolled round the backyard near the kitchen where a few rabbit traps were stored. It was forbidden ground to the students. I pulled out an old trap, set it to see if it would work, when from nowhere appeared the Rector. 'What are you doing here?' he blurted out in no pleasant voice. 'Trying to catch a rat', I casually replied. 'We have no rats, so get out', he said. I set the trap again, sprung it and said to John that it would work all right. 'Get out', he said, and from the tone of his voice, I knew what he meant! I set the trap in the dormitory that afternoon, and in the evening when I disturbed the blanket, a rat ran out, and stepped into the trap. The butt end of a rifle, which we Territorials were provided with, finished off the rat. And next morning I threw trap, with rat still attached, onto the back door where everyone could see. I do not know what happened to the trap and rat, but both disappeared, and from the looks that I got I understood that I won that round. Or did I?[77]

In his unpublished memoirs, Bishop John Mackey tells how Liston expelled Edward ('Ted') Lyons from Holy Cross 'because, I think, he came back late having stayed on at home for family reasons – a funeral possibly'. Bishop Cleary, to whose diocese the student belonged, refused to accept this judgement on Lyons. Cleary funded Lyons to study at Manly, and Lyons went on to have a long career as an Auckland diocesan priest.[78] There was also some private criticism of Liston's expulsion of the Auckland student Hugh Magill, although in this case Cleary did not want Magill for his diocese.[79] Bishop Leonard Boyle reports an elderly priest telling him that students in Liston's time found Liston a demanding master. Approximately once a fortnight he would visit a friend in South Dunedin, and whenever he paid such visits he would wear, under his soutane, different trousers from his everyday wear. Students watched out eagerly for his 'South Dunedin' trousers, knowing that this was the signal for at least one evening of relaxed horseplay. Years later, after Liston had founded *Zealandia* newspaper, one mischievous Holy Cross alumnus supplied his privy with 'Zealandia' brand lavatory paper whenever Liston was visiting him.[80]

Rather more cutting are the veiled criticisms in Edmund Lynch's apparently eulogistic account. Lynch says that at Holy Cross 'there was present what one may describe as a reverential apprehension of doing ought that might displease him'. (Does this mean that students and staff were scared of Liston?) 'The staff and main body of the students were caught up in the whirlwind of his enthusiasm. That his collaborators were ever willing did not admit of any doubt.'

(Does this mean that Liston made too many demands?) 'Although Father Liston was always kind and considerate . . . he was a strict disciplinarian. The rules of the college were there to be kept and with this understanding there was never any compromise.' (This presumably means what it says.)[81]

Liston (like Verdon) seems essentially to have been shy and withdrawn in his demeanour. He had at least one area of great sensitivity, likely to burden any teacher in an all-male establishment. This was his supremely imitable voice, lifelong butt of rude mimicry, with its strange falling sonority and lengthened vowels. He had an operation on his nose, apparently in the summer holidays of 1918-19. To Cleary in 1920, Liston declared, 'I have had no trouble with my voice since the nasal operation 18 months ago'.[82] But the voice remained subject for comment. In typically double-edged fashion, Edmund Lynch wrote that Liston's lectures at Holy Cross were –

> . . . delivered in a voice that was always subdued, even-toned, unemotional, such lectures demanded a degree of attention and alertness that engaged all the physical and mental energy of students bent on getting them down, so far as possible, word for word in their notebooks.[83]

This appears to be a sly way of saying that Liston's voice made his lectures hard to follow.

Peter Norris's conclusion is that Liston 'did not win the hearts of the College students'.[84] While this may well be true, it is worth asking how many seminarians felt a warm regard for rectors in those days anyway. As John Mackey has observed, pre-Vatican II seminaries aspired to be 'total communities', cutting students off as much as possible from the world and subjecting them to a standard pattern of discipline.[85] Was Liston harsh even by those standards? Possibly. One commentator implied criticism by noting that Liston's successor, Cecil Morkane, deliberately relaxed discipline in the belief that it was better for students to learn 'self-control'.[86] Even so, it is probably fairest to see Liston's approach as of a piece with his generally paternalistic conception of church authority and of what a seminary should be.[87] Like Manly, Holy Cross in its early days had to accommodate young schoolboys. In its first 20 years of existence, only 32 per cent of its students reached ordination, as compared to 52 per cent of students in the 1930s.[88] This suggests the extent to which the junior school accommodated youngsters who were not really set in a vocation to the priesthood. Some senior students became impatient with a rector whose pattern of discipline was as much intended for naughty adolescents as for maturing young adults. Their impatience would have been exacerbated by physical conditions which, as even one sympathetic observer recalled, continued to be Spartan.[89]

Teaching, acting as rector and ministering to neighbouring parishes were not Liston's only official duties in these years. By 1911, he was part of Bishop Verdon's diocesan Council of Vigilance, whose brief was to examine any matters potentially harmful to Catholic faith and morals as well as having a veto over what appeared in Catholic newspapers and periodicals.[90] In the same spirit, Liston was, in 1913, part of a special diocesan committee of the Catholic Federation charged with drawing up 'a suitable list of Catholic works' to recommend to librarians.[91] He was also becoming a familiar name to a wider public than his parishioners or students. He provided the *Tablet* with apologetic material, theological expositions and the occasional controversial article. In 1908, he wrote two articles replying to a book on the doctrine of Atonement by the Presbyterian clergyman Gibson Smith of Wellington.[92] Six years later he contributed a negative review of the (silent) film version of Max Reinhardt's spectacular play production, *The Miracle*, criticising it on the theological grounds that it did not adequately emphasise remorse.[93]

There is the strong possibility, too, that it was Liston who used the signature 'Ghimel' for the apologetic series, 'Stand Fast in the Faith' ('A Weekly Instruction') which began appearing in the *Tablet* in 1912.[94] Ghimel is a letter of the Hebrew alphabet used to introduce some of the Lamentations of Jeremiah. Until the Second Vatican Council, priests chanted the Lamentations, and their introductory letters, in the Tenebrae of Holy Week. Ghimel is usually pronounced with a hard 'G'. But if pronounced with a soft 'G', 'Ghimel' would be a very appropriate pseudonym for James Michael Liston, 'Jim L.' or 'J.M.L.'. In the years 1916 and 1917, apologetic articles by 'C.M.' (Cecil Morkane) and 'C.J.C.' (Cornelius Collins) frequently appeared in the *Tablet*, but there are none by 'J.M.L.'. It would be odd if Liston did not make contributions similar to those of his two Holy Cross subordinates.

The Sectarian Setting

In the later years of the First World War (1916 to 1918), Liston, with Verdon's approval, defended the church's position on a number of issues in the letters columns of the *Evening Star* and the *Otago Daily Times*, as well as in the *Tablet*. The tone and full import of his letters can be understood only in the context of sectarian tensions that were at their worst in New Zealand about that time. Religious controversy and anti-Catholic feeling were not new to these years.[95] Protestants took exception to the papal *Ne Temere* decree on marriage.[96] Catholics opposed the Protestant Bible-in-Schools movement, which aimed to introduce Bible instruction into state schools.[97] Prohibition of alcohol was supported by some Protestant churches but opposed by most Catholics.[98] There were Protestant rumours about the supposed favouritism of the Catholic prime minister Sir Joseph Ward (1906-12) towards Catholics in the civil service.[99] There was also what amounted to a crisis in Protestant self-definition. Among Protestants, real church-going was declining drastically and it was becoming problematic to describe New Zealand as a 'Protestant nation'.[100] The most notorious anti-Catholic polemic of this period, J. Dickson's *Shall Ritualism and Romanism Rule in New Zealand?* (1912) spends as much space attacking 'Catholic' tendencies in Protestant churches as it spends attacking Catholicism.[101]

Before the First World War, there were also the beginnings of a shift in Catholic political sympathies away from the Liberal Party. After 1916, this led Catholics to identify more with the Labour Party.[102] Some Catholic spokesmen, like Liston, took Leo XIII's encyclical *Rerum Novarum* as a charter to embrace the interests of the working class.[103] The New Zealand Labour Party was never a Catholic fiefdom, but Catholics had little inclination to support the Reform Party, which harboured some anti-Catholic sentiment. Catholic clergy maintained a diplomatic neutrality during the industrial dispute in Waihi in 1912.[104] Catholic bishops kept on good terms with the strike executive during the maritime dispute of 1913-14.[105] For the extreme fringe of Protestantism, this conjured up the phantasm of an alliance between Catholicism and revolutionary socialism.

But it took the peculiar stresses of the First World War to make sectarianism really raucous. The Catholic Federation had been set up in 1913, but only in 1917 did the militantly anti-Catholic Protestant Political Association grow out of the Orange Lodge. A war of words ensued between the PPA's Howard Elliott and James Kelly, newly-appointed editor of the *Tablet*.[106] Given the martial language that was then a staple of religious rhetoric, it is easy to exaggerate the depths of religious animosities in these years.[107] There is little evidence of strife between different congregations in local communities, leaders of the mainstream churches maintained cordial relations with one another, and few Anglicans or Presbyterians supported the PPA, which attracted members from smaller, marginal Protestant groups.[108] Nevertheless, in the wartime atmosphere, there was some Protestant unease over the limited reach of Protestantism as a factor in world affairs.[109] Militant Protestants chose to see the Catholic church as potentially disloyal to the war effort on the three interlocking issues of papal neutrality, the Irish struggle for self-determination, and the long drawn-out controversy over conscription and military service.[110] On each of these issues, Liston made polemical contributions to Dunedin's secular press.

New Zealand Catholics, still largely of recent Irish descent, had always celebrated their cultural heritage in many harmless and non-controversial ways.[111] More chauvinistic Irish utterances were rare. This cultural landscape changed with Ireland's Easter Rising and then with the dogged resistance to the introduction of conscription in Ireland.[112] At first, the *Tablet* reflected official Catholic opinion by vigorously denouncing the Rising. Father Coffey preached in St Joseph's Cathedral against the rebels and a *Tablet* editorial, headed 'The Made-in-Germany Rebellion', rebuked the 'insane plot' of Casement, Connolly and 'the notorious Larkin'.[113] Up to this time, the *Tablet* was as patriotically pro-war as other New Zealand newspapers.[114] But New Zealand's Catholic attitude towards the Irish rebels changed gradually in the later months of 1916. Writing from a hospital bed in Dublin, Bishop Cleary said in June 1916, 'the repressive measures taken by the Government have won [the rebels] wide sympathy and probably made ten Sinn Feiners where there was one before'.[115] In Dunedin, an Irish Relief Fund was set up for those Irish who had suffered in the Rising and repression. Liston was among the hundreds of clergy and laity who made a contribution.[116] More significantly, James Kelly became editor of the *Tablet* early in 1917 and moved to a more Sinn Fein-oriented outlook.[117] In March 1917, he produced an article, 'Easter Week in Dublin', giving a positive account of the insurgents and the policies of Sinn Fein.[118]

Much of the Catholic community shifted from its pre-war support for the Irish parliamentary nationalists. A more assertive Irishness was evident when the Dunedin Diocesan Synod of priests (of which Liston was a member) passed a resolution in January 1918 calling for the teaching of Irish history in Catholic schools, and another endorsing the new editorial policies of the *Tablet*.[119] The way was being prepared for Archbishop Redwood's declaration, at the Australasian Irish Race Convention in late 1919, in favour of de Valera and complete Irish independence.[120] And while respectable

Catholic opinion was changing, there was the matter of *Green Ray*, the anti-conscription Sinn Fein paper which lasted in Dunedin from November 1916 until it was suppressed by the police in July 1918 and its owner and editor were jailed.[121] For more militant Protestants, it was further evidence of Catholic revolutionism.

Apart from his obvious support for relief funds and for the resolutions of the diocesan synod, what was Liston's position over the Irish question at this time? One student claims that 'although a born New Zealander, he devoted himself to the Sinn Fein cause with an intensity that contrasted with the austerity of his personal manner'.[122] Ireland seems to have been a major element in his shift of sympathy to the Labour Party, which at this time was quite consciously courting Catholic Irish support in its declarations of solidarity with the Irish struggle.[123]

All this was a red rag to the Protestant bull, especially given the strong Ulster-Orange connections of the Protestant Political Association (and of William Ferguson Massey).[124] The years 1917-18 were the awful climax of the First World War, and as casualty lists grew and patriotism intensified, 'expressions of support for the Irish rebels became more dangerous'.[125] Among the handful of draft-dodgers in New Zealand were at least some Irish Catholics.[126] The press filled with letters denouncing disloyal Irish Catholics who subjected themselves to a pope who would not take sides in the great world struggle.

It was in this heated context that Liston's letters to the daily press appeared, from 1916 to 1918, with Verdon's tacit approval. In August 1916, he wrote a series of them to the Dunedin *Evening Star*, refuting the Rev Stanley Jenkin's anti-papal correspondence. Jenkin had objected to Benedict XV's peace proposals as anti-British, claimed that there were far more Catholics in the Central Powers than among the Allies and wondered why the pope was neutral when right was so obviously on Britain's side. Liston's replies made a number of shrewd points, referring to the pope's quiet diplomacy and to his public protests at German atrocities in Belgium. In referring to the pope's philanthropic works, he raised an issue that had often irked Irish nationalists in New Zealand – the partiality of cable reports:

> It may be that several facts mentioned here are new to the Rev. Mr. Jenkin, for they have not appeared in the cables. But after two years of war news most people know that the cables don't report everything, and, to put it mildly, don't always give the exact truth . . . The simple truth is that neither side would at present brook

interference in this life-and-death struggle, and Benedict XV, wise with the accumulated wisdom of the Papacy during nineteen centuries, sees that any pronouncement about its justice would not stop the war, and would for long ages irritate and place in a more war-like condition than ever those against whom the decision might be given.[127]

In March 1917, Liston wrote to the *Otago Daily Times* defending the new editorial tone of the *Tablet* and protesting at the *Times*'s editorial assertion that Ireland now 'stinks in the nostrils of all decent people' for its rebelliousness and disloyalty to the empire. Liston referred in detail to the large number of Irish serving as British imperial troops, 'conveniently forgotten except when their names appear in casualty lists'.[128] In November and December of the same year, Liston duelled verbally with John Dickie, Professor of Systematic Theology at Knox College. Antagonistic towards Catholicism and (since the outbreak of the war) profoundly anti-German, Dickie was at this time wont to make sneering comments about the Irish. Ireland was, said Dickie, 'pampered and spoon-fed at the expense of Great Britain, and like other spoiled children becoming more unreasonable the more it is indulged . . . seething with intrigue and disloyalty'. Again, Liston wrote to the *Otago Daily Times*, refuting Dickie by chronicling Irish service in the war, and calculating the numbers of Catholics serving the Central Powers and the number serving the Allies.[129]

In June and July of 1918, as resistance to conscription in Ireland became more evident, Liston was again in the correspondence columns. In this case, he faced a group of enraged Protestants. Alex Finlayson asserted that Ireland's Cardinal Logue had no right to make statements about conscription. 'Obvious' commented that 'the powerful sect' of the Jesuits was headed by a German and 'the inference that may be drawn is obvious'. S.G. Griffith (a Church of Christ evangelist and prohibitionist) claimed that all the pope's diplomacy was aimed at advancing German interests, and that if (as Liston said) Catholic Belgians had suffered heroically in the war, it had nothing to do with their Catholicism. P. Mulroy called the Catholic church in Ireland a 'stumbling block' to the war effort. To all of these charges, Liston wrote long and temperately-worded replies. He claimed that there was 'no Catholic principle at stake' in the issue of conscription in Ireland. He replied to other correspondents' declared concern for the welfare of oppressed small countries by quoting Sydney Smith on the blindness of the British to their own misdeeds in Ireland, the oppressed small country at their back door. As evidence that the Irish had every right to reject conscription, he also referred to the two defeats of conscription referenda that had taken place in Australia. In this exchange of letters, Liston had only one supporter, who signed himself 'Bonnie Play'.[130]

Lest the views of his opponents be thought marginal to Dunedin Protestantism, it is instructive to read the report on a 'Special Protestant Service' that was held at Knox Church at about the same time. Before a large congregation, Dickie and the Rev R.E. Davies denounced from the pulpit 'the Church of Rome' which 'had never known any principle except her own self-interest', condemned the Catholic 'dupes and tools' who had followed the bishops' lead in resisting conscription in Ireland, and declared that 'it could not be disproved that the Vatican was behind the Central Powers' in the war. The Catholic church had 'paraded her disloyalty' in Australia and would 'use' the Labour movement to win advantages.[131] As a very public spokesman for the church in Dunedin, Liston was answering this level of accusation as the question of Ireland meshed with questions of the ongoing conduct of the war.

The Conscription Controversy

Since 1912, there had been compulsory territorial training for Mosgiel's senior seminarians. James Allen, the Minister of Defence, had early refused a request for the exemption of ecclesiastical students.[132] Mosgiel students did an evening of military drill each week and had to attend an annual training camp. The bishops' protests were muted. Once war broke out, despite aspersions some Protestants cast on the pope's neutrality, the Catholic church in New Zealand had a conventionally patriotic attitude. *Tablet* editorials waxed patriotic over the departure of the New Zealand Expeditionary Force (NZEF).[133] Requiem masses for fallen Catholic soldiers were routinely reported.[134] By 1917, there were 14,000 Catholics in uniform (about half of them overseas on active service).[135] Many column inches were being devoted to Bishop Cleary's eyewitness accounts (with a strongly patriotic tone) of his experiences as a chaplain on the Western Front.[136] Seven of the 14 serving New Zealand Catholic chaplains were Mosgiel graduates. College staff and students suffered bereavements. Chaplain-Major James McMenamin, one of Mosgiel's first ordinands in 1909, survived Gallipoli but was killed in France (at Messines) in 1917, while ministering to forward trenches.[137] Bishop Verdon said the requiem mass for him at Holy Cross in the presence of Liston and the whole student body.[138] Lt Michael McKeefry, elder brother of the Mosgiel student Peter McKeefry, was killed in France in 1918.[139] On the whole, Catholics, including those at Holy Cross, 'march[ed] to the same drum as most of their compatriots'.[140]

It was in 1917, however, that wholehearted Catholic participation in this patriotic consensus came under threat. In the Military Service Act, clergy, religious teachers and theological students were not exempted from conscription, even though clergy and members of religious orders were routinely exempted in other British Empire countries. In the first conscription ballot in November 1916, a number of priests and other clergy were called up, including Liston, James Kelly and Bishop Brodie.[141] Allen, the Minister of Defence, met with the Catholic hierarchy and assured them that priests and theological students would receive certificates of exemption which they could present to the local Military Service Boards. Liston, Brodie, Kelly and other conscripted clergy went through the performance of presenting themselves to their local boards and were duly exempted. But the Military Service Boards were independent and not obliged to honour the certificates of exemption, as Allen tactlessly reminded them in a public speech. In February 1917, appeals of two Mosgiel students against conscription were turned down by the Wellington board. In March, two more were turned down by the Dunedin board. To Archbishop O'Shea, as to Liston and others, it seemed that Massey's government was intent on destroying the church's major source of personnel. Loud protests were lodged by O'Shea, by the *Tablet* and by Liston. In April 1917, the government, in conference with the chairmen of the Military Service Boards, agreed that clergy and theological students in their last four years of training would be exempted automatically from conscription.

While this ruling applied equally to all religious denominations, it seemed to more zealous Protestants that Catholics had won an unfair concession. This was especially so as Catholics pushed for the exemption from conscription of Catholic teaching brothers, for whom there was no Protestant equivalent. For the first time in his career, Sir Joseph Ward bestirred himself on behalf of Catholics, and pressed in parliament for the exemption of all teachers.[142] Protestant jeers were heard about what they called the 'Marist Brothers Protection Bill'.[143] Ward's proposal passed the House of Representatives, but was rejected by the upper house, the Legislative Council, which was more firmly controlled by Massey's Reform Party.

It was in this context that sectarianism took on a new vehemence in New Zealand. The conscription question was added to the Irish question and to long-standing suspicions about Catholic 'loyalty'. As conscription was being hotly debated, Howard Elliott's PPA was formed in July 1917. Although it had no basis in fact, there was a Protestant myth that New Zealand Catholics were 'shirkers' and had not volunteered for military service as readily as their Protestant compatriots.[144] There was also the fact that Protestant churches had not objected to their theological students, or even their clergy, volunteering for military service. Some Protestant theological colleges had virtually emptied for the duration of the war.[145] And all this was played out against the background of Australia's two referenda on conscription.[146] Twice, conscription was defeated. Sectarian tensions were raised, and militant Australian Protestants could believe that Catholics (and revolutionary trade-unionists) had frustrated the will of loyal British imperialists. The Australian Howard Elliott was ready to persuade his followers that New Zealand's difficulties with conscription were of a piece with the vast Catholic conspiracy he believed was engulfing his native country.

In the midst of this debate, Liston, as rector of Holy Cross, attempted to keep his public utterances civil. In a letter to the *Otago Daily Times* in February 1917, replying to Rev W. Finlayson, he emphasised the idea that, while honouring patriotism, the church also had to answer to a higher calling:

> The highest authorities of our Church have taught us not that the flag of our country is a commercial asset of fluctuating value, and to be treated accordingly; but that we are all bound by our very law of nature to love and cherish our native land. If I may speak for myself, I was born here, have lived here and worked here – not to make money, but, according to the measure of my abilities, simply and solely to further the spiritual interests of my parishioners and to educate Christian youth for the priesthood . . . In doing all this – others have done far more – I consider I have done the state no mean service – enough at any rate to fling back the insult conveyed in the suggestion that priests are aliens. Indeed it is just because we are subjects that we claim, and will continue to claim, that the Government of the day shall respect the religious feelings and instincts of ourselves and our Catholic people in this matter . . . Of course I have ties and duties other than those most sacred ones that bind me to the country and the King. But what of that? Hasn't a Christian minister, like Mr. Finlayson, duties to laws higher than the civil law, and obligations to God which must be fulfilled at every sacrifice? . . . all of us, non-Catholics as well as Catholics, have duties to God as well as to Caesar.[147]

Liston noted that, despite charges to the contrary, there was no preferential treatment for Catholic clergy in the matter of certificates of exemption. All denominations could avail themselves of them, 'miserable and humiliating' though the procedure was.

Certainly Liston did not publicly endorse James Kelly's (privately-expressed) view that the Catholic hierarchy had brought trouble upon itself by not pressing harder for exemptions when conscription legislation was first debated.[148] But once the refusal of exemptions for theological students had happened, his tone became more militant. In a letter on conscription to the *Tablet* in late March, he wrote:

> It seems all too true that, thanks to a policy of bigotry, political cowardice and treachery, we are at the present moment threatened with the conscription of theological students at Greenmeadows and Mosgiel. Within the past week, four of our students called up in ballot have been refused exemption by Military Appeal Boards . . . Some of these students will be ordained this year, others next year, a third batch in 1919, and a fourth in 1920 . . . They mean much to us in this corner of the globe; they mean nothing, absolutely nothing, to the Allied army of twelve millions . . . If the theological students of Mosgiel are conscripted . . . it will mean that the sacrifices made in men and money for the past seventeen years to build up an ecclesiastical college are to be without their due reward . . . It would be a cruel blow to see the seminary turned into a preparatory school for Trentham.[149]

In the following issue of the *Tablet*, there was a report of devotions held in Mosgiel parish church for the general intention of preventing 'the terms of the Military Service Act being applied to the priests, brothers and ecclesiastical students'.[150] Liston's more pugnacious tone at this time was in keeping with his private views as expressed in a letter to Monsignor Mahoney in Auckland. Liston wrote:

> Edward Lyons's appeal was dismissed today. Father Coffey had a big battle of an hour's length with the Board. The Labour member was favourable, the farmer's rep not unfavourable, but the Magistrate (a wowser) lead against us. . . . they seem to be smarting under the treatment they received from Allen – first being told to exempt on the strength of the certificate, and then being told they were not bound to follow it . . . Isn't it up to us to take no more notice of the whole business, and if they want these students let them come and take them?[151]

After the government's decision (in April 1917) about senior theological students, Liston took practical steps to prevent Holy Cross seniors being marched off to Trentham. Some students in the philosophy classes were called up and served in the medical corps. But those in the last years of arts studies were promoted into theology classes so that they met the government's criterion of being within the last four years of their studies.[152] Ordination for some was sped up. As Liston wrote in his final report as rector in 1920, 'the Conscription menace forced us to give Tonsure and Minor Orders in 1917 to all the Theologians'.[153]

What was the outcome of this whole controversy for Mosgiel? Not one single recruit was netted for New Zealand's Expeditionary Force. For members of religious orders, appeals against conscription were adjourned *sine die*, in effect offering a blanket exemption. Even the threat hanging over the Marist brothers passed once the government agreed that it was better to leave all schools open.[154] By April 1918, Liston was writing to Bishop Cleary that 'the danger is over for the present and we are not likely to be worried by the Defence authorities'.[155] In 1940, when conscription again became an issue during the Second World War, a Labour government automatically exempted staff and students of Holy Cross from military service, and there was no replay of the controversies of 1917-18.[156]

The Making of Bishop Liston

As rector of Holy Cross, Liston had weathered a very public controversy, but he was now about to be plunged into a more intense struggle that was to have longer-term consequences for him. On 23 November 1918, at St Gerard's Redemptorist monastery in Wellington, Bishop Verdon died.[157] His health had been sinking for a number of years.[158] James Coffey had had his own quarrels with Verdon over the years, but the consultors put him in charge of the diocese as Vicar-Capitular as soon as the bishop died.[159]

The loss of Verdon was a great blow to Liston, who wrote the 'Appreciation' that appeared in the *Tablet*.[160] He was widely believed to be Verdon's chosen successor. This was the impression that the Apostolic Delegate Cerretti had gained in his visit in 1916.[161] He would have endorsed Bishop Cleary's judgement when, in 1913, Cleary had picked Liston as a possible future Bishop of Dunedin and had described him as a 'really excellent man ... an old Propagandist, an outstanding man, pious, brainy, prudent, learned: just the man'.[162] Liston had been one of the two trustees of Verdon's will since 1906, when he was already being groomed for the role of seminary rector.[163] But it was to be over two years from Verdon's death to the consecration of a new bishop of Dunedin, and that successor was not Liston. From November 1918 to the middle of

1920, prolonged negotiations took place between the bishops, the clergy of Dunedin, the Apostolic Delegate in Sydney and the Vatican. Until the *Tablet* and the *Month* carried announcements about the new appointee in April and May of 1920, these manoeuvres were officially confidential, but Liston was fully aware of the rumours and gossip that circulated about him in the small clerical circles. One history states that 'the senior priests [of Dunedin] opposed the appointment [of Liston] and succeeded in having their own candidate replace him'.[164] This is only half true. The senior priests of Dunedin rejected Liston, but the new bishop was not their choice either.

In December 1918, while still mourning the loss of Verdon, Bishop Brodie confidently expressed the belief that either Liston or Coffey would win the Dunedin priests' *terna* voting.[165] The bishops' own preference was for Liston. Voting, delayed by the 'flu epidemic, took place after the 'month's mind' for Verdon on 15 January 1919.[166] Dunedin priests named Michael O'Farrell, an Australian missioner who had given retreats at Mosgiel, as their first choice (*dignissimus*) with 10 votes.[167] Coffey was second (*dignior*) with four votes. Liston came a poor third (*dignus*) with only three votes.[168] If we are to believe a letter he wrote at the end of 1919, Coffey effectively ruled himself out of contention, declaring that by education and disposition he was 'absolutely unfit' for the position of bishop.[169] But the voting was still a resounding rejection of the heir apparent, with added insult in the priests' selection of a complete outsider.

What caused this rejection? At this time, James Kelly was still a friend of Liston's. He had long planned to visit Liston from his parish in Taranaki and had finally had a happy reunion with him at Mosgiel in 1916.[170] Kelly was defended by Liston when Bishop Cleary first brought his charges against the aggressive tone of the new editor of the *Tablet*.[171] A year and a half later, Kelly was still citing Liston as his ally when the *Tablet* was criticised.[172] Yet in his private correspondence with the Irish College rector John Hagan, Kelly, the indefatigable gossip, tore apart his friend's character, providing his explanation of why Liston had been rejected. Before the Dunedin *terna* voting, he wrote of Liston,

> . . . he is a very old friend of mine and I admire him very much; but Coffey would be my selection if I were compelled to select the man likely to make the best bishop. You know the old story about the narrow horizon of a man who has never been out of College. That is the danger with Liston. Unknowingly he is narrow and obstinate . . .[173]

In March 1919, Kelly was telling Hagan that Coffey would not make a good bishop either ('he has a knack of putting his foot in it and rubbing people the wrong way'), but he elaborated on his objections to Liston:

> For many reasons Liston would hardly be the right man in the right place. He is honest and straight and he has the ability, but he is narrow and obstinate. I must say I don't find him so but that is the opinion of all the men who live with him in the college.[174]

Later, when Coffey was plainly no longer under consideration and the bishops were still lobbying for Liston, Kelly wrote:

> My view is that for his own sake I would not like to see him elected. He has the ability (I think). He is a strong character. He is a pious man. But those who live with him say he is pig-headed when he takes a notion and he is a very bad judge of character. More for his own happiness than for anything else I hope it won't come his way.[175]

One of the 'men who lived with [Liston] in college' was his colleague Edmund Lynch, who was probably Kelly's chief informant in making these judgements. Lynch was the nephew of Dean William Burke. It was the circle of priests around Burke that most clearly rejected Liston: John Mackay, Patrick O'Donnell, George Hunt, James O'Neill and Patrick O'Neill. By mid-1919, they were petitioning the Apostolic Delegate with the claim that the choice of Michael O'Farrell was 'the intention and desire of the great majority of the responsible clergy of the diocese'.[176] Over 20 years earlier, some of these same priests (notably Burke and James O'Neill) had opposed the appointment of Patrick Maguire Lynch as Bishop Moran's successor in 1896. History appeared to be repeating itself, to the consternation of the bishops who still insisted on Liston as their first choice.

As correspondence preserved by Propaganda Fide shows, Liston's clerical opponents attempted to discredit him by spreading unsavoury news about his family, referring especially to the alcoholism of his deceased brother John and the problems of his elder sister Mary Maud. In a letter signed by all the bishops, and written in Archbishop Redwood's erratic French, the hierarchy had to answer this gossip as they responded to the Apostolic Delegate's standard queries about Liston's qualifications. With euphemistic understatement, they declared that it was true that Liston's brother 'drank a little too much in his last years'.[177] They then launched into a defence of Liston's elder sister:

Twelve years ago the elder sister Mary married a Protestant called Kempston. A dispensation was obtained for the priest to celebrate the marriage. The married couple went to England. They had a child. The marriage was not happy and the couple separated. Later, in her distress, Mrs. Kempston became addicted to morphine. Twice she voluntarily admitted herself to Good Shepherd convent near Christchurch to break this evil habit. In this institution she was treated as a guest. She had a private room and spent her time painting and doing needlework. She had a remarkable range of skills. She also asked if she could look after any of the sisters and penitents [reformed prostitutes] who were ill. For some time she did not honour her religious duties, but at present she practices the faith of her childhood. Nobody has ever accused her of [sexual] immorality. In young countries like this one, it is quite normal to find excellent Catholic families with one or two members who leave something to be desired. The unworthy reputation of one member of a family is not seen in the same light as it would be in older nations. We firmly believe that the established facts concerning Father Liston's sister in no way sully his good reputation or influence, and will in no way hinder the good he would be able to do as Bishop of Dunedin. Understand, then, why we repeat our recommendation in favour of Father Liston, and we regard with horror the attempt to harm him by claiming that he is illegitimate, or suggesting that his sister is a penitent – that is, a woman of ill repute – staying with the sisters of the Good Shepherd.[178]

It is hard to believe that Liston would have been unaware of the coarse and aggressive tactics being used against him by some of his fellow priests. They had described him as illegitimate, his sister as a former prostitute and his brother as an alcoholic. Only the last part of this gossip was true. To add to his worries, this was a time when Protestant sectarian propaganda seized eagerly upon any irregularities in Catholic custodial care. Two years later, Bishop Brodie was writing to Liston warning him that Howard Elliott 'is interviewing former Mt Magdala inmates' with a view to lobbying for government inspection of Catholic convents. Brodie advised 'precautionary measures' to head off this offensive.[179] It would at the very least have been an embarrassment to Liston to have his name linked to the institution. Liston's isolation was heightened by his lack of any close family support. His only other surviving sibling, his mentally-unstable younger sister Catherine Anne Josephine ('Anne'), had by this stage left for Britain on a nursing career from which she was never to return.[180] As far as family was concerned, Liston was on his own.

The eventual solution to Liston's (and Dunedin's) difficulties came from a not entirely unexpected source. By coincidence, there was another episcopal vacancy to be filled at this time. Late in 1918, Bishop Cleary made a formal request for a coadjutor-bishop (assistant bishop with right of succession) in Auckland.[181] Bishop of Auckland since 1910, Cleary had long been in delicate health. He had been absent from his diocese for much of 1915 undergoing operations in Sydney. In 1916-17, he sought cures in Europe, but further damaged himself by his two months of active service as a front-line military chaplain in France. He had intended to resign his see. Of the genuineness of Cleary's afflictions there can be no doubt. They were variously described as 'neuritis' and 'nerve overstrain' complicated by a weak heart and a tendency to crippling (perhaps migraine) headaches. The state of Cleary's health, the cures and operations he underwent in Australia, England and Ireland, were reported at length in the *Tablet*, as well as being noted in detail in Cleary's own regular bulletins to interested correspondents.[182] Cleary's autobiographical notes say that his health 'broke down' many times during his priestly training, he had 'recurrent peritonitis' after a youthful accident, and 'acute pleurisy' and 'trench mouth', necessitating the extraction of all his teeth, as a result of his front-line chaplaincy.[183] By 1918, it was widely believed that he had not long to live.[184]

Cleary's request was not the first time a New Zealand bishop had sought a coadjutor for reasons of ill health. In 1895, Luck of Auckland made the same request, but died before it was granted.[185] It was widely understood, however, that the position of coadjutor was a difficult one, sometimes making for divisions among the diocesan clergy. Cleary himself had turned down the opportunity to become Coadjutor-Bishop of Adelaide in 1913.[186] Bishop Brodie wrote to Cleary advising caution. In January 1918, Brodie suggested Cleary go easy in his work and 'be very slow in coming to the conclusion that you must resign or even seek a coadjutor'.[187] Eight months later, Brodie elaborated on his belief that 'the appointment of a coadjutor should be a last resource on account of the difficulties usually arising'. He told Cleary that wartime conditions were abnormally stressful anyway and were therefore no time to be thinking of making such a decision.[188] At this time, Cleary's diocesan consultors had already advised against a coadjutor. From another perspective, once Cleary had made his request, the Apostolic Delegate showed how aware he was that anyone serving as coadjutor under Cleary would have much to bear. He wrote:

Above: An apprehensive Liston, on the day of his consecration as bishop in 1920, poses with Dunedin clergy and Mosgiel staff. Some of these men had actively prevented his becoming Bishop of Dunedin.

Below: Jubilee celebrations, Holy Cross, Mosgiel, 1925. New Zealand's six Catholic bishops with college staff and alumni. Liston is seated between Cecil Morkane and Bishop Matthew Brodie, four bishops away from his Auckland superior Henry Cleary.

Cleary is a good and brave bishop, but we must not ignore the fact that especially in recent years, because of the various illnesses he has suffered, he is as nervous [nerve-wracked] and irritable as he is impulsive.[189]

After Cleary had gained the Holy See's permission, *terna* voting for a coadjutor took place in Auckland on 26 February 1919.[190] *Dignissimus* was the 40-year-old Jeremiah Cahill, 37-year-old William Ormond was *dignior* and 62-year-old William Mahoney *dignus*. Four other priests received stray votes, including a solitary vote for James Michael Liston, who was then largely a stranger to Auckland.[191] The hierarchy ruled out Mahoney and Cahill.[192] Ormond was acceptable but he was later to make it clear that he did not want the responsibility of the episcopate.[193] The bishops reported to the Apostolic Delegate that Ormond could be Coadjutor-Bishop of Auckland. But Cleary provided the hierarchy with a way out of its impasse over Dunedin by saying that he was willing to have the rejected Liston as his coadjutor.[194] By March, within weeks of the Auckland *terna*, Cleary was checking on Liston's family background to verify his worthiness for the role.[195]

Not only was Cleary willing, he was even eager to have Liston as his coadjutor. In the late 1920s, when their relationship had soured, Cleary petitioned Rome to have Liston removed from his diocese. The legend grew that Cleary had never wanted a coadjutor and that he especially had not wanted Liston. Nothing could be further from the truth. All the relevant correspondence shows that in 1919-20, it was Cleary who pressed his fellow bishops to send Liston to Auckland. On his own initiative, he wrote to the Apostolic Delegate refuting the slanderous remarks that had been made about Liston.[196]

Cleary was to give Liston a series of generous public welcomes to Auckland. In July 1920, he described him as 'by far the ablest Catholic ecclesiastic in this dominion' and 'one whose zeal, piety and intellectual ability will be assets of enormous and fructifying benefit to this diocese'.[197] In December 1920, he asked a cathedral congregation to thank God for 'the precious Christmas gift of so holy, learned and able a Bishop'.[198] Such words could be taken as expected tactful rhetoric for such public church occasions. More to the point, however, Cleary and Liston had enjoyed a warm mutual regard since the days when Cleary edited the *Tablet* and consoled Liston at his brother's funeral. Correspondence shows Liston in 1909 congratulating Cleary on his 'brilliant' polemical work in the Bible-in-Schools debate.[199] In 1913, Liston researched technical questions on canon law (relating to marriage annulments) at Cleary's request.[200] In 1914, Liston wrote to Cleary for advice on how a Catholic politician should answers questions about education. He also passed on to Cleary a folk-remedy for Cleary's persistent insomnia ('a pillow-case of dried hops used as the lower pillow at night').[201] In 1915, Liston again wrote to praise Cleary's polemical skills and to urge him to take a much-needed holiday.[202] In 1918, at Cleary's request, Liston researched a detailed reply to a PPA charge that Catholics were permitted to 'break faith with heretics'.[203] In all this, Cleary regarded Liston as his friend and ally, and also as a useful resource in his polemical work. They did not always see eye-to-eye. Liston's stubborn defence of James Kelly's editorship of the *Tablet* could be read as a foretaste of later differences.[204] But this in no way negates the fact that Liston was Cleary's chosen coadjutor.

By the end of 1919, the hierarchy was still noting its preference for Liston as Bishop of Dunedin and were giving the Apostolic Delegate a glowing account of his virtues. He was, said Redwood, O'Shea, Brodie and Cleary,

> ... in good health, patient, frugal and ... successful in all his acts of administration ... He shows strength of character, but this strength is accompanied by great tact, constant good humour and great discretion. He enjoys a remarkable reputation for piety and nothing has ever been alleged against his morals.[205]

Reluctantly they conceded, in the light of the Dunedin priests' opposition to Liston, that William Ormond could become Bishop of Dunedin and Liston could go to Auckland.

It appears to have been the Apostolic Delegate himself who suggested James Whyte be appointed Bishop of Dunedin. Bartolomeo Cattaneo shrewdly remarked that as Dunedin priests had themselves chosen a complete outsider (O'Farrell), they could not very well object to the bishops choosing another complete outsider for them.[206] As in 1896, clergy had rejected one of their own, and had been given an Irishman from Australia instead. In his early fifties, Kilkenny-born James Whyte had been a priest in Sydney since his ordination in 1892. He was archdiocesan chancellor under Cardinal Moran and Archbishop Kelly. He had directed the *Catholic Press*, been inspector of Catholic schools and taught at Manly, where Liston was one of his pupils.[207]

The Apostolic Delegate formally notified Whyte of his appointment in April 1920.[208] At the same time, Cardinal Gaspari of Propaganda wired Cleary that Whyte had been appointed to Dunedin and Liston to Auckland. Cattaneo wrote and confirmed the details.[209] The appointments were announced in the *Tablet* on 29 April 1920. The *Tablet* made the best of the situation, playing up Whyte's meagre New Zealand connections. He was –

> . . . a personal friend of the late Bishop Verdon, and has several times visited New Zealand, being present at important religious functions, including the consecration of his Lordship Bishop Brodie.[210]

A welcoming address to him in Dunedin, however, more honestly called him 'a stranger in this Dominion'.[211]

Liston, still caught up in the middle of the academic year at Holy Cross, began to make arrangements for his consecration. At first, he believed Whyte would be consecrated in Sydney.[212] Once Whyte decided to have the ceremony in Dunedin, Cleary and James Coffey both suggested that it should be a dual ceremony.[213] Liston readily acquiesced. He would welcome being consecrated in Dunedin as then 'I can slip into Auckland with as little ceremony as possible and take up my work there quietly'.[214]

Liston looked to his spiritual preparation. He planned to cross to Sydney to make a retreat in the company of Patrick O'Neill (one of the clergy who had petitioned the Apostolic Delegate against him) and James Delaney.[215] This he did over five weeks in July and August. At a college reunion, he briefly met again some of his acquaintances from Manly. He made his retreat with the Vincentian Fathers at Ashfield, writing that it was 'bracing and encouraging, even if it does make me pause and fear'. He also once again met Whyte ('a very fine man – prudent, affable, energetic') who returned to New Zealand with him. And he sent Cleary a design for his personal coats of arms, explaining:

> The Cross represents the arms of the Liston tribe and incidentally reminds me of Holy Cross while the chalice etc. tells me of what must be the main feature of my future work.[216]

Later, in October and November, he made another retreat to Mt Magdala in Christchurch. He described it as 'a lovely place for recollection and prayer'.[217]

Already by June, it had been decided that he would, as coadjutor-bishop, take over the parish of St Benedict's in Newton in Auckland; but he had to wait until September before official authorisation of his appointment arrived.[218] Meanwhile, both before and after his trip to Australia, he was thrown into a round of farewells from

Dunedin. Staff and students of Holy Cross subscribed to buy him a pectoral cross, while Coffey and the diocesan clergy bought his episcopal ring.[219] In July, he was formally farewelled by Mosgiel parish in the presence of the mayor and Holy Cross staff. His diocesan farewell in the same month was chaired by Mr T.J. Hussey (an old classmate from the Christian Brothers' School). Fr Coffey spoke the major tribute, declaring with regional pride that 'when they wanted a good man in the north they always sent to the south for him'. Liston was presented with an address inscribed on vellum and a personal grant of £630. At St Philomena's in South Dunedin, there were more speeches and he was given a 'a solid silver Bougie [ornamental candlestick], suitably inscribed'. At St Dominic's, the nuns presented him with another illuminated address of their own devising and 'a very serviceable leather writing-case'.[220]

A week before his consecration, Liston was eased into his new role by acting for the first time as secretary to a meeting of the hierarchy in Dunedin.[221] Finally, on 12 December 1920, Whyte and Liston were consecrated in a unique dual ceremony in St Joseph's Cathedral.[222] Redwood was assisted by Cleary and by Bishop Carroll from Lismore in New South Wales. All diocesan priests were in attendance, all religious orders were represented and there was a large lay congregation in spite of the rainy weather. O'Shea preached the occasional sermon, describing a Catholic bishop, in accordance with the triumphalist theology of the day, as 'Prophet, Priest and King' with the power to legislate for his flock. It was two months short of 17 years since Liston had been ordained priest in the same cathedral after his return from Rome. Conducting the choir of Holy Cross students was his friend from Rome, Daniel Buckley. Liston accepted and signed the anti-Modernist oath, as all Catholic bishops then did.[223] Dean William Burke, who had so much contrived against Liston, had the satisfaction of presenting the address of welcome to Whyte as the new Bishop of Dunedin.[224]

Between the death of Bishop Verdon and the consecration of Liston and of Verdon's successor, there had been two years of unpleasant and acrimonious bargaining among the clergy, unknown to the laity and unreported in the press. Liston could not help being affected by the harsh judgements on his character that were made. He had a negative attitude towards Dean Burke from this time onwards. In 1921, he wrote to Brodie that it would be a 'real disaster' if Burke were allowed to teach at Mosgiel as he planned to do.[225] On the other hand, there is no evidence that he felt any ill will towards his former teacher who had become Bishop of Dunedin in his stead. A large file of letters from early in his episcopate shows Liston enjoying a chatty – almost slangy – friendship with his brother-bishop James Whyte.[226]

The difficulties in the making of Dunedin's bishop and Auckland's coadjutor were not unique in New Zealand's church history. Sometimes, the appointment of a bishop was a simple matter, and the hierarchy was in complete accord with the wishes of the diocesan clergy. This was the case with the appointment of Cleary to Auckland in 1910. He was *dignissimus* in the *terna* voting (Matthew Brodie was *dignior*), and the printed *Relazione* of his appointment in the archives of Propaganda Fide is a mere four pages long.[227] On the other hand, the *Relazione* of Brodie's appointment to Christchurch in 1916 runs to many pages, outlining the bitter contentions between the Marist and secular clergy in that diocese. The Aucklander Brodie featured nowhere in Christchurch's *terna* voting, and was strongly favoured, not by the local diocesan clergy, but by Redwood and Cleary.[228] James Kelly disliked Brodie and privately accused Cleary of 'wire-pulling' to place his ally in another see. The priests' voting he dismissed as 'only a farce' when it could so easily be overridden.[229] *Terna* voting was – and still is – purely advisory, and the bishops would have been within their canonical rights to impose their choice, Liston, upon Dunedin without further ado. But after strife over episcopal succession in Christchurch and Wellington, the hierarchy was reluctant again to ignore the wishes of diocesan clergy.[230]

There remains the matter of Liston's own attitude towards his appointment to Auckland. Repeatedly, he expressed fears about his unworthiness and his unsuitedness for the role. As the prospect of becoming Cleary's coadjutor loomed, he wrote, 'I am trying to think and pray over my coming duties and I find it all very humbling and terrifying'.[231] 'Feel quite unequal', he wired to Cleary on the day of his appointment.[232] In a letter he elaborated:

> I still feel deep down in my heart and conscience that I do not possess the gifts requisite for this office. It seems to me that it is one thing to have to train a few select students with the assistance of very capable and most loyal professors, but quite another to face the vast charge of a diocese.[233]

To Michael Curran in Europe he wrote:

> This change is about the last thing I could wish for. College life has always suited me . . . I have been intensely happy here always and if I had my choice would stay on forever. And now I have to face

a position for which I feel unequal. I cannot find in myself any of the gifts that must surely be required. All I have are good health, toughness, a stout heart, some faith (that comes from Clonliffe and Roman training) and deep respect and affection for Bishop Cleary, my old friend: that's the lot. I can only go on hoping that my friends will pray very hard for me.[234]

When he arrived in Auckland in December, he told a large gathering of –

... the painful sacrifice of separation from the diocese and work and friends I loved and love so tenderly . . . I confess that I should have been glad to spend all my life in the work of training aspirants to the priesthood.[235]

Such humble professions could be read as purely conventional.[236] Yet Liston seems sincere in his expressions of reluctance to leave Dunedin, where he said he was 'as happy as any man on Earth could be with my work and my friends'.[237] He privately acknowledged that both Brodie and Cleary had had to talk him into accepting the Auckland appointment.[238] Even Edmund Lynch noted Liston's mixed feelings as he left Holy Cross.[239]

At 38 years of age, James Michael Liston was not the youngest Catholic bishop consecrated in New Zealand. George Lenihan had also been 38 at the time of his consecration and Francis Redwood (reputed to be the youngest bishop in the world) had been 35. However, Liston was, after Matthew Brodie, only the second New Zealand-born priest to become a bishop. For 17 years, he had been teacher and rector in the national seminary. Gradually, with his bishop's approval, he had taken on a public role as spokesman for the church in a number of public controversies. Parochial duties had come second to these roles. Even while taking responsibility for Mosgiel parish, he had not been a parish priest in the usual sense. Some of the hostile criticisms, made at the time he was mooted as a possible bishop, would suggest that his pastoral skills were underdeveloped. Yet with Cleary's illness, he was now effectively being placed in charge of the second most populous diocese in the country. His abilities were about to be tested, and to find their limits.

CHAPTER III

COADJUTOR AT WORK

1920-29

Auckland and Its Welcome

Auckland diocese embraced the northern half of the North Island, including Northland, Auckland, the Waikato, the East Coast parishes around Gisborne and some of the King Country west of Lake Taupo. In number of Catholics, Auckland was much more populous than either of the South Island dioceses and stood second to Wellington. In the early 1920s, there were between 40,000 and 50,000 Catholics in Auckland diocese, and between 50,000 and 60,000 in Wellington. Nevertheless, Auckland was growing fast. There had been 33 Auckland parishes at the beginning of Cleary's episcopate. There were 57 by the time of his death. Cleary and Liston regularly opened new churches, laid foundations for new schools and blessed new presbyteries.[1] To meet pastoral needs, the Marist Fathers were reintroduced into the diocese and took responsibility for Mt Albert and Whangarei.[2]

Population growth meant more work for teaching orders. In the 1920s, the Marist Brothers were the only male teaching order in the diocese. But of the six orders of nuns in Auckland, five were dedicated to teaching. Between 1920 and 1929, the number of sisters in the diocese grew from 281 to 395. The number of children in Auckland's Catholic schools grew from 5,600 in 1920 to approximately 7,200 in 1930, and while there were only eight Catholic secondary schools in the diocese, there were 51 Catholic primary schools.[3]

One feature unique to Auckland diocese was its extensive Maori Mission, run by priests of the Missionary Society of St Joseph (commonly known as the 'Mill Hill' Fathers after their society's headquarters in north London). Although an English order, most of their priests in New Zealand at this time were Dutchmen, headed by Dean van Dijk. In his 1924 report, van Dijk claimed that there were about 4,000 Catholics among the 25,000 Auckland Maori, but he lamented the lack of effective catechesis and remarked that for Mill Hill priests living in the backblocks 'the presbyteries are all humble and poor, quite missionary-like'.[4] Primitive conditions in outlying districts were underlined by letters from Mill Hills asking for power generators and water-drilling equipment.[5] Travel was also a problem where sealed roads gave way to mud tracks. Cleary made disparaging remarks about 'the roadless North', above Auckland. A wide audience heard how he toiled over muddy unsealed roads while on pastoral visitations in the country, and later how he became the first bishop to fly around his diocese, piloted by pioneer aviators George Bolt and Vivian Walsh.[6]

Throughout the 1920s, there was another major problem. There were not enough priests.[7] Priests regularly complained that they were not allowed to take adequate holidays because there was nobody to relieve them.[8] More than once, as coadjutor, Liston wrote to other dioceses requesting the temporary placement of priests to help fill gaps.[9] In 1924, Cleary wrote to the Apostolic Delegate,

> There is a great strain upon our finances; we are in pressing need of some ten priests more with only two in prospect; and owing to old age, ill-health, and other causes, this shortage of priests will be accentuated by the loss of three more . . .[10]

Similarly, he wrote in 1927,

> We are rather seriously embarrassed in this diocese through lack of priests, partly because of death and sickness, partly because of the rapid increase in population, still maintained, which has led to the formation of 23 new parishes in my short episcopate, with four more ready and waiting as soon as we can staff them.[11]

Cleary made many trips to recruit clergy. His visit to Ireland in 1927 netted seven new priests. By the end of his episcopate, there were about 85 priests in the diocese, a quarter of whom ministered to Auckland city and suburbs. Liston was officially vicar-general as well as coadjutor, but the size of the diocese demanded a second vicar-general. This was Monsignor William Henry Mahoney, who died in 1925. In June 1924, Cleary appointed his replacement Jeremiah Cahill. He had known Liston since a visit to Mosgiel in 1911-12, remained vicar-general until Liston's own retirement in 1970 and was always one of his closest associates. Auckland's cathedral administrator was John Bradley, who transferred to Remuera parish in 1925 and was replaced at the cathedral by Leonard Buxton.

This was the growing diocese to which Liston came. Cleary and a large crowd met his train on 23 December 1920. The official welcome was in St Patrick's Cathedral, where Liston celebrated high mass two days later on Christmas Day. He expressed tactfully the widespread belief that Cleary had not long to live, and his own sense of inadequacy:

We all pray, I for one pray with a full heart, that God may spare him [Cleary] as long as it is good for his people – surely a long, long time – and that the evening of his days on earth may be radiant with peace . . . I stand in need of all the sympathetic help you can give me. I have no high gifts of intellect or wisdom or eloquence or character with which to serve you. All I have is a heart that is determined to devote itself to your best interests . . .

There was a garden party in Liston's honour at Sacred Heart College in Ponsonby, and on Boxing Day he ordained a priest for the first time. Ironically, the ordinand was the same Edward Lyons whom he had expelled from Mosgiel and who had been one of the students at the centre of the conscription debate.[12]

All Liston's correspondence shows that he was made to feel welcome in Auckland, but that his feelings of acceptance were mixed with intense homesickness. Publicly he admitted 'the painful separation from the diocese and work and friends I loved and love so tenderly'.[13] Privately he wrote to Bishop Whyte, in January 1921,

Bishop, priests and people have . . . fully carried out Dr. Cleary's promise of the open door to their hearts . . . I still dream about Dunedin and my friends and the other day when I came across 'Dunedin Street', I felt inclined to pack up for Mosgiel.[14]

On the same day, he wrote to Bishop Brodie, 'when I came across "Dunedin Street" the other day, I could have sat down and wept'.[15] At a welcome in Gisborne, he repeated that he would have been happy to continue at Mosgiel.[16] Later in life, Liston used many public occasions to express his attachment to Dunedin and likened his coming to Auckland to 'pulling up the roots of a well-established tree'.[17] In the 1920s, Dunedin friends often visited him and he sometimes took holidays there.[18] He still had family responsibilities in Dunedin. On behalf of the daughters of his remarried sister-in-law, Catherine (sometimes Katherine) Boyle, he administered the estate of his late mother until it was wound up in 1928.[19] When James Coffey died in 1923, Liston settled his affairs and wrote to Bishop Whyte requesting some of Coffey's paintings, including a copy of Raphael's 'Transfiguration', and a miniature (dated 1549) of 'Our

Lady and the Divine Child'.[20] To add to his sense of separation, he learnt once again in Auckland that friendships could be short-lived. The octogenarian Monsignor John Golden, chaplain to the home of the Little Sisters of the Poor, died in November 1922. He had welcomed Liston with cheerful doggerel verse in January 1921, and enjoyed Liston's friendship for the next two years.[21] Liston expressed his bereavement, remarking that Golden's death was 'singularly holy and edifying' and that 'I miss the old man very much . . . He was my confessor and I valued his counsel very much'.[22]

In the first years of Liston's coadjutorship, all Cleary's utterances expressed enthusiasm for his presence. He told the Apostolic Delegate, 'the new Coadjutor-Bishop is winning golden opinions on all sides, both among clergy and laity, and is relieving me both of much work and much anxiety'.[23] As he was about to leave on his extensive overseas trip, Cleary granted Liston wide powers of attorney, including the right to open accounts, auction or sell church land, buy land and buildings for the diocese, dispose of Cleary's stocks, borrow against diocesan property and transfer diocesan mortgages.[24] From Europe, Cleary wrote back to Liston, commending him for his ministrations to the dying Father John Carran, 'It is so good to have you there to act for both of us'.[25] Later he added,

> I thank God, with all my heart, that you are on the spot in Auckland, and you know how fully I trust in your goodness and your prudence in all matters of diocesan administration. I therefore have no worries whatsoever about such things, knowing well that you . . . will do everything for the best. So I rest easy.[26]

In Rome, Cleary undertook a favour for Liston, getting new episcopal vestments made for him there, and praised the *relatio* of the diocese that Liston had forwarded as 'a model'.[27]

Episcopal Secretary, Parish Priest and Coadjutor

As the youngest member of the hierarchy, Liston appears to have enjoyed similarly cordial relations with the other four bishops, especially Whyte and Brodie, with whom he corresponded regularly. His familiar letters with Whyte were another link with Dunedin. Brodie, the only other New Zealand-born bishop, was nearest in age to Liston. Liston sometimes sought Brodie's advice on practical administrative matters, such as the market values of diocesan properties, the reliability of Jeremiah Cahill and the least disruptive way of collecting the diocesan levy.[28] Throughout the 1920s, Liston acted as secretary to the hierarchy's meetings. These were held irregularly until 1925, when Whyte suggested the arrangement was insufficient. Thenceforth the six bishops always held an annual meeting in Wellington on the third week of Easter. Through illness, Liston missed one meeting in the decade (that of 3 May 1928), but the minute book for the whole period is kept in his handwriting.[29] He was delegated to special projects, being chief organiser of New Zealand participation in the 29th Eucharistic Congress held in Sydney 6-9 September 1928. In February of that year, he suggested a joint pastoral letter to drum up lay support and interest.[30] The other bishops consulted him about their liturgical requirements for the congress.[31]

While acting for the national church, Liston also had a specific local care. On 13 February 1921, he was officially installed as parish priest of St Benedict's, Newton, and he lived in the parish presbytery until Cleary's death. He replaced the elderly Monsignor Gillan, who died early in 1922. Later that year, Liston unveiled a memorial tablet in his honour in St Benedict's and preached a panegyric.[32]

St Benedict's large brick church had been completed in 1888, after fire destroyed an earlier impressive wooden church. Originally run by the Benedictine order, the parish came under secular control in 1899 when Gillan became parish priest. Gillan supervised the building of churches in Balmoral and Avondale. As population grew, new parishes were formed out of what had once been a geographically larger Newton parish. For nearly a century (until 1982), the Josephite order of nuns ('Brown Joes') ran the parish's convent school and adjoining secondary school for girls. During Liston's time as parish priest, the parish choir was conducted by Signor Constantini, one-time conductor of the Sistine Chapel choir, and gained a city-wide reputation.[33]

A parish history generously praises Liston's qualities as parish priest in the 1920s:

> At St Benedict's, the Bishop was not unmindful of the temporalities; the present seats and stained glass windows are of his initiative. But of deeper significance, he was a pastor of souls of rare quality. Those who knew him will attest his gift of prayer and quiet courtesy, combined with firmness; of the radiance of holiness. But to the laity no one could have been more discerning and tender. A few calm words from some unexpected angle had a healing touch. Countless households in bereavement or other distress knew his presence and blessed him. In spiritual gifts [he] had not a little in common with Cardinal Newman.[34]

Right: Official portrait of the 39-year-old Liston, newly-consecrated coadjutor-bishop of Auckland, 1920.
Below: The impressive Saint Benedict's church and presbytery, Newton, Auckland, where Liston was parish priest from 1920 to 1929.

There is no doubt that Liston took seriously such parish duties as
he could perform. A later bishop of Auckland, who was a schoolboy
in the parish at the time, remembers Liston personally training altar
boys in their responses to the mass and other liturgical duties.[35]
Even so, it is clear that at Newton Liston was once again part of a
pastoral team and could not be said to have shared the quotidian
experience of most parish priests. In early 1921, Monsignor William
Joseph Ormond was installed as Newton parish 'administrator'.
Philip O'Malley and Matthew Joseph Curley were his assistants
until 1923, Francis Joseph Skinner was also an assistant from 1922
to 1932, and Alfred Ernest Bennett joined the parish in 1928. This
team of three or four priests was large enough to 'supply' other
parishes at need.

Liston took a leading part in many parish matters. Under his
direction, the presbytery was extensively renovated in mid-1921. In
1928, he directed the refurbishing of the church in time for its fortieth
anniversary, which was celebrated by a special mass on 22 April
1928 at which Liston rejoiced that 'over 30,000 masses' had been
said there since April 1888.[36] His own sacerdotal silver jubilee was
celebrated in a crowded St Benedict's with a mass on 31 January 1929.
Representatives came up from Dunedin, and Liston was reported
as saying that he wanted no public function in his honour – only
the mass.[37] In 1924-25, Liston also took charge of determining the
boundary between St Benedict's parish, Newton, and Good Shepherd
parish, Balmoral, after Dean Murphy of Balmoral had complained
that Mgr Ormond had conducted a funeral for a parishioner who
properly belonged to Balmoral.[38] Cleary congratulated Liston for
settling the matter, but said that responsibility for Catholic pastoral
care of the Avondale Mental Hospital was still a problem, 'and I
shall be glad to have any suggestions from you as to the best method
of solving it'.[39]

Yet in spite of all this, the day-to-day running of the parish was in
the hands of Ormond, especially when Liston's duties took him far
from the city. Ormond was one of Liston's closest friends among the
Auckland clergy. He was of similar background. Born on the West
Coast in 1882, he too was the New Zealand son of Irish parents.
The influential businessman Michael Joseph Sheahan was his uncle.
Like Liston, Ormond had had a role in the church's bureaucracy,
having been secretary to the Apostolic Delegate in Sydney for six
years. After Liston's departure, Ormond was officially parish priest
of St Benedict's until his death in 1949.[40]

Far from being primarily a parish priest, then, Liston in the

1920s was pre-eminently Cleary's substitute. Cleary was frequently absent from the diocese on trips related both to his health and other matters. He left on a major trip to Britain and Europe in September 1921 because 'his health was completely shattered . . . his life was despaired of . . . he [was] practically an invalid'.[41] This trip doubled as his official *ad limina*, and he had the private intention of lobbying at the Vatican against James Kelly's editorship of the *Tablet*.[42] There was a farewell dinner at Bishop's House, and Liston accompanied Cleary on part of his journey to Wellington to catch the steamer.[43] Cleary was away for 21 months, returning to Auckland only in June 1923 on the steamer *Manuka*. He was met at the wharf by Liston and proceeded to a welcome in the cathedral where he addressed the Maori portion of the congregation in Maori, a skill that Liston was never able to replicate.[44] Cleary was overseas for another six months between March and August 1927, partly for his health but also to recruit priests in Ireland and Rome. 'His sudden and hurried departure left no time for his flock to meet and say farewell to him', reported the *Tablet*.[45] When he came back, with new priests in tow, he declared to a welcome in the cathedral, 'nearer and dearer to me than the jewels of the East are the faces of my coadjutor-bishop, my faithful clergy and my dearly beloved people'.[46]

He made a trip to America, for his health, between November 1928 and February 1929, by which time he had the additional motive of making a case against his coadjutor. The steamer *Aorangi*, on which he travelled to America, also carried the papal legate Cardinal Cerretti, who was en route for Rome from the Eucharistic Congress in Sydney and had stayed in Auckland for two days, laying the foundation stone for extensions to the Mater hospital.[47] This was an influential person with whom Cleary could discuss his discontents.

These absences from the diocese were added to by Cleary's illnesses and accidents. Almost as soon as his coadjutor arrived, Cleary spent two months in the Mater.[48] He was again hospitalised in 1927, shortly after his return from Europe. He had left his bed to open a fête being run by the hospital but had collapsed and was operated on by Dr Casement Aitken.[49] Liston undertook some of Cleary's engagements at this time, saying mass in the cathedral on Christmas Day and opening a new church in Kaikohe.[50] Yet Cleary still insisted on making such diocesan visitations as he could, sometimes with unhappy results.[51] In July 1928, he was involved in a collision while driving through the Waikato with his friend, the well-known English Jesuit apologist, C.C. Martindale. Some weeks later, the *Tablet* said:

> Dr. Cleary has made such rapid recovery after his severe motor accident that he has been able to be removed from the Waikato Hospital to his home in Ponsonby. His Lordship had the unique experience of being conveyed by hammock in the guard's van to Auckland, and arrived home none the worse after the journey. Dr. Cleary will be laid up for several weeks, but there is every prospect that he will be able to attend the Eucharistic Congress in Sydney.[52]

In fact, while Martindale recovered rapidly, Cleary was still too ill to go to Sydney.[53] He was on crutches for some months after his discharge from hospital.[54] He was then involved in another road accident in February 1929 when he crashed his car into a bridge outside Colville in the Coromandel. This time, however, he suffered no ill effects and was able to walk some miles for assistance.[55]

In the nine years that Liston was coadjutor, Cleary was out of the diocese for a total of 29 months. When Cleary's other periods of ill health and hospitalisation are added, it is fair to say that Liston was effectively in charge of the diocese for something over three years of this period. Liston threw himself into diocesan visitations when Cleary was indisposed. In April 1921, he set off on a six-week pastoral tour of the diocese from Whangarei to Gisborne. Early in 1923, he visited the remoter East Coast parishes. In December 1921, it was Liston (together with Matthew Brodie) who accompanied the Apostolic Delegate on his tour of the diocese.

Yet Liston, too, had his illnesses. In late 1925, he had acute appendicitis and spent some months recuperating after an operation.[56] He later claimed that this prevented him from working effectively from September 1925 to August 1926, and that his trip to America in 1926 was partly for his health.[57] Illness kept him from the 1928 bishops' Easter meeting and a severe bout of influenza sent him off to Dunedin to rest for three weeks in 1929. He also took brief periods of leave. Shortly after Cleary returned in 1923, Liston had a fortnight's holiday in Sydney.[58] In February 1926, in late 1927 and again in July 1928, he went to Dunedin.[59]

Liston's longest period outside the diocese was his four-month journey to North America, in the company of Ormond and James Delaney, from April to August 1926. Their chief object was to attend the Eucharistic Congress in Chicago, but Liston also regarded it as a health trip. He was farewelled by St Benedict's parish and presented with a cheque.[60] They sailed for Canada on the *Aorangi* on 13 April 1926. Entering Vancouver, Liston confided in his diary how ill-treated New Zealand's Union Steamship Company passengers were by Canadian immigration authorities ('like cattle being penned for the slaughter').[61] After meeting the Archbishop of Vancouver, Liston bought rail passes to New York, Chicago and Los Angeles. He also visited Winnipeg and Minnesota, saw the Niagara Falls, watched a baseball match, met some distant American relatives and was received by the Bishop of Baltimore. But the highpoint was the Congress. Liston noted enthusiastically, 'many priests spoke to me of the crowds at confession – of returns of sinners etc. – greatest mission ever held'. Of a mass for children held in the Chicago stadium, he wrote, 'Stadium packed – 60,000 children, over 300,000 adults. Indescribable. Prayer, reverence, quietness of people most striking. Obviously they are bent on things above'. A rally of 200,000 men under the auspices of the Holy Name Society particularly impressed him and helped decide him to establish the sodality in Auckland.[62] He was intensely moved by the sheer scale of the Catholic congress. 'I'm afraid I wept most of the time on Sunday in the [Chicago] Cathedral', he wrote to Mother Helen Lynch. 'Yesterday, the vision of 60,000 children in white dresses and gold ribbons was a dream. . . .'[63] In the completest contrast, Liston was unimpressed with Prohibition and depressed by Los Angeles – 'noisy, cheap, vulgar city – every second building a picture theatre – eat houses everywhere – everybody selling something!'[64] He enjoyed a concert in the Hollywood Bowl, visited San Francisco and the Californian missions and jotted down some current jokes (on the silence of President Calvin Coolidge). He also dined with New York's Governor Al Smith and remarked favourably on his Catholicism.[65] (Two years later, Smith was the Democrat Party's unsuccessful presidential candidate.) Liston, Ormond and Delaney sent back reports on American hospitality and on the Congress. They arrived home on the *Niagara* in early August, having travelled across the Pacific with members of the Australian hierarchy who had also been at the congress, Archbishops Mannix and Clune of Melbourne and Perth, and Bishop McCarthy of Bendigo.

Mannix declared the Chicago event had set a sound benchmark for the Eucharistic Congress to be held in Sydney.[66] Attendance at that congress, in September 1928, became Liston's second major absence from the diocese.[67] During it, he took responsibility for lay visitors from New Zealand and caught up with old contemporaries from Manly and with Monsignor Michael Curran from the Irish College in Rome, who was travelling as part of Cardinal Cerretti's entourage.[68]

If Cleary was absent or indisposed for about three years between 1920 and 1929, Liston himself was absent or hospitalised for a total of about ten months. Despite his slight frame, however, his health was more robust than Cleary's and his appointment as coadjutor was vindicated. This was illustrated by both his personal initiatives as coadjutor, and by his continuing role as a spokesman to a wider public for distinctively Catholic causes.

Liston's Initiatives

Much that Liston undertook in the 1920s had to do with fostering an informed and disciplined Catholic laity. Upon his arrival in Auckland, he declared –

> Catholic laymen feel that they stand in the light of a new and prophetic dawn . . . they are growing in the realisation of their rights and even more of their responsibilities . . . They recognise that the Church has been too often, is too often, one-handed in her mighty struggle against the powers of evil . . . and so, as becomes educated and loyal sons, they are offering themselves to the Church – their talents, energies, and personal service – in her onerous mission to men.[69]

Whether there was such a groundswell of lay support for church service is open to question. Nevertheless, Liston busied himself with building up, or establishing, lay societies in the diocese. The son of a Dunedin Hibernian, he was described by the *Tablet* as an 'enthusiastic member' of the Hibernian Australasian Catholic Benefit Society, a branch of which he had founded in Mosgiel. Hibernians welcomed him to Auckland in a meeting in the old St Patrick's schoolroom on Hobson Street, and he replied 'feelingly' with a speech on Ireland's destiny.[70] He moved to establish a parish branch at St Benedict's. Of this he was an honorary member.[71] Later, he presided at the foundation of a Hibernian branch in Devonport and at the first meeting of the Hibernians held in the new St Patrick's School.[72]

More specifically his own creation was the Auckland Catholic Students' Guild which gradually transmuted into the University Catholic Society. Founded under his patronage in 1922, it met for monthly papers or debates and welcomed university staff, clerics and such secondary school students as were interested.[73] Closely linked with this was his foundation of the Guild of St Luke, open to all Catholic professional men (doctors, lawyers and academics) and intended to clarify Catholic teaching on public issues. In the initial invitation he sent out, Liston proposed they discuss such matters of concern as divorce laws and the incidence of surgical abortion.[74] This 'important innovation' met monthly in St Benedict's presbytery for a lecture followed by questions and discussion.[75] It may have been concern about non-Catholic (or irreligious) teachings on marital and sexual matters that led Liston to suggest, in 1926, that a salaried nurse be attached to the St Vincent de Paul Society to offer advice to mothers.[76]

A much wider membership was intended for the Holy Name Society, soon the largest devotional sodality for Catholic laymen in New Zealand. Although a contemporary press report gave Bishop Cleary the credit, it was Liston who introduced the Holy Name Society into Auckland in October 1926, after he had been impressed by its organisational skills at the Eucharistic Congress in Chicago. Holy Name members were pledged to the regular reception of the sacraments, and wore a distinctive (but inconspicuous) badge when they attended mass as a group to receive communion.[77] A similar concern for sacramental involvement by the laity had led Liston to circularise diocesan priests early in 1922, promoting a more detailed version on the Forty Hours' Adoration.[78]

Catholic education of a special sort also concerned Liston as he took responsibility for correspondence catechism lessons for children in remote country areas.[79] In 1921, he discussed the possibility of setting up a specifically Catholic schools journal to supplement (or supplant) the state school journal that was then used in Catholic schools.[80] This scheme had been suggested before at conferences of Catholic teachers, but did not come to fruition until Liston himself was Bishop of Auckland.[81] Liston also promoted a method of teaching singing in Catholic schools.[82] When he was in America in 1926, he sounded out many possibilities for Auckland. With Dr Leonard, the Director of Charities in Baltimore diocese, Liston discussed fund-raising, the Big Brother and Big Sister movements for Catholics in trouble with the courts, how to assist impoverished parishes financially, a regular parochial levy to avoid the intrusiveness of charity drives and a Catholic Bureau to find foster parents for orphans. He also discussed the religious education syllabus with Dr Barrett, Baltimore's director of Catholic schools.[83] He made notes on American Catholic hospitals, the conduct of liturgy, and the decoration and furnishing of American churches, this last with an eye to improvements at St Benedict's.

In other initiatives, Liston was simply responding to needs as they arose. These included the establishment of a Marist Brothers' school in Hamilton and of a new parish at Frankton, and the provision of a Catholic chaplain to the Devonport naval base.[84] When the Catholic boys' orphanage at Takapuna was gutted by fire on 3 March 1923,

Liston at once called a public meeting and set up an appeal for funds to rebuild.[85] He organised some of the orphans to write letters to the Catholic press appealing for support.[86] The orphanage was run by the Mercy Sisters, one of whom years later described Liston, on the day of the fire, presiding at an emergency meeting in St Benedict's Hall and persuading a crowd to provide temporary billets for all the 50 boys who had been rendered homeless.[87] Thanks in large part to Liston's efforts, the orphanage was rebuilt and reopened exactly one year later, on 2 March 1924, in the presence of the Apostolic Delegate and the Governor-General, Lord Jellicoe. In his speech on that occasion, Liston was able to point out that Catholics were not alone in contributing to the appeal.

Liston did, however, have a vision of a better-staffed diocese that went beyond mere *ad hoc* initiatives. At various times in the 1920s, he suggested that Auckland foundations could be made by Dominican Sisters and by the Sacred Heart Fathers from Australia. Cleary opposed some of these initiatives. But in one enterprise the two bishops were in accord. This was the plan to provide Auckland's Croats (Dalmatians) with a priest who could actually speak their own language. As far back as 1903, Bishop Lenihan had asked the diocesan council how he could respond to 'an appeal from the Austrians in the North' for a Croatian-speaking priest.[88] The Croats, especially the single men working in the gumfields north of Auckland, were not well-integrated into the religious life of the diocese. Nevertheless, Lenihan's papers on the refurbishing of St Patrick's Cathedral, between 1901 and 1909, do include a letter from M.A. Ferri of the Auckland Croat newspaper, *Napredak* ('Progress'), enclosing a cheque from the Croat community which was intended to provide the cathedral with a Calvary group near the altar.[89] Father Josephus Zanna whom Lenihan provided was in fact a German-speaking Italian from the Tyrol, who learnt to preach in the Croat tongue only with great difficulty.[90] During the First World War, the Croats in the north had fallen under suspicion as 'enemy aliens', though they clearly regarded Austria as their enemy. A commission of enquiry cleared them of disloyalty charges, but a number were still interned between 1917 and 1919.[91] At the request of their families, Cleary had interceded on behalf of some of these internees.[92]

Providing a genuine Croat priest was Cleary's initiative. In 1924, he wrote to Monsignor Marchetti-Salvaggiani at Propaganda seeking permission to find a priest to minister to the unchurched Yugoslavs.[93] In 1927, he told Liston that in his audience with the pope he had suggested Auckland needed *two* Yugoslav priests.[94] Eventually he secured the services of Milan Pavlinovich, who took up his duties in Auckland early in 1928.[95] Auckland's Yugoslav Reading Room committee contained a strongly left-wing anti-clerical element, which passed a motion against offering any sort of welcome to Pavlinovich. This led to a split in the executive and the emergence of the first real Yugoslav Club and Library (Jugoslav Dom), which associated itself with the church. In return, Pavlinovich organised the club's first Tamburica Band, performances of Croat national dances and other cultural activities.[96]

None of this had been Liston's initiative, but Liston joined Cleary in welcoming Pavlinovich to Auckland.[97] Years later, it was Liston who was honoured by the Yugoslav government of King Peter II 'in recognition of the keen and helpful interest he has always taken in the Jugoslav members of his flock'. In 1936, he was presented by the Yugoslav consul, at a public ceremony, with the Order of St Sava (Second Class). That King Peter was an Orthodox Serb, St Sava an Orthodox saint and the award was not First Class, appears to have caused some mild amusement to Auckland's Croats. Pavlinovich spoke at the ceremony and praised the work of Catholic schools in educating 'over 300' children of Croat families.[98]

Publicist for Catholic Causes

Bishop Cleary was the Catholic apologist *par excellence* at this time. As the ordinary, he was always the official spokesman of his diocese. Nevertheless, Liston had many opportunities to publicise church causes between 1920 and 1929. Sermons and speeches on church occasions were sometimes intended for a public wider than their immediate audience. Most commonly broached was the government's failure to provide state aid to Catholic schools. On his arrival in Auckland, Liston asserted:

> Once a true Christian education is secured to our children in the school and out of the taxes we ourselves pay, we are ready to fall in with whatever arrangements authority may provide.[99]

In blessing and opening the school at Good Shepherd parish in 1923, he protested that Catholic children were not allowed to take up state scholarships in Catholic secondary schools.[100] There followed further broadsides against the payment of Catholic parents' taxes into state schools.[101] Such concerns mingled with the view that education without religious instruction 'made children indifferent to God'; and 'a life without God was a failure'.[102] On the other hand, Liston joined Cleary in publicly opposing the Bible-in-Schools movement, which was viewed by the Catholic hierarchy as a Protestant means of proselytising Catholic children who *were* in state schools. He endorsed Cleary's 1925 pamphlet against Leonard Isitt's Bible-in-Schools bill.[103] He preached at St Benedict's against the Religious Exercises in Schools bill when it was being presented to parliament in 1927, and circularised diocesan priests to mobilise the faithful to write to their MPs against the bill.[104]

Other familiar Catholic concerns were also voiced in Liston's sermons. One was the secular materialism that was encroaching on the celebration of Christmas.[105] Another was Catholic teaching on marriage. In mid-1927, Liston gave a series of sermons at St Benedict's on divorce and annulment, partly in response to press reports about a sensational Anglo-American divorce case (the Vanderbilt-Marlborough case) that had involved a Vatican ruling.[106] 'Mixed marriages' (between Catholic and non-Catholic) were the subject of another sermon.[107] Only occasionally was the viewpoint of a wider, non-Catholic, world admitted, and then in controversial tones. Early in 1928, Liston addressed some of the matters raised in the current Anglican Prayer Book debate by delivering a special Lenten series of sermons at St Benedict's on 'church re-union'. Naturally, the inadequacy of Anglican theology was taken as axiomatic.[108] So, too, was the invalidity of Anglican Orders, on which Liston talked to the Catholic Students' Guild in June 1928.[109]

Liston was publicist for the wider international Catholic church, in which capacity he was occasionally involved in diplomatic public relations. When Admiral Gillet and officers of the French warship *Jules Michelet* paid a courtesy call in 1923, Liston escorted them to the convent of the Sisters of the Sacred Heart, and the home run by the Little Sisters of the Poor, two orders of French origin.[110] At St Benedict's, he preached in 1927 on the political situation in Mexico, the persecution of the church there and the unreliability of cabled news reports from Mexico.[111] A year later, all six of New Zealand's bishops signed a pastoral in sympathy with the Mexican hierarchy.[112] When he was answering Cleary's charges against him in 1929, Liston claimed that he had managed to build good relations with the *New Zealand Herald*, after an unfavourable beginning, and the newspaper had been willing to publish his contributions on schools funding, the Bible-in-Schools, Mexican persecution, decisions of the Roman rota (concerning divorce) and 'The Settlement of the Roman Question'.[113] This last-named was a series of articles which appeared in the *Herald* on three successive days, 14-16 February

1929, explaining the setting up of the independent Vatican state and the signing of an accord between Mussolini and Pius XI.[114] Some weeks later, the *Herald* reported Cleary presiding at a solemn Te Deum in St Patrick's Cathedral in honour of this Lateran Treaty.[115] As the *Herald* had adopted a hostile and critical view of Liston during his trial for sedition in 1922, it was indeed remarkable that a few years later they opened their columns to his specifically Catholic polemic.

The Discipline of the Clergy

In all these controversial matters, Liston and Cleary were in accord. They were in accord, too, in matters relating to the discipline of diocesan clergy. The rebukes they sometimes had to administer were remarkably similar. Judging from surviving memoranda and diocesan parish files, it is not possible to argue that either bishop was more or less disciplinarian than the other. Later, Liston was sometimes represented as the unreconstructed seminary rector who too often treated adult priests as if they were still adolescent students. If this were indeed the case, then another psychological explanation will have to be found to account for Cleary's identical ideas of proper discipline. The fact was that both men applied standard criteria in what was still essentially a Tridentine church.

Priests then were under the very direct control of their bishop. Subjects of Sunday sermons were specifically prescribed in annual catechetical instructions.[116] Liston, afraid chronic shortages of priests meant that catechesis was being neglected, arranged early in 1922 for a monthly 'day of recollection' to be held in Bishop's House, to refresh priests' catechetical skills.[117] He expected all to be present at the regular priests' conferences, upon which they were subsequently examined, and sternly rebuked those who had been absent without a specific exemption. He also expected priests to send him a copy of their weekly sermons.[118]

Very strict rules on the eucharistic fast bore heavily upon priests, who were expected to fast from Saturday evening until after they had said their last Sunday mass. This could mean a fast until well into Sunday afternoon for rural priests who ministered to a number of widely-separated communities. Occasionally, elderly or infirm priests were granted partial exemptions, although these had to be referred to the Vatican.[119] More commonly, requests for dispensation were simply turned down.[120] Priests were also expected to police the boundaries between Catholics and non-Catholics. There were some lodges and fellowships which the church permitted Catholics to join:

Druids, Oddfellows and Foresters (but definitely not Freemasons or the Orange Lodge). Sometimes, officials of such groups requested that they be allowed to say a few words at the funeral of a deceased Catholic member. Liston always turned down such requests on the grounds that 'the Catholic [funeral] service is quite sufficient – no other'.[121] Priests were not permitted to dispense Catholic parents from sending their children to Catholic schools. That authority was reserved to the bishops.[122] But they were expected to discourage 'mixed marriages' between Catholics and non-Catholics. According to the circular Liston sent to diocesan priests early in 1922,

> [Mixed marriages] have worked and are working incalculable evil to the church in New Zealand, and no bounds should be set to the zeal of a pastor in stopping them. If they must take place, every endeavour should be made to get the non-Catholic to take a course of instruction . . .[123]

In 1920, the hierarchy laid it down that no music was to be played for the weddings of mixed couples, which were not to be performed before the altar.[124] Bishop Brodie suggested that performing such weddings before the altar 'might add solemnity to the Marriage ceremony and leave a favourable impression on non-Catholics', but the other bishops disagreed and the ban remained in place.[125]

Priests also had their pastimes strictly limited. Attendance at the theatre was forbidden without special permission. When, in 1928, Father Shore of Morrinsville asked permission to see a grand opera performance of *La Traviata* in Auckland, Bishop Cleary told him that a dispensation could only come from the Holy See and was unlikely to be granted anyway. Any priest's presence at the opera would be 'a HOWLING scandal' and Shore would be suspended if he dared to go.[126] Particular vigilance was taken over attendance at the races, which had a greater attraction for more priests than the opera did. The hierarchy decreed that priests could not attend the races. Individual priests were sternly rebuked if they ignored this ruling.[127] But the frequency with which the matter came up in circulars and bishops' meetings suggests that priests often either ignored the ruling or found ways of circumventing it. Bishop John Mackey recalls that in the 1920s his uncle, Father John O'Byrne, would watch races at Ellerslie from Ladies' Mile, a nearby street outside the racecourse, and get members of his family to lay bets for him.[128] Similar evasion of the ruling is implied in the wording of Liston's 1922 circular to priests:

RACES. May I remind some priests that the law promulgated some years ago by all the Bishops of New Zealand forbidding priests to go to the races still holds in this diocese. I shall be disappointed if I hear of any priests breaking this law, and will consider its violation a grave fault.[129]

The law varied slightly from diocese to diocese. Some priests went to the races when visiting another diocese. The bishops agreed to forbid such priests to say mass in their host diocese.[130] This cannot be taken merely as evidence of a killjoy spirit. Races were occasions for gambling and priests were in no position to wager with funds most of them did not have. In 1923, Cleary had to deal with a priest who had incurred over £1,000 worth of gambling (and drinking) debts that he could not cover.[131] The prohibition did, however, mean that to be consistent Cleary had to turn down requests for the appointment of a Catholic chaplain to race clubs.[132]

In the financial administration of their parishes, priests were supposed to act in concert with a parish committee of six elected laymen. They were also to take their bishop's advice on the maintenance of church buildings and sale of church property. Liston and Cleary at different times wrote to individual priests condemning unauthorised property deals.[133] Both also had to determine where the boundaries of city parishes were when neighbouring priests came into dispute over their jurisdiction.[134] Most Auckland parochial correspondence from the 1920s deals with such routine administrative matters.

There were, however, a significant number of priests who did not meet the high standards expected of them. The most visible problem was alcohol. In Auckland, both Liston and Cleary had to discipline drunken priests.[135] One South Auckland priest caused a scandal in 1928 by appearing in court on a drink-driving charge, and was suspended from his duties by Cleary. But a large petition from his parishioners attested to his popularity, and he was temporarily restored to his parish on condition that he abstain from drink.[136] Less publicly visible were sexual indiscretions, sometimes connected with drink. At least two Auckland diocesan priests in the 1920s had to be removed from parishes for having affairs with women, one of them being also notorious for his heavy drinking.[137] One of the English Mill Hill fathers was rumoured to have fathered a child. As he forbade the priest to continue living with lay friends in Auckland, Cleary told him that his 'mode of life and actions' had been a 'hindrance' to the church.[138] A few priests left the diocese under a cloud.[139]

There were priests who antagonised parishioners by their absence and neglect of duties. Thomas Lynch would clearly have preferred to be a farmer rather than a priest. Parish priest of Puhoi 1919-22, Lynch deigned to visit the parish only on Sundays, neglected to keep a baptism or confirmation register, never taught catechism, was unfamiliar with the daily office and never went to Silverdale, which was supposed to be in his pastoral care. Instead, he ran a farm in Te Awamutu, which he said was on behalf of his nephew. The nephew did not exist. Liston followed Cleary's instructions, removed Lynch from the parish and assigned him elsewhere.[140] But in 1924-25, Cleary was having to deal with parishioners' complaints that Lynch was neglecting the Kumeu area of his assigned parish of Helensville.[141]

At the opposite extreme from neglect, some priests fought with their parishioners. Cleary twice received deputations from Cambridge of parishioners who were angry at Fr John Kirrane's contemptuous dismissal of his financial council, and his habit of ridiculing individuals from the pulpit.[142] In 1925, Thomas Buxton (father of Leonard Buxton) threatened legal action after Michael Joseph O'Carroll, the assistant at Remuera, publicly upbraided him for not contributing enough to a church bazaar. Cleary made O'Carroll send a formal apology.[143] That same year, Stephen Farragher of Waiuku was called to account by Cleary for naming parishioners from the altar for non-payment of dues. In his own defence, Farragher said that this was customary in his native Ireland. He left the diocese in 1925 and did not return until Cleary was dead.[144]

Priests were not the only church personnel for whom the bishops took some responsibility. Sometimes nuns had to be granted dispensations from their vows and permitted to return to secular life. It is noticeable, however, that requests for such dispensation came from women who were in danger of severe mental or nervous disorders, or who were unhappy in the communal life of the convent, rather than in contention with church discipline. There is a suggestion that those sisters who belonged to teaching orders led more circumscribed lives.[145]

Apart from generic problems such as drink, there were some individuals whose relationship with the bishop was fraught. In 1925, Cleary fell out with Archdeacon Henry Francis Holbrook. Early in the year, Holbrook had claimed that some money from the Fynes Estate should have gone to the Pt Chevalier section of his parish rather than to the new Mt Albert parish for which the Marists were then taking responsibility. Liston and the Marist

Bernard Joseph Gondringer disagreed. So did Cleary.[146] Later, Cleary dismissed Holbrook from the diocesan council and sacked him as the diocesan Chancellor. This appears to have been related to Holbrook's friendship with the editor of the *Tablet*, James Kelly. Cleary suspected that Holbrook had provided Kelly with some of the gossip which enabled sly remarks about the Auckland diocese to appear in the Dunedin newspaper.[147] Undaunted, Holbrook stayed in the diocese and had a distinguished career until his death in 1952.

While Cleary was overseas, he wrote to endorse Liston's protracted series of struggles, between 1921 and 1923, with James McGuinness, parish priest of Te Aroha and former Dean of Ohinemuri.[148] It began when McGuinness complained that Liston had diverted funds intended for refurbishing a church into a school building project in Te Aroha. McGuinness left the diocese but returned when he could not find work elsewhere. His heavy drinking increased. He refused to hand over financial records. Cleary ordered him to write a letter of apology for his rudeness to Liston. McGuinness complied. Cleary attempted to steer him into a less demanding position as chaplain but McGuinness refused the post. In late 1923, when he was back in Auckland, Cleary wrote a memo on McGuinness's drunken behaviour and brawling in a number of Auckland pubs. Under threat of arrest, McGuinness was confined by Cleary to the Ellerslie presbytery and threatened with the permanent withdrawal of his faculties (i.e. withdrawal of his right to say mass or administer the sacraments) unless he went through a long programme of drying out. The correspondence on this case shows Cleary in complete accord with Liston, although Cleary was later to claim that the problem was stirred up by Liston's antagonism towards McGuinness.[149]

The most notorious contest between priest and bishop began long before Liston's arrival, but Liston was directed to discipline the priest concerned. This was the case of Joseph Croke Darby of Hamilton, who had studied with Liston at Manly. Darby was a member of a prominent Auckland family. His father was Patrick Darby, a wealthy philanthropist who had donated much property, land and money to the church.[150] Patrick was described as the 'trusted adviser' to a series of bishops of Auckland.[151] Joseph derived his middle name from Bishop Croke, who baptised him in 1872. He had once been regarded as one of the more promising priests in the diocese. Together with Matthew Brodie, he was a 'prefect of discipline' at the Auckland annual synod in 1912.[152] He was parish priest of Hamilton from 1901 to 1921, served on the diocesan council and was made Dean of the Waikato in 1916. But according to the very evasive obituary that appeared in the diocesan newspaper *Zealandia*, Darby suddenly 'retired' at the age of 50 in 1921 and lived in retirement in Ponsonby until his death in 1941.[153] Unmentioned by *Zealandia* was the contest of wills between this volatile priest and two bishops.

Darby's first major blunder was in 1906, when he sent an abusive letter to the Minister of Lands when the Liberal government failed to lease some land off him in the Waikato. He threatened that local Catholics would get their 'revenge' in the next election. This was exactly the sort of church interference in government that could embarrass the Catholic prime minister, Sir Joseph Ward. Ward intervened with Bishop Lenihan, who made Darby apologise to the minister concerned.[154] In 1917, when he was writing his report on the diocese, the vicar-general William Henry Mahoney described Darby as having a 'spirit of uniform discourtesy and selfishness . . . This has been manifested in a marked degree towards Mgr Gillan V.G. and in a lesser degree towards myself'.[155]

One cause of this hostility related to the will of Andrew Casey, who died in October 1915. Casey left the bulk of his large estate to St Mary's church in Hamilton East. While he provided for his widow and elder children, he did not provide adequately for his younger children. They contested the will in a case dragging on from 1915 to 1918. Finally, under the Families Protection Act of 1908, the Supreme Court considerably altered the will in the younger children's favour and greatly reduced the amount payable to the church. Darby saw himself as an intermediary between the church and aggrieved members of the Casey family. But he had contracted large debts for a church building programme in the expectation of a payout from the will. By 1919, with a £3,000 overdraft in the Hamilton Church Building Fund, Bishop Cleary was getting nervous about the church's ability to service the debt, and berated Darby for not adequately looking after the church's interests. He believed that Darby had in fact antagonised the younger members of the Casey family and driven them to litigation. In 1920, the church did receive a substantial payout from the Casey estate, but not enough to cover the large interest on the loans Darby had raised. In October 1920, the Apostolic Delegate wrote to Cleary querying whether they could bring an action for damages against Darby for mishandling church finances. Meanwhile, in 1918, Cleary deprived Darby of his position as Dean of the Waikato.

Above left: A young Fr James McGuinness. In the 1920s, his drinking and disorderly behaviour were to cause problems for both Cleary and Liston.

Above right: Joseph Croke Darby, the priest whose major argument with Cleary had to be brokered and resolved by Liston in the early 1920s.

Left: James Kelly (with camera), editor of the *New Zealand Tablet* and indefatigable gossip, with his Auckland friend Fr W.J. Murphy of Balmoral. Kelly's private correspondence includes a malicious version of the conflict between Liston and Cleary.

Below: New Zealand's Catholic hierarchy at the jubilee celebrations of Holy Cross College, Mosgiel, 1925 – Liston, James Whyte, Francis Redwood, Thomas O'Shea, Henry Cleary and Matthew Brodie.

In addition to problems arising from the Casey estate, Cleary
believed that he had been slandered by Darby (and Dean Michael
Edge).[156] Darby took to describing Cleary as 'insane'.[157] By January
1920, Cleary had suspended Darby from his parochial duties and
issued a decree removing him from Hamilton parish. Darby was
able to ignore it for some months, and it was not until August 1921
that he left Hamilton.[158] Outraged at losing both his deanship and
his parish, Darby threatened to 'expose' all those he claimed were
working against him, and loudly protested. He made an appeal to
the Vatican contesting Cleary's judgement. Presenting his side of
the case appears to have been yet another item in Cleary's very full
agenda as he headed overseas in September 1921.[159]

This was the situation upon Liston's arrival in the diocese. It
was Liston who, in Cleary's absence, received the final judgement
from Rome in August 1922, which upheld Cleary's removal of
Darby from Hamilton, and ordered Darby to pay a fine of £200 and
make a religious retreat to atone for his sins. The bishop was told
to provide for Darby but not to give him any work.[160] Hence what
Zealandia was to deem Darby's 'retirement'. Liston wrote to Bishop
Whyte in Dunedin, 'I will let you know later how J.C.D. takes the
sentence. A week ago he was still talking in a very airy fashion
about victory and episcopal humiliation'.[161] He formally appointed
Michael Bleakley as parish priest of Hamilton in Darby's place.

The Vatican's judgement against Darby was written in Latin.
Complaining that Darby's understanding of Latin was hopeless,
Liston gave his account of the strained one-hour-and-40-minute
interview between them on 18 October 1922, in which he got Darby
to submit to the Holy See:

> Fr. D. explained that the point in 'cohabitatio' amused him greatly,
> that he had to laugh heartily over it and he proceeded to laugh etc.
> I rebuked him severely and told him there was no need to laugh at it
> or at anything that came from the S[acred] Cong[regation], that he
> did not know the meaning of the word in the document.[162]

Darby submitted, paid his fine, made a retreat at Greenmeadows
and effectively ended his career as a priest.[163] Cleary wrote from
London congratulating Liston and the diocesan council on doing
'the best possible in the circumstances' in assigning Bleakley to
Hamilton.[164]

This case interested other members of the hierarchy, especially
because Darby had publicly defied his ordinary and because Bishop
Brodie had still been an Auckland diocesan priest, and had fallen

out with Darby, at the time the trouble over the Casey will began. James Coffey wrote to Bishop Whyte,

> The Darby Case will teach a lesson to those who want law and who appeal to Rome. Bishop Brodie gave me a hint as to the result and Bishop Liston merely said I 'congratulate you on the result' so I presume poor Joe has got enough of law.[165]

Brodie himself wrote to Liston,

> Many thanks for the good news of Joe's submission; grace is evidently beginning to work . . . If our priests would realize that the . . . attacks of outside enemies are nothing compared with the harm done by their own, they would be more ready to live and work for the good of Holy Faith.[166]

Throughout his life, Liston had a very elevated idea of the role of the priest. It was typically expressed in a speech he gave in Dunedin at the time of the silver jubilee of Holy Cross College, where he remarked on Verdon's plans for an indigenous clergy:

> Consider if only for a moment the dignity and powers of the priesthood. Uncover and bow your heads before it, statesmen, soldiers, kings. At best your dignities and gifts are human, born of this world, confined in their reach to this world, whereas the priesthood is divine in its origin, its power and its aim. It is created by the Breath of the Incarnate God, the priest is another Christ, and his mission is Christ's own.[167]

By 1929, however, as he answered Cleary's charge that he had not adequately cooperated with him, Liston ruefully remarked on the diocese's *scandala clericorum*:

> During the past eight years six priests have been dismissed from the diocese on account of scandal, in some cases of the gravest kind. We seem to have a super-abundance of them. It has been my sad duty to deal wholly or in part with them and thus relieve the Bishop to some extent. This duty as well as that of dealing with other clerical failings meant much reference to the Bishop.[168]

Cooperation of the Bishops

By the mid-1920s, Coadjutor-Bishop Liston was regularly engaged in a busy yearly schedule of official duties. This entailed attending and acting as secretary for the regular bishops' conferences, making pastoral visitations to both city parishes and outlying areas of the diocese, presiding at clergy and religious teacher conferences in Auckland and Hamilton, presiding at meetings of lay organisations and sodalities, ordaining priests, witnessing the final vows of sisters and sometimes being present at the election of religious superiors, making regular pastoral visits to the Little Sisters of the Poor home for the infirm and elderly, being the guest of honour at Catholic school prizegivings, celebrating mass or presiding at a gathering on St Patrick's Day, attending AGMs of the Catholic Federation (before its demise in 1923), participating in the annual Corpus Christi procession at Sacred Heart Convent, saying the annual memorial mass for deceased clergy at Panmure, and also presiding at the main Holy Week and Christmas ceremonies. In 1929, Liston claimed that because of Cleary's frequent absences and sickness, it was he, rather than Cleary, who throughout the 1920s had celebrated all the Easter and Christmas pontifical high masses in the cathedral.[169] He remained, in his leisure time, a voracious reader.[170] By the 1920s, he had given up smoking but was rumoured to enjoy playing cards with some of his clerical friends.[171]

In an interview in 1964, Liston described his years with Cleary in idyllic terms. He said he was 'guided by [Cleary's] counsel and prestige' and that he 'realised it was a privilege to serve under the bishop, whom I greatly admired'.[172] Certainly both bishops appeared together at public occasions involving the whole hierarchy, such as the silver jubilee of Holy Cross College in Dunedin in 1925 or the opening of the Christian Brothers' new college 'Redcastle' in Oamaru in 1927.[173] When they were both in Auckland, they also undertook many official duties together.

Quite apart from those events that were recorded in the press, the bishops' private correspondence also gives solid evidence of their cooperation. In 1925, Cleary delegated Liston to resolve the problems that had arisen in the parish of Avondale between the parish priest Fr Colgan, and the Mercy superior Mother Mary Josephine, who deeply resented having members of her order asked to take part in parish fundraising when they were already fully engaged in running the parish school. She threatened to withdraw the order from Avondale. It is indicative of the heavy burden placed upon some teaching orders then that the sisters were expected to run a school of 160 pupils with a total staff of three. At Cleary's direction, Liston, who tended to see things Mother Josephine's way, worked a reconciliation.[174] In the same year, Cleary, under doctor's orders not to travel, lent Liston his mana for a hui on the Hokianga when a church was to be opened 'in the recently converted village near Whangape'. Cleary wrote,

It is important that this date be kept as the local Catholic converts are making great preparations for the hui, and involving themselves in a very heavy expenditure running probably into several thousand pounds . . . I personally am very keen on going there, in view of the circumstances of the conversion and the importance of the occasion in the eyes of the natives . . .[175]

Cleary also continued to give Liston considerable powers of attorney, informing one assistant priest, whose parish had incurred heavy debts, that in future all parish-related cheques had to be counter-signed by Liston.[176]

If one were to judge solely from the way events were publicly reported, and from a very limited number of archival memoranda, one could draw a picture of cooperation between the two bishops every bit as harmonious as that implied in Liston's 1964 statement. But such a picture would be quite false. The reality was that relations between Cleary and Liston deteriorated between 1923 and 1929 until, in 1929, Cleary petitioned the Vatican to have Liston ejected from his diocese. In Dunedin, Liston had been involved in the public controversy over conscription, and the private (and more bruising) debate over the episcopal succession. In Auckland, too, he was involved in a public controversy and a private struggle. The first was the spectacular affair of Liston's trial for sedition in 1922, the effects of which were relatively short-lived. Much longer was the private and growing conflict with Cleary, which was to have a more lasting impact on Liston. They were respectively Liston's lesser and greater trials.

CHAPTER IV

THE LESSER TRIAL

1922

Liston's Trial for Sedition

On Saint Patrick's Day, Friday 17 March 1922, James Michael Liston presided at a concert in the Auckland Town Hall.[1] Before the interval, he spoke to the audience of about 3,000. His speech was a wide-ranging one, lasting over 20 minutes. He deplored the 'foreign masters' and 'snobs of empire' who had driven his parents from their native Ireland. He protested his love of New Zealand. He referred to the recent treaty that had ended three years of guerrilla warfare and reprisals between Irish insurgents and British forces. He said that everyone of Irish descent would rejoice that Ireland had won 'some measure of her freedom' and that she might yet hope for 'complete deliverance from the house of bondage'. Ireland had got 'the first instalment of her freedom and was determined to have the whole of it'. Much of his speech was taken up with an expansion of the image of Ireland as the land of saints and scholars, but in its concluding moments he returned to current events. Clearly referring to Eamon de Valera, he said it was 'providential' that he was there to ensure that 'the rulers of Ireland are not duped by England'. Finally, he referred to the various groups of Irish who had died in the independence struggle since what he called the 'glorious' Easter Rising of 1916. One group, he said, had been 'murdered by foreign troops'. He concluded his speech by calling for forgiveness. The audience applauded enthusiastically a number of times. Two people walked out but there was no disorder in the hall and, after the interval, the concert proceeded peaceably with musical items and recitations.

But the following morning, the *New Zealand Herald* printed a garbled version of Liston's speech, reproducing only a small part

110

and emphasising his most contentious points. The report misled readers to believe Liston said it was the rebels of 1916 who had been 'murdered by foreign troops'.[2] It noted that the national anthem had not been sung at the Irish concert, and that instead the audience had sung 'God Save Ireland'. That afternoon, the *Auckland Star* produced an almost identical report.[3] The *Herald* account was written by Gordon Leith Stanbrook, who later admitted that he knew no shorthand and had taken only limited notes from the speech. The *Star* account was written by Laurence O'Brien, who had simply cribbed the *Herald*'s report.[4] Both newspapers delivered editorial rebukes to Liston. The *Herald*'s editor, Robert Hackett, called his speech 'sneering', 'bitter' and 'provocative', and opined, 'it is certain that such utterances do much to disturb the peace of New Zealand and to encourage religious intolerance and racial antagonism'.[5] For the *Star*'s editor, Thomas Wilson Leys, it was 'a rasping and bitter address'.[6]

Why should a speech on Irish matters provoke such an angry reaction in New Zealand at that time? Partly because, in his reference to de Valera, Liston appeared to be taking the side of the more extreme republicans in the debate still going on in Ireland over acceptance of the treaty. A few months later, that debate led to civil war between the new Irish Free State and Republican 'irregulars'. The same partisanship seemed implied by Liston's reference to Ireland having won the 'first instalment' of her freedom and being 'determined to have the whole of it'. Did this mean that he was advocating an undivided 32-county independent Ireland, against the wishes of those Ulster Unionists who had persuaded the British government to grant them their new six-county statelet of 'Northern Ireland'? It was provocative to refer to the 1916 rising as 'glorious' when imperialists still saw it as a stab in the back during the world war. Most provocative was the characterisation of British as 'foreign' in Ireland, then seen by imperialists as an integral part of the United Kingdom. The phrase causing most outrage was 'murdered by foreign troops'.

The mayor of Auckland, James Gunson, having read the Saturday *Herald*'s version of the speech, obtained an affidavit from Gordon Stanbrook vouching for its accuracy. He sent a note to Liston asking him to clarify his attitudes. Liston received it in Monday's post. But before he could reply, Gunson had already gone to the press deploring what Liston had said. In a statement printed in the *Herald* of Monday 20 March, Gunson said the speech was 'disloyal' to king and country, 'an affront to our citizenship', 'seditious' and 'designedly calculated to cause disintegration of all that Britishers hold dear'. The reference to British soldiers as 'foreign murderers' was 'especially offensive and unwarrantable'. Gunson said the Town Hall and all city council facilities should henceforth be closed to any such 'seditious and ruinous' speeches. He questioned whether those holding Liston's views had the right to be protected by the British flag, and said he was informing the attorney-general of Liston's seditious intent.[7] Liston replied to the mayor with his own brief statement that appeared in the *Herald* on Wednesday 22 March:

> Seeing as Your Worship has not had the courtesy, not to say the sense of fair play, to await my reply to your question before handing your condemnation of me to the press of New Zealand, it seems to me quite unnecessary that you should have written to me at all, and it is certainly unnecessary that I should answer your question. As Your Worship has made this matter public, I am handing this letter to the press.

Editorially, the *Herald* praised Gunson's attack on Liston as a splendid piece of public-spirited patriotism. 'There can', it said, 'be no suspicion of the motives that have led Mr. Gunson to issue a public protest.'[8] In fact, there could be at least some suspicion. Although noted for his moderation on religious matters, the Methodist Gunson was in search of a popular issue in election year. In 1919, he had failed to move into national politics after defeat by Vivian Potter, a fiercely anti-Catholic PPA-endorsed Reform Party candidate in the Roskill electorate. From this point, Gunson began to beat the 'loyalist' and imperialist drum more loudly.[9]

On Thursday 23 March, Gunson's council resolved that Liston must publicly disavow his speech before either the Town Hall or the Domain would be made available for Catholic functions. Other Auckland local bodies made similar decisions. By this time, every major daily in the country was reviling Liston's 'disloyalty'. On Saturday 25 March, the *Herald* ran a cartoon depicting Liston, dressed in a shamrock-covered shirt and wielding a shillalegh, trampling furiously on the Union Jack. Liston was, according to Leonard Buxton, 'the most talked-of man in New Zealand'.[10] Among those who wrote to the press to dissociate themselves from Liston's speech was a small number of 'loyal' Catholics, including a Catholic Maori group, William Joseph Napier of the Navy League and Patrick Darby, brother of the much-disciplined priest Joseph Croke Darby. George Earwood, vice-president of the PPA, praised Gunson as 'a Protestant with backbone'.[11] Replying to the 'loyal'

Catholics, priests under Mgr Hackett and Fr Brennan affirmed their loyalty to Liston and condemned 'certain self-constituted spokesmen of our community'.[12]

On Friday 24 March, in a close vote, cabinet decided to prosecute Liston for sedition. Prime Minister Massey and Attorney-General Dillon Bell were opposed to proceeding. But the Minister of Justice, Ernest Page Lee, and the Minister of Agriculture, William Nosworthy, both of them sympathetic to the PPA, urged the case.[13] Affirming that the most offensive section of his speech was the phrase 'murdered by foreign troops', the lawyer Patrick Joseph O'Regan (head of the Irish Self-Determination League) wrote to Liston on 25 March advising him that if he were to be prosecuted it would be under Sections 118-119 of the Crimes Act. These very catch-all clauses made it an offence 'to raise discontent or disaffection amongst His Majesty's subjects OR to promote feelings of ill-will and hostility between different classes of such subjects'. The act, under which socialists, pacifists and Irish nationalists had been prosecuted during the war, threatened two years' imprisonment for seditious utterances.[14] As the first serious account of the 'Liston affair' shrewdly remarked,

> An element of the farcical now pervaded proceedings as the heavy political artillery ranged together to answer the paltry challenge of a Catholic prelate who had not once mentioned disloyalty to New Zealand. The distinction was not appreciated at the time and seems to have been deliberately confused by all manner of persons in an attempt to make political capital out of the *Herald* report.[15]

As Liston travelled to Wellington for the ceremonial opening of St Mary of the Angels on Sunday 26 March, his friend the Dunedin lawyer John Callan formed the opinion that Liston's words really had been seditious. He advised Liston to make a guilty plea and bargain with the Crown.[16] Liston did not retract his speech, but under legal advice he sent a conciliatory message to the government in which, according to the later account in the *Month*, 'he affirmed his own loyalty and defined the obligation and loyalty which the Catholic Church lays upon her children'.[17] He released his letter to the press. Some newspapers were now satisfied that the Crown Law Office had no case to answer. Publicly, the *Tablet*'s editor James Kelly said nothing. Privately he fumed, later writing to John Hagan in Rome that Liston had apparently gone back on his stirring Irish nationalism:

> Liston used to be a friend of mine, but he has developed into a snob pure and simple since he got a little authority – dignity he will never

have. His crawl to Massey was the most awful thing ever happened here. It just illustrated the difference between being pig-headed and courageous, for he lost his head completely. He also lost the respect of clergy and laity throughout New Zealand and it was a common saying that he ought to get gaol for writing such a letter instead of sticking to his guns.[18]

The solicitor-general William MacGregor still urged the prime minister to prosecute. On Friday 7 April, a policeman came to St Benedict's presbytery and served Liston with a summons. Aware that prosecuting a bishop in the Easter season would create some unfortunate symbolism, the Crown delayed the preliminary hearing until 1 May. Accompanied by Jeremiah Cahill, Liston appeared in court before the magistrate, J.W. Poynton. His defence counsel John Laurence Conlan faced the crown solicitor Vincent Meredith. Conlan's performance before the magistrate was deemed to be mediocre, and by the time the hearing was over Patrick O'Regan had come to Auckland and agreed to be Liston's senior. The magistrate agreed with the crown that there was a case to answer under Section 118 of the Crimes Act, bail of £100 was set and the case was committed to the Supreme Court for trial.[19]

Between his summons and his trial, Liston's letters to Bishop Whyte in Dunedin show his mood to be confident – almost cocky – in contrast with his letter of conciliation to Massey's government. He wrote, 'the whole affair is doing our Catholics here immense good – I can feel it in the air'.[20] He asserted, 'I'm not conscious of having done anything to be ashamed of and we are in God's hands'.[21] Of the preliminary hearing, he remarked,

> I was treated with perfect consideration – a special room, a seat alongside counsel and every mark of courtesy. The S.M. and the Crown Prosecutor and the chief witness gave me the unmistakable impression that they were sorry to have anything to do with the business.[22]

A week before his trial he declared,

> What is most consoling is that our people here are discovering or have discovered themselves and resurrected their Catholic pride and loyalty. They are just splendid. What a change from 7 or 8 weeks ago.[23]

No matter how 'splendid' the Catholic spirit may have been, however, both Catholic newspapers were very cautious in their reporting of the case until the verdict was in. Before the trial, the *Tablet*, which had not even mentioned Liston or his speech in its first report of the

Auckland St Patrick's Day concert, confined itself to a bare account of the preliminary hearing.[24] The *Month*, in its April issue, made no mention whatsoever of the controversy. But both reported the trial itself in comprehensive detail.[25] So did Auckland's two daily newspapers.[26]

In the supreme court on Tuesday 16 May, before Mr Justice Stringer, Vincent Meredith opened for the prosecution. He asserted the essential accuracy of the reported version of the speech and called five witnesses. But under cross-examination by O'Regan, Gordon Stanbrook had to agree that he did not take shorthand, and that his version of the speech was a three-minute condensation of over 23 minutes of talk. He also admitted that he had taken only 'a longhand note of what I wanted' before writing up his version. Although the matter was not pursued in court, the phrase implied a pre-determined bias. The crown's other witnesses were unimpressive. None of the large Town Hall audience would speak against the bishop. The crown was unable to get any police witnesses to Liston's speech. A 'conspiracy of silence' was suspected of those few off-duty Catholic police who heard the speech. The prosecution was reduced to a handful of low-level council employees who made little impression in court and added nothing to the prosecution's case.[27]

O'Regan opened the case for the defence. He emphasised the distorted nature of the *Herald*'s report. He was able to prove that in uttering the words 'murdered by foreign troops', Liston had been referring only to those 57 Irish men and women who had been killed by the notorious Auxiliaries and Black-and-Tans between 1919 and 1921. The phrase had occurred in a lengthy catalogue of those Liston said had died for Ireland's freedom at different times. The catalogue was based on a report that Liston had received on the very afternoon of the speech. Under examination, Liston declared:

> I . . . have never in my life attended a political meeting. I don't remember giving any public speech in Auckland before. I have spoken in Dunedin in public and in patriotic gatherings in Mosgiel.[28]

He disclaimed any sympathy for the use of force in furthering national ends. He explained his use of the phrases about the 'first instalment' of Ireland's freedom, and about Ireland 'determined to have the whole of it', as being analogous to New Zealand's constantly readjusting its relationship with London. Liston's handwritten defence notes show that he and O'Regan had worked out this defence before the trial. Liston had noted that Michael Collins said Ireland negotiated in London as a sovereign independent nation, that it had the right to seek further freedom and that Arthur Griffith called the Anglo-Irish Treaty 'no more the final settlement than this is the final question'.[29] He had also noted points on New Zealand's constitutional development from crown colony to dominion. All of this justified his use of the word 'foreign' for the British in Ireland. It also explained why it was necessary that one party not be 'duped'. With regard to how the words 'murdered by foreign troops' had been presented in the *Herald* report, Liston said –

> The words in the indictment do not in that case set out correctly what I did say. The report is inaccurate, misleading and hopelessly bungled. I think it was taken down by a man who was as competent, however honest, to report this lecture on Irish affairs as I would be to report a lecture on engineering.[30]

He disavowed any seditious intent and said the speech had been delivered in a calm fashion to an orderly audience. Cross-examined by Vincent Meredith, Liston agreed that 'strong exception' could have been taken to his remarks as reported by the *Herald*, but said he was subsequently unable to clarify his position to the public as there had been the threat of legal action hanging over him. Meredith attempted to coax Liston into expressing admiration for the 1916 Easter Rising. Liston objected to being asked to give an opinion on this and the judge agreed with him.

On Wednesday 17 May 1922, the second day of the trial, the defence called three witnesses. Jeremiah Cahill gave evidence that 'murdered by foreign troops', as used in Liston's speech, had referred only to the activities of the Black-and-Tans. Alfred Hall Skelton, the president of the Auckland branch of the Irish Self-Determination League, was allowed to say that seven months before, in August 1921, Liston had cautioned him against saying anything inflammatory about the Irish situation. The timber merchant J.J. O'Brien attempted to give a general character reference for the bishop.

O'Regan spent over an hour making the closing speech for the defence. He stressed the inaccuracy of the newspaper reports. He quoted evidence to illustrate Lloyd George's deviousness, and hence the validity of Liston's statement about the need for Ireland not to be 'duped'. He referred at length to all those members of the British establishment who had deplored the murders perpetrated by the Black-and-Tans and he cited rebels throughout history whose illegal actions were subsequently acknowledged to be 'glorious'. He provoked laughter when he pointed out that Michael Collins, one of the rebels of 1916 and later IRA commander, was now a respectable minister of the crown in the Free State government. Would he not be welcomed with all due ceremony by the crown prosecutor and even by Mayor Gunson were he to visit Auckland? His conclusion was that there was no seditious intent and Liston's address was a permissible exercise in free speech.

Vincent Meredith's closing speech for the prosecution was much more terse, taking less than half-an-hour, insisting on the accuracy of the *Herald*'s report, criticising Liston for not publicly clearing up the matter in his statement to the prime minister and suggesting that Liston's refusal to give an opinion on the 1916 Easter Rising betrayed his basic sympathy for the rebels. Before the jury retired to consider its verdict, the judge then spent over an hour in his own summing-up of the case.

One of the most notable features of the trial was Stringer's understated sympathy for the defence. Most of his interventions benefited the defence. Only once, when he prevented J.J. O'Brien from making a voluntary statement on Liston's behalf, did Stringer assist the prosecution case. He overruled Meredith when Meredith objected to Skelton's being allowed to say what Liston's attitude to public statements about Irish affairs had been, months before the speech in contention. He supported Liston's objection to having to state his opinion of the 1916 Easter Rising. Most damagingly, he referred to the murders committed by crown forces in Ireland as 'actual facts', and remarked 'when the reprisals were in progress the Black and Tans committed murders. Everybody knows that'.[31] Meredith was 'stunned' by Stringer's admission of murders by British forces in Ireland. Already hamstrung by the poor performance of crown witnesses, the heart went out of his prosecution case from this point onwards.[32] To all intents, Stringer's hour-long summing-up was a direction for acquittal. He endorsed Liston's view of Irish history, spoke of the clear lack of seditious intention, asked the jury to consider the difference between the reported version of the speech and the version sworn to by the bishop *which the prosecution had not disproved*, and asked them to remember that 'the speech was made to Irishmen' and was appropriate to its audience.[33]

The all-male jury, which contained no Catholics, spent an hour-and-a-quarter considering its verdict. Unanimously they voted 'Not Guilty'. When the foreman Thomas Henry Chapman read the verdict out in court, there was a burst of cheering from Liston's supporters, quickly quietened by the judge. Chapman also read out a carefully-worded rider to their verdict which the jury had devised:

> We consider that Dr Liston was guilty of a grave indiscretion in using words capable of an interpretation so calculated to give offence to a large number of the public of New Zealand, and we hold that he must bear the responsibility in part at least for the unenviable notoriety that has followed his utterance.

The judge said, 'Thank you gentlemen, that is a very sensible rider'. The court was cleared. Some of Liston's supporters wanted to 'chair' him outside the court, but he avoided them and left quietly by a side door.[34]

Cheated of its prey, the *Herald* attempted to make the most of the jury's rider. Its editorial concerning Liston's acquittal still declared his statements to have been 'foolish'.[35] But after the trial, in conversation with O'Regan and Conlan, members of the jury said they had written their rider only as a sop to some of their friends 'who were very unfriendly to the bishop'.[36] The *Month* took the opportunity to censure Mayor Gunson for his 'touching faith in the disinterested accuracy of the Auckland daily press'. It went on to berate those Catholics who had not stood by the bishop.[37] Both Catholic papers advertised a testimonial to be presented to Liston, and a collection on his behalf, as 'a tangible mark of their resentment of the bigoted attack' made upon him, and as 'a token of their joy in his victory over the enemies of our Holy Church'.[38] Mgrs Hackett and Holbrook were among the organisers of this tribute, but the generous wording of the testimonial seems to have been Liston's own.[39]

Chief unfinished business after the trial was the Auckland City Council's continued ban on Catholic use of the Town Hall or the Domain. Liston hoped to enjoy the irony of having the testimonial ceremonially presented to him where he had made his offending speech. James Gunson continued to insist that the ban would not be lifted until Liston made some show of 'loyalty', and he harped on the jury's rider about Liston's 'grave indiscretion'. Throughout June and July, there was an acrimonious correspondence between them.[40] Once again, Liston's letters to Whyte showed him in a gleeful mood:

> I am having a happy time . . . toasting Gunson by letters. He started it himself – very respectfully and friendly too. He evidently sees that he is in a corner and wants to get out – at my expense. So I have given him a dirty right and an upper cut in the shape of two letters . . . Our people have applied for the Town Hall in order to have a demonstration for this criminal – but so far the request has been declined. That can't continue. I am pressing Gunson hard, first, to

grant the hall unconditionally and, second, to expunge the famous city council resolutions.[41]

Later he added,

> If Gunson doesn't move for the rescinding of the Council's resolutions about me, the Labour members will. Our correspondence is over and he is sorry (I believe) he spoke.[42]

Liston discussed with the diocesan lawyer Robert McVeagh the possibility of bringing a libel action against Gunson.[43] It was not until November that a compromise was worked out that lifted the ban, deemed the council's resolutions inoperative and allowed both parties to declare the whole incident closed.[44]

The Trial and the Times

In one sense, the most apt comment on the whole 'Liston affair' was the heading of James Kelly's editorial in the *Tablet* after Liston's acquittal: 'Much Ado About Nothing'.[45] It is easy to join Kelly in seeing the outcry against Liston as a piece of Jingo (and Orange) foolery that said little about the greater New Zealand public. But in another sense, the affair does tell us something of the nature of New Zealand society then. Condemnations of Liston revealed an identity crisis about the 'British' nature of New Zealand. As O'Regan made clear, and as Liston confirmed in his defence notes, British newspapers such as the *Manchester Guardian*, and prominent British figures such as the Archbishop of Canterbury and Lord Asquith, were less squeamish about denouncing British military terrorism in Ireland than was the New Zealand press.[46] During the Anglo-Irish war, the New Zealand press, like the Australian press, was 'more pro-British than the British'.[47] British colonials, distant from the Mother Country, declared their uncertain status by wrapping themselves in the Union Jack, the flag Liston was said to have trampled. In the mainstream press, there was reluctance to believe anything negative of Britain and her Empire. Catholics in Australia and New Zealand had, since the 1880s, frequently protested at the biased and one-sided nature of news reports about Ireland. The same week that it berated Liston, the *Herald* rebuked Bishop Whyte for his own St Patrick's Day speech in Dunedin, in which he had said that many news cables from Ireland were 'lies'.[48] This attitude of the press was in tension with the close involvement of New Zealand Catholics in the Irish struggle, especially members of the clergy, many of whom were themselves Irish-born.[49]

Yet Liston's speech and trial occurred at a time when the attitude of the colonial Irish was about to change radically. Ireland was drifting towards civil war between those who accepted and those who rejected the Anglo-Irish Treaty that Michael Collins and Arthur Griffith had signed in December 1921. Part of the offence Liston gave by his speech sprang from his apparent refusal to accept the finality of this treaty, and his apparent siding with Eamon de Valera's Republican criticisms of it. The Irish Civil War lasted for just under a year, from June 1922 to May 1923, and managed to kill more people than the Anglo-Irish War.[50] The former apparent unanimity of Irish nationalism was shattered. According to Patrick O'Farrell, among Catholics in Australia and New Zealand, the civil war 'almost totally destroyed the Irish cause' so that 'lack of interest was the best reaction to be hoped for from the handful of Republican enthusiasts'.[51] The Catholic hierarchy in Ireland unambiguously sided with the new Free State and roundly condemned lawless Republicans for creating 'a domestic strife as disgraceful as it is criminal and suicidal'.[52] In Australia and New Zealand, too, with the sole exception of Daniel Mannix of Melbourne, Catholic church leaders endorsed the new Free State.[53] The Catholic press followed suit. The civil war caused the Hibernian Society in New Zealand to withdraw from any further Irish political debate and confine itself to being a friendly society.[54] In September 1922, in the presence of much of the diocesan clergy, Liston celebrated a requiem mass for Arthur Griffith and for Michael Collins, whose recent assassination was deplored as one of the worst of Republican crimes.[55] In Dublin, Cleary attended the funerals of Griffith and Collins. So did James Duhig, who was an outspoken supporter of the Free State.[56] Cleary witnessed some of the Irish fighting at close quarters, and narrowly missed being shot in an accidental volley in Enniscorthy.[57]

By the mid-1920s, it was common for even sympathetic New Zealand Catholic clergy to speak in exasperated tones of Irish political matters. In 1925, Fr Forde of Te Aroha wrote to Cleary, from Bray in Ireland, about a debate over the Irish Boundary Commission that he had witnessed in the Dail in Dublin. His caustic comment was –

> When I return to New Zealand I want never more to hear of the 'Irish Question'. I have made a good study of the people here during my holiday and I am convinced they don't know what they want.[58]

If this was all a fairly immediate sequel to Liston's speech, a larger context was the beginnings of the de-Hibernicisation of the Australasian church. Like other Pakeha, most New Zealand Catholics by the 1920s were New Zealand-born.[59] Over in Australia, some younger priests criticised the church's Irish leadership and adopted a distinctively Australian nationalism, such as those who were in the Manly Union (founded 1914) with its motto 'Pro Deo et Australia'.[60] The Apostolic Delegate sympathised with their hopes for an Australian church to evangelise Australian people. In like fashion, he had a hand in promoting the appointment of Matthew Brodie as New Zealand's first native-born bishop.[61] There were minor Irish-flavoured incidents later, but Liston's trial was the last major 'Irish' controversy in New Zealand Catholicism. In the later 1920s, there was a distinct reluctance among Auckland Catholics to celebrate St Patrick's Day with the same fanfare and fervour as previously.[62] It was no longer a venue for contentious statements about the political state of Ireland.

Within a few years, Liston made his peace with both the *Herald* and James Gunson. In later life, he showed a pronounced disinclination to recall anything controversial about Ireland. In 1963, an obituary by Liston celebrated Archbishop Mannix's greatness as a church leader, but scarcely touched on his attachment to Ireland and made no mention of his arrest at sea in 1920 (an affair which had created the same sort of Irish-related controversy in Australia as Liston's trial had done in New Zealand).[63] At about the same time, he was said to have rebuked Rolland O'Regan (son of his defence counsel) when, at a private function, O'Regan referred to Liston as a famous 'rebel'.[64]

In another light, Liston's trial could be seen as the last major episode in the sectarian tensions that had divided New Zealand since the time of the conscription debate. As it happened, Howard Elliott had been sick during the first six months of 1922. Without his demagogic leadership, the PPA had not exploited the Liston controversy as vigorously as they might otherwise have done.[65] In 1921, sectarian tensions were such that the accidental destruction of the Grey Lynn convent by fire could still lead some Catholics to suspect, wrongly, that it was the work of PPA-inspired arsonists.[66] There were still examples of the apparent exclusion of Catholics from public competitions.[67] In 1925, Bishop Cleary could still express concern over possible Protestant criticisms of Catholic events, such as the way the Mill Hill fathers ran a fund-raising lottery.[68] Nor did a triumphalist Catholic interpretation of church history cease to be the norm, as when Patrick O'Regan delivered a stirring address (in Liston's presence) on the centenary of Catholic Emancipation in 1929; or when Liston himself, speaking to the Catholic Students' Guild, dismissed Martin Luther's life work as 'purely of a revolutionary nature, without reform or improvement [for the Christian church]'.[69]

Yet it remains fair to say that the 1920s witnessed the decline in that bigotry which had reached its peak in the last years of the war. Visiting Poverty Bay and the East Coast in 1923, Liston rejoiced that 'the wretched plague of sectarianism' had not taken root there, and that 'the most cordial relations existed among all creeds'.[70] In the same year, the Catholic Federation was wound up. When the PPA's publication the *Sentinel* denounced the new convent school at Puhoi as 'creeping Romanism' that was destroying the state school system, local Protestants wrote sympathetic letters to the Catholic parish priest deploring the *Sentinel*'s stand.[71]

The PPA had its one legislative victory in 1920, when it persuaded the Reform government to add a clause to the Marriage Amendment Act making it an offence to question the validity of legally-contracted marriages. This was intended as a hit at the papal *Ne Temere* decree.[72] But after that point, the PPA began to wither away. It was a 'shadow of its former self' by the late 1920s.[73] Cleary described it as 'pretty nearly defunct' when, in 1929, a bemused Minister of Education in Sir Joseph Ward's United government forwarded him a piece of PPA outrage at the minister's having attended the opening of a convent school.[74] As early as 1922, the *Sentinel* had declined to a tiny circulation of about 1,000 and Massey's Reform government was beginning to see Howard Elliott's associates as a political liability.[75] Massey maintained a courteous correspondence with Bishop Cleary and on a number of occasions refused to meet PPA delegations. He did not seek PPA endorsement for Reform candidates going into the 1922 election, and Catholics were delighted to note that some prominent government supporters of the PPA (such as E.P. Lee) lost their seats in that election.[76] In return, members of the PPA took to denouncing Massey as a mere 'place-holder'.[77] When Massey died in 1925, the new Reform prime minister Gordon Coates specifically repudiated the PPA.[78] Finding an Irish connection, James Kelly rejoiced to his friend John Hagan in Rome,

> Events here are tame. The new prime minister is a decent man and not a bigot. As a matter of fact he is a cousin of Roger Casement. He is well disposed to us, and he put his foot down on bigots who wanted to arouse anti-Catholic feeling during the elections.[79]

By this stage, the PPA was well on the way to being a tiny crank group, disdained by all political parties. It ceased to exist in 1932. The Bible-in-Schools movement also declined to comparative insignificance. Bible-in-Schools bills were repeatedly rejected by parliament in the late 1920s and early 1930s. The movement limped on into the 1940s before giving up the campaign and switching to acceptance of the voluntary 'Nelson system' of religious instruction.[80] Politicians no longer saw support for this Protestant campaign as a potential vote winner. The larger background to this was the rise of Protestant nominalism. In 1921, 56 per cent of those who listed themselves in the census as Catholic were regular churchgoers, but only 36 per cent of Presbyterians and 23 per cent of Anglicans were. In 1921, Methodists were ahead of Catholics in this table (59 per cent), but they had slipped behind Catholics by the 1926 census.[81] The 1926 census also suggested that only 55 per cent of Protestant children of Sunday School age were actually attending, whereas the figure had been nearer 90 per cent at the turn of the century.[82]

If Liston's trial may be seen in a context of declining bigotry, and declining Protestant commitment, it occurred in that of friendly relations between the Catholic church and the Labour Party.[83] Labour courted Irish Catholic votes with an 'Irish campaign' during the Anglo-Irish War. They gave it credibility by making their chief spokesmen on the issue the conspicuously non-Irish Harry Holland and Peter Fraser.[84] Seeking to broaden its support base, Labour stepped back from the doctrinaire socialism that had been anathema to most church leaders. Michael Joseph Savage formed a friendship with Liston in the early 1920s. The two of them often went for Sunday drives together. Savage made a point of never missing Sacred Heart College sports days.[85] In 1929, he appeared with Liston at the formal opening of the new blocks of St Mary's College in Ponsonby and spoke generously of the work of the Mercy Sisters.[86]

Labour spokesmen defended Liston before, during and after his trial for sedition. Savage had been a member of the Auckland City Council at the time it censured Liston, but he had been absent during the relevant debates. It was left to another Labour councillor, Tom Bloodworth, to oppose James Gunson, John Allum and others.[87] In the week that the *Herald* misreported the St Patrick's Day speech, John A. Lee wrote to Liston interpreting the controversy as conservative electioneering:

> ... 90% of our movement are with you without qualification. We have so frequently been accused of disloyalty by similar groups and factions and know so well what their 'loyalty' means.[88]

Lee later added, 'everything that is young and clean and decent is on your side'.[89] In one of his replies to Lee, Liston wrote,

Your letter goes right to my heart and I will treasure it and your warm heartfelt support always. If I were to talk for a month I could not sufficiently say how much I appreciate the goodness of yourself and your friends these days. We shall meet again.[90]

On his acquittal, Liston was sent over 200 congratulatory messages from clergy and laity, but also from many Labour supporters.[91] Bloodworth and George Davis were the two councillors who now attempted to have the council's ban lifted.[92] Combining Biblical with socialist imagery, Bloodworth wrote to Liston,

I almost wish that their hearts may be hardened as was the heart of Pharoah of old, and with the same results i.e. overwhelmed in a Red Sea of votes.[93]

Labour MPs reviled the vehemently anti-Catholic member Vivian Potter, one of them describing Potter to Fr Holbrook as 'a piece of political filth'.[94] As secularists, Labour members were also tactical allies with the Catholic church in opposing the Bible-in-Schools. In 1927, John A. Lee wrote to Liston acknowledging Liston's thanks for his efforts in this area. Lee opined that at that date Reform and other conservative MPs were only going through the motions of supporting the Protestant pressure group.[95]

In all its formal statements, the New Zealand Catholic church was politically neutral and non-partisan. But in the same year as his sedition trial, Liston made a second public utterance that outraged some political conservatives, suggested an official Catholic bias towards Labour and led to another flurry of denunciatory letters to the editor.[96] Labour made considerable gains in the election of 1922, getting 17 members into the House. Like other Catholics, Liston believed that the Labour Party was more friendly to the church in the matter of Catholic education. In his speech at the Sacred Heart College prizegiving, closely reported in the *Auckland Star*, he applauded the election result:

I have full confidence in the sense of fairness among my fellow countrymen. I believe that they will in time come to see the justice of our claims in this matter of education, and when they have seen the justice they will soon undo the grave wrong. The minds of men move. We saw last week that the people of New Zealand have at last awakened to the true state of affairs in the political life of this country. In the same way we feel that the people of New Zealand will one of these days awaken to the injustice that is being done daily to Catholics in the matter of education. Thanks be to God the Labour people, our friends, are coming into their own – a fair share in the government of the country. They were not long since a minority, now their claims are being listened to. So too, please God, we Catholics, a minority, will come into our own and have our claims in the matter of education listened to with respect.[97]

It could be argued that the speech was mainly about Catholic education, but what stuck in people's minds was the phrase, 'Thanks be to God the Labour people, our friends, are coming into their own'. Years later the septuagenarian John A. Lee claimed that Liston had made a similar comment upon Labour's becoming government in 1935. He recalled the words, 'Praise be to God our friends, the Labour Party, are coming into office'.[98] As there is no other evidence that Liston made any such statement in 1935, this is presumably Lee's misremembering and misreporting of the 1922 comments. In itself, that is testimony to their notoriety.

Liston's trial can been seen, then, in the context of Labour's strategic alliance with the Catholic church. The political opportunism of some Reform members and of the mayor of Auckland provoked both the controversy and the trial. In the period after the trial, sectarian bitterness faded away but so did Catholic enthusiasm for Irish political causes. It remains pertinent, however, to ask why it was Liston who was prosecuted for his remarks in 1922. Others in New Zealand had been far more outspoken about British outrages in Ireland. With great regularity in the period 1919-21, James Kelly's *Tablet* described British actions in Ireland as 'murder'. 'Civilians Murdered by British Soldiers', 'Murder by the British Military', 'Bashi Bazouk Government in Ireland: Murder, Fire, Loot', 'How Lloyd George Murders Ireland', 'Government by Murder', 'Wanton Butchery – Crown Forces Shoot Youths They Were Ordered to Bring Home' – these are all headlines from the *Tablet* in the period of the Anglo-Irish War.[99] Such stories were often accompanied by Kelly's bellicose anti-imperialist editorials. Though more restrained, Cleary's *Month* also regularly denounced the Black-and-Tans' 'reign of terror' or 'militarist terror' in Ireland, sometimes comparing it with 'Prussianism' in occupied Belgium during the war.[100] A romantic mythology presents the sober 41-year-old Liston as a 'turbulent young priest' and firebrand over the Irish issue.[101] In the 1980s and 1990s, *Saoirse – New Zealand Irish Post*, a tiny-circulation publication with a Marxist-Sinn Fein editorial policy, three times reproduced abridged versions of Liston's speech as a stirring specimen of Irish patriotism.[102] It also showed a marked hostility to any attempts to interpret the speech in a more balanced fashion.[103]

One contention of *Saoirse* may be true – that after Liston's acquittal it became possible for New Zealanders to comment more freely on British policies.[104] But the notion that Liston was an ardent Republican is very wide of the mark. Perhaps Ernest Simmons, in his diocesan history, came nearest to explaining the phenomenon of Liston receiving the opprobrium that others better deserved. After recording that Bishop Cleary had sometimes been outspoken on Irish affairs, Simmons noted that Cleary (OBE) was a more familiar figure to Aucklanders. He had made patriotic imperialist statements during the war and, as a former front-line military chaplain, could be seen as a returned serviceman. But 'the almost unknown Liston, rather cold and precise in speech, was both more offensive to the patriotic and an easier target'. Simmons concluded that Liston was 'deeply hurt' by the trial and that it fuelled his suspicions of ill-will towards the church.[105]

Seen together in 1934, two prelates who had both caused a stir by their involvement in Irish nationalism – Liston with Archbishop Daniel Mannix of Melbourne.

CHAPTER V

THE GREATER TRIAL

1923-29

Bishops in Conflict

Overseas throughout the period of Liston's trial, Cleary sent back messages of complete support for his coadjutor.[1] He interceded on Liston's behalf with government leaders. But almost as soon as he returned, their relationship began to sour. There followed six years of unpleasantness between the two bishops. This came to a head in 1929 when Cleary petitioned Propaganda for Liston's removal.

In June 1928, Cleary wrote to Liston formally delineating their respective responsibilities. Cleary decreed that thenceforth he would look after all diocesan temporalities, parochial properties, finance, accounts, archives, Curia (marital) cases, orphanages, irremovable rectorships and the *Month*; and provide direction for all men's societies, retreats and missions. Liston's responsibilities were confined to visitations, clergy conferences, diocesan education, chaplaincies of religious orders, preparing students for ordination and representing Cleary with the Fynes Trust.[2] In January 1929, when he was in America for a couple of months, Cleary sent the Apostolic Delegate an indictment of Liston in 28 numbered paragraphs, prefaced by his contention that –

> Monsignor Liston has never yet been a coadjutor . . . as contemplated by the Church and required by Her laws and the terms of his appointment. On the contrary he has all along and persistently acted – and still continues to act – in a spirit of opposition and hostility to the undersigned Bishop of Auckland.[3]

The Apostolic Delegate forwarded a copy of these charges to Liston, and in April-May 1929 Liston formulated a defence.[4] To Cleary's comment that Liston had only four times invited him to St

Benedict's since 1921, he issued a flat denial and added, 'If during the past five years the Bishop had shown one mark of genuine courtesy it would have been eagerly welcomed and wholeheartedly responded to'.[5] In June, Cleary formally petitioned for Liston's removal from his diocese, and in July, Liston had his complete defence of himself typed up. It is a very long document (320 pages) including copies of letters, memoranda and other matter as corroborating evidence for Liston's view of the situation. When he retired in 1970, Liston destroyed all his personal correspondence, but he kept materials relating to his trial for sedition and he kept three large files on his differences with Cleary.[6] They contain both rough handwritten drafts and final typed copies of his defence of himself, and such correspondence as supported his case.

Like the processes surrounding the appointment of the Bishop of Dunedin in 1918-20, the contention between Cleary and Liston was not played out in public. It is noticeable, however, that many press photographs taken of Cleary and Liston at public functions in the late 1920s show two men standing far from each other, as if studiously ignoring each other's presence.[7] We are justified in feeling some scepticism about that high mutual praise they sometimes expressed in public situations at this time.

All this began upon Cleary's return to the diocese in June 1923. The formal address of the clergy stated,

> You will have learned abroad how ably his Lordship Bishop Liston
> has conducted the affairs of this diocese, and now upon your return
> you will see first hand how it has progressed under his care.[8]

Cleary, however, chose to see no such thing. A diocesan historian opines that Liston had come to regard Cleary's long absence as a signal that the diocese was to be gradually handed over to him.[9] Instead, Cleary reasserted his authority and found fault with much that Liston was doing. In November 1923, Cleary wrote to complain that Liston had not arranged for the debt on the Vermont Street boys' school to be met.[10] In March 1924, he claimed that some priests had protested to him about Liston's organising too many missions in their parishes.[11] By 20 May 1924, matters were such that Liston began to keep a memorandum book of all the things in dispute.[12] Liston attempted to set up a Catholic Buying Association to supply food to diocesan colleges, schools and orphanages at cheaper rates than they were currently enjoying. Cleary forbade further meetings on this proposal. Fr Holbrook believed Cleary was afraid that such an agency, not involving some companies which the church patronised,

Above: Bishop Henry William Cleary as he liked to be seen – about to make a pastoral visitation in one of the Walsh Brothers' flying boats.

Below: At Bishop's House in Ponsonby in 1926, Cleary and his coadjutor Liston host the eminent Archbishop Daniel Mannix of Melbourne, and the less eminent Bishop John McCarthy of Bendigo.

might hurt the advertising revenue of Cleary's beloved *Month*.[13] Cleary sent Liston a letter claiming that a delegation of priests had come to him complaining of Liston's high-handed manner. To his minute book Liston confided his 'disappointment to think that such a letter co[uld] be written'. A friend (possibly Mgr Ormond) commiserated with him that it was an 'extravagant production, full of idle gossip', said that he had heard nothing of any delegation to the bishop and suggested it was a 'myth'.[14] Liston had a 25-minute meeting with Cleary. Liston apologised if he had, inadvertently, seemed to usurp some of Cleary's authority and denied that he had invited religious orders to make foundations in Auckland without Cleary's knowledge. In his minute book he reported Cleary as being 'much milder and quite courteous' in comparison with his letter, but as saying that, while he thought he had got 'the pick of the bunch' when Liston was appointed his coadjutor, he now believed Liston's authority should be restricted because 'the majority of the priests and a considerable section of the laity had very strong feelings of indignation' against him.[15] A few days later, on 25 May 1924, Liston met with the Marist provincial Charles O'Reilly, who refuted Cleary's claim that it was 'common gossip' in Wellington that Liston had attempted to bypass Cleary in inviting orders into the diocese.[16] Liston added a memo that 'in order to keep peace in the diocese' and 'for the sake of my own soul', he would not pursue Cleary's further accusations.[17] But in June, when Mt Albert parish was formally handed over to the care of the Marist order, Liston was hurt that Cleary did not invite him to the ceremony at which the Marists were installed, especially as he had been responsible for Mt Albert up to that time. Liston agreed with Ormond that the appropriate procedure was to make his formal farewells to his Mt Albert parishioners the week before the ceremony.[18]

Three months later, Cleary had a major disagreement with Liston about how diocesan sustenation funds should be invested. Cleary curtly told Liston that he was not a trustee and should defer to the advice of a 'zealous and successful Catholic businessman in the city', by whom Cleary probably meant Donald McDonald.[19] In December, Liston wrote that Cleary 'didn't seem a bit interested' when he reported on the state of catechetics and of Auckland students attending Holy Cross, Mosgiel.[20]

Some tension between the bishops was becoming a habit by the end of 1924. When Cleary made his indictment of Liston in 1929, his numbered paragraphs accused Liston of general mismanagement, encouraging financial disorder, usurping the ordinary's authority, showing disrespect for church and civil authorities, and misusing the Catholic press for partisan political statements. Bearing in mind that many documents survive only because Liston chose to preserve them, it is still instructive to assess what substance there was in each of these charges.

Concerning general mismanagement, Liston did make administrative errors. In early 1923, he had to write to the Director of Education to apologise for failing to have a new Catholic school in Avondale registered as a private school, and inspected by the Department of Education, before it was opened. He admitted to 'a similar infringement' with two other schools.[21] In the management of priests, Cleary charged that there was an 'indignant protest' by some priests at Liston's 'follies and tyrannies', and that Liston had threatened to suspend some of the protesting priests. Particularly, Cleary claimed, Liston had dictated the letters threatening suspension to a '16-year-old schoolboy'.[22] Liston replied,

> It is true that on one occasion I made a twofold mistake in threatening with suspension some junior priests because of their delay in attending to a legitimately prescribed duty (the writing of sermons) and in causing the notices thereof to be dictated by an ecclesiastical student, aged 21. I at once regretted the foolish mistake, due to my inexperience, and tried later to show my regard and affection for these good priests.[23]

While Cleary's statement of the case here may have been exaggerated, Liston had acted imprudently and in a manner calculated to antagonise some priests. Other of Cleary's charges are less probable. Cleary claimed that Liston refused to make parochial visitations, forcing Cleary to undertake arduous tours of the diocese himself.[24] Liston replied,

> I have not even once refused a request made by his Lordship the Bishop to go to any parish for Visitation or Confirmation . . . Not one priest has on any occasion whatsoever asked that I should go to his parish for Confirmation or Visitation and been refused.[25]

He substantiated this by giving details of all the parishes he had visited since 1921. He had made three or four visitations to every parish, and was able to produce letters of thanks from priests. He did admit that some years his visitations were fewer than they could have been. In 1923, he was preoccupied with raising funds for the fire-damaged orphanage, while in 1925-26 he was recovering from his operation for appendicitis and visiting America. Rather mischievously, he could not forebear to include in his response a letter from the Mill Hill Father Devolder, complaining of the nuisance Cleary's much-publicised visitations by air actually caused, implicitly in comparison with Liston's more orderly visitations.[26]

Cleary accused Liston of abandoning educational clergy conferences.[27] More defensively here, Liston replied that the Codex did not define running such conferences as one of his duties, that he had run 12 clergy conferences between 1921 and 1923, but later 'I could not feel I possessed the confidence of His Lordship the Bishop and I thought it better to take no action'.[28] He also noted that Cleary had attended no clergy conferences at all between 1914 and 1921.[29]

In many responses, Liston's trump card was Cleary himself. Liston was able to produce a letter from October 1923 in which Cleary urged Liston to slow down, saying that he might suffer –

> ... a serious breakdown through overwork, aggravated by a high capacity for absorbing, and reacting to, worry of every kind ... I shall ever most gratefully remember that you have taken all this varied mass of work and worry upon your shoulders with a view to relieving me as far as possible.[30]

There was also Cleary's friendly note of February 1925, thanking him for undertaking pastoral visitations in the north of the diocese, and a letter from July 1928 in which Cleary said it was quite acceptable for Liston to quiz priests by mail about the state of their religious knowledge rather than at conferences.[31]

Cleary's indictment of Liston's financial disorder is rather more prolix, as are the necessary responses. Cleary charged that Liston had indulged in 'unauthorised and irregular sales of church property', dismissed the regular diocesan lawyer, found a more pliable one and disposed of properties at under market value; that he had trusted an 'adventurer' (i.e. property speculator) with valuable city properties, and attempted to override the expert advice of the lay members of the diocesan administrative council. Liston 'imposed excessive financial burdens upon small and poor congregations' in the mortgages and loans he had arranged. He also maladministered the Fynes Trust, which was responsible for providing teachers' salaries in 11 Catholic schools. Hence any control of church property by Liston 'would result in calamitous mismanagement of the temporalities of the Diocese'.[32]

In his lengthy reply, Liston was able to list all ten parishes for which he had arranged loans and mortgages, always after extensive consultation with the parish priests and parishioners, and in all cases on terms that meant the mortgages were easily paid off. He produced letters of commendation from parish priests to substantiate these claims. By contrast, he counter-charged, Cleary himself had loaded much larger burdens of debt on some parishes without any consultation at all. He noted that, in resuming control of temporalities in October 1923, Cleary had made no charges whatsoever against Liston's administration, and had not thought to do so until years later. More tellingly, Liston remarked, much of the work of which Cleary now complained was done early in their association:

> During my first nine months in Auckland before the Bishop's departure in 1921 I attended to, with his full knowledge and consent, various temporal matters. I did so all the more eagerly because during these months the Bishop was a very sick man and spent many weeks in the Hospital. In brief, I was given a very large and effective share in the government, temporal as well as spiritual, of the diocese. The Bishop encouraged and approved my work before his departure and in letters from Europe . . . I had no idea how long the Bishop was to be absent: he often spoke as if he were not going to return. During his absence the work of the diocese had to go on and parochial activities fostered.[33]

Liston expressed complete confidence in the lay members of the administrative council, Robert McVeagh, J.J. O'Brien, Thomas Mahoney and Henry Kavanagh. The only one he did not fully endorse was Cleary's favourite, Donald McDonald. He defended himself from the charge of entering into a compact with an Australian 'adventurer' by noting that the proposals of the man in question (M.S. Dunne of Melbourne) were always considered by the diocesan council, and few of them had been taken up. As for substituting a more pliable lawyer for the diocesan solicitor Robert McVeagh, Liston noted that his lawyer John Laurence Conlan was already retained in diocesan work before Cleary's departure overseas, the work of the two lawyers overlapped and Conlan had taken on some of McVeagh's work only when McVeagh had not been available. Further, he noted, Cleary had never answered his own correspondence about the Fynes Trust. The secretary of the trust (A.A. Dignan) endorsed Liston's administration. Liston remarked that when Cleary had been a trustee (1916-23), he had not attended any meetings.[34]

Another of Cleary's major accusations relating to finance was that Liston had misapplied trust funds 'to a purpose of his own choosing' in a number of parishes, that this was 'an offence of very great gravity under our criminal law' and that in one case Liston had 'succeeded in scaring the parish priest into committing a criminal misapplication of the local Trust funds'. The parishes to which Cleary referred were Pukekohe and Te Aroha. In the latter case, Cleary claimed, the priest in question required considerate treatment 'on account of certain facts in his family's mental history'. But Liston's 'extreme bitterness' had driven the man to drink.[35] The priest was James McGuinness, Liston's discipline of whom had been fully endorsed by Cleary in the period 1921-23. Liston's reply said that Cleary's account of matters in Te Aroha was 'simply imagination run riot'. In the case of Pukekohe, Liston noted that his decision to divert funds (from extending the parish church to building a proper parish school) had been taken when the Education Department was hostile to Catholic schools and severe in their criticisms of their shortcomings. The existing parish school was below standard, being a couple of rooms in the local convent. Liston had had the unanimous approval of the diocesan consultors for this diversion of funds.[36] Other correspondence shows that in early 1922, Liston urged Pukekohe's parish priest, James Molloy, to see the building of a proper school as imperative:

> Bare justice to the children and teachers demands a proper school building, and the facts that the Sisters have given for many years to the Parish free school rooms and have taught the parish children for all these years for a mere pittance call aloud for recognition in the shape of decent classrooms.[37]

When Molloy pleaded that the parish was too poor to contribute to the Cathedraticum, Liston sent him a blank cheque to cover it.[38] Molloy appears to have been offended that his parish church was not extended. Two years later, in April 1924, he wrote to Jeremiah Cahill complaining that Liston had caused the church to lose a promised legacy, by interfering and causing to be modified a design for an addition to the church that had been approved by Cleary. He also said that he had been 'up against it' ever since Liston had been in charge.[39] When an angry Cleary questioned Molloy about this, however, Molloy was not able to offer any proof that the church had lost a legacy. It was merely 'the word of old Mr. Goodwin' that he might have contributed more money.[40] This seems to have been the sum of Liston's maladministration of Pukekohe.

In formulating his indictment, Cleary appears to have been working out his annoyance with a number of people. The wording comes close to suggesting a 'conspiracy' against his authority. Cleary had pronounced disagreements with others about temporalities. In 1921, he was piqued that the Marist Brothers decided to buy a property in Tuakau for their juniorate (training centre) rather than one in Papakura which had been offered for sale by Patrick Darby.[41] In 1928, he was still harping on this matter in one of his verbose two-part letters, when he took the Marist Brothers to task for suggesting that Auckland diocese did not adequately support them.[42] Interestingly, Liston is not mentioned in the paragraph of his indictment where he condemned 'a very small and rapacious group' of property speculators and unskilled lawyers who, Cleary claimed, were trying to defraud the diocese. But he did claim in the next paragraph that they were 'close personal friends' of Liston's.[43] Cleary also persistently defended his friend Donald McDonald. In September 1926, he warned Fr Michael Edge of Te Awamutu that he would support McDonald in a threatened action for slander, after Edge said that McDonald had personally profited from generous fire insurance policies he had arranged for church properties.[44] In 1929, Cleary published 'for private circulation only' an account of the diocesan administrative council. This gave his view of every member of that body. He lavished particular praise on Robert McVeagh and Donald McDonald.[45] In August 1929, he sent a copy of this publication to Mgr Marchetti-Salvaggiani of Propaganda, with a covering note especially commending McDonald who was, he said, 'assailed, unjustly and untruthfully, by a very small group of personal enemies' including Fr Holbrook and Fr Forde who were 'light-headed and incurable gossips'.[46] In his indictment, Cleary accused Liston of unwisely trusting an agent in financing a church building project in Morrinsville. The agent offered 'generous' loans which were secured against his own mortgages. Cleary did not acknowledge that the agent was in fact McDonald and that he too had trusted him implicitly in this matter. Liston pointed this out in his reply.[47]

Reading the surviving evidence, and admitting that Liston has been the archivist, it is still hard to avoid the impression that where financial matters are concerned, Cleary's accusations make very much out of very little. Even harder to take seriously are Cleary's accusations of Liston's usurping his authority and showing disrespect for church and state. Cleary complained that Liston regularly occupied the episcopal throne in the cathedral, bore the pastoral staff, wore the mozzetta, and had been heard to use the formula, 'My dear people, I am now speaking to you *as your Bishop*', as if he were the ordinary. Further, said Cleary, Liston had forbidden

Mgr Cahill to take a health trip which Cleary had authorised, and had shown 'dire offensiveness and hostility . . . and bad manners' towards Cleary at diocesan council meetings.[48] Denying that he had ever claimed to be Bishop of Auckland, Liston said he used the episcopal throne, staff and mozzetta only during Cleary's long absence. As a teacher of liturgy, he was uncomfortable about doing this, but Cleary had insisted. He quoted a letter Cleary wrote in November 1921, in which he reflected on the outcome of his serious illness:

> But (*entre nous soit dit*) if I consulted my own feeling in the matter, I would have preferred a very different issue to the malady. I felt that I had had my day and, if it were God's will, would have vastly preferred the Great Rest. However, if there be a complete recovery 'non recuso laborem'. But when I return, and you are better acquainted with the Diocese, you will increase and I shall diminish – I shall be steadily less and less (I hope) Bishop of Auckland, and you more and more the ruling power there. The younger shoulders must bear the burden; only, I fervently hope, you will not, either now or then, follow those phases of my career, in which I unskilfully (v. often, I fear, stupidly) made the work needlessly hard for flesh and blood . . . I thank God with all my heart you are in Auckland.[49]

The complaint about Liston's disrespect for church and civil authorities arose from a single incident. Cleary claimed that at the reopening of the boys' orphanage in 1924, Liston had inconvenienced the Governor-General, Lord Jellicoe, by beginning the event half-an-hour later than planned, and had then prevented the Apostolic Delegate from properly performing the religious ceremony.[50] Aware that he was addressing one of the dignitaries he was supposed to have insulted, Liston told Cattaneo that Cleary's 1929 indictment was the first time he had heard any complaint about this. He denied intending any disrespect in having to delay the ceremony slightly, and took the opportunity to remark –

> In connection with the Orphanage Building . . . priests and people generally felt that the Bishop might very fittingly have made some public acknowledgement of my work in providing homes for the orphans after the fire, in rebuilding and in raising within twelve months the greater part of the rebuilding fund (about £23,000).[51]

Harder to dismiss were Cleary's accusations of Liston's political partisanship. According to Cleary, Liston was a 'strong and highly indiscreet partisan of a particular political party', too friendly with the Labour Party, whose journal was notorious for its 'aggressive

Cleary and Liston stand behind the Marist Superior Fr Rieu, and the Apostolic Delegate Cardinal Cattaneo, 1929. It is possible that Liston's body language reflects the behind-the-scenes conflict between the two Auckland bishops. He appears to have aged by many more years than the eight or nine that have passed since the official portrait reproduced on page 89 above.

atheism'. This was 'to the grief and shame' of New Zealand Catholics, especially as Liston had shown a marked hostility to Cleary's publication the *Month*:

> The Diocese of Auckland is kept in a state of anxiety and tension on account of Monsignor Liston's notorious tendency to highly indiscreet (and at times highly sensational) public and semi-public utterances and actions.

Cleary instanced not only Liston's 1922 St Patrick's Day speech and remarks at the Sacred Heart College prizegiving, but also two editorials which had appeared in the *Month*, when it was under Liston's direction, at the time of the 1922 general election. These, claimed Cleary, had allowed a propagandist in 1928 to launch an attack on the political partisanship of the Catholic church.[52]

The editorials to which Cleary referred appeared in the *Month* on 15 September and 15 December 1922. The first was mainly an attack on Howard Elliott and the PPA. It stressed Catholics' freedom of conscience to vote for whichever party they chose, but did criticise the Reform government for 'its general tendency to show anti-Catholic bias', including its marriage legislation, its education policy and 'its attitude in regard to Bishop Liston'. Clearly, this could be interpreted as an incitement not to vote for Massey's party.[53] The second noted happily that some PPA-friendly candidates had been defeated. The anti-Catholic propagandist to whom Cleary referred was the Anglican Canon Percival James. In June 1928, after the defeat of yet another Bible-in-Schools bill, James wrote to the *Herald* denouncing the Labour Party as a tool of the Catholic church.[54] As evidence, James referred to Liston's speech from six years previously. This charge was refuted by the Labour Party.[55] It was also refuted by Cleary in a sermon at the beginning of July and in an exchange of letters with the Anglican Bishop Averill, which appeared in the *Herald* July-August 1928. Cleary later had them printed in the *Month*, together with further refutations of Canon James, and also in pamphlet form.[56]

Replying to Cleary's accusation, Liston flatly denied political partisanship:

> I am not a strong and highly indiscreet partisan of a particular political party in New Zealand. Such a statement is false through and through. I have never in all my life attended even one political meeting. I have never seen or spoken to the leader of the New Zealand Labour Party.

While strictly true (Liston had never met Harry Holland), this statement overlooked Liston's friendship with Michael Joseph Savage and the sympathetic notes he exchanged with John A. Lee and Tom Bloodworth. Liston claimed that his 1922 speech at the Sacred Heart College prizegiving had been misreported, that most people had happily forgotten it, and that if Canon James chose to use it as polemical ammunition six years later, it was only because he was a noted anti-Catholic bigot, taken seriously by few people outside his own Bible-in-Schools movement. As for the two editorials in the *Month*, Liston disowned them as the work of an unreliable editor, J.C. Gill, 'a confirmed drunkard and drug-taker', who had been appointed by Cleary and who had written them when Liston had been too busy with visitations to supervise the paper closely.[57]

Years earlier, before real editorship of the *Month* passed to the newly-ordained Father Peter McKeefry, Cleary had indeed approved the appointment of Gill. He had later been aware of Gill's shortcomings before the editor was sacked.[58] In February 1923, Cleary wrote to Liston from Rome, acknowledging that Gill had written the editorials and declaring –

> I do not intend to face the worry of intemperance on his part. I already notified to him my vehement objection to the party-political attitude taken by him in 'The Month', the diocesan organ, contrary to my known and expressed directions. In the same letter, I informed him of the probability of his dismissal, for this cause, on my return.[59]

Nevertheless, Liston's answers to charges of political partisanship are among his feeblest. Even if Liston's prizegiving speech was made years previously, it had been undeniably partisan. Even if Liston had not written the *Month* editorials, the publication had been part of his responsibility at that time. In this instance, it was harder for Liston to use Cleary's earlier words to refute him. Careful political neutrality was one issue on which Cleary was very consistent. It made him a successful apologist for the church.[60] When he first read reports of Liston's Sacred Heart College prizegiving speech, Cleary was appalled. In the same letter in which he deplored Gill's editorials, he told Liston –

> I have to confess, frankly, that I am greatly perturbed by this alleged report. As it stands (I may add) it is very likely to embarrass me soon and seriously here [in Rome]. *It even makes me feel troubled about the relations between you and me in the future.* So you will

understand how anxiously I await the qualification or correction of this alleged report.[61]

Later, Cleary explained that he was sympathetic to Labour and usually voted for them, but he was troubled by their 'purely secular' education policies. He pointed out that, despite its rhetoric, the only party to provide some concessions to Catholic schools was the Reform Party – at least until the PPA goaded it into undoing some of its helpful work. From his personal contacts, Cleary also noted that neither Massey nor his attorney-general Dillon Bell had wanted to prosecute Liston for sedition. That was solely the will of the 'rabbit-brained section' of the Reform cabinet.[62] Upon his return to Auckland in June 1923, Cleary was careful, in his reply to speeches of welcome, to stress the principles which he believed should govern the Catholic press. It should 'keep itself . . . free from alliances or entanglements either with or against any political party'.[63] In 1928, Cleary wrote to the Apostolic Delegate saying that 'not more than two party-political ecclesiastics' had been in a position to endanger the Catholic position regarding the 'protestantising' measure that might pass through parliament; and that 'one of these is now reformed'.[64] Presumably he was referring to James Kelly at the *Tablet* and implying that Liston was the 'unreformed' political priest.

In all this, Cleary's quiet, non-partisan diplomacy and willingness to make friends with MPs across the political spectrum were at odds with Liston's more confrontational approach. Nevertheless, there was still something forced in Cleary's suggestion (in 1929) that Liston's statements (in 1922) could be used to bring on a new round of sectarianism. Not only had the heat gone out of sectarian issues by this date, but Cleary himself was in as good a position as anyone to know what sort of an opponent Canon Percival James was. He had himself had to face James's criticisms when, in 1924-25, James attacked Cleary's evidence against a Bible-in-Schools initiative.[65] Furthermore, some of Cleary's ire at the two editorials in the *Month* could be related to touchiness over his pet publication. Bishop Brodie was later to suggest that clerical careerists in Auckland knew they could win the bishop's favour if they flattered the *Month*.[66] There is archival evidence to support this contention.[67] There is also evidence that, despite Cleary's claims that the magazine made a healthy profit, it was partly underwritten by the sale of diocesan assets.[68]

Further vitiating the effectiveness of Cleary's indictment was his attempt to revive the odium of two controversies that were already passing from public consciousness. In both cases, Cleary's 1929 accusations of Liston flatly contradicted Cleary's earlier views.

The first of these was the matter of Liston's sedition trial in 1922. Cleary now claimed that it was 'a singularly ill-timed and indiscreet political public speech' and that Liston had only 'narrowly escaped' a guilty verdict through 'the brilliancy of his lawyer'. Like the *Herald* seven years previously, Cleary now chose to emphasise the jury's rider.[69] In his reply, Liston remarked that the whole affair had sprung from the mayor's political ambitions; that the jury had very quickly declared him not guilty; that the few Catholics who had written against him in the press were now on friendly terms with him; and that he had been supported by the Catholic community at large *including Cleary*. 'I shall always remember this action of the Bishop with a sense of most grateful appreciation', said Liston. He also noted that since 1926 he had been on friendly terms with James Gunson ('we meet now and again and write one another pleasant letters') and that the *Herald* now frequently opened its columns to him. Instancing the wide Protestant help he had received in rebuilding the boys' orphanage in 1923, Liston described the action against him as 'the beginning of the end for bigotry in New Zealand'. He concluded,

> It appears, then, that the only one in Auckland to attach importance to the Sedition Case after these seven intervening years is His Lordship the Bishop.[70]

Cleary's attitude in 1922 had been completely supportive of Liston. Not only had he sent an encouraging telegram; in Dublin, he had also urged Michael Collins to intervene with Winston Churchill at the British Foreign Office on Liston's behalf, in order to halt the pending prosecution. He apparently drafted the message that Collins sent. But the Foreign Office merely forwarded it to the governor-general and to Massey, both of whom replied that public opinion supported the case's proceeding.[71] Liston was able to compile a large file of letters proving that Cleary, in 1922, said the opposite of Cleary in 1929. In April 1922, as Liston's possible prosecution was being debated, Cleary wrote to say he would intercede 'without a moment's delay' on his behalf.[72] In May 1922, Cleary said he had spoken to Dillon Bell in Europe and knew that Liston would not be convicted. The whole affair had only arisen in reaction to the offensive editorial policy of the *Tablet*.[73] Liston rejoiced to Bishop Whyte in July 1922, 'I am very blessed, am I not, in having such a wholehearted friend as my Bishop'.[74] In August 1922, Cleary forwarded to Liston a copy of a letter he was sending to Gunson, rebuking the mayor for passing judgement on Liston and continuing to close the Town Hall to Catholic meetings.[75] Cleary later sympathised with Liston over the council's refusal to lift the ban.[76] When he prepared to return to Auckland in June 1923, Cleary stipulated that nobody associated with 'the soi-disant "Maori Catholic" attack' upon Liston could participate in his welcome home.[77] In 1929, it was easy for Liston to rebut Cleary over this matter when he could quote Cleary, in 1922, writing the following:

> I read, and re-read, with very great pleasure, your description of your attitude and action towards Mr. Gunson since the happily abortive trial. Your attitude is kind, friendly, charitable, dignified, yet firm and in all respects proper and worthy of your position as Catholic Bishop. I would myself act towards him, in the same circumstances, in the same way, if the Lord gave me as much wisdom.[78]

The other case Cleary resurrected in 1929 had caused a brief sensation in September 1924. This was the so-called 'Martin Case'. Margaret Martin, a 17-year-old schoolgirl at Epsom Girls' Grammar School, ran away from home. She said she wanted to become a Catholic, but that her widowed mother would not let her. She was influenced by one of her teachers, Miss Terry, who was a Catholic. For a week Margaret Martin's whereabouts were unknown until it was discovered that, without her mother's knowledge, Leonard Buxton had arranged for her to be living with a Catholic family. Finally, Bishop Cleary brokered a meeting between the girl, her mother and the family solicitor. Margaret was brought, by taxi, from an unknown location to the bishop's residence. She went home with her mother on the understanding that, at some later date, she would be free to decide whether or not she became a Catholic.

The matter was followed eagerly by the *Herald* and the *Auckland Star*. There were reports of a meeting of the Grammar School board at which it was discussed whether a teacher should be dismissed for unduly influencing a pupil's religion.[79] There was the suspicion that Margaret Martin had been incarcerated in some Catholic institution. Had the sectarian atmosphere been more heated, and had the PPA been stronger by that time, the matter could have been inflated into a *cause célèbre* like the Liguori affair in Australia in 1920-21.[80] As it was, Cleary wrote a long personal statement in the *Month* refuting the *Herald*'s suggestion that the girl had been either abducted or secreted in a Catholic convent and vindicating his part in the affair.[81] He later arranged to have this statement reprinted in Catholic publications overseas, where the case had been cited in sinister terms by some Protestant sectarian journals.[82] He also expanded his statement into a pamphlet.[83]

Liston had very little to do with this affair. He is mentioned nowhere in either the contemporary newspaper reports or in Cleary's apologia. But in his 1929 indictment, Cleary claimed that Liston and Leonard Buxton had jointly arranged for Margaret Martin to be removed from her mother's home, and that Buxton had then refused to give Cleary information about the matter. Cleary had not spoken to Liston about this, but he attempted to 'prove' Liston's complicity thus:

> Rev. Dr. Buxton was a former pupil of Monsignor Liston in the Provincial Seminary of New Zealand ... he is known to consult frequently his former teacher and personal and family friend – Monsignor Liston is a very frequent visitor to the Buxton family ...

He also sought to impart a sense of moral horror by saying that the whole case had arisen as a result of Miss Terry's lesbian attraction to the schoolgirl (the term he used was 'sexual perversion'). This, he said, had been clear to the girl's mother ('a remarkably cultured and ladylike widow') and was clear to him when he interviewed Miss Terry. He promised a 'secret and inner history' of the affair should the Vatican request it – presumably meaning one that would expand on such personal and sexual details.[84]

Liston's major reply was that he had never met or even heard of Margaret Martin until the whole case was over. The girl had gone to Leonard Buxton, who had put her in the hands of Cleary's solicitor, Robert McVeagh. Liston did admit that he had interviewed Miss Terry, who had come to talk to him about 'one of her pupils' who wished to become a Catholic. But he said he had then 'strongly advised her . . . to be very prudent in such a delicate matter'. Given Miss Terry's devout Catholicism, Liston said he was shocked at Cleary's suggestion of 'sexual perversion'. Rhetorically, he asked, 'If the Bishop really believes this charge, why did he allow her brother to be ordained a priest in Rome last November?' He added,

> The sensation was largely a creation of the bigoted newspaper the *Herald*. The same paper followed the same line of action last year during the Eucharistic Congress by making a sensational feature of an unfortunate incident on the part of one of our priests.[85]

There are some dubious elements to Liston's defence of himself here. His characterisation of the *Herald* as 'bigoted' is at odds with his explanation elsewhere that he enjoyed cordial relations with the editor and had been allowed to contribute articles. To a later generation, too, there is something naïve at least in his rhetorical question about Miss Terry's brother. It seems to assume that homosexuality is a communicable disease. Referring to a priest's misbehaviour as an 'unfortunate incident' is indicative of a church that was not forthcoming about the shortcomings of its clergy.[86] Nevertheless, Liston's final point about the Martin case reflects more badly upon Cleary than it does upon Liston:

> The case occurred in 1924. Neither during the case nor at any time since did the Bishop discuss my conduct with me, or ask me for any explanation, or inform me, directly or indirectly, of these grave charges. The very first I hear of them is four-and-a-half years later . . .

If Cleary's attempts to replay matters from seven and five years previously were fairly questionable, they were not as questionable as his most personal level of attack upon Liston. This was Cleary's attempt to show that Liston was mentally unbalanced – perhaps even insane. Cleary was aware that since 1921, Liston's younger sister Anne had been in a psychiatric hospital in Ireland.[87] In a letter to Liston in mid-1929, Cleary claimed that he had shown his coadjutor special consideration because of this fact.[88] More than once, part of the two bishops' duty had been to consult each other about the mental health of priests and of candidates for the priesthood.[89] Cleary, a polymath in many ways, even claimed some expertise in matters of mental illness 'as the result of a keen interest taken by me . . . during five years' experience as chaplain to two very large public mental hospitals'.[90] There is strong circumstantial evidence that, in 1929, Cleary made a covert attempt to find out more information about Anne Liston, the better to suggest a congenital mental abnormality in Liston himself. In June 1929, Captain T.C. Donne, apparently one of Liston's trustees in the matter of his sister, wrote from London to tell Liston that he had not disclosed Anne's whereabouts when a publishing company sought information about her on behalf of 'one of our customers who lives abroad'. Liston conveyed to Donne his 'cordial thanks'.[91]

Throughout his indictment, Cleary repeatedly describes Liston's actions in terms of 'hysterics or semi-hysterics'. Speaking of their interview in May 1924, Cleary says –

> . . . means had to be adopted by the undersigned Bishop to soothe his Coadjutor as if the latter were a sobbing baby, and to restore to him some partial degree of mental calm and send him home. In a

long and varied experience of men in very many countries, I have never before, and never since, witnessed such exhibitions of violent and uncontrolled emotionalism, and such manifest loss of balance, in an adult male.[92]

On the occasion of the reopening of the orphanage in 1924, says Cleary,

> Monsignor Liston acted offensively towards the undersigned Bishop in the presence of a crowd of people (making 'ugly faces' at me, after the manner of a rude schoolboy) . . . one of the priests surrounding the Apostolic Delegate said aloud 'Look! Look! Look at Bishop Liston. He's acting like a madman!' As a former chaplain to two large mental hospitals, with five years' experience, it was then (and it still is) my firm and decided conviction that Monsignor Liston's mind was temporarily unbalanced on that occasion.[93]

Replying to such accusations, Liston could only dispute Cleary's version of these events, deny that he was mentally unbalanced and refer to the opinion of the rest of the hierarchy.[94] What he failed to note, however, was that in alleging fears of Liston's 'hysterics', Cleary was providing himself with a convenient excuse for having never previously approached Liston (or anybody else) about some of the things of which he was now accusing him. Explaining, for example, why he had never, prior to 1929, said anything to Liston about the Martin case, Cleary pleaded,

> . . . the utter futility of approaching Monsignor Liston for any statement of his part in these transactions, and the complete certainty that the writer of these lines would not only fail to secure any such information, but would also add to his own great anguish of mind the racking spectacle of yet another exhibition of hysteria by Monsignor Liston.[95]

It would be easy to dismiss Cleary's charges as the baseless accusations of a man who was, by 1929, wracked with permanent sickness. But surviving evidence suggests that one of Cleary's accusations may have had some merit, and another might be regarded more sympathetically by later generations of Catholics.

Cleary complained that Liston had not kept records of meetings of the diocesan administrative council during the bishop's absence 1921-23. This does indeed seem to have been the case; no minutes of such meetings survive in the archives. By 1927, aware that he would be subject to Cleary's criticisms, Liston withdrew from attending the council's meetings and referred Robert McVeagh to Cleary on any matters with which the council dealt. At the same time, Cleary, having made his complaint, had to explain why he himself had kept no minutes of administrative council meetings from 1923 to 1925. He said that the meetings were informal, and that he had not recovered the minute book from Liston.[96]

The issue upon which later generations of Catholics may have agreed with Cleary was the issue of the Knights of the Southern Cross. It was part of Cleary's indictment that Liston had introduced a 'secret society' into the diocese without Cleary's knowledge. In this instance, Liston appears to have done nothing irregular, but nevertheless to have offended one of Cleary's best-established and most sincerely-held beliefs. Like nineteenth-century Irish bishops who had condemned Fenianism, Cleary was opposed to secret societies of any sort. He waged particular war upon Freemasonry and the Orange Lodge. As a young priest in Australia, he regularly wrote to the press refuting scandal stories about the church that had been spread by the Orange Lodge.[97] In 1899, he produced a 400-page exposé of the lodge, explaining its origins, its oaths and its proclivities to violence.[98]

Founded in Australia, the Knights of the Southern Cross was a Catholic men's organisation which had much in common with the American Knights of Columbus.[99] Membership forms asked each applicant 17 questions, designed to prove he was a practising Catholic, would keep all society matters confidential, and was willing to 'defend Catholicity and Catholics against bigoted and ignorant attacks wherever made, and against insidious rationalist and materialist propaganda'.[100] Some Australian bishops welcomed the organisation as 'a vehicle of information, influence and action'.[101] The bishops appointed chaplains to the knights, although some did later express misgivings about having in parishes a society that was independent of the parish priest, and potentially a rival source of authority.[102]

At a meeting with a group of laymen in Auckland in 1921, Liston approved the formation of a similar, but home-grown, organisation called the 'Senator's Lodge'. By 1923, there were 70 members, and Jeremiah Cahill was acting as chaplain.[103] Members of this organisation approached other New Zealand bishops with a view to establishing the Senator's Lodge in their dioceses, but Bishop Brodie told Bishop Whyte he found it too much like 'a kind of Catholic Freemason's Lodge', and said he would prefer the Australian Knights of the Southern Cross instead.[104] By late 1923, Liston had come to agree, membership of the Senator's Lodge in Auckland was pruned back and made more exclusive, and it finally became a branch of the Knights of the Southern Cross with J.McD. Coleman as the first Supreme Knight.

All this was very much Liston's initiative, but Cleary never approved of it. Although it was pledged to obedience of the ordinary, for Cleary it was still a 'confidential' Catholic group in his diocese that was not under his direct control or supervision. Cleary was especially galled to hear non-Catholics refer to the Knights as 'Catholic Freemasons'. In 1929, he deluged Liston with letters explaining his objections to the Knights, their secrecy, exclusivity and potential to undermine the legitimate authority of local priests. On 21 March 1929, he ordered Liston to disband the organisation in Auckland and drafted the circular that was to be sent to Auckland members explaining his decision.[105] Unhappy, Liston complied, reporting that the Knights had disbanded 'with the most perfect loyalty and respect'. More disingenuously, he ignored the prior existence of the Senator's Lodge by adding, 'I was not in any way the founder or inspirer of the Order in this Diocese', and he claimed that it was founded with Cleary's knowledge and tacit approval five months after Cleary's return from Europe, in December 1923.[106]

The rest of the hierarchy was aware of these developments in Auckland and sympathised with Liston. On 24 April 1929, at a bishops' meeting which all attended, the minutes reported –

> Dr. Brodie spoke of his recent establishment of the Knights of the Southern Cross in his Diocese. Archbishops Redwood and O'Shea and Dr. Whyte agreed with him in their cordial approval of the work, which had been operating in their dioceses with hugely successful results.[107]

Liston (who kept the minutes) and Cleary said nothing to these remarks, but it is hard to interpret them as anything other than a deliberate rebuke to Cleary. They were cited by Liston as he refuted Cleary's charge that he had devised a dangerous secret society. He went on to remark that no other New Zealand bishop had heard the rumour, which Cleary retailed, that the existence of the Knights was going to be used as the basis for an anti-Catholic attack in parliament.[108]

Post-Vatican II Catholics tend to share Cleary's distaste for a secretive men's society that reported to the bishop on parochial matters. Nevertheless, Liston had neither committed any impropriety nor done anything that was not approved by the whole hierarchy – with the exception of Cleary.

Significance of Cleary's Indictment

A survey of all Cleary's accusations, and all Liston's documented replies, has to reach the conclusion that Cleary's indictment was mainly unbalanced, unfair and unjustified. But it remains to ask why Cleary made his case in the first place. It is very easy to slip into psychological speculation and see the mercurial genius and polemicist at odds with the pious methodical plodder. Given Cleary's initial enthusiasm for Liston's assistance, it could be interpreted as a 'marriage that went wrong'. Perhaps Cleary resented it when Liston ceased to be merely the unassuming research assistant and subordinate he had once been, and became instead a rival centre of power and attention. Perhaps Liston, in his relationship with some priests, really did become the schoolmasterly precisian and pedant whom James Kelly had criticised in 1919. Cleary exaggerated the evidence, but Liston's manner and approach did antagonise some priests. Under much of Cleary's indictment and Liston's response there lurks what a later cliché would call a 'personality clash'.

Quite apart from their age difference of 22 years, there were two issues which may serve to show the different ways Cleary and Liston thought and reacted to the world: Prohibition and responses to Ireland.

Cleary stood out from the rest of the Catholic hierarchy by supporting the prohibition of alcohol. He was a welcome propaganda prize to the New Zealand Alliance for the Abolition of the Liquor Trade, which had few Catholic friends. In 1918, Cleary had a long and friendly correspondence with John Dawson and R.S. Gray of the Alliance, accepting their assurances that communion wine would not be affected by their proposals and being congratulated on having declared, 'Mount the water-waggon and stay there'.[109] Before each liquor poll, his editorials in the *Month* reassured Catholics that they could vote for Prohibition.[110] The Alliance used his statements in newspaper advertisements, notably his proclamation that 'The Church of the Living God is Built on a Rock – not on a Vat'.[111] A handful of other Catholic public figures supported Cleary's stance. They included the Dunedin Catholic businessman Charles Todd, who was for a short time president of the Alliance, and a few crusading priests from overseas.[112] Some local priests, however, appear to have gone through the motions only of supporting Cleary on this issue.[113]

Archbishop Redwood disapproved openly of Cleary's stance. He denounced 'the fanatical and gallingly inquisitorial tyrants, the

Prohibitionists', and his own pastorals urged Catholics to oppose the movement at each liquor poll.[114] Similarly, Whyte described Todd as 'unreliable' and 'dangerous'.[115] Whyte thanked Monsignor Pesorari in Rome for preventing Todd from getting a papal blessing. He also noted that Redwood and Cleary regularly issued pastorals of opposing tendencies on the liquor question.[116]

Cleary's association with prohibitionists can be seen as part of his tendency to win friends across sectarian divides. He also served to undermine Protestant mutterings about the Catholic church's being in the pocket of the brewing interest. It was, after all, true that Archbishop Redwood's nephew Vernon Charles Redwood was a member of a brewing family.[117] Brewers did sometimes make very friendly overtures to the church.[118] Irish Catholics were over-represented among New Zealand's publicans.

Unlike Cleary, Liston was convinced by the argument that Prohibition would lead rapidly to restrictions on altar wine. He confided these fears to Bishop Whyte when he expressed disapproval of one Auckland priest (George Wright) who appeared on a Prohibition lecture platform.[119] He also asked Whyte jocularly if he had 'any powerful exorcisms for scotching . . . Prohibition'.[120] Liston, the publican's son, the alcoholic's brother, the teetotaller by choice, knew the damage that alcohol could do. Like another abstemious celibate, his friend Michael Joseph Savage, he 'disliked the excessive consumption of alcohol and the squalid conditions in which it was often consumed'.[121] But he was unconvinced by the Prohibition argument.

Liston was fully aware of his ordinary's views on the matter when he visited the United States in 1926. In his diary he recorded extensive observations on how Prohibition was not working there. Liston remarked that some bishops had formerly been in favour of the Volstead Act, but were now all against it. Prohibition had corrupted public officials, had put police officers in the pay of bootlegging gangsters and had increased disrespect for the law. Liston was impressed by the sight of Catholic men in a packed Chicago stadium taking a pledge of sobriety. But he saw this as being in line with the American bishops' policy of encouraging voluntary Temperance rather than compulsory Prohibition. Irish priests in Chicago, 'old Thurles Men', were all scornful of Prohibition. To Liston, Archbishop Matthew of Regina, Archbishop Sinnott of Winnipeg and Mgr Moynihan of St Paul's seminary –

> ... all described Prohibition as a failure, impossible to enforce, millions spent on enforcing, crime a result, 1,750,000 stills in USA, drunkenness in homes where none before. No difficulty re Altar Wine in St Paul, but has been difficulty in some Southern States.

Every bishop to whom Liston spoke described Prohibition in negative terms, although none had any difficulty in obtaining altar wine. The Archbishop of Baltimore 'said he never had champagne in the house until Prohibition came in! A farce'.[122]

Posterity is likely to agree with Liston rather than with Cleary on this issue. Even in the 1920s, New Zealand support for Prohibition was waning. There followed decades of an increasingly pointless liquor poll at each general election, until it was eventually abolished in 1987.[123] Nevertheless, unlike the publicist Cleary, Liston did not air his views publicly. His private difference of opinion with Cleary was not a matter for Cleary's indictment.

The matter of the two bishops' shared Irish heritage is more complex. Cleary was Irish-born and Irish-raised, but from a middle-class Wexford family. He was proud of the fact that some of his ancestors were Protestants. His father Robert Cleary was Catholic but his mother Susan Wall was a convert from Anglicanism. Some of her Sutton relatives had connections with Trinity College, stronghold of the Anglo-Irish establishment in Dublin.[124] Cleary tended to conceive of Irish nationalism in terms of justice for Ireland *within the British Empire*. In other words, he was a Home Ruler, looking to make Catholics the legal and economic equals of their Protestant masters. In 1909, his 400-page book *An Impeached Nation* indicted aspects of British rule in Ireland since the Act of Union – rack-renting, coercion, jury-packing, suspension of Habeas Corpus as applied to Irish patriots, the 'closed shop' of the Protestant Ascendancy in leading professions, and the unbalanced way violence in Ireland was reported in the British and colonial press. But nowhere did he suggest that complete independence from Britain was the answer for Ireland. His appeal was to the British legal system and sense of justice and his ideology was implicitly Home Rule.[125]

A necessary Home Rule strategy was the constant courting of approval from the ruling British (and British colonial) elite. Cleary's care not to outrage non-Catholic opinion was seen in his banning of all Sinn Fein paraphernalia, banners, badges and posters from any Irish meeting in his diocese, and his insistence that 'God Save the King' be played at public gatherings of Catholics.[126] Such an attitude could be interpreted as obsequious or 'shoneen' by more determined Irish nationalists like Cleary's fellow Wexford-man

James Kelly. 'Through thick and thin Cleary waves a khaki flag and recks as little of Ireland as did his land-grabbing ancestors', wrote Kelly scornfully of Cleary's war service, taking an additional shot at Cleary's Protestant forebears.[127] Indeed, there is something condescending in Cleary's reports on the Irish troubles. Not only was he a supporter of the Free State in the Irish Civil War, but he took pride in the fact that his brother Christopher Cleary (a 'dead shot' who 'knows no fear') was organising the defence of his home town against 'Dev's and Childers' robber and murder gangs'.[128] The Republican 'irregulars' under de Valera and Erskine Childers were 'organized gangs of robbers and assassins'.[129] Cleary told Liston, 'Ireland has learned to her bitter cost not to trust her fortunes to ill-born outside adventurers who find their natural level among the criminal gangs'.[130] While such language was not unusual among disapproving clergy, the choice of 'ill-born' as an epithet for de Valera seems significant. The haughty Free Stater looks down on the foreign and peasant Republican rabble. Cleary is at his very worst when he writes to the Bishop of Killaloe describing how he was caught, between Dublin and Kilkenny, in an ambush of Free State troops by Republicans. While telling how he 'rescued and removed one man under pretty active fire', he continues, 'neither I nor my car was hit – the firing was the firing of amateurs, which is about the best feature of all the fighting witnessed by me'.[131] Irishmen with guns in their hands are 'amateurs', not the 'real' imperial soldiers whose hardships Cleary has shared on the Western Front.

The New Zealander Liston was born and raised far from his parents' Irish homeland. They were 'farmers' (that is, descendants of peasants) from the overwhelmingly Catholic West of Ireland. Their cultural formation and mythology differed from that of the Wexford middle class. Despite spending student years in Ireland, Liston still took the more romantic view of Irish nationalism typical of children of the exiled. He was never an ardent Republican. But, until the aftermath of his 1922 speech taught him prudence, he clearly advocated complete independence for Ireland. It is not always possible to make a simple causal link between ancestral background and political views. Like Cleary, Archbishop Redwood was the child of Anglican converts, but unlike Cleary he was also an outspoken supporter of Sinn Fein during the Anglo-Irish War.[132] Even so, the different Irish backgrounds of Liston and Cleary were a factor in their different temperaments and outlooks.

Cleary was always preoccupied with what New Zealand's non-Catholic majority would think of Catholic affairs. Most notoriously he had printed an edition of the catechism which omitted questions on Catholic marriage that might be considered offensive to Protestants. This was at the time of the controversy over the proposed Marriage Amendment Act in 1920.[133] Cleary was inclined to overstate the dangers of sectarian strife. This is evident throughout his indictment of Liston. Justifying his suppression of the Knights of the Southern Cross, he told Liston he feared a Protestant campaign against 'secret societies' and he referred to the reaction to the Martin case:

> I thank God that the then rising tide of anti-Catholic passion did not reach the level which I (and others as well) feared during those weeks of agony and (for our people) persecution – namely the wrecking of St. Patrick's Cathedral and Presbytery and of this house by enraged and 'worked-up' mobs. Here are easily possible results of a combination of guarded secrets and wild sensations that have so deeply afflicted the Diocese.[134]

One wonders whether Cleary's accusations of Liston's 'hysteria' would not have been better self-directed.

Was Cleary over-concerned with the church's public 'image' at the expense of its day-to-day working? This was the way Liston chose to present the matter when he wrote –

> . . . it is, in fact, the common impression among the priests that the Bishop takes no deep interest in parochial problems that touch the spiritual life of the priest and people. For myself, I cannot, for example, recall the Bishop's ever speaking about the St. Vincent de Paul Society in spite of its extensive devoted work. Since I came to Auckland eight-and-a-half years ago he has not attended one meeting of the Society, though its quarterly meetings are as a rule held in public. Again, he has never shown any interest in the Students' Guild . . . he once promised to present a paper, but it did not materialize.[135]

Elsewhere he remarked that priests had said Cleary –

> . . . hurries thro' the work of Visitation, preaches at irregular intervals, never hears confessions in the Cathedral and but seldom in country parishes, gives the impression of taking but slight interest in the priests' spiritual well-being and problems etc.[136]

This contest of wills between the two bishops was not public knowledge, but Catholic clergy could not help knowing that something was amiss. Rumours spread, including the rumour that Liston might be transferred to Hobart. 'There seems to be some trouble in the Auckland diocese, for the Apostolic Delegate paid a private visit there', a puzzled Sister Mary de Sales Grennell wrote to her cousin John Hagan in July 1929.[137] Cattaneo came in the middle of the year in an attempt to mediate between Cleary and Liston. Auckland clergy did take sides.[138] Recalling his time as a young curate in the 1940s, Bishop John Mackey spoke of some older priests who 'had a bond in that they were known as "Cleary's men"'. He listed Michael Bleakley of Hamilton, Bill Dore of Tuakau, Joe Murphy of Te Aroha, Bill O'Meara of Paeroa and his own parish priest Edward Lyons.[139] It may be significant that, many years after Cleary's death, Liston had not transferred any of these men into Auckland city parishes.

The clash of personalities between Liston and Cleary was not the only falling-out that occurred in the diocese in the 1920s.[140] But it was the most demoralising. There were individual priests whom Liston had offended or irritated.[141] The group most openly at odds with him were the Mill Hill Fathers. Occasionally they had their difficulties with Cleary. In 1929, one of them, Father Bruning, expressed his anger at what he saw as Cleary's underfunding of their Maori Mission by declaring, 'I thoroughly dislike working in Bishop Cleary's diocese'.[142] More often, however, the order preferred the Maori-speaking Cleary to Liston. Dean van Dijk wrote in his confidential report in 1924,

> The bishop of the Diocese (Dr. Cleary) is our great friend and admirer . . . The auxiliary Bishop (Dr. Liston) is unsympathetic towards the Maori Mission. I have been forced on occasion to fight him in order to protect our interests. The fact that he came out second-best has not lessened in any way his antagonism.[143]

Possibly in the same year, Father Jansen wrote to the Superior-General in London –

> Our Bishop has truly proved himself a father to us and has helped and encouraged us in every possible way. The auxiliary bishop (*cum jure successionis*) has shown himself not so favourable to us. I would almost call it hostile and we all fear the day when death shall call our Bishop away.[144]

Both Cleary and Liston had had to discipline two Mill Hill priests over drunkenness.[145] In 1929, Cleary also had to defend himself against Dean van Dijk's accusation to the Vatican that the diocese was not adequately supporting the society.[146] Nevertheless, it was clearly Liston who was most out of sympathy with the Mill Hills. Defending himself against Cleary's accusation that he was not helping the Maori Mission, Liston was reduced to citing Dean van Dijk's conventional Christmas greetings as evidence of their good will.[147]

On the other side, there were significant individuals with whom Cleary had quarrelled, such as Fathers Holbrook and Forde whom he accused of being incurable gossips. In 1917, Mother Aubert's order, the Sisters of Compassion, had withdrawn from Auckland diocese. After Aubert's death late in 1926, Cleary wrote to them in Wellington saying they were welcome to return, but they preferred not to do so until well after Cleary's death.[148] There was sharp correspondence between Cleary and a member of the diocesan council, J.J. O'Brien, when O'Brien objected to Cleary's failure to consult him over the purchase of land on the North Shore.[149]

With his habitual rancour, James Kelly sent gossipy letters to John Hagan in Rome commenting on the bishops' dispute. Kelly wrote negatively of both of them. 'A year of Liston's schoolmaster methods and tyranny has sickened them', he wrote of the Auckland clergy in 1923, 'but they deserve it, for a greater gang of sycophants God never made.'[150] A year later he called Liston 'powerless and spineless' in failing to oppose Cleary's expensive schemes to expand the *Month*, and claimed the Auckland clergy 'detested and despised' Liston for treating them like schoolboys.[151] In late 1925, he wrote –

> In Auckland Cleary has been ill since the elections and the defeat of prohibition. His treatment of Liston has been cruel and brutal. But the latter lost all sympathy by his own bullying and browbeating of the clergy, who all detest him cordially, the Irish particularly. His health is not good. No doubt humbled pride and mortification help to retard his recovery after an operation for appendicitis. He was down here before I came back, and I hear he cried over his treatment by Henry W.C. But even that can never teach him a lesson.[152]

Later he retailed a malicious anecdote about Cleary 'staging' a collapse in order to divert the Vatican's attention from the diocese's 'dreadful financial muddle', and described Cleary as a 'tyrant' while still calling Liston a 'coward' and a 'bully'.[153] Kelly's version of events would be more convincing if it were not for his habit of slandering the whole hierarchy, with the sole exception of Archbishop Redwood.[154]

The rest of the hierarchy sided with Liston and regarded Cleary's indictment as irrational and unjustified. In May and June 1929, Brodie wrote to Liston telling him that he and Whyte were twice interviewed (in Sydney and in Wellington) by the Apostolic Delegate about the Auckland situation. Brodie reassured Liston, 'you must not be worried – you have gone along on safe lines and it is about time the position of Coadjutor Bishop was put on a proper footing'.[155] At about the same time, Whyte wrote to Liston –

> You are aware, of course, that Dr. B[rodie] and I paid a hasty visit to Wellington. We saw a certain formidable document. The more formidable the better. Good must result from the Delegate's visit. Your answer to that document ought to write 'finis' to the whole dissension. Nobody could give an answer to some points except yourself. From the conversation you and I had in Wellington I have no doubt as to which account is the more reasonable.[156]

Brodie was asked by the Apostolic Delegate to write his estimate of both Liston and Cleary. The result offers a complete vindication of Liston. Brodie criticises Cleary's rashness in making such a large issue out of the editorship of the *Tablet*, foolishly siding with the prohibitionists, quarrelling with the Catholic Federation, producing a 'mutilated' catechism and causing strife by founding the *Month* in opposition to the *Tablet*. He criticises Cleary's pompous verbosity as a polemicist ('writing a hundred pages where one would suffice'). Most important, however, he attributes Cleary's indictment of Liston to Cleary's own shattered health. 'His state of nerve exhaustion overwhelmed him with terror at the *imagined* consequences of *imagined* hostile attacks.' This, says Brodie, is the result of Cleary's 14 years of continual illness. By contrast, Brodie refuted Cleary's suggestion that Liston was mentally unsound. He declared –

> To my mind the most conclusive proof of the mental soundness of Bishop Liston is the fact that he has had to endure painful and public humiliations. He has borne them as a strong-minded man, as a man of God. I do admit that the strain of the last seven years of discouragement and humiliation has proved a severe physical strain, but this admission is a strong argument that the present sad condition should be immediately adjusted.[157]

Despite such valuable support, Liston found it necessary to seek allies in Rome. Michael Curran, vice-rector of the Irish College, had been in Sydney with Liston for the Eucharistic Congress in 1928 and paid a brief visit to New Zealand.[158] Liston sent him copies of Cleary's indictment and of his defence. Curran replied,

> I shall carefully read the contents . . . I shall have a talk with Cardinal Cerretti on his return and the Rector [John Hagan] I am sure will interest a high official in Propaganda . . . At any rate anything that can be done on your behalf by friendly influence and discussion will be done . . . I hope the affair will be ended soon. It is a trying position, but I have every confidence that your attitude will be

vindicated. Fortunately the Bishop's [Cleary's] abnormality is well known. Mgr. Ormond enjoys the absolute confidence of Cardinal Cerretti who counts as everything on Australasian affairs.[159]

In a personal memorandum, Curran suggested that 'some kind of separation' was likely for Cleary and Liston, implying that Liston might be sent to another diocese (possibly Hobart).[160] A year later, at the end of a letter of routine news, Liston commented, 'By the way, would you be good enough to destroy all those papers I sent you last year?'[161] One can infer, too, that when he was in America in 1926, Liston confided his problems in some trusted individuals. 'We can pray for each other', he wrote to Mother Helen Lynch. 'I shall go back to my work in Auckland and its at times strange difficulties with lighter heart knowing that I can count on prayers from new friends.'[162]

Apparently Liston's personal friend and fellow priest at St Benedict's, William Ormond, had the ear of Propaganda. It may be significant that Cleary, despite his greater authority as ordinary, also felt the need to seek allies. In July, he wrote to his old antagonist James Kelly, congratulating him on a short story he had written and receiving an uncharacteristically gracious reply.[163] But Kelly later sneered to John Hagan that he 'took no notice' of Cleary's friendly gestures 'because I felt they were only due to the row with Liston'.[164]

Bishop Cleary Dies

While Rome was still considering the evidence, the dispute was resolved in the most definitive way possible. On 9 December 1929, at the age of 71, Bishop Cleary died in the Mater hospital. He was bed-ridden for the last fortnight. To judge by the report that Liston promptly sent to the Apostolic Delegate, there appears to have been at least some sort of death-bed reconciliation. After describing how Cleary's health had sunk so rapidly, Liston continues that they decided –

> ... it better he should receive the help of the Sacraments. The Bishop welcomed the suggestion and in a state of full consciousness received most devoutly the Viaticum, Extreme Unction and the Last Blessing. He was very weak but managed to give many of the responses. This was the afternoon of Thursday December 5th. Monsignor Cahill, Monsignor Ormond, Father McKeefry and the Sisters were present. After I suggested to the Bishop that he should receive the Sacraments, I was very glad to have had and to have used the opportunity of referring to past difficulties and I felt the

bishop welcomed what I said. A couple of hours later the Bishop began to wander again and he had a restless night. At 5 a.m. Friday December 6th a cerebral haemorrhage occurred, and the Bishop fell into a state of deep coma, which remained to the end. As the heart was very strong and he had previously taken much nourishment, he just lived on, free from pain, peaceful to the end. The priests of the City and Suburbs, at my invitation, came in often during these days to pray and give the Bishop a blessing. Prayers and Masses and the Holy Communions were offered by all our priests, religious and people, especially on the Sunday. The end came very peacefully at 2:45 p.m. on Monday, December 9th, the sisters, Monsignor Cahill, Monsignor Ormond and several other priests being present with me.[165]

Liston noted Doctor Gunson's report that Cleary had suffered for a long time from arterio-sclerosis and the cause of his death was lethargic encephalitis. It is probable that Liston heard Cleary's last confession. It is at least ironical that Cleary died surrounded by priests (Ormond, Cahill) who had conspicuously sided with Liston in the dispute between them.[166]

Before his end came, Cleary realised the need to avoid scandal. In a handwritten addition to his will (of which Liston and Ormond were the executors), he noted, 'In order not to cause adverse comment, I have left everything absolutely to my successor'. He also directed,

> I *strictly* require that my funeral shall be simple and free from all shadow of ostentation, so far as the undertaker's part of it is concerned: the coffin is to be of plain timber, *without cloth, stain, varnish, polish or ornaments. No flowers*. Grave is not to be in Cathedral, but in Waikumete Cemetery. My Executors will have Masses celebrated for my soul without delay.[167]

At least part of this request was met. Cleary was not buried in the cathedral, but in the cemetery of St Patrick's, Panmure, already the graveyard of diocesan clergy. Liston said his requiem mass in the cathedral and conducted the graveside rites, but it was Bishop Brodie who preached the eulogy.[168] Neither Archbishop Redwood nor James Kelly was at the funeral. To John Hagan, Kelly sourly wrote that he personally had boycotted it while –

> Redwood also refused to attend, telling me that people would interpret his presence as approval of things he did not approve. There is one honest bishop anyhow.[169]

They would, however, have been among the few church dignitaries and representatives of other denominations who were not at the very

Left: The funeral procession of Bishop Cleary in Queen Street, December 1929.

Below: Burying the man who would have ejected him from his diocese. Liston leads Cleary's coffin to its final resting place in the Panmure cemetery. At left are Brodie, O'Shea and (back to camera) Whyte. Archbishop Redwood was not present.

large and very public funeral. Donald McDonald was aggrieved that Liston did not ask him to be a pall-bearer.[170] Next month, on 17 January 1930, Bishop Whyte celebrated a requiem in the cathedral for Cleary's 'month's mind'. This time, Liston preached. It is notable that, in the presence of Cleary's brother and nephew, Liston took as his text 1 Timothy 16: 'Fight the good fight; lay hold on eternal life whereunto thou art called and hast confessed a good confession before many witnesses'. His panegyric emphasised Cleary as a public figure – his skills as a polemicist and educator in Catholic causes. In the field of education, 'he gave most out of his intelligence, zeal and energy and has the largest claim upon our gratitude'. Liston spoke of Cleary's wartime chaplaincy, public service during the influenza epidemic of 1918, love of country, great gifts as a journalist and manner of death. 'A good death, we know, is a masterpiece and the Bishop's death was peaceful and sanctified.'[171] The eulogy was a model of courtesy and praise, but clergy in the know would have noticed that Liston said virtually nothing about Cleary as a private man or Cleary's pastoral duties as a priest. These were the areas on which Liston had written negative assessments in response to his superior's accusations.

Liston celebrated an annual requiem mass on the anniversary of Cleary's death.[172] As a memorial, Liston dedicated to Cleary the new chapel at the Star of the Sea orphanage in Howick.[173] He also arranged for the architects Tole and Massey to create an impressive gravestone, in the shape of a prone Celtic cross, over Cleary's grave. This was paid for by the diocesan clergy.[174] He negotiated (through Father Peter McKeefry) with Cleary's nephew John for those personal effects that could be separated from the episcopal inheritance and sent to the family in Ireland.[175] Six years later, when he was passing through Ireland on his *ad limina*, he made a courtesy call on Cleary's brother Chris and his family.[176]

As coadjutor, Liston automatically succeeded to the see of Auckland. On 4 March 1930, with J.J. O'Brien presiding and E. Casey speaking for the laity, the Catholic community held, in the Auckland Town Hall, a formal *conversazione* and reception for the new ordinary. Speaking on behalf of the clergy, Jeremiah Cahill –

> ... assured His Lordship of their unfailing loyalty. There would be no human difficulties to mar their relations. They had known him for the past ten years and had admired his zeal and high ideals. They accepted his appointment without the slightest reservation and welcomed him not only as bishop of the church but also as a guide, a counsellor and an ever-faithful friend.[177]

Conceivably some in the audience may have seen Liston's succession in another light, but he was now quite clearly the bishop in charge. At the gathering, he announced formally that Ormond would take his place as parish priest of St Benedict's, while Michael Edge became parish priest of Parnell.

Officially, Cleary's complaints and Liston's replies were still under review at the Vatican. The Apostolic Delegate wrote congratulating Liston on his succession and informing him that he had not yet received the Vatican's judgement. He also offered a word of caution:

> You will, I am sure, permit me to say that in view of recent happenings you should proceed very slowly and very cautiously. While following the prescriptions of Canon Law, you should be extremely careful and prudent in your dealings with all, but in a particular manner with those who enjoyed the intimate confidence of the late Bishop. On the other hand the request of advice, especially from the senior priests of the Diocese, and the benevolent consideration of the advice given by them, will be a valuable assistance to you in the administration of the Diocese and a powerful safeguard against adverse criticism.[178]

This clearly advised Liston not to conduct a 'purge' of Cleary's conspicuous allies. The Vatican produced its judgement in April 1930. Writing in Latin, Cardinal van Rossum, Prefect of Propaganda, vindicated the new bishop. The key phrases implied that Bishop Cleary's judgement had been unbalanced:

> From the acts and evidence set before us it is patently clear that nothing serious can be imputed to you. It is evident that the accusations made against you were not made out of ill will, but ought to be attributed either to error or to an unfavourable construction being put on your own reasons for acting as you did.[179]

Van Rossum delicately suggested Liston might have been over-zealous in his discipline of diocesan clergy (*severitas erga Sacerdotes Dioceseos in ecclesiastica disciplina tuenda*). Like Cattaneo, he urged Liston to make sure that he sought the advice of the senior clergy in the diocese – in other words, that he treated Cleary's friends reasonably. Liston replied, accepting Propaganda's judgement and assuring the cardinal that all was now well in Auckland. [180]

John Hagan died in early 1930, leaving one fewer person to whom James Kelly could address his gossip. In his place, Liston's old classmate Michael Curran now became rector of the Irish College in Rome. To Curran, Liston wrote in June 1930,

The incident of Auckland has been closed with a very satisfactory and fatherly letter from Propaganda. The stand taken by all the Bishops of New Zealand threw light on many things. All goes well and we are a very happy family. Nothing could exceed the goodwill and affection of the priests and people alike.[181]

In the end, not only the New Zealand hierarchy but also the Vatican saw things Liston's way. Throughout the dispute between the bishops, Cleary himself was Liston's best ally against Cleary. To refute many of his accusations, Liston merely had to quote words of high praise Cleary had written about him in earlier years. Brodie noted how enthusiastically Cleary lobbied for Liston as his coadjutor a decade previously. This may have been a factor in forming Propaganda's final judgement.[182] Given Cleary's reputation as a temperate apologist, it is tempting to agree with Brodie's assessment that Cleary's accusations were the result of his own mental unbalance after years of painful physical sickness. Yet a suspicion lingers. Even if Cleary's specific charges against him were unwarranted, Liston's manner and methods irritated more church personnel than Cleary alone. Mill Hill fathers and specific parish priests were apprehensive when Cleary died. In turn, Liston had had to relive some of the old attacks upon his character. The orphaned seminarian became the aloof, scholarly rector, isolated as his siblings disappeared into alcoholism and madness. The aloof, scholarly rector became the coadjutor distrusted and criticised by the superior who should have been his chief support. Liston had real and long-lasting friends among Auckland's clergy. But as he became Bishop of Auckland in his own right, caution, suspicion of colleagues and a retreat into magisterial isolation were potent temptations.

CHAPTER VI

CHURCHMAN AT WORK

Bishop Liston 1930-54

The Bishop and his Diocese

Between 1930 and 1954, when the Vatican awarded Liston the personal title of Archbishop, the Catholic population of Auckland almost doubled. By 1954, it stood between 70,000 and 90,000. The diocese had overtaken Wellington. Thirty new parishes were created in Auckland, 43 new churches and 29 new schools were built, and the number of resident priests doubled from 85 to 171. There had been 395 teaching sisters in 1930. There were 692 in 1954. Auckland's Catholic school population rose from 7,000 to 13,886.[1]

A major part of Liston's life in these years was the regular ceremonial launching of churches, convents, schools, presbyteries and parish facilities, all triumphally reported in the Catholic press. Liston introduced 16 new congregations of priests and religious into his diocese. Most were engaged in social work or the giving of retreats. They included the Sisters of Compassion, the Good Shepherd Sisters and the Missionary Sisters of the Society of Mary. Carmelite nuns, Carmelite priests and Redemptorists also made small Auckland foundations.

For giving retreats to men, Liston introduced the Australian-based Franciscan friars, whose Hillsborough friary was occupied in October 1939 and ceremonially opened in 1940. After the Second World War, he gave similar attention to retreats for women. Liston negotiated with his old friend Mother Helen Lynch for Cenacle Sisters to come from America. Lynch's many letters to Liston were playful and affectionate (she habitually addressed him as 'Dear Bishop O'Mine'). The Cenacle Sisters' commanding convent and retreat house in Glen Innes was opened 1953.

162

The greatest number of sisters and brothers, however, were still engaged in education, including the well-established Sisters of St Joseph of the Sacred Heart ('Brown Joes'), the Marist Sisters, the Mission Sisters and the Mercy order, all of whom ran many elementary schools. To do similar educational work, Liston brought in smaller groups of Brigidine Sisters and Sisters of St Joseph of Cluny.

Shortly after he became bishop, Liston wanted to introduce to Auckland two orders whose educational work he had known in his native Dunedin, the Dominican Sisters and the Christian Brothers. The former were established in a convent at Henderson in 1932, and later opened a primary school in Northcote, where St Dominic's College for secondary girls was also developed. In inviting the Christian Brothers to Auckland, however, Liston provoked opposition from a rival order. The Marist Brothers were afraid that a new boys' school would take students away from Sacred Heart College and would diminish their revenue. Unmoved by their misgivings, Liston wrote to his old schoolmate Michael James Hanrahan (Brother Benignus) requesting Christian Brothers to provide staff for the proposed school.[2] A contractor cleared the Mountain Road site in 1931 and it was expected that the school would open in 1933.[3] But financial problems caused delays. The Marist Brothers continued to protest until the Apostolic Delegate ruled 'that the Bishop is free to make whatever provision he may decide in this matter'.[4] The Marist Brothers accepted this ruling, but unhappily. The first Christian Brothers school outside the South Island, St Peter's, opened in January 1939.[5]

Part of the Marist Brothers' annoyance arose from their own scheme to re-develop Sacred Heart College. As early as 1928, land was bought on the North Shore with the aim of relocating the college there, and architects' plans were drawn up in 1938, but the scheme was allowed to lapse.[6] In the postwar period, the North Shore land was exchanged for crown land at Glen Innes, and serious fund-raising for a rebuilt college began in 1947. Undeterred by his previous contention with the Marist Brothers, Liston made a personal gift of £1,000 to the fund.[7] The foundation stone was laid in 1953.[8] Sacred Heart College was officially transferred to Glen Innes in 1955, its old site now becoming the Marist Brothers' St Paul's College. No contention surrounded the De La Salle Brothers when Liston invited them to establish a boys' school in south Auckland.[9] With scant resources and spartan facilities, De La Salle College was opened in mid-1953.[10]

Catholic primary and secondary schools in Auckland usually

received favourable reports from government inspectors, but concern was expressed about overcrowding and poor facilities. When the 'Brown Joes' set up school in Three Kings in 1946, they ran classes in the parish hall. Severe overcrowding of their Whangarei school led to its being rebuilt in 1951.[11] As a new state housing development opened in Panmure, Fr Singleton Gardiner begged Liston for new classrooms, writing that 'each week new families are moving into the district' and noting that the Mission sisters were attempting to teach 74 new entrants in a single classroom.[12] The complaints of M.J. O'Connor, diocesan director of Catholic schools, about the overcrowding in Pukekohe convent school in 1951 were typical of many of his communications to Liston in those years.[13] Liston attempted to deal with such problems with renewed building programmes and increased recruitment.

His most notable educational achievement in these years was in the training of teachers. In 1945, Liston began considering a training college for religious sisters, who were the backbone of the Catholic primary system.[14] The Mother General of the Sacred Heart Sisters agreed that the college could be situated in the grounds of Baradene in Remuera.[15] After delays caused by a carpenters' strike, Loreto Hall opened in March 1950.[16] Being a college with a national intake, it included among its first students four sisters of St Joseph of Nazareth ('Black Joes'), an order that had no foundation in Auckland at that time.[17] As lecturers and tutors for the new institution, Liston invited to the diocese Dominican priests who made a foundation in Remuera.[18] Loreto Hall functioned for over 30 years until its closure in 1984. It developed as a training centre for lay teachers as well as religious after 1960.[19]

Like the Franciscan friary, the Cenacle retreat house, the new Sacred Heart College and St Michael's church in Remuera, Loreto Hall was for generations of Auckland Catholics a sign of the church's power and presence. But one institution was a visible Catholic presence to all Aucklanders. Over its development Liston was specially vigilant. This was the Mercy order's Mater Misericordiae Hospital. As early as 1928, Liston began lobbying members of parliament for recognition of qualifications that nurses earned in private hospitals. Against the opposition of the New Zealand Trained Nurses' Association (which feared for the international status of their members), a bill was passed in September 1930 to allow such recognition. Michael Joseph Savage had personally assured Liston of the support of the Labour opposition, and Liston wrote to thank the conservative Minister of Health, A.J. Stallworthy.[20] Only in

Right: Bishop Liston in mid-life in the grounds of Saint Mary's, Ponsonby.
Below: Liston at Bishop's House, Ponsonby, his home and official residence from 1930 to 1970.

1936 did the Mater's superintendent Sr Gonzaga apply to have the hospital recognised as a training school. This was approved in November 1937.[21] The following year Liston blessed and opened the hospital's new nurses' home, and in 1941 he presided at the Mater's first graduation ceremony for sisters and nurses.[22] He later endorsed the setting up of the Sir Carrick Robertson Travelling Scholarship to enable Mater-trained nurses to go abroad for postgraduate studies.[23] His speeches at the nurses' graduation ceremonies became a regular feature of his yearly calendar. In 1937, he also organised a voluntary Auxiliary Service Guild to raise money for the care of patients in the hospital's free beds.[24] This became the focus for many charitable fund-raising events in which he was involved.

The Mater undertook an extensive building programme. There was an impressive opening ceremony for a new wing in March 1936. Liston acted as master of ceremonies to the huge crowd. He spoke at length of the hospital's 'ministry of healing' before Archbishop O'Shea performed the official opening in the presence of the Apostolic Delegate, John Panico.[25] In March 1952, Liston blessed a new annexe to the hospital – a maternity block under the supervision of Dr H.P. Dunn.[26] In August, he opened the hospital's hospice for the dying.[27]

As a close associate of the Mercy order, and in a climate in which the hierarchy lobbied against contraception and promoted specifically Catholic medical ethics, Liston was very protective of the Mater. He would allow no criticism of it from within the church, as was shown after the Hamilton parish priest Michael Bleakley printed a thinly-disguised attack upon the Mater in his parish magazine, the St Mary's Gazette in June 1944. Bleakley criticised raffles organised for 'various [Catholic] institutions in the guise of charity'. Pointedly, he claimed that the only two truly charitable Catholic institutions in Auckland were the Home of Compassion and the Little Sisters of the Poor, and he condemned the Mater's 'class distinction . . . pandering to the wealthy . . . de luxe suites for the people who have big banking accounts'. He suggested such institutions gave ammunition to Communists in their attack on 'our alliance with wealthy Capitalism', and wondered how 'Christ and his badly-dressed, uncouth-looking rabble of Apostles' would be welcomed if they attempted to enter the Mater.[28]

Liston was furious. He at once issued a pastoral to all Hamilton parishioners, commending to them eleven diocesan charitable institutions and movements, and placing the Mater at the top of his list. He remarked,

Speaking as your Bishop whose duty it is to watch over these holy works for God and man, and to foster the purity and zeal of their spirit, I wish you to know that I am day by day edified by the sight of the charity of Christ that fills the hearts of the religious and laity, men and women.[29]

He wrote to Bleakley saying he had 'read with a sense of humiliation' the editorial in the *St Mary's Gazette*, and directed him to print the pastoral on the front page of the next issue.[30] Bleakley complied.

The Bishop in Health and Travel

Unlike his predecessor, Liston was rarely hospitalised or absent from the diocese.[31] Only as he neared his seventieth birthday were there signs of trouble. In 1948, he complained of a persistent 'tired feeling' to Bishop Hugh O'Neill, who suggested he think about requesting a coadjutor or auxiliary.[32] Shortly afterwards, the young Felix Donnelly witnessed the first of what were to become Liston's 'regular collapses'. The nuns of St Mary's, claimed Donnelly, 'thought he was going to die, and cut him out of his vestments as he lay on the floor'.[33] In 1950, Leonard Buxton and Bishops O'Neill and Kavanagh congratulated Liston on his recovery after hospitalisation, but urged him to slow down.[34] The following year, after Dr Basil Quin gave Liston a clean bill of health, Archbishop McKeefry wrote,

> I have been deeply concerned for quite a while for everybody knows just how you give yourself to everything. It can be overdone, but that thought never had a place in your mind and yet it is one that you should not lose sight of . . . You must learn to spare yourself, to conserve your energy, and not to be prodigal as though life's work was just beginning . . . Nature's warnings are to be noticed.[35]

By this stage, Liston was 70. He did not entirely ignore 'Nature's warnings'. Near the time of his collapses in 1949, he amended his will making special provision for his younger sister Anne who was still in psychiatric care in Dublin.[36] There was another intimation of mortality in 1948, when his long-time housekeeper 'Louie' collapsed and died.[37]

Liston tended to limit his overseas journeys to essential church business. The most common destination was Australia. He went with Leonard Buxton to the Eucharistic Congress in Melbourne at the end of 1934 and spoke at the children's mass in the showgrounds.[38] Three years later, he was with the whole hierarchy at the Plenary Council of all Australasian bishops in Sydney, and used the occasion to visit the grave of Bishop Steins, his predecessor as Bishop of Auckland, and to win support for his planned celebration of New Zealand's Catholic centenary.[39] Thanks to air travel, later trips to Australia were swifter. He flew to Melbourne for its Catholic centennial celebrations in 1948 and to Sydney for a Eucharistic Congress in 1953.[40] In 1951, he preached in Sydney at the golden jubilee celebrations of Australian federation.[41]

In his whole episcopate, Liston's 1935 *ad limina* was his longest single absence. It was also the first time he had visited Ireland, Britain and Europe since he was a seminarian. He had planned to take this trip in 1931, but postponed it. He explained to the Apostolic Delegate Bartolomeo Cattaneo that he did not feel it was right to leave Auckland during the distress and unrest caused by the Depression.[42] He did not renew serious planning until the beginning of 1935.[43]

Leaving the diocese in the care of Jeremiah Cahill, Liston was farewelled in March. He was presented with 'a portable altar and a quantity of altar linen'.[44] There was a civic farewell in the Town Hall at the beginning of April, at which the mayor paid extensive tribute to Liston's public spirit and calming influence when the Depression had led to extensive protests by the unemployed.[45] On the 5 April, Liston sailed for Australia with his Dunedin friend James Delaney. After stops in Hobart and Melbourne, they rendezvoused in Sydney with William Ormond.[46] Still one of Liston's closest friends, Ormond was his frequent travelling companion.[47] By May, the three clerics had landed in Naples and made their way to Rome via a visit to Monte Cassino. The *Tablet* enthused that Pius XI spoke to Liston for 'over half an hour' at their first informal meeting.[48] Liston sent back to his diocesan newspaper appropriately favourable remarks on his more formal meeting with the 'gracious and paternal' pope, when he presented his diocesan report.[49] His remarks were tailored to New Zealand Catholics of Irish descent. The pope, said Liston,

> . . . rejoiced in that we had such a goodly supply of vocations to the priesthood and the religious life, and in that so young a country was already producing vocations for the missions of the Far East . . . When I was explaining that most of our Catholic people in New Zealand were of the Irish race by birth or descent, he said, 'Ah! That is how it comes to pass that they are so fervent in approaching the Sacraments and in works of religion. The Irish it is said are almost like the presence of God, everywhere and everywhere bringing blessings . . .'[50]

Above left: Liston with a young Fr Edward Lyons, whom he had expelled from Mosgiel, but who went on to ask Liston awkward questions at Auckland clergy conferences.
Above right: During their 1935 trip to Europe, William Ormond and Liston enjoy a gondola ride in Venice.
Below: Liston (third from right) and clergy give a shipboard farewell to Cardinal MacRory of Ireland after his brief stay in Auckland in 1935. On the right, tall Peter McKeefry, known jocularly as the 'high priest'.

After his visit to the Vatican, some of Liston's subsequent travels in Europe were sheer tourism. He attended a reception for the singer John McCormack in Rome, then went with Ormond and Delaney to Florence, Venice, Milan and Turin and over into France.[51] Having renewed his acquaintance with the Irish College in Rome, he wrote frequently to his friend the rector Michael Curran. He gave him his impressions of passing through the Dolomites – 'a glorious drive . . . I'm weakening in my allegiance to New Zealand!'[52] But much of this journey was taken up with practical church business, as his 1926 trip to America had been. He visited the Mill Hill Fr Zanna in the Italian Tyrol. He had discussed the Maori Mission with the Apostolic Delegate in Sydney, and in Rome he conferred about the Mill Hills with Cardinal Fumasoni Biondi, the Prefect of Propaganda, and Dr Schute, Procurator for Mill Hill in Rome. He later visited, in England, the superior general of the order.[53] He requested Michael Curran's advocacy in having three Auckland priests made monsignori.[54]

Even the tourism resembled a pilgrimage as Liston attended solemn church functions and visited the burial places of founders of religious orders that were represented in Auckland. In Rome, he said mass at the tomb of Pius X, who had blessed him in 1903. He attended the canonisation ceremonies for Thomas More and John Fisher, symbols of English Catholicism's resistance to the Church of England. In France, he visited Lourdes ('it reveals as never before Our Lady's place in the church and in the hearts of Catholics'); said mass at the tomb of St Therese at Lisieux; visited Blois and Cambrai to meet Little Sisters of the Poor who had served in New Zealand; and said mass with Ormond at Jette St Pierre, the shrine to the founder of the Sacred Heart nuns, St Madeleine Sophie Barat. He also prayed at the tomb of Frederick Ozanam, the founder of the St Vincent de Paul Society, and visited the mother house of the Marist order. Perhaps his most significant visit in France was to the grave of Bishop Pompallier at Puteaux. Finding it neglected, he arranged to have it tidied and renovated.[55]

After a short time in England, Liston spent two months (August-September) in Ireland. Delaney and Ormond followed their own separate itineraries in Ireland while Liston stayed mainly in Dublin. It is probable that he visited his afflicted younger sister in St Vincent's psychiatric hospital at this time. Liston accepted the hospitality of Archdeacon McMahon at Holy Cross College in Clonliffe.[56] To Curran he wrote nostalgically, 'Every tree & walk & stone & picture of Clonliffe is well remembered – I think I could have found my way around blindfolded'.[57] In London, he had visited many Catholic centres that were associated with his predecessors Luck and Lenihan.[58] In Ireland, too, he showed comparable filial piety, visiting the family of Bishop Cleary's brother Chris at Bagnalstown, Bishop Verdon's nephews and nieces, and the grave of Bishop Croke. He also travelled to the County Meath birthplace of Thomas Poynton, the pioneer of Catholicism in New Zealand, and addressed the Sisters of Mercy in the same room at St Leo's, Carlow, where Bishop Pompallier had first invited the order to accompany him to New Zealand. Together with his visit to Pompallier's grave, and his (1937) visit to Bishop Steins' grave in Australia, this meant that before the New Zealand Catholic centennial in 1938, Liston had visited and prayed at places connected with all six previous Bishops of Auckland. In Ireland, Liston, Delaney and Ormond visited many clergy who had served in New Zealand, and Liston attended the sacerdotal golden jubilee celebration for Cardinal MacRory. He also looked in on the six Irish seminaries that had students promised for Auckland diocese, enquired whether the monks at Roscrea wished to establish a house in Auckland and consulted Frank Duff about the possibility of setting up Auckland branches of the Legion of Mary.[59]

Finally, in October, Liston returned to England, took ship to Galway, where he was joined by Ormond and Delaney, and headed across the Atlantic to Boston aboard the *Lancastria*. The parting from Ireland was difficult. Referring to his visit to the church of the Irish College's special patron, Blessed Oliver Plunkett, Liston wrote to Curran,

> It was not easy to leave Ireland – but of course there is always the hope of return. I think I was most impressed by the spirit of the people: their sense of confidence in themselves and in their destiny; and their determination to give Ireland its due place in the world. Even on top of all that one knew, or had imagined, one was amazed at the strength and fervour of the Faith. The thought keeps coming to my mind that a widespread devotion to Blessed Oliver, culminating in his canonization, would be the best means of healing divisions.[60]

The letter reflected Liston's idealised view of his parents' homeland and its Catholicism. Indeed, much of his journey encouraged a backward-looking, perhaps sentimental, view of the church in Europe. But modern political realities did intrude. Liston looked in on a debate in the House of Commons, calling it 'a rather unreal affair', but judging Sir Stafford Cripps an impressive speaker.[61] Visiting the Catholic pavilion at the international exposition in Brussels, Liston spoke of a coming confrontation between German Catholics and the Nazi government.[62] It was in the year of his *ad limina* that Mussolini's Italy invaded Abyssinia, to the impotent condemnations of the League of Nations. Returned to New Zealand, Liston had to reply to criticisms that the pope had not adequately denounced the invasion. He argued defensively that the pope had often spoken against Fascism, but could not imperil Italian Catholics by making his denunciations more forceful.[63]

Liston came home through America, where he made contacts that would later result in Auckland foundations. He disembarked from the *Niagara* in Auckland on 27 November. A large contingent of diocesan clergy met him at the wharf and Catholic schoolchildren lined his route to St Patrick's Cathedral. He had been away for a little under eight months. His friend Michael Joseph Savage had just been elected prime minister at the head of the first Labour government. Liston now undertook a round of welcoming-home functions. The diocese presented him with a 'sedan motor car', an Austin Six.[64] Given the interruptions of the war years, he did not begin to contemplate his next *ad limina* until 1950.[65]

The Bishop and the Hierarchy

Between 1930 and 1954, Liston went from being the youngest member of the hierarchy to being, in effect, the patriarch of the New Zealand church. Throughout the 1930s and 1940s, he continued as secretary of the bishops' conference and was delegated to special tasks.[66] In late 1943, he convened a conference of Catholic schools in response to major changes in the secondary curriculum that were being proposed by the Ministry of Education.[67] The resulting Dominion Catholic Education Conference was held in Wellington in 1945. He was chief organiser of pilgrims attending the Holy Year celebrations in Rome. He also wrote, in 1950, to Holy Cross College, Clonliffe, and to the Irish College in Rome, seeking their official messages of congratulations for the golden jubilee of Holy Cross College, Mosgiel.[68] In his own diocese, he frequently hosted visits by senior church dignitaries from overseas. Archbishop Daniel Mannix of Melbourne passed through Auckland in 1934, as did Cardinal MacRory of Ireland and Archbishop Clune of Perth in 1935.[69] Both Cardinal Spellman and Bishop Fulton Sheen of New York visited in 1948, and gave well-publicised lectures and sermons.[70] Bishop John Heenan of Leeds accepted Liston's hospitality for a week in

1952.[71] Archbishop McQuaid stopped over in 1953, blessing a new novitiate for the Mercy Sisters.[72]

Liston fitted easily into the ranks of senior churchmen. But early in his episcopate he was involved in two controversies that revealed tensions in the hierarchy. The first was not of his making. The second largely was.

In 1930, the Bible-in-Schools League still sought to introduce Bible readings into state primary schools. For the first time, League advocates entered into direct negotiations with the Catholic hierarchy.[73] They said they would now accept the late Bishop Cleary's admonitions to respect Catholic consciences and to allow Catholic teachers and pupils to be excluded from their proposed programme. They wished to ensure that the Catholic hierarchy did not speak against any future League-proposed bill before the parliamentary Education Committee. League representatives met with the bishops in Wellington on 29 April 1930. Subsequent accounts agree that the conference was cordial. Nevertheless, all the bishops, with the exception of Archbishop O'Shea, did express reservations. Bishop Brodie took the lead, while Bishop Liston pointedly suggested that any concessions to the League by the hierarchy should be reciprocated by League support for state aid to Catholic schools.[74]

After this meeting, the three suffragan bishops (Brodie, Liston and Whyte) held their own conference in Christchurch. On 2 May, Liston, on his way back to Auckland, called in on O'Shea in Wellington to report on the suffragans' deliberations. What Liston reported to O'Shea became a major bone of contention in everything that followed. Liston later insisted that he told O'Shea the suffragans were prepared to 'consider' the League's proposals, but only on condition that the League would issue a public 'goodwill statement', and would 'help us in the matter of such things as bus transport for our Catholic children, [and] dental clinics and [would] do at least something for securing grants for our schools'.[75] Whyte and Brodie readily affirmed that this was indeed what their Christchurch meeting had decided. One historian asserts that O'Shea was 'transparently direct and unswerving' in his version of what transpired. He further remarks that 'the only realistic conclusion' is that 'Liston dissembled in some way' or that 'the suffragans later changed their minds without telling him'.[76] But this is not 'the only realistic conclusion' from the archival evidence. It is just as probable that O'Shea, who was determined to reach an agreement with the League, heard what he wanted to hear from Liston's accurate report to him. O'Shea understood Liston to be saying that the suffragan bishops had agreed unconditionally not to oppose the League's next attempt at legislation.

Without the other bishops' advice or knowledge, O'Shea wrote to the League on 12 May giving his own interpretation. He consulted with Archbishop Redwood (who was not involved in any of the negotiations), then on 25 July he released to the press a statement from the two archbishops. It said that the hierarchy and the Bible-in-Schools League had reached an agreement.[77] The League rejoiced, believing that all Catholic objections to their plans had now been answered. Over the next year, they set about energetically lobbying and framing a new bill for state schools' Bible reading.

But on 24 June 1931, nearly a year after O'Shea's press announcement, Bishop Brodie publicly repudiated any agreement with the League. Liston and Whyte followed suit, and eventually Redwood declared he had made a 'mistake' in endorsing O'Shea's press release in the first place. Tactfully not emphasised by most chroniclers of the affair is the fact that Redwood (who was 91 in 1930) was by this stage sliding into senility. It seems clear that he had signed O'Shea's statement on 25 July 1930 without having read it.[78]

O'Shea was now isolated in the hierarchy. On 19 October 1931, with O'Shea vigorously dissenting, the bishops' conference agreed that Whyte would appear before the parliamentary committee and present a prepared statement opposing the League's bill.[79] On its second reading, the League's latest initiative failed to pass into law. Of course, it was not Catholic lobbying *alone* that had defeated it. Sympathy for the League's aims was never as strong among MPs as League propagandists liked to believe. Nevertheless, some Protestants saw the whole affair as illustrating the Machiavellian untrustworthiness of Catholic bishops. For a whole year, it seemed to them, the Catholic hierarchy had let the League believe it would face no Catholic opposition, had let them put in the hard work of mounting a new campaign, and then at the last moment had double-crossed them. Much bitter comment followed. Years later, E.O. (Ernest) Blamires, one of the League's chief negotiators, wrote his own version of the affair in which he condemned this 'black ... betrayal of faith', and praised O'Shea's 'honest dealing and straightforwardness' only the better to condemn the duplicity of the other bishops.[80]

His words, however, were mild compared with what O'Shea was saying about the other bishops behind closed doors. Voices were raised. Minutes of the bishops' meetings on 29 April and 19 October 1931 (all kept in Liston's handwriting) show O'Shea loudly contesting with Whyte, Liston and Brodie and finally 'withdrawing from further consideration of the matter'.[81] A year later, at the meeting of 26 October 1932, O'Shea 'drew attention to some statements made by Abp. Redwood in recent pronouncements which he considered incorrect'. He argued with the three suffragans and stormed out. Liston's minutes delicately remark, 'sharp differences of opinion were now revealed and the Secretary was unable to take any proper record. Abp. O'Shea withdrew from the meeting'.[82]

O'Shea felt that he had been made to look a fool publicly. By this stage Brodie, by approaches made through Redwood's secretary Fr P.J. Smyth, had persuaded Redwood to repudiate O'Shea's press release.[83] On 8 November 1932, O'Shea wrote to Redwood giving his frank characterisation of Fr Smyth and the three suffragans:

> The Church in New Zealand has far more important matters to face just now, than to have me pursuing three men whose incapacity and prevarications are long since public property. It would be like shooting clay pigeons with cannon. I said mass for Your Grace after the meeting that God might protect you against evil advisers.[84]

In 1933, both O'Shea and the suffragan bishops appealed to the Apostolic Delegate over what the suffragans called a 'division in the ranks of the Catholic hierarchy of New Zealand . . . of a most serious nature'. To the Apostolic Delegate they explained,

> The division is public; it has been a matter of public reference in the press; and has also been referred to in parliament. The division has reached a regrettable stage since it has brought about such scenes as Archbishop O'Shea leaving the meeting of the hierarchy; again on another occasion the attitude of Archbishop O'Shea towards Archbishop Redwood brought about the intervention of Bishop Brodie to terminate a most distressing exhibition. It is known that Archbishop O'Shea has referred to the Suffragan Bishops as 'three men whose incapacity and prevarications are long since public property'.[85]

This suggests that O'Shea had been browbeating the aged Redwood over his faulty memory, about which O'Shea had complained to the Apostolic Delegate in earlier letters.[86] It also suggests that O'Shea's private letters to Redwood were now being passed on to the suffragans by Redwood or his secretary.

Only in early 1934 was the affair patched up. In March, a Vatican official wrote to Brodie rejoicing at the 'complete restoration of harmony among the hierarchy'.[87] Brodie wrote to Liston that 'it is gratifying to have come to finality on this unpleasant difficulty'.[88]

It appears that O'Shea apologised to the rest of the hierarchy for having misrepresented their views in his letter to the Bible-in-Schools League and in his press release. It further appears that he was advised to make this apology by Daniel Mannix during Redwood's episcopal diamond jubilee in Wellington in February 1934.[89] Knowing that the 95-year-old metropolitan would not be with them much longer, the coadjutor O'Shea probably calculated that it would be unwise to begin his own term of office in contention with the other bishops.

What is a fair judgement on Liston's role in this affair? Liston has received some criticism for breaking precedent and linking Catholic opposition to the Bible-in-Schools League with Catholic requests for state aid.[90] Liston must also share with Brodie and Whyte the blame for failing to react to O'Shea's press statement for nearly a year, and thus giving the Bible-in-Schools lobbyists legitimate cause for complaint. But the suffragans were at first unaware of O'Shea's private communication with the Bible-in-Schools people, and did have reason to think that Redwood was going to qualify O'Shea's public announcement.[91] Besides, O'Shea was probably at fault in misinterpreting (or ignoring) Liston's report of the suffragans' Christchurch meeting, and misreporting their intentions to the League. In one respect, however, O'Shea was more far-sighted than the suffragans. In terms that would have made Protestant lobbyists wince had they known about them, he told the Apostolic Delegate that the suffragans were really fighting yesterday's battle because the age of Protestant bigotry was over in New Zealand and Protestant fervour was in decline. Catholics now had far more important enemies to confront. He wrote,

> The three bishops do not seem to have any conception of the great changes in feeling that have been taking place during the last few years. Their policy seems to be to have no parley whatever with non-Catholics, no matter what concessions the latter are prepared to make. They cannot understand that the issue in the future is not between Catholicism and Protestantism, for the latter is disintegrating, but between the Church and secularism, communism and irreligion. There is at present a wave of tolerance mixed with considerable admiration for the Church among a large section of the non-Catholic people of New Zealand. A little sympathy and a little understanding shown by the Catholic authorities would do tremendous good.[92]

By 1937, O'Shea as metropolitan was expressing his belief in the Bible-in-Schools League's good faith in not pressing Catholic consciences, now that they had won five minutes' prayer time in the state school day.[93] As the League metamorphosed in the late 1940s into the New Zealand Council for Christian Education, it was no longer either a formidable group or a promoter of anti-Catholic sentiments.

Most of the acrimony between the bishops had been kept 'in house'. In the early 1930s, however, the second controversy involving Liston landed him in a courtroom. In this case, it is hard to excuse his intransigent attitude.

In 1926, Dalton Henry Campbell, Marist parish priest of Whangarei, arranged to borrow money from his father to build a new parish church. Between 1926 and 1928, Thomas Campbell lent £3,500 in instalments and the Whangarei church was built. But Dalton Campbell had gained from Bishop Cleary only the vaguest spoken assent to this project. He had been granted no formal permission to raise a substantial loan, and his own parish book-keeping practice was inadequate. He was later unable to account specifically for all the money he had borrowed. St Francis Xavier's church was opened in October 1928. Dalton Campbell was transferred out of the diocese at the beginning of 1929. The incoming Marist priest, Henry Joseph Herring, took up with his bishop the matter of the parish church's finances and the extent of the parish debt.[94] In the strongest possible terms, Cleary repudiated the loan that Dalton Campbell had raised. 'This loan was NOT authorized by me; I was NEVER consulted about it; I would NEVER have agreed to it; AND I REFUSE TO RECOGNIZE IT.'[95]

Thomas Campbell attempted to recover his money from the new Bishop of Auckland. In January 1930, Liston's lawyers advised that the diocese was not responsible for debts which priests contracted without the bishop's permission.[96] The diocesan council concurred.[97] Thomas Campbell was not reimbursed. In November 1931, his lawyers wrote that –

> The Church in general and Whangarei Parish in particular have beyond doubt had the benefit of our client's money and it is a matter of astonishment to us that the Parish and the Church authorities should deny liability.[98]

Eventually, in January 1932, Thomas Campbell sued Liston for recovery of £3,500.[99] Liston checked with the Apostolic Delegate to make sure that Cleary had left no formal written agreement in the matter with Dalton Campbell. He again had his accountants check the ill-kept records of Whangarei parish. Then he refused to pay.[100]

The action came to court in Wellington on 1 and 2 June 1932, before Mr Justice McGregor, and received considerable attention from the press. Liston's counsel H.E. Barrowclough was able to prove that it was a parish debt, not a diocesan debt; that Dalton Campbell had kept poor accounts; and that the priest had not even informed the parishioners of the source of the loan or the size of the debt. But Thomas Campbell's lawyer Watson made it clear in cross-examination that Dalton Campbell had not misappropriated any of the money and that Liston was not accusing him of so doing. The Marist provincial David Kennedy gave it as his opinion that the bishop and the parish were jointly liable for repayment.[101]

Both the *Dominion* and the Wellington *Evening Post* gave full accounts of the case, drawing attention to the judge's impatience at the prevarications of clergy under examination. At one point, exasperated at Fr Herring's fencing, McGregor burst out, 'Oh, do try to be frank!' The press also reported this exchange between Liston and Campbell's lawyer:

> Counsel: 'As head of the Roman Catholic Church in Auckland, do you approve of the church seeking to take advantage of a legal technicality to avoid liability?'
>
> Liston: 'I am fully entitled to use every legal means to decide whether there is liability.'
>
> Counsel: 'Are you content to take refuge behind a technical defence apart from any meritorious defence?'
>
> Liston: 'Yes, I am perfectly entitled to do that.'[102]

Despite his evident annoyance, McGregor found in Liston's favour. The bishop, the diocese and the parish were not legally liable for a debt Dalton Campbell had contracted on his own initiative. McGregor did, however, add as his personal opinion that the diocese had a moral debt, and that Liston's attitude was questionable. After first checking with his lawyers, Liston sent a confidential letter to Whangarei parishioners dissenting from the judge's concluding remarks.[103] Thomas Campbell's further appeals for repayment were ignored.

In a strictly legal sense, Liston was right, as the court had found. The Bishop of Auckland had not authorised the loan Dalton Campbell had contracted. Liston did not wish to set a precedent whereby other priests could burden the diocese with unapproved debt. Nevertheless, there was a case in natural justice for repaying Thomas Campbell. Dalton Campbell was not an embezzler, and the

Whangarei church *had* been built with Thomas Campbell's money. Liston adamantly refused to concede this point. Not only the press, but many Catholics were scandalised by his attitude. The Rotorua solicitor M.H. Hampson wrote to O'Shea protesting that Liston, in his evidence, had maligned Cleary's reputation by implying that the late bishop was lax in his application of canon law.[104] O'Shea himself (concurrently in angry contention with Liston over the Bible-in-Schools matter) wrote to Archdeacon Holbrook claiming that Catholics were 'incensed' by Liston's courtroom manoeuvres.[105]

The Marist order was clearly embarrassed by Dalton Campbell's behaviour.[106] The priest's father Thomas Campbell (who was not a Catholic) was unimpressed by Liston's performance and was still determined to recover his money. He now threatened to sue Archbishop Redwood, as being ultimately responsible for debts contracted by bishops and other Catholic clergy. Redwood feared adverse publicity at the time of his forthcoming episcopal diamond jubilee. Slowly and painfully, in 1932-33, Redwood's secretary and Bishop Brodie put together an out-of-court settlement. Fr Smyth came to Auckland, checked the Whangarei accounts and confirmed that Dalton Campbell's book-keeping left much money unaccounted for.[107] Smyth then summoned Dalton Campbell before Redwood. They persuaded him to write to his father, taking personal responsibility for the loss of his money.[108] Having thus firmly disavowed any legal liability, they were able to present any compensation to Campbell as being in the nature of a gift. Finally, Thomas Campbell agreed to accept, as full settlement, £2,000, of which £1,000 were contributed by the Marist order and £250 by each of the four Catholic dioceses.[109]

Liston was grudging in acceding even to this payment. In a letter to Redwood, he insisted that Dalton Campbell had 'allowed the Bishop of Auckland to suffer all the indignity of a court case', that the Marist order had not adequately disciplined Campbell, and that 'I have publicly declared that I recognize no moral responsibility in the matter; hence I could not in honour make any compromise'.[110] Brodie had written to Liston soothingly agreeing to his descriptions of Dalton Campbell.[111] Later, Liston professed to be 'deeply hurt' by the tone of a letter in which Redwood urged him to agree to the settlement. 'I had not expected that you would write to a brother bishop in that way.'[112]

In December 1933, the *New Zealand Herald* reported that 'the dispute . . . has been amicably settled . . . to the satisfaction of all parties'.[113] But it was not to Liston's satisfaction. Within church circles he doggedly insisted that all liability lay with Father Campbell's Marist order. By March 1935, he had persuaded the Marist fathers to agree that the whole Whangarei debt was theirs. They authorised him, on his *ad limina*, to tell the Marist Superior General in Rome that they would repay the full sum to Mr Campbell.[114]

Given the nature of Cleary's emphatic reply to Fr Herring, it is possible that he would have acted similarly to Liston in these circumstances. Even so, in handling the Campbell case Liston was oblivious to the church's need for good publicity, which Cleary had cultivated so industriously. A church leader who so often taught moral lessons was not the right person to hide behind legal niceties when money was owing.

O'Shea and Redwood criticised Liston for his handling of the Campbell case, and Liston had been fully involved in the strife between the bishops over the Bible-in-Schools negotiations. After the early 1930s, however, there were no comparable controversies to disrupt his relationship with his brother bishops. As he continued in sole charge of Auckland, sickness and death changed the leadership of the other three New Zealand dioceses.

In Dunedin, Whyte's health faltered from the late 1930s. He suffered a major stroke at the end of 1941 and remained bed-ridden until his death in December 1957.[115] Officially he was still Bishop of Dunedin, but in 1943 a coadjutor was consecrated. This was Hugh O'Neill, a former pupil of Liston's at Mosgiel and, like Liston, an alumnus of the Christian Brothers' Dunedin school. O'Neill frequently acknowledged his many debts to Liston, and Liston preached at his consecration. But by 1948 O'Neill admitted, 'I have been a bad investment as a bishop from a health point of view'.[116] Subject to duodenal ulcers and cerebral arterial diseases, he was frequently hospitalised.[117] In March 1949, Whyte announced the resignation of the man who was supposed to have relieved him for health reasons.[118] Another bishop had to be found. John Patrick Kavanagh, another of Liston's former students, was appointed Dunedin's new coadjutor in July 1949.[119] He was consecrated in Wellington in December by Liston.[120]

Meanwhile, there had been successive changes in the leadership of the archdiocese. Redwood died in January 1935. His coadjutor O'Shea automatically succeeded as metropolitan. For a decade, O'Shea led effectively. He presided at the 1940 national Eucharistic Congress that coincided with the national centennial celebrations.[121] But by the late 1940s, O'Shea, who had endured the senility of Redwood, was himself showing signs of decay. 'For some time past he has become forgetful and has in some ways lost his grip of things', wrote Liston to the Apostolic Delegate in early 1947, reporting the views of a meeting of the suffragan bishops.[122]

The man who became O'Shea's coadjutor was in every respect Liston's protégé. His appointment strengthened Liston's predominance in the New Zealand church. Peter Thomas Bertram McKeefry had been an Auckland diocesan priest since his ordination in Rome in 1926. For over 20 years he had edited Auckland's diocesan magazine and newspaper, and he was Liston's private secretary. In March 1947, Liston advised the Apostolic Delegate that McKeefry and Leonard Buxton were 'episcopabile'.[123] McKeefry was appointed O'Shea's coadjutor in July. Liston described himself as 'one who has day by day watched his life and has his confidence'.[124] Like Kavanagh and O'Neill, McKeefry was a former student of Liston's at Mosgiel.[125] In October 1947, Cardinal Gilroy consecrated him archbishop in Liston's cathedral in Auckland.[126] McKeefry was the first New Zealand-born archbishop and became the first New Zealand-born metropolitan when O'Shea (who had been bed-ridden in the Calvary Hospital since 1950) died in 1954. Yet while officially outranking Liston in the hierarchy, McKeefry continued to address Liston as 'Carissimo Padre' and to sign himself 'your obedient son' or 'your devoted child'. One letter in 1948 goes far beyond routine pleasantries:

> Your strength has ever sustained me just as your own life has been my inspiration – and the joy of thinking ever to be with you, ah, that was the dread of all those days last year, but I am not going to dwell on all that again. As I once said – I refuse to think of separation and I still see myself your secretary – we are still working together, and thanks be to God for the joys of letters and phone calls for these give reality to our united work, and make the distance seem negligible.[127]

Liston came very near to having a similarly close bond with a new bishop of Christchurch. Matthew Brodie celebrated his episcopal silver jubilee in February 1941. Shortly thereafter, he began to be seriously troubled by a malignant tumour on the lymphatic gland.[128] His health broke down rapidly and Liston paid him a visit of sympathy in August 1943.[129] Brodie died in October 1943. Liston celebrated his requiem mass in Christchurch.[130] In January 1944, the man chosen to succeed Brodie was Liston's close friend and travelling companion William Ormond.[131] The Vicar-Capitular of Christchurch wrote to congratulate Liston, saying 'his [Ormond's] appointment strengthens the ties that unite Your Lordship to us'.[132] Of Ormond, Bishop O'Neill playfully remarked, 'Poor man! If he feels as I felt at this time last year, he needs a lot of sympathy'.[133] In fact, Ormond needed far more sympathy than O'Neill realised. The responsibilities involved in becoming a bishop overwhelmed and scared him. The Auckland diocesan newspaper reported in February that he was 'at present indisposed, and acting on medical advice is taking a complete rest'.[134] Ormond plunged into deep depression, out of which Liston was unable to coax him.[135] By late February, doctors were advising Liston that Ormond would have 'a complete breakdown' if he forced himself to take up the appointment as bishop of Christchurch.[136] In March, he was released from his appointment.[137] Unfortunately, this did not ward off his nervous breakdown. By 1947, he was under psychiatric care for 'melancholia' and was being sedated to prevent 'suicide or self-injury'.[138] He died in 1949. Liston preached his eulogy.[139]

As this private and unreported tragedy was being played out, Christchurch still needed a bishop. Hastily the Vatican appointed an outsider.[140] Patrick Francis Lyons was Daniel Mannix's vicar-general and secretary in Melbourne.[141] He was consecrated bishop in Melbourne in July 1944, with just one representative of the New Zealand hierarchy present.[142] In August, he was enthroned in Christchurch in the presence of all the hierarchy except Whyte.[143] Though a comparatively young man, Lyons lasted a mere six years as bishop of Christchurch. Even by the standards of pre-Vatican II bishops, he had 'a difficult and authoritarian personality'.[144] He opposed such initiatives as Liston's attempt to extend exemptions from the eucharistic fast to nurses working in Catholic hospitals.[145] Christchurch had a history of tensions between Marist and secular priests. Lyons managed to exacerbate them when he demanded that the Marists vacate a number of parishes.[146] The dispute reached Rome, which decided to have Lyons transferred. In 1950, he resigned as bishop of Christchurch and became Cardinal Gilroy's second auxiliary bishop in Sydney. There he gained a name as one of the more aggressively 'political' bishops in the anti-Communist crusade that was about to split the Australian Labor Party.[147] His successor was the Lyttelton-born Edward Michael Joyce, consecrated in July 1950 by McKeefry with Liston and Kavanagh assisting.[148] Joyce was installed in time to host the Catholic celebrations in November 1950 at the time of Christchurch's centennial, when Liston preached at the high mass.[149]

Perhaps because of the uncertainties of Christchurch's leadership in the 1940s, Liston took a decisive role in the planning, funding and construction of the junior seminary, Holy Name, which was located there in the suburb of Riccarton. This was opened by the Apostolic Delegate John Panico in February 1947.[150] The post-Vatican II church views the formation of priests differently. It is no longer considered appropriate to recruit seminarians by institutionalising them in their younger teenage years. Tales were later told of Liston applying unfair psychological pressure on parents as he urged them to send their young sons to Riccarton.[151] Holy Name ceased to be exclusively a minor seminary in 1959 and its high school closed down in the 1960s.[152] Nevertheless, its creation was regarded as a major achievement in the 1940s, and much of the credit was Liston's.

In 1954, the bed-ridden Archbishop O'Shea died. Bishop Whyte remained an invalid. Liston's protégé McKeefry was metropolitan, his former pupil Kavanagh was Bishop of Dunedin and Joyce was Bishop of Christchurch. The hierarchy had undergone a major transformation. As the *Marist Messenger* noted in 1950, 'our four active bishops are all native-born'.[153] Of these four New Zealanders, Liston was much the senior and it was to him, rather than to the metropolitan, that the others commonly deferred.

The Bishop and his Clergy

In his 1935 *relatio* to the Vatican, Liston wrote of his diocesan clergy, 'All paroci fulfil their strict obligations, nearly all are noted for their true priestly zeal and many are living models of zeal and holiness'.[154] This did not mean, however, that he had no real problems with his clergy. The proportion of New Zealand-born priests was growing. In 1945, Auckland's Sacred Heart College was celebrating the ordination to the priesthood of its fiftieth old boy.[155] By later standards, Liston's diocese was fully staffed and was able to join Dunedin in lending priests to understaffed Christchurch.[156] Philip Purcell remarks that Liston 'had sufficient priests' in the 1940s, but also notes that canon law forbade priests to say more than two masses on a Sunday. Hence many parishes needed more than one curate.[157] Liston made regular appeals for vocations. He also relied on recruits from Ireland. In 1937, he tabulated the ethnicity of the Auckland clergy. Of the 119 priests, 54 were Irish-born, 32 were New Zealand-born, 17 (all Mill Hill missioners) were Dutch and the remaining 16 were smaller groups of Australians, English, Germans and one Croat. There were no Maori priests.[158] Irish seminarians were regularly 'promised' to Auckland, and the Catholic press regularly welcomed new Irish priests. Senior clergy visiting Ireland

Above left: Monsignor Henry Holbrook, parish priest of Grey Lynn 1914-52, and major organiser of Catholic charities. He innocently antagonised Bishop Cleary, but served the diocese well for the first two decades of Liston's episcopate. *Above right:* The young William Ormond, Liston's close friend, colleague and successor at St Benedict's, but a man not cut out to be bishop. *Below left:* Daniel Silk, who lectured briefly at Mosgiel when Liston was rector, and later became one of Auckland diocese's most enduring identities. *Below right:* Bishop (later Cardinal) Peter McKeefry, the metropolitan who remained Liston's protégé. In his private correspondence to Liston, he continued to style himself 'your most obedient son'.

Above left: Fr Martin Alink, Mill Hill provincial from 1934 to 1960. His missioners were for many years in contention with Liston over matters of finance, organisation and evangelisation. Above right: John James Bradley, long-serving parish priest of Remuera (1925–59) and trusted member of Liston's diocesan council. He left a very mixed reputation among younger priests. Below left: Leonard Buxton, cathedral administrator, parish priest of Parnell, benefactor to the diocese, diocesan councillor – and one of Liston's most trusted lieutenants. Below right: Jeremiah Cahill, long-serving vicar-general of the diocese and effectively Liston's second-in-command. The man whom priests would approach first. He died after Liston's retirement.

were commissioned to report on how the 'promised' students were progressing.[159] Liston also made it his habit to send Holy Cross (Clonliffe), All Hallows (Dublin), Maynooth, St Patrick's (Thurles) and St Kieran's (Kilkenny) regular reports on how their graduates were progressing in Auckland, and obituaries of those who had died.[160]

What was true of priests was true of religious. The great majority of sisters and nuns in Auckland were not New Zealand-born but had emigrated from Ireland or Australia.[161] Two Mercy Sisters were sent to Ireland to seek postulants for Auckland in 1937, 1948 and 1951.[162] Liston smoothed their way with letters of introduction to Archbishop McQuaid.[163] Mother Genevieve O'Donnell brought out 24 Irish postulants in 1949. The majority of those postulants who met Liston in a ceremony of reception at St Mary's in 1952 were Irish.[164] In 1948, Liston organised the recruitment of ten Cluny Sisters from Ireland to act as domestic staff in the two national seminaries (outside Auckland diocese).[165] He also, in 1951, enquired of the Irish College in Rome whether any sisters from 'displaced communities' in postwar Europe could be persuaded to come to Auckland.[166]

Having so large a proportion of Irish clergy did create some problems. Liston was particularly exercised by homesick priests who spun out to inordinate length their periods of leave in Ireland.[167] It also appears that, of those priests who had to be disciplined for drunkenness or an overbearing attitude, a disproportionate number were Irish. In 1938, Stephen Farragher, in the Waikato parish of Cambridge, quarrelled with the sisters over how they ran the local convent school, and moved parishioners to complain to Liston when he denounced individuals from the pulpit. Liston was relieved when Farragher returned to Ireland in 1940.[168] In Huntly, the racecourse debts and drinking of Matthew Curley caused a scandal in 1931. He was removed from the parish in 1932.[169] In Waihi, the aged Irishman John Peter O'Hara nearly provoked a riot when he insulted non-Catholic relatives at a family funeral. Liston 'invited' him to retire. Instead, the old man died.[170] In Coromandel in 1935-36, Philip Fitzpatrick was so homesick that he eventually produced a medical certificate to say he was near breakdown. Liston allowed him to return to Ireland.[171] John Thomas Taylor was removed from Paeroa parish by Liston in 1930 after repeated episodes of drunkenness. When Taylor was dismissed, he wrote scurrilous letters about other clergy and attempted to steal the parish car. Liston temporarily suspended him from his duties. In 1932, Liston gave Taylor charge of Northcote parish, but the Irishman's drinking and abusive letters continued. In 1934, Liston intervened when Taylor began a long quarrel with Sr M. de Pazzi over the Dominican Sisters' conduct of the parish school. Taylor was ejected from the diocese in 1936.[172] 'I would like to get out of this place to be somewhere where I can see a fellow priest once in a while', wrote Cormac Joseph Brady from Opotiki in 1941, when Liston was in the midst of protracted disciplinary action over his drunkenness and verbal abusiveness.[173] It is significant that most of these unhappy men felt isolated in rural parishes outside metropolitan Auckland. Their stories suggest at least some loneliness and disappointment among those who were used to far more prestige and respect in highly-clericalised Catholic Ireland.

For all his priests (Irish and non-Irish), Liston maintained strict rules. Since the Second Vatican Council, priestly faculties are granted for life. In the 1930s and 1940s, they still had to be renewed annually. Liston re-licensed each priest at the annual clergy retreats, to conduct which he usually contracted Jesuits or Vincentians from Australia.[174] Attendance was compulsory. He kept a careful record of priests present, and disciplined those who were absent without leave.[175] Each retreat ended with Liston's own exhortations before faculties were distributed. Liston 'strictly enforced' the wearing of clerical garb.[176]

Subjects for the parish priest's programme of sermons and homilies were prescribed by the bishop for every Sunday of the year. Liston had this homiletic programme printed as a booklet and distributed. His idea was picked up by other bishops and after 1952 his leaflets were distributed in all dioceses.[177] Liston instructed that sermons had to be between 15 and 20 minutes long, and warned –

Never preach for display.

Never say anything you don't mean.

Never point to heights of virtue you yourself have no idea of touching.

Shun all self-satisfaction over your sermons.[178]

Younger priests had to submit sermons to the bishop's scrutiny, and even more experienced hands could expect a reprimand if their sermons drew the wrong sort of attention. 'There was too much of self in the preaching', complained Liston to Fr Francis Terry, on a notorious occasion in 1940 when Terry had asked members of an Auckland congregation to raise their hands to show they were true followers of Jesus. 'One reproof was offensive; some things were imprudently said; your earnestness ran to excess.'[179] Liston took a close interest in liturgy and its proper performance. He delighted in promoting the correct use of Gregorian chant, and he attempted to encourage laypeople to learn and sing parts of the Latin mass rather than singing hymns during the ordinary, which was too common a pre-Vatican II habit.[180]

Long eucharistic fasts were still mandatory for priests. Despite some querying of the rule, priests were still officially banned from theatres and racetracks. They also had to gain permission from the bishop to read or consult 'books and periodicals and magazines that are written against or contain attacks upon the Faith'. The university chaplain Thomas Ryder was granted such permission in 1948 when he wanted to enter more effectively into debate with non-Catholic student groups.[181] Liston preferred to supervise personally all diocesan publications. In 1931, he expressed some unease over the *Marist Messenger*, which he feared would develop into a magazine outside the bishop's control.[182] In 1946, he rebuked John Downey at Morrinsville for starting a parish newsletter without his permission, although he made no objection to the newsletter once he had seen it.[183] In a similar spirit, he wished, in 1945, to remove Whangarei parish from the care of the Marist order and place it once again under diocesan control. But he did not pursue this matter when the Marist provincial Fr Heffernan showed how important the parish was in the Marist mission.[184]

Liston's sacerdotal management was often autocratic. Younger priests were addressed in curt commands. Bishop John Mackey, a curate in the 1940s, recalls receiving from Liston a one-word message – 'Desist!' – when Liston learnt that he was taking unauthorised flying lessons. Later, when Mackey requested a car to get him around a large pastoral area, Liston remarked dryly, 'We have an excellent bus service'.[185] Liston expected to be obeyed when he assigned a priest to a new parish. In 1932, a large petition was signed by parishioners who wanted Maurice Hunt to remain in Cambridge. Liston ignored the petition and sent Hunt to Takapuna anyway.[186] More questionably, in 1948, when the ageing Michael Bleakley asked to be transferred from Hamilton to a more manageable Auckland city parish, Liston first made him resign his cure. He then appointed the man who had criticised the Mater to a small-town parish, Te Puke.[187] At the same time, Liston could show considerable concern for aged and infirm clergy. In 1935, he offered a curate for the elderly Thomas Lane at Ellerslie. Lane proudly turned the offer down, arguing that there was not enough work in the small parish for two priests.[188]

There were also priests who saw Liston as a preferable alternative to other ecclesial authorities. In 1939, John Alexander Higgins, a Marist polemicist in the archdiocese of Wellington, had a major quarrel with the Marist provincial Victor Geaney when Geaney told him to cease some of his public educational work. Higgins at once petitioned Liston to be accepted as a secular priest for Auckland.[189] Twice, Liston and his council courteously turned Higgins down, on the grounds that he would do better to patch up his quarrel with his superiors.[190] Higgins was later incardinated for the archdiocese, but thanked Liston for his concern.[191] A far more quarrelsome former Marist was James Eccleston. Successively at Tuakau and Tauranga, Eccleston quarrelled with his former Marist colleagues, fought with parishioners over a fund-raising ball, denounced the moral condition of the local township as 'dreadful . . . a sink of filth', upbraided the Cluny Sisters from the pulpit about the state of their finances and argued with Liston over the leadership of the local Legion of Mary branch. Nevertheless, Eccleston was an effective parish priest, and Liston preached at his funeral in 1952.[192] In like fashion, Liston sided with James Molloy when some Pukekohe parishioners complained in 1938 of Molloy's personal denunciations from the pulpit.[193]

As the years passed, Liston began to outlive some of his priestly colleagues. In 1936, he presided at the funeral of Ferdinand Dignan, the middle-aged priest of Thames who had contracted pneumonia. He spoke the eulogy at Henry Francis Holbrook's funeral in 1952. A year earlier he attended the Dunedin funeral of his close friend James Delaney. Some priests died tragically young. In 1951, James Shore, curate of St Benedict's, was killed in a road accident while returning from the funeral of Joseph Patrick Murphy of Te Aroha. Liston officiated at both funerals.[194] On the other hand, some priests seemed to go on forever. Michael Furlong at Devonport was celebrating his sacerdotal golden jubilee in 1952 and still had many years ahead of him as parish priest. He seemed a permanent fixture to generations of Auckland Catholics.[195]

Though Liston was the ultimate authority as bishop, he could not administer on his own. Surrounding him was a phalanx of senior clergy. The Vicar-General Jeremiah Cahill was the second man in the diocese, and Liston's voice during his absences. His durability matched Liston's own. 'In learning, virtue and prayer he stood at the heart of the diocese for some fifty years', wrote Liston after Cahill's death in 1971.[196] Increasingly, after William Ormond's death in 1949, Cahill became Liston's closest personal confidant as well. Michael

Above left: Liston happy to help celebrate the sacerdotal golden jubilee of Devonport's long-serving parish priest Michael Furlong.
Above right: A studio portrait from the 1940s.
Left: A familiar sight at Auckland diocesan functions for many years – Archbishop Liston shadowed by his private secretary Fr John Flanagan.

Kennedy (parish priest of Ponsonby, 1932-57) and John Bradley (parish priest of Remuera, 1925-59) were long-time members of the diocesan council. So were Leonard Buxton (cathedral administrator, 1925-42; parish priest of Parnell, then of Hamilton, 1942-64) and Michael Edge (parish priest of Parnell, 1930-42) and Henry Francis Holbrook (parish priest of Grey Lynn, 1914-52).[197] Liston advanced their careers, placing them on his council and having them named 'domestic prelates' and monsignori by the Vatican. Sometimes even members of his trusted circle had disagreements with the bishop. Holbrook complained in 1942 of delays in making him a diocesan councillor, which he saw as very unfair after all his years managing the diocesan orphanages.[198] Generally, though, the councillors were Liston's firmest support.

The careers of younger men were being fostered, too. In 1939, Reginald John Delargey returned from Rome with a doctorate, and Francis Terry from Dublin, where he had studied educational administration. Liston had earlier petitioned Rome to have Terry's doctorate recognised.[199] He put Delargey to work with the Catholic Youth Movement and Terry with the school inspectorate. Young Adrian Curran became cathedral administrator in 1942 when Leonard Buxton was transferred to Parnell.[200] A decade later, Liston arranged for Francis Wright to study Catholic social teaching in Ireland.[201] Some of the younger men were restive under Liston's leadership. The Irishman Thomas Ryder, who had arrived in the diocese in 1937, credited himself with being the first priest to introduce 'JOCist' Christian worker ideas into Auckland. He later complained that Liston overburdened him with work when he had been suffering from tuberculosis, and unfairly deprived him of his university chaplaincy; but he was compensated by being appointed to lead the Marian Year pilgrimage to Rome.[202]

It is noticeable that there was an influx of younger intellectual priests immediately after the Second World War. Many of these men had acquired extensive life experience during the war. They had considerably more maturity than raw seminarians. A late vocation, Ernest Richard Simmons served in the British Navy during the war before being ordained in 1953 at the age of 31.[203] He later edited the diocesan newspaper. John Joseph Flanagan and Owen Noel Snedden were newly ordained when the war trapped them in the Vatican in 1941. Together with the Irish Monsignor O'Flaherty, they secretly organised escape networks for Allied prisoners of war and downed pilots. For this work they were thanked by General Freyberg. They were both awarded MBEs in 1945, after the prime minister Peter

Fraser had personally arranged their repatriation. In 1947, when Peter McKeefry became coadjutor-archbishop of Wellington, Liston made Flanagan his private secretary and gave Snedden the editorship of the diocesan newspaper.[204] Leo Vincent Downey was also trapped in Italy by the war, but was smuggled out through neutral Portugal with the help of the Swiss consul. His letters back to Liston provide a frank and alarming critique of Italian Fascism.[205] Liston later made Downey responsible for diocesan social work.

The priest most publicly identified with his war experience was Edward Archibald ('Ted') Forsman. He had been ordained in Rome in 1936 and was a curate in Auckland before the war. Evading Liston's ruling against priests playing competition sport, Forsman sometimes played club cricket under the pseudonym F.A. Edwards.[206] He befriended a wide circle of intellectual friends. These included political foes of Catholicism such as S.W.('Sid') Scott, the secretary of the New Zealand Communist Party, who later wrote of Forsman, 'we walked the streets until the midnight hours, discussing the world as it was and as we would like it'.[207] Writing to Liston in 1938, the young Forsman cheerfully reported how he had worn down and won over a group of Communist workers when he challenged them to an all-night discussion in a work-camp.[208]

Forsman was a military chaplain during the war. En route to North Africa, he made a lasting friendship with the soldier-novelist Dan Davin, who had by that stage long since renounced his family's Catholicism.[209] Forsman won the respect of the troops and, when he was made a prisoner of war, he was able to pass on information that allowed New Zealanders to disable their vehicles and prevent them falling into enemy hands. This soldierly man was an obvious person for Liston to choose to preach the Anzac Day sermon in the cathedral in 1946.[210] He was parish priest of Parnell from 1949 to 1975. Apart from this, however, Liston did not quite know what to do with him. Between 1945 and 1949, together with another former army chaplain John Charles Pierce, he was set to work editing the short-lived *Catholic Review*. Later, Forsman, 'a man of considerable culture and ability', lectured in philosophy at the University of Auckland.[211] In an unpublished memoir, Forsman's brother Henry wrote that as a curate –

> Ted was required to submit regularly his sermons to Bishop Liston for criticism. I know Ted appreciated greatly the comments of his erudite Bishop who, despite a poor oral delivery, wrote extremely well.[212]

Of Ted's postwar adjustments, Henry wrote that Liston was 'most understanding' and showed 'caring and perceptive awareness' of Ted's needs. 'Rightly or wrongly, I believe Bishop Liston's kindness and his concern for his priests were not always recognized in the Auckland diocese.'[213]

Liston's relationship with priests like Simmons, Snedden, Flanagan, Pierce, Downey and Forsman was the relationship of an institutional superior to well-educated, mature men. They obediently did the bishop's bidding, but they were not schoolboys cowering before the college rector. It may be significant, however, that outside his trusted circle of diocesan councillors, Liston was more likely to seek intellectual companionship in tertiary-educated nuns, such as Sacred Heart Sister Dorothea Loughnan, than in junior diocesan clergy.[214]

At the other end of the scale from such mature obedience, there was the minority of priests who were genuinely delinquent. In 1933, Liston sent home the hard-drinking, gambling Australian priest Thomas Hilly, but he was still being bothered by Hilly's creditors years later.[215] The elderly Francis Buckley had been deemed incapable of administering a parish by Bishop Cleary. Liston shared this view.[216] Buckley later accused Liston of stealing his life savings when Liston took charge of some trust funds for him.[217] Liston's treatment of one sad misfit was deemed rather cruel by later clergy. George Jowett Lockwood had been active in the diocese from 1934, but he wavered in his vocation and was restive under Liston's authority. Liston temporarily withdrew Lockwood's faculties in 1936 when Lockwood took an unauthorised holiday. Lockwood considered leaving the priesthood, then he considered leaving the diocese and joining the Redemptorist order. But they rejected him.[218] Lockwood had the temerity to complain that he had been left too long in the same appointment. A major argument with Liston followed. Lockwood left the diocese without permission in 1952 and went overseas. He returned but was permanently deprived of his faculties. Lockwood, in his old age, told Bishop Patrick Dunn that Liston sent an apologetic John Flanagan down to the wharf to meet Lockwood's incoming ship, and to tell him that he was 'no longer wanted as a priest' in the diocese. For many years, Lockwood continued to live in Auckland, dressed in clerical garb but forbidden to say mass or function as a priest. 'This is the shadow side of the archbishop', says Dunn. 'I find it hard to understand how a bishop could leave a priest in limbo like that.'[219]

Considerably more delinquent than Lockwood were the few

documented cases of sexual misconduct by priests. When a mother complained in 1934 that a drunken priest had sexually harassed her teenage daughter, Liston reprimanded the priest concerned, but also wrote to the mother, 'I am sure you will see to it that the incident is not spoken of'.[220] In 1943, an angry husband complained of a priest's sexual advances to his wife. Liston attempted to persuade the priest to go to Australia.[221] In such cases, silence, discretion and the shuffling of delinquent clergy to other parishes were later to earn the church much opprobrium. But they were standard practice for bishops at the time.

Quite apart from the delinquents, the 'big men' and the younger intellectuals, there were some priests who managed to turn themselves into distinct diocesan identities. Edward Lyons, expelled by Liston from Mosgiel and then ordained by him in Auckland, continued for many years as parish priest of Thames. John Mackey was his curate for some years in the 1940s and describes him as 'one of the kindest and wisest men I've ever met'. But Lyons knew he could not resist sparring with Liston. Before one of Liston's parish visitations, Mackey recalls Lyons saying to him, 'For heaven's sake stop us quarrelling'.[222] On one occasion, Lyons argued with Liston about the historical facts relating to Bishop Pompallier's role at the signing of the Treaty of Waitangi. Lyons paid an artist to produce a painting depicting his version of the historical event, and then hung it in a prominent place in his presbytery so that Liston had to see it whenever he visited.[223] To the vast amusement of younger priests, Lyons' specialty was to challenge Liston, at clergy conferences, with awkward theological questions which he knew Liston could not answer. Lyons' nephew, John Lyons, says –

> It's interesting to describe the relationship between the two of them because when I was a young priest it was quite famous. Rather like two people who really didn't agree on many things but were actually not going to meet head-on . . . The [Hamilton] clergy conference went well if Father Edward arrived because sooner or later he'd take on James Michael by either asking or answering a question that he'd keep nagging away at. And this would meet with all the priests' approval.[224]

Bishop Mackey concurs, saying that at clergy retreats a few priests like Edward Lyons and Michael Bleakley, already stationed outside Auckland city, 'would stand up and express an opinion and then sit down because they knew that to some extent they were immune'.[225] After all, having sat his concursus in the late 1930s, Edward

Lyons was an 'irremovable' priest.[226] In managing clergy, episcopal autocracy had its limits.

The Maori Mission

In the 1920s, Mill Hills had expressed anxiety at the prospect of Liston's becoming bishop. In the 1930s, many of their worst fears seemed realised. The bishop and the missionary order clashed over finances, administrative method and the allocation of parishes.

In 1936, the provincial's official report said that of the region's 50,000 Maori, 9,068 were baptised Catholics. There were 12 Mill Hill stations run by 22 priests with the help of two lay brothers and 34 sisters of various orders.[227] (In the Wellington archdiocese at this time, a smaller Maori mission was in the hands of the Marist fathers.) Liston's public demeanour towards the missioners was courteous. He wrote prefaces to their publications.[228] He preached at the funerals of Mill Hill priests.[229] In 1937, he hosted a farewell dinner for the Mill Hill provincial, Martin Alink, as he set off to England.[230] Later, he smoothed the way for the Dutch government to present Alink and the Mill Hills with the Order of Orange-Nassau, for the Dutch priests' 'excellent behaviour and individual good qualities [that] have contributed to the good name in New Zealand of their fatherland'.[231]

Under the surface courtesies, however, a different story was being played out. Much of it had to do with finance. Even in Cleary's episcopate, Mill Hill missioners were already complaining that they were not eligible for the funding that was given to 'necessitous white parishes', and that they had to 'beg' for contributions in special annual appeals.[232] Shortly after Liston became bishop, he seemed to show indifference to the Mill Hills' endeavours when he sold off land near Te Awamutu that had once been earmarked for an expanded Maori mission.[233] Liston's priority was assimilation. His ideal was that, as much as possible, Maori parishioners should be absorbed into the Pakeha church, though perhaps being sometimes addressed in special 'missions'.[234]

This meant that throughout the 1930s and 1940s, as Pakeha became the majority in some parishes, Liston withdrew those parishes from Mill Hill control and turned them over to the diocesan clergy. Thus the Mill Hills were withdrawn from Opotiki (1931), Whakatane and Tolaga Bay (1933), Tauranga and Kihikihi (1935), Te Puke (1946) and Ohura (1948).[235] To the Mill Hills, however, these new arrangements exacerbated their financial woes. They were becoming more dependent on smaller, poorer rural Maori congregations that could not financially support them.[236] Sometimes, too, there was Maori resistance to being absorbed into the general Pakeha community. The most notorious example was in the parish of Whakatane. In April 1934, Liston's pastoral letter to the Maori of Whakatane (it had been translated into Maori for him) stressed their oneness and unity with their fellow-parishioners.[237] This was because the previous month, Liston had rebuked the Mill Hill missioner van Beek for saying mass at the local pa, explaining that –

> The good Maoris at the Pah can easily come to the church at Whakatane and have been doing so, as well as taking their proper part in the activities of the parish.[238]

Maori, however, preferred to worship at their own little church at Wairaka. Liston had the church closed. A struggle developed as Mill Hills tried to have the Wairaka church re-opened and explained how culturally significant it was to the Maori congregation. There was a lengthy exchange of letters on the subject between Liston and Martin Alink in 1939. Liston contended that 'local conditions' necessitated the closure of the Maori church, but he was not prepared to elaborate on what these 'local conditions' were. Alink was moved by the scandal of Catholic Maori passing a locked church where their parents had prayed.[239] The Mill Hills attempted to sidestep Liston's action by saying a monthly mass for Maori at the local meeting house. Liston forbade this practice too. In 1950, he also banned a rosary crusade at the meeting house and had the Wairaka church moved elsewhere.[240] Maori were to worship like other Whakatane parishioners or perhaps not worship at all.

There was much acrimonious correspondence between Liston and the Mill Hills, or *about* Liston between local Mill Hills and their superiors in London. In 1930, Dean van Dijk told Liston how badly in debt the Maori mission was, how *ad hoc* appeals could not make up its losses and how an annual grant that used to come from Propaganda Fide should be restored. 'At present the task is wearing me down . . . the Maori mission might manage to STRUGGLE on.'[241] In response to this plea, Liston did indeed write to the Apostolic Delegate asking for the Propaganda grant to be restored. But he also pleaded diocesan poverty as a reason for not supporting the mission more.[242]

The Mill Hills had signed a formal agreement with Bishop Cleary in 1923. It was due for renewal in 1933. At the beginning of 1931, the Mill Hill Superior-General Bishop Biermans visited, conferred with the missioners, and then held talks with Liston and van Dijk.[243]

Memoranda were drawn up and a new formal agreement between the bishop and the order seemed imminent. But Liston was unwilling to reach such an agreement before the transfer of some parishes was concluded. Van Dijk complained to Biermans,

> ... the only thing that is worrying him is how and when to get certain parishes away from our Fathers and hand them over to his diocesan clergy. Apparently he is quite content that we should starve in the meanwhile as long as we do so quietly. We are rather of a different opinion.[244]

Accusations of attempted 'starvation' are quite common in the surviving archival material. After the death of van Dijk in 1931, the new provincial O'Callaghan conceded that Liston was entitled to remove Mill Hills from Kaitaia, Whakatane and Putaruru. But he reported a description of this move as a 'bombshell' and a 'breach of faith' when the Mill Hills were so dependent on revenue from these parishes. He went on,

> It does seem outrageous that these things can be settled behind our backs. We are over 20 priests doing the most difficult work in the Diocese, and yet having no voice on the Bishop's Council – no opportunity to express even an opinion on matters that affect us and our work very closely. This surely should be one of the many matters for settlement . . .[245]

Later he added, '[Liston's] policy seems to be one of slow strangulation of the Maori mission'.[246] Mill Hills in the field regularly wrote to Liston saying how harsh their working conditions were. 'Since the bottom fell out of these things', Everard Bruning wrote from Waitaruke parish in 1936, with reference to the Depression, 'it has been scraping, scraping and biting of fingernails to make ends meet'.[247]

Underfunding, transfer of parishes without consultation and lack of representation upon the diocesan council were the missioners' main charges against Liston. But Liston had some counter-charges. In a long report to the Apostolic Delegate in 1934, he claimed some Mill Hills were not even bothering to learn Maori, some were attempting to work in largely Pakeha parishes rather than sticking to their proper missionary work, and –

> One cannot but feel that the national temperament of the Dutch Fathers does not make them very acceptable to our people of the White race. Parishioners often make known their feelings to me in this respect and ask that they be given one of our own diocesan priests.[248]

Liston was here presumably referring to the case of the 'grumpy' Mill Hill Fr Bressers about whom Pakeha had complained, or the drinking problems of Fr van Westeinde, about which O'Callaghan had himself commented.[249] It is, however, notable that Liston's concern is with the Pakeha congregations. He made no comments on 'national temperament' when it came to maladjusted Irish members of his clergy. Alink later complained to the Apostolic Delegate that Liston was insisting new Mill Hill recruits be either English or Irish, but not Dutch.[250] Liston did, however, have reason to suspect the motives of Fr Spierings when he unsuccessfully petitioned the diocesan council in 1932 to be accepted as a diocesan priest rather than be transferred by his order to missionary work outside New Zealand.[251]

To offset charges of underfunding the mission, Liston told the hierarchy in early 1935 that he and Archbishop O'Shea had applied to Rome to have most of the proceeds from the annual missions appeal handed over to the Mill Hills.[252] Liston made several consultations about the order while on his 1935 *ad limina*, but it was not until May 1938 that he reached a more amicable accommodation with the Mill Hills. Negotiating with the new provincial Martin Alink (who remained in the position from 1934 to 1960), Liston confirmed that predominantly Maori parishes would continue to be in Mill Hill care. Putaruru, though largely a Pakeha parish by this stage, would remain a Mill Hill base for the Waikato. Rotorua was to remain in Mill Hill care, but a future diocesan parish might have to be carved out of it. A Mill Hill station would remain at Kaihu, near Dargaville, and Liston would approach the South Island bishops to authorise Mill Hill appeals in the southern dioceses.[253] Despite a suggestion by the Apostolic Delegate, Liston refused to make the Mill Hill provincial a diocesan consultor or *ex officio* member of the diocesan council. But he did agree that the provincial would be given the title Dean, and would always be invited to council meetings when the Maori Mission was discussed. With some encouragement from Jeremiah Cahill, Alink acquiesced.[254]

After this 1938 agreement, the heat went out of the contention between the bishop and the missioners. In 1943, Alink wrote to his Superior-General in London,

> I am very pleased to say that our relationship with J.M.L. has . . . greatly improved these last few years. He is very helpful in many things and is even a regular visitor to St Peter's. Just to show by one example: the other day, in conversation with him, he himself came out with the proposal that I should apply for more priests! Formerly one dreaded to go and approach him with such proposals.[255]

A year later, Alink told O'Callaghan how upset he had been when one Mill Hill priest deserted the order and got married; but 'the bishop was most sympathetic, and I must say I felt a lot less discouraged after I left him'.[256] In 1948, Alink said Liston was 'most sympathetic and anxious to help' in the matter of obtaining visas for two new Mill Hill priests.[257] The same letter described Liston at the funeral of the young Mill Hill priest Michael Joseph McNally: 'The bishop spoke beautifully and everyone could see that he felt the loss of such a young and zealous priest keenly'. Liston later took the side of the Mill Hills when they complained of the uncouth and insulting behaviour of an Irish priest at Kaikohe.[258] At his worst, some of Liston's comments on the Mill Hills implied that they should expect to put up with harsh conditions and had no right to complain. In 1934, he had written –

> Surely as the Fathers are Missionaries they should be prepared to sacrifice, and point the way to the Diocesan priests. They joined the Society and were ordained for this difficult work and should not shrink.[259]

Given this attitude, it is little wonder that the Marist provincial too could describe Liston as 'not an easy man with whom to do business', and a Mill Hill historian could assert, 'it was . . . sometimes even impossible . . . to deal with Bishop Liston'.[260] Yet having asserted his diocesan leadership, Liston became cordial and generous towards the Mill Hills.

To later generations, Liston's attitude towards Maori themselves would seem paternalistic and culturally insensitive. He never spoke Maori. A much later Mill Hill Provincial, Peter Ryan, opines –

> Liston didn't really understand what mission meant in the eyes of the church . . . He didn't understand that to be a missionary meant to understand the faith in their ways and in their language. His ideal was for a Maori to be as like an Irish Catholic as possible . . . He judged them as he would judge a Pakeha.

Ryan says that Liston once greeted a Maori congregation with the incorrect singular form *tena koe* rather than the correct plural *tena koutou*. The congregation giggled and Liston never attempted a Maori greeting again. Occasionally missioners would take playful advantage of Liston's lack of *te reo*. In the 1930s, Liston sometimes asked Theo Wanders to translate the spiritual instruction he had just been giving to a Maori congregation. Instead,

> Wanders would get up and give a lovely talk . . . nothing at all to do

with what the bishop had said . . . [Wanders] would say, 'if you're ever in Auckland, don't forget to call round at the bishop's house, and the least he'll give you is a cup of tea'.

The rural congregation would nod its approval of an invitation none of them could take up. And Liston, having not understood a word, retained the happy illusion that his theological teaching had been conveyed.[261]

Yet by his own assimilationist lights, Liston did make an effort to accommodate Maori. In 1936-37, he took advice on how to devise a 'rule' for a non-European order of nuns, and he established the diocesan Sisters of Mary for Maori women. It had a novitiate at Waitaruke and was affiliated to the Marist Sisters. Liston himself wrote the ceremony for the Sisters of Mary's profession of first vows in 1940, in which they pledged 'service to the salvation of the Maori race'. But in his correspondence with the Marist Sisters Francisca and Anselm in the 1940s, Liston discovered that Maori postulants did not take easily to convent life. There were few recruits. In 1952, when they had only seven members, the Sisters of Mary were wound up and the order was absorbed into the Marists. Liston personally interviewed each of the Maori nuns, who said they were happy to become Marist Sisters so long as they could still be engaged in Maori work.[262]

Sometimes, Liston displayed awareness of Maori sensitivities. In 1931, when Fr van Westeinde told Liston that Maori were 'sentimental' about bells that had belonged to Bishop Pompallier and did not want them removed from a certain parish, Liston telegrammed, 'If removal likely to cause worries to Maori, please do not disturb them'.[263] Becoming aware, by the late 1940s, that Maori were moving increasingly into the cities, Liston invited the Missionary Sisters of the Society of Mary into the diocese. They were to assist the Mill Hills in social work among Maori in Auckland city.[264] Liston's association with Whina Cooper proved beneficial in the care of urban Maori. She threw herself into fund-raising work for a Maori girls' hostel in Auckland.[265] Michael King argues that all too often Liston treated Maori as troublesome children, and yet it is clear that he frequently consulted Cooper about urban Maori problems.[266] In return, she was happy to enhance her own mana by her association with the bishop. In 1948-49, negotiating with her good friend Theo Wanders, she generously donated six acres at Panguru as the site for a convent school. An old school was moved to the new site and a residence was built for the teaching sisters.[267]

Since the collapse of its first mission to the Maori in the 1860s, the Catholic church had been far behind other major Christian denominations in the ordination of Maori clergy. The first Maori priest, Wiremu Te Awhitu SM, was not ordained until December 1944.[268] He sang his first high mass in St Patrick's Cathedral, with Alink preaching the occasional sermon in Maori. Liston presided and announced, 'Catholic New Zealand shares fully in the pride and joy of the Maori people on this wonderful day'.[269] Liston did hope that improved secondary education for Maori Catholic boys would produce some candidates for the priesthood. With a tiny roll of 20 students, St Peter's Rural Training College in Northcote had begun secondary classes in 1936.[270] In 1941, Liston began negotiating with the Marist fathers for the expansion of this facility into a full secondary school.[271] However, it was the Marist Brothers who took charge in March 1946, when extensions to the existing college were opened and it became St Peter's Maori College, with a roll of about 50 students.[272] Later, it became more generally known as Hato Petera.

Liston's paternalistic attitudes are temptingly easy to judge in retrospect. As a priest he had an essential and proper indifference to race. It was irrelevant to the process of salvation. If he believed in racial assimilation, it was no more than other equivalent authorities believed at the time. Among his papers he kept a cutting about the Anglican Bishop Bennett who, in 1932, praised the work of Princess Te Puea but declared,

> Another century will see the passing of the Maori people as a nation. There can only be one end, and that is absorption into the European population.[273]

At the time, government social policy was based on similar assumptions. Further, considering Liston's firm application to Maori of rules against religiously-mixed marriages, Peter Ryan concedes that these rules were first strictly applied by the Mill Hill priests themselves. 'The old priests [such as Fr Zangerl] did want it like that.'[274] Besides, Liston was right to see that some Mill Hills were drifting from their original missionary purpose, and that Maori required new forms of evangelisation in an urban setting.

The fairest judgement is that Liston applied to the Maori Mission the standards of his own age. At his worst, his treatment of the Mill Hills was parsimonious and legalistic. But it is unhistorical to judge him according to bicultural ideals that were scarcely articulated before the 1960s.

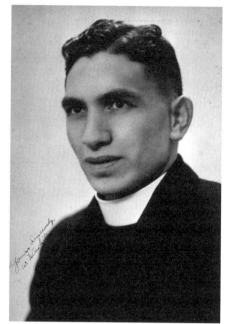

Above left: Whina Cooper's *mokopuna* Henare Tate, whose ordination to the priesthood had a Maori dimension in which Liston was happy to be involved. Above right: Marist Fr Wiremu Te Awhitu. Liston was delighted when he became the first Maori Catholic to be ordained, in 1944; but as this was after over a century of Catholic evangelisation, it was also a sign of how far behind other denominations' missions the Catholic mission had fallen. *Left:* Concessions to Maoritanga – newly-ordained Henare Tate's vestments and the cloak on the statue of the Blessed Virgin.

Above: Archbishop Liston chats with past pupils of Hato Petera (St Peter's Maori) College. Despite his lack of *te reo*, his easy affability and ability to socialise at public functions set him apart from some of his fellow bishops.

Below: Archbishop Liston outside St Patrick's Cathedral with the university chaplain and Catholic graduates. An educated laity was one of the chief aims of his episcopate.

CHAPTER VII

THE PUBLIC FIGURE

Bishop Liston 1930-54

The Bishop and the Laity

In his 1935 *relatio*, Liston reported on the Auckland Catholic laity. After noting that there were '12 excellent Catholics' among members of parliament, he continued,

> The Christian life of the majority of our Catholic families is excellent and, considering the pagan thought and atmosphere around them, is marvellous. A great deal of freedom is allowed, too much, and outward respect for parents on the part of grown-up children has declined, but on the whole children and youths are pious and good. The evil of contraception, chiefly because of mixed marriages, is spreading.[1]

A number of anxieties are evident here. By close analysis, one historian argues that Catholics did not inhabit a cultural 'ghetto' and were largely integrated into general New Zealand society in the interwar years.[2] Nevertheless, at the official level many boundaries were set between Catholic and non-Catholic.

There was, said Liston in 1933, no church law to compel Catholic parents to send their children to Catholic secondary schools.[3] But he was, in 1948, very grudging in giving parents permission to withdraw their daughter from the local convent school and send her to a state primary school, even though they were able to prove that she had been neglected in a Catholic classroom of 43 pupils.[4] As more Catholic secondary schools were built, Liston became firmer in applying the rules. From very early in his episcopate, he showed concern for Catholic children outside the Catholic school system and promoted schemes to give them religious instruction.[5] On Anzac Day, Catholics were still expected to shun combined religious services.[6]

In 1953, the bishop's secretary was advising boy scouts to stay away from a 'non-Catholic service' for Scouts and Guides, and to go to the Christ the King procession instead.[7] Catholic funerals were for the faithful, and not for merely nominal Catholics. In 1937, Liston instructed all priests in Northland that they could not officiate at funerals of 'people of the Yugoslav race . . . who during life have not carried out their proper duties as Catholics'.[8]

Greatest anxiety was expressed over religiously-'mixed' marriages which, it was feared, would lead to religious indifferentism. In a general population where Catholics were only 13 per cent, it was inevitable that many found spouses outside their church. In the period 1930-34, over a third of the weddings celebrated in Liston's diocese were 'mixed'.[9] In 1937, the bishops tightened their regulations.[10] Non-Catholics who wished to marry Catholics had to take a 12-part course of instruction and promise to raise their children as Catholics. A 'mixed' marriage was performed with maimed rites. It was without candles, flowers or a final blessing of the couple, and vows were exchanged away from the altar. Liston intended these rules to be applied strictly. Distant from his more vigilant supervision, however, some priests in country parishes quietly ignored them. Mgr Paul Cronin recalls that 'past the Bombay Hills' priests like Eugene O'Connor would claim that their sacristies were under repair, so that they could perform 'mixed' weddings before the altar.[11] Some priests even protested at the rules. George Colgan wrote to Liston in 1950 condemning the 'useless insult to non-Catholics' which the regulations implied.[12] Only at the end of 1951 did the hierarchy begin to ease these rules.[13]

Much concern arose from the fear that married Catholics would become accustomed to practices that were condemned by the church. In 1935, Liston wrote –

> We look upon Mixed Marriages as more than ever an evil, because of the practice of contraception now much in vogue amongst non-Catholics, and we ask ourselves at times if it would not be well to prohibit all Mixed Marriages.[14]

The official Catholic campaign against contraception and abortion was consistent and prolonged. In a 1930 sermon, Liston described birth control as 'intrinsically and eternally wrong'.[15] Revelations in 1935 about the frequency of abortion led the bishops' conference to warn priests 'to be vigilant in instructing penitents in materia contra-conceptarium'.[16] A parliamentary enquiry heard that there were between 5,000 and 6,000 illegal abortions annually in New Zealand. In 1937, Liston said that government and doctors should join the church in combating the practice.[17] With Archbishop O'Shea and John Higgins, he corresponded in 1938 over the question of whether Catholic women should be advised to withdraw from organisations (such as the Women's Division of Federated Farmers) which advocated birth control and relaxed abortion laws.[18]

With a sceptical and dismissive attitude towards Catholic teaching, one historian notes that in statistical terms, New Zealand Catholic women were as likely to have abortions as other women at the time.[19] However, another historian shows that Catholic teaching differed only in degree, and not in kind, from the teaching on sexual matters of other mainstream Christian churches. What Liston and the rest of the hierarchy taught was New Zealand's ethical orthodoxy, and not a 'conspiracy' against conscience as it has sometimes been represented in later polemical writings.[20] By 1946, parliament's Dominion Population Committee was calling for parents and religious leaders to help in the 'raising of the moral and spiritual tone of the community' to eliminate the evil of abortion.[21] For all that, Liston's zeal could make some Catholics uneasy. In September 1931, Liston's *Month* sarcastically commented on a 'practising Catholic' who edited the *New Zealand Artists' Annual*, and who had allowed a disgraceful cartoon to appear in it. This was a reference to the orthodox and conservative Pat Lawlor. Under his editorship, the *Artists' Annual* had run a David Low cartoon, 'Attempted Revolution in Dublin', which ridiculed the Irish ban on information about contraception. Lawlor was so upset by the *Month*'s reference that he threatened to sue, and was dissuaded from doing so only by the fact that his mother became 'sick with worry' at the thought of his being in contention with a bishop.[22]

Observant laity were supposed to be careful about what they read. In 1949, a Catholic trade unionist wrote to Liston asking how seriously he was meant to take an American cleric's direction that 'Catholics sin grievously if they read a Communist publication, even for information, professional reasons or curiosity'. Liston supported this rule, but granted the unionist permission for two years to continue his current research practice.[23] Liston was also concerned about what was read by those Catholic children who attended state schools. In 1944, he joined in a campaign with other Christian leaders (including the heads of the Presbyterian church in Dunedin) to protest against the Education Department-approved social studies textbook, *Man and His World*, which gave a totally humanistic view of the origins of Christianity.[24]

In America, Catholic pressure groups had led a successful campaign to introduce stricter censorship into the film industry, generally with the full approval of their Protestant equivalents. By 1934, the Legion of Decency, Catholic trade publisher Martin Quigley, the Jesuit Daniel Lord and the bureaucrat Joseph Breen had persuaded film producers that a 'production code' was preferable to state-imposed censorship.[25] Liston was impressed by this American campaign. In 1933, he sent a circular warning parents 'to take care not to allow their children to be contaminated' by the 'disgusting exhibition' of Roman orgies in Cecil B. de Mille's film, *The Sign of the Cross*.[26] In 1934, he was a member of a deputation suggesting stricter film censorship to the government.[27] He joined Bishop Lyons in condemning the sexual suggestiveness of Otto Preminger's *Forever Amber* in 1948, and he declared King Vidor's *Duel in the Sun* was 'to be avoided in strict conscience by all members of every Catholic home'.[28] Liston had not seen any of these films himself, but was relying for his directives on advice from American Catholic sources.

Beyond prohibitions, Liston was concerned to raise Catholic self-confidence in the midst of surrounding non-Catholic society. When he encouraged Catholic laymen to participate in 'Catholic Action' in late 1935, Liston held up the newly-canonised Saints John Fisher and Thomas More as models for faithful Catholics defending the church against the encroachments of the state.[29] 'Catholic Action' or the 'apostolate of the laity' was never specifically defined in New Zealand. It certainly did not imply a confessional political party, as was the case in some European countries. In 1936, Liston said 'Catholic Action' disavowed any 'concern with party politics, with the sponsoring of a legislative and governmental programme'. He implied it meant faithful obedience by the laity to the hierarchy's instructions. 'Catholic Action' was –

> . . . the participation of the laity in the hierarchical apostolate . . . The call is to the laity without distinction of sex or social position; the appeal is to their sense of responsibility towards Christ and their neighbour, Catholic and non-Catholic . . . They are bidden to supplement the work of the clergy by their holiness of life, prayer, activity . . . The Church is not a society of equals; there are grades and there is authority . . . the parish is the first unit . . . The diocese is the second unit.[30]

Despite this conception of the laity's subordinate place, Liston knew that more Catholics had to be encouraged into tertiary education and the professions if they were to make any impact on society. He worked on building up a Catholic intellectual élite. The diocesan press publicised the achievements of Catholics, with regular stories on Catholic scholarship winners, Catholic qualifying lawyers, doctors and architects and Catholic literary figures. Liston also hoped to encourage a distinctive New Zealand Catholic literature. He gave some journalistic work in Auckland to the novelist Ruth Park, and offered her hospitality at bishop's house when she visited with her Australian husband D'Arcy Niland.[31] The poet Eileen Duggan had privileged access to him, writing frequent personal notes to him, and often commenting at length on the books he lent or gave her.[32] An Auckland Catholic Repertory Society was set up in 1932 and was encouraged by Liston to produce 'plays of a religious nature'.[33] By 1938, Liston was writing on the society's behalf to the Catholic Theatre Conference in New York, looking for suitable plays of more contemporary significance to produce.[34] The society had some successes, but faded away in the 1940s.

Among intellectuals at this time, Liston's closest personal friend was another former classmate from the Christian Brothers' School in Dunedin, Mr Justice John Bartholomew Callan.[35] A later High Court judge, Sir Ian Barker, recalls that Callan was 'the only man ever to call [Liston] by his Christian name . . . In a way [Liston] was a lawyer manqué – he rather liked lawyers'.[36] Quite apart from his two courtroom appearances as defendant, Liston was fond of legal processes and disputation. Sir Maurice Casey concurs. But Callan differed from Liston when he decided to disregard a statement by Pope Pius XII and 'stick by his judicial oath' in administering the law of the land with respect to granting petitions for divorce. This seems to have caused no breach in his friendship with Liston, who felt the loss keenly when Callan died in February 1951.[37] In a eulogy, Liston spoke of 'our friendship from boyhood to death'. There was nobody else left to call the bishop 'James'. Like Callan, Liston enjoyed public speaking and wanted to encourage Catholic men in rhetorical skills. Under his patronage, a Catholic Men's Luncheon Club was set up and held regular Thursday meetings throughout the 1940s.[38] Liston often presided.

There were more durable intellectual enterprises. Longest-lasting were Liston's approved diocesan publications. A monthly *Schools Journal* for Catholic primary schools was established in 1932, and was joined by a journal for Catholic secondary schools in 1939. The monthly magazine the *Month* was turned into the fortnightly broadsheet *Zealandia* in 1934. It became a weekly in 1937 and was

Above: At the Vatican in 1945 with New Zealand military personnel – John Flanagan (left) and Owen Snedden (right), two priests whose careers Liston helped to advance.

Below left: John Flanagan, for many years Liston's private secretary, wearing the medal the New Zealand government awarded him for helping Allied prisoners to escape through the Vatican.

Below right: Justice John Bartholomew Callan, classmate and friend of Liston, and possibly the only man to regularly call him by his Christian name.

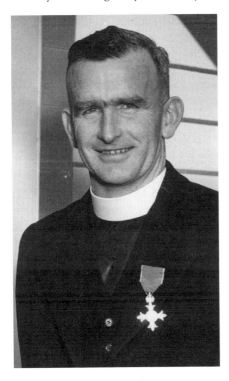

edited successively by two trusted, Roman-educated priests, both of whom later became bishops – Peter McKeefry from 1934 to 1947, and Owen Snedden from 1947 to 1962. The highbrow monthly *Catholic Review* was shorter-lived. Launched in 1945 and edited jointly by Fathers Forsman and Pierce, it failed to find an audience and folded in 1949. Liston was fully aware that priests jokingly referred to the *Catholic Review* (or *Zealandia*) as 'the Liston-er'.[39] Concern for appropriate Catholic reading matter extended to a central city Auckland Catholic Library, which Liston launched in 1938. It was always badly under-patronised and lasted a little over 20 years. Liston's desire to have an educated and literate laity was also seen in the Catholic Study Association, set up in 1938, 'to extend the present facilities for lectures and study of Catholic subject'.[40] Its aim was to have laymen discuss theological topics.[41] The same year, the Catholic university students' guild was replaced by a more formally-organised club. The chaplain Michael Lavelle rejoiced to Liston that Catholic students were –

> ... making it known to all and sundry that there was a traditional Christian belief and many non-Catholics were pleased that the noisy pseudo-intellectual Leftist minority were at last challenged.[42]

For some years in the later 1930s, Catholic students dominated the editorial board of the student newspaper *Craccum*, and in 1947 Liston and the rest of the Catholic hierarchy approved the constitution for a nationwide University Catholic Society.[43]

Besides intellectual associations, the diocese also supported sporting and youth clubs. Liston was chief patron of the women's Auckland Catholic Basketball Association, and opened extensions to their courts on Mountain Road.[44] The Marist rugby union and rugby league clubs sometimes joined with the basketball association at functions where he presided.[45] With Liston's approval, Catholic boys began to join the Scouting Movement in 1932-33, with a strand being organised into parish troops by George Joseph and Fr Francis Quinn.[46] By the mid-1930s, Liston presided at a cathedral mass for Catholic boy scouts on the feast of Christ the King.[47] A general Catholic Youth Movement coordinating different clubs and activities was first mooted in 1938-39.[48] Liston put it under the direction of Reginald Delargey in 1940, and began a quest for appropriate clubrooms in 1941.[49] Leonard Buxton gave to the diocese a property at Oratia which he named Knocknagree after his mother's Irish birthplace.[50] It became the venue for youth retreats and Catholic schools activities.

Some lay organisations in the diocese were well-established before Liston's time. Others were set up on his initiative. In 1930, he blessed a statue of St Vincent de Paul in the sanctuary of the cathedral, and spoke of the progress of the charitable St Vincent de Paul Society in the 21 years since its establishment in the diocese in 1909.[51] The venerable Hibernian Australasian Catholic Benefit Society suffered a major 'split' in 1932-34 when its national headquarters moved from Auckland to Wellington. Nineteen branches broke away and declared themselves to be a new Northern District of the society.[52] Liston refused to recognise this new organisation.[53] He instructed priests to forbid the use of church halls to Northern District canvassers, to forbid them to wear society regalia in church, and to 'exercise your zeal and tact in trying to bring these men back to a sense of what is due from them as Catholics'.[54] Only the established New Zealand District was to be recognised as a Catholic society.[55] Liston patronised extensions of the New Zealand District in Auckland, and was present at the inauguration of their new cathedral branch.[56] He forbade members of the Northern District to have any part in the Catholic centennial celebrations of 1938. Attempts at the reconciliation of the two branches of Hibernianism were unsuccessful in 1941, 1946 and 1952.[57]

More definitely Liston's creature, the Knights of the Southern Cross were reconvened and reactivated by Liston shortly after Cleary's death. Membership was by invitation only. Liston apparently found many recruits among the Hibernians.[58] The Knights have been much criticised by Catholics since the Second Vatican Council.[59] 'They were sort of the secret police of the diocese', says Sir Ian Barker, who gave an excuse not to join when he was invited.[60] Common rumour said the Knights' main purpose was to 'spy' for Liston on clergy and religious. Knights were said to report secretly to him on controversial or otherwise unwelcome sermons, and to promote a great sense of unease among diocesan priests. Documented information on such cases is unavailable. The Knights did, however, help organise one regular public function in the diocesan calendar. This was the annual Catholic Charity Ball, inaugurated in 1931 and continuing until the 1970s, though suspended during the Second World War. Yearly, Liston was curtseyed to by debutantes from the city's more affluent Catholic families, and the event was reported in detail in the Catholic press.[61]

The Knights' role in this was unreported. More overtly associated with charity balls was the women's movement that was a very durable part of Liston's legacy. The international Catholic Women's

League (CWL) had been founded in England in 1906 by Margaret Fletcher, a convert from Anglicanism.[62] Liston was responsible for introducing it into New Zealand. An Auckland branch was set up by Liston in July 1931.[63] It was very much under Liston's authority and he hand-picked the first executive.[64] Jeremiah Cahill was made the organisation's spiritual director. With his most senior clergy, Liston was present when the Catholic Women's League's meeting rooms were ceremonially opened.[65] Later, he conveyed a pontifical decoration to Mrs M. Pilling as the league's first president.[66]

Other dioceses were slow to follow Liston's initiative. The CWL was introduced into Christchurch only in 1936, into Wellington in 1944 and into Dunedin when a national executive was set up in 1948-49. Liston was as protective of the league as he was of Catholic schools and the Catholic press. When Huntly's parish priest set up a women's social club in 1947, Liston urged him to convert it into a branch of the CWL.[67] At various times in the 1940s and 1950s, Liston declared it was his goal for *all* Catholic women to join. This aim was never achieved, and despite the existence of some country branches, the CWL remained essentially a movement of urban, middle-class Catholic women.[68]

Liston saw the CWL as he saw other lay organisations. It was there to support initiatives of the hierarchy, as he told the dominion conference in 1949:

> ... the work of the Catholic Women's League is the collaboration of you, layfolk, in the apostolate of the Bishops ... your faith and goodness are your gifts to the world. [69]

He had envisaged 'voluntary social work' as the CWL's main sphere of activity when he set it up in the midst of the Depression.[70] Later, at the outbreak of war, he encouraged the league to organise wartime relief activities, but also to show concern for 'the spiritual needs of the Catholic men in camp'.[71] As a body affiliated to national women's organisations, however, the CWL did take part in debates on social policy. In 1949, in reply to a CWL questionnaire, Liston urged that restrictive immigration policies be opposed. It was, he said, 'a very good thing' that Chinese wives be allowed to join their husbands in New Zealand, and that Greek refugees be made welcome. He was 'all for exclusion' of violent crime serials from New Zealand commercial radio, and he instructed the CWL to oppose moves to reintroduce capital punishment which 'says to the multitudes – human life has no dignity. I have a strong aversion from capital punishment'.[72]

Sir Maurice Casey, husband of the long-time CWL president Stella Casey, confirms that the league was 'very much [Liston's] creature', but quotes his wife as saying that 'one of the big things in favour of the league was that [in Liston's eyes] they were just women and their views didn't count'. In other words, Liston allowed the CWL considerable freedom in proposing to the National Council of Women remits on secular matters, because he thought such remits were less 'official' than the hierarchy's views.[73]

Liston held a traditional view of women's proper place. In 1937, in opening a conference of the non-denominational League of Mothers, Liston exalted women's 'devotion, purity and self-sacrifice' in 'sanctifying' the lives of their husbands and children. He declared that women without children could become 'in the care of others . . . the great spiritual mothers of the race'.[74] Motherhood of some sort was women's essential destiny. For young mothers, the Catholic 'Young Married Homemakers' Groups' were established in Christchurch in the 1940s. Liston rapidly approved the introduction of Homemakers into Auckland in 1949.[75] Homemakers were to be an auxiliary of the CWL.[76] It seems clear, however, that many younger women preferred the supportive club activities of Homemakers to the earnest social activism of the league, and Homemakers began to become an independent organisation.[77] Thomas Ryder claims that 'the Catholic Women's League executive became jealous of this new movement and had it quashed'.[78] At all events, by 1954 Liston was reminding Homemakers that they were to function as 'branches' of the CWL only.[79]

Homemakers and the CWL were not the only organisations with female membership. In 1935, Liston had spoken enthusiastically of the Grail, which coordinated a 1940 conference of Catholic youth groups.[80] But the Grail soon disappeared from the diocese. The Legion of Mary, however, became as familiar as the Holy Name Society. With Liston's approval, Mgr Holbrook investigated this devotional group when he visited Dublin in 1932.[81] Liston himself conferred with its founder Frank Duff in 1935 and in 1938 he set up the Legion's first Auckland *praesidium*, with Mgr Bradley as its chaplain.[82]

The Bishop's Public Profile

As the head of a large religious body, the Bishop of Auckland acquired a high public profile. He was the hierarchy's representative in 1940 centennial celebrations at Waitangi. He conferred frequently with successive mayors of Auckland and he became patron or honorary vice-president of a number of non-denominational charitable and welfare organisations. He received foreign decorations. In 1936, the Yugoslav government awarded him the Order of St Sava (second class), and in 1938, the French government honoured the memory of Bishop Pompallier by giving Liston the Cross of a Chevalier of the Legion of Honour.[83] Throughout his episcopate, Liston regularly wrote letters of introduction for Catholic clergy and laity who were visiting Rome. But he also arranged papal audiences for non-Catholic figures such as Queen Salote of Tonga.[84] Some secular events with which he was involved had a strong Irish and Catholic flavour, such as his appearance at Auckland's public reception for Eamon de Valera in 1948.[85] Other occasions were quite unrelated to traditional New Zealand Catholic concerns. It is a measure of Liston's stature as a public figure that, in 1950, he led the official Auckland welcome to the visiting British Lions rugby team.[86]

Liston offered the use of Catholic facilities to the wider community. In 1931, after the Napier earthquake, and in 1939, after the Glen Afton mining disaster at Huntly, he offered to provide accommodation for those rendered homeless and cooperated in the mayor's fund-raising campaign. He was invited to be part of various secular initiatives, sometimes with controversial results. In 1930, he was one of many academics, intellectuals and churchmen who signed a petition calling for a commission of enquiry into New Zealand maladministration in Samoa.[87] The following year he was part of a conference on disarmament sponsored by the League of Nations union.[88] The mayor invited him, in 1943, to be on a committee investigating the illegal consumption of alcohol in the city, and on another committee planning a war memorial in 1946.[89] But in 1945, both he and the veteran Protestant campaigner J.J. North objected when their names were used, without their permission, in an open letter urging the British prime minister Clement Attlee to approve unrestricted Jewish settlement in Palestine.[90]

The Second World War saw some controversial statements from Liston. Like Catholic prelates worldwide, he protested in 1943 and 1944 at the Allies' bombing of Rome.[91] In 1945, he made an even more vigorous protest at the first use of nuclear weapons.[92] His sermon after the dropping of the Hiroshima bomb was heartfelt. 'How evil and bitter a thing it is for us', he said,

> ... to have put God out of sight and to have flouted his commandments, has been seen even by the spiritually blind in the fearful and portentous events of the past few days. Because we have so much forgotten him and misused the gifts with which he has

filled the earth for all his children, we have come to this last act of destruction that strikes terror into the hearts of men. Today for thee, tomorrow for me, men are rightly saying. Our good and just cause has, let us confess it in sorrow, been dishonoured in the sight of God and men. In our humiliation we find some comfort in the thought that the few alone, and not the common man amongst us in his millions and millions, have done this evil thing; we find some balm in the hope that the common man will now rise in his just anger and power, to demand that the human family of all peoples shall never again be stricken with the suffering and hatred of war.[93]

Liston also composed a message of sympathy to the Polish government in exile in London in 1945, as its authority was usurped by a puppet government installed by the Red Army.[94] He had some role in the bringing of Polish and Dutch refugee children to New Zealand, just as earlier he had been involved in the placement of Catholic children from England.[95]

On the whole, though, the Second World War in New Zealand was a time for national solidarity. There was no return to the sectarian strife of the First World War. In 1940, Archbishop O'Shea and Liston received government assurances that seminarians and teaching brothers would not be liable for conscription.[96] Liston wanted the Department of Defence to change its policy and allow *resident* chaplains in military camps. But the other bishops disagreed and were willing to accept the government policy of having chaplains attached to echelons only. No campaign was mounted on the issue.[97] Liston did, however, have money raised for a Catholic 'hutment' at Papakura military camp.[98]

In sermons, Liston offered the traditional consolations to bereaved families of servicemen who had been killed.[99] He also made sure that Catholic participation in the war effort was well-publicised. Speaking at the general requiem mass at Panmure in 1945, he estimated that about 900 of the dead of the Second New Zealand Expeditionary Force were Catholics.[100] For the living, he got the CWL to organise hospitality for servicemen on leave, and had a Catholic Services Club established.[101] In the immediate post-war period, Liston assigned two former military chaplains, Fathers Forsman and Pierce, to assist Catholic servicemen back into civilian life.[102] He set up a social club and rehabilitation centre for the demobilised.[103] CWL members were organised to offer hospitality to 'overseas wives of servicemen'.[104]

By the late 1940s, Liston was familiar to a large non-Catholic listenership through his regular religious broadcasts. Drafts of his frequent Easter and Christmas talks show that he avoided denominational references as much as possible and always strove to present the Nativity in vivid descriptive terms, emphasising the wonder of the Incarnation.[105]

Much of Liston's relationship with local and national government was simply courteous formality. Yet Liston took his civic duties very seriously and was shocked at the more pragmatic attitude others adopted towards public occasions. Writing to a friend in 1953, Archbishop McKeefry summed up his experience of Liston's attitude thus:

> Bishop Liston has been conscientious in attending all functions sponsored by government and civil authority, and he feels that in his position he has a grave obligation to show good example in this way. I accompanied him often to such functions in Auckland and he frequently remarked how leading people were absent from these functions simply because they were of a popular nature. He was particularly critical of audiences that would turn up to farewells to Governors-General – their fewness of numbers and lack of leading figures, in contrast to the numbers that would be there when a new Governor-General was being welcomed. He used to feel, though only I would express it, he being so charitable, that the crowds at a welcome indicated favours expected, and the fewness at the farewell – well, the one going could give no more.[106]

To participate in public affairs with representatives of other churches implied a sense of equality between denominations with which Liston was not always comfortable. He sometimes found it necessary to assert Catholic distinctiveness, telling Catholic teachers in 1946 that they stood 'almost alone in our land in giving children the saving knowledge of Christ Jesus'.[107] In 1948, he berated the Presbyterian General Assembly for being 'out of step with the assembly's spiritual home, Scotland' in opposing state grants to Catholic schools.[108] A judge was corrected when he made *obiter dicta* comments about supposed Catholic beliefs.[109] In 1951, Liston and McKeefry fielded complaints from Protestant representatives that some Catholic contributors to religious broadcasting had become too aggressively denominational. Their private comments on 'the parsons' were not complimentary.[110] During the war, Liston opposed a suggestion by Anglican bishops that a morale-boosting interdenominational movement should be formed, like the 'Sword of the Spirit' in England that was jointly convened by the Archbishop of Canterbury and Cardinal Hinsley. Liston reasoned that the Catholic church in New Zealand had itself gained 'in recent times a position commanding respect for and interest in our teaching and outlook'. It did not require an alliance with other denominations to make its influence felt.[111] Sometimes there was a tension between Liston's desire to express solidarity with non-Catholic Christians and his promotion of a distinctly Catholic view of history. In one Ascension Day speech to the CWL, he praised non-Catholic churches for joining Catholics in combating materialism and secularism, yet still traced the beginnings of 'the unbelief and scepticism of present times' to the Protestant Reformation.[112]

For all that, with hard sectarianism now a fading memory, Liston did make an effort to accommodate other religious groups. He thanked Te Aroha's Anglicans and Presbyterians for the respect and sympathy they showed at the time of the death of the parish priest.[113] He addressed a 'Crusade for Social Justice' luncheon in 1937 on the church's social policy in the presence of the Governor-General Lord Galway and the Anglican Archbishop Averill.[114] In 1934, the Yugoslav consul wanted to organise a requiem mass for King Alexander II, who had been assassinated in France. Liston replied that, as the king was an Orthodox Serb, he could not celebrate such a mass, but he helped the consul organise an appropriate memorial service in the Anglican cathedral.[115] State and civic occasions brought Catholic, Anglican, Presbyterian, and other clergy and laypeople together frequently, and Liston readily socialised. Like Archbishop Redwood, he enjoyed a particularly good relationship with the Jewish community.[116] Rabbi Astor was a personal friend and sent him notes of sympathy when prominent Catholics died.[117] Liston felt comfortable enough with Astor to gently joke with him. 'No, Rabbi, after you – Old Testament before New', he is reported to have said when the two of them arrived at a door at the same time, and were courteously attempting to usher each other through.[118]

Despite the civic, secular and interdenominational occasions in which Liston participated, however, he was still best known to the non-Catholic public in the context of Catholic ceremonial. A requiem mass for a public figure would be widely reported.[119] Some church celebrations were organised as grandiose public spectacles, or shows of Catholic strength. In April 1932, 'the largest religious gathering ever held in Auckland' took place when Liston organised a eucharistic procession to synchronise with the eucharistic congress in Dublin.[120] Two years later, he hosted Archbishop Daniel Mannix in Auckland when Mannix came to publicise the forthcoming Eucharistic Congress in Melbourne.[121]

For Aucklanders, these events were dwarfed by the Catholic

centennial celebrations in 1938. The interior of St Patrick's was refurbished. A special fund was set up and contributions solicited. Liston arranged for the French government to be involved, in honour of France's original Catholic mission to New Zealand.[122] He solicited a congratulatory message from Eamon de Valera. The Irish leader obliged Liston with the phrase, 'the Motherland is deeply proud of the splendid story of one hundred years progress now to be celebrated'.[123] Cardinal MacRory agreed that Archbishop Gilmartin of Tuam could come to represent the Irish hierarchy.[124] Liston invited most of the Australasian hierarchy and persuaded the *Auckland Star* to print a special Catholic centennial issue giving a programme of the events, held between 25 February and 6 March 1938.[125]

There was a packed civic reception in the Town Hall presided over by the mayor Sir Ernest Davis and the Apostolic Delegate John Panico, with Mr Justice Callan and Mr Justice O'Regan representing the laity. Prime Minister Savage, some of his cabinet, Archbishops Gilmartin and Mannix and Duhig and many of the Australasian hierarchy heard Liston read out de Valera's message to 'long and sustained applause' from the hall. 'I hope that it will be read out at our next centenary celebrations', Liston added. A contingent of French naval officers accompanied Captain Auphan, of the cruiser *Jeanne D'Arc*, up to the podium, where he gave a patriotic speech linking Bishop Pompallier to New Zealand's alliance with France in the Great War. Later, the undersecretary for housing, John A. Lee, led visiting prelates on a tour of new state housing in Orakei. The bishops made a pilgrimage up to Totara Point, where a high mass was celebrated by Liston, 1,700 Holy Name Society men received communion and a banquet was held for laymen. In the last days of the celebrations, *Credo*, a spectacular Catholic theatrical pageant, was staged at Western Springs under the direction of the Australian theatrical producer George Duke Walton.[126] On 6 March 1938, Liston carried the Blessed Sacrament in solemn procession through the streets of Auckland.[127]

The centennial celebrations had been staged at a very slight financial loss to the diocese.[128] Much of the organisation had been the responsibility of the bishop's secretary Peter McKeefry. Liston saw it as excellent publicity for the Catholic church in New Zealand and for his diocese within the Catholic church. He arranged for copies of the centennial publication *Fishers of Men*, and the centennial issue of *Zealandia* (both of them edited by McKeefry), to be sent to a wide range of public figures. Not everyone was impressed with this ostentatious display. A few Protestants grumbled. J.J. North preached a furious sermon against the 'Roman church' at the time *Credo* was being staged.[129] For the *New Zealand Herald*, however, 'the concourse of people, the enthusiasm of the children, the splendour of the procession of prelates' at the civic reception were 'unsurpassed in the history of Auckland'.[130] It is notable that many Catholic lay organisations were mooted or founded in 1938 as Liston sought to build on the enthusiasm the centennial had generated.

During the war years, one feature of Liston's public liturgical activities was the large involvement of American, Australian and other overseas Catholic personnel. When Liston gave benediction at the Christ the King procession in 1942, his canopy was carried by 'four members of the medical staff attached to the United States Mobile Hospital'.[131] Liston preached to a large congregation of Americans when he said requiem mass for Rear-Admiral Daniel Callaghan in 1942.[132] His altar-servers were American and Australian soldiers for the cathedral mass on the Feast of the Assumption in 1945, celebrated amid rejoicings for the Japanese surrender.[133] Liston was impressed by the quality of American military chaplains, and noted with approval their willingness to make retreats with Auckland diocesan clergy at the Franciscan friary in Hillsborough. In turn, Bishop John O'Hara wrote from the Military Ordinariate in New York, saying, 'our chaplains are constantly telling me of your kindness to them, and your great interest in their work'.[134] In some ways this offset questions about the validity of some Catholic marriages that American servicemen had contracted with New Zealanders.[135]

The Bishop's Politics – The Labour Connection

From the 1930s to the 1950s, Liston was also a public figure on account of his political pronouncements. His early reactions to the economic depression were purely penitential. In 1931, he declared that he would offer benediction and Stations of the Cross every day for those in distress, and in 1932, he called for calm, stoical acceptance of the time of trouble.[136] He also conducted religious retreats for the unemployed.[137] Archdeacon Holbrook set up a charity shop for poor relief.[138] Nevertheless, with a larger working-class constituency than other mainstream churches, the Catholic church had to propose more thorough-going solutions.[139] The very few extreme right-wing ideologues, who offered quasi-fascist solutions to New Zealand's problems, came from conspicuously non-Catholic backgrounds.[140]

Liston was signatory to the hierarchy's pastoral on 'Present Economic Distress' in 1931. It gave a mixed message. Among other things, it called upon Catholics to support private charities and turn back to God and to true Christian education. Women were urged to return to their 'proper sphere of life' in the home. However, the pastoral used Leo XIII's encyclical *Rerum Novarum* to criticise the existing economic order, although without clearly advocating socialism. It called for government intervention:

> The present industrial economic system, like the great machine that it is, has got beyond the control of those who guide it . . . Governments should check by wise laws the exploitation of the people by the great and the powerful. They should aim at bringing about a better distribution of wealth, for instance by developing the land which contains the real riches of the country, and by encouraging the private ownership of small businesses and industries.[141]

That same year Archdeacon Holbrook asked Liston not to allow a statement on the economic distress by conservative prime minister George Forbes to be read in churches a few weeks before the general election. Holbrook argued that Forbes's message could be interpreted as anti-Labour propaganda and would 'fill a large proportion of our people with indignation'.[142] Clearly, many Catholics were already voting for the Labour opposition, but it would have been imprudent for the clergy to advertise this fact if they did not wish to provoke a sectarian backlash among the conservative political parties. Just before the 1931 election, Holbrook wrote to John A. Lee to wish him well, apologising for not attending any of his electoral meetings 'not to show my hand or to give them the catchcry "Rome" which would do you more harm than good'.[143]

Like the other bishops, Liston supported labour-intensive work schemes for the unemployed.[144] 'In view of the prevailing unemployment the parish is anxious to go on with the erection of the church as soon as possible', he wrote to the Apostolic Delegate in 1932, regarding St Michael's church in Remuera.[145] Such schemes have been criticised as 'slave labour', exploiting for low pay workers who had no other work opportunities at the time.[146] It seems true, too, that Depression-era cost-cutting made some church construction ventures less durable than they could have been.[147] For all that, providing paid employment was a necessary and practical measure, and the church was less niggardly in its treatment of workers than other employers.[148]

Liston's rhetoric became radicalised, often linking solutions to the problem of unemployment to larger questions of charity and social justice.[149] In a 1932 editorial, he declared –

This is not the time for discussion or theorizing, but for facing the facts and for prompt, generous action ... The government of the land has a strict duty to see that the unemployed do not go hungry, and that homes are not ruined by starvation, and if it would take courage to do its duty to the full it could rest assured of the whole-hearted support of the public ...[150]

In April of that year, the conservative coalition, in line with its retrenchment policies, passed an Industrial Conciliation and Arbitration Amendment Act. This has been interpreted as part of a long-standing conservative anti-union agenda, aimed at decreasing workers' access to collective bargaining.[151] Liston was alone among church leaders in realising the workplace implications of the act and in voicing a protest at its attack upon workers' rights.[152] In a *New Zealand Herald* symposium on unemployment relief, in which Anglican, Salvation Army and government figures also took part, Liston opined that international spending on armaments might have had something to do with the world's economic woes, and he quoted Pius XI on the rights of both capital and labour.[153] Unemployed workers rioted in Auckland in April 1932, smashing shop windows and looting. Liston's diocesan press made no direct comment on these events, but in December 1932 the *Month* ran an American article (by Walter Farrell) defending those who were driven to desperate measures by poverty. This was interpreted as veiled retrospective justification for the rioters.[154] By mid-1933, Liston was advocating a huge government-sponsored 'internal loan' to stimulate business and industry and to drive down unemployment.[155] In July 1934, Liston (together with the Rev Colin Scrimgeour, the Rev W.W. Averill and others) took part in a public meeting in the Town Hall, organised by the Auckland Citizens' Committees, 'to urge the adoption by the Government and the Unemployment Board of a more generous attitude to the unemployed'.[156] Liston declared –

Many families are struggling almost without hope to maintain the ordinary decencies of life. Discontent and resentment dwell in the hearts of thousands ... a remedy must be found and found quickly for their plight ... So far, in spite of the praiseworthy efforts of the Government and other public authorities, no adequate remedy has been found. The support of the unemployed, their restoration to work in the proper sense, is only being played with, argued about, restricted, and there is not one in the Dominion who claims that our present system of providing for them is doing what we should all wish it to do. If that be so, are we not bound, I ask, to try some other system?

Above: The public figure – assisted by senior clergy, Bishop Liston conducts the graveside rites for his friend, prime minister Michael Joseph Savage.

Below: In the Auckland Town Hall in 1954, celebrations of Liston's sacerdotal golden jubilee bring to the same stage the Catholic hierarchy, the mayor, the prime minister Sid Holland (centre), and the leader of the opposition Walter Nash (right).

Liston called on the government to 'take courage to strike out on bold lines' in creating work. A member of the Unemployed Workers' Association, F.E. Lark, cautioned the meeting that work should not be created in such a way as to threaten conditions of employment for those who were still in work. But Liston still drew loud applause when he suggested a programme of slum-clearance.[157] Throughout the rest of 1934 and 1935, editorials in *Zealandia* routinely complained of government inaction and the poor way unemployment relief was being administered.[158] Regular fortnightly *Zealandia* articles on 'Catholic Social Science', by Fr John Higgins, proposed such radical economic solutions to the depression that John A. Lee said 'they would decorate any Labour paper'.[159]

The election of a Labour government in 1935 did not silence the Catholic church's criticisms of government policy. In May 1938, as the Labour government proposed its general social welfare legislation, the hierarchy sought to give constructive criticism in a memorandum, drafted by Higgins, which praised many of the government's aims but warned of the necessity for economic freedom and limitations to government power.[160] The official attitude of the Catholic press remained non-partisan. Priests were still forbidden to offer churchgoers advice on how to vote.[161] Nevertheless, the hierarchy tended to approve of the Labour government.[162] The Labour Party, by and large, shed its earlier doctrinaire socialism. In return, Catholic bishops softened their anti-socialist stance.[163] Five of the 14 members of Savage's original cabinet were at least nominal Catholics. In 1936, Catholic university students in Auckland met with the campus Labour Club to discuss the social implications of papal encyclicals.[164] In 1937, one of the reasons Archbishop O'Shea gave Liston for not opposing a Bible-in-Schools initiative was that he did not wish to destabilise the government and provide an opening for the conservative National opposition:

> We must carefully guard against . . . doing anything which would offer the least excuse for raising the sectarian cry. This is not only in our own interest but in that of the present government. Adam Hamilton [leader of the National Party] is in the offing. Secondly, we must avoid anything that would make us appear to be in any way helping the secularists and enemies of religion.[165]

The following year, with a general election in prospect, O'Shea wrote privately to the editor of the *Tablet* advising him not to accept any more 'anti-socialist' condemnations of Labour policy. His reasoning now was that amicable Catholic relations with the

Labour government were keeping the Party's more radical elements in order.[166] Part of the Catholic accommodation with Labour arose from Liston's close personal friendship with Michael Joseph Savage, which began in the days of Liston's trial for sedition in 1922. In opposition or in government, Savage was always happy to appear with Liston at Catholic social functions. He was an honorary vice-president of the Ponsonby Catholic Tennis Club.[167] In 1930, as an opposition front-bencher, he spoke at length on the value of Catholic education at the opening of the residential block of St Mary's College.[168] As prime minister he regularly visited Auckland's Catholic orphanages and the Ponsonby Home of the Little Sisters of the Poor.[169] He also took part in the Catholic centennial celebrations in 1938. 'It is a pity that the principles outlined are not more widely practised today', Savage wrote to Liston in 1932, when Liston had sent him copies of an encyclical of Pius XI. In return, Savage sent Liston Labour Party electioneering material.[170] Liston was a major influence in Savage's return to his early childhood Catholicism in the last months of his life. Savage's last public engagement in 1940 was a meeting with the Apostolic Delegate. In death, he was surrounded by Catholic ceremonial. Archbishop O'Shea and Fr Robinson, superior of St Gerard's Monastery in Wellington, gave him the last rites. O'Shea conducted his funeral mass in Wellington. In Auckland, Liston said a requiem mass for him and conducted the graveside service.[171] 'The devotion, dignity and solemnity of the ceremonies impressed us all', the new prime minister Peter Fraser wrote to Liston.[172] Later, when a memorial mausoleum was being prepared for Savage at Bastion Point, Savage's coffin was sealed into the sacristy of St Patrick's from June 1941 to March 1943. Liston officiated at the reinterment.[173]

If all this was a symbolic association of Liston and the hierarchy with the Labour, a more practical association involved Labour's attitude towards Catholic education. In 1930, when the conservative coalition was still in power, Liston had drafted the hierarchy's memorandum objecting to the government's Education Committee Report for ignoring Catholic schools and advocating the creation of intermediate schools.[174] Under the first Labour government, however, Catholic schools gained a number of concessions, even if they did not amount to the full funding that was desired. Bus services, health inspections, visual aids, teacher refresher courses, free milk and apples, primary school textbooks and the *School Journal* were all provided to Catholic schools on the same terms as to state schools.[175]

When Labour was re-elected in 1938, Liston wrote to the Minister of Education Peter Fraser,

> Your grasp of the educational needs of the country and devotion to the immense amount of work command the confidence of all, and your consideration for our Catholic schools is greatly appreciated by us.[176]

In 1939, a parish priest wrote to Liston to complain that convent school pupils were being turned away from the local state dental clinic. Liston at once contacted the Minister of Health, Peter Fraser, who put matters right.[177] By 1944, at a cordial meeting with the hierarchy, Prime Minister Fraser was assuring the bishops that he would personally reprimand any state school inspector who made negative or injudicious remarks about the Catholic school system.[178] Fraser, his Minister of Education, H.G. Mason, and the Director of Education, Dr Beeby, were welcomed by Liston to the Catholic hierarchy's conference on education in 1945.[179] Later that year, Liston lauded the courteous approach the government and Department of Education were now adopting towards Catholic schools.[180] This does not mean that the church and the Labour government always saw eye-to-eye on education. Within the Labour Party, there was a strong rationalist strain and strong support for the state school system as opposed to private ones. In 1948, Archbishop McKeefry was warning the bishops of the 'secularist and unsympathetic' attitude of the Labour government's new Minister of Education.[181] Even so, education was one factor that made a liberal-left political alignment a logical one for Liston.

The Bishop's Politics – The Anti-Communist Crusade

Yet this alignment was strained by the hierarchy's campaign against Communism. On one level, this can be seen as shadow-boxing. The Communist Party in New Zealand was a pitifully small thing. Sid Scott, its former general secretary, estimated that in 1938 there were about 300 card-carrying members, many of them idealists with little skill in practical politics.[182] The New Zealand Labour Party was very suspicious of Communists. They had been forbidden membership of the Labour Party since 1925.[183] Throughout the Depression, Labourites and the tiny group of Communists held one another in mutual contempt. Members of the Communist-front group the Friends of the Soviet Union were expelled from the Labour Party by 1931 and were refused readmission in 1937.[184]

The New Zealand Catholic crusade, however, had as much to

do with international as with local concerns. From the 1930s to the 1950s, there were regular anti-Communist articles in the Catholic press, and publicity for anti-Communist lecturers. In 1938, a pastoral of the whole New Zealand hierarchy condemned the Soviet-sponsored Anti-God Congress in London, and called Catholics to a day of prayer in response.[185] In 1948, Liston circularised priests to publicise the Auckland Town Hall reception for Cardinal Spellman and Monsignor Fulton J. Sheen, 'convert-maker of Communists'.[186] One early high-point in the international church's campaign was Pius XI's anti-Communist encyclical *Divini Redemptoris* issued within weeks of his anti-Nazi encyclical *Mit Brennender Sorge*, in April 1937. In September of that same year, the Australian and New Zealand hierarchies all signed their own anti-Communist pastoral.[187] Liston reassured the Apostolic Delegate that the pope's encyclical would be given 'the fullest publicity' in Auckland, and that he had formed a committee of six priests to distribute anti-Communist pamphlets from American Catholic sources.[188] Liston's zeal for this work, however, almost brought him to the courtroom for the third time. In November 1937, *Zealandia* printed the text of a fiercely anti-Communist talk which had been broadcast from Wellington by the Redemptorist K.D. (Kevin) Crowe. There was a complaint to the broadcasting service about this misuse of a religious slot for political purposes. A *Zealandia* editorial described the complainant, F.L. Turley of Greymouth, as a 'cheap Red agitator'.[189] Turley threatened to sue Liston for defamation.[190] The case was settled out of court in mid-1938 when *Zealandia* apologised for implying that Turley was a Communist.[191]

Even among New Zealand's 'Left' intellectuals, Communism lost its savour during the period of Stalin's alliance with Hitler, 1939-41. Communists essentially backed Hitler in his war with 'imperialist' France and Britain.[192] The small-circulation left-wing journal *Tomorrow* was shut down in May 1940 for opposing the war effort.[193] Catholic anti-Communist polemic at this time was in tune with the national mood. But it became harder to sustain after mid-1941, when Hitler's attack on Russia forced the Soviet Union into the war. For New Zealand Communists, says Nancy M. Taylor, 'overnight, the imperialist war became a holy war'.[194] A Society for Closer Relations with Russia was promptly formed to do propaganda work, and an Aid to Russia Committee set about influencing trade unions.[195] Sympathy for Russia brought New Zealand Communist Party membership to a wartime peak of between 1,000 and 2,000, Communists were able to take over some leading trade union positions, and the Communist newspaper the *People's Voice* claimed to sell 14,000 copies weekly.[196] Contrary to the facts, propaganda presented Russia's war effort as a willing defence of the Soviet regime and said that there were few Russian 'quislings'.[197]

From Ngaruawahia military camp in late 1941, a chaplain wrote to Liston of the propaganda war he was waging against Communist ideas among the troops, and thanking Liston for sending relevant materials.[198] Catholic newspapers remained hostile to Communism. Privately, the government's Director of Publicity cautioned *Tablet*, and rebuked *Zealandia* for describing Stalin as a 'bloodthirsty Georgian bandit'.[199] One admirer of Stalin, the New Zealand Rationalist Association, opportunistically argued that Catholics were disloyal for not supporting 'our great friend and ally'.[200] Even in this wartime climate, the Catholic attitude was not far from the New Zealand mainstream. Aware that Communists were tardy supporters of the war, the Labour Party still shied away from allowing them to affiliate.[201] Despite sympathy for Soviet wartime suffering, general attitudes towards Communism remained highly sceptical.[202]

In the postwar and Cold War period, some of Liston's anti-Communist statements took on an apocalyptic tone. Our Lady of Fatima was promoted in conservative Catholic circles as a counterweight to materialistic, atheistic Communism.[203] 'O Mother of all mankind, lead Russia back home again', went one of the hymns in 1949, when a statue of Our Lady of Fatima was welcomed by Liston into St Patrick's Cathedral. 'Our Lady of Fatima, preserve us from the dangers of Communism', said one of the invocations.[204] 'Brethren, might we not be pardoned for thinking that anti-Christ has come and the final issue is to be decided?', Liston asked in 1950 at the consecration of Bishop Joyce.[205] Catholic missions were being closed down in newly-Communist China, and Catholic church leaders were being subjected to show trials in Eastern European countries that were now Soviet satellites. These matters were given prominence in *Zealandia*. Liston obeyed the Apostolic Delegate's instructions and arranged formal protests at the arrest of the Hungarian Cardinal Mindszenty in 1949, and at Communist attacks upon the church in Czechoslovakia in 1951.[206]

For Liston, the most painful of such matters concerned the imprisoned Croat Archbishop Alojzijc Stepinac, accused by the Yugoslav government of collaboration with the wartime Fascist regime.[207] This situation had local repercussions. In private communications, Liston had long been critical of nominal Catholicism among Auckland's Croat community. In his 1935 *relatio*, he described the '4,000 natives of Dalmatia . . . who should all be Catholics' as 'indifferent . . . many of them contemn religion and are fiercely Communistic', and he said the ministry of Father Pavlinovich 'has had little effect on them'.[208] Now, in the postwar period, the Yugoslav Benevolent Society which Pavlinovich had set up was taken over by left-wingers. There was a split between the conservative Yugoslav Club, with Catholic affiliations, and the Yugoslav Club 'Marshal Tito', which passed resolutions condemning the Catholic press's comments on Stepinac.[209] Liston complained in 1946 that 'with rare exceptions the 4-5,000 Jugo-Slavs in this diocese are very bad Catholics, ignorant of their Faith, unfriendly or hostile to the Church, and fervidly Stalin-Tito'.[210]

He was aware that some anti-Communist publicity had to be handled with caution. In 1936, he lent the Australian priest M.D. Forrest material on Communism so that Forrest, on a mission in Huntly, would be well prepared to deliver a sermon pre-empting an address by the Auckland Communist Harold Brown.[211] The following year another priest, Francis Columb, became concerned at Forrest's inept handling of hecklers and talent for 'abuse'. He wrote to Liston expressing his fear that this would upset the mining community in another address on Communism that Forrest was planning.[212] Liston wrote to Forrest urging him, should he be heckled, to –

> . . . deal with good humour and unruffled courtesy with these miners: they are not given to logic and hold strong views, but for many years past have been quite well disposed. If your address leaves them on good terms with you, your successor will find it much easier to talk to them on this or other subjects, and the parishioners more pleasant to live in their midst [sic].[213]

In the event, Forrest spoke to a capacity audience for two hours with no interruptions.[214]

In 1941, Liston wrote to the chairman of the *Catholic Worker* in Melbourne, saying that distribution of the paper 'has been a big factor in throwing the Communist menace out of one of our mining centres [Huntly]'. But at the same time he warned that the newspaper's tone was rancorous, verging on the un-Christian, and was 'too personal, especially when dealing with Government and companies'.[215]

Events in Australia bolstered Liston's attitude towards Communism. There its influence among the trade unions led

Above left: Liston setting out for a brief visit to Australia, 1953.
Above right: Liston greets Cardinal Francis Spellman of New York on his brief stopover in Auckland in 1948. They were equals as committed ideological foes of Communism.
Below: On his last trip to Ireland in 1954, Liston chats with Archbishop McQuaid (left) while the Apostolic Delegate and mayor look on.

to a counter-attack by the Catholic 'Movement' that eventually helped split the Australian Labor Party. Liston received material from Archbishop Mannix of Melbourne, the 'Movement's' chief episcopal promoter, advising on Communist trade union activity and fomentation of strikes.[216] Bishop Lyons of Christchurch arranged for B.A. Santamaria's News-Weekly to be sent to New Zealand bishops.[217] Santamaria himself regularly wrote to Liston, advising him of 'Catholic Action' developments and of the efforts of the Young Christian Workers movement in Australia.[218] Liston passed on News-Weekly and other Santamaria publications to parochial Catholic Men's Study Groups.[219] At this time, he advised the St Vincent de Paul Society that Catholic participation in the relief agency CORSO might be inadvisable 'owing to the state of affairs in China'.[220] Suspecting Communist tendencies, he told the Catholic Women's League that the agency had 'not been fair in its distribution of funds'. He also described the left-wing Labour ideologue William Sutch as 'a most obnoxious person . . . a thorough planner with all the fellow-traveller attitude'.[221]

At the same time, Liston and the rest of the hierarchy were aware that Communism was not as robust in New Zealand as it was in Australia. Sid Scott noted that Communist-influenced organisations like the New Zealand Peace Council gained some favourable propagandist publicity, but real Communist power in New Zealand trade unions was both limited and superficial. 'From 1947 onward it was not difficult for the opponents of the Communist Party to organize their forces and throw us out of one position after another.'[222] In 1950, John Flanagan's diocesan report (authorised by Liston) noted that while there was some Communist leadership in the unions, there were few Communists in the rank-and-file, 'and one can see a general anti-Communist feeling steadily growing'.[223]

Perhaps because of this, Liston did not make public pronounce- ments about the waterfront dispute in 1951. Some interpreted the dispute, between February and May 1951, as the work of Communists.[224] Yet there was no editorialising on it in Liston's Zealandia. The Catholic press's only reaction was an exchange between pro- and anti-watersider correspondents in the Dunedin Tablet.[225] Liston's lack of enthusiasm for this particular dispute may have sprung from his mixed feelings about the stance of the new leader of the Labour opposition, Walter Nash, who could not bring himself either to support or condemn the watersiders or the government. Referring to the recently-deceased Peter Fraser, Liston wrote to the Apostolic Delegate late in 1951,

Some of us think that if Mr Fraser had been alive, he would, at an early date, have said that his party was standing in with the Government in its acceptance of the challenge to the authority of the State; such a statement would have helped to end the strike much more quickly and would have meant political gain to the Labour Party.[226]

Liston was still a Labour supporter, but in the fight with Communism he thought that 'fellow-travellers' and a pusillanimous leader were weakening Labour's backbone.

The Bishop's Politics – Overtones of Fascism

For at least some people of left-wing sympathies, any firm opposition to Communism equated with sympathy for Fascism. The Catholic hierarchy was especially vulnerable to such charges in the 1930s. The Catholic press was staunchly on the side of Franco in the Spanish Civil War.[227] Even before it started, Catholic newspapers showed marked hostility to anti-clerical and secularist tendencies in the Spanish republic, and lauded the rise of the Spanish Right.[228] A month after the 1936 election of a centre-left coalition in Spain, the *Tablet* and *Zealandia* were both reporting violence against the church and strife in Spain already amounting to a state of civil war.[229] Once the Francoist uprising began in July 1936, it became the main front-page story of the Catholic press.[230] Liston campaigned for a Francoist view of the war not only in the Catholic press but also in letters to daily newspapers. He sparred in the *New Zealand Herald* with Jack Langley, editor of the *Rationalist*.[231] The other bishops praised him for this stance.[232] But it put the Catholic press at odds with most other newspapers. Apart from the small-circulation Communist *Workers' Weekly*, the press generally adopted a non-interventionist, vaguely pro-Republican and anti-Franco view of the war. More significantly, the Catholic attitude caused tensions within the Labour Party. Savage's government was sympathetic to the Spanish republic, but feared alienating its own Catholic support. Catholics campaigned against the Spanish Medical Aid Committee's scheme to send an ambulance unit to the assistance of the republic.[233] The Labour paper the *Standard* was forced to close correspondence on the Spanish situation after complaints from Catholics. In October 1937, *Zealandia* warned Christchurch Labour MP Ted Howard that he would face electoral retribution for making an anti-Franco speech. Early in 1938, Catholic members of the Labour Party in Upper Hutt publicly protested against 'a recent lecture by Dr Sutch casting slurs on the church in Spain'.[234] Whatever its sympathies may have been, the government became very cautious about expressing them. To that extent the Catholic campaign was a success.

In the 1930s, Liston's newspaper, along with Catholic journals elsewhere, expressed some guarded sympathy for regimes that could loosely be seen as 'Fascist' – Salazar's in Portugal and Dollfuss's in Austria.[235] Yet the attitude of the Catholic press towards Fascism itself was highly disapproving. Relations between the Vatican and Mussolini's regime degenerated rapidly after the Lateran accords. By 1930, the church in Italy was locked into a struggle over the control of Catholic schools and youth movements. Pius XI's encyclicals *Quadragesimo Anno* and *Non Abbiamo Bisogno* denounced the inflated powers of the state that Fascism assumed.[236] In July 1931, Liston preached on the conflict, saying 'men today are being led in wrong directions by a group of pernicious theories which teach that the state is supreme in spiritual as well as in temporal matters'.[237] Later in the decade, the church press felt obliged to repeat some of these arguments, apparently goaded by the suggestion that support for Franco equated with support for Fascism.[238] 'Statism' was regularly condemned by *Zealandia* and the *Tablet*. In 1937, Fr Higgins wrote an attack on the whole philosophical basis of Fascism.[239] In 1939, the *Tablet* reprinted *Non Abbiamo Bisogno* as a three-part series.[240] Meanwhile, Liston was several times obliged to explain that the Vatican was quite a separate political entity from Fascist Italy. In 1935, he announced that the pope believed Italy 'to be engaged in an immoral, unjust war' in its invasion of Abyssinia.[241] In 1940, when Mussolini entered the Second World War, *Zealandia* published on its front page a map showing the independent Vatican state and emphasising the pope's neutrality.[242]

However ambivalent his judgement on Italian Fascism may sometimes have appeared, Liston unwaveringly condemned Nazism. When the Nazi government signed a concordat with the Vatican in 1933, Liston told Auckland daily newspapers that, while Hitler had been baptised a Catholic, 'his ideals, principles and methods are opposed to all that the Catholic church holds dear'.[243] Throughout the 1930s, *Zealandia* ran regular exposés of Nazi brutality, usually concentrating on Nazi anti-Christian 'paganism' while mentioning Nazi persecution of the Jews in subordinate paragraphs.[244] In 1940, Liston told the Catholic Men's Luncheon Club –

> German racialism leads to doctrines and practices incompatible with Christian teaching and morals. It is a fundamental law of Christianity that all human beings, as children of God and equal in origin and destiny, possess essential personal rights, which they

do not lose because they happen to belong to a race regarded as inferior.[245]

In hindsight, some of Liston's judgements on international politics appear both naïve and ill-informed, although no more so than those of his contemporaries. If he welcomed the Munich agreement in 1938, and took part in church and civic acts of thanksgiving, he was at one with both the mayor of Auckland and leaders of all the main Christian denominations.[246] If his newspaper's criticisms of Italian Fascism were sometimes more muted than they could have been, he was not the enthusiastic supporter of Mussolini that the *New Zealand Herald* sometimes was.[247] During the war, *Zealandia*'s determination to support a 'Catholic' outlook could lead to anomalies, such as the front page which at once praised the conservative social legislation of Marshal Pétain's collaborationist regime in France and yet displayed a photograph of General de Gaulle, splendid Catholic leader of the anti-Pétainist Free French, in conversation with Cardinal Hinsley in London.[248]

Liston's basic political judgement on international affairs was not Fascist, but clericalist. This resolve to protect the church's interests and standing made him a tactical ally of some right-wing movements, but not their wholehearted apologist. In this he was like other notable English-speaking church leaders of the era. In England, Cardinal Hinsley supported Franco, whose signed portrait he kept on his desk throughout the Spanish Civil War. But Hinsley also denounced the Italian invasion of Abyssinia and later earned the distinction of being placed on a Nazi death-list when he appeared on the same platform as England's Chief Rabbi to protest the Nazis' Kristallnacht pogrom in 1938.[249] Hinsley berated the Irish press and bishops for not adequately publicising the pope's anti-Nazi pronouncements.[250] In Australia, Archbishop James Duhig's diocese contained many Italian immigrants and Duhig sponsored some of their Fascist social clubs. But, like Hinsley, he was swift to denounce both Mussolini's Abyssinian adventure and Hitler's anti-Jewish violence.[251]

Despite left-wing assumptions of the 'Popular Front' era (and the assumptions of some later left-wing historians), opposition to Communism and support for Franco did not automatically make one a Fascist.[252] Addressing a medical group in November 1952, Liston gave a rationale for seeing Franco's continuing regime as a separate case from Fascism. He noted that 'the purpose of the state is the furtherance of human welfare in regard to those things which the individual and family, left to [themselves] could not attain'. He went on to remark that the pope had written encyclicals critical of Communism, Nazism and Fascism, then said of Spain,

> A dictatorship the Franco regime may be: but most assuredly it is not a totalitarian dictatorship. To begin with – the natural law and the moral principles of Christianity are admitted as supreme, intangible beyond the reach of political manipulation. Nobody in Spain, certainly not Franco, holds the fundamental totalitarian tenet held by Hitler and Mussolini, and held to this day by Stalin, that the state is the sole source and arbiter of right.[253]

James Michael Liston and John Alexander Lee

Liston's particular line of argument here was a standard trope in the Cold War, especially when American policy-makers sought to distinguish their dictatorial right-wing allies from their dictatorial Communist foes. Not everybody was convinced. Liston's most outspoken critic was John A. Lee, who cast himself as the conscience of the left wing of the Labour Party. Like Savage, Lee regarded himself as Liston's friend since the sedition trial in 1922. The pair exchanged many friendly notes in the early days of Liston's episcopate. 'What a big and well-deserved win the Party in Auckland has scored! Good!', wrote Liston in December 1922, congratulating Lee on an electoral victory.[254] Often they lent each other books.[255] When he became bishop in 1929, Liston thanked Lee for his good wishes:

> I should like to feel when the end of the road approaches that whatever influence I may possess has been exercised – and wisely – for the benefit of all the needy of both soul and body, Catholics and non-Catholics. This, as I view it, is a Bishop's work. May I add that I hope you will help me – for you have the experience and the heart – to do this work by a visit from time to time or by a letter?[256]

Some of the surviving exchanges between Lee and Liston are routine politeness. But in the Depression, they were close ideological allies. In 1931, Liston thanked Lee for his positive response to articles about the crisis that were appearing in the *Month*, and invited him around to discuss them.[257] In April 1932, Lee wrote to Liston from parliament, praising Liston's protests at the conservative government's attack on industrial conciliation:

> My Lord and I know my friend, may I thank you sincerely for your courageous statement on Arbitration. It was sincere and timely.

> The smugness of this House irritates me to the point of explosion.
> Untold suffering beyond the walls seems to evoke only sneers . . .

Lee predicted that government parsimony might provoke violence among the unemployed.[258] Liston agreed, but hoped they might both be wrong.[259] The day after Auckland unemployed did riot, Lee called on Liston, the Anglican Archbishop Averill and others, suggesting they join him in asking the government to make extra food distributions to relieve the distressed.[260] Liston's memorandum of Lee's visit said, 'Consider this likely to have good effect, be welcomed by all and help in solution of grave problem'.[261]

Throughout the 1930s, Lee was as willing as Savage to appear at Catholic social functions. In November 1937, he was present at the opening ceremony for the golden jubilee celebrations for Mosgiel parish, when Liston preached at length.[262] He often accompanied Savage on his visits to Catholic orphanages and hospitals, and he conducted visiting Catholic bishops around the new state housing estate at Orakei during the Catholic centennial celebrations in 1938. Afterwards he wrote to Liston lauding –

> . . . the tremendous celebrations that have been unique in New Zealand's history. It is rarely that religion parades its organization publicly, and the huge congregations of Catholics who paid public testimony to their faith must have stirred Auckland and New Zealand.

He thanked Liston for placing the Orakei tour on the visiting bishops' itinerary, praised the church's organisational skills and said how impressed he was by the 'magnificent personality' of Archbishop Mannix of Melbourne.[263]

Years later, in his unpublished essay, 'Myself and the Catholic Church', Lee claimed that he was the Labour Party's special intermediary with Liston:

> Liston and myself became closer friends during the depression. He made many splendid statements opposing the depression policies of the coalition conservative government. I cannot say we ever discussed religious matters or that any effort was made to win me, but Liston warmly endorsed our anti-depression fight . . .[264]

Probably underrating Liston's friendship with Savage, he added –

> I had many a cup of tea with Liston at his house in Ponsonby. The friendship was closer that that of any other Labour politician. It became so that if he wanted to convey some message to members of the party hierarchy I was often the bearer . . . I liked the radicalism

of the man. I appreciated what he had done for the great Jewish organist Karoli Moor . . . I can fairly say that no MP was on better terms with James Liston than John A. Lee.[265]

Yet Liston and Lee fell out spectacularly and the breach was never healed. Lee claimed that the cause was his distaste for Liston's right-wing sympathies, and the way *Zealandia* praised the regimes of Mussolini, Dollfuss, Salazar and Franco. 'I haven't the slightest doubt that James Liston continued to favour the Labour Party', wrote Lee, but 'Liston was a zealot who would follow the Vatican line, and the Vatican line under Roncalli and Pacelli was Fascist, not democratic'. Lee argued that Catholic influence had caused the Labour leadership to compromise its democratic principles over support for the Spanish republic.[266] Elsewhere, he called Liston's *Zealandia* 'the dirtiest political paper in New Zealand', and remarked of Liston, 'He came to see me as Satan when I opposed Catholic fascism'.[267]

Yet, while his opposition to right-wing regimes was genuine, there is something anomalous in Lee's claims. He remained on good terms with Liston throughout the 1930s, including the period of the Spanish Civil War when *Zealandia* ran its pro-Franco polemic. It was only after his expulsion from the Labour Party in 1940, for his criticisms of the ailing prime minister Savage, that he openly criticised the journal's politics. He half admitted as much when he wrote, 'Liston and myself remained close friends until I fell out with Savage'.[268] In his account of his relationship with the Catholic church, he claimed there was a Catholic plot to expel him from the Party. Historians have found no evidence of such a plot.[269] By the mid-1940s, Lee blamed hostile Catholic propaganda for the poor electoral showing of his 'Democratic Soldier Labour Party', but he later tacitly admitted that this explanation was nonsense.[270] He also claimed that Catholics had ensured he, as a freethinker, was excluded from the Labour cabinet between 1935 and 1940. Erik Olssen remarks, 'It seems unlikely that the Church had any strong objections to Lee which could not have been urged against some who were included'.[271] In the version of events that Lee now promoted, Savage only returned to Catholicism because he was becoming feeble-minded. He 'would be a rationalist until his mind gave way in his fatal illness at which point he received instruction from a Catholic priest'.[272]

In this context, Lee's criticism of Liston's 'Fascism' was part of his desire to find scapegoats for his own political misfortunes. In the war and post-war period, *Lee's Weekly* and its more modest successor, *Lee's Fortnightly* (which folded in 1953) offered a regular diet of anti-clerical articles.[273] With the Rationalist Association, Lee arranged New Zealand distribution of anti-clerical pamphlets, and he fought a wartime ban on Edith Moore's anti-Catholic polemics, *No Friend of Democracy* and *The Vatican in War and Peace*.[274] By this time, his public hostility to Catholicism was such that he was willing to court the Orange Lodge and the remnants of Howard Elliott's defunct Protestant Political Association.[275] This alliance embarrassed the Rationalist Association, whose historian notes that Lee's publications now carried advertisements for bigoted Protestant publications, and remarks that Lee 'in the end had outrun the Rationalists when it came to anti-clericalism'.[276] It is possible that it later embarrassed Lee too. In the 1960s, *Simple on a Soapbox*, Lee's gossipy account of his political career, made 19 references to the Catholic church, to the hostility of priests, to the (unnamed) 'high Catholic dignitary' who persuaded Savage to keep him out of the cabinet and to the 'Catholic Action' plot to have him expelled from the Labour Party.[277] Nowhere does it mention his friendship with Liston. But nowhere does it mention his wartime alliance with the Orange Lodge either.[278]

It would be possible to dismiss Lee's criticisms of Liston as part of a general animus against those who had cast him out. But this might be to underrate Lee's case. Even if Catholics were not responsible for his expulsion from the Labour Party, it seems that Catholics were indirectly responsible for his not being readmitted once he had embarked on his course of anti-Catholic polemics. Arnold Nordmeyer believed that Peter Fraser did not want to risk Catholic electoral support by welcoming Lee back.[279] By the early 1950s, the Labour leadership was unwilling to have any dealings with Lee without Liston's blessing.[280]

Lee also took offence at Liston's friendship with a former Mayor of Auckland, Sir Ernest Davis. Davis was generous in selling some of his Auckland properties to Catholic religious orders at very reasonable rates.[281] He made a very large cash donation to Liston for the upkeep of St Patrick's Cathedral.[282] Davis also took what Conrad Bollinger called a 'fatherly interest' in the Labour Party and had paid to have Michael Joseph Savage's portrait painted in 1937.[283] But for Lee, Davis was the 'arch corrupter' of the Labour Party who had bribed and compromised politicians in the interests of the brewing industry.[284] Lee later attacked Davis as 'Sir Ernest Booze' in his novel *For Mine is the Kingdom*. Russell Stone remarks, 'Lee was right in describing Ernie Davis as the chief of the barons'.[285] By association, Lee came to see Liston as moving with the same sinister cartel he believed Davis controlled.

Once their friendship had ended, Liston did authorise the occasional attack upon Lee in *Zealandia*. In 1941, when Lee claimed his criticisms of Catholic 'Fascism' were in the interests of true Christianity, the newspaper ridiculed him with an item headed, 'A New Champion of Christianity! J.A. Lee Strikes a Pose'.[286] Liston soon decided, however, that it was best to deal with Lee by simply ignoring him. In 1946, J.C. Reid wrote a series of articles on New Zealand literature for the *Catholic Review* which included favourable comment on John A. Lee's novels. Liston wrote a memo to the editor:

> On reflection I am perturbed by the reference, any reference, to Lee's books in JCR's article: it seems out of place to have a Review such as our's treating of him at all and many readers would feel hurt ... N.Z. literature's story wouldn't suffer by leaving him out.[287]

In 1950, the diocesan report to the Apostolic Delegate remarked on the 'limited circulation' of anti-Catholic publications such as those of the Rationalist Association and the Communist Party. It noted that there was –

> ... a fortnightly published by an individual named John A. Lee, which occasionally attacks the Church under the guise of protecting the workers. This publication, it is understood, is subsidised by the Protestants' Organization in America and has little influence and a falling circulation. It is used of late most to advertise the proprietor's product of contraceptive and sex books of the pseudo-scientific type. It is read mainly by the curious type of person who is intrigued by a catch-line on posters for the paper ... It has been found that the greatest injury one can do to these anti-Catholic papers is to ignore them even when they make allegations against the Church. To start a controversy would only raise their circulation. Any answers are given in *Zealandia* without reference to the anti-Catholic paper concerned.[288]

No further items about Lee appeared in *Zealandia* until the eve of Liston's retirement in 1970.[289]

The Making of an Archbishop

Whatever Lee might have thought of him, by the late 1940s Liston was an unignorable feature of the Auckland landscape. His annual round of public engagements included confirmations and pastoral tours; ordinations of priests; professions of nuns; saying masses at clergy and lay retreats; opening churches, schools, convents, presbyteries and parish halls; visiting orphanages and old people's homes; presiding at special 'Forty Hours Adorations'; being the main celebrant in the cathedral at Easter and Christmas; attending *praesidia* of the Legion of Mary; opening conferences of the Catholic Women's League; presiding (usually with Sir Carrick Robertson) at nurses' graduation ceremonies at the Mater Misericordiae Hospital; attending the Catholic Men's Luncheon Club; supervising board meetings of *Zealandia*; attending civic functions; welcoming sports teams; making religious broadcasts; and presiding at Catholic school prize-givings.

Every January, he celebrated a beginning-of-year mass for Catholic primary teachers (most of whom were at that time religious sisters). In March, there was the St Patrick's Day concert and the academic mass for Catholic university staff and students. April saw both the Holy Week ceremonies and the Anzac Day requiem mass. There was the charity ball in May, the Christ the King procession at Sacred Heart Convent and the rally for Catholic boy scouts in October, the general requiem at Panmure for the deceased of the diocese in November and the orphans' picnic in December. A typically busy Sunday saw Liston say morning mass at the cathedral, drive to Mt Albert for confirmations, continue on to Howick for the orphans' picnic, and return to the cathedral to preach and conduct more confirmations.[290]

As a prominent public figure, Liston was sometimes the target for cranks, like the savant in the late 1930s who wanted him to endorse a cure for cancer.[291] He was also widely entrusted with the administration of private wills and bequests. Every day, on top of his public engagements, he followed a 'carefully devised routine'. He always began by saying mass either at St Mary's Convent or in his private chapel at Bishop's House. He then proceeded to look at the birth and death notices – and the examination results – in the morning's *New Zealand Herald*, and to write notes of condolences or congratulations. Almost every day he would visit patients at the Mater or at other private or psychiatric hospitals.[292] He would also find time, every day, to read extensively – especially devotional works or works of theology, but also history, sociology and political theory.[293]

Among Catholic families, he was known for his elaborate courtesy and his habit of calling on anyone who was ill.[294] His 'prodigious memory and great humanity' are illustrated by John Sumich in the following anecdote:

Left: Liston blessing a new presbytery at Devonport with Fr Michael Furlong. Below: Diocesan priests and most orders of religious are represented in this shot of Liston (standing next to Fr Ted Forsman) taken at Loreto Hall in the 1950s.

In the early 1930s when St Mary's College accepted both boys and girls in the primers, both my sister and I . . . were pupils . . . One morning whilst on our way walking to school the bishop's car drew up and he offered us a lift to school whereupon my sister Pat answered 'My mother told us that we must not ride in cars with strange men'. Many years later (about 12 years) my sister Pat was to be a debutante at the charity ball and the old girls who were to be debutantes assembled at the school to be presented to the bishop. When my sister was presented, Bishop Liston said to her 'Does your mother let you ride in cars with strange men yet Pat?'[295]

Sir Ian Barker first met Liston when he was an altar boy in Taumaranui. He recalls the bishop's visitations to the parish thus:

He used to stand outside the church after the confirmation service in the evening and he would personally greet everybody and he seemed to know everybody . . . He seemed to pick up the conversation from three years previously and the people thought it wonderful.[296]

Some Catholic families had a special social attachment to the bishop. Sister Margaret Browne, whose parents were married by Liston in 1930, recalls that he would always visit her family on Christmas afternoon and encouraged the children's religious vocations.[297] Mary Elizabeth Hales (née Simson) says that Liston was a frequent guest who enjoyed 'the informality of the family . . . he had a good sense of humour and enjoyed family humour'. She recalls him once adjudicating in a family dispute about the children's choice of career. As a schoolgirl at Baradene, however, her impression was of more formal visits:

The arrival of the bishop for a ceremony or event was on a scale of specialness similar to that accorded to the Governor General or any other dignitary . . . If the bishop came to some ceremony he would generally mingle with the girls afterwards, but always very formal, stiff and proper with respectful children around him.[298]

Sister Judith Leydon remembers Liston's regular Friday night visits to the boarders at St Mary's College in the 1940s:

He would sit down and talk and tell us what was happening in the diocese – I'm sure it was very edited, but he had an interest in us and he knew a lot of our people.[299]

By this stage, Liston's strange and distinctive speaking voice was familiar enough throughout Auckland to be the punchline of innumerable jokes and the butt of practical jokers. In an obituary tribute, D.W. Lochore commented –

His part-cadenced, part-staccato speaking style, with emphasis on consonants that ended phrases, was unorthodox and a target for mimics, but Archbishop Liston made it an asset because it was distinctive; moreover, the more people listened the more they knew that what he said was worth attention.[300]

If Liston was a familiar 'character' by now, he was also outliving other members of the hierarchy and becoming the *de facto* patriarch of the New Zealand church. In March 1946, Pius XII sent him late acknowledgement of his silver jubilee as a bishop. In 1950, as his thirtieth episcopal anniversary approached, he was awarded the symbolic titles of Assistant at the Pontifical Throne and Count of the Apostolic Palace. Finally, in November 1953, the Vatican awarded him the personal title of Archbishop, acknowledging that while Auckland was not the nation's archdiocese, Liston was the most senior active bishop. At the end of January 1954, there were church celebrations for Liston's 50 years in the priesthood. McKeefry preached at his golden jubilee mass in the presence of 160 priests, 500 members of religious orders and all the active members of the hierarchy. Liston here described the clergy as 'my right hand and my left hand'.[301] He wrote to Cardinal Fumasoni-Biondi of Propaganda, thanking the pope for making him an archbishop and announcing that he would set out on his second *ad limina* to Rome in May.[302] There was a programme of official celebrations for his sacerdotal golden jubilee on 23-25 March 1954, two months after the actual date of the anniversary. These also served as farewell functions. Two pontifical high masses were said, then there was a public reception in the Town Hall in the presence of the metropolitan McKeefry, the prime minister Sid Holland, the leader of the opposition Walter Nash, the deputy mayor and a large group of invited guests.[303]

When he departed for Rome, Archbishop Liston was 73 years old and well beyond what was regarded as retirement age in the secular world. It was widely assumed that his recent honours were twilight honours and that he was near the end of his ecclesiastical career. In fact, ahead of him lay another 16 years as Bishop of Auckland.

CHAPTER VIII

BEFORE VATICAN II

Archbishop Liston 1954-62

The Last *Ad Limina*

Thanks to air travel, Liston's 1954 *ad limina* was brisker than his 1935 one. He was out of Auckland for a little over five months, leaving the diocese in the care of Jeremiah Cahill. His itinerary took him briefly to Ireland, via Paris to Rome, then back to England and Ireland before returning by way of the United States.[1]

He passed through Hawaii on the outward journey. In Dublin, he stayed with Archbishop McQuaid, whom he accompanied to Marian Year celebrations for Irish industrial workers. He negotiated with Dublin publishers Brown and Nolan for a New Zealand edition of their junior catechism.[2] He met various Irish seminary rectors. It is probable that he once again visited his sister Anne in the psychiatric hospital. Passing through France en route to Rome, he prayed for a second time at the grave of Bishop Pompallier, this time in the company of the papal nuncio to France.[3] He also visited the mother-general of the Cluny Sisters.[4]

In Rome, he stayed at the Irish College. As McKeefry's exchanges with the rector, Donal Herlihy, make clear, Liston once again revelled in the nostalgic associations the college had for him.[5] He presented his diocesan report to Propaganda, but the highlights of his trip were the canonisations of Pius X (29 May) and of Peter Chanel (13 June). He sent back to New Zealand a relic of Pius X and promised to make a novena of masses at the papal altar.[6] On 15 June, he preached on Chanel in the church of St Louis of the French.[7] Frank Wright, who had served as his chaplain in Rome, returned to New Zealand after these ceremonies.[8] Liston undertook other business in Rome. He wrote to McKeefry asking him to lobby the Immigration Department to allow some refugee nuns from Croatia to settle in

New Zealand.[9] This request was unsuccessful. Archbishop O'Shea having died shortly after Liston's departure, Liston took delivery in Rome of the pallium to be bestowed on McKeefry as the new metropolitan.[10]

In England, Liston stayed with the Mill Hill fathers for three days and called at St Augustine's Abbey, Ramsgate, which was associated with his predecessor Edmund Luck. He visited priests of the Institute of Charity (Rosminians) and enquired about their making a New Zealand foundation.[11] He accepted hospitality from the former Governor-General Lord Freyberg.[12] He visited the mother house of the Mission Sisters, where he spoke to nuns who had been expelled from Vietminh-held areas of Vietnam.[13] He reported that in England there was 'dread of the future and horror of what another war might do', but that 'men were now fully aware of what the bear-hug of Communism had done to many enslaved nations in Europe', hence there was less credulity given to favourable reports by travellers to Russia and China.[14]

He returned to Ireland for a 'holiday' of two months, but official business was rarely neglected. This included attending the ordination at All Hallows of 80 young priests, four of whom were promised to New Zealand dioceses. In Dublin, he also attended the concilium of the Legion of Mary and sent back a report to New Zealand branches. In Cork, he had a civic reception. At the beginning of September, he joined Bishop Kyne of Meath in unveiling a plaque in the parish of Ballivor in honour of Thomas Poynton, New Zealand's pioneer Catholic settler. Liston visited five seminaries in search of priests for New Zealand, and at McKeefry's request contacted the provincial of the Brothers of St John of God about whether they would be interested in making a foundation to care for 'difficult boys' in Christchurch.[15]

As in his 1935 trip, Liston chose to see what was positive in Irish life. He claimed that –

> . . . the changes in Ireland since the country obtained the management
> of its own affairs are most impressive in housing, roading, better
> cultivation of land, the promotion of small industries and the very
> large distribution of electrical power into every corner of the land.[16]

Unfortunately, continued mass emigration from a sluggish economy was still a fact of Irish life. Liston reluctantly noticed that Ireland's population had only 'slightly increased' since independence. Far more attractive to him was the image of the Irish people at prayer. He wrote to McKeefry,

Above: Members of the hierarchy, 1949. Liston stands between two of his protégés and former pupils, Peter McKeefry and John Kavanagh. At left Bishop Patrick Lyons, whose tenure of Christchurch was brief and troubled.

Below: Members of the hierarchy meet at Sacred Heart College in 1958, at the time of the consecration of the Sacred Heart old boy Reginald Delargey as Liston's auxiliary. Bishops Joyce, Kavanagh and Delargey, and Archbishops Liston and McKeefry.

... in Tuam for three days during the past week and one day in Galway: both prelates very, very pleasant ... I looked on the face of Croagh Patrick for some three hours on a perfect day and was on its sacred ground for an hour, the Archbishop an enthusiastic guide. Next day he took me to Knock, which he loves and is bent on keeping simple ... Some 60,000 were at CP this year on the big Sunday in July, some 30,000 at Knock for Aug. 15th and some 25,000 Pioneers are expected there on a Sunday in September. Every day large numbers.[17]

Liston left Ireland for the last time on 14 September and flew to New York, where he visited the Cenacle Sisters. With the assistance of the New Zealand ambassador, he watched one sitting of the Security Council of the United Nations, reacting badly to a 'disagreeable' speech by the Soviet representative and describing the council's deliberations as 'fatuous'. He approved of the American 'determination to resist Communism'.[18] He returned across the Pacific from San Francisco, making a brief stop-over at Canton Island where he said mass at the Pan-American Airways base.[19] He landed at Whenuapai on 4 October, and was greeted by his vicar-general and the three active members of the hierarchy.[20] On 10 October, there was a solemn liturgical reception in St Patrick's Cathedral and on 14 October, the mayor presided over a civic reception in the Town Hall.[21]

Liston's 1954 *ad limina* was the last time he saw Europe. It was also the last time he was out of his diocese for an extended period. In the 1950s, he did make briefer visits to other parts of the Pacific. In mid-1955, he visited Fiji and Samoa for a fortnight, attending both the funeral of Bishop Dieter at Apia and a mass said by Cardinal Gilroy for the sacerdotal golden jubilee of Bishop Joseph Darnand. To *Zealandia* readers he reported,

... the Samoan villages are Christian communities of faith and piety ... One is struck by the serious bearing of the men, by the perfect modesty of the women. These two things combined with a charming manner on the part of the people, who seem anxious to please the visitor, leave an indelible impression on one's mind.[22]

Later that year, Liston and the rest of the hierarchy were the guests of James Duhig at an episcopal conference in Brisbane.[23] Little tourism was involved in Liston's other brief overseas journeys. Unlike Cleary or Redwood, in his old age he was never a 'Bishop of Tours'.

The Archbishop and his Diocese

The Auckland diocese to which Liston returned was still a growing one. It contained 86 parishes in 1954. Ten years later there were 101. The number of diocesan clergy increased from 171 to 225, the number of religious brothers from 72 to 147, and the number of religious sisters and nuns from 692 to 789. In 1954, 13,886 pupils were enrolled in Auckland's 85 Catholic primary and secondary schools. By 1965, the number was 18,108.[24] Much of the archbishop's official calendar still involved the ceremonial opening of new churches and other parish facilities – presbyteries, parish halls, chapels and parish centres.[25]

The Catholic school system was under increasing pressure. State inspectors' reports on Catholic schools continued to draw attention to understaffing and overcrowding.[26] In 1957, C.E. Beeby, the Director of Education, pointed out that the post-primary department of St Michael's school, Rotorua, was being run by a total of two sisters when a state school with the same number of pupils would be entitled to six teachers. Liston replied that he had decided 'reluctantly' to close the school for lack of staff.[27] Yet this was a time when Liston spent many weekends opening new schools, additions to schools or convents for teaching sisters.[28]

Liston was still inviting religious orders to make foundations in Auckland. He negotiated unsuccessfully for the Little Company of Mary to run a maternity home in Hamilton.[29] At his invitation, a community of Passionist priests opened a monastery and retreat house in Fairfield in 1960.[30] Three English Rosminians arrived in Takapuna in 1961, and the first classes of Rosmini College commenced in 1962.[31] The Sisters of St Joseph of Nazareth ('Black Joes') entered the diocese in 1961 when Liston invited them to run the convent school in the new East Coast Bays parish.[32] Liston also recruited the Irish Sisters of the Holy Faith to staff the convent school of Glen Innes and they later staffed the convent school at Point Chevalier.[33]

Despite these arrivals, the later 1950s were less a time of new foundations than a time when established religious orders consolidated their position. The 'Brown Joes' had new convents and schools in Whangarei, Three Kings, Owairaka and Otorohanga; the Marist Brothers ran the new Sacred Heart College in Glen Innes, Marcellin College in Mt Albert and St John's College in Hamilton; and the Christian Brothers started the new Edmund Campion College in Gisborne and Edmund Rice College in Rotorua. The Mission Sisters built a new Sacred Heart College for girls in Hamilton, and the Mercy Sisters completed Carmel College in Milford. The Mater hospital was also growing. In 1956, Liston opened a new hostel for its domestic staff. A hospice for the dying was expanded in 1959 and the maternity unit enlarged between 1959 and 1962. In 1961, a board of governors was established for the hospital, with Liston as chairman, to raise funds and promote the hospital as a charitable institution.

A Diocesan Building Fund was set up in 1957. The *Tablet* noted in 1960 that extensive building projects around Auckland diocese were being undertaken at a cost of £350,000.[34] The old slate roof of St Patrick's Cathedral was replaced with aluminium three years before the cathedral's golden jubilee in 1958.[35] Not all Liston's projects regarding church property were successful, however. The Catholic Library, and offices of the Catholic Women's League and Catholic Youth Movement, were shifted in early 1957 to a building on Victoria Street East. In 1958, the Auckland City Council compulsorily purchased this property under the Public Works Act. It was demolished and a car-park was built on the site. Liston's protests were unavailing.[36]

The Archbishop and his Clergy

In the 1950s, Auckland was still well supplied with priests. 'It was a boom-time in the church then', says Frank Roach:

> There were new parishes being opened, new churches being built. Schools were staffed by brothers and sisters ... We had a great sense of confidence ... the morale was high amongst the clergy because of the numbers pouring out of the seminaries.[37]

By the end of the decade, George Marinovich, director of diocesan vocations, reported that while young Catholic women were losing interest in the convent life, respectable numbers of young men were still enquiring about the seminary.[38] Indeed, Liston had an abundance of priests. It was not unusual for him to officiate at ordination ceremonies for five or six priests at a time.[39] This could be seen as the high tide of the pre-Vatican II institutional church, although even at the time organised religion was in decline in New Zealand. In 1960, at a ceremony for the new Mosgiel chapel, Liston stressed the need for religious vocations by declaring –

> Things are not as they were in 1900. The situation for religion now is tragic: the retreat from the spiritual is rapid because of the comforts of life and the confusion of ideas; we live an abstract sin because of materialism and the denial of the supernatural.[40]

Even so, there were still ample priests. Laurence Sakey suggests Auckland diocese was overstaffed. Curates then had to wait an average of 14 years to gain their own parishes.[41] Much of this abundance, however, still came from recruitment in Ireland. 'We never have had an adequate supply of priests in New Zealand', according to James Shannahan.[42] For some, over-supply meant redundancy. 'Frankly, I think we probably had too many priests', says Mgr Vincent Hunt. 'We had a priest in parish work for every 717 people in New Zealand. In Ireland it was one for 1300.' Hunt notes that many rural parishes in the 1950s were served by three priests. 'What they did all the time I'm not sure.'[43]

Liston continued to exercise strong formal control. Extensive summaries of each parish's yearly accounts were kept in Liston's own handwriting.[44] Younger priests were not consulted about the parishes to which they were assigned. John Lyons reports:

> You got a letter at Christmastime to be at such-and-such a place on January the First . . . That's what happened to me the first three or four times . . . You got two or three weeks to get out of the place and that was it. You were very, very disposable.[45]

Curates still submitted sermons to the archbishop's appointed scrutineers, and changes to parish mass timetables were personally approved by the archbishop. Priests needed the archbishop's permission to buy motor vehicles. Laurence Sakey, assistant at Gisborne in the 1950s, says he was 'dobbed in' by other clergy when he bought a car on his own initiative, and was ordered by Liston to sell it.[46] Priests also required Liston's permission to read any 'forbidden books', such as those which Vincent Hunt needed to pursue his philosophy studies.[47] Policing the boundaries of the Catholic world remained a high priority. James Shannahan recalls Liston giving the one-word answer 'Numquam!' ['Never!'] whenever priests relayed parishioners' requests to attend weddings or funerals in non-Catholic churches. He does, however, also remember Liston offering the advice, 'It's your duty to go!' when a man sought permission to be pallbearer at the funeral of his non-Catholic long-time employer.[48] General rules could be bent to accommodate the specific pastoral situation.

Liston expected priests to perform extra duties without reward. The Mill Hill Peter Ryan says he personally arranged the broadcast of a sung mass from St Michael's in Rotorua. The choir included 'all the Morrisons' (the family of Howard Morrison), most of whom were not Catholic. The broadcast was very well received by the public, but Liston's only response was to complain to Ryan that some Latin prayers had been omitted.[49] James Shannahan received only a curt 'Thank you' when he explained to Liston how he had arranged for the archbishop's car to be panelbeaten after it was involved in a slight accident.[50] Des Angland complains that he received 'no commendation at all' from the archbishop after he had arranged for a church to be built in Mt Wellington and had been involved in fund-raising in Dargaville.[51]

The hierarchical ethos was strong. James Shannahan remarks,

> [Liston] had a concept of the episcopacy which in a way was divorced from himself as a person because ... when I was bold enough to venture something that was a little controversial, he would say 'But *the bishop* says this'. Not *I* but *the bishop*.

Shannahan believes Liston preferred to deal only with parish priests rather than with their subordinates.[52] Of curates, Bruce Bolland says,

> Once we got out into the parishes we were exposed to the mindsets of the parish priests, which varied quite a lot ... Some of them did not like [Liston] ... They felt uneasy ... They went to him almost cap in hand ... Letters of those days were signed 'Your Most Obedient Servant' ... The hierarchical thing was very strong ... Some of the parish priests were very anti-Liston.

Bolland's own first parish priest, Frederick Walls, was convinced that Liston 'had it in for him' as he had not been appropriately advanced in his career; but he also notes that promotion always was difficult when the diocese was so over-supplied.[53] In some cases, an informal competition for the archbishop's attention was in progress among careerist priests. Peter Ryan characterises senior clergy in the 1950s as being 'like lot of schoolboys trying to get something out of the teacher or trying to get around the teacher'. Some became adept at 'smoothing down' the archbishop by consulting him over matters of theology or Latin translations, where he was only too happy to display his expertise. Others, such as the Mill Hills in Rotorua, learnt not to make major requests, but to seek only minor concessions. Thus, bit by bit, Mill Hills persuaded Liston to let them construct the type of church they wanted in Rotorua by asking for a series of minor modifications only rather than by submitting one master-plan.[54]

The archbishop could rejoice that some of his priests served uncomplainingly for years in the same parish. In 1955, he presided at a special golden sacerdotal jubilee mass for James Molloy, who had been parish priest of Pukekohe since 1912.[55] In the same year, Michael Furlong celebrated the fiftieth anniversary of his appointment to Devonport.[56] Liston continued to reward his trusted senior clergy with honorary titles. John Kelly and Adrian Curran were both named 'Domestic Prelates' to the pope.[57] At the other end of the spectrum were delinquent priests who had to be reined in. The heavy drinking of Michael McCormack made Liston remove him from Otorohanga parish in 1955 for 'the hurt to the parishioners . . . caused by your conduct'.[58] Personal circumstances of a few priests created problems quite innocently. When Michael Bleakley died in 1954, he left some of his private belongings to his housekeeper. She caused anxious correspondence from Liston when she took this as a signal to make off with the furnishings of the presbytery.[59] Mgr Leonard Buxton was the chief beneficiary of his wealthy parents' inheritance, much of which he donated to the church. Buxton did not die until 1964, but already in the late 1950s the archbishop was receiving letters from Buxton's siblings, who demanded a larger share of the family estate.[60]

The most dissatisfied clergy tended to be curates and junior assistants, who were made to feel they were of little account. Vincent Hunt recalls Liston concluding an address at one clergy conference by asking, 'Are there any questions?' A young curate was brash enough to ask a question. Liston studiedly ignored him and rephrased himself: 'Do the *senior* clergy have any questions?'[61] While admiring the archbishop's personal piety, Des Angland gives this reminiscence of his time as a curate:

> I often wonder why [Liston] wasn't more human. Had he been human I would have been one of the first to push for his canonisation . . .
> He fawned over us when we were seminarians, but once we were ordained and in parishes he would come on visitations and virtually ignore [us] and make a fuss of the wealthy and prominent people of the parish . . .

Angland says the archbishop was 'unfair' in the way he made some appointments. He recalls one young priest, assigned by Liston to a rural 'dump', saying with weary resignation, 'I suppose it's God's will – bugger it'.[62]

Peter Ryan gives an equally unfavourable view of Liston's pastoral visitation to the rural parish where he was curate:

> It was like the [school] inspector. It wasn't like a pastoral visit at all, it was like the inspector coming to make sure you had the sanctuary lamp, the special kind of oil you had to buy . . . and don't you dare

use anything else or you'd be excommunicated. If you were saying the right prayers at the end of mass . . . *Sub grave* was the phrase he liked to use, which meant 'under the pain of mortal sin'. Bloody stupid! . . . He was niggling, niggling, niggling.[63]

Others took a more positive view of the archbishop's pastoral skills. Bishop John Mackey says that when he was a young priest, 'the visitation of the area of the parish' was what Liston stressed to young curates. 'He was very strong on the need for us to know the people for whom we had to care', and on the need for accurate parochial statistics.[64]

Greatest tensions between members of diocesan clergy tended to be between younger curates and older parish priests. The archbishop usually sided with the parish priests. In 1960, Daniel Silk, ageing pastor of Matamata, made it plain that he disliked his assistant Ewen Derrick. Liston's advice was for the younger man to bear patiently and uncomplainingly with Silk's eccentricities.[65] More notorious, and potentially more embarrassing, was a dispute in Epsom in 1956. The curate, Edward Russell Gaines, wrote to Liston complaining that the parish priest, Joseph Dunphy, was becoming mentally unbalanced. Gaines said there was 'unrest and upheaval' in the parish because of Dunphy's obsession with sexual sins. Dunphy's lurid and sexually-explicit homilies were forcing parents to remove their children from mass, or to withdraw to other parishes. Gaines also wrote of Dunphy's 'tantrums, even physical violence' in the presbytery and his habit of criticising his curate from the pulpit.[66] Liston interviewed Dunphy about these matters, but then banished young Gaines to the distant northern parish of Kaitaia.[67] Yet Gaines' observations would appear to have been accurate. The following year Dunphy's new curate, Ray Green, was also writing to Liston to outline similar difficulties with the old priest.[68] The rustication of Edward Gaines became notorious among the clergy, especially as Gaines himself was later a respected bishop. Brian Arahill recalls that priests would jokingly say they would be 'sent to Kaitaia' if they said anything that displeased Liston.[69]

Unexpected embarrassment was created by Mgr John Bradley of Remuera, a trusted lieutenant. Liston paid generous tribute to Bradley when the 25th anniversary of St Michael's church was celebrated in 1958.[70] He preached at the monsignor's requiem mass in 1959, lauding Bradley's personal 'austerity'.[71] But after Bradley's death, the archbishop was forced to change the rules about how 'house accounts' were managed by parish priests. He decreed that henceforth 'house accounts' would automatically be frozen and revert to the parish upon a priest's death. They could not be bequeathed or distributed in any way. This was because Liston was shocked to discover that Bradley had amassed a considerable personal fortune – £78,000 – out of parish funds, and had bequeathed it to his brother and two sisters in Ireland. As parishes were then largely self-funding, with no fixed diocesan clergy allowance, priests in wealthier parishes like Remuera were in a position to grow rich.[72]

If priests, living and dead, were under Liston's unquestioned authority, religious brothers had to be reminded that they functioned in the diocese only at the archbishop's pleasure. In 1961, Liston wrote to the Marist Brother principal of St John's College in Hamilton, ordering him to reinstate a boy who had been expelled. He remarked –

> . . . you have no authority to expel a boy from school without consultation with the parish priest, who in turn refers the matter to myself. I ask you further to understand that you and the other Brothers teach in our schools by authority of the Bishop of the diocese and according to his directions. He naturally looks to the teachers to act in full harmony and counsel with the parish priest in matters that come within the priest's circle.[73]

With nuns, however, his attitude was more truly paternal. He still witnessed the final vows of sisters and presided at the funerals of Mothers Superior.[74] He continued to cross New Street from his residence to visit the community of Mercy Sisters opposite. Sister Judith Leydon, a novice in the 1950s, recalls his weekly visits as being rather strained affairs, not because of the archbishop but because of the Mercy rule that the younger sisters were not allowed to speak. 'He always seemed rather remote', she says, 'but he wasn't. He had a very warm heart.' She says he was 'brilliant' at remembering the families of St Mary's students and following up bereavements. He was a very close friend of Sr Mary Ambrose, who was a classical scholar 'and he really did favour those people'. He also encouraged superiors of religious orders to allow sisters to study for university degrees.[75]

The Archbishop and the Laity

Older lay sodalities and service groups continued in the 1950s, with the Holy Name Society, the Legion of Mary, the St Vincent de Paul Society and the Hibernians all still having large memberships. Sports groups and Catholic lobby groups were encouraged. In

1956, Liston said masses of thanksgiving for the 25th anniversaries of both the Catholic Women's League and the Auckland Catholic Basketball Association.[76] His particular concern, though, remained professional groups. Medical ethics were a special interest. A Catholic Nurses' Guild was set up in 1960 and Liston addressed their first meeting.[77] For doctors, the Guild of St Luke and SS Cosmas and Damian was founded in Auckland in 1955.[78] Addressing it in 1957, Liston rejoiced that there were now about 150 Catholic doctors of medicine in New Zealand, 50 of them in Auckland.[79] Sexual morality remained a large motive for this interest in the medical profession. In August 1958, the archbishop told the doctors' guild that they could not unreservedly recommend the 'rhythm method' of contraception to patients.[80] In 1961, Dr H.P. Dunn asked whether it would be advisable to open a clinic at the Mater to give advice on 'safe periods' and the 'rhythm method' to Catholic women who had difficulties with child-bearing. Dunn reasoned that such women would otherwise be attracted by propaganda of the Family Planning Association. At first Liston demurred, saying the scheme was 'not advisable' and would 'open the door' to a contraceptive mentality. But the following year he agreed to Dunn's request.[81] A Catholic Marriage Guidance Council had been inaugurated by Liston in 1957 in consultation with Catholic Social Services.[82]

For Catholic lawyers, there were monthly meetings of the St Thomas More Society, although Sir Ian Barker recalls that such meetings also included numbers of Catholic businessmen who were not lawyers.[83] Sir Maurice Casey notes with approval that the archbishop observed strict probity in paying lawyers appropriate professional fees for diocesan work, and never assumed that he could gain the services of Catholic lawyers at lesser rates.[84] Barker was chairman of the university students' Catholic Society (CatSoc) for some of the 1950s. He says that Liston always came to CatSoc conferences, often held at Knocknagree, and mingled affably with the students. 'He was a great one for the one liners', says Barker, who remembers the hilarity that followed when the archbishop described Marist priests as 'wonderful men', but then added in a very audible undertone, 'But what leaders!'. For Barker, Liston made a stronger impression at student conferences than the 'gaunt, uncharismatic' Peter McKeefry, who had no small talk and tended to forget people's names.[85]

Liston attempted to strengthen a Catholic identity at Auckland University by sponsoring a students' centre. The Glenalvon private hotel, on Waterloo Quadrant near the main university campus, was part of the family inheritance which Leonard Buxton donated to the church. In 1959, Liston announced that Dominican priests would be taking over the Glenalvon as a Catholic students' centre and hall of residence.[86] Details were worked out in 1961-62 when the Glenalvon became Newman Hall under the direction of Fathers Peter Durning and David Sheerin, later joined by Leo Clandillon.[87] The archbishop opened Newman Hall in 1962, with the mayor of Auckland and the Anglican Bishop Gowing among the invited guests.[88]

Liston mainly left the Catholic Youth Movement to Fr Reginald Delargey.[89] Sometimes there was a new consultative attitude to the laity. Liston took part, in 1959, in an open discussion with architects and an audience on desirable designs for the proposed new church in Parnell.[90] Yet lay intellectuals were becoming restive at their exclusion from 'official' Catholic opinion. In 1956, a group of Catholic tertiary lecturers petitioned Liston for a correspondence column in *Zealandia*, saying it would be a 'very valuable step forward in the encouragement of mature Catholic Lay opinion'. Liston denied the request, arguing that Catholic opinion was better influenced by 'experts' than by letters to the press.[91]

If the Knights of the Southern Cross reported to the archbishop on the activities of priests, there were still some priests who thought it their right to denounce members of the laity to the archbishop. In 1956, Dr J.C. Reid, back from postgraduate studies at an American university, gave an interview to *Zealandia* in which he praised American Catholic schools and the large role they had for lay teachers. It was good, he said, that Catholic pupils were sometimes able to talk to mature Catholic adults who were not in religious orders.[92] The Irish Fr Michael Lavelle chose to interpret this as an attack upon the way clergy still dominated New Zealand's Catholic schools. He wrote to Liston denouncing Reid and, for good measure, condemning what he interpreted as Reid's anti-Irish attitudes.[93] Liston ignored Lavelle's outburst. Besides, within a short time he accepted that demand for teachers in Catholic schools was outrunning supply. Lay teachers were a growing presence, and in 1960 Liston approved a Catholic Education Board 'to administer the lay teacher scheme in the diocese'.[94] The school system was becoming more like the American one that Reid had praised.

In various ways, the composition of the Auckland Catholic laity was changing. Maori urbanisation meant that Liston was more likely to be present at such ceremonies as the first communion celebrations of Maori children at Knocknagree in 1955.[95] In the same year, he had to defend himself against an anonymous accusation that he practised 'unjust racial discrimination' in making it difficult for Maori to get dispensations for interdenominational marriages. Liston replied that he simply followed the protocols which had been established by Bishop Cleary, and with which the Mill Hill fathers were satisfied. The Apostolic Delegate accepted this explanation.[96]

A new factor at this time was the influx of immigrants from the Pacific Islands. At the end of the 1940s, Liston arranged for the Cluny Sisters to run a convent school at Avarua in the Cook Islands. Bishop Robin Leamy recalls, from his own time there, that Liston had a high reputation for having generously sent materials for the school's construction and maintenance. He also recalls Liston's solicitude for the growing Pacific Island community in Auckland. The archbishop organised Father Huia Hyde (of St Benedict's) and the Marist Fathers Louis and Peter Schwer to run Samoan and Tongan language chaplaincies in Auckland. The Dutch Picpus priests preached to Auckland's Cook Islands community.[97] Liston arranged with the Marists in Wellington for the solitary Maori priest, Te Awhitu, to say mass and preach at a special day for Maori and Pacific Island Catholics at the end of the Catholic Exhibition in 1956.[98] He took part in the celebrations for the ordination of a Samoan priest and a Tongan priest in 1959, and drank from the kava bowl.[99] A priest of a later generation, Neil Darragh, believes Liston left most Auckland Polynesian matters to the initiatives of Reginald Delargey.[100] Even so, the septuagenarian was beginning to experience the cultural diversity of his congregations.

Yet the 1950s were still a time of more traditional Catholic triumphalism. In 1954, the 'Rosary Crusade' of the visiting Fr Patrick Peyton attracted a crowd of 30,000 Catholics to Western Springs and another 8,000 to Hamilton.[101] Liston still presided at huge Christ the King processions at Baradene. Census figures were already showing a large decline in mainstream Protestant churches, while the Catholic church still enjoyed a modest growth. In his official report to the Apostolic Delegate in 1956, John Flanagan wrote,

> The big change in the relations between Catholics and Protestants is the growing lack of interest in any religion on the part of Protestants. There is less bigotry because there is more indifference. Conversions are slow but the number is increasing slowly. There is an average of 460 each year in the diocese.[102]

For Liston at this stage, ecumenism was essentially something for non-Catholic churches to practise among themselves. He was reported as telling a men's luncheon club in 1956 –

... he was glad ... to see a number of non-Catholic bodies striving toward union. The Catholic Church was divine and could not compromise by taking any part in the movement, since this would be equivalent to saying that one religion was as good as another. But if these bodies were sincere, which we take for granted, God's blessing must one day come upon them.[103]

There were nevertheless some genuine examples of early ecumenical activity. Liston took part in an interdenominational gathering to bless the renovated chapel of the Auckland Psychiatric Hospital.[104] Jocelyn Franklin, received into the Catholic church in 1945, recalls that the archbishop was fully understanding of her family situation and made no objections to her attending non-Catholic weddings, funerals and baptisms.[105] Yet the climate of the age was such that Liston saw all Protestants as potential converts. Frs Alfred Bennett and Frederick Walls had studied the proselytising methods of the Catholic Evidence Guild in England. Throughout the 1950s, under Liston's patronage, they operated a 'Mission House' in Vermont Street and ran missions and outreach programmes for converts. They were sometimes joined in this work by Ernest Simmons, Terry Leslie and Leo Downey.[106] Liston saw it as a routine part of his duties to educate non-Catholics about the church. In 1960, he broadcast a sermon in which he described the film *The Nun's Story* as 'beautiful but fiction', and proceeded to give a detailed account of the practical work of New Zealand's 2,500 nuns and religious sisters.[107] Clearly, this information was not aimed primarily at a Catholic listenership. At the same time, Catholics were warned off any Protestant attempts as proselytising. Liston told the faithful in 1959 that they could not attend rallies of the visiting Billy Graham, which were 'a Protestant mission for Protestants'.[108]

Auckland's Catholic congregations were becoming ethnically more diverse. Some lay intellectuals were more assertive. But the official place of the laity in the pre-Vatican II institutional church was still vividly illustrated by the Catholic Exhibition of 1956. Heavily publicised by Liston, and widely reported in the daily press, the exhibition was essentially an attempt to promote religious vocations. Its aim, said Liston, was to give 'a vivid picture of the life and works of priests and religious communities'.[109] Over eight days, in the concert chamber of the Auckland Town Hall, 50,000 visitors came to see 22 religious orders presenting exhibits for the edification of potential recruits.[110] Implicitly, real Catholic life entailed religious vows.

The Archbishop's Public Profile

The 1950s consolidated Liston's unofficial seniority within the hierarchy. Archbishop O'Shea died in 1954. Hugh O'Neill died in 1956. Bishop Whyte finally died at the end of 1957. In a *Zealandia* editorial, Liston emphasised the penitential nature of Whyte's long suffering. It was the 'supreme test' in which the bishop's nature was 'coming to perfection' and by which all were 'edified, comforted, encouraged'.[111] The whole hierarchy attended Whyte's Dunedin funeral and John Kavanagh became *de jure* Bishop of Dunedin, which he had been *de facto* since 1949. Other contemporaries of Liston's were also dying. In 1958, he attended the funeral of Mgr T. Connolly, who had long been vicar-general of the archdiocese of Wellington.[112]

Liston still often undertook secretarial duties for the bishops' conference and initiated projects. In 1962, he took charge of the production of a leaflet explaining the sacrament of penance to the laity. At the same bishops' meeting, he arranged for Australian women's representatives to address the CWL on pending changes in the church.[113]

Inevitably, Liston was most visible to the general public at ecclesiastical events in his own diocese. These included the annual debutante ball, the blessing of the sick at the Fatima shrine in Meadowbank, and his attendance at celebrations such as the 75th anniversary of St Benedict's church in 1959.[114] The church press reported in detail his reception of major church dignitaries – the new Apostolic Delegate Romolo Carboni in 1956, Cardinal Gilroy in 1958, the Prefect of Propaganda Cardinal Agagianian in 1959 and the Apostolic Delegate Maximilian de Furstenberg in 1961. He was also the most distinguished participant in a number of church events outside his own diocese. His long association with the Mercy Sisters led to his preaching their praises at a special celebration in Wellington in 1961. Similarly, it was Liston who presided and preached at the diamond jubilee of Holy Cross, Mosgiel, in 1960, and who laid the foundation stone for the Bishop Verdon Memorial Chapel.

As a respected and ageing public man, Liston accompanied the Governor-General, Lord Cobham, on a visit to the Little Sisters of the Poor's home for the aged in 1959.[115] He guided the Ministers of Health and Housing around the Mater hospital in 1961.[116] Perhaps mindful of lingering denominational bigotries, there was still the determination to present the Catholic community as law-abiding and respectful of civic authority. Of the 4,000 secondary school pupils who took part in the Empire Day procession to the Town Hall in 1955, approximately half were Catholic. Mayor John Luxford and Archbishop Liston jointly took the salute before the Catholic contingent fell out and marched up to St Patrick's Cathedral for a special mass.[117] That same year, Liston issued a public statement on a young man, a nominal Catholic, who had just been executed for murder. He carefully explained that the young man had neglected all religious observance until the last days before his execution, and compared him with the 'good thief' asking pardon at the crucifixion. But the clear message was that young murderers did not really represent the Catholic community.[118]

There were still broader public issues on which Liston made controversial statements. He was reported as listing some of them at a communion breakfast for Catholic students in 1957, where he spoke of –

> . . . the problems of the world today, notably the growth of world population, and the question not only of how the world would support so many, but how the great majority of the world's population could be lifted up from the bare subsistence level on which they were struggling. Racism, state policies hostile to family life, inequalities of wealth, emphasis on luxury and secularism were other problems. The Church was deeply interested in all these problems, and students should also be interested and use whatever gifts God had given them in a spirit of apostolate.[119]

Two issues in particular made up the bulk of Liston's controversial statements in the 1950s. One was the hierarchy's ongoing quest for state aid to Catholic schools. The other was the continuing animus towards Communism and its fellow-travellers.

In 1954, the metropolitan McKeefry was reported as saying that if another war were to break out, he would advise Catholics not to volunteer for service until justice had been done to Catholic schools.[120] Two years later, W.S. (Walter) Otto of the Holy Name Society organised the 'State the Case' petition calling for state aid to Catholic schools. Widely publicised in the Catholic press, it was presented to parliament but was rejected by a parliamentary committee after extensive submissions and hearings. The status quo prevailed, Catholic schools remained unfunded by taxation, and the hierarchy was able to win no more concessions from a National government than from a Labour one.[121] Like other Catholic bishops, Liston took every possible opportunity to remind the general public of the financial sacrifices Catholics were making in maintaining their school system. Openings of Catholics schools provided the ideal platform, especially as they were usually attended by the press, the local mayor and the local member of parliament. It was these public figures, as much as the parents he was ostensibly addressing, who Liston hoped would mark his words when he said in 1959, 'Since 1877 you have been providing religious schooling for your children wholly out of your own resources, even whilst you are paying your full share for the schooling of other children in state schools'.[122] He made similarly pointed statements in opening schools at Orakei, Glen Innes and New Plymouth.[123] Aware of the hostile questioning presenters of the 1956 petition had endured from state-school bodies, Liston gave the rest of the hierarchy the following advice in 1958, when they again considered approaching the government over state aid:

> Considerations in favour of submitting a written statement rather than presenting it: it tells the story adequately, it is not open to cross-examination by an unpleasant protagonist of a Public Body, and it escapes the publicity that the Press would give to an appearance.[124]

Even as building programmes continued, Catholic schools were under increasing financial pressure. They were often kept afloat only by their staffs of underpaid (or unpaid) religious sisters, brothers and priests. At the end of 1959, the whole hierarchy signed a pastoral in which they explained that parish priests would now have to institute a regular system of fees for convent schools, although pupils would not be turned away if their families were experiencing hardship.[125]

The wartime bubble of Communism had burst by the mid-1950s. By 1956, Stalin's successor Khrushchev was denouncing him and his regime, the Soviet invasion of Hungary disillusioned as many western Communists as the 1939 Nazi-Soviet Pact had done, and in both Australia and New Zealand small Communist parties became even smaller.[126] Nevertheless, in these Cold War years, Liston and the rest of the New Zealand hierarchy regularly spoke against the influence of Communism. A pastoral of 1955 called for prayers for 'the peace and unity of peoples, for the overthrow of Communism and for the coming of God into the hearts of men'.[127] A former Communist Douglas Hyde, now a convert to Catholicism, made regular appearances in New Zealand's Catholic press with analyses of events behind the Iron Curtain and advice on Communist tactics. For Liston the chief concern was the persecution of the church in Communist countries. He greeted Catholic Hungarian refugees to Auckland in 1956 and preached on the trials of Cardinal Mindszenty.[128] He called for prayers for 'the victims of tyranny in Poland and Hungary'.[129] In 1959, he ceremonially received a report from Lithuanian bishops on the suppression of the church in the Baltic states.[130] At the same time, he played host to church personnel who had been mistreated by Communist forces in Asia, including Bishop Thomas Quinlan, who had been imprisoned in North Korea.[131]

In all this, however, neither Liston nor his paper could be called Cold Warriors. *Zealandia*'s condemnations of Communism came from a distinctly Catholic and moralistic perspective and did not entail an unquestioning acceptance of any particular foreign policy. Western follies, such as Britain's and France's Suez adventure in 1956, were as promptly condemned by *Zealandia* as they were by left-wing journalists. Unsavoury aspects of Western life were criticised. Nor was the attack on Communism un-nuanced. The claims of indigenous nationalists in colonial territories were readily admitted and, surprisingly, at first both the *Tablet* and *Zealandia* greeted Fidel Castro as a hopeful force in overthrowing a corrupt dictatorship.[132]

Nevertheless, suspicion of Communism still qualified Liston's approval of some local aid schemes. Correspondence in late 1956 shows Liston and McKeefry both suspecting that CORSO could be use as a left-wing 'front', diverting aid funding for ideological purposes.[133] In 1958, however, Liston and the Catholic bishops were commended by CORSO's dominion secretary for their wholehearted support for the organisation's World Refugee Year appeal.[134] By the late 1960s, Liston regularly sent the aid agency large Lenten appeal cheques 'for the needy and in admiration of the many splendid things done by CORSO'.[135]

In the 1950s, Communism was by no means the only international matter upon which Liston pronounced. At his sacerdotal golden jubilee reception in 1954, he drew attention to the plight of the world's refugees.[136] The following year he issued a circular condemning the South African government for forcing mission schools to pay African teachers at lesser rates than European teachers.[137] This was the first of many protests he made against the apartheid regime. Nevertheless, no matter how nuanced his comments were, fear of Communism remained a preoccupation even as it became increasingly unrealistic.

Above: Liston with
Auckland Catholic primary
schoolchildren.
Below: Liston conferring
with his gardener at
Bishop's House, Ponsonby.

Age, Ill Health and the Appointment of an Auxiliary

By the late 1950s, James Michael Liston was nearing his 80th birthday and was beginning to be treated as a 'grand old man'. In 1958, he sat in his episcopal robes at Bishop's House as his portrait was painted by the Australian Royal Academician William Dargie. The portrait was commissioned by the brewing millionaire Sir Henry Kelliher.[138] Buildings were now named after Liston. At the time of his 40th episcopal anniversary in 1960, he consented for the new diocesan centre, built around the offices of *Zealandia*, to be called Liston House.[139] He blessed and opened it in 1961.[140] He became an honorary member of the Passionists in 1960.[141] His episcopal jubilee was celebrated with a public banquet, after which the diocesan clergy presented him with a new A99 Austin car with automatic transmission.[142] Though sometimes chauffeured by younger priests, the archbishop still insisted on doing most of his own driving. Staff at Bishop's House became used to hearing the 'fearful racket' he made as he habitually applied the accelerator too hard in backing out of his garage.[143]

The archbishop was ageing. One year, after saying his annual memorial mass for Bishop Cleary, he lamented that the congregation was so small, and that people seemed to be forgetting the late bishop. He had to be reminded that most of Cleary's contemporaries were now dead and that most Auckland Catholics had been born since 1929.[144] Ageing also brought health problems. Liston was briefly hospitalised in early 1957 after a collapse, but he promptly returned to his duties.[145] He then had a heart attack while preaching in the cathedral on Easter morning.[146] He was rushed to the Mater. John Flanagan asked Archbishop McKeefry to come to Auckland and, after visiting Liston, McKeefry decided that he and the other bishops would have to undertake some of Liston's diocesan duties, especially his scheduled confirmations. 'I think if he made the year a little light for himself it would do him a world of good', McKeefry told Bishop Joyce.[147] In a typically playful letter to Mother Helen Lynch of the Cenacle, Liston made the best of his condition; but he acknowledged that he was having to rest.[148] He took his medical problems seriously enough to alter his will again late in 1957, gifting his life insurance policy to the Dublin psychiatric hospital where his sister was a patient, and asking his secretary to draw up a list of clerical and laypeople to whom bequests could be made.[149]

It was increasingly evident that he could no longer run his large diocese on his own. An assistant was needed. But, perhaps mindful of his own unpleasant experiences with Bishop Cleary in the 1920s, Liston sought an auxiliary bishop only, rather than a full coadjutor with automatic right of succession. There would be no misunderstandings over precedence and authority. In his memoirs, Felix Donnelly claimed that Liston's first choice for an auxiliary was his cathedral administrator Adrian Curran.[150] There appears to be no truth to this claim. In his first formal request to Rome in May 1957, Liston specifically named the assistant he wanted. 'Should the Holy Father deign to grant this petition I beg to submit the name of the Rev Reginald Delargey as a suitable Auxiliary.'[151] Later, when the Apostolic Delegate asked Liston to nominate three *episcopabiles*, Liston named Delargey as his first choice and Curran as his second. (The editor of *Zealandia,* Owen Snedden, was third.)[152] Contrary to Donnelly's suggestions, the archbishop had been aware of Delargey's qualities for a number of years, and had actively advanced his career. As early as 1949, Reginald Delargey was second (to Leonard Buxton) in the diocesan clergy's *terna* voting.[153] In 1950, the Apostolic Delegate Paul Marella forwarded to Liston anonymous complaints that Father Delargey lacked prudence, forgot appointments, showed levity in his conversation and had been observed to yawn during mass. Liston promptly gave a spirited defence of a man who was temperamentally very different from himself. The charges against Delargey, wrote Liston, were all 'news to me'. Liston said he resented being questioned about Delargey in this way when the bishops had all already shown their confidence in the younger priest. The complaints showed that there was –

> . . . little or no humour in some. [Delargey] is full of fun, in the right way and place, and practises perfectly the give and take of friendly talk among priests. They welcome his company and hold him in high respect. For myself I think prudence is his middle name.[154]

In 1954 and 1955, Archbishop McKeefry had expressed some misgivings about the direction of the Catholic Youth Movement, which Delargey had managed since 1942. Delargey drew up a detailed *apologia* of himself.[155] Liston had no part in this brief dispute. Indeed, in 1957 Liston gave Delargey permission to spend six months overseas studying the lay apostolate and attending the world congress of Catholic youth movements in Rome.[156]

Delargey's appointment was confirmed by the Apostolic Delegate in December 1957 and publicly announced on 12 January 1958.[157] With Archbishop McKeefry and Bishop Kavanagh assisting, Liston consecrated Delargey in St Patrick's Cathedral on 27 February

1958. At the public reception that followed, he praised Delargey's work in the Catholic Youth Movement and the lay apostolate.[158] The new auxiliary took over Remuera parish in mid-1959 when John Bradley died.[159] Archbishop Liston and Bishop Delargey now regularly appeared together at major church functions. More to the point, Delargey began to relieve Liston of some of his more onerous duties. The most pressing was the *ad limina* which the 79-year-old Liston was scheduled to make in 1960. Liston petitioned the Vatican and gained permission for Delargey to take his place.[160] 'Rome has graciously freed me', he wrote. 'Our good bishop is to take my place. He will do it well and find experience in it for the years to come.'[161] Delargey left in May and returned in September, having presented the diocesan report in Rome, conferred with Cardinal Agagianian, attended a Eucharistic Congress in Munich and made the final arrangements for the Rosminian foundation in Auckland that Liston had planned. To McKeefry, Liston described Delargey as a 'treasure'.[162] He confirmed an earlier judgement on his own work habits which he had made to Sister Helen Lynch:

> By doing the day's work at less pace than formerly and by piling on things to a wonderful Auxiliary and the capable, generous Dr Flanagan, I manage to scramble along.[163]

It would have been easy to mistake these for the words of a man who was contemplating retirement.

CHAPTER IX

THE CRISIS OF AUTHORITY

Archbishop Liston 1962-70

The Impact of Vatican II

Pius XII died in 1958 and his successor John XXIII called an ecumenical council of the world's Catholic bishops. Between 1960 and 1962, the New Zealand Catholic press prepared readers with background articles on earlier church councils and speculation on the issues that might be addressed. Archbishop Liston welcomed the council, telling Aucklanders that 'the Spirit of God is clearly seen guiding the Church' in John XXIII's plans.[1] Possibly he expected the council to reaffirm the status quo. He told the Holy Name Society that the pope was 'trying to realize the prayer of Our Lord that there should be one fold and one shepherd'.[2] But such Christian unity would presumably be under Catholic leadership. In 1962, he remarked –

> Today Protestantism has come almost to a standstill . . . It is not sure of itself. Many of the greater minds among Protestant theologians today seem hardly Christian at all. They have embraced a rationalist philosophy or a form of criticism destructive of all faith. But others, anxious to keep the Faith, are feeling the need of a Church with teaching authority. The hour has come for a Catholic synthesis to show the reality of the Church and give light to the men of our time.[3]

In such expectations, Liston was possibly at one with that third of the Australian hierarchy who had no recommendations to make to the council's Antepreparatory Commission and suggested that they were quite happy with the church as it already was.[4]

It was expected that the octogenarian archbishop would attend the council. Early in 1962, McKeefry wrote to the Irish College

Liston's smile, more common in life than in surviving portraits.

in Rome to arrange accommodation for the *whole* New Zealand hierarchy.[5] But when the Second Vatican Council opened, Liston was conspicuously absent. Declining health had intervened. After Dr H.P. Dunn had declared him fit, he collapsed while saying mass. 'The privilege of being at the council is not to be mine', he wrote. 'Such is God's way and it is always wise and loving.'[6] In August 1962, he reminded the Apostolic Delegate of the heart attack he had suffered five years before and begged to be excused.[7]

During the three years of the Vatican Council, Liston did sometimes wish he could be in Rome. He was, wrote McKeefry to Donal Herlihy, 'sufficiently intrigued with all the side-gossip' of the council to be 'tempted' to travel to Rome.[8] Others of a conservative temperament also wished he could be there. 'I can't help wishing you could go to the council', wrote Eileen Duggan. 'It could do with your type.'[9]

Archbishop McKeefry and Bishops Delargey and Joyce regularly sent personal reports back to Liston. Without guessing at the major liturgical changes that lay ahead, Joyce wrote to him in the council's earlier stages, 'The talk – endless talk – goes on. The "pro" vernacular taking a beating this week: all the big men and good speakers "anti" '.[10]

The very aged Daniel Mannix (born 1864) and James Duhig (born 1871) were the only members of the Australian hierarchy not to attend Vatican II.[11] Liston, their slightly younger contemporary, was the only New Zealand bishop absent. As the 1960s advanced, there were changes in the hierarchy, so that some of Liston's brother bishops were now considerably younger than he. In 1962, Owen Snedden was consecrated as McKeefry's auxiliary in Wellington. Bishop Joyce of Christchurch died suddenly in 1964. His successor was Brian Ashby who, aged 40, was half Liston's age. In 1969, Liston's protégé McKeefry became New Zealand's first cardinal. The Apostolic Delegate, Domenico Enrici, announced that an apostolic delegation for New Zealand and the Pacific would now be separated from Australia and established in Wellington. Liston wrote to Enrici saying that he did not see this change as necessary. Besides, he argued, in making the announcement without first consulting New Zealand's bishops, the Apostolic Delegate was violating the spirit of episcopal collegiality which the Second Vatican Council had sought to promote.[12]

That Liston could cite the principles of Vatican II in this way raises the question of how he responded to all the changes the council encouraged. He left a mixed impression among younger contemporaries. Sir Ian Barker believes Liston was 'obedient' to Rome but 'uncomfortable' with the vernacular mass.[13] Sir Maurice Casey says Liston complied with change 'out of loyalty to the Vatican', but that he 'cannot at all have been comfortable with the diminishing of local episcopal authority that was implied'.[14] For others, however, Liston anticipated the church's transformation. 'It was remarkable that he was able to go with the flow', says Sister Margaret Browne. 'He was quite ahead of Vatican II and the changes it called for.' She instances his early support for the institution of a shorter eucharistic fast for nursing sisters who were on night duty.[15] Similarly, Jocelyn Franklin calls Liston 'far-sighted' in his consistent sponsorship of the Catholic Youth Movement. He did censor all material that was published about the CYM; but he was 'really a very forward-thinking person . . . because the things we were branching out into in the youth movement were really fore-runners of the Vatican Council'.[16] Kevin Hackett recalls that Liston was ahead of all other New Zealand bishops in announcing the abolition of the traditional Friday abstinence from meat. The more conservative McKeefry 'was not amused' by Liston's announcement.[17]

At the same time, according to Bernard Dennehy, Liston was 'very gradual' in introducing the vernacular into the mass, and was slow to grant priests permission to say their breviary in English. He 'thought that too much change too quickly would have a disastrous effect'.[18] Mgr Vincent Hunt emphasises that Liston's gradualism 'didn't mean reluctance, but could have good pastoral reasons'.[19] Some priests note that Liston seemed very well-informed about the theological bases of Vatican II, but was not in office long enough to see the full consequences of council initiatives in practice. 'He was very well-read and very up-to-date', says Paul Cronin, 'but I think the effect of Vatican II would have shocked him more than Vatican II principles.'[20] John Lyons concurs, saying that Liston spent the 1960s coming to grips with 'the ideological material [that] came out of the council', but that 'the practicalities of it didn't affect him' as he had already retired before they could do so.[21] Joseph Grayland, a liturgist of a later generation, speculates that Liston expected the changes of Vatican II to be 'a movement from one rubrical system to another', permitting of no further developments.[22] He believes Liston's greatest achievement was to allow his enthusiastic auxiliary Delargey to proceed with bold liturgical reform.[23]

Some of these impressions of Liston are contradictory and mutually-exclusive. But there is one point of consensus. However conservative some of Liston's impulses may have been, he in no way obstructed changes brought about by the council. In 1963, he may have written an admiring obituary of the rock-fast conservative Daniel Mannix.[24] But he was not himself a reactionary. Some liturgical changes endorsed by Liston pre-dated Vatican II. He presided at a new, shortened form of the dedication ceremony (a mere two hours long) when the church of Our Lady of Perpetual Help was opened in Herne Bay in mid-1962.[25] Some pedagogical change sponsored by Liston was quite independent of the council. Felix Donnelly says there were 'angry reactions' in some quarters when a new religious education programme was devised by Donnelly and Joyce Williams; but the archbishop gave it his full support.[26] Whenever change was sanctioned by the Vatican, Liston accepted it unquestioningly. The journalist Dorothy Coup recalls Liston becoming incensed at articles advocating 'mass facing the people' and for this reason vetoing some stories in *Zealandia*.[27] But once Pope Paul VI, in 1965, celebrated mass facing the congregation, the issue was decided.[28] In 1969, the archbishop sent a circular to all parish priests introducing the new prefaces that were now available for the eucharist.[29]

Contrary to memories of his 'caution', it was Liston who, early in 1964, urged the hierarchy to bypass the Apostolic Delegation and directly approach Propaganda for approval to introduce English into the liturgy. 'Our main concern is to encourage the people, who have had great expectations built up, and to avoid their being disappointed and let down', wrote McKeefry to the rector of the Irish College, Dominic Conway, as he explained Liston's initiative.[30] The first English-language mass in Auckland was celebrated in August 1964. In 1967, Liston endorsed Christian Life Week which was designed to educate Catholic clergy and laity about liturgical renewal. Out of Christian Life Week came the Catholic Publications Centre, permitting the easier dissemination of new liturgical material.[31]

Sometimes Liston consciously dissociated himself from determined conservatives. In 1963, he rejected the conservative George Duggan's criticisms of a progressive Jesuit theologian.[32] Four years later, he wrote that he was 'not in favour' when Gavin Ardley, lecturer in philosophy at Auckland University, asked if a Latin Mass Society could be established.[33] To the hierarchy, Liston suggested some changes in liturgy and was reserved about others. At the bishops' meeting of July 1967, he proposed the British form of the 'prayers of the faithful' that was eventually adopted for mass in New Zealand. But he also supported McKeefry's argument for retaining the kneeling posture for reception of communion. At the same meeting, he suggested the bishops issue a pastoral 'giving encouragement and confidence for the future' while explaining recent liturgical change.[34] Nowhere was he as conservative as McKeefry, who opposed the loss of altar rails, and who wrote anxiously to Bishop Ashby,

> I have little respect for these priests who are so anxious for innovations. If they gave more time to wearing out boot leather on door to door visitation, they would be doing far better work for the souls of their congregations.[35]

For Liston, post-Vatican II liturgical changes were orderly. When a Vatican survey asked him if there had been 'arbitrary liturgical experiment' in his diocese, he wrote 'Happily, none'.[36] In early 1969, he described positively the processes of renewal and self-scrutiny that religious congregations were then undertaking, saying they were growing in 'openness' and 'loyalty to the Holy See (*sentire com Ecclesia)*'.[37]

There were limits to Liston's acceptance of innovation. In 1967, Norbert Berridge was denied permission for an evening mass with folk music and a layman addressing the congregation.[38] Anton Timmerman also had to apologise for allowing a layman behind the lectern.[39] Liston told the Redemptorist R.W. Dobbs how reluctant he was to 'enlarge for pastoral reasons' permission to celebrate 'house masses'.[40]

One major change fostered by Vatican II was in attitudes towards non-Catholic denominations. Suspicion faded. In 1963, Liston was happy to write to a wide variety of civic and non-Catholic church leaders and newspaper editors, thanking them for the sensitive way they had responded to news of the illness and death of John XXIII.[41] He was a signatory to the hierarchy's pastoral on ecumenism which declared that while there must be 'no formal acceptance of error', nevertheless Catholics should show 'honour to the separated brethren for the truth which they do possess'. In conformity to Vatican II, most barriers to Catholics praying in common with non-Catholics were now dissolved.[42] Liston permitted Catholic university students to attend services at the university's McLaurin Chapel.[43] Kevin Hackett remembers being rebuked by Liston for conducting a funeral service for a non-Catholic. But the archbishop relented, and had the good humour to see it as a great joke when Hackett reminded him that he had himself conducted such a service in a funeral parlour the previous week.[44] Paul Cronin, naval chaplain for most of the 1960s, recalls that Liston participated silently in Anzac Day ceremonies in earlier years; but now became a full

Above left: Ernest Simmons, priest, journalist and editor of *Zealandia* for most of the 1960s. His thoughts on a changing church were often ahead of Liston's. *Above right:* Felix Donnelly, who worked harmoniously with Liston in religious education, but later wrote an angry critique of the archbishop's pride. *Below left:* Tom Ryder, one of many priests who sometimes found themselves unhappy with assignments Liston gave them. *Below right:* Michael Bleakley, long-term parish priest of Hamilton. Liston was enraged by his remarks on the Mater Misericordiae hospital and never did assign him to an Auckland city parish.

Above left: Fr Reginald Delargey ('full of fun' according to Liston) who succeeded Liston as Bishop of Auckland. Despite rumours to the contrary, he was Liston's personal choice. Above right: Whina Cooper, friend of Mill Hill missionaries and benefactor of the Auckland diocese, who regarded Liston as her ally, and took up his suggestion to do social work among Auckland's urban Maori. Below left: Eileen Duggan, poet, frequently wrote to Liston with advice and queries, and regretted that he could not attend the Second Vatican Council ('It could do with your type,' she wrote). Below right: Surrounded by admirers, Cenacle Mother Helen Lynch, one of Liston's most regular correspondents, who playfully addressed him as 'Dear Bishop O'Mine'.

participant as a more ecumenical tone was established for these events. He was always invited to attend significant naval days.[45] He was increasingly present at interdenominational gatherings and services, joining the Anglican bishop of Auckland and the Presbyterian moderator in opening prayers for the conference of New Zealand hospital chaplains.[46] In 1968, the archbishop attended the opening, by rabbis Israel Porush and Alexander Astor, of the new synagogue and social complex in Grey's Avenue.[47] He hosted an interdenominational gathering of ministers at Bishop's House and, just before his retirement, accepted an invitation to preach in St Mary's Anglican Cathedral, quoting extensively from Vatican II documents on ecumenism.[48] By the late 1960s, he was also regularly invited to be an observer at the Anglican synod. Bishop Gowing had prayers said in Anglican churches for Archbishop Liston's 85th birthday, and Liston made the gift of a cope to the Anglican Bishop of Aotearoa, Manu Bennett, at the time of his consecration.[49] This was also a time when Liston and Gowing publicly supported each other in seeking state assistance for denominational schools.[50]

Yet a policy of ecumenism did not mean a surrender of Catholic distinctiveness. In 1965, Liston sent a representative to a reception for the visiting Archbishop of Canterbury; but he declined an offer for a Catholic priest to lead prayers in an Anglican church on Queen's Birthday.[51] While approving the laity's attendance at combined religious services in 1968, Liston still 'emphasized the need for adequate instruction of people concerned'.[52] In an exchange of letters with the Marist John Mannix, he approved the building of an interdenominational chapel at Marsden Point, but he argued against a policy of joint tenure of country churches with other denominations. This, he said, would lead to 'a lessening of the real differences between us'.[53]

He was most concerned to defend theological orthodoxy. When Lloyd Geering offended the Presbyterian General Assembly with his heterodox views on the Resurrection, Liston responded with a sermon in which he cited St Paul and called the Resurrection 'a fact, beyond all question'.[54] He assured the Holy Name Society that 'Catholic teaching remains eternal'.[55] In 1968, he turned down an invitation to attend a Presbyterian 'People's Night' at which Geering was going to preach. (A month later, however, he did attend a reception for the new moderator, Ian W. Fraser.)[56]

In the 1960s, there were still awkward situations where the pastoral practices of different denominations were not compatible. One such occurred in 1967 when the daughter of Bishop Holland, Anglican bishop of the Waikato, married a Catholic in the Catholic church. In conformity with Catholic practice at the time, Archbishop Liston allowed Bishop Holland no formal part in the ceremony. In silent protest at his exclusion, the Anglican bishop attended his daughter's wedding in 'gaiters' – formal social wear.[57] But most often now, sectarian differences were approached with respectful tact. In 1968, G.R. Montieth, Anglican Dean of Auckland, was compelled by his parishioners to release a press statement on the pope's encyclical on birth control, reminding general readers that Anglicans were not bound by Catholic teaching. He forwarded a copy of his statement to Liston with a very apologetic covering letter explaining why he had had to take issue with some of Liston's own statements. 'Please believe me', wrote Montieth,

> . . . there is nothing I wish to do less than to harm the friendly and charitable relations that exist between us and which I so much value. I only wish I could have kept out of this controversy entirely.

In reply, Liston wrote that he was –

> . . . deeply moved by the kind consideration you show in your presentation of the Anglican position . . . How sad that these divergencies should be, but you and I and so many others hold to our trust in the action of the Holy Spirit to lead us into one heart and soul.[58]

An Oversized Diocese?

The 1966 census reported 176,197 Catholics in Auckland diocese, now considerably more than the 143,339 Catholics in the Wellington archdiocese.[59] There were 91 Auckland Catholic schools in 1962. By 1970, there were 118, catering for 23,000 pupils. Mass attendance was still high. In South Auckland, Liston created the parish of Mangere out of parts of Onehunga and Otahuhu parishes, and he invited Franciscans to staff it. To the north of Auckland, he set up the new parish of Massey and put it in the care of the Oblate Fathers. New churches were opened at Huntly and Raglan, existing facilities continued to be upgraded and new Catholic secondary schools were established. The Christian Brothers' Edmund Rice College was opened in 1963, and the Josephite Sisters' MacKillop College in 1966. The Marist Brothers planned a college in Tauranga and the Marist Fathers planned a college in Whangarei. In the year of his retirement, Liston blessed and laid the foundation stone for the emerging Pompallier College.

Growth continued, but at a lesser rate than in the previous decade. Church-building and the creation of new parishes slowed. New religious communities were invited to make foundations. Franciscan Sisters came to run the convent school in Otara. Later they also ran a geriatric hospital in Hamilton.[60] At the same time, others were withdrawing. The Carmelite priests left the diocese in 1970.[61] Dominican Sisters withdrew from Northcote in the late 1960s, and re-established St Dominic's College in Henderson.[62] Intake levels for Loreto Hall began to falter, although it continued to function until after Liston's episcopate. Liston sponsored the new Chanel Institute (modelled on the Xavier Institute in Sydney), which shared some facilities with Loreto Hall.[63] It was placed under the direction of Grahame Connolly SM, who says it was set up 'to provide theological and scriptural training to young religious' for their own formation rather than to train them directly as religious teachers. He recalls how Liston tested him for his leadership role by getting him to write a critique of a liturgical document. Liston, he says, personally ordered the books for the institute's library.[64]

But other establishments seemed to have outlived their usefulness. Bosco House in Ponsonby had been founded in 1953 as a hostel for delinquent boys. But (while praising the talents and methods of the former chaplain Felix Donnelly) James MacRory and Leo Downey now called the hostel's efficacy into question. Liston permitted it to be closed and the site was sold in 1967.[65] The Parnell parish school was closed for lack of teaching staff in 1964.[66]

Liston now had an auxiliary to relieve him of much official business, and on the whole, he functioned in his last decade as if Auckland had the ability to continue as an undivided entity. For all that, the diocese was still a huge care for the old archbishop. It was divided in two in 1980, four years after Liston's death, with the creation of the new Hamilton diocese. How seriously was such a division discussed in the last years of Liston's episcopate? The question had been raised as early as 1947, when the Apostolic Delegate mooted the feasibility of a third North Island diocese,[67] and there is some evidence that the division of the diocese was tentatively broached in the 1960s. In 1965, there were suggestions from Christchurch that intake into Catholic primary schools should be deliberately limited, to force the government to recognise how stretched Catholic schools' resources were. Liston rejected this idea, and declared that a large building programme of extra classrooms was underway, and teacher-training in hand, in Auckland.[68] In 1966, he issued a circular soliciting contributions to the Diocesan

Development Fund in the light of 'the extraordinary expansion in the population of the diocese (six thousand new Catholics per year)'.[69]

'It was certainly talked about', says Sir Ian Barker.[70] Paul Cronin says many priests believed that when Leonard Buxton died (in 1964) some administrative change would be made to Hamilton.[71] In the overlarge dioceses of Auckland and Wellington, claimed Tony Peterson, 'it was virtually impossible for bishops to have sufficient contact with priests and people'. But Ernest Simmons, editor of *Zealandia*, was rebuked by Liston when he suggested that the diocese was unwieldy and that Catholics should emulate the Anglicans in having seven New Zealand dioceses. Liston retorted that 'those who are competent to discuss this matter as yet haven't'.[72] Both Frank Roach and Kevin Hackett claim many priests were opposed to any division, fearing the unnecessary replication of existing services.[73] Bishop John Mackey, who eventually engineered the creation of the new Hamilton and Palmerston North dioceses, says –

> It was talked about for years – everybody said Auckland was too big . . . I think it was five times the size of Dunedin . . . But to talk to Liston or McKeefry about cutting up their dioceses would be like Solomon holding up the baby.[74]

Whatever criticisms there may have been, the large diocese remained intact so long as it was Liston's.[75]

The Changing Laity

In the 1960s, lay societies, too, looked to a less certain future. Liston could still be photographed with a Catholic tennis team, and the Marist Rugby Club named their Ellerslie property after him. Debutantes, although in diminishing numbers, continued to curtsey to him at the Charity Ball. The third (lay) order of Franciscans set up a national centre in the diocese in 1964.[76] The Catholic Women's League reached its peak of membership (12,500 members nationally) in 1965, with Liston continuing to address its diocesan conferences.[77] In 1965, Liston brokered the reconciliation of the two competing Hibernian societies, and was applauded for having 'recognized the Northern Society as a Catholic body'.[78]

Yet some lay sodalities were disintegrating. Membership of the Holy Name Society fell rapidly. An attempt to divide it into regional groups failed in 1964, and by 1965 half Auckland's 33 branches had ceased to function. In 1969, there were not enough active members of the society in Northcote to organise the Christ the King procession.[79] The Knights of the Southern Cross were beginning to transform themselves from an exclusive society into a club. Despite talk of 'openness', though, Liston and the other bishops were not yet prepared, in 1967, to let the Knights 'come out into the open' and publicly disclose their identity, as was happening in Australia.[80]

The Catholic Youth Movement was looked after by Liston's auxiliary Delargey. The archbishop did, however, receive reports from CYM president Jim Anderton on attitudes of young Catholics and on the availability of indecent literature in Auckland. CYM records were kept by Terry Leslie in the mid-1960s. Liston authorised the purchase of property at Orewa for the organisation in 1968, by which time the Catholic Youth Movement was attempting to become Young Christian Workers.[81]

While changes were going on in established diocesan societies, the laity at large was also changing. Catholics were rapidly becoming less exclusive. Liston reported to the Apostolic Delegate in 1964 that over 40 per cent of marriages contracted in Auckland diocesan churches were now religiously 'mixed'.[82] Responding to the Vatican council, committed Catholic laypeople expected to participate in discussion of theological matters. In 1964, the university Catholic Society inaugurated a three-year course in theology for the laity, conducted by David Sheerin OP. Liston declared, 'the study of theology is a fascinating study, not only for Bishop and priest, but also for layman'. His further comments, however, suggested that he saw this as another opportunity for the proclamation of traditional truths:

> The great need today is to bring the thought of God into every walk of life. To say that it is a trivial thing that at least 50,000,000 people died in the last war because death awaits us all and that after death, oblivion, is an insult to the dignity of human nature. But that, of course, follows if there is no God and no life after death. It is the dignity of man today which is attacked by the denial of God. Men must learn to occupy their minds with the thought of God – the study of God in his existence and nature and the role of God in our lives. This is the highest use to which the mind can be applied.[83]

Opportunities for lay retreats were expanded when Liston presided and said mass at the first National Retreat Conference at the Cenacle in 1964.[84] Courses on marriage preparation were also improved.[85]

Meanwhile, with the setting up of an Auckland Diocesan Education Council, the lay-dominated Parent-Teacher Association, under its president Desmond Piggin, urged Liston to find more equitable ways of raising finance for Catholic schools.[86] Liston still clung to the hope that the Catholic school system would be able to find a place for every Catholic child. He was reluctant to lift the ban on Catholic parents' sending their children to state schools. In 1966, one Cambridge parishioner complained that he and his wife were being denied the sacraments after they had removed their children from the local, grossly-overcrowded, convent school. Liston replied to him tartly, 'There is a simple solution: obey the law of the Church of God'.[87] Yet already, Fr Brendan Sherry of Henderson was telling Liston, 'next year we are going to have far more [Catholic] children at state primary schools than at our own school'. The local teaching order was forced to turn applicants away for lack of space and staff.[88] In 1967, the Catholic Education Office at last rescinded denial of sacraments to those parents who failed to send their children to Catholic schools.[89] Three years later, Liston told Fr George McHardy SM that the old ruling was 'no longer enforceable; the situation has just developed beyond control'.[90] Even so, the archbishop ordered Tom Ryder to read to Kawerau parishioners a pastoral on the importance of Catholic schools when a local newspaper article implied that Ryder advocated non-denominational religion classes in state schools.[91] As Catholic schools faced a financial crisis, in 1966, Liston and the Catholic Education Office polled schools on the effectiveness of a school journal separate from the state school journal. Responses were overwhelmingly negative and *Catholic School Journals* ceased publication.[92]

By the end of the decade, it was clear that the laity would no longer be passive recipients of clerical teaching but were partners in the church. The setting up of a Commission of the Laity in 1970 was essentially Bishop Delargey's initiative, but it was Archbishop Liston who officially launched it.[93]

The Question of Cultures

As the number of Pacific Islanders in his diocese grew, Liston was inevitably part of their life and ceremonies. According to Fr Theobald Broekman, there were 500 Catholic Cook Islanders in Auckland by 1966.[94] The archbishop presided at the opening of their social centre in 1969.[95] He took part in a requiem mass for Queen Salote of Tonga in 1965.[96] He also made the gift of a crozier to Pio Taofinu'u, bishop-elect of Apia, in 1968, but was unable to comply with the bishop's requests for clergy for Samoa.[97]

As always, a more prominent cultural question for Liston was how to relate most properly to Maori congregations. Mill Hill Fathers counted 19,000 Catholics among the 120,000 Maori of the Auckland diocese in 1966.[98] Liston supported regular appeals for the Maori Mission, and sponsored the ordination of Auckland's first Maori diocesan priest.[99] Henare Arekatera Tate was *mokopuna* of Whina Cooper (the great-grandson of her uncle Himi).[100] He recalls that it was Liston who confirmed him in Panguru, who frequently visited his family in the Hokianga and who 'took a great interest in me while I was at the seminary' at Mosgiel. Liston also encouraged him to take Maori studies at university.[101] Tate's ordination in mid-1962 was a major cultural and liturgical event, involving large numbers of Catholic and non-Catholic Maori.[102] Another major project encouraged by Liston was the establishment of a Catholic Maori centre in Auckland. Tate recalls that Liston persuaded Whina Cooper to come to Auckland to work for urban Maori with the argument, 'there are far more souls there than in Panguru'.[103] Together with Fr van Enkevort, she set up an Auckland Catholic Maori Society specifically to raise funds for the proposed centre. An old bakery was bought on Manukau Rd in Epsom, and converted to this new purpose. At Whina Cooper's suggestion, it was named Te Unga Waka (the Meeting Place of the Canoes), and was opened by Archbishop Liston and the Governor-General, Sir Bernard Fergusson, on 5 March 1966.[104]

On occasion, the archbishop could show great sensitivity to Maori needs. He advised McKeefry in 1964 that he had approved the Mill Hills' proposal to say parts of the mass in Maori for Maori congregations.[105] Without altering his decision, he dealt tactfully and courteously with Hepi Hoani Te Heu Heu when he organised a petition to protest Liston's closure of the convent school at Waihi village on the western shore of Lake Taupo.[106] He tried to sponsor a credit union for Auckland Maori, and he at first argued against celebrating the bicentenary of the French explorer De Surville 'in view of De Surville's treatment of the Maoris'.[107]

Yet it is hard to escape the impression that Liston's attitude to Maori culture remained perfunctory and paternalistic. Having attended the opening of its chapel in 1967, there is no evidence that he ever again set foot on the Te Unga Waka marae.[108] He still expected Maori to merge into mainstream parishes. The Mill Hill superior, Fr Aarts, explained to him the social aspect of Maori worship, and the fact that many urbanised Maori gave up religious practice altogether and never found their way into a suburban church because it was unconnected with their community or marae. For this reason, Aarts suggested Maori be allowed to marry at Te Unga Waka.[109] Liston gave permission very grudgingly, and urged Aarts to provide more priests for the city.[110] He did not respond well to Aarts' suggestion that some urban 'Pakeha' parishes might go into Mill Hill care, now that the urban Maori population was growing.[111] He was capable of ignoring Maori contributions to religious ceremony. In January 1967, he said requiem mass and conducted the graveside ritual for the Mill Hill priest Anselm Joseph Wardle. But, says Brian Arahill, 'once the Maori people came to do their cultural thing the archbishop didn't see that [as a legitimate part of the ceremony] and so he walked away'.[112] Not wishing Catholic Maori to drift into non-denominationalism, he forbade a priest to participate in an interdenominational service at Ngaruawahia, even though he had been requested to do so by the Maori queen.[113] Nor would he countenance anything that looked like preferential treatment for Maori. He vetoed a proposal to establish a bursary for Maori candidates to the priesthood.[114]

Peter Ryan recalls that Liston underfunded Hato Petera College, and was deaf to Dean Alink's pleas for greater assistance: 'Dean Alink was really upset a number of times when he'd been to see Liston . . . his life was made agony by Liston's refusal to see common sense'.[115] When Liston opened extensions to Hato Petera in 1969, his speech suggested that he still conceived of Maori education in terms of preparation for rural life:

> It seems to me, and I speak my thought in the light of what I learn from many competent to judge, that whilst some Maori are clearly qualified for professional careers through university training, most will do best for their own good estate, their homes and country in the technical fields and in agriculture, both fine ways of life, calling for high skills and characters creative, valuable, indispensable.[116]

Peter Ryan remarks, 'He didn't like the later Maori at all – they had begun to acquire the vocabulary of the protester'.[117] Liston happily accommodated Maori into existing church structures, but did not contemplate alternatives.

The Old Archbishop and his Clergy

In 1969, when he conducted the requiem for John Joseph O'Connor, former parish priest of Tokoroa, Archbishop Liston spelled out his ideal of the priest as Christ's representative.[118] Not all priests attained his standard. In the 1960s, Liston was confronted, not only by delinquent priests, but also by committed younger priests who questioned Tridentine expectations of priestly obedience. Here was a crisis of ecclesial authority that coloured the archbishop's last active decade.

Above: Liston as 'patriarch' of the New Zealand hierarchy in the 1960s. He was outranked by the metropolitan Archbishop McKeefry (right), but was still much the senior man. From left – Owen Snedden, Reginald Delargey, John Kavanagh, Liston, Brian Ashby, McKeefry.

Below: In 1964, the archbishop cuts a cake marking his 60 years as a priest while his auxiliary Reginald Delargey looks on.

The older guard of Liston's contemporaries were becoming inactive or dying. Jeremiah Cahill remained busy, and celebrated his sacerdotal diamond jubilee in 1964, the same year as Liston.[119] But Michael Furlong of Devonport died, aged 85, in 1962 after 57 years' service to the parish.[120] Leonard Buxton died in 1964, leaving his relatives to write the archbishop more letters concerning his estate.[121] In 1969, Liston wrote a tribute for the aggrieved Frederick Walls, whose funeral he was unable to attend.[122]

Considerable numbers of young men were still enrolled in the seminaries, but the peak of the 1950s was never again attained. Tony Peterson claimed that there were half as many seminarians in 1970 as there has been in 1960.[123] Nationally, 21 priests were ordained in 1962, but only 15 in 1968.[124] Liston personally encouraged some vocations, such as that of the middle-aged William Sidney ('Bill') Jordan MC MBE, journalist and war hero, who entered a seminary in Rome at the age of 57 and served Auckland diocese in the years after Liston's retirement.[125] Large numbers of defections from the priesthood were still in the future.[126] According to some later observers, the diocese in the 1960s had more than enough priests. Liston 'was always saying we need more priests', says Bernard Dennehy. 'We were overstaffed really.' He notes that Ponsonby parish was served by four priests, one of whom realised he was really redundant and asked to be transferred elsewhere.[127] Yet Liston sometimes wrote to McKeefry begging 'a loan' of priests from Wellington to cover perceived shortages.[128]

Liston was always concerned with the corporate image of the church, and the edification of a laity presumed to be easily scandalised. 'His idea of the church', says Bishop Robin Leamy,

> . . . was that the church came first and priests just served the church. In other words, the hierarchical and structural church was the church he thought of. He didn't think of the people of God, the Vatican II model . . . he would prefer a priest or [other] person to be treated unjustly rather than scandalise the church . . . His top priority was that we must not cause scandal.[129]

Leamy recalls that his fellow-Marist Kevin Roach was 'scolded' by Liston for writing a thesis critical of Bishop Pompallier, and was for years discouraged from developing as a church historian. Similarly, Liston denied John Roberts access to diocesan archives to research Pompallier's dispute with the Marists. A bishop's reputation was not to be questioned. Con (Joseph Consedine) Kiernan, a young priest in the 1960s, says that Liston's 'one controlling pattern of thinking was 'Is this going to be for the betterment of the church?' He believed 'the people had to be preserved from anything dangerous, and he didn't believe they had the knowledge to assess things'.[130]

According to Grahame Connolly, Liston was efficient but formal. Priests knew he had built only very limited 'free time' into his busy weekly schedule, and he was to be telephoned only at certain very specific hours 'unless it was life or death. . ... If you really had to see him, it was rare that he didn't see you that day or the next day'.[131] Formality governed Liston's written communications. 'There were three types of letter you received', says Mgr Paul Cronin. 'The first was "Dear Father", the second was "Father", the third was "Memo" . . . that was the dangerous one'. The archbishop did not like anyone anticipating his official announcements. Once, his annual clergy appointments were 'leaked' before the official letters had been sent out to the priests concerned. So Liston 'changed them all'.[132] He could act with good humour, but still made it clear appointments were his prerogative alone. He 'grinned' when he told John Mackey that he could not take on a position in Zambia which Mackey had been offered by the Zambian bishops' conference without Liston's knowledge.[133] Priests received mixed messages in Liston's pastoral of 1967, where he urged them to encourage a Parent-Teacher Association and a Confraternity of Christian Doctrine in every parish, but also sternly warned them against wearing secular garb at church functions, and admonished 'only for special, quite special, reason' could priests ever share a car with a religious sister or laywoman.[134]

For some younger priests, it seemed that Liston was out of touch with pastoral realities. David Price says his generation of seminarians at Mosgiel received letters from Liston instructing them, in their first appointments as curates, never to call the parish priest by his first name, and to report everything they did to the parish priest. 'It took me only three weeks in Dargaville to realize how unrealistic and out-of-date this advice was.' Older parish priests simply were not interested in detailed accounts of their curates' doings. Price notes that clergy retreats would 'bring out the old rector' in Liston. Every year, Liston still warned priests against granting too easily dispensations for 'mixed' marriages. Hence in seeking such dispensations, priests 'would virtually write down what they thought the archbishop wanted to hear'.[135] Mgr Paul Cronin concurs, recalling Liston saying 'Ugh! Ugh! Ugh!' at the number of dispensations he was asked to endorse:

We felt as though perhaps (having never been a parish priest himself) the nuances of relationships between young people and so forth [were] a bit in his past and he didn't realize the pressures of the peer group of the age.[136]

There were still, according to Neil Darragh, 'rumours' that priests who had offended Liston were rusticated, although the only one Darragh can recall is Tom Ryder 'exiled' to Kawerau.[137] Certainly there were priests who felt that Liston had mistreated them in assigning them to country parishes. Transferred by Liston from Hauraki Plains to Ruawai, the elderly Laurence O'Neill complained in 1963 that he was being sent 'from one swamp to another swamp'.[138] He died in 1971, having never been given a city appointment.[139] Before he was transferred to Hamilton, Frank Wright complained of the vastness and frequent flooding of his Huntly parish.[140] On the other hand, Kevin Hackett recalls only Liston's 'tremendous compassion' and concern for the welfare of the parish when he was sent to administer Matamata in place of the ailing Daniel Silk.[141]

Liston still had to deal with a few eccentrics. In 1967, the parish priest of Waihi, Frank Sheerin (described by John Lyons as 'a peppery little Irishman') decided that the easiest way to dispose of his old presbytery, before building a new one, was to burn it down under the supervision of the local fire brigade. This he proceeded to do, without first asking Liston's permission. 'But that's arson!' protested Liston.[142] He later wrote to Sheerin, 'I am disappointed in your disobedience and confused ways'. Nevertheless, he allowed the priest to proceed with a legal contract to build a new presbytery.[143] As Michael Lavelle gave way to drink and clinical depression, Liston removed him from Henderson parish, replaced him with Brendan Sherry and sent him to what he hoped would be the easier berth of Epsom.[144]

Liston was genuinely puzzled about how he was meant to treat priests who decided to quit active ministry. When one priest left to marry a divorced woman, and two others left because they had been 'caught up in unsavoury situations', Liston wrote anxiously to the rector of the Irish College in Rome, asking him to investigate how the Congregation now expected laicisation to be handled in such cases.[145] He was equally puzzled by seminarians who decided to discontinue studies. To the rector of Holy Name, Christchurch, he wrote in 1965, complaining that some Auckland seminarians said they did not 'feel' any longer like becoming priests. 'It is this "I feel" that troubles me', wrote Liston, as he deplored the subjectivism of the students and their failure to discern that a vocation was a special invitation from God.[146] There is evidence of his applying psychological pressure. 'How sad. How very sad. How disappointing', he wrote shamingly to one seminarian who decided to leave in 1966.[147] But in 1967, he refused to ordain a deacon who publicly questioned the nature of authority in the church.[148] Mosgiel students believed Liston 'clipped' one student in the 1960s for showing too much interest in the controversial theologian Teilhard de Chardin.[149]

In 1968 the archbishop personally commended the American archbishops' pastoral on the nature of true authority in the church, and had it printed as a nine-part series in *Zealandia*.[150] But some priests were becoming restive under Liston's authority. In late 1969, Ewen Derrick resigned as diocesan education advisor after Liston rebuked him for sending out a questionnaire which searchingly quizzed religious orders on their role in education. Derrick said he found it hard to comply with Liston's ban on his making press statements.[151]

One incident in particular seemed to dramatise the gulf that could now open up between the Tridentine-formed archbishop and his younger post-Vatican II priests. On 28 August 1968, Archbishop Liston joined mayors, community leaders and churchmen of various denominations in an orderly march through central Auckland to protest against the Soviet invasion of Czechoslovakia.[152] A few weeks later, on Labour Weekend, Tony Peterson and Con Kiernan joined an Auckland demonstration against New Zealand's involvement in the Vietnam war. A third young priest, Bernard Dennehy, had planned to join them but happened to be out of town at the time. Liston was furious. He disapproved of the young priests' Catholic Peace Movement. Dennehy says, 'He was against Communism, but he wasn't against colonialism'.[153] The priests' involvement in the anti-war demonstration was reported on both national and BBC news, which readily noted that the archbishop had participated in another demonstration a few weeks earlier. Con Kiernan recalls that both he and Peterson believed they had 'covered themselves' by this fact. But it cut no ice with Liston in what Kiernan calls a 'very, very difficult session' when the two priests were summoned to explain themselves. Liston's secretary John Flanagan was in attendance to take down every word they said. 'I've never heard of that before', says Kiernan 'where priests would be interviewed by the archbishop and actually have his secretary in attendance'. Both priests were suspended from their duties and ordered to make a retreat at the Hillsborough friary. (Bernard Dennehy says they were 'imprisoned in the friary to consider their sins'). Three days later they were summoned back by Liston and told they would be assigned to parish duties outside Auckland city. A few months later, Tony Peterson was sent to Te Aroha and Con Kiernan to Tauranga. For Kiernan, the worst part of the affair was the archbishop's failure to contact or reassure Kiernan's parents during the period of disciplinary proceedings.[154]

There were some priests who heartily approved of Liston's actions. 'You have my wholehearted support', wrote Philip Bartholomew Purcell, adding, 'It is high time these fellows got a taste of lawful authority'.[155] William Wood wrote to thank Liston for 'giving us such necessary true leadership during these days of unrest and stupid thinking, speaking and acting'.[156] There were others in the late 1960s who discerned a compassionate side to the archbishop. Kevin Hackett recalls Liston 'weeping inconsolably' when he learned that a priest who had begun to behave oddly had been diagnosed as having terminal cancer.[157] In retrospect, Con Kiernan is able to speak of the archbishop with considerable affection. He recalls times when Liston showed him great consideration, and was willing to discuss frankly the theology and spiritual reading that interested the younger man. 'As far as I was concerned, I had really quite good episodes with him.'[158] Even so, as he approached 90, Liston too often showed the strain of a man fighting yesterday's battles, and failing to connect with a generation whose priestly formation was very different from his own.

As always, his relationship with the nuns of the diocese was radically different from that with the priests. Sister Margaret Browne remarks,

> . . . we were more fortunate than the priests . . . I think he didn't have the responsibility for us, the way he did with the clergy . . . he often came over to St Mary's and would sit in the community room and appeared to be quite relaxed and friendly and enjoyed a good joke . . . It was nice to see him in that setting.[159]

Pauline Engel comments,

> I never lost my view of this somewhat pernickety old man who had been really tough on the young priests . . . and often seemed to make pretty irrational and highly conservative decisions . . . but underneath all that the reality of his pastoral care was quite extraordinary.

She recalls the archbishop steadying her shaking hand as she put on the ceremonial ring in taking her final vows in 1966. She also remembers his careful handling of one troubled member of the

Mercy community who was having difficulty with her fellows.

Liston was a connoisseur of art, a benefactor to the Loreto Hall library and a man who encouraged all the religious sisters to study the documents of Vatican II.[160] Among sisters as among priests, however, some of the archbishop's older friends were dying. Dorothea Loughnan, the scholarly Sacred Heart expert on liturgy, died in 1968, and Liston wrote a personal tribute to her for *Zealandia*.[161]

How the hierarchy related to religious communities changed in the 1960s. There were conferences of religious superiors once the Association for Religious was set up in the diocese in 1967.[162] But Liston was not in favour of anything resembling a trade union for priests. 'Ugh! No answer', he scrawled in 1970 on a letter from Fr John Broadbent, who wrote from Wellington enquiring about the setting up of a National Association of Priests.[163] His attitude to clergy remained monarchical.

The Old Archbishop and the Press

At this time, Archbishop Liston was troubled by a new tone in the Catholic press. For Liston, the Catholic press existed to publicise and promote loyally the interests of the church. He had a veto over the contents of *Zealandia*. He frequently chose to contribute articles and editorials. Typically, he would write an article explaining the new rite of ordination, or order the editor to print retractions to mildly facetious comment on Catholic schools.[164] He resented any attempts by *Zealandia* to pre-empt official announcements. In 1968, he rebuked the editor for publicising the agenda of a bishops' meeting, and reporting a religious superiors' conference, without his prior permission.[165]

Anathema to him was any publication in his diocese which purported to be Catholic but which did not have his imprimatur. In 1966, a group meeting at Newman Hall attempted to establish the quarterly *Insight* to replace the (cyclostyled) Catholic students' magazine *Ikthyus*. Edited by Peter Gibbons, with John Daly-Peoples as his assistant and Michael King as its Wellington representative, *Insight* had a minuscule circulation and a combative liberal tone. 'The Catholic community is rigid and conservative', declared Peter Gibbons in his first editorial, condemning the laity as 'quite apathetic'. The fourth issue ran letters-to-the-editor criticising the concept of the Legion of Mary, and a provocative article, 'Are Catholic Schools Desirable?' As 'balance' there were articles by the conservative Pat Lawlor; but James K. Baxter and Tom Ryder were more typical contributors with their criticisms of the institutional church.[166] Liston detested *Insight*. He wrote to the university chaplain Leo Clandillon deploring its 'superficial and brash' writing, but he refused to answer Michael King's letter which asked him to specify which articles were superficial and brash.[167] Liston argued that the magazine violated the church's hospitality. It could not be produced from Newman Hall.[168] *Insight* was shut down at the end of 1967.

At the same time, the archbishop was becoming increasingly uneasy about *Zealandia* under the editorship of Ernest Simmons, who had taken over in 1962. An urbane and scholarly man, Simmons embraced the teachings of Vatican II, took to heart John XXIII's encyclical *Pacem in Terris* and stepped back from the fervent anti-Communism *Zealandia* had displayed in previous decades. In 1962, at the time of the Cuban missile crisis, Simmons had to explain himself when he produced an editorial critical of the American position.[169] Liston said he had received a complaint from the American ambassador. Simmons replied that that was the ambassador's job, and he stood by his editorial.[170] The Catholic press in New Zealand was as divided as the Catholic press in Australia over a proper response to the Vietnam War.[171] Simmons ran some material supportive of the New Zealand's government's position. But his own editorials, and articles by Roderick Finlayson, were largely opposed to the war. It is clear that by early 1968, Liston was considering removing Simmons from his post. In February of that year, he discussed the matter with Bishop Delargey who defended Simmons' editorship, noted that the newspaper's circulation had held up very well in a trying decade, and said that despite an occasional 'annoying patronising tone', Simmons' Catholicity was 'thoroughly orthodox'.[172] For the moment, Liston left Simmons alone.

Even less to Liston's taste now was the Dunedin *Tablet* under the editorship of John Kennedy. Although the layman Kennedy was essentially a conservative, he believed in the strong participation of the laity in the Catholic press and the right to criticise decisions by the hierarchy. Just before he took up his editorship, he told Catholic graduates that Catholic newspapers should avoid being 'Catholic *Pravdas*'. Without mentioning *Zealandia* by name, he pointedly noted the *Tablet*'s freedom from episcopal control.[173] Unlike *Zealandia*, the *Tablet* now ran a correspondence column and Liston was said to be 'horrified' by the divisions of Catholic opinion displayed there.[174]

In his reaction to both newspapers, much of Liston's disquiet centred on the issue of artificial contraception. Throughout the 1960s, there were increasingly open pronouncements on this issue by Liston and his subordinates. A 1963 *Zealandia* editorial (presumably by Ernest Simmons) reaffirmed the traditional Catholic teaching.[175] Liston clearly condemned the new contraceptive pill.[176] In 1967, he drew the attention of the bishops' conference to prevalent 'confused and dangerous thinking', and urged that bishops 'insist with their priests on the absolute need of fidelity to the authoritative magisterium'.[177] He ordered the St Vincent de Paul Society to cease selling a 'Living Parish' pamphlet by Rosemary Haughton, saying it contained 'pernicious teaching' on birth control.[178] He issued a pastoral telling the laity not to speculate on the Vatican's deliberations, nor to pursue 'selfish satisfaction' by making 'a choice for themselves against God'.[179]

It is no coincidence that Liston's problems with the Catholic press came to a head in late 1968, when Paul VI's encyclical *Humanae Vitae* reaffirmed the ruling against artificial contraception, and much of the Catholic laity publicly dissented. In August 1968, the New Zealand hierarchy declared that the pope's teaching was authoritative.[180] For good measure, Liston added his own pastoral in which he warned that noisy public opinion was not the magisterium, and made *Humanae Vitae* a test of 'loyalty' to the church's authoritative teaching.[181] 'Loyalty' featured in another statement a few weeks later where Liston said conscience was 'not a thing of feeling' but 'fashioned before the face of God in the light of . . . the guidance of the Church of God'.[182] In such statements, Liston was at one with many bishops of his generation and formation. At about the same time, Archbishop John Charles McQuaid of Dublin was writing a pastoral whose 'shrill, terse tone', according to one commentator, 'betrayed his anger, frustration and bemusement' at Dubliners' negative response to *Humanae Vitae*.[183]

Throughout late 1968, the correspondence column of the *Tablet* included much dissident reaction to the encyclical. At the beginning of September, Liston sent a 'strictly confidential' circular to parish priests, telling them to cancel parish orders for the *Tablet*. 'It is to be a simple cancellation with no reason given', wrote Liston.[184] The directive became front page news for the *New Zealand Herald*, which reported John Kennedy saying that 'some people' found 'disturbing' his publication's freedom in presenting opinions.[185] Predictably, the *Tablet* itself for three weeks ran extensive comment on the 'ban'. An editorial by Kennedy declared 'we were cutting too heavily into the sales of the controlled Auckland organ [*Zealandia*]'. Letters to the editor compared Liston's heavy-handedness to the Communist government in Czechoslovakia; said he was disobedient to the pope's suggestion that bishops should retire at the age of 75; and reported the protests of the university Catholic Society, Catholic journalists and (anonymous) Auckland priests. There were a few voices raised in Liston's defence. One letter compared him with Christ 'who, when every voice was raised against him, said nothing at all'.[186] But lay reaction was more typified by Fr Frank Roach's elderly mother, who said of Liston, 'Who does he think we are? Children?'.[187] A current joke said that while the pope had banned the pill, the archbishop had banned the *Tablet*. In the controversy, Auckland subscriptions to the *Tablet* increased. But the archbishop refused to either comment upon, or rescind, his directive.

John Kennedy's remarks about *Zealandia* were unfair inasmuch as they did not admit that *Zealandia* continued to have a much larger circulation than the *Tablet*; and Ernest Simmons' editorship was at least as broad-minded as Kennedy's own, save for the one particular that Simmons was not permitted to run a correspondence column. At the beginning of 1969, Liston dismissed Simmons, reassigned him to parish duties and replaced him with his deputy-editor Patrick Murray. Simmons went quietly, although in a parting interview he implied that the archbishop no longer trusted the press. Patrick Murray, however, continued with Simmons' editorial policies. In late July 1969, Liston dismissed Murray too, and replaced him with his own, very conservative, appointee, Pierre Denzil Meuli. This time there were protests. Most of *Zealandia*'s staff resigned. University students organised a 'pray-in' in the cathedral to protest the archbishop's action. On Sunday 3 August, about 120 demonstrators, under the nominal leadership of Maurice Casey, gathered with placards outside the archbishop's residence in New Street. Hastily, Dr H.P. Dunn had organised a counter-demonstration of about 80 people to support the archbishop. The two groups stood grinning at each other from opposite sides of the road.[188] Two hundred and fifty two laypeople signed a petition expressing 'our disappointment at the manner in which authority is being exercised in Auckland diocese'. This was forwarded to Cardinal McKeefry, as were many other letters of complaint. Loyal to his mentor, McKeefry replied that he had no authority to interfere in another bishop's diocese, and besides, the proprietor's decision to replace an editor had nothing to do with dialogue with the laity.[189]

The demonstrations were fully reported in the *Tablet*, which also ran pages of letters concerning *Zealandia*'s woes.[190] More embarrassingly for Liston, the demonstrations and staff resignations were front page news for both of Auckland's dailies.[191] This was just the type of public scandal he had sedulously avoided since his trial for sedition in the 1920s and the Campbell case in the 1930s.

The affair generated much folklore. Hyperbolically, Tony Peterson declared that the dismissal of Patrick Murray provoked 'the biggest internal explosion in the history of the New Zealand church'.[192] It was hardly that. Those who came to the New Street demonstration did so with considerable diffidence. Sir Ian Barker recalls, 'I decided not to go on either side because my sympathies were with the Maurice Casey-led rebels . . . but I didn't want to hurt the old man'.[193] The lawyer Maurice Flynn came to New Street, but then went home without joining either demonstration as he saw so many friends on both sides of the street. Sister Judith Leydon recalls that the archbishop's secretary John Flanagan was reported to have quipped, 'Don't worry – we've barricaded the doors with unsold Zealandias', when Liston jocularly wondered whether the demonstrators were going to storm Bishop's House.[194] Dr Dunn's son, Bishop Patrick Dunn, has a memory of the two groups of demonstrators shaking hands, chatting and laughing before dividing for a few perfunctory moments of protest for the press cameras. It was said that Archbishop Liston watched from the windows of Bishop's House muttering 'Silly people! Silly people!'.[195] Sir Maurice Casey says he was 'talked into' leading the protest. He felt he had to resign from the Commission of the Laity, and Liston sent him a letter rebuking him for his disloyalty 'which was pretty sad'. Later, however, at a national conference, the archbishop made a point of speaking cordially to Maurice and Stella Casey in public, as a clear sign that the incident was closed.[196] As a sop to reader demand, a correspondence column was at last introduced into Zealandia; but Liston retained his conservative editor and for some months sales of the newspaper fell dramatically.[197]

Despite the good humour some of this evokes years later, the Zealandia affair was for many people another sign that the archbishop was out of touch, too authoritarian and, at the age of 88, much too old to be heading the country's largest diocese. In the Waikato Times, the young journalist Michael King devoted a long feature article to cataloguing Liston's shortcomings, from banning folk music at masses to suspending a priest (Kevin Donnelly) who had dissented from the magisterium's teaching on contraception.[198]

Grand Old Man

Yet whatever strife he attracted within the church, Liston was undoubtedly a 'grand old man' to most Aucklanders. His longevity meant he had been Catholic Bishop of Auckland for as long as most people could remember. His continuing stamina and apparent ubiquity made him a figure of respect, affection, awe and sometimes envy. Anecdotes abounded. It was said that when he attended garden parties at Government House, a separate reception line would form of all the people who wanted to greet him.[199] One newspaper profile told of his still regularly hearing confessions in the cathedral on Saturday nights. It recounted how a young boy, watching him absent-mindedly eat sandwiches on a train journey one Friday, had asked him, 'Do you always eat ham sandwiches on a Friday?' It also reported that he 'still chuckled over' the incident of an old man in hospital who, after the archbishop had spent some time at his bedside, said, 'Thank you very much for coming to see me, Jasper'.[200] In another profile, Liston's charitable interests and following of rugby were recorded, as was the anecdote of an old woman enthusiastically thanking him for the 'wonderful comfort' she had derived from his 'lovely broadcasts', and then asking, 'You *are* Uncle Tom, aren't you?'[201] That Liston could be mistaken for the popular religious broadcaster Tom Garland, or for the Anglican city missioner Jasper Calder, is a tribute to how much he had become associated in the minds of the non-Catholic public with a general idea of religious benevolence.

A rich mythology circulated. In one popular tale, a priest, annoyed that his homilies were judged negatively by the archbishop, surreptitiously took a tape-recorder into the cathedral, recorded one of Liston's own sermons, transcribed it and submitted it to the archbishop as his own work. It was returned to him heavily scored out in the archbishop's hand, and with the marginal comment 'Utter rubbish!'.[202] Another story said that in 1965, when the American prizefighter 'Sonny' Liston was definitively defeated in the world heavyweight championship by Cassius Clay, the archbishop declared, 'I'm afraid it has been a sorry day for the Listons'.[203] The elderly Liston's approach to drink caused some wry comment. He remained a committed abstainer but, says Sir Ian Barker, 'like all teetotallers he was sort of lethal with pouring the whisky'.[204] Paul Cronin says, 'he was very heavy-handed when he poured drinks [considering he was] a man who didn't believe in it'.[205] It was noted with amusement that at public dinners he enjoyed eating trifle infused with brandy.[206]

Apart from the anecdotes, there was Liston's documented interest in the arts. He conducted a dedication service for the 1968 Auckland Festival of the Arts in the presence of the Governor-General Sir Arthur Porritt. His homily linked the arts – especially music – to his deepest religious instincts.[207] Although he never gambled, the old archbishop was also known for his interest in horse-racing. David Tonks, who entered the seminary in 1968, recalls,

> I was accepted in one interview, which . . . was extraordinary. Part of the reason that I was accepted was that he had a great respect for my father [race commentator Sid Tonks] because of his love of horse-racing . . . He would have listened to all the races on a Saturday and would know all the horses that had won and the jockeys that had won and how much they had paid. This love of horse-racing that he had stood by me a little later on.

Tonks also recalls that young seminarians, on retreat at Bishop's House, had to pretend that they had spent an afternoon in prayer when they had really been watching a rugby test-match on television. Liston generously pretended to believe them.[208]

The archbishop could now be celebrated for his length of service. His sacerdotal diamond jubilee in 1964 involved a number of public events including a banquet at which toasts were proposed by the Governor-General Sir Bernard Fergusson, the prime minister Sir Keith Holyoake, the assistant Anglican Bishop of Auckland Bishop Caulton and J.C. Reid for the Catholic laity.[209] Felix Donnelly later claimed the prime minister's speech showed he knew virtually nothing about Liston.[210] Nevertheless, the archbishop's eminence was suggested by the company. The *Auckland Star* called him 'one of the greatest churchmen New Zealand has had'.[211] Bishop Gowing, the Presbyterian moderator, Auckland's rabbi and the mayor Sir Dove-Myer Robinson all spoke for him at a civic reception which attracted a crowd of 7,000 to the Ellerslie racecourse.[212] There were other, specifically church, celebrations for him at about the same time, in Hamilton and Dunedin.[213] The New Year's Honours list in 1968 made him a Companion of the Order of Saints Michael and George.[214]

As a churchman, Liston's newsworthy public appearances were mainly church-related. He joined the rest of the hierarchy in travelling to Dunedin for the blessing of the new Holy Cross chapel and seminary auditorium, and to Christchurch for the opening of extensions to Holy Name, Riccarton.[215] He was at Whenuapai to greet Cardinal Spellman as he made a brief stop-over en route

Above: The public figure – Liston with Governor-General Bernard Fergusson and prime minister Keith Holyoake (John Flanagan, as always, hovering over Liston's shoulder), celebrating Liston's diamond jubilee as a priest, 1964.
Below: Having become a member of the Order of St John, Liston chats with the Governor-General Sir Arthur Porritt.

to McMurdo Sound.[216] Although the Holy Name Society was evaporating, Liston, Delargey and Mgr Curran welcomed the governor-general to the cathedral for a celebration of the society's 40th anniversary in 1966.[217] Traditional sentiment could draw him to the Irish Society to welcome visiting Gaelic footballers.[218]

By now, his endorsement was sought for many non-denominational causes – campaigns for road safety, famine relief in India, the Auckland Alcoholism Trust Board or better care in psychiatric hospitals.[219] He was expected to pronounce on public matters, such as the assassination of President John F. Kennedy.[220] The *New Zealand Herald* gave him the space to contribute three articles giving the Catholic perspective on abortion, birth control, conscience and wealthy nations' obligation to provide for the world's poor.[221] Towards the end of his episcopate, a trust was set up to build the James Liston Hostel for destitute men on a strictly interdenominational basis. The board was composed of two laymen from each of the Anglican, Methodist, Presbyterian and Catholic churches.[222] Liston's presence was expected at such functions as a McLaurin Chapel service to mark the centenary of the Auckland Supreme Court, or a special Gisborne celebration for the bicentenary of Captain Cook's visit.[223] Non-denominational organisations sought him as a member. In 1964, at the governor-general's invitation, he was made chaplain and sub-prelate of the Order of St John.[224] He became an honorary member of Rotary in 1965.[225]

Despite all this, he remained a committed spokesman for Catholic schools. When the hierarchy had suffered yet another reverse, in 1966, in their quest for state aid, Liston wrote to them,

> I have a suggestion: invite some 10-12 non-Catholic men of standing in the country's life to join our committee, sound friends of religious schools, this mostly for prestige purposes *coram publico et membrii Gubernii*, but also for advice on how to approach government, opposition and press.[226]

School prizegivings were still used by Liston as an appropriate forum for complaints about the lack of government assistance.[227] For all his non-denominational admirers, the archbishop did not forget what body he was primarily serving.

The Archbishop Retires

Whatever fanciful tales may have been told about him, the aged Liston retained his mental vigour. There were rare moments of forgetfulness. Brian Arahill recalls going to Bishop's House in 1967 and being mistaken for somebody else.[228] Grahame Connolly, however, remembers Liston at that time skim-reading theological works every day. He once cross-examined Connolly over a speed-reading course he had attended, before saying, 'Yes, I think I've acquired most of those [skills] over the years'.[229] As always, it was McKeefry who gave the most favourable report. To the rector of the Irish College he wrote in 1967,

> I had the bishops down for a meeting. Archbishop Liston seemed to be the brightest and most alert of all, despite his 86 years. As Bishop Kavanagh and I so often say, he is now reaping the reward of an early virtuous life.[230]

Time was, however, catching up with him. He sometimes suffered 'turns' and 'blackouts' and had to be replaced at the last minute for important functions.[231] He was, according to the *Tablet*, 'indisposed' and was thus one of two distinguished old boys of the former Christian Brothers' High School in Dunedin who could not attend his alma mater's 90th anniversary celebrations in 1966. (The other was McKeefry, who had managed to break his arm that week.)[232] His most dramatic collapse happened in 1967 at the opening of the Te Unga Waka marae chapel. Fr Henare Tate recalls:

> We thought we were going to have a first-hand relic because he collapsed during the mass and had to lie down on the floor, so we thought 'Oh yes. Here we are. We've got our first martyr' . . . But he soon recovered so we didn't get our relics for the chapel . . . It's a pity in a way he didn't die, because we would have claimed him there and then.[233]

There were rumours that the archbishop was no longer contributing fully to the bishops' conference. One such rumour, attributed to Terry Leslie, was that the other bishops would sometimes meet a day in advance and settle matters on the agenda before Liston arrived, so that they could present him with a 'united front'.[234] While official records of meetings can be deceptive, the record does not appear to bear this rumour out. Many of the bishops' decisions were still Liston's initiatives. In 1962, it was he who drafted the bishops' response to possible government offers of financial relief to Catholic schools.[235] He presided in 1969 at meetings to set up the Chanel Institute.[236]

He was absent from a 1964 meeting where the bishops considered how much vernacular to use in the liturgy.[237] But he was present at most of the bishops' liturgical deliberations, raising the matter of the colour of vestments for requiems and the appropriate posture for reception of communion, and providing the rest of the hierarchy with liturgical articles from *L'Osservatore Romano*, which the bishops decided to have translated and circulated.[238] Bishop Dunn suggests, however, that the non-drinking Liston would retire for a reasonable night's sleep while the other bishops talked, socialised and had a nightcap; and it was probably then that McKeefry, Ashby, Kavanagh, Snedden and Delargey made some decisions.[239]

How much was Liston's diocesan workload now being borne by Delargey? The verdict is mixed. One priest says Delargey 'dutifully submitted' to Liston's directives, but was 'grooming himself' for his own episcopate, and the diocese 'would have been at a standstill if Delargey hadn't been there'.[240] Another says that, by the late 1960s, Delargey did most of the confirmation visitations, although he did not ordain any priests until well after Liston's retirement.[241] Neil Darragh believes Delargey increasingly tended to the practicalities of the diocese, and made the decisions regarding ethnic communities. Nevertheless, Delargey was a 'visionary' rather than the organiser that Liston was. Darragh judges Liston an 'autocrat'. He sees a symbol of Liston's approach to life in the way he witnessed the archbishop leave a Newman Hall function, get into a very large car the laity had given him and pull confidently away from the kerb without bothering to check for oncoming traffic. 'A kind of parable of what he was at the time', says Darragh.[242]

Archival records show that by the late 1960s, Liston regularly consulted Delargey on capital expenditure and maintenance.[243] Nevertheless, says Delargey's secretary Jocelyn Franklin, 'the archbishop was the archbishop'. Delargey was not allowed to sign anything in the name of the diocese, and more than once Liston overruled Delargey's decisions on property.[244] For some observers, this was not necessarily a bad thing. Delargey 'thought he was a bit of a property magnate on the basis of his father's having been a bank manager', says Sir Ian Barker. Delargey was incapable of giving clear instructions 'whereas the old man was very focused'. Barker describes Liston as 'an ideal client' who took professional advice seriously and never assumed he knew more than his hired advisors.[245]

In the face of age, adverse criticisms and some ill health, there was speculation that the archbishop would retire as he approached

90. Liston seemed resolutely opposed to retirement. According to Bernard Dennehy, he once told a priest who wanted to retire, 'good priests never retire', with the clear implication that good bishops never retire either. 'He did have that idea of long-term commitment . . . you died with your boots on.'[246] But in December 1969, on the 40th anniversary of his succeeding to Cleary, Archbishop Liston petitioned the Vatican for permission to retire. Paul VI's official acceptance of Liston's resignation arrived in March 1970.[247] Between December 1969 and April 1970, Delargey and the rest of the hierarchy knew of the archbishop's retirement, but it had not yet been made public. The bishops accepted Liston's resignation with expressions of regret.[248] 'I am content in the decision to retire and happy in knowing there will be some share in the brotherhood of the bishops', wrote Liston to Ashby.[249] Later, Delargey wrote to McKeefry,

> We manage to keep the flag flying here in the North although I think the archbishop finds the waiting a bit wearisome. On the other hand I really think it has helped him adjust to the changeover. He has been able to gradually look over his old files and do the sorting he wants to do calmly.[250]

To the frustration of future biographers, Liston now destroyed the bulk of his private correspondence. Ironically, about this time, he also received treasures for the diocese treasures when Mlle Aunier, grand-niece of Auckland's first bishop, sent him Pompallier's episcopal ring and pectoral cross.[251] Finally, in April, Liston publicly announced his retirement.[252] He declared:

> It seemed to me wise to have a time of retirement during which to thank God for the graces of my priesthood, for the privilege of serving you and our country, and for the intimate preparation of soul for God's judgment.[253]

In his retirement, the Vatican made him titular head of the defunct Irish see of St Secundus, Domnach Sechlainn.[254] To a farewell gathering of 200 priests, Bishop Delargey remarked, 'The Pope is aware that it is indeed the Patriarch of the church in New Zealand, almost the father of the church, who is retiring'.[255] Liston was now 89. Delargey was Liston's auxiliary, not his coadjutor. Hence his succession was not automatic. For some months he was termed Vicar Capitular and, when he was briefly in Rome, the diocese was in the hands of the cathedral administrator Adrian Curran.[256] There were some complaints over the length of time it took Rome to confirm his appointment.[257] Only in September was Delargey officially appointed Bishop of Auckland.[258] He was not enthroned until December 1970, a whole year after Liston had requested to retirement.[259] By that stage, *Zealandia* was celebrating Liston's 50 years as a bishop [260]

Meanwhile, Liston had left Bishop's House. On 29 September, as he waited for John Flanagan to drive him to his new address, he wrote his last letter from his long-time residence. Fittingly, it was to McKeefry, in honour of 'your support and comfort, enriched for my life by your friendship'.[261] Farewell functions occupied him in the latter half of the year.[262] One of the most public was receiving an honorary Doctorate of Laws from the University of Auckland.[263] It was conferred in a dual ceremony on 8 July, where the historian Andrew Sharp was similarly honoured.[264] The university orator, Professor Sidney Musgrove, extolled the archbishop's administrative and pastoral achievements, but he also included a personal anecdote:

> I remember, some years ago, being at an official function in Auckland which was heavily attended by various dignitaries. As it broke up, the official cars came and went with their honourable loads, until someone thought to ask what had happened to the Archbishop. He was found outside, quietly waiting for the bus to take him home. This unobtrusiveness, this tendency to do good by stealth and to wish that no fuss should be made of it, is a well-known quality of which the university has often felt the beneficent effects.[265]

Such unobtrusiveness could, though, co-exist with presumption. After the conferral of the honorary degree, Catholic lawyers arranged a celebratory dinner for Liston at the Northern Club. Without forewarning his hosts, the archbishop brought along as his guest Bishop de Coq of the Cook Islands. All the careful seating arrangements had to be hastily reorganised.[266]

At a re-dedication of Saint Patrick's Cathedral, Liston ritually marks with a cross the grave of one of his predecessors Bishop Lenihan.

Liston at prayer in his private chapel at Bishop's House, Ponsonby. For 72 years, from 1904 to within the last weeks of his life in 1976, Liston said his daily mass and office.

CHAPTER X

IN RETIREMENT

1970-76

The address to which John Flanagan drove the retiring archbishop was a flat attached to the Mater Misericordiae Hospital. Here Liston lived for the last six years of his life. He made 'intimate preparation of soul for God's judgement', but not in solitude. Until the last few months, his life remained busy with public engagements, the sponsorship of worthy causes, and many personal visits and consultations.

His own anniversaries were still noted. His golden jubilee as a bishop was celebrated in December 1970 at the time his successor was enthroned. The Knights of the Southern Cross organised a major function for him in the passenger terminal of Prince's Wharf. The whole hierarchy attended, as did Bishop Gowing, many MPs and the president of the seminary at Manly. Paul Temm Q.C. delivered an address praising Liston for urging Catholics to seek their 'civil rights' and tactfully noting the firmness with which he had guided the diocese:

> Throughout the long years of his term of office there has been constantly present the steady, even discipline that one finds in many a well-ordered but loving family; where parents, anxious that their children will grow to maturity responsible, independent, well-developed and reliable, use their best efforts to see that the rules that govern the home remain enforced, evenly and continually, for the mutual benefit of all within its walls. Not for the seventh Bishop of Auckland a policy of self-expression and waywardness.[1]

The archbishop's birthdays were reported in the Catholic press.[2] So was his seventieth sacerdotal anniversary in 1974 but no official celebrations were scheduled.[3]

In addition to Liston House, other institutions were now named after him. In October 1972, the James Liston Hostel for indigent men was opened with an inter-denominational service in which Liston participated. Work began in 1973 on a new Christian Brothers' college for boys in Henderson, to be called Liston College. The archbishop was in the official party when it was opened in November 1975. Later that month, at a concert for St Cecilia's Day, Liston inaugurated an appeal for the Archbishop Liston Presentation Organ.

Public engagements still involved travel. In late 1970, he was briefly in Australia during the visit of Pope Paul VI.[4] The following year he went to Dunedin for its Catholic centennial and spoke in the Town Hall on the faith of Bishop Patrick Moran. He challenged Catholics to uphold humane virtues in a secular world:

> We must join with the Christian, the Jew, the unbeliever, men of good will, in upholding the dignity of every man and in promoting social justice and peace among men.[5]

A month later, he joined McKeefry in travelling to Whangarei for the opening of Pompallier College. He went to Ngaruawahia for a reception by the Maori queen, wearing Bishop Pompallier's episcopal ring, chain and pectoral cross for the occasion. In 1972, at the age of ninety-one, he was in Christchurch to celebrate the silver jubilee of Holy Name seminary.[6] Closer to home, the archbishop said jubilee masses for the Mission Sisters and the Dominican Sisters. He opened the new chapel of St Mary's College. With Bishop Delargey he blessed the new parish church at Papatoetoe. He also honoured significant individuals. In 1975, at a ceremony organised by the Guild of St Luke, he personally invested Dr H.P. Dunn with a papal knighthood.[7] He attended the diamond jubilee celebrations of Marist Brother Stephen Coll.[8] Some people he sought out with advice. He invited the censorship campaigner Patricia Bartlett to visit him when she was circulating a petition seeking a statutory definition of indecency. As a gift he gave her a carved image, from Vietnam, of the Virgin Mary, which she treasured. She was still writing him detailed accounts of her campaign to within a month of his death.[9] In 1976, he was reappointed a patron of the Ryder Cheshire Foundation.[10]

Despite his age and fragile health, there is no evidence that Liston's intellectual powers were dimmed. An eminent Hungarian historian visited him at the Mater, and came away marvelling at how well-informed he was about European current affairs.[11] Kevin Hackett recalls being regularly sent by Liston to Auckland residences of the Governor-General, and to the Anglican bishop's house, with material from Liston to help Sir Bernard Fergusson and Bishop Gowing in the preparation of speeches.[12] Liston kept up a lively correspondence with Sir Bernard.[13] He also undertook various writing commissions, including a foreword to a special New Zealand issue of the American Catholic medical journal *Linacre Quarterly*.[14] He was part of the successful campaign to have Blessed Oliver Plunkett canonised.[15] He provided a personal commendation when *Zealandia* ran a feature on the one-hundred-and-twenty-fifth anniversary of the Mercy Sisters.[16] On the other hand, in 1973 Liston declined John Kennedy's invitation to write something for the centenary of *Tablet*, and something about the late Fr Edmund Lynch. He gave no reason, but it is possible that he still disapproved of Kennedy's editorship, and had perceived how ironically Lynch had written about him in the golden jubilee publication of the Mosgiel seminary.[17] His judgements upon people could be impish and subversive. In 1973, Mother Theresa of Calcutta visited Auckland. To Bishop Snedden, Liston wrote, 'Mother Theresa's visit stirred hearts at a gathering – some 10,000 . . . It was my privilege to have a 15-minute visit from her, a favour indeed'.[18] Later, however, somebody lamented to him that the revered nun had refused a small gift that had been bought for her, on the grounds of her commitment to lived poverty. 'Oh well, it's all part of the act, isn't it?', Liston is reported to have said in commiseration.[19]

In retirement, the archbishop almost had the busy schedule of an active churchman, but some invitations he turned down. He sent a message of goodwill to, but did not attend, the 1974 Catholic Women's League conference.[20] Illness prevented him from attending the centenaries of Mosgiel-Allanton parish, and of the Dominican Sisters, in Dunedin. His prepared address to the Dominicans was read for him by Mgr Curran.[21] Three months before his death, he could send only written greetings to the golden jubilee celebrations of a Gisborne convent school.[22] Infirmity explains most of these situations, but as his retirement began, he appears to have decided consciously not to undertake engagements more properly undertaken by the Bishop of Auckland. 'Age is age at 90', he wrote tactfully in 1971 as he declined to attend both the Catholic Charity Ball and the nurses' graduation ceremony at the Mater.[23] Not interfering in his successor's leadership was one of his priorities. For many people this was the most edifying thing about his retirement. He did not aspire to be an 'alternative bishop' or bishop-in-exile, even when things happened in the diocese of which he might have disapproved. Not only was a Commission on the Laity set up in the first year of

Delargey's episcopate; so too was the senate of priests, which Liston had opposed.[24] A possible division of the diocese was now openly discussed.[25] Liston made no public announcements, but spoke his mind privately. To the Apostolic Delegate he expressed distress in 1971, when a group of Christchurch priests discussed whether celibacy should be optional.[26] A letter to Bishop Ashby in 1972 gave his views on the current state of the New Zealand church:

> Some things good, very good: respect for the Church and in many hearts some feeling (is that the word?) of having the answers in matters of real moment: the stability of our lay folk, their sense of realising their strength, the emergence of many, very many, into important commercial positions and therein witnessing to the right things: priests speaking of a noticeable return to sanity in the ways of many young people; and of course the shining goodness of priests, brothers and sisters, the excellence of our schools and the eagerness of parents (non-Catholic ones too) to have their children in the Catholic school.
>
> Sadnesses? Defections – what comes into the heart of these men? The Maori in the city – forty thousand of them. This is a decisive hour for their Faith, and in this city – country too? – they have much to bear.
>
> I am wholly content in life here and day by day marvel in seeing the goodness and at times the saintliness of patients.[27]

To the very end of his episcopate, the archbishop did much of his own driving. Michael King had a memory of Liston in 1970 'driving the length of [Victoria Street, Hamilton], his head just visible over the dashboard and his eyes enlarged by his glasses so that he looked exactly like Toad of Toad Hall'.[28] Only in his ninetieth year did Liston desist. As he went into retirement, Felix Donnelly wrote to him, 'I understand you aren't driving yourself at this stage', and offered his services as chauffeur.[29] Bruce Bolland, a chaplain at the Mater in the early 1970s, drove the archbishop on a number of occasions, but recalls that his most regular drivers were Adrian Curran, John Flanagan and Kevin Hackett.[30]

Liston's personal piety was noted by all. Paul Cronin says, 'Liston was a man of God, irrespective of how we looked at him', and expresses a common view when he adds that the old archbishop blossomed as a human being once he was relieved of the burden of being an 'autocrat'.[31] He was a 'good presence' in the years of his retirement, doing pastoral work among hospital patients.[32] Maurice Drumm recalls taking Liston to a nursing home. Liston's presence there, he says, seemed to animate even the semi-comatose inmates, so that they all looked up and responded to his prayers and blessings. This effect was noted and remarked upon by the nursing staff.[33] At the Mater, he said morning mass in the hospital chapel and spent much of the day visiting the wards. Sr Margaret Browne recalls the archbishop having to be summoned once when an elderly woman was in tears because 'the old man' had missed his usual evening visit. 'He was kind of disciplined. He had his day mapped out', she adds, noting that he loved books and regularly lent books to, or bought books for, patients, and every day received many visitors. One of the most frequent was Rabbi Alexander Astor.[34] The rabbi's affection for the archbishop was long-standing. Upon Liston's retirement he had written,

> In all the years that I have been in Auckland I have enjoyed and greatly cherished your warm-hearted and generous friendship and have deeply appreciated the kindness and sympathetic understanding you have always shown towards the Jewish people.[35]

To some, Liston's retirement brought out in him a new strain of humility. David Price was on the diocesan marriage tribunal from 1971. He says that Liston sometimes sent down articles critical of the apparent ease with which annulments were being granted. With the encouragement of Huia Hyde, Price in return sent Liston more up-to-date and scholarly articles on canon law, and Liston readily acknowledged the limitations of his own knowledge in this area. 'He was always most gracious', says Price, 'once he was no longer in the seat with heavy responsibility.'[36] Similarly, Bernard Dennehy calls Liston 'a very different person after he retired . . . far more human and tolerant and flexible and understanding'. He recalls how well-informed Liston was about trends in the South American church which Dennehy had observed.[37] It was still a matter of amusement to some visitors that Liston remained so well-informed about major rugby matches and race meetings, spending Saturday afternoons listening to the broadcasts.[38] Visiting him in 1974, the newspaper columnist Noel Holmes noted that his quarters at the Mater were 'comfortable enough, if a trifle austere. Shelves and shelves of books. A desk with a telephone which seems pretty busy'.[39] There were still many people who wished to talk with Archbishop Liston.

But to live into a tenth decade is to be reminded constantly of death. 'Most weeks, he'd be off to somebody's funeral', says Sr Margaret Browne.[40] Familiar old identities in the diocese were dropping away. Jeremiah Cahill died in 1971 at the age of 92. Liston was a concelebrant at his requiem.[41] The next year he was present at the funeral of T.J. Sheahan, who had managed advertising at the *Month* and *Zealandia* for over 40 years.[42] In 1975, he was told of the death of his long-time correspondent, Mother Lynch of the Cenacle.[43] He also wrote obituaries or sent condolences on the death of Irish public figures he had known – Archbishop McQuaid in 1973 and Eamon de Valera in 1975.[44] What reinforced Liston's public image as the 'ancient of days' was the fact that so many who pre-deceased him were many years younger than he. In 1972, he attended the funeral of Professor J.C. Reid, who died at the age of 56.[45] His most eminent protégé, Cardinal McKeefry, died late in 1973 at the age of 75. Liston was in the sanctuary of St Mary of the Angels in Wellington when the Apostolic Pro-Nuncio Archbishop Raymond Etteldorf celebrated the requiem for McKeefry, and Bishop Snedden preached the panegyric.[46] Reginald Delargey succeeded to the primacy of the New Zealand church and John Mackey took over as Bishop of Auckland.[47] Liston's immediate successor had had his Auckland position for barely four years. One of Liston's successors as rector of Holy Cross, Mosgiel, also died before him. He wrote a tribute to Bernard Courtenay in 1974.[48] 'You contradict the saying that only the good die young', Mayor Dove-Myer Robinson said to Liston late in 1975, at the official opening of the square next to St Patrick's Cathedral.[49]

The archbishop was still attending social functions in the last year of his life. He went to David Tonks' ordination party in 1975.[50] Sir Ian Barker says Liston 'still had all his marbles' in March 1976 when he helped celebrate Barker's appointment to the Bench.[51] Even so, life was increasingly a matter of farewells. Liston suffered a severe blow in February 1976 with the sudden death of his long-time secretary, the diabetic 59-year-old John Flanagan.[52] Sr Judith Leydon visited Liston at this time with Mgr Curran:

> I have this great recollection of him sitting in a big chair in the little sun-porch that was part of the flat and he was crying. The tears were literally rolling down his cheeks and down the front of his soutane, but at the same time he was laughing at all the funny things that John Flanagan used to do because John Flanagan had a great gift of repartee and wit and he was always able to make the archbishop laugh or to break the ice at some stage when things were getting a bit cool.[53]

It was a little after this that Liston had his last meeting with Edward ('Ted') Forsman, who was to die a mere six weeks after Liston. According to Forsman's brothers,

It was a happy occasion where each bared his soul as they reviewed their lives, their aspirations and their differences. Sometimes they touched on sensitive issues. These moments, I understand, were accompanied by distinct moistening of the eyes. They took their farewells in an emotionally-charged embrace, Ted swearing loyalty to the end and the Bishop assuring Ted of his appreciation of his work.[54]

At the end of 1975, Liston surrendered the cash value of his life insurance policy to the Dublin hospital which had cared for his insane sister for over forty years.[55] By May 1976, his successor Bishop Mackey was calling for prayers for Liston's failing health.[56] Finally, on 8 July 1976, Archbishop Liston died in the Mater hospital.[57] He was 95 years and one month old. His body lay in state in the cathedral from 9 July, and Bishop Mackey said his requiem to a packed congregation on 11 July. Brian Arahill was part of the team organising the obsequies. He recalls:

It was a very emotional time having to take the ring from his finger and the pectoral cross from around his neck because he was lying in state in the cathedral . . . And telling the funeral director to put the lid on.[58]

James Michael Liston was buried on the other side of the Panmure cemetery from the time-worn concrete monument to Bishop Cleary. Later, Ted Forsman was buried near him, and a large black cross was raised over him.

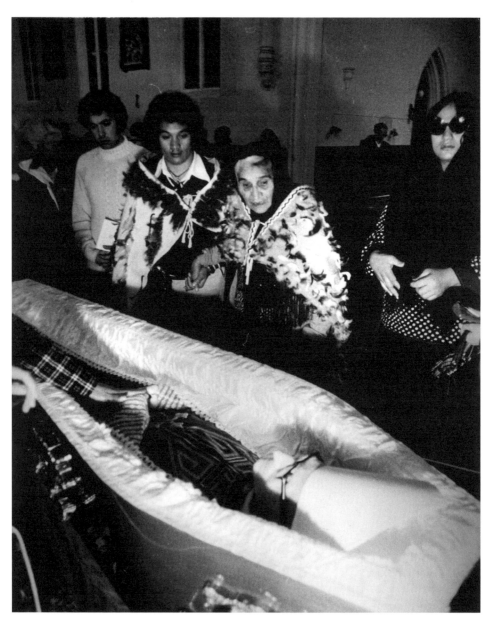

Whina Cooper sees Liston for the last time as he lies in state in Saint Patrick's Cathedral.

Right: Part of the funeral cortège for Archbishop Liston.
Below: Reginald Delargey (assisted by John Mackey) conducts the graveside rites for Liston in the Panmure cemetery.

AFTERWORD

James Michael Liston's values and deepest impulses were derived from his environment and background. Like any significant historical figure, he lived much of his life transcending his environment and background. Liston's forebears were West-of-Ireland Catholic peasantry. His first conceptions of church were shaped by the Cullenite 'devotional revolution' as conveyed to the New Zealand fragment of the Irish diaspora by Bishops Patrick Moran and Michael Verdon. Irish Catholics did not constitute a ghetto in New Zealand in any meaningful way. Yet their defensive sense of group identity was shaped in a largely non-Catholic society.

James grew up in strongly Presbyterian Dunedin, and there were times when the young man was a pugnacious controversialist in the cause of his Irish Catholic inheritance. During the First World War, his press campaign against the conscription of seminarians was influenced by events in both Australia and Ireland. He was a champion of Irish independence from the British Empire. The most notorious New Zealand echo of the Irish struggle was his 1922 trial for sedition. In some respects, he could be compared with his senior, Daniel Mannix of Melbourne, and his junior, John Charles McQuaid of Dublin, two Irish churchmen whom he admired. A sentimental regard for Ireland was reinforced both by his years there as a seminarian, and by his visits in 1935 and 1954.

Yet it would be wrong to interpret Liston's formation solely in terms of his inherited Irish identity, as can happen if too great an emphasis is placed on his 1922 trial. Liston was a New Zealander. At least some of his life was devoted to putting Irishness behind him. Moreover, Irish Catholicism was not a national sect, and the Catholicism of Liston's upbringing was ultimately more important than the Irishness. Paradoxically, one of the strongest Cullenite influences was the quality of 'Romanita', meaning devoted obedience to the authority of the pope and the culture of Rome. This Liston observed in Michael Verdon, after whom he consciously strove to model himself. 'Romanita' meant that, throughout his priestly career, Liston obediently relayed the directives of the Vatican, was a consistent apologist for papal policies, and did not obstruct the major changes in teaching and liturgy which the pope had approved in the Second Vatican Council. When the church's highest authority sanctioned change, so did James Michael Liston.

Liston was a product of his environment in a more intimate sense, too. While his relationship with his parents seems to have been affectionate and respectful, scanty records also suggest a troubled family. His elder brother was an alcoholic who died young. His elder sister had severe domestic problems. His younger sister was clinically insane and spent the last forty-six years of her life in a psychiatric hospital. To add to his isolation, James was separated early from his family, going into the seminary before he was an adolescent. Both his parents died in middle age, when James was studying in Rome. The institutional church, in which he was so early immersed, could be seen as his substitute family. Clonliffe and the Irish College were what provoked his most sentimental recollections.

In becoming a priest, he simply passed from one seminary to another. He went straight from ordination to a teaching position at Holy Cross, Mosgiel, and stayed there for sixteen years. The college man, the corporation man, Liston was intellectually bright and received the extraordinary plaudit of being made head of the national seminary at the age of twenty-eight. But he never had the experience of being a real parish priest. At different times, he had official charge of parishes (Mosgiel and Newton), but their care was essentially an adjunct to other positions he held at the time. To some observers, this meant that he missed exercising an important level of pastoral care, and it told in his later rigid management of clergy and laity. As seminary rector, Liston was a disciplinarian and precisian. This appears to have made the Dunedin clergy reject him when it came to finding a new bishop for the diocese in 1918, even though Liston was Verdon's heir apparent. Ironically, his transference to Auckland, with which he was identified for over half a century, was almost accidental. Cleary's request for a coadjutor furnished the expedient solution to the problem of Liston's rejection by the Dunedin clergy, which had embarrassed the hierarchy.

Liston's personal communications were often wary, correct, courteous and distant. His reserve may have been exacerbated by the church's culture of confidentiality. In both 1918-20, as he was rejected by the Dunedin clergy, and 1923-29, as he was subjected to the accusations of Bishop Cleary, he had to bear the burden of gossip and personal criticism which he could not answer publicly. Upon examination, few of Cleary's charges against Liston have any merit. They are most charitably regarded as expressions of Cleary's own obsessions and chronic ill health. This, at any rate, was the way both the Vatican and the rest of the New Zealand hierarchy came to regard them. But for all their deficiencies, the charges do suggest that young Bishop Liston really had antagonised a number of people and 'rubbed them up the wrong way'. His endorsement of the Knights of the Southern Cross (a 'spy' system, according to his critics) might suggest a desire to control clergy rather than to persuade them to share his views. Liston's part in the bishops' 1932 dispute over the Bible-in-Schools issue remains very much open to question. The problem may have been caused by Archbishop O'Shea's wilful misunderstanding of what Liston accurately reported to him. But Liston's handling of the contemporaneous Campbell case does show stubbornness pushed to an unreasonable degree. Here Liston's determination not to yield took no account of the damage he was doing to the church's public reputation.

On their own, all these things could suggest a repressed, legalistic personality without warmth, humour or easy familiarity. But against them must be set the many deep and lasting friendships Liston enjoyed – with his Dunedin colleague James Delaney, with Jeremiah Cahill, William Ormond, Leonard Buxton, John Bradley and later John Flanagan. Liston's letters to Bishop Whyte in the 1920s are filled with slangy chatter and happy wisecracks, his long correspondence with Sister Helen Lynch is a matter of affectionate sparring, and with Peter McKeefry he adopts the tone of a concerned father who can exchange notes in the face of shared problems. With his ecclesiastical equals he was at ease. With his ecclesiastical subordinates he was correct. He would socialise with adult laity, teaching sisters, students and schoolchildren more readily than some of his fellow bishops.

To analyse Liston's personal relationships in terms of background and psychological make-up may be to miss a more important extrinsic factor. The church Liston served was essentially hierarchical, hence so was Liston's own ecclesiology. Propriety and correct regard for rank were the keys. This may be reflected in Liston's life-long fondness for lawyers and judges: rational people with a necessary sense of their own status, like his boyhood classmate John Callan. It was certainly reflected in his management of the clergy. A bishop was *ipso facto* an autocrat, and Bishop Liston's attitude towards his priests is best described as monarchical. They were there to obey his instructions, convey his pastorals, police the boundaries of the Catholic world for the laity and be rebuked by him, without complaint, if they offended. Liston did not invent this approach. Archival evidence shows that his predecessor, Bishop Cleary, was just as unwilling to compromise with delinquent clergy as Liston was. If Liston had critics and enemies among priests, so too (as the

case of Henry Holbrook shows) did Cleary. There were instances
where priests, like the Marist John Higgins, saw service under Liston
as a preferable alternative to service under another church authority.
Even so, much of Liston's long strife with the Mill Hill missioners
seems to have arisen from his unease about having in his diocese an
order that was not fully his to command.

Liston's hierarchical ecclesiology was essential to his relationship
with the Catholic laity too. In a largely non-Catholic society, Liston
saw the need for an influential, well-educated Catholic elite. He
sponsored many movements to encourage the growth of one. An
autonomous Catholic hospital was as important in the promotion
of Catholic ethics as an autonomous Catholic school system. Liston
defended the Mater Misericordiae Hospital against all critics,
and founded guilds for Catholic nurses and doctors. Under his
patronage were societies of Catholic lawyers, businessmen and
university students. He established devotional sodalities like the
Holy Name Society, but he also established the Catholic Women's
League. Yet in his public statements there is often the assumption
that the 'apostolate of the laity' is a matter of the laity's faithfully
transmitting the directives of the hierarchy. In the 1960s, change
with regard to the status of the laity was harder for him to grasp
than liturgical change.

Inevitably, many of the judgements Liston made and the positions
he adopted were of their age. After the controversies of the First
World War and the early 1920s, he rarely said anything that could
be construed as sectarian. The diocesan press that he controlled
only occasionally attacked statements made by non-Catholic
churches, and on the whole studiedly ignored them. Nevertheless,
the superiority of the Catholic church was usually assumed. To later
generations, the 1938 Catholic centennial could be seen as an exercise
in triumphalism. As he aged, Liston did become more comfortable
with ecumenical endeavours. He established excellent relations with
the leaders of other Christian churches and with Jews. It may be
that he had somewhat tardily caught up with Archbishop O'Shea's
perception that the rivalry of Catholic and Protestant would be less
important to a future New Zealand than the tension of secular and
religious.

Liston's long and vigorous campaigns against Communism and
contraception are unexceptionable in terms of the prevailing Catholic
teaching that he faithfully conveyed. They are on a par with the long
campaign for state funding for Catholic schools. Beside them can
be set his commitment to economic justice during the Depression in

the 1930s, his genuine abhorrence of nuclear weapons and capital punishment, and his many statements against apartheid and other forms of racial discrimination. If his attitude towards Maori was assimilationist, and sometimes patronising and paternalistic, it had the virtue of being not essentially racist. It reflected the received wisdom of informed Pakeha of his age. So, too, did his views on the domestic and subordinate role of women.

Retrospective articles on Liston were right to emphasise his achievements as a diocesan administrator. Bishop of Auckland when it became the country's most populous diocese, he oversaw unprecedented growth, invited in many religious orders, and built a formidable number of schools, churches, convents and other facilities. Like the durable American prelate Cardinal Dennis Dougherty of Philadelphia, he could easily have been given the sobriquet 'God's bricklayer'. The exercise of authority in this large diocese remained highly centralised, and Liston would not consider suggestions that the diocese might have to be divided.

Liston's longevity was in itself one of his most notable characteristics as a leader. Although he never became metropolitan, he was, by the 1950s, the oldest member of the hierarchy and was widely regarded as the church's patriarch. Most of his fellow bishops were either his protégés or his former students. The career of his auxiliary Reginald Delargey had been actively encouraged by him. Liston was by now a 'character' – an admired public figure and the recipient of civic honours. By the 1960s, however, there was growing exasperation within the church at his continued leadership. Highly-publicised differences with some younger priests, and with the editors of the diocesan newspaper, seemed to epitomise a man who, despite obedient study of the Second Vatican Council, had not worked through its practical implications. That he did not retire until the age of 89 is another sign of the times he inhabited. Subsequently, canon law made it mandatory for bishops to retire at the age of 75.

Liston's six years of retirement were gracious and serene. Should they be seen as a coda to his life, or as his life's fulfilment? He was widely admired for not interfering in his successors' episcopates, and for devoting himself to prayer and pastoral work. This may point to the single most important fact about him. In passing judgement on his personal relationships, ecclesiology, political pronouncements or managerial style, it is easy to forget that he saw himself first and foremost as a man of God, praying and offering mass daily, and following a lifelong regime of devotional and theological reading. The personal piety was not an extra component added on to his busy public life. For him, it was the essence of his life.

In the early 1960s, the Catholic church in New Zealand still had a 'forward'-building mentality. Pages of the Catholic press were still taken up with photographs of the many newly-ordained seminarians. Holy Cross College was building extensions to accommodate new recruits. In Northcote, the new St Mary's church was built, its external walls decorated with mosaics of Marian scenes, its altar canopied by a modern baldacchino, the underside of which showed the Holy Spirit, as a dove, brooding over the clouds.

Forty years later, the mosaics have fallen off and been replaced with functional whitewash. The underside of the baldacchino has been painted over and the dove has disappeared. Forty years later, the national seminary has relocated to Auckland. Its courses attract more interested laypeople than potential priests. The Marist juniorate at Tuakau is history, the Franciscan retreat house in Hillsborough is often empty and a Eucharistic Congress means a gathering by a roomful of enthusiasts. In the early twenty-first century, the Catholic church in New Zealand has succeeded better than the other old 'mainstream' churches (Anglican, Presbyterian) in maintaining membership and filling churches. It is still building. Even so, in popular memory, the optimism and renewal of the first years after the Second Vatican Council are as much ancient history as the church that preceded the Second Vatican Council.

In the 1960s, James Michael Liston often seemed at odds with an inevitable, progressive historical process. Now that process has been as much superseded by subsequent history as he has. To pass judgement on Liston is to pass judgement on a church that no longer exists. Liston served that church as well as any other bishop and better than most. That is his most fitting epitaph.

NOTES

Prologue: After the Funeral, 1976

1   See editorial, 'Death of a Priest', *NZH*, 9 July 1979, p. 9; editorial, 'Leader and Servant', *AS*, 9 July 1976, p. 6; also news reports, 'Bigotries Died in Bishop's Lifetime', *Evening Post* (Wellington), 12 July 1976, p. 12; 'City Pays Tribute to Humble Shepherd', *NZH*, 13 July 1976; 'A Funeral Father Liston Could Not Have Foreseen', *AS*, 12 July 1976. The last of these spoke not only of the ecumenical nature of the mourners, but also of the fact that the requiem mass was now said in English rather than the Latin in which the young Father Liston was trained. See also feature articles, 'The Moods They Remember', *AS*, 9 July 1976, p. 6; 'Tremble? Yes. Falter? No', *NZH*, 9 July 1976, p. 6.

2   Editorial, 'A Great Leader', *Tablet*, 14 July 1976, p. 2. *Zealandia* issues of 18 and 25 July 1976, and *Tablet* of 14 and 21 July 1976 contain much retrospective material on Liston.

3   Erik Olssen, *John A. Lee* (Dunedin, 1977), p. 52, p. 204 and pp 175 ff. Barry Gustafson, *From the Cradle to the Grave – A Biography of Michael Joseph Savage* (Auckland, 1986), p. 122, pp 212 ff and p. 272. However, Liston does not rate a mention in biographies of other eminent Labour Party figures such as his contemporaries Walter Nash and Peter Fraser, perhaps because they were not so grounded in Auckland. See Keith Sinclair, *Walter Nash* (Auckland, 1976); and Michael Bassett and Michael King, *Tomorrow Comes the Song – A Life of Peter Fraser* (Auckland, 2000).

4   See Carolyn Moynihan, *A Stand for Decency – Patricia Bartlett and the Society for the Promotion of Community Standards* (Auckland, 1995), p. 21; Margaret Lovell-Smith (with Luisa Shannahan), *The Enigma of Sister Mary Leo* (Auckland, 1998); K.J. Walsh, *Yesterday's Seminary – A History of St Patrick's Manly* (Sydney, 1998), p. 116; Diane Strevens, *In Step With Time – A History of the Sisters of St Joseph of Nazareth, Wanganui, New Zealand* (Auckland, 2001), p. 109 and p. 124; Rory Sweetman, *Faith and Fraternalism – A History of the Hibernian Society in New Zealand 1869–2000* (Dunedin, 2002); Rory Sweetman, *'A Fair and Just Solution?'* *– A History of the Integration of Private Schools in New Zealand* (Palmerston North, 2002).

5   Peter Joseph Norris, *Southernmost Seminary – The Story of Holy Cross College, Mosgiel (1900–97)* (Auckland, 1999), pp 22–24.

6   Michael Belgrave, *The Mater – A History of Auckland's Mercy Hospital 1900–2000* (Palmerston North, 2000). For Liston's involvement, see especially pp 51 ff, pp 66–68, p. 76, pp 84 ff and pp 118–120.

7   Nicholas Evan Reid, *The Bishop's Paper – A History of the Catholic Press of the Diocese of Auckland* (Auckland, 2000). See, especially, chapters 3 and 4.

8   Michael O'Meeghan, *Steadfast in Hope – The Story of the Catholic Archdiocese of Wellington 1850–2000* (Wellington, 2003).

9   E.R. Simmons, *In Cruce Salus – A History of the Diocese of Auckland 1848–1980* (Auckland, 1982), p. 249.

10   Ibid., footnote, p. 268.

11   Ibid., p. 265.

12   Ibid., p. 239.

13   Ibid., p. 223 and p. 238.

14   See entry on Simmons in 'Deceased Priests', ACDA.

15   Felix Donnelly, *Big Boys Don't Cry* (Wellington, 1985) (reprint of book first published in 1978), p. 14.

16   Ibid., p. 117. Donnelly commits a factual error here. Liston tendered his resignation at the age of 89.

17   Felix Donnelly, *One Priest's Life* (Auckland, 1982), p. 104 and p. 107.

18   See anecdote, ibid., pp 15–16.

19   Ibid., p. 36.

20 Ibid., pp 45–46.
21 Ibid., p. 48.
22 Ibid., pp 93–101.
23 Ibid., p. 162. It is worth noting that Donnelly made a similar attack upon Liston's 'pride' within a fortnight of Liston's death, in a column which he wrote at that time for the *Auckland Star*'s Saturday supplement, the *8 O'clock*. (Comments quoted in Robert Gilmore's 'Give and Take' column, *AS*, 24 July 1976.)
24 Bradley was parish priest of Remuera from 1925 to 1959. See entry on Bradley in 'Deceased Priests', ACDA. In *One Priest's Life* (p. 33), Donnelly claims to have 'feared' him.
25 Felix Donnelly, *Father Forgive Them* (Auckland, 1990).
26 Thomas J. Ryder, *Following all Your Ways, Lord – Recollections of Fr Thomas J. Ryder* (transcribed and compiled by Margaret Paton) (privately published, no date), p. 51.
27 Ibid., p. 53.
28 Ibid., p. 57 and p. 60.
29 Ibid., p. 61.
30 Ibid., pp 70 ff.
31 Ibid., p. 101.
32 Michael King, *God's Farthest Outpost – A History of Catholics in New Zealand* (Auckland, 1997), p. 170.
33 Michael King, *Whina – A Biography of Whina Cooper* (Auckland, 1991) (originally published in 1983), p. 143.
34 Ibid., p. 151.
35 Ibid., p. 161 and p. 193.
36 Ibid., p. 169.
37 Ibid., p. 194.
38 Patricia Brooks, *By the Name of Mary – Tauranga Catholic Church 1840–2000* (published by the author, 2000), esp. pp 73–74.
39 Rory Sweetman, *Bishop in the Dock – The Sedition Trial of James Liston* (Auckland, 1997).
40 Rory Sweetman, entry on James Michael Liston, *DNZB*, Vol. 4 (1998), pp 288–289.
41 See Allan K. Davidson and Peter J. Lineham (eds), *Christianity Transplanted* (Auckland, 1987), pp 262–263; Allan Davidson, *Christianity in Aotearoa – A History of Church and Society in New Zealand* (Wellington, 1991), p. 90. See also David McGill, *The Lion and the Wolfhound – The Irish Rebellion on the New Zealand Goldfields* (Wellington, 1990), p. 151; Tim Pat Coogan, *Wherever Green is Worn – The Story of the Irish Diaspora* (London, 2000), p. 494 (Coogan's main source of information was apparently Sweetman's *Bishop in the Dock*, which he erroneously cites as *Bishop in the Dark*).
42 James Belich, *Paradise Reforged – A History of the New Zealanders* (Auckland, 2001), p. 114; Michael King, *The Penguin History of New Zealand* (Auckland, 2003), p. 316.
43 B.A. Santamaria, *Daniel Mannix – The Quality of Leadership* (Melbourne, 1984), chapter 8, 'Arrest on the High Seas'; Patrick O'Farrell, *The Irish in Australia* (revised edition, Sydney, 1993), p. 282.
44 T.B. Boland, *James Duhig* (Brisbane, 1986), especially chapter 8, 'Archbishop in War and Peace'.
45 Jeff Kildea, *Tearing the Fabric – Sectarianism in Australia 1910–1925* (Sydney, 2002).

Chapter I: Young Liston, 1881–1904

1 *Month*, 15 June 1922 (issue giving full account of Liston's trial, and acquittal, on charges of sedition), p. 6.
2 Ibid., p. 12. Liston's testimony regarding his family's origins was also reported, although in less detail, in the article 'Trial of Bishop Liston – Prosecution Opens', *Tablet*, 18 May 1922, pp 22–24.
3 National Archives, Wellington, death certificate James Liston (died 25 August 1900), call number 1818; death certificate Mary Liston (née Sullivan) (died 14 July 1902), call number 1951.

4   Obituary of James Liston, *Tablet,* 30 August 1900, p. 18; obituary of Mary Liston, *Tablet,* 17 July 1902, p. 19.

5   Birth certificate of James Michael Liston, ANZ.

6   *Tablet* obituary.

7   Letter, private communication, Basil Minihane to Nicholas Reid, 28 July 2003.

8   Letter, Terence Liston to Liston, 1 December 1927. CLE 129–3, ACDA.

9   See entries for 20 June and 20 July 1926 in Liston's 1926 appointment diary. LIS 15, ACDA.

10   Letter, Liston to Mother Helen Lynch, 28 October 1935. In A183 Fr John Flanagan Papers (Folder 6), ACDA.

11   Letter, Bishop John O'Hara to Liston, 8 May 1943. LIS 111–3, ACDA.

12   News item, 'U.S. Cousin's Gift – Plaque for Archbishop', *Zealandia*, 1 December 1966, p. 7.

13   Letter, Sr K. Liston to Liston, 30 April 1970. LIS 12–3, ACDA.

14   Lyndon Fraser, 'Irish Migration to the West Coast, 1864–1900' (in Lyndon Fraser, ed., *A Distant Shore – Irish Migration and New Zealand Settlement,* Dunedin, 2000), p. 92.

15   Rory Sweetman, *Bishop in the Dock*, Auckland, 1997, p. 94.

16   Letter, Liston to Bishop Henry William Cleary, 19 March 1919. CLE 84, ACDA.

17   On the Famine Irish who mainly went to America, see Patrick O'Farrell, *England and Ireland Since 1800*, Oxford, 1975, p. 29.

18   See precise figures, Donald Harman Akenson, *Half the World From Home – Perspectives on the Irish in New Zealand*, Wellington, 1990, p. 12.

19   Ciaran O'Carroll, 'The Pastoral Politics of Paul Cullen' (in James Kelly and Daire Keogh, eds, *History of the Catholic Diocese of Dublin*, Dublin, 2000), p. 302 and p. 308. The cholera outbreak would have occurred after Liston's father had emigrated.

20   See, for example, comments on the lower social status of Catholics in Dunedin diocese, Carmel A. Walsh, 'Michael Verdon 1838–1918, Second Bishop of Dunedin and Founder of Holy Cross College, Mosgiel, New Zealand', MTheol. thesis, Melbourne College of Divinity, 1994, pp 60–61.

21   The phrase comes from Akenson, *Half the World From Home*, p. 14. On New Zealand government attempts to limit Irish immigration, see also chapter 2 of Richard P. Davis, *Irish Issues in New Zealand Politics 1868–1922*, Dunedin, 1974, especially pp 24–32; and James Belich, *Making Peoples*, Auckland, 1996, p. 316.

22   See Donald Harman Akenson, 'No Petty People – Pakeha History and Historiography of the Irish Diaspora' (in Fraser, ed., *A Distant Shore*), p. 21.

23   See Patrick O'Farrell, *The Irish in Australia*, revised ed., Sydney, 1993, pp 61 ff.

24   Sweetman, *Bishop in the Dock*, pp 92–93.

25   Akenson, *Half the World From Home*, p. 24, for statistics on the long-term impact of immigration in the Vogel years.

26   Ibid., p. 43 and p. 47.

27   Ibid., p. 66.

28   Lyndon Fraser, 'Irish Migration to the West Coast 1864–1900', *NZJH*, 34, (2), October 2000, pp 203–205.

29   Akenson, *Half the World From Home,* p. 79.

30   News item, 'Right Rev. Dr Liston's Arrival in Auckland', *Tablet,* 30 December 1920, pp 21–23.

31   Details of the career of Fr Michael Walsh (1845–1910) may be found in Deceased Priests File, DCDA. Walsh was a Maynooth graduate who had a long career in Dunedin diocese, mainly in Invercargill and Southland.

32   See tribute to Mgr William Henry Mahoney (1857–1925), the first New Zealand-born priest, who had been serving as vicar-general of Auckland diocese, *Tablet*, 16 February 1922, p. 23.

33   See Patrick O'Farrell, *Vanished Kingdoms – The Irish in Australia and New Zealand*, Sydney, 1990, pp 221 ff.

34   *Zealandia*, 7 November 1935, p. 4, reports Liston's visit to Poynton's birthplace in the parish of Ballivor, County Meath. He unveiled a memorial to Poynton there in 1954 (see *Tablet*, 29 September 1954, p. 11) and was happy to show Poynton's personal Bible to visitors as a prized possession (see *Zealandia*, 13 January 1966, p. 7).

35   As evidence of his later readiness to identify with general 'Christian' values of New

Zealanders, see his sermon on the occasion of Otago's Catholic centenary, reported in *Zealandia*, 8 April, and *Tablet*, 14 April 1948.

36   See David McGill, *The Lion and the Wolfhound*, Wellington, 1990.

37   On 1 January 1975, John Sullivan wrote to Liston on the death of his father Michael Joseph Sullivan 'who treasured so much your long-standing and constant friendship'. LIS 7–3/1, ACDA.

38   Fr Aimé Martin SM was 'born in the Lower Alps, France, but . . . was to spend 45 years in New Zealand, 35 of them as parish priest of Hokitika' (Neil Vaney, 'The Dual Tradition – Irish Catholics and French Priests in New Zealand – the West Coast Experience, 1865–1910', MA thesis, University of Canterbury, 1976, p. 156).

39   Marriage Certificate, ANZ. The witnesses to the marriage, Michael and Margaret Houlihan, are also identified as 'brewers'.

40   In a handwritten autobiographical note, which appears to be instructions for a sacerdotal diamond jubilee article to be written by the journalist Brian Healy for *Zealandia* in 1964, Archbishop Liston says his parents' 'first born died as a babe' (Historical File, ACDA).

41   Baptismal certificates provided by Christchurch Catholic Diocesan Archives.

42   This advertisement ran in the *Tablet* through most of 1881, e.g. issues of 17 June, 22 July etc.

43   The date given on his baptismal certificate is 2 June 1881 (DCDA), as it is on his gravestone. It is also '2 June' in the news report introducing the new coadjutor-bishop to Auckland, *Month*, 13 December 1920, p. 19; in the official programme for his vigil mass of requiem at St Patrick's Cathedral, Auckland, 11 July 1976.

44   Unsigned article, 'The Pastor Who Loved and Served his People', *Zealandia*, 18 July 1976. When Liston wrote to the registrar of births asking for his birth certificate in 1951, he said he was born 'June 2 (or 9) 1881', Letter, 11 July 1951, Liston to registrar. LIS 166, ACDA. His birthday was given as 2 June 1881 when he was enrolled at St Patrick's, Manly. 'St Patrick's Ecclesiastical College, Manly – Register' (entry provided by Kevin Walsh).

45   See Bernard Cadogan, 'The Bar-Room Church of Early Dunedin', *Tablet*, 13 March 1985, p. 9. See also reference to Fr Seon saying mass in the Royal Hotel in Christchurch, B.S. Allom, 'Bishop Grimes: His Context and Contribution to the Catholic Church in Canterbury', MA thesis, University of Canterbury, 1968, p. 18.

46   Letter, M.J. Sullivan to Liston, 9 May 1973. LIS 7–1, ACDA.

47   For a pious account of the life of Moreau, see Mary Catherine Goulter, *Sons of France – A Forgotten Influence on New Zealand History*, Wellington, 1957, chapter 5.

48   For historical details on St Joseph's, see John Broadbent's lecture, 'Catholicism', in *The Farthest Jerusalem – Four Lectures on the Origins of Christianity in Otago*, Dunedin, 1993; also notes on cathedral, 'Information About Priests', DCDA.

49   Liston confirmed these details in many retrospective articles over the years, including his 1964 autobiographical note (Historical File, ACDA). See also Liston's reply to a farewell function, *Tablet*, 15 July 1922, pp 22–23. The phrase about his 'receiving the call' in St Joseph's comes from an article celebrating his 25th sacerdotal anniversary, *Month*, 19 February 1929, p. 17.

50   See 1964 note, Historical File, ACDA.

51   Liston's Pontificio Collegio Irlandese Memories (note written in August 1975), in LIS 14–3, ACDA.

52   Letter to the Apostolic Delegate, signed by Archbishops Redwood and O'Shea and Bishops Cleary and Brodie, dated 5 March 1919, included in documents relating to *Relazione* on choice of a bishop for Dunedin. CEP Nuova Serie 1921 160 707, Archives of Propaganda Fide, Rome. The letter is in French, the original description of Liston's parents being 'parents Irlandais Catholiques qui menèrent une vie sainte; c'étaient des colonnes de l'Église, et un bon exemple pour tout le monde . . . très-connus des Évêques'.

53   Handwritten note from Liston to Bishop Delargey, dated 25 September 1970. Included in Historical File 1969–70, ACDA.

54   Obituary, *Tablet*, 17 July 1902, p. 19.

55   His career has much in common with a slightly later generation of Irish-Catholic Dunedin publicans who began as country licensees but ended up proprietors of salubrious city pubs. See Bernard Francis Cadogan, 'Lace Curtain Catholics – The

Catholic Bourgeoisie of the Diocese of Dunedin 1902–1920', BA Honours dissertation, University of Otago, 1984, pp 21–22.

56   The will of James Liston is dated 29 March 1900. ANZ, Dunedin.

57   The will of Mary Liston is dated 21 June 1902. ANZ, Dunedin.

58   Patrick O'Farrell, 'Varieties of New Zealand Irishness – A Meditation' (in Fraser, ed., *A Distant Shore*), p. 34.

59   Erik Olssen, *A History of Otago*, Dunedin, 1984, p. 40 and p. 56.

60   Figures quoted from Appendix B of Hugh Laracy, 'The Life and Context of Bishop Patrick Moran', MA thesis, Victoria University of Wellington, 1964.

61   For wry comment on the naming of this church, see *Christian Brothers' Educational Record*, Necrology, 1955, vol. Dublin, p. 309, where the naming of the Cromwell Church is called 'a dedication unique in annals ecclesiastical'. The naming of the church is also the subject of pointed comment in news items in the *Tablet*, 26 November 1907, p. 22; 19 March 1908, p. 24; and 22 April, 1909, where there is a three-column report of Bishop Verdon blessing and opening the church.

62   For details on the foundation of the Catholic diocese of Dunedin, see John Broadbent, 'Catholicism', in *The Farthest Jerusalem*. See also Lillian G. Keys, *Philip Viard – Bishop of Wellington*, Christchurch, 1968, p. 190 and pp 216–220.

63   Letter, Verdon to Archbishop William Walsh, 30 June 1897. Letter file in Walsh Papers 370/8 1897, DAA.

64   Ernest Simmons, *Pompallier, Prince of Bishops*, Auckland, 1984, p. 5, notes the vastness of Pompallier's original Pacific cure ('a sixth of the globe'); Felice Vaggioli noted that Auckland diocese was 'more than one third the size of Italy', *A Deserter's Adventures – The Autobiography of Dom Felice Vaggioli*, John Crockett trans., Dunedin, 2001, p. 15.

65   Laracy, 'The Life and Context of Bishop Patrick Moran', p. 113. Much of the information about Moran in the preceding paragraph is also drawn from Laracy.

66   Hugh Laracy, 'Paranoid Popery: Bishop Moran and Catholic Education in New Zealand', *NZJH*, 10 (1), April 1976. See also Vaney's characterisation of Moran, 'The Dual Tradition', p. 79.

67   Akenson, *Half the World From Home*, p. 176.

68   For one such challenge, see Ambrose Macaulay, *William Crolly – Archbishop of Armagh 1835–49*, Dublin, 1994, especially pp 11 ff, p. 233 and pp 237–38, which argue that evidence of a 'devotional revolution' is much exaggerated.

69   Charles R. Morris, *American Catholic – The Saints and Sinners Who Built America's Most Powerful Church*, New York, 1997, p. 40.

70   Ibid., p. 44. A traditional and admiring view of Cullen may be found in chapter 3 ('Cardinal Cullen, Founder of Holy Cross College') of Richard Sherry, *Holy Cross College, Clonliffe, Dublin – College History and Centenary Record 1859–1959*, Dublin, 1962.

71   This is the very unsympathetic judgement implied throughout Desmond Bowen, *Paul Cardinal Cullen and the Shaping of Modern Irish Catholicism*, Dublin, 1983. See especially Bowen's conclusion, pp 297–99.

72   O'Carroll, 'The Pastoral Politics of Paul Cullen', p. 297, p. 298, p. 300, p. 302 and p. 305 (for Cullen's repeated condemnations of Fenianism) and p. 304. Cullen was instrumental in defining the dogma of the Immaculate Conception in 1854.

73   For comments on Cullen's Australasian influence, see Sherry, *Holy Cross College, Clonliffe, Dublin*, p. 69; and Bowen, *Paul Cardinal Cullen*, p. 146 and p. 168. See also Akenson, *Half the World From Home*, p. 163. Because of his influence in Australia, Cullen is one of only two people who never lived in Australia to gain an entry in the *Australian Dictionary of Biography*.

74   There are major retrospective articles on Verdon's career in *Tablet*, 28 November 1918 (five days after Verdon's death); 'A Scholar Bishop' in *Tablet*, 24 March 1948, pp 12–13 (the Dunedin Catholic centennial issue); on opening of Verdon Memorial Chapel at Holy Cross College, Mosgiel, *Tablet*, 13 March 1963, pp 30–31. For Verdon's teaching career at Clonliffe, see also Sherry, *Holy Cross College, Clonliffe, Dublin*, pp 60 ff.

75   K.J. Walsh, *Yesterday's Seminary*, Sydney, 1998, p. 94.

76   Ibid., p. 106.

77   In a letter dated 8 March 1914, Verdon wrote to O'Riordan, the rector of the Irish

College in Rome, asking him for this reason to intercede on his behalf with the Congregation, seeking this privilege for a Dunedin convent. O'Riordan Papers, Box 15, ICR.

78 Sherry, *Holy Cross College, Clonliffe, Dublin*, p. 38.
79 O'Carroll, 'The Pastoral Politics of Paul Cullen', p. 302.
80 Bowen, *Paul Cardinal Cullen*, p. 163.
81 Deirdre McMahon, 'John Charles McQuaid, Archbishop of Dublin, 1940–72' (in Kelly and Keogh, eds, *History of the Catholic Diocese of Dublin*), p. 366.
82 Father Edward Lynch, 'Most Rev. James Liston D.D.' (in Rev B. Mannes, ed., *Golden Jubilee – Holy Cross College, Mosgiel, New Zealand 1900–1950*, Dunedin, 1949), p. 33. A modified version of this same article ran in *Zealandia*, 28 January 1954.
83 *Tablet*, 28 November 1918, pp 25–26.
84 Carmel Walsh, 'Michael Verdon 1838–1918', pp 189–195. The chapel at Mosgiel was designed by Commadore Leonardo with a carved altar by Aristide Leonari. See also pp 58–59 for Verdon's self-image as a *Roman* bishop.
85 Letter, Verdon to O'Riordan, 22 February 1906. O'Riordan Papers, Box 5, ICR.
86 For examples, see Liston's contribution, 'Bishop Verdon – Founder', pp 5–10, in Mannes, ed., *Golden Jubilee – Holy Cross College*. Also Liston's 'Michael, Bishop of Dunedin, An Appreciation', *Tablet*, 28 November 1918, pp 26–27; Liston's speech on the diamond jubilee of Mosgiel seminary, reported in *Tablet*, 21 September 1960, and *Zealandia*, 25 September 1960; Liston's sermon at the opening of the Verdon Memorial Chapel, reported in *Tablet*, 13 March 1963, and *Zealandia*, 14 March 1963.
87 Liston, 'Bishop Verdon – Founder' (in Mannes, ed., *Golden Jubilee – Holy Cross College*), p. 5. See also Sherry, *Holy Cross College, Clonliffe, Dublin*, p. 83. A photograph of Liston working at his desk next to the photograph of Verdon is reproduced in *Zealandia*, 30 January 1964, p. 18, and 18 July 1976, p. 7.
88 For further explorations of the concept of 'Romanita' and its impact on Australasian bishops, see John N. Moloney, *The Roman Mould of the Australian Catholic Church*, Melbourne, 1969, which concentrates on the formation of the Australian hierarchy in the pontificate of Pius IX.
89 Information on Christian Brothers from *To All Parts of the Kingdom (Christian Brothers in New Zealand 1876–2001)*. Sesquicentennial publication (no author or publisher given), p. 5.
90 'Christian Brothers' School Register 1885–1934', Hocken Library, Dunedin.
91 J.C. O'Neill, 'The History of the Work of the Christian Brothers in New Zealand', Dip. Ed. thesis, Auckland, 1968, p. 36.
92 Unsigned article, 'The pastor who loved and served his people', *Zealandia*, 18 July 1976.
93 Details on Hanrahan taken from *Christian Brothers' Educational Record*, Necrology, pp 313–315.
94 The term was used, with only a little irony, by Father Pat Crawford, grand-nephew of Michael Hanrahan (interview, 27 November 2001). He also used the term in his interview with Peter Norris, *Southernmost Seminary*, Auckland, 1999, pp 22–23. He advances the view that the Christian Brothers were determined to get one of these two talented pupils as a member of their order, and 'kidnapped' Hanrahan in retaliation for Liston's being recruited to the priesthood.
95 See, for example, *Tablet*, 9 February 1927, p. 35, where Liston briefly recalls his own schooldays at the opening of the Christian Brothers' College 'Redcastle' in Oamaru; Liston's address on the centennial of the death of Edmund Rice, founder of the Christian Brothers, *Zealandia*, 24 August 1939, p. 15; report of Liston blessing an outdoor crucifix at the Christian Brothers' St Paul's High School as part of his sacerdotal diamond jubilee, *Tablet*, 26 February 1964, p. 38. Also Liston's celebrating mass for the newly-formed Christian Brothers' Old Boys' Association, *Tablet*, 27 May 1920, p. 28, and 3 June 1920, p. 27. The association had recently congratulated him on his recently having been appointed coadjutor-bishop of Auckland, *Tablet*, 6 May 1920, p. 27.
96 Mentioned *Tablet*, 26 February 1964, p. 34 and p. 38. By 1968, 70 old boys of the school had been ordained priests. J.C. O'Neill, 'The History of the Work of the Christian Brothers', p. 39. See also photos of ordained old boys of the school, *Tablet*,

31 March 1943, p. 5, and 29 October 1947, p. 5.

97   Unsigned article, 'Archbishop Liston's Sixty Years of Faith and Service', *NZH*, 29 January 1964.

98   Unsigned article, 'Catholic Bishop Resigns From See of Auckland', *NZH*, 8 April 1970.

99   Interview article by Allan Cole, 'Misuse of Alcohol Serious Problem', *NZH*, 28 April 1970, p. 6.

100 Lynch is specifically mentioned by Liston in interview, *NZH*, 28 April 1970.

101 See, for example, biographical outline in Deceased Priests File, DCDA.

102 Ibid. The material on Lynch in DCDA derives mainly from articles in *Tablet*, 20 October 1882, p. 17; 4 March 1898, p. 18; and 19 October 1927, pp 30–31.

103 Carmel Walsh, 'Michael Verdon 1838–1918', pp 6–8.

104 Lynch also appears to have maintained a fatherly interest in Liston's career. In 1919, when Lynch was a Redemptorist stationed in Australia, he visited Holy Cross College in Mosgiel, of which Liston was then rector, and spoke to the junior students at Liston's request. File on Fr Patrick Maguire Lynch, DCDA.

105 Liston later recalled that before he went to Manly, he was sent by his mother 'to receive a blessing from [the Dominican superior] Mother Mary Agnes'. *Tablet*, 3 February 1971, p. 13.

106 K.J. Walsh, *Yesterday's Seminary,* pp 102–103.

107 For example, in his account of Bishop Verdon in Mannes, ed., *Golden Jubilee, Holy Cross College, Mosgiel*, Liston tells how Verdon sent him to Clonliffe, but simply does not mention that he would first have known Verdon as rector of Manly. A similar omission is evident in D.P. O'Neill, ed., *Mosgiel '75*, Dunedin, 1975.

108 See biographical detail on Whyte, *Tablet*, 1 January 1958, pp 1 ff.

109 K.J. Walsh, *Yesterday's Seminary,* p. 116.

110 Manly, 'Rector's Year Book', entry provided by Kevin Walsh.

111 Letter from Verdon to Murphy dated 4 February 1897, quoted K.J. Walsh, *Yesterday's Seminary,* p. 116.

112 See Carmel Walsh, 'Michael Verdon 1838–1918', pp 156–159; Sweetman, *Bishop in the Dock*, pp 99 ff; and Norris, *Southernmost Seminary*, pp 11–13.

113 See K.J. Walsh, *Yesterday's Seminary,* p. 116.

114 Letter, Verdon to Walsh, 30 June 1897. In Walsh Papers 370/8 1897, DAA.

115 Contemporary *Tablet* report, quoted in *Tablet,* 22 May 1968, p. 3.

116 Letter, Liston to St Mellary president, 23 February 1951. LIS 153–2, ACDA. In another letter, Liston said Lynch received a 'rapturous welcome' from the monks. Letter, Liston to Fr P.R. Mee, 19 August 1969. LIS 59–9, ACDA.

117 Information from enrolment register supplied by Clonliffe College archivist.

118 See Sherry, *Holy Cross College, Clonliffe, Dublin*, p. 98.

119 Letter, Liston to Fr McCarthy, rector of Clonliffe, November 1958. Reproduced Sherry, *Holy Cross College, Clonliffe, Dublin*, pp 97–98. Many of the teachers and students whom Liston mentions here he also recalls in a letter he wrote to Archbishop Walsh of Dublin at the time he was appointed coadjutor-bishop of Auckland. Letter, Liston to Walsh, 16 May 1920. Abp William Walsh Papers, Box 392 II, File 350/3, DAA.

120 'An Appreciation of the Late Monsignor O'Leary', *Tablet*, 7 December 1916, p. 30.

121 Sweetman, *Bishop in the Dock*, p. 100. The quotation (per Sweetman) is from a report on Liston from the (Sydney) *Catholic Press*, 30 March 1922.

122 'Late Archbishop Had Clare Connections', article in *Clare Champion*, 30 July 1976, p. 9. The article describes Liston as 'the son of East Clare emigrants' and makes extensive comparisons between his career and that of Bishop Fogarty of Killaloe.

123 Letter, Fr Cornelius to Liston, 1 August 1959. LIS 127, ACDA.

124 Letter, Liston to Bishop Cleary, 19 March 1919. File CLE 84, ACDA.

125 Report of letter from Lynch, *Tablet,* 7 September 1899, p. 18.

126 See comments on the judgements of the Gaelic Athletic Association, Tim Pat Coogan, *Wherever Green is Worn*, London, 2000, p. 179.

127 Entry on Liston in 'Student Accounts – Holy Cross College, Dublin 1899–1900', DAA.

128 There is a report on his umpiring a match between diocesan priests and the Marist Brothers, *Month*, January 1932, p. 23.

129 See interview, *NZH*, 28 April 1970, p. 6.
130 The Irish College did not move to its present site near St John Lateran until 1926. See *The Irish College, Rome*, Irish Heritage Series pamphlet no. 64, Dublin, 1989.
131 Information on entrants from (1901 document) 'Entrance of Students', Kelly File 1901, ICR. Italics in the original.
132 This information is taken from chapter 3 of T.B. Boland, *James Duhig*, Brisbane, 1986. Duhig was a student at the Irish College in the 1890s, leaving in 1896.
133 Ibid., p. 45.
134 The Irish College Roll Book, ICR.
135 Further information on Curran is found in Sean T. O'Ceallaigh, 'The Late Rt Rev Mgr M.J. Curran', in *Reportorium Novum – Dublin Diocesan Historical Record*, 3 (1), Dublin, 1962. O'Ceallaigh emphasises Curran's Irish patriotism and support for Sinn Fein at the time of the Irish War of Independence, and notes that he was in Sydney in 1928 with Cardinal Cerretti for the Eucharistic Congress. Liston also attended.
136 James Michael Liston, 'Pontificio Collegio Irlandese Memories' (written 1975). LIS 14–3, ACDA. Years after their first acquaintance, Liston was to say a requiem mass for Kelly, *Tablet*, 20 March 1940, p. 33.
137 Results recorded in 'Esam.1901–1903' (record of examination results), Collegio Urbano archives, Rome.
138 Letter dated 4 December 1919, signed by Archbishops Redwood and O'Shea, and Bishops Cleary and Brodie, in *Relazione*, Archives of Propaganda Fide, Rome.
139 Letter, Verdon to William Murphy, 9 May 1902. Murphy File 1901–06, ICR.
140 Irish College Roll Book.
141 The outbreak is discussed in a letter from Archbishop William Walsh of Dublin to the rector, Murphy, 28 December 1902. Murphy File 1901–06, ICR.
142 Liston, 'Pontificio Collegio Irlandese Memories'.
143 Letter from Liston to Monsignor Eamonn Marron (rector of the Irish College) dated 15 January 1975. Marran Papers 1976 (box not numbered), ICR. For further material on New Zealand interest in the 'cause' of Oliver Plunkett, see the photographic supplement relating to St Plunkett's beatification (on 23 May 1920) in *Tablet*, 16 December 1920.
144 Liston's 1964 autobiographical note (Historical File, ACDA).
145 *Zealandia*, 5 December 1935, p. 6.
146 Liston's 1964 autobiographical note (Historical File, ACDA).
147 Boland, *James Duhig*, p. 146.
148 Their (brief) death notices appeared in the *Otago Daily Times*, 25 August 1900, p. 6, and 15 July 1902, p. 4. Information on causes of death are in their death certificates (ANZ, Wellington). Information of their funerals in the fuller obituaries that appeared in the *Tablet*.
149 Liston, 'Collegio Pontificio Irlandese Memories'.
150 Cadogan, 'Lace Curtain Catholics', p. 32.
151 Letter from Liston to Dr Murphy, 21 December 1903. Murphy File 1901–06, ICR.
152 Will of Mary Liston, ANZ, Dunedin.
153 Interview article, *NZH*, 28 April 1970, p. 6.
154 See chapter 11, Ernest Simmons, *Pompallier, Prince of Bishops*.
155 'On the Requisites for Ordination to the Priesthood', Book 3, Part 1, Article 1, *Code of Canon Law*, 1917.
156 Irish College Roll Book.
157 Propaganda granted Verdon the appropriate faculties just before Liston returned to Dunedin. This is mentioned in Liston's letter to Murphy, 21 December 1903. Murphy File 1901–06, ICR.
158 Cleary's diary for 1904 (written in Italian) is included in CLE 6, ACDA. Pleasure excursions with Liston and others are recorded on 2, 13 and 21 January 1904.
159 *Tablet*, 4 February 1904, p. 19.
160 Liston to Murphy, 9 May 1904. Murphy File 1901–06, ICR.

Chapter II: Father Liston, 1904–1920

1   Cadogan, 'Lace Curtain Catholics', p. 5.
2   Figures per Bishop Verdon's hand-written 'Relatio Status Diocesis Dunedinensis in Nova Zelandia' (1908), included in Bishop Verdon Box, DCDA.
3   Carmel Walsh, 'Michael Verdon', p. 88.
4   See Ernest Simmons, *Pompallier, Prince of Bishops*, pp 127 ff.
5   Carl Telford, *'In Their Descendants Remains a Rich Inheritance' – The Centenary of Mount St Mary's, Greenmeadows*, Wellington, 1990, pp 4–5. See also Michael O'Meeghan, *Steadfast in Hope*, Wellington, 2003, pp 132–133.
6   A general account of the foundation of the seminary may be found in *Tablet*, 6 March 1963, p. 4, 'Bishop Verdon Returns to Mosgiel'; also article by Archbishop Liston, 'In the Steps of the High Priest', *Zealandia*, 17 November 1974.
7   Programme of Holy Cross Jubilee Concert, 1950, included in Holy Cross College Boxes, DCDA.
8   Fullest details on property and land purchase are found in a Memorandum from Owen Toomey to Bishop Leonard Boyle, 31 January 1997; the report 'Canonical Status of Holy Cross College' by David Price, 25 April 1997; and the account 'Holy Cross College – Mosgiel, Land and Buildings', by Monsignor F.D. O'Dea, October 1986. All in Holy Cross College Boxes, DCDA.
9   See Norris, *Southernmost Seminary*, chapter 2. Vincentians did eventually staff the college from 1934.
10   Letter, Verdon to Murphy, 28 August 1901. Murphy File 1901–06, ICR.
11   Letter, Verdon to Murphy, 9 May 1902. Murphy File 1901–06, ICR.
12   Letter, Verdon to O'Riordan, 3 June 1906. O'Riordan Papers, Box 5 (October 1905–August 1906), ICR.
13   An original roll of 11 students is the figure given in *Zealandia*, 2 March 1950, p. 9, 'Fifty Years of Holy Cross College, Mosgiel'; Verdon mentions 18 students in his letter to Murphy at the Irish College, 28 August 1901; and *Tablet*, 22 February 1906, p. 19, speaks of 25 students enrolling for the new year.
14   Carmel Walsh, 'Michael Verdon', pp 116–122. Also Norris, *Southernmost Seminary*, pp 19–20. Ryan died in 1906 after having spent some time as parish priest of Queenstown. *Tablet*, 4 October 1906, Obituary, p. 23.
15   Carmel Walsh, 'Michael Verdon', p. 122; see also Liston, 'Bishop Verdon – Founder', in Mannes, ed., *Golden Jubilee*.
16   *Tablet*, 4 February 1904, p. 19.
17   Letter, Liston to Murphy, 21 December 1903. Murphy File 1901–06, ICR.
18   *Tablet*, 10 May 1906, includes a photographic supplement on extensions to Holy Cross. It includes a photograph of Verdon with the teaching staff (Delaney, Liston, Michael Ryan and Buckley). Interestingly, Delaney is identified as rector. Kavanagh's arrival is noted in Michael Scanlan's article, 'Early Memories of Holy Cross College', in Mannes, ed., *Golden Jubilee*, p. 24.
19   Scanlan, 'Early Memories', p. 21.
20   Verdon's Holy Cross notes for 1906. In Holy Cross College Box, DCDA.
21   Scanlan, 'Early Memories', especially p. 17 and pp 21–22.
22   Scanlan, *Early Memories*, p. 16 and pp 19–20. Father John Pound, in his article 'Sport and Entertainment Through the Years', in Mannes, ed., *Golden Jubilee*, says that cricket had only a brief vogue, p. 141.
23   Father Edmund Lynch, 'Most Rev. James Liston D.D.', in Mannes, ed., *Golden Jubilee*, pp 36–37. This description (or at least part of it) is quoted in the unsigned *Auckland Star* article, 'The Moods They Remember', 9 July 1976; by 'Pippa' (Eileen Duggan) in *Tablet*, 31 January 1968, p. 14; in Sweetman, *Bishop in the Dock*, p. 101; in Sweetman's *DNZB* entry on Liston; and in Norris, *Southernmost Seminary*, p. 21.
24   Ibid., p. 39.
25   *Tablet*, 31 March 1954, p. 32.
26   *NZH*, 28 April 1970, interview, p. 6.
27   Brian Healy, 'An Interview with Archbishop Liston – Sixty Years in the Priesthood', *Zealandia*, 30 January 1964.
28   In a letter to Brodie in 1921 (by which time they were both bishops), Liston said, 'I

was thinking of you all the way from Paeroa and recalling the drive you and I made together over the same road in January 1905'. Letter dated 11 March 1921, Brodie Papers, Box 12 A, CCDA.

29   Letter, Coffey to Cleary, 26 February 1918. CLE 84–1, ACDA.

30   For reports on St Patrick's celebrations involving Liston, see, for example, *Tablet*, 31 March 1904, p. 19; 23 March 1905, p. 19; 24 March 1910; 21 March 1918, p. 28.

31   For the involvement of Liston and other Holy Cross staff and students in Holy Week ceremonies, see, for example, *Tablet*, 7 April 1904, p. 18; 10 April 1906, p. 19; 4 April 1907, p. 32; 15 April 1909; 31 March 1910; 20 April 1911; 11 April 1912, p. 35; 29 March 1917, p. 35; 12 April 1917, p. 36; 4 April 1918, p. 27.

32   For sisters' reception ceremonies (at which Liston was present), see, for example, *Tablet*, 11 January 1906, p. 19; 9 July 1908, p. 22; 29 December 1910; 22 June 1911; 1 April 1915, p. 34.

33   *Tablet*, 21 December 1911; 27 January 1916, p. 23; 17 October 1918, p. 28.

34   Noreen Pearce, *The Catholic Parish of Mosgiel 1900–2000*, Mosgiel, 2000, p. 3.

35   *Tablet*, 8 November 1906, reports Liston making a presentation to a parish choir member on the occasion of her approaching marriage; *Tablet*, 22 April 1920, p. 28, has Liston as one of the people making farewell speeches at a function for a departing parishioner; *Tablet*, 30 October 1919, p. 27, reports Liston granting the use of college grounds for the parish fete.

36   1964 autobiographical note (Clippings File, ACDA).

37   Brian Healy's interview article, 'Sixty Years in the Priesthood', *Zealandia*, 30 January 1964.

38   See *Tablet*, 17 November 1937, pp 1–2 and 24–25. See also *Zealandia*, 25 November 1937, p. 5.

39   *Tablet*, 29 April 1920, p. 23; *Tablet*, 8 July 1920, p. 28.

40   *Tablet*, 8 July 1920, p. 28.

41   Diocesan Reports on Parishes, 1908–1916, DCDA.

42   *Tablet*, 11 February 1909, simply noted that there had been 'a solemn requiem mass for the repose of the soul of the late Mr. J. Liston at the cathedral', and did not note his family relationship, even though James Michael was in the sanctuary. The memorial notice inserted in the *Tablet* by John's widow one year later gives no particulars of John's death. In his 1964 autobiographical note (Clippings File, ACDA), Archbishop Liston merely remarked that he had 'an older brother and sister, both dead', and gave no further particulars of them.

43   Death certificate of John Patrick Liston, ANZ, Wellington.

44   John Patrick's marriage to Catherine Lynch on 14 February 1903 is noted in the file, 'Catholic Marriages in NZ Tablet', DCDA. DCDA has baptismal records of Margaret Mary (b. 1904); Patrititia Johanna (b. 1905); Catherine Josephine (b. 1906); Eileen (b. 1907); and Florence Agnes (b. 1909). Florence Agnes may have died in infancy as there is no mention of her in later correspondence relating to Catherine (née Lynch)'s daughters.

45   The widow Catherine Liston's marriage to John Boyle, on 25 November 1911, is noted in 'Catholic Marriages in NZ Tablet', DCDA. Apparently, the Boyles were for a long time in straightened financial circumstances. In the 1920s, James Michael Liston's former sister-in-law wrote to him a number of times (via her solicitor) seeking larger payments from John Liston's share of Mary Liston's estate, which Bishop Liston was administering. See correspondence between Liston and the firm of Callan and Gallaway, 1925–28, LIS 9–1, ACDA.

46   Those of Archbishop Liston's nieces who were still alive attended his funeral in 1976. See references to 'Miss E. Liston of Dunedin, Mrs. P. Sewell of Karori and Mrs. M. Wood of Milton', all of them John Liston's daughters, in article on Liston's funeral, *Zealandia*, 18 July 1976, p. 3. Eileen Liston's will (ANZ, Dunedin), dated 2 September 1987, shows her leaving her estate to church charities and to the families of her married sisters.

47   Letter, Liston to Cleary, 7 February 1909. CLE 86, ACDA.

48   *Tablet*, 28 December 1955, p. 23.

49   *Zealandia*, 7 September 1967, p. 12.

50   Allan Cole's interview article, 'Misuse of Alcohol Serious Problem', *NZH*, 28 April 1970, p. 6.

51 Comment on ordination of Holy Cross graduates found in Liston's 1964 autobiographical notes (Clippings File, ACDA). See also Liston's article, 'In the Steps of the High Priest', *Zealandia*, 7 November 1974.

52 Scanlan, 'Early Memories', in Mannes, ed., *Golden Jubilee*, p. 27.

53 See, for example, the golden anniversary article, 'Fifty Years of Holy Cross College, Mosgiel', *Zealandia*, 2 March 1950, p. 9, which assumes that Liston was the second rector after Verdon.

54 See *Tablet*, 3 February 1910, which says Ryan 'has been rector of Holy Cross College, Mosgiel, for three years'. Farewell articles for Ryan appeared in *Tablet*, 25 February and 17 March 1910, and the solemn requiem mass for him (said by Liston) was reported in *Tablet* on 26 December 1912. He is referred to as 'rector' in all cases.

55 The term 'president' is used of Verdon in the preface (page not numbered) of Mannes, ed., *Golden Jubilee*.

56 *Tablet*, 15 July 1920, pp 22–23. Coffey was speaking at a farewell function as Liston was leaving for Auckland.

57 Rev B. Courteney speaking at formal dinner on the college's diamond jubilee. *Zealandia*, 22 September 1960, front page.

58 Letter, Bishop Cleary to Fr James Coffey, 5 March 1918. In Holy Cross College Box, DCDA.

59 Letter, Cleary to Silk, 13 March 1918. In Holy Cross College Box, DCDA.

60 Letter, Liston to Silk, 14 March 1918. In Holy Cross College Box, DCDA.

61 The description comes from pp 114 ff, Father Francis Finlay, 'Some Reminiscences', in Mannes, ed., *Golden Jubilee*.

62 Information on courses taught is taken from Liston's report to the Bishop of Dunedin dated 30 June 1920. In Holy Cross College Box, DCDA.

63 Letter, Liston to Curran, 12 November 1920. In Curran Papers, Box 1 (1914–1926), ICR.

64 1954 speech included in Clippings File, ACDA.

65 Francis Finlay, 'The Young Fr. Liston', *Tablet*, 21 July 1976, p. 4.

66 Document dated 4 December 1919 in Nuova Serie 1921 160 707, archives of Propaganda Fide, Rome. The original is written in French and declares that Liston has acted 'avec un succès remarquable au point de vue spirituel et scholastique aussi bien qu'au point de vue financiel' and also that 'il a été pendant quelque temps directeur spirituel au séminaire provincial et il a rempli cet office avec grand succès'.

67 Apparently in Liston's time, about half the students came from Dunedin diocese, most of the rest being from Christchurch and Wellington. Auckland was very poorly represented. See Liston's report to Bishop Whyte, 30 June 1920. In Holy Cross College Box, DCDA.

68 James Maguire, 'Mosgiel of the Middle Ages – Random Recollections', in Mannes, ed., *Golden Jubilee*, p. 75.

69 Liston's report to Bishop Whyte, 30 June 1920. In Holy Cross College Box, DCDA.

70 See Scanlan, 'Early Memories', pp 27–31.

71 Maguire, 'Mosgiel of the Middle Ages', pp 78–79.

72 Letter, Vespa Miller to her friend Eileen Oswald, on the occasion of Liston's death, 12 July 1976. Letter deposited in LIS 6–5, ACDA.

73 The death of Yirrell is reported in *Tablet*, 15 August 1918, p. 28.

74 Letter, Liston to Whyte, 22 February 1921. Whyte Papers, DCDA.

75 Letter, Liston to Whyte, 10 May 1922. Whyte Papers, DCDA.

76 Letters, Boyd to Whyte, 12 January 1921; Whyte to Boyd, 1 February 1921. Holy Cross College Box, DCDA.

77 A copy of Father Martin's typewritten reminiscences was provided by Peter Norris, who gives his own summary of Martin's anecdote in *Southernmost Seminary*, p. 23.

78 Unpublished typescript, 'Memoirs of Bishop John Mackey' (written in 2001), p. 17, ACDA.

79 Letter, Fr D.V. Silk to Cleary, 19 May 1925. CLE 119–2, ACDA. Silk's letter criticises Liston for expelling Magill from Holy Cross, and then later (when he was coadjutor-bishop of Auckland) sending Magill back to Holy Cross, even though Bishop Cleary had made it clear that he could not find work for Magill in his diocese.

80 Anecdotes related by Bishop Leonard Boyle to Nicholas Reid, 28 August 2001. Similar anecdotes, about students watching out for the rector's absence as a signal for

a night's relaxation, were told about the rectorship of Bishop Verdon. See Scanlan, 'Early Memories', p. 14. Both stories probably reflect as much upon the schoolboy age of many of the students as upon the severity of the rector.

81   All quotations from pp 39–42 of Edmund Lynch, 'Most Rev. James Liston D.D.', in Mannes, ed., *Golden Jubilee.*

82   Letter, Liston to Cleary, 31 May 1920. CLE 84–1, ACDA.

83   Lynch, 'Most Rev. James Liston', p. 40.

84   Norris, *Southernmost Seminary*, p. 23.

85   Bishop John Mackey, 'The Vincentians and the Diocesan Clergy – A Working Partnership', in D.P. O'Neill, ed., *Mosgiel '75*, pp 23–24.

86   T. O'Brien's article on Cecil John Morkane in Mannes, ed., *Golden Jubilee*, p. 65.

87   See, for example, Liston's 1932 sermon in which seminarians (with Biblical authority) are characterised as the bishop's 'children'. *Tablet*, 16 November 1932, pp 1–2.

88   Figures given in Fr Nicholas Rossiter's article 'Transition', in Mannes, ed., *Golden Jubilee*, p. 83.

89   Francis Finlay, who arrived as a student at Holy Cross in 1915, later wrote, 'I remember that while I was there I was cold and hungry. Oh, how cold! and how hungry! Present day students can have no idea of what Spartan conditions existed in earlier times. I have never been so hungry or so cold before or since and I hope I never shall be'. 'Some Reminiscences', in Mannes, ed., *Golden Jubilee*, p. 108.

90   Carmel Walsh, 'Michael Verdon', p. 126.

91   *Tablet*, 17 July 1913, p. 31.

92   Articles 'A Much-Discussed Book', 'Doctrine of the Atonement', 'Statement of the Catholic Position', in *Tablet*, 27 August 1908, pp 11–12, and 3 September 1908, pp 10–11.

93   *Tablet*, 2 April 1914. Hugh Benson's review of the stage play, 'The Miracle – How It Impressed Mgr. Benson' (reprinted from the English *Tablet*) was printed opposite Liston's comment on the film ('The Cinematograph Presentation'), pp 23–24.

94   The series began in *Tablet*, 17 October 1912, p. 3.

95   See clippings from the *New Zealand Herald* of June 1903 concerning sectarian incidents in Auckland (included in LEN 6, ACDA). See also Michael O'Meeghan, *Held Firm by Faith – A History of the Catholic Diocese of Christchurch 1887–1987*, Christchurch, 1988, pp 202–203, for an account of the 'Temuka Tournament', a controversy between a Marist priest and a Presbyterian minister.

96   O'Meeghan, *Held Firm By Faith*, p. 257. See also Nicholas Anthony Simmons, 'Archbishop Francis Redwood – His Contribution to Catholicism in New Zealand', MA thesis, Massey University, 1981, pp 40–44, on reactions to *Ne Temere*. See also Akenson, *Half the World From Home*, pp 105–106, for an account of how *Ne Temere* influenced the social behaviour of some Catholics.

97   The Bible-in-Schools movement was supported by sizeable sections of the Anglican and Presbyterian churches, and by the Women's Christian Temperance Union and the Orange Lodge. But it was opposed by Baptists and Unitarians who, among other things, were afraid that the larger Protestant churches would dominate the smaller ones in the instruction proposed for state primary schools. Rev Howard Elliott, a Baptist, was the most reckless and vociferous anti-Catholic propagandist, but he opposed the Bible-in-Schools and supported the National Schools Defence League. See chapter 3 of D.V. MacDonald's thesis, 'The New Zealand Bible in Schools League', MA in Education thesis, Victoria University, 1964. See also Christopher van der Krogt's *DNZB* entry on Elliott. Bishop Cleary was the most indefatigable Catholic opponent of the Bible-in-Schools. See materials in CLE 178–1, ACDA. Of Cleary, O'Connor said, 'Dialectically he was a match for the whole of Knox College, and the newspaper controversies in which he demonstrated this would fill several volumes'. P.S. O'Connor, 'Sectarian Conflict in New Zealand, 1911–1920', *Political Science*, 19 (10), July 1967, p. 3.

98   Grigg argues that Prohibition demonstrated the failure of non-episcopalian Protestant churches to come to grips with necessary social reforms, and their predilection for a 'safe' issue of personal morality instead. He suggests this had something to do with the middle-class orientation of such churches, which had been steadily losing working-class support since the late nineteenth century, whereas 'the Roman Catholic Church drew on a much wider cross-section of the community than did any other

denomination . . . it had a particular appeal to the poorer classes, among whom alcohol was also thought to have a greater appeal'. See A.R. Grigg, 'Prohibition, the Church and Labour – A Programme for Social Reform, 1890–1914', *NZJH*,15 (2), October 1981. Elsewhere, Grigg argues that Prohibitionists grossly over-estimated the appeal of Prohibition to women. See A.R. Grigg, 'Prohibition and Women: The Preservation of an Ideal and a Myth', *NZJH*, 17 (2), October 1983. Archbishop Redwood and most of the Catholic hierarchy feared that Prohibition would limit access to altar wine. Redwood's strongly worded anti-Prohibition pastoral of 1919 is included in the Whyte Papers, DCDA. Of the hierarchy, Bishop Cleary alone supported Prohibition. Cleary's own pastoral of 1919 is included in CLE 77, ACDA.

99   For suspicions of Catholic favouritism in the civil service, see R.P. Davis, *Irish Issues*, Dunedin, 1974, p. 124. See also Michael Bassett, *Sir Joseph Ward*, Auckland, 1993, p. 117 and p. 200.

100 Only 20 per cent of declared Protestants were regular churchgoers, according to Grigg, 'Prohibition, the Church and Labour', pp 138–139. The dominance of the Reform Party, which most often articulated a 'Protestant' outlook, was based on the unrepresentative system of the 'country quota'. See W.J. Gardner, 'The Rise of W.F. Massey, 1891–1912', *Political Science*, 13 (1), March 1961, p. 23.

101 J. Dickson, *Shall Ritualism and Romanism Capture New Zealand? – Their Ramifications in Protestant Churches*, Dunedin, 1912.

102 See Michael Bassett, *Sir Joseph Ward*, chapter 14, for the declining fortunes of the Liberals. Gustafson notes in this connection that the Catholic church had more working-class adherents than other major denominations, and hence Labour held increasing attraction for Catholics. Barry Gustafson, *Labour's Path to Political Independence*, Auckland, 1980, p. 125.

103 *Tablet*, 20 March 1919, p. 11 and p. 13, reporting Liston's opening of the Catholic Federation conference on 5 March 1919, gives his words on the church's need to identify with 'the toiling masses'.

104 Waihi's Catholic priest, Matthew Brodie, made it clear that he did not support the 'scab' union that had been brought in to break the strike. 'The Church and Labour', *NZH*, 20 May 1912, p. 8, reports the Waihi sermons of Father Brodie and the Rev White. See also Gustafson, *Labour's Path to Political Independence*, p. 126.

105 Bishop Cleary told the Irish College rector of his good relations with the leaders of the strike. Letter, Cleary to O'Riordan, 6 January 1914. O'Riordan Box 15, ICR. He also sent a circular to his priests (dated 8 November 1913) telling them to remain neutral in the dispute. CLE 86–3, ACDA.

106 Bishop Cleary in 1913 interpreted the new Catholic Federation as a response to the Bible-in-Schools League. He produced an 'occasional letter' justifying its establishment entitled *Rights of Conscience in the School – A League of Attack; A Federation of Defence* (CLE 79, ACDA). P.S. O'Connor shared this view of the Catholic Federation's genesis in 'Sectarian Conflict in New Zealand, 1911–1920'. But O'Connor also called the Catholic Federation 'an extremely aggressive organization, much pointed to by the defenders of the later Protestant Political Association'. P.S. O'Connor, 'Storm Over the Clergy – New Zealand 1917', *Journal of Religious History*, 4 (2), December 1966, p. 132n. The militant New Zealand Protestant Defence Association as a stimulus to the formation of the Catholic Federation is mentioned in chapter 1 of Max Satchell, 'Pulpit Politics – the Protestant Political Association in Dunedin from 1917 to 1922', BA Hons. History dissertation, University of Otago, 1983. James Michael Liston was on the inaugural Dunedin diocesan council of the Catholic Federation in 1913 (see report in *Tablet*, 17 July 1913, p. 7). For the genesis of the PPA, see H.S. Moores, 'The Rise of the Protestant Political Association – Sectarianism in New Zealand Politics during World War One', MA History thesis, University of Auckland, 1966.

107 For martial language used in a controversial context, see report of Liston's address, 'The Duties of Catholic Laymen', *Tablet*, 20 March 1919, p. 11 and p. 13. See also editorial denouncing government policies and Bishop Whyte's reply to his formal welcome to Dunedin, *Tablet*,16 December 1920, p. 26 and pp 22–23.

108 This is the conclusion of Satchell's analysis of Dunedin membership of the PPA, 'Pulpit Politics', especially chapter 5. In a heavily Presbyterian city, the PPA's membership comprised Church of Christ people and Methodists more than Presbyterians and Baptists, even though Howard Elliott himself was (nominally) a Baptist. It is fair to

note, too, that despite having no love for Catholicism, other publicists of the Baptist church disowned Elliott when his reckless falsehoods became intolerable. In the October 1917 issue of *New Zealand Baptist*, Rev J.J. North, a veteran anti-Catholic polemicist, denounced Elliott. According to Gustafson (*Labour's Path to Political Independence*, p. 129), 'Elliott's religion by that time had become anti-Romanism and anti-Socialism rather than Christianity'.

109   Dickson, *Shall Ritualism and Romanism Capture New Zealand?* p. 139, written before the war, lauds the growing power of Protestant Germany. Such sentiments became embarrassing after 1914, especially as the editor of the *Tablet* took to taunting Protestant zealots over the Protestantism of Germany's leaders. For the duration, the portrait of Martin Luther was taken down from the walls of Knox College in Dunedin. See Ian Breward, *Grace and Truth – A History of the Theological Hall, Knox College 1876–1975*, Dunedin, 1975, p. 29.

110   Protestant fantasies of papal collusion in the German war effort are touched on in Hugh Laracy, 'Priests, People and Patriotism: New Zealand Catholics and War, 1914–1918', *Australasian Catholic Record*, 70 (1), January 1993, p. 16. For an account of the Vatican's diplomatic position in the war, see also Jerome aan de Wiel, 'Monsignor O'Riordan, Bishop O'Dwyer and the Shaping of New Relations Between Nationalist Ireland and the Vatican During World War One', *Archivium Hibernicum – Irish Historical Records*, 53, 1999.

111   Generally speaking, the hope of expatriate Irish was for Home Rule within the British Empire. Home Rulers were the 'Irish Nationalists' who feted Bishop Lenihan on his visit to Liverpool in 1908 'for his services to the cause of Irish Nationalism', *Tablet*, 19 November 1909, p. 12. In chapter 4 of 'New Zealand Catholicism' (PhD History thesis, University of Cambridge, 1990), Rory Sweetman points to Henry William Cleary's temperate Home Rule position when he was editor of the *Tablet*, and notes his role in organising the tours of Irish Nationalist MPs. He interprets the high tide of Home Rule sentiment as 1913–14.

112   For Irish resistance to the introduction of conscription in Ireland, see Patrick Callan, 'Ambivalence Towards the Saxon Shilling: the Attitudes of the Catholic Church in Ireland Towards Enlistment During the First World War', *Archivium Hibernicum – Irish Historical Records*, 41, 1986. The most outspoken Irish bishop opposing enlistment was Bishop Edward O'Dwyer of Limerick. In some of his pastorals, he adopted a strictly neutralist attitude towards the world war, scrupulously in line with Benedict XV's position. See O'Dwyer's *Pastoral Letter to the Clergy and Laity of the Diocese of Limerick, for Quinquagesima Sunday 1917*, a copy of which is preserved in Mgr M. Curran – Political Papers, DAA.

113   The report of Coffey's sermon appeared under the heading 'Revolt in Dublin', *Tablet*, 4 May 1916, p. 25 and p. 27. The editorial appeared in the same issue, pp 29–31.

114   For example, it happily publicised such Irish heroism in the war effort as the achievement of Sergeant Michael O'Leary (of the Irish Guards) in winning the Victoria Cross. *Tablet*, 15 April 1915, pp 17–19.

115   Letter, Cleary to O'Riordan, 25 June 1916. O'Riordan Papers, Box 17, ICR. James Kelly expressed similar sentiments to Michael O'Connor, 27 June 1916, Hagan Papers, Box 6, ICR. Anger at British repressive policy was expressed by anonymous Catholics in New Zealand, too. In 1917, Bishop Cleary, who very publicly supported New Zealand's war effort, wrote a pamphlet on 'Prussian Militarism at Work', an exposé of German atrocities against civilians in Belgium and France. On the cover of one copy that was sent back to him, an anonymous hand has scrawled, 'Why not write something on England's atrocities in your native land, 1916?' Copy preserved in CLE 77, ACDA.

116   The fund is publicised in *Tablet*, 21 September 1916, p. 36. Liston's name (with a record of his £2 donation) appears seventh in the list of 100 subscribers. The fund was regularly reported in the *Tablet* for the rest of the year, and Liston made other contributions. In the Irish Affairs Box of DCDA, there is a notebook recording Donations for Irish Relief. *Tablet* donated £50, Bishop Verdon £20 and Liston (like five other diocesan priests) £5. After Verdon's death, a funeral panegyric praised him for having organised relief for Dublin after Easter Week, *Tablet*, 28 November 1918, p. 25.

117   J.A. Scott's resignation as editor, and a letter of appreciation for his editorship, appear in the *Tablet*, 9 November 1916.

118 *Tablet*, 8 March 1917, pp 13 ff. Kelly also regularly included anti-imperialist jibes such as 'What England Has Done for India', *Tablet*, 24 April 1919, pp 42–43, cataloguing the millions who had died of famine under British rule.

119 *Tablet*, 24 January 1918, p. 22. See also Cadogan, 'Lace Curtain Catholics', p. 69.

120 *Tablet*, 20 November 1919, pp 9 ff.

121 Information on *Green Ray* from Moores, 'Rise of PPA', pp 59 ff; Cadogan, 'Lace Curtain Catholics', p. 65; Gustafson, *Labour's Path to Political Independence*, pp 126–127; and Sean Brosnahan, 'Shaming the Shoneens', in Fraser, ed., *A Distant Shore*.

122 Cadogan, 'Lace Curtain Catholics', p. 58.

123 See chapter 9, 'New Zealand Labour and Irish Self-Determination', in Davis, *Irish Issues*.

124 It is significant that much of the 'evidence' of Catholic tyranny in Dickson's *Shall Ritualism and Romanism Capture New Zealand?* is taken from Belfast and Scottish sources, and the book ends by quoting 'Fenian' plans to overthrow the British government in Ireland. In other words, like much extreme Protestantism in New Zealand at that time, its parent is the Orange fear of losing ascendancy over Catholic Ireland.

125 Brosnahan, 'Shaming the Shoneens', p. 120.

126 O'Meeghan, *Held Firm by Faith*, p. 139. See also Laracy, 'Priests, People and Patriotism', p. 20.

127 *Evening Star* letters column, 9 August 1916. Other letters from Liston refuting Jenkin appeared in the *Evening Star*, 12, 16 and 21 August 1916. All letters were reproduced by *Tablet*, 10,17 and 24 August 1916 (Liston probably sent copies to both publications), and on 17 August 1916, *Tablet* made its own editorial criticisms of Jenkin's factuality (p. 17).

128 Liston's letter, 'Treatment of the Irish Question', *ODT* letters column, 31 March 1917, p. 4.

129 Liston's letters in *ODT* letters column, 23 November and 15 December 1917. Both letters were reprinted in *Tablet*, 29 November and 20 December 1917. The quotation from Dickie is cited in a letter by Liston's colleague at Holy Cross, Fr E.J. Lynch, refuting Dickie in *Tablet*, 6 December 1917, pp 11–12. Biographical details on Professor John Dickie, and his anti-Germanism, are found in Breward, *Grace and Truth*, pp 27–33; also in *DNZB* entry on Dickie by W. John Roxborough, which notes that Dickie did some theological study in Germany but he was 'a fierce patriot whose love of Germany soured'.

130 Letters by Liston and by Finlayson, 'Obvious', Griffith, Mulroy , 'Home Ruler' and 'Bonnie Play' included in the letters column of *ODT*, 25, 26, 27, 28, 29 June and 2, 5, 6, 8 July 1918.

131 Report, 'Special Protestant Service', *ODT*, 15 July 1918, p. 2.

132 O'Connor, 'Storm Over the Clergy', p. 130.

133 See *Tablet* editorial, 'A Just War', 27 August 1914.

134 See, for example, *Tablet*, 3 August 1916, p. 31, for requiem masses for soldiers in St Joseph's Cathedral.

135 Norris, *Southernmost Seminary*, pp 23–24.

136 *Tablet*, 8 February 1917, pp 23 ff, prints a Cleary letter from the front covering seven columns.

137 See McMenamin's letter to Liston, dated 11 July 1915, written from Gallipoli, where McMenamin says, 'I am writing this on my knee and the shells are screaming along overhead'. LIS 166, ACDA.

138 *Tablet*, 21 June 1917, p. 27.

139 Unsigned profile of Peter McKeefry in Mannes, ed., *Golden Jubilee*, pp 71–72.

140 Laracy, 'Priests, People and Patriotism', p. 15.

141 See Paul Baker, *King and Country Call – New Zealanders, Conscription and the Great War*, Auckland, 1988, p. 125, on the balloting of clergy. O'Meeghan, *Held Firm by Faith*, p. 257, mentions the balloting of Brodie.

142 Michael Bassett, *Sir Joseph Ward*, says that over the conscription of the teaching brothers, Ward 'for the first time in his political life . . . fought directly and publicly on behalf of his co-religionists', pp 229–230.

143 At this time, there were ten schools (only one of them post-primary) run by the Marist

brothers in New Zealand, who became a religious province separate from Australia only in 1917. At most, about 30 brothers would have been the right age for military service. See Brother John Paul Kane, 'The Marist Brothers in New Zealand Education 1917 to 1967', Dip. Ed. dissertation, Massey University, 1972, p. 2, pp 8–9 and p. 17.

144 The myth has gained a certain respectability. In *King and Country Call*, Baker comments that there was a 'lower Catholic rate of volunteering in New Zealand (12 per cent of volunteers but 17 per cent of conscripts)'. He seems unaware that the Catholic rate of volunteering (in fact 12.6 per cent) was, as Laracy remarks ('Priests, People and Patriotism', p. 20), 'only marginally below the part occupied by Catholics in the total population'. If 17 per cent of conscripts were Catholic, this reflects the more working-class nature of the Catholic church in New Zealand. Fewer Catholics were in reserved occupations. A formal enquiry in 1917 showed that of religious denominations, Baptists rather than Catholics were the most under-represented in the armed forces. See O'Connor, 'Religious Conflict in New Zealand 1911–1920', pp 9–10. The mythology of Catholic 'shirking' was believed by militant Protestants in other parts of the British Empire, too. The Irish College archives (O'Riordan Papers, Box 17, ICR) contain the 12 October 1916 issue of the *Canadian Freeman* in which Catholic correspondents in the *Ottawa Journal* had to answer charges that the war was a Jesuit conspiracy, Catholics were under-enlisting and so forth.

145 From the Presbyterian Knox College, 'even [John] Dickie was called up in 1918, but was rejected on his medical. A number of promising students were killed in action'. Breward, *Grace and Truth*, p. 32.

146 For general accounts of the Catholic part in these referenda, see Michael Hogan, *The Sectarian Strand – Religion in Australian History*, Melbourne, 1987, chapter 7; Patrick O'Farrell, *The Catholic Church and Community in Australia*, Brisbane, 1977, pp 324–325; and Edmund Campion, *Australian Catholics*, Sydney, 1988, pp 82–84.The Australian Catholic hierarchy had been neutral in the lead-up to the first referendum (August 1916), but Catholic lay and working-class opinion swung them more against conscription before the second referendum (November 1917).This is the general thesis of Michael McKernon, 'Catholics, Conscription and Archbishop Mannix', *Historical Studies*, University of Melbourne, 17 (68), April 1977. In 'Religion, Race and Conscription in World War I' *(Australian Journal of Politics and History*, University of Queensland Press, 20 [2], August 1974), D.J. Murphy argues that the Australian Labor Party and the Catholic church became more firmly joined over the conscription debate because of the attacks made upon them by Protestant imperialists. Before the first conscription referendum, W.M. 'Billy' Hughes had sought allies in the Catholic church, but after it, he ran a noisily anti-Catholic sectarian campaign. This general overview is endorsed by B.A. Santamaria in *Daniel Mannix*, Melbourne, 1984, chapter 6. See too Jeff Kildea, *Tearing the Fabric*, Sydney, 2002, especially chapters 8 and 9.

147 *ODT* letters column, 25 February 1917. This letter was reprinted in the *Tablet* under the heading, 'Father Liston Hits Back', 1 March 1917, p. 45.

148 In a letter to his friend Hogan at the Irish College in Rome, Kelly scorned the hierarchy's 'idiotic policy of conciliation', said they were 'accepting assurances from men who are professional liars' and ridiculed the 'whining platitudes' of Bishop Brodie who had been negotiating over the conscription of students with the government. Letter, Kelly to Hogan, 14 September 1917. Hogan Papers, Box 6, ICR.

149 Liston's letter headed 'Conscription and Theological Students', *Tablet*, 22 March 1917, pp 26–27.

150 *Tablet*, 29 March 1917, p. 36.

151 Letter, Liston to Mahoney, 15 March 1917. CLE 95–3, ACDA. Bishop Verdon's sorrows about the strains being placed on priests and theological students during this controversy were expressed in a letter to O'Riordan dated 18 April, 1917. O'Riordan Papers, Box 18, ICR. Similar sentiments are expressed in Mgr Mahoney's end-of-year report on Auckland Diocese 1917, in CLE 2–3, ACDA.

152 See Scanlan, 'Early Memories of Holy Cross College', in Mannes, ed., *Golden Jubilee*, p. 30. One theologian so exempted was Joe Martin, as related in his typescript reminiscences.

153 Rector's report to bishop on Holy Cross College, dated 30 June 1920. In Holy Cross College Box, DCDA.

154 O'Connor, 'Storm Over the Clergy', pp 145–147.
155 Letter, Liston to Cleary, 20 April 1918. CLE 95–3, ACDA.
156 Norris, *Southernmost Seminary*, p. 43.
157 A full report of Verdon's death is given in *Tablet*, 28 November 1918.
158 James Coffey wrote to his friend O'Riordan at the Irish College (31 January 1919) explaining how Verdon had been ordered north by his doctor for his health's sake, but had taken ill in Wellington while hurrying home to open a church in Oamaru. Coffey was at Verdon's deathbed and reported, 'He died as he lived a true Saint'. O'Riordan Papers, Box 19, ICR. Archbishop O'Shea had sent Bishop Cleary progress reports as Verdon sank (see O'Shea to Cleary, 21 November 1918, in CLE 84–1, ACDA).
159 John Mackay had been administering the diocese during Verdon's trip north (see *Tablet*, 28 September 1918, p. 27). Coffey wrote to Cleary that the diocesan council was making him administrator in accordance with Verdon's wishes (see Coffey to Cleary, 3 December 1918, in CLE 84–1, ACDA). An example of Coffey's differences with Verdon is found in a letter he wrote to Fr Delaney, 2 September 1910 (Bishop Verdon Box, DCDA), in which Coffey rages against 'the old man' who was tempting him to apply for a transfer to another diocese.
160 'Michael Verdon, Bishop of Dunedin, An Appreciation', *Tablet*, 28 November 1918, pp 26–27.
161 In a letter of 4 December 1919, Cerretti said Liston 'completely won the confidence of the late bishop' ('gagna éminemment la confiance de feu évêque'). CEP Nuova Serie 1921 160 707, Propaganda Fide archives. Another letter of Cerretti's, dated 12 August 1919, speaks of Liston as Verdon's intended successor. It is quoted in the *Relazione* (concerning the appointment of bishops) of March 1920, Acta de Sac. Cong. de Propaganda Fide 1920 291.
162 Cleary writing to O'Riordan, 15 September 1913. O'Riordan Papers, Box 14, ICR.
163 Verdon's wills of 1906 and 1911, and records of Liston's trusteeship (which he eventually shared with James Coffey), are preserved in Bishop Verdon Box, DCDA.
164 Norris, *Southernmost Seminary*, p. 23.
165 Letter, Brodie to Cleary, 12 December 1918. CLE 84–1, ACDA.
166 Coffey had first sought an assurance from the Apostolic Delegate that all Dunedin priests (including the rector of Holy Cross) had the right to vote. Coffey to Cattaneo, 13 December 1918 (Bishop Verdon Box, DCDA). Coffey advised Cleary that the 'month's mind' for Verdon, and the *terna* voting, would be delayed until 15 January 1919 because of the holiday season and the 'flu epidemic. Letter, Coffey to Cleary, 3 December 1918. CLE 84–1, ACDA.
167 In his report to Propaganda Fide, the Apostolic Delelgate briefly outlined O'Farrell's successes as spiritual director in Australian seminaries. *Relazione*, 1920, p. 4.
168 Results on *terna* voting in *Relazione*, 1920.
169 Letter, Coffey to Archbishop O'Shea and Bishops Cleary and Brodie, 15 December 1919. Monsignor J. Coffey Boxes, DCDA.
170 Kelly described it to John Hagan as 'a very enjoyable session, quite a bit of old times'. Letter, Kelly to Hagan, 7 July 1916. Hagan Papers, Box 6, ICR. Letters to Hagan in which Kelly expresses the intention to visit Liston are dated 20 September 1913 and 6 May 1914. Hagan Papers, Box 4, ICR.
171 Liston wrote to Cleary explaining his 'warm friendship' for Kelly, and excusing Kelly's editorial policies on the grounds of the 'vulgar and offensive' anti-Catholic jibes of the bigoted 'Civis' in the *Otago Daily Times*. Letter, Liston to Cleary, 25 November 1917. CLE 97–1, ACDA.
172 In a letter to John Hagan of 24 April 1919, Kelly said he had told Cleary that Liston was one of the 'men . . . more capable of advising me' over *Tablet* matters than Cleary was. Hagan Papers, Box 7, ICR.
173 Letter, Kelly to Hagan, 4 December 1919 (apparently in mistake for 1918). Hagan Papers, Box 8, ICR.
174 Letter, Kelly to Hagan, 18 March 1919. Hagan Papers, Box 7, ICR.
175 Letter, Kelly to Hagan, 3 August 1919. Hagan Papers, Box 8, ICR. It should be noted that Kelly had been 'lent' to Dunedin diocese by Archbishop Redwood specifically to edit the *Tablet*. He himself had no part in the *terna* voting.
176 Burke et al to the Apostolic Delegate, 3 July 1919. It is clear, however, that the Apostolic Delegate gave little credence to the claims of Burke and his associates.

Relazione, 1920, pp 8–9.

177 The original reads 'dans ses dernières années [il] buvait un peu trop'. Letter from hierarchy to Apostolic Delegate, 5 March 1919. In Documents from CEP Nuova Serie 1921 160 717, Propaganda Fide.

178 Ibid. The original reads, 'La soeur ainée Marie a pris en mariage un Protestant, nomme Kempston, il-y-a douze ans. Le mariage a été célébré par un prêtre avec dispensation. Les deux époux allèrent en Angleterre. Ils ont eu un enfant. Le mariage n'a été pas heureux. Plus tard, dans ses embarras, Madame Kempston a pris l'habitude de morphineuse. Deux fois elle est entrée volontairement dans le couvent du Bon Pasteur, près de Christchurch, afin de se corriger de sa mauvaise habitude. Dans cet institut on l'a traitée en hôte. Elle avait un chambre privée, et passait son temps à peindre, et a travailler artistement avec l'aiguille. Elle avait des connaissances remarquables. Elle aussi demandé à soigner les malades parmi les soeurs et les pénitentes. Pendant quelque temps elle ne pratiquait pas bien ses devoirs réligieux, mais à présent elle pratique la foi de son enfance. Aucune accusation, aucune suggestion d'immoralité ne s'est jamais portées contre elle. Dans les pays nouveaux, comme celle-ci [sic], il est assez ordinaire de trouver des familles Catholiques excellentes avec un où deux membres qui laissent a desirer. Et l'indigne réputation d'un seul membre n'est pas regardée du même oeil que dans les contrées plus agées. Nous croyons très fermement que les faits avérés à l'égard de la soeur de l'Abbé Liston ne peuvent nullement nuir à la bonne réputation, ni à l'influence de l'Abbé, et ne pourraient empêcher le bien qu'il voudrait faire comme évêque de Dunedin. Voilà pourquoi nous répétons notre recommendation de l'Abbé Liston, et nous regardons avec horreur la tentative de lui faire tort en le déclarer [sic] illégitime, où en suggérant que sa souer est une pénitente – c'est-à-dire, une femme de mauvaise vie – chez les soeurs du Bon Pasteur.'

179 Letter, Brodie to Liston, 1 August 1921. CLE 83–2, ACDA. A good brief account of the Good Shepherd home at Mt Magdala, where Liston's sister was a voluntary resident, is found in O'Meeghan, *Held Fast by Faith*, pp 151–155. The sisters continued to provide custodial care until 1968.

180 Anne Liston was a nurse at St Thomas's Hospital, London, during the First World War. By the 1960s, she was being described as an 'invalid' in Dublin, where she had been since at least 1921. See Liston's 1964 autobiographical note (Clippings File, ACDA). See also 'Archbishop is Foremost a Pastor Among his People', retrospective article in *Auckland Star*, 29 January 1964. In fact, the term 'invalid' was a euphemism. Anne Liston had suffered a complete mental breakdown and was the inmate of a psychiatric hospital for the last 46 years of her life. James Michael regularly sent remittances for her maintenance. See correspondence between Liston and staff of St Vincent's Hospital, Dublin, included in LIS 9–1, ACDA. Anne Liston's death certificate, dated 13 October 1967, is filed in Irish National Archives, Dublin. It erroneously gives her age as 87. In reality, Anne Liston was 84 at the time of her death.

181 Cleary's correspondence with the Apostolic Delegate, Cattaneo, relating to this request (October-November 1918) is filed in CLE 82–2, ACDA. The letter of 25 October 1918 in which Cattaneo informs Cardinal Van Rossum of Propaganda of the request is filed in CEP Nuova Serie 1921 160 707, Propaganda Fide.

182 Reports on Cleary's health are found in *Tablet* on 29 July 1915, p. 35; 12 August 1915, p. 35; 19 August 1915, pp 33 and 40; 26 August 1915, p. 35; 2 September 1915, p. 35; and 7 October 1915, p. 35. Cleary's visit to Europe for his health in 1916 is noted in *Tablet*, 23 March 1916, p. 35, and 27 July 1916, p. 19, as is his return, 1 November 1917, p. 35. The *Tablet* was still exercised by his health in 1919, *Tablet*, 21 August 1919, p. 27. Cleary himself, as an inexhaustible letter writer, wrote to many correspondents about his health, including O'Riordan at the Irish College, to whom he wrote from his hospital bed in Dublin, 25 June 1916. O'Riordan Papers, Box 17, ICR.

183 Autobiographical notes (written in August 1921) in CLE 3–2, ACDA.

184 At the same time, Cleary was egotistical enough to take a perverse pride in his ill health and to boast of his industry and forbearance under suffering. See, for example, Cleary's description of himself as 'one of the wounded soldiers' of the church. Cleary's Christmas speech of welcome to Liston, reported in the *Month*, 22 January 1921, p. 11. See also his claim to the Apostolic Delegate that he was 'the seventh recorded case in medical history and the first to recover' of 'that happily very rare malady myoctonis

multiplex'. Letter, Cleary to Cattaneo, 17 September 1918. CLE 82–2, ACDA. On the title page of a copy of his 1920 pamphlet on the Marriage Amendment Act, Cleary has written that it was composed in a surgical bed in the Mater hospital while he was having 'violent convulsions'. Copy preserved in CLE 84–1, ACDA. See also the 68–page *Report of his Consecration with Biographical and Other Details* which he has reprinted in 1919 when he thought his death was near. Copy preserved in CLE 80–12, ACDA.

185 Luck's letter to Bishop Grimes of Christchurch, 18 July 1895, in which he reports that Archbishop Redwood has given him permission to seek a coadjutor, is preserved in Grimes Papers, Box 12 B, CCDA.

186 Correspondence relating to Cleary's rejection of this offer (July-September 1913) is found in CLE 86–3, ACDA. He also wrote to O'Riordan about it, letters of 31 July, 14 August and 15 September 1913. O'Riordan Papers, Box 14, ICR. There was the unhappy example of the former rector of the Irish College, Michael Kelly, who had been coadjutor-archbishop to Cardinal Moran in Sydney from 1901 until Moran's death in 1911, but had been treated by Moran as an 'unwelcome adjunct', thus creating 'two rival centres of influence' in the diocese. K.J. Walsh, *Yesterday's Seminary*, p. 126.

187 Letter, Brodie to Cleary, 4 January 1918. CLE 97–1, ACDA.

188 Letter, Brodie to Cleary 17 September 1918. CLE 83–5, ACDA.

189 Cattaneo, quoted in *Relazione*, 1920. The original reads, '[Cleary is] un ottimo e valoroso Vescovo, ma non si puo negare che in questi ultimi anni particolomente, a cagione della varie malattie sofferté, e nervoso e irritabile alquanto e forse anche un po' impulsivo'.

190 Cleary wrote to Archbishop Redwood seeking permission to hold *terna* voting for a coadjutor, 22 January 1919. On the same day, Cleary wrote to the Apostolic Delegate to ensure that he could exclude the Mill Hills from the process. Both letters in CLE 82–2, ACDA.

191 Report on Auckland's *terna* voting in CED Nuove Serie 1921 160 707, Propaganda Fide.

192 Mahoney was 'trop âgé et trop faible', and Cahill unacceptable 'à cause de son éducation sérieusement défectueuse, son manque d'érudition nécessaire et son impuissance de bien parler en public'. Quoted in *Relazione*, 1920.

193 Letter, Ormond to Brodie, 3 June 1920, in which he expressed relief over Liston's appointment to Auckland. Brodie Papers, Box 12 A, CCDA.

194 Letter of Cleary quoted in Cattaneo's correspondence with Cardinal Van Rossum, 6 June 1919. By this stage, Cleary was claiming his need for a coadjutor was urgent because of his declining health. CEP Nuova Serie 1921 160 707, Propaganda Fide.

195 Letter, Cleary to Liston, 19 March 1919. CLE 84, ACDA.

196 *Relazione*, 1920, pp 20–21.

197 Cleary writing to the Bishop Liston Reception Committee, 5 July 1920. CLE 89–2, ACDA.

198 Christmas sermon reported in the *Month*, 22 January 1921, p. 11.

199 Letter, Liston to Cleary, 8 June 1909. CLE 11, ACDA.

200 Letter, Liston to Cleary, 1 September 1913. CLE 86–3, ACDA.

201 Letter, Liston to Cleary, 1 April 1914. CLE 83–4, ACDA.

202 Letter, Liston to Cleary, 25 May 1915. CLE 87–1, ACDA.

203 Letter, Liston to Cleary, 6 July 1918. CLE 93, ACDA.

204 See Liston's defence of Kelly, to Cleary, 25 November 1917. CLE 97–1, ACDA.

205 Report of hierarchy to Cattaneo, 4 December 1919. CEP Nuova Serie 1921 160 707, Propaganda Fide. The original reads: [Liston is] 'de forte santé, patient, frugal et . . . il a été heureux dans toute son administration tempérelle. Il est ferme de caractère, cependant sa fermeté est accompagnée d'un grand tact, d'une bonne humeur constante et d'une grande délicatesse. Il jouit d'une haute renommée de sainteté et rien n'a jamais pu allongé contre ses moeurs'.

206 ' . . . non dovrebbe offendersi se vien scelto un estraneo alla Nuova Zelanda come il loro candidato'. Cattaneo reported in *Relazione*, 1920.

207 Biographical details on Whyte drawn from *Tablet*, I January 1958, and *Zealandia*, 9 January 1958 (obituaries). Also *Catholic Press*, 29 April 1920 and 2 December 1920, for reports of Whyte's appointment to Dunedin. There is also a brief biography in Bishop Whyte Boxes, DCDA.

208 Communication from Cattaneo dated 23 April 1920. In Whyte Papers, DCDA.
209 Gaspari's wire (dated 28 April 1920) and Cattaneo's letter in CLE 82–2, ACDA.
210 'The New Bishop of Dunedin', *Tablet*, 29 April 1920, p. 28.
211 *Tablet*, 16 December 1920, p. 21.
212 Letter, Liston to Cleary, 29 April 1920. CLE 84–1, ACDA.
213 Letter, Coffey to Brodie, 28 May 1920. Brodie Papers, Box 12 A, CCDA. Also Liston to Cleary, 31 May 1920. CLE 84–1, ACDA.
214 Letter, Liston to Cleary, 29 April 1920. CLE 84–1, ACDA.
215 Letter, Liston to Brodie, 8 June 1920. Brodie Papers, Box 12 A, CCDA.
216 Liston's comments to Cleary on retreat and Sydney in letters of 25 July and 28 July 1920. CLE 84–1, ACDA. Liston's comments to Brodie on Sydney in letter of 25 July 1920. Brodie Papers, Box 12 A, CCDA.
217 Letter, Liston to Cleary, 12 November 1920. CLE 113, ACDA.
218 Liston mentions to Bishop Brodie in a letter of 18 June 1920 his gratitude at being assigned the Auckland parish. Brodie Papers, Box 12 A, CCDA. On 26 September 1920, he wrote to Cleary apologising that he still did not have his 'papers' from the Vatican, and hoping he was not inconveniencing Cleary. CLE 95–2, ACDA.
219 Letter, Edwin Anderson to Brodie, 7 June 1920. Brodie Papers, Box 12 A, CCDA. Fifty ex-Manly priests, proud of one of their own being raised to the episcopate, also contributed to buy his cross. *Tablet*, 26 August 1920.
220 Farewell from Mosgiel parish reported *Tablet*, 8 July 1920, p. 28; diocesan farewell and South Dunedin farewell reported *Tablet*, 15 July 1920, pp 22–23; Dominican farewell reported *Tablet*, 23 September 1920, p. 32.
221 On 4 December 1920. See 'Minute Book for Meetings of Archbishops and Bishops of New Zealand', in CLE 1–5, ACDA.
222 For Bishop Whyte's later recollection of the occasion, see 'Pastoral Letter of Bishop Whyte on the Occasion of His Episcopal Jubilee' (December 1945). Whyte Papers, DCDA.
223 Liston's *Formula Professionis Fidei* and *Formula Iurisiurandi*, countersigned by Redwood and including the anti-Modernist oath, are included in CEP Nuova Serie 1921, 160 707, Propaganda Fide. Liston became 'titular bishop of Olympus', thus conforming to the legal fiction of canon law that every bishop has his own territorial see. Olympus is a defunct Catholic diocese in Greece.
224 Information on the dual consecration taken from *Tablet*, 16 December 1920, pp 18–19 and 21–23; and the *Month*, 22 January 1921, p. 15.
225 Letter, Liston to Brodie, 11 March 1921. Brodie Papers, Box 12 A, CCDA. Dean Burke's part in denying Liston the Dunedin see was not to be the last time Burke's family played a contentious role in the diocese. In 1929, Burke's nephew Father James Lynch was angrily contesting decisions made by Bishop Whyte's church court regarding the disposition of Burke's estate. See letters of James Lynch to John Hagan dated 17 May, 21 June and 10 July 1929. Hagan Papers, Box 27, ICR.
226 Twenty-three friendly letters from Liston to Whyte, written in 1921–22, are included in Whyte Papers, DCDA.
227 *Relazione* Propaganda Fide, 1910, Rubrica 151–162, Vol. 492. In O'Riordan Papers, Box 11, ICR, there is also a letter from Bishop Grimes to Cleary, dated 30 March 1910, telling him of his being *dignissimus* in Auckland's *terna* voting.
228 The *Relazione* on Brodie's elevation to the episcopate runs to 30 pages. CEP Nuova Serie 1916, 160–161 582, Propaganda Fide.
229 Letter, Kelly to John Hagan, 31 December 1918. Hagan Papers, Box 6, ICR.
230 Imposition of a bishop against the local clergy's wishes was not unique to New Zealand. In 1940 in Dublin, John Charles McQuaid figured nowhere in the *terna* voting when Archbishop Edward Byrne died, but was manoeuvred into the see mainly after lobbying by de Valera and the Papal Nuncio. See chapter 10 of John Cooney, *John Charles McQuaid – Ruler of Catholic Ireland*, Dublin, 1999.
231 Letter, Liston to Cleary, 19 May 1920. CLE 84–1, ACDA.
232 Telegram from Liston to Cleary, 26 April 1920. CLE 83–5, ACDA.
233 Letter, Liston to Cleary, 26 April 1920. CLE 84–1, ACDA.
234 Letter, Liston to Curran, 16 May 1920. William Walsh Papers, Box 392II, File 380/3, DAA. The letter, filed among Walsh's correspondence, is presumably addressed to Curran, but Liston's salutation is simply 'My dear Friend'.

235 Liston's speech reported in *Tablet*, 30 December 1920, p. 22.

236 To Mother Mary MacKillop, George Lenihan expressed similar misgivings upon his appointment as bishop, claiming 'the sweet hope that Rome will retract [its] mistake'. Lenihan to MacKillop, 29 October 1896. LEN 28–3, ACDA.

237 Letter, Liston to Michael Curran, 12 December 1920. Curran Papers, Box 1, ICR.

238 See Liston's letters to Brodie, 1 May and 8 June 1920. Brodie Papers. Box 12 A, CCDA.

239 Edmund Lynch, 'Most Rev. James Liston D.D.', in Mannes, ed., *Golden Jubilee*, pp 44–45.

Chapter III: Coadjutor at Work, 1920–1929

1   From just the first two years of Liston's coadjutorship, see, for example, report on Liston presiding at meeting of the newly-formed Good Shepherd parish in Mt Roskill, *Tablet*, 5 May 1921, p. 23; opening new presbytery at Matamata, *Tablet*, 13 October 1921, p. 22; blessing and opening new church at St Helier's, *Tablet*, 23 March 1922, p. 22; blessing foundation stones for new school and presbytery at Mt Roskill, 28 September 1922, p. 22; blessing foundation stone of new school in Pukekohe, *Tablet*, 21 December 1922, p. 27. From later in the decade come reports of Liston's opening the church of St Vincent de Paul in Mt Albert (*Tablet*, 6 December 1923, p. 26); blessing and opening the new St Joseph's convent in Good Shepherd parish, Mt Roskill (*Tablet*, 1 May 1924, p. 15); opening the new Papatoetoe church (*Tablet*, 23 September 1925, p. 35); opening the new church of Our Lady of the Sacred Heart in Epsom (*Tablet*,16 September 1925, p. 35); and opening the new church of St Peter Chanel in Hikurangi (*Tablet*, 9 March 1927, p. 30).

2   See Cleary's letter to Liston concerning the Marists' re-establishment in the Auckland diocese, 4 February 1921. LIS 16–1, ACDA. See also *New Zealand Herald*, 21 June 1926, report of the opening of the Marist presbytery in Mt Albert. The Marists also ran a 'mission station' at St Helier's for some of the 1920s. See 1928 correspondence in CLE 113–2, ACDA.

3   Statements on numbers and orders derived from *Tablet*, 15 April 1970, p. 5 (summary of Auckland diocese at time of Liston's accession as bishop); from Liston obituary in cuttings box, ACDA; and Ernest Simmons, *In Cruce Salus*, Auckland, 1982, p. 219.

4   Dean Van Dijk, 'Report on the Maori Mission' (1924), Box NZL3 (1913–34), Archives of Missionary Society of St Joseph, Mill Hill, London.

5   See, for example, letters from the Mill Hill priests in the Hokianga and Panguru areas. CLE 110–3, ACDA.

6   An example of Cleary's visitations to the 'far north' over atrocious roads is reported in *Tablet*, 28 January 1915, pp 17 and 19. Some of his flying exploits are recorded in *Tablet*, 25 March 1920, p. 23; and *Month*, April 1919, p. 7, and April 1922, p. 7, p. 9 and p. 11.

7   Returning from Rome, Leonard Buxton said, 'I find the shortage of priests acute', and related how, after only one night home, he had been assigned to a parish in the place of a priest who had died. Letter, Buxton to Michael Curran, 9 April 1922. Curran Papers, Box 1, ICR.

8   See letters of Dean W.J. Murphy of Balmoral parish, August 1923, where he asks Liston for overdue holidays. Liston turns him down 'owing to the shortage of priests'. CLE 106–2, ACDA. Also letter from Fr John Kirrane of Cambridge, 21 February 1927, complaining of how few holidays he has had since 1911. CLE 107–2, ACDA.

9   See Liston to Bishop Whyte, 11 November 1921, asking for two priests. Whyte Papers, DCDA. And Liston to Mgr Ryan in the archdiocese of Sydney, 14 December 1923, asking for three or four priests. LIS 16–1, ACDA.

10   Letter, Cleary to Cattaneo, 30 April 1924. CLE 82–3, ACDA.

11   Letter, Cleary to Hagan, 15 February 1927. Hagan Papers, Box 23, ICR.

12   Details of Liston's round of welcomes in Auckland, and his speech in reply, drawn from 'Bishop Liston in Auckland', *Month*, 22 January 1921, pp 11 and 13; and 'Right Rev. Liston's Arrival in Auckland', *Tablet*, 30 December 1920, pp 21–23.

13   Speech reported in *Month*, 22 January 1921.

14   Letter, Liston to Whyte, 10 January 1921. Whyte Papers, DCDA.

15   Letter, Liston to Brodie, 10 January 1921. Box 12 B, CCDA.

16   Report on Liston's welcome to Gisborne, *Tablet*, 26 May 1921, p. 23.
17   Letter, Liston to Mother Helen Lynch, 10 June 1926. In A183, Fr John Flanagan Papers, File 6, ACDA.
18   See, for example, Liston's account of a visit from 'Jim' Delaney ('a sheer joy to me') in his letter to Whyte, 20 August 1921. Whyte Papers, DCDA. Also notice of Liston's forthcoming visit to Dunedin, *Tablet*, 31 July 1929, p. 49.
19   LIS 9, ACDA, contains correspondence July-September 1923 between Liston, Mrs Boyle and their respective solicitors. Having fallen on hard times, the Boyles requested more funds from Mary Liston's estate. There is detailed correspondence on the payments that were made to each of Liston's nieces until they came of age.
20   Letter, Liston to Whyte, 24 March 1923, in Coffey Papers, DCDA.
21   *Tablet*, 6 January 1921, gives a report of Liston's visit to the home at p. 21, including Golden's verse of welcome describing Liston's task, Sunday, 19 March 2006: 'To help our Bishop in his needs / And succor him in noble deeds. / Uncertain health and burdens great / His heavy lot have been of late. / To him thou'lt be a tower of strength / And ample succor bring at length'.
22   Letter, Liston to Cattaneo, 24 November 1922. CLE 82–2, ACDA. Letter, Liston to Whyte, 20 November 1922. Whyte Papers, DCDA.
23   Letter, Cleary to Cattaneo, 24 January 1921. CLE 82–2, ACDA.
24   Document dated 1 September 1921. CLE 1–2, ACDA. Many passages of this document have been marginally marked, suggesting that it was scrutinised very carefully by Liston when he was later accused by Cleary of maladministration.
25   Letter, Cleary to Liston, 23 November 1921. LIS 16–1, ACDA.
26   Letter, Cleary to Liston, 16 February 1922. LIS 16–1, ACDA.
27   Letters, Cleary to Liston, 6 February 1923 and 27 February 1923. LIS 16–1, ACDA.
28   See letters Brodie to Liston, 4 July and 1 August 1921. CLE 83–2, ACDA.
29   CLE 1–5, ACDA, contains the 'Minute Book for Meetings of Archbishops and Bishops of New Zealand', 1920–31. The first of the regular Easter meetings was held on 6 May 1925.
30   Correspondence relating to this is included in LIS 17, ACDA.
31   The bishops' meeting of 3 May 1928 includes a memo from the other bishops asking Liston about the vestments they needed for congress functions. Minute Book CLE 1–5, ACDA.
32   *Tablet*, 7 December 1922, p. 15.
33   Historical details from Gavin Ardley, *The Church of St Benedict, Newton, Auckland – A Centennial Narrative 1988*, Auckland, 1988. For a personal account of the earlier years of St Benedict's parish, clearly informed by the author's hostility to his fellow Benedictine priests, see Vaggioli (Crockett trans.), *Deserter's Adventures*.
34   Ardley, *The Church of St Benedict*, p. 32.
35   Bishop John Mackey, interview, 19 January 2003.
36   *Tablet*, 9 May 1928, p. 15.
37   *Tablet*, 6 February 1929, p. 45; *Month*, 19 February 1929, p. 17.
38   Murphy's letter of complaint is dated 1 July 1924. Liston replied on 3 July 1924 that Ormond had conducted the funeral because nobody could find Murphy at the time. CLE 106–2, ACDA.
39   Letter, Cleary to Liston, 14 August 1925. CLE 113–3, ACDA.
40   Biographical details on Ormond from obituary, *Zealandia*, 15 September 1949, p. 3. Also Deceased Priests File, ACDA.
41   *Tablet*, 11 August 1921, p. 23, announcing Cleary's forthcoming trip.
42   See Nicholas Reid, *The Bishop's Paper*, Auckland, 2000, chapter 2, for Cleary's indictment of Kelly. Liston sent a pastoral to Auckland clergy explaining that Cleary was going for his health, and to present the diocesan report to Benedict XV. *Tablet*, 18 August 1921, p. 23.
43   *Tablet*, 8 September 1921, p. 22; *Tablet*, 22 September 1921, p. 21; *Month*, 15 September 1921, p. 3.
44   *Tablet*, 14 June 1923, p. 27; *Tablet*, 21 June 1923, pp 26–28; *Month*, 15 June 1923, p. 3.
45   *Tablet*, 9 March 1927, p. 30. *Tablet* also reported the progress of his trip in Ireland, 29 June 1927, p. 29.

46 Speech reported *Tablet*, 24 August 1927, and *Month*, 16 August 1927 (special supplement).
47 *Tablet*, 28 November 1928, p. 45; *Tablet*, 6 February 1929, p. 45.
48 *Tablet*, 27 January 1921 and 17 March 1921.
49 *Tablet*, 28 December 1927, p. 29.
50 *Tablet*, 11 January 1928 and 22 February 1928.
51 *Tablet*, 29 February 1928, reported Cleary setting off for a pastoral tour of Northland, shortly after coming out of hospital.
52 *Tablet*, 1 August 1928. This report is next to a news item about Father Martindale's recovery.
53 *Tablet*, 22 August 1928, p. 45.
54 *Month*, 29 September 1928, p. 67, has a report of Cleary on crutches; while *Tablet*, 6 February 1929, p. 45, declares, 'His Lordship no longer walks lame'.
55 *Tablet*, 27 February 1929, p. 46.
56 *Month*, 20 October 1925, p. 22; *Tablet*, 7 October 1925, p. 31; *Tablet*, 11 November 1925, p. 31; *Tablet*, 25 November 1925, p. 30.
57 Liston's reply (dated May 1929) to Cleary's charge that he had not undertaken parish visitations. LIS 16–3, ACDA.
58 *Month*, 15 October 1923, p. 16, and 15 November 1923, p. 16; *Tablet*, 11 October 1923, p. 28, and 1 November 1923, p. 27. Liston was away 5–23 October.
59 *Tablet*, 31 August 1927, p. 29; *Month*, 17 July 1928, p. 41.
60 *Month*, 20 April 1926, p. 17; also *Tablet*, 21 April 1926, p. 30. Other reports of preparations for the journey and the journey itself are found in *Month*, 16 March 1926, p. 28, and 15 June 1926, p. 33; and *Tablet*, 30 June 1926, p. 29.
61 Liston's appointment diary for 1926 (filed in LIS 15, ACDA) was kept by him as a special travel diary.
62 Ibid. See entries for 20, 21 and 22 June 1926.
63 Letter, Liston to Lynch, 22 June 1926. A183 Flanagan Papers, File 6, ACDA.
64 Diary entry for 3 July 1926.
65 Letter, Liston to Mother Helen Lynch, 21 October 1926. A183 Flanagan Papers, File 6, ACDA.
66 *Tablet*, 25 August 1926, p. 29.
67 The announcement that Liston and his large party were to leave for Sydney was made in *Tablet*, 5 September 1928. A major report on the Sydney congress takes up most of *Month*, 29 September 1928.
68 Sean T. O'Ceallaigh, 'The Late Rt. Rev. Mgr. M.J. Curran P.P., P.A.', in *Reportorium Novum – Dublin Diocesan Historical Record*, 3 (1), Dublin, 1962, p. 11.
69 Liston's speech, 25 December 1920, reported in *Month*, 22 January 1921.
70 'Bishop Liston Honoured by Auckland Hibernians', *Tablet*, 3 March 1921, p. 23.
71 Rory Sweetman, *Faith and Fraternalism*, Dunedin, 2002, p. 73 and pp 96–97.
72 *Month*, 14 April 1923, p. 10, and 17 May 1927, p. 31.
73 Reports of Liston's meetings with the Catholic Students' Guild are found in *Tablet*, 12 April 1923, p. 27, and 14 April 1926, p. 30; and *Month*, 14 April 1923, p. 10. See also general statement on students' association in Ardley, *Church of St Benedict*, p. 32.
74 Form letter sent by Liston, 28 July 1921. LIS 17, ACDA.
75 *Tablet*, 8 September 1921, p. 23.
76 *Month*, 16 March 1926, p. 28.
77 Liston gives his own account of establishing the Holy Name Society in Auckland at p. 14 of the 24–page document answering Cleary's charges about the Knights of the Southern Cross. LIS 16–3, ACDA. The 22 June 1926 entry of his diary has already been cited for his impressions of the society in Chicago. LIS 15, ACDA. *Tablet*, 10 November 1926, p. 29, notes the society's establishment in Auckland. So does *Month*, 19 October 1926. It is in relation to this latter report that van der Krogt notes that credit was given to Cleary. Christopher John van der Krogt, 'More a Part than Apart – the Catholic Community in New Zealand Society 1918–1940', Doctoral thesis, Massey University, 1994, p. 83 and note. See also 5 and 20 June 1928, exchange of letters between Liston and Cleary on setting up the Holy Name Society. LIS 209–2, ACDA.
78 Liston's circular of 26 January 1922. CLE 76–13/5, ACDA.

79   Responding to a Mr Patience of Kaikohe, who had complained of inadequate catechesis for Catholic children in the country, Bishop Cleary referred him to Liston. Letter, Cleary to Patience, 30 September 1927. CLE 90–2, ACDA.

80   Letter, Liston to Whyte, 20 August 1921. Whyte Papers, DCDA.

81   Monsignor Mahoney's October 1917 report on the diocese said a proposed 'Catholic School Magazine' had been raised at Catholic teachers' conferences. CLE 2–3, ACDA.

82   A letter from Mother Colgan (of the Sisters of the Sacred Heart) to Cleary dated 23 July 1926 showed that Liston had proposed hiring for a year from overseas a teacher to train children in 'the Justine Ward method of singing'. CLE 127–6, ACDA.

83   Entry for 11 June 1926 in Liston's 1926 diary. LIS 15, ACDA. Later in the diary, Liston shows a concern for how priests are paid. He writes, 'Priests salaries. Minneapolis. No distinc. made bet. Pastors – all receive 1300 dollars a yr. (if poss.) Thus: Sunday collections, Xmas and E. dues (if made), Stole fees etc. go into Parish a/c'.

84   Pat Gallagher, *The Marist Brothers in New Zealand, Fiji and Samoa 1876–1976*, Marist Brothers Trust Board, 1976, says at p. 91 that the opening of a Marist school in Hamilton in February 1922 was 'as a result of an urgent request from Bishop Liston'. A letter from Fr Michael Bleakley to Cleary, 24 March 1924 (CLE 109–3, ACDA) suggests that Liston and Bleakley had begun considering a site for the Frankton church before Cleary had fully accepted the idea of a separate Frankton parish. Liston's undated letter (possibly 1928 or 1929) making arrangements for a Catholic naval chaplain at Devonport is filed in CLE 108–2, ACDA.

85   Liston's circular to priests, 6 March 1923. CLE 93, ACDA.

86   'The Little People's Page' of *Tablet*, 30 August 1923, p. 39, prints letters from the orphans which had been forwarded by Liston.

87   [Sister Veronica Delaney] *Gracious is the Time – Centenary of the Sisters of Mercy Auckland New Zealand 1850–1950*, Auckland, 1952, pp 104–105.

88   On 21 November 1903, Lenihan placed clipping about 'Austrians' before the council. LEN 6, ACDA.

89   LEN 29, ACDA.

90   In July 1904, Zanna wrote to Lenihan to say the Croats had been 'disappointed' that he was not one of their own, and that he was about to preach his first sermon in Croat. LEN 48, ACDA.

91   Judith Bassett, 'Colonial Justice – The Treatment of Dalmatians in New Zealand During the First World War', *NZJH*, 33 (2), 1999.

92   Correspondence between Cleary and the affected families is included in CLE 89–1, ACDA.

93   Letter, Cleary to Marchetti-Salvaggiani, 24 October 1924. CLE 82–4, ACDA.

94   Letter, Cleary to Liston, 30 April 1927. CLE 97–3, ACDA. Cleary had already suggested the need for two Yugoslav priests in a letter to John Hagan at the Irish College, 15 February 1927. Hagan Papers, Box 23, ICR. In this letter, he described Auckland's Dalmatians as 'about 3,000, scattered about in small groups'.

95   'Dobro Dosao – The Jugo-Slavs Welcome Their Pastor Father Milan Pavlinovich', *Month*, 15 May 1928, pp 18–19.

96   Andrew D.Trlin, *Now Respected, Once Despised – Yugoslavs in New Zealand*, Palmerston North, 1979, p. 174.

97   Tablet, 9 May 1928, p. 45; *Month*, 15 May 1928, pp 18–19.

98   Report on the presentation ceremony, hosted in the Manchester Unity Hall by the Yugoslav consul, J.M. Totich, and including the mayor of Auckland, Sir Ernest Davis, *Zealandia*, 23 April 1936, p. 5; and *Tablet*, 22 April 1936, p. 37.

99   Speech reported in 'Bishop Liston in Auckland', *Month*, 22 January 1921, p. 13.

100 *Tablet*, 8 February 1923, p. 31; *Month*, 15 February 1923, p. 9.

101 See, for example, Liston's speech on the opening of the new St Patrick's School in Wellington Street, *Month*, 17 May 1927, p. 13. Also speech on Catholic education at the opening of the new Grey Lynn convent, *Month*, 15 November 1922, p. 13. At other times, Liston told audiences of the money Catholic schools were saving the government. See his speech at St Michael's, Remuera, *Tablet*, 10 September 1924, p. 8. He also spoke of the 'secular efficiency' and high educational standards of Catholic schools. See his speech at the Sacred Heart College prizegiving reported in *Month*, 15 December 1923, p. 18.

102   Liston at opening of convent school in Te Awamutu, report reprinted from *Auckland Star* by *Tablet*, 14 July 1921, p. 21.

103   Cleary's letter asking for Liston's endorsement, 20 July 1925, together with Liston's reply, is included in LIS 16–1, ACDA.

104   Report on Liston's sermon, *Tablet*, 3 August 1927, p. 27. Liston's circular dated 20 July 1927, LIS 17, ACDA.

105   See report of Liston's Christmas sermon at St Patrick's, *Tablet*, 9 January 1929, p. 45.

106   *Month*, 21 June 1927, p. iii; *Tablet*, 27 July 1927, pp 25 and 27. These sermons were subsequently printed as a series of articles in the *New Zealand Herald*.

107   *Tablet*, 25 January 1928.

108   *Month*, 21 February 1928, p. 37; *Tablet*, 7 March 1928, p. 48.

109   *Month*, 21 August 1928, p. 37; *Tablet*, 11 July 1928, p. 43.

110   *Tablet*, 1 February 1923, p. 31.

111   *Tablet*, 11 May 1927, p. 29.

112   *Tablet*, 16 May 1928, p. 23.

113   Liston's (mid-1929) answer to Cleary's charge No. 23. LIS 6–6, ACDA.

114   Liston's three articles were all headed 'The Roman Question' and bore the successive sub-headings, 'Civil Power of the Popes', 'Basis of the Papal States' and 'Attitude of the Popes', *NZH*, 14, 15 and 16 February 1929.

115   *NZH*, 6 March 1929.

116   File CLE 81, ACDA, contains the catechetical instructions for 1922, 1923 and 1924. In 1922 and 1923, Liston instructed priests each Sunday to preach on each clause of the Apostles' Creed, the nature of each sacrament, and the Our Father and Hail Mary. In 1924, Cleary's programme for Sunday sermons was based on the ten commandments.

117   Liston's circular to clergy instituting monthly 'days of recollection' dated 26 January 1922. LIS 17, ACDA.

118   Undated (1923) circular from Liston to diocesan priests mainly concerned itself with arrangements to welcome back Bishop Cleary, but contained a warning to priests who had absented themselves from conference. CLE 81, ACDA. On 9 December 1922, Liston wrote to Fr George Kelly of Tuakau rebuking him for failing to send a copy of his weekly sermon and failing an examination on conference matters. CLE 123–2, ACDA.

119   On 12 December 1924, Cleary wrote to Propaganda informing them that Fr Michael Furlong 'in very delicate health, suffering from stomach troubles and insomnia' had been given relief from his fast (CLE 82–3, ACDA). On 16 March 1926, Cleary granted Fr Mansfield of Howick partial dispensation from his fast because of his ill health (CLE 111–1, ACDA).

120   Cleary was enraged by one housekeeper who demanded that the parish priest be allowed 'an egg-flip between masses', even though the priest's last mass did not conclude until 1 pm on Sunday. See correspondence between Cleary and Fr O'Carroll of Puhoi, 10, 14 and 16 March 1926. CLE 119–2, ACDA. Also letter of 3 April 1926. LIS 16–1, ACDA.

121   See correspondence between Liston and Fr William Christopher Dunphy of Paeroa concerning the funeral of a Druid member, 21 July 1922. CLE 117–1, ACDA. Also Liston's response to Fr O'Doherty concerning an Oddfellow's funeral, 15 June 1921. CLE 122–4, ACDA. Also Liston's response to Fr John O'Hara of Waihi, concerning the funeral of an Oddfellow and a Forester, 15 June 1921. CLE 122–4, ACDA.

122   Minuted in bishops' meeting, 3 May 1928. Minute book of bishops' meetings, CLE 1–5, ACDA.

123   Liston's circular to priests, 26 January 1922. LIS 17, ACDA.

124   Minutes of bishops' meeting for 4 December 1920. CLE 1–5, ACDA.

125   Minutes of bishops' meeting for 6 May 1925. CLE 1–5, ACDA.

126   Letter, Cleary to Shore, 8 September 1928. CLE 73–5, ACDA. Capitals in the original.

127   On 24 June 1924, the curate Matthew Curley had to write to Cleary from Hamilton justifying his attendance at races. He was, however, a multiple sinner, having also to justify attending the pictures and driving a female parishioner in his car. CLE 109–3, ACDA.

128 Unpublished 'Memoirs of Bishop John Mackey' (written 2001), p. 7.
129 Liston's circular to priests, 26 January 1922. LIS 17, ACDA.
130 Minutes of bishops' meeting, 7 February 1927. Minute book CLE 1–5, ACDA. This was after Bishop Brodie asked for a clarification of the rules against priests attending theatre or the races.
131 Letters, Cleary to Fr Finn of Te Kuiti, 11 and 14 September 1923. CLE 122–2, ACDA.
132 See the exchange of letters between the Catholic jockey J.M.B. Buchanan and Cleary, 14 June and 17 June 1924. CLE 108–3, ACDA.
133 See, for example, Liston to Fr George Kelly of Tuakau, 9 December 1922, threatening him with suspension for incurring heavy debts and engaging in unauthorised property transactions. CLE 123–2, ACDA. On the other hand, Cleary wrote to both Liston and the Apostolic Delegate in August 1921, vindicating Fr O'Flynn of Te Kuiti for ignorantly, but in good faith, contracting debts to build a church without first consulting the bishop. CLE 122–2, ACDA.
134 In 1928–29, Cleary had to determine the exact boundary of Avondale and Mt Albert parishes. CLE 106–1, ACDA. Liston's determining of the boundary between Newton and Balmoral parishes, in 1924–25, has already been noted.
135 On 18 February 1922, Liston threatened Fr Dominick O'Brien of Tuakau with suspension for drunkenness (O'Brien left the diocese later in the year). CLE 123–2, ACDA. On 10 March 1926, Cleary to Fr Van Westeinde in Whakatane, rebuking him for his drinking and also complaining of the untidy state of his presbytery. CLE 112–3, ACDA. In March 1926 and March 1928, Fr Silk of Matamata had to defend himself on the charge of being drunk and also of deserting his parish for three days to attend a cricket match. CLE 112–2, ACDA. On 28 January 1930, Marist superior Kennedy wrote to Liston of the 'weakness for drink' of the parish priest at Whangarei. CLE 113–2, ACDA.
136 Letter, Cleary to Fr Joseph Duffy of Papakura, 30 October 1928. CLE 129–1, ACDA.
137 Letter, Cleary to Fr John Taylor of Matamata, 14 September 1924. CLE 112–2, ACDA. On 19 December 1926, Bishop Brodie wrote to Cleary asking him to forbid Taylor to visit Christchurch as he was too familiar with a young woman there. In November 1927, Cleary rebuked Taylor for his heavy drinking. CLE 123–5, ACDA. In 1926–27, Liston's correspondence with his former student from Mosgiel, Fr William Skinner of Otahuhu, rebuked Skinner for his sexual dalliance with a woman.
138 Letter, Cleary to Fr Aloysius Bowen, 24 August 1924. CLE 106–3, ACDA.
139 See Liston's letters to the Apostolic Delegate, 14 April 1934 and 18 June 1936, concerning Fathers Dominick O'Brien and Philip O'Malley, both of whom had left Auckland for Australia in 1927. LIS 53–2, ACDA.
140 Correspondence between Cleary and Lynch, 29 June 1921 and 31 August 1921; and report on Lynch by Liston, 5 January 1922. CLE 119–2, ACDA.
141 Letters between parishioners, Cleary and Lynch, 8 August 1924, 7 April and 10 April 1925. CLE 110–1, ACDA.
142 On 21 March 1926 and 25 May 1926. In the former instance, Kirrane was present to hear the parishioners' complaints. CLE 107, ACDA.
143 Letter, Buxton to Cleary, 21 December 1924. Letters, Cleary to O'Carroll, 28 April and 11 May 1925. CLE 119–5, ACDA.
144 The 1924–25 correspondence between Cleary and Farragher. CLE 123–5, ACDA.
145 File CLE 126 (Mercy Sisters), ACDA, contains correspondence relating to dispensations granted by both Cleary and Liston.
146 Correspondence February-March 1925, Cleary and Holbrook. CLE 113–2, ACDA.
147 The long correspondence between Cleary and Holbrook is a good example of Cleary's propensity for wanting to have the last word in all circumstances, in this case about a long-ago conversation Holbrook was supposed to have had. Even after Holbrook had made his apology, Cleary continued to write. Letters between them are dated 7, 15, 17, 20, 22 and 23 December 1925. CLE 109–2, ACDA.
148 McGuinness is identified as Dean of Ohinemuri in a note from Mgr Mahoney dated 10 October 1918. CLE 81, ACDA.
149 The long correspondence, mainly between Cleary and McGuinness, with some comments by Liston, dated 1921–23, is filed in LIS 17/1, ACDA.

150 See, for example, [Delaney], *Gracious is the Time*, pp 148–49, on Patrick Darby's donations to the Mercy Sisters.
151 Deceased Priests File, ACDA.
152 Minutes of synod,18 January 1912. CLE 2–2, ACDA.
153 'Death of a Priest', *Zealandia*, 22 May 1941, p. 4.
154 Correspondence between Ward and Lenihan, December 1906 and January 1907. LEN 28–5, ACDA.
155 Mahoney's 1917 report on diocese. CLE 2–3, ACDA.
156 This related to moneys which Cleary believed he was owed by the Catholic Federation to cover his expenses in the campaign against the Bible-in-Schools movement. Letter, Cleary to Apostolic Delegate concerning Darby, 24 July 1918. CLE 87–1, ACDA.
157 See summary of events in folder CLE 129–1, ACDA.
158 See Cleary to Apostolic Delegate, 12 January 1920. CLE 82–2, ACDA. And Cleary to Darby, 31 August 1921. LIS 16–1, ACDA.
159 Most of the information in the preceding paragraph is derived from the folder concerning the Casey estate, LIS 21–3, ACDA. Aftershocks from the affair continued for a number of years. In the late 1920s, the new parish priest of Hamilton, Michael Bleakley, was still being confronted by members of the Casey family with claims on church properties. See letter, Bleakley to Cleary, 26 October 1926. LIS 21–3, ACDA.
160 Letter, Liston to Whyte, 10 August 1922. Whyte Papers, DCDA.
161 Letter, Liston to Whyte, 22 August 1922. Whyte Papers, DCDA.
162 See Liston's minute of meeting with Darby, 18 October 1922. CLE 129–1, ACDA.
163 Letter, Liston to Cardinal Prefect of Propaganda, 30 October 1922. CLE 129–1, ACDA. Letter, Liston to Whyte, 20 November 1922. Whyte Papers, DCDA.
164 Letter, Cleary to Liston, 29 September 1922. LIS 16–1, ACDA.
165 This unsigned letter *appears* to be from James Coffey to Bishop Whyte. It is undated but is apparently from the end of 1922. It is included in the Deceased Priests C box folder on James Coffey, DCDA.
166 Letter, Brodie to Liston, 31 October 1922. CLE 83–2, ACDA. An alternative version of the case of Fr Darby, which presented him as the innocent victim, passed into priestly folklore. Fr John Edward Lyons, interview, 29 December 2002.
167 Liston's sermon reported in *Tablet*, 13 May 1925, pp 15, 17, 19.
168 This is point 23 of Liston's concluding 28–point defence of himself, mid-1929, included in LIS 16–4, ACDA.
169 Liston's 28–point defence of himself. LIS 16–4, ACDA.
170 Liston used his personal diary for 1926 to write summaries of books he was currently reading, such as William Pember Reeves' *Long White Cloud*. LIS 15, ACDA.
171 Felix Donnelly, *One Priest's Life*, Auckland, 1982, p. 163, says that Liston in the 1920s was a 'card gambler'.
172 'Sixty Years in the Priesthood', Brian Healy's interview with Liston on the occasion of his sacerdotal diamond jubilee. *Zealandia*, 30 January 1964, p. 3.
173 *Tablet*, 6 May 1925, pp 29 ff; *Tablet*, 2 February 1927, p. 29; *Month*, 18 January 1927.
174 Correspondence of June-July 1925 relating to this matter is filed in LIS 16–1, CLE 106–1 and CLE 126–2 (Mercy Sisters File), ACDA.
175 Letter, Cleary to Liston, 8 February 1925. CLE 110–4, ACDA.
176 Letter, Cleary to Fr Eugene O'Connor of Takapuna, 3 March 1927. CLE 120–3, ACDA.

Chapter IV: The Lesser Trial, 1922

1   Liston's speech and subsequent trial for sedition have been written about more than any other single episode in his life. They have been the subject of many articles, of passing references in general texts and of two full-length studies. The first was Michael Brian Laws's unpublished dissertation, 'The Sedition Trial of Bishop Liston', University of Otago, 1980, which confines itself to a narrative of the trial itself. The second was Rory Sweetman's much more detailed *Bishop in the Dock*, Auckland, 1997, which contextualises the trial and makes use of much original material. Speech and trial were very fully reported in the press at the time. In its issue of 15 June 1922,

the *Month* devoted 21 closely-printed pages of wide double columns to the affair, giving both the defence and the prosecution cases with the minimum of additional editorialising. Unless otherwise stated, it is the *Month*'s account of the trial itself that is followed here.

2   'Ireland in Bondage – Catholic Bishop's View', *NZH*, 18 March 1922.
3   'Ireland – Past and Present – Bishop Liston's Address, *AS*, 18 March 1922.
4   On Stanbrook and O'Brien, see Sweetman, *Bishop in the Dock*, chapter 2.
5   Editorial, 'The Irishman's Coat Tail', *NZH*, 18 March 1922.
6   Editorial, 'A Deplorable Attitude', *AS*, 18 March 1922.
7   *NZH*, 20 March 1922.
8   Editorial, 'The Mayor's Protest', *NZH*, 20 March 1922.
9   On Gunson's political background, see Sweetman, *Bishop in the Dock*, chapter 3. It is notable that Gunson had been among those, caught in wartime patriotic zeal, who had insisted on Dalmatians being made to do war work. See Judith Bassett, 'Colonial Justice', p. 170.
10 Letter, Buxton to Michael Curran, 9 April 1922. Curran Papers, Box 1, ICR.
11 Letters from Darby and Earwood both appeared on the *Herald*'s letters page, 23 March 1922.
12 *Month*, 15 June 1922, p. 6.
13 Sweetman, *Bishop in the Dock*, chapter 10.
14 Letter, O'Regan to Liston, 25 March 1922. LIS 6–1/20, ACDA.
15 Laws, 'The Sedition Trial of Bishop Liston', p. 32.
16 See Sweetman, *Bishop in the Dock*, chapter 12.
17 *Month*, 15 June 1922, p. 6.
18 Letter, Kelly to Hagan, 7 August 1922. Hagan Papers, Box 13, ICR.
19 For contemporary accounts of the preliminary hearing, see 'Committed for Trial', *NZH*, 2 May 1922, p. 9; 'Charge of Sedition', *AS*, 1 May 1922; and *Month*, 15 June 1922, p 7. Sweetman, *Bishop in the Dock*, chapters 15 and 16, gives an account of the lawyers' performances as well as the crown's decision not to hold the trial over Easter.
20 Letter, Liston to Whyte, 8 April 1922. Whyte Papers, DCDA.
21 Letter, Liston to Whyte, 12 April 1922. Whyte Papers, DCDA.
22 Letter, Liston to Whyte, 3 May 1922. Whyte Papers, DCDA.
23 Letter, Liston to Whyte, 10 May 1922. Whyte Papers, DCDA.
24 The *Tablet*'s first report of the concert simply said it was a 'decided success'. *Tablet*, 30 March 1922, p. 23. Report of the preliminary hearing, *Tablet*, 4 May 1922, pp 21–22.
25 *Tablet*, 18 May 1922, pp 22–24; and 25 May, pp 18–19, 21–23. *Month*, 15 June 1922 (21 pages of report).
26 'Bishop Liston's Trial' and 'The Bishop Acquitted', *NZH*, 17 and 18 May 1922; 'Charge of Sedition – Bishop in Court', *AS*, 16 and 17 May 1922.
27 On the feebleness of the prosecution's witnesses, and on the police 'conspiracy of silence', see Sweetman, *Bishop in the Dock*, chapters 11 and 17.
28 *Month*, 15 June 1922, p. 12.
29 Liston's defence notes, LIS 6–1/3(i), ACDA.
30 *Month*, 15 June 1922, p. 13.
31 *Month*, 15 June 1922, p. 14.
32 Laws, 'Sedition Trial', p. 77 and chapter 5.
33 *Month*, 15 June 1922, pp 23–25.
34 Ibid., p. 7.
35 Editorial, 'The Trial of the Bishop', *NZH*, 18 May 1922.
36 Sweetman, *Bishop in the Dock*, pp 249–50.
37 *Month*, 15 June 1922, p. 3.
38 Advertisement, *Tablet*, 6 July 1922, p. 6.
39 A draft version of the testimonial, in Liston's handwriting, is filed with his defence notes. LIS 6–5, ACDA.
40 Letter, Gunson to Liston, 24 June, 28 June, 3 July, 10 July 1922. LIS 6/1–47, ACDA.
41 Letter, Liston to Whyte, 3 July 1922. Whyte Papers, DCDA.
42 Letter, Liston to Whyte, 18 July 1922. Whyte Papers, DCDA.
43 Letter, Liston to Whyte, 1 August 1922. Whyte Papers, DCDA.

44   See van der Krogt, 'More a Part than Apart', p. 339; and Sweetman, *Bishop in the Dock*, pp 259–260.

45   *Tablet*, 25 May 1922, p. 25.

46   See O'Regan's speech, *Month*, 15 June 1922, pp 17–22. Also Liston's defence notes. LIS 6–1/3(I), ACDA.

47   O'Farrell, *The Irish in Australia*, p. 281.

48   Editorial, 'A Question of Fact', *NZH*, 20 March 1922.

49   News reports from Ireland sometimes literally involved their kith and kin. Fr Watters, shot dead 'accidentally' by British troops during the Easter Rising, had been the first rector of St Patrick's College in Wellington. See Nicholas Simmons, 'Archbishop Francis Redwood', p. 122. In March 1921, Liston said requiem mass for the brother of a local nun, who had been killed by the military in Drogheda; see *Tablet*, 10 March 1921, p. 21. Also in March 1921, one of the priests at St Benedict's parish received news that his parents' home in Ireland had been burnt down by the Black-and-Tans; see *Month*, 15 March 1921, p. 7.

50   Approximately 1,500 died in the Anglo-Irish conflict 1919–21. Approximately 4,000 died in the Irish Civil War 1922–23, including 77 Republican prisoners executed by the Free State government. J.J. Lee, *Ireland 1912–1985, Politics and Society*, Cambridge, 1989, chapter 2, esp. pp 56–69.

51   Patrick O'Farrell, *Vanished Kingdoms – Irish in Australia and New Zealand*, Sydney, 1990, p. 224.

52   Pastoral letter signed by Cardinal Logue and the whole Irish hierarchy, dated 22 October 1922. Filed in Box Mgr M. Curran – Political Papers, DAA. This pastoral appeared when the civil war was already in progress. Before the outbreak of hostilities between Free State forces and 'Irregulars', Logue and the hierarchy had already written a pastoral (dated 7 May 1922) condemning both the Protestant violence in Belfast and the threats of civil war being made by the republican military council. LIS 6–1/37 (I), ACDA.

53   See Kildea, *Tearing the Fabric*, pp 245 ff. For Daniel Mannix's attitude, more complex than a simple endorsement of the Irish Republicans, see Santamaria, *Daniel Mannix*, chapters 10 and 11.

54   Sweetman, *Faith and Fraternalism*, pp 22–23.

55   *Month*, 15 September 1922, p. 9; and *Tablet*, 21 September 1922, p. 23.

56   *Tablet*, 26 October 1922, p. 27, notes Cleary's presence at the funerals. See Boland, *James Duhig*, chapter 8 for Duhig's reaction to the Irish Civil War.

57   *Tablet*, 16 November 1922, p. 27.

58   Letter, Forde to Cleary, 6 December 1925. CLE 121–2, ACDA.

59   Van der Krogt, 'More a Part than Apart', pp 7 ff.

60   See K.J. Walsh, *Yesterday's Seminary*, chapter 6.

61   O'Meaghan, *Held Firm by Faith*, p. 248.

62   There were debates over whether there should be a full procession or only the Town Hall concert on St Patrick's Day; see *Tablet*, 18 February 1925, p. 30; 1 April 1925; and 9 March 1927, p. 30. One correspondent complained of apathy about the celebration; see *Tablet*, 2 March 1927, p. 30, and 23 March 1927, p. 31. This may have been wilful overstatement, as in 1928 both Cleary and Liston presided at a major St Patrick's Day event in the Domain (at which both the Free State flag and the Union Jack were flown); see *Tablet*, 28 March 1928. Next year, *Tablet* was rejoicing at the 'revival' of a full St Patrick's Day programme; see *Tablet*, 3 April 1929, p. 44. But after 1930, the celebration was confined to children's events only; see *Month*, September 1930, p. 18.

63   Editorial (by Liston), 'A Great Leader', *Zealandia*, 14 November 1963.

64   Unsourced anecdote recalled in Sweetman, *Bishop in the Dock*, p. 317 (n. 56). The incident took place at a meeting of the Guild of Saints Cosmas and Damian. Liston was not the only person who preferred not to recall the 1922 trial. In reminiscences of his 'famous cases', Vincent Meredith makes no mention of it. Sir Vincent Meredith, *A Long Brief – Experiences of a Crown Solicitor*, Auckland, 1966.

65   Max Satchell, 'Pulpit Politics', BA Hons History thesis, University of Otago, 1983, chapter 4, especially p. 51.

66   See file of letters between Cleary and the Minister of Justice, E.P. Lee (who was sympathetic to the PPA), in which Cleary calls for an investigation into the possible

incendiarism at Grey Lynn, March-April 1921. CLE 109–2, ACDA. See also *Tablet*, 4 April 1921, p. 15, where, reporting Liston's appeal on the burnt-out sisters' behalf, reference is made to 'the horse-whipped parson and his foul-minded followers' who might have incited the incident. Much of the *Month* for 15 April 1921 is taken up with the fire at Grey Lynn, with Cleary remarking on a PPA meeting which had taken place in the near vicinity before the fire. In fact, in large wooden buildings at that time, fires were particularly common. Both of Auckland's Catholic orphanages were gutted by fire in the 1920s, the boys' orphanage in 1923 and the girls' orphanage in 1929. See [Delaney], *Gracious is the Time*, pp 101–105.

67 Such as the dispute over the Payne Trophy in Christchurch 1923–24. O'Meeghan, *Held Firm by Faith*, pp 140–141.

68 See Cleary's correspondence with Dean Lighthead (especially the letter of 22 October 1925) concerning this 'art union', which had been attacked in print by the Baptist polemicist, J.J. North. CLE 120–1, ACDA.

69 *Tablet*, 8 May 1929, p. 50; and 8 October 1924, p. 28.

70 *Tablet*, 26 April 1923, p. 27.

71 *Sentinel*, 1 June 1923. This article, and replies to it by Fr Silk and local Protestants, are preserved in CLE 119–2, ACDA. See also Silk's refutation of Howard Elliott, *Month*,17 March 1925.

72 The real purpose of the *Ne Temere* decree was to get Catholics to solemnise their marriages in church. Evidence of the effect it had on some Catholics is seen in the letters (16 February 1921 and 18 July 1922) of Fr William Christopher Dunphy (of Paeroa) to Cleary, in which Dunphy seeks to regularise the 'irregular' marriages of some of his parishioners.

73 H.S. Moores, 'Rise of the PPA', MA History thesis, University of Auckland, 1966, p. 312.

74 The July-August 1929 exchange between Cleary and Minister of Education, Harry Atmore. CLE 121–2, ACDA.

75 See Van der Krogt, 'More a Part than Apart', p. 340, on *Sentinel*'s circulation.

76 Moores, 'Rise of the PPA', pp 319–20.

77 W.J. Gardner, 'W.F. Massey in Power', *Political Science*,13 (2), September 1961, pp 25–26. For a very sympathetic reading of Massey's extrication from PPA involvement, see Sweetman, 'New Zealand Catholicism', pp 342–346, and *Bishop in the Dock*, chapter 9.

78 Gardner, 'W.F. Massey in Power'. For further evidence of Coates' negative attitude towards Protestant zealotry, see Michael Bassett, *Coates of Kaipara*, Auckland, 1995, pp 16, 59 and 134. Also Bruce Farland, *Coates' Tale – J.G. Coates*, Wellington, 1995, pp 28 and 72.

79 Letter, Kelly to Hagan, 31 December 1925. Hagan Papers, Box 21, ICR.

80 See D.V. MacDonald, 'The New Zealand Bible in Schools League', MA thesis, Victoria University of Wellington, 1964, chapters 4 and 5. In July 1925, all six Catholic bishops were signatories to a statement declaring their opposition to what they called the 'State Religion' bill, on the usual grounds of fear of proselytism, lack of an effective conscience clause for parents and teachers, and the (Protestant) sectarian nature of proposed Bible readings. Statement included in Education Box 375, WCAA.

81 Figures according to James Watson, 'Were Catholics Over-Represented in the Public Service During the Early Twentieth Century?', *Political Science*, 42 (2), December 1990, p. 32.

82 Ian Breward, *Godless Schools*, Christchurch, 1967, p. 78.

83 Howard Elliott had earlier attempted to present the Labour Party as a Catholic 'front', but was refuted by Labour's representation committee which pointed out that there was not one practising Catholic on the Labour Party executive or on the staff of the *Maoriland Worker*. Moores, 'Rise of the PPA', pp 273–76. By contrast, in 1920 in New South Wales, Catholics were 25 per cent of the population, but made up 60 per cent of the Labor caucus and held 40 per cent of the Labor state government's cabinet positions. Kildea, *Tearing the Fabric*, p. 227.

84 R.P. Davis, 'The New Zealand Labour Party's 'Irish Campaign' 1916–1921', *Political Science*,19 (2), December 1967. Also Davis, *Irish Issues*, chapter 9.

85 Gustafson, *From the Cradle to the Grave*, pp 122 and 128.

86 *Tablet*, 24 July 1929.

87   Laws, 'Sedition Trial of Bishop Liston', pp 34–35. Tom Bloodworth kept a file of newspaper cuttings on the trial which he later donated to the Catholic diocese. DEL 37, ACDA.
88   Letter, Lee to Liston, 24 March 1922. LIS 6–2, ACDA.
89   Letter, Lee to Liston, 27 March 1922. LIS 6–2, ACDA.
90   Letter, Liston to Lee, 24 March 1922. Lee Papers, NZMS 828, Series 9, Folder 1, Auckland Public Library.
91   Letter, Tom Bloodworth's letter of congratulations to Liston, 18 May 1922. LIS 6–2, ACDA.
92   Reports on the council meeting at which they voiced their opposition to the ban appeared in the *Herald* (28 July 1922) and the *Auckland Star* (29 July 1922). Cuttings preserved in LIS 6–1/50, ACDA.
93   Letter, Bloodworth to Liston, 14 August 1922. LIS 6–1/54, ACDA.
94   Letter, Fred Bartram to Holbrook, 27 July 1923, explaining why Labour MPs had not bothered to reply to some of Potter's anti-Catholic rhetoric in parliament. Bartram said Labour was adopting a policy of publicly ignoring him. CLE 109–2, ACDA.
95   Letter, Lee to Liston, 26 July 1927. LIS 17, ACDA. Lee and Savage also at different times wrote to Cleary congratulating him on his efforts against the Bible-in-Schools and the Marriage Amendment Act. Letter, Lee to Cleary, 11 July 1923. CLE 83–5, ACDA. Letter, Savage to Cleary, 12 October 1920. CLE 95–2, ACDA.
96   See letters column, *NZH*, 14–22 December 1922.
97   'Labour Party's Success and the Education System – Bishop Liston's Remarks', *AS*, 13 December 1922.
98   Lee in a letter to R.P. Davis dated 16 March 1965. Reported in Davis, 'NZ Labour Party's 'Irish Campaign'', footnote p. 23.
99   *Tablet*, 29 July 1920, p. 21; 5 August 1920, p. 31; 25 November 1920, p. 25; 2 December 1920, p. 25; 16 December 1920, p. 31; 12 May 1921, p. 32.
100   *Month*,13 December 1920, pp 5–6; 22 January 1921, pp 8–10; 15 February 1921, p. 15.
101   McGill, *The Lion and the Wolfhound*, p. 149.
102   *Saoirse – NZ Irish Post*, 2 (4) (March/April 1983), 5 (1) and 8 (3).
103   See Denis Edwards' negative review of Sweetman's *Bishop in the Dock* in *Saoirse*, 13 (5) (July-August 1998), basically accusing it of not being racy enough and of not acknowledging Michael Laws's thesis as a source. A more generous assessment of the book (by the present writer) appeared in *New Zealand Books*, October 1997.
104   Denis Edwards, 'Sedition!', *Saoirse*, 8 (3).
105   Ernest Simmons, *In Cruce Salus*, p. 227.

Chapter V: The Greater Trial, 1923–29

1   'In the present circumstances and always, you have my kindliest wishes, fraternal affection and full confidence' read the telegram Cleary arranged to have reproduced in the press. See *Month*, 15 June 1922, p. 5.
2   Letter, Cleary to Liston, 20 June 1928. LIS 6–6, ACDA.
3   'Notes' sent by Cleary to Apostolic Delegate, January 1929. LIS 6–6, ACDA.
4   Letter, Liston to Cattaneo, 18 May 1929. LIS 6–6, ACDA.
5   Liston's reply to Cleary's charge no. 27. LIS 16–4, ACDA.
6   LIS 6, LIS 16 and LIS 17, ACDA.
7   See, for example, the photograph accompanying the story about the hierarchy's attending the opening of the Christian Brothers' college in Oamaru, where Liston stands at the other end of the group from Cleary. *Tablet*, 23 February 1927, p. 41. See also *Month*, 19 June 1928, p. 23, where a snap of the two bishops at the opening of St Peter's (Rural) Maori College shows Liston looking away from Cleary, who is smiling at the camera. It is, of course, very easy to read too much into such body language.
8   Address of clergy to Cleary. CLE 90–1, ACDA.
9   Ernest Simmons, *In Cruce Salus*, p. 225.
10   Letter, Cleary to Liston, November 1923. CLE 103, ACDA.
11   Letter, Cleary to Liston, 10 March 1924. LIS 17, ACDA.
12   Liston's minute book comprises LIS 6–4/1, ACDA.
13   Ibid., pp 2–8.

14 Ibid., p. 10.
15 Ibid., pp 12–24.
16 Ibid., p. 26.
17 Ibid., p. 38.
18 Ibid., pp 40–44.
19 Exchange of letters between Cleary and Liston, September 1924. LIS 16–1, ACDA.
20 Note attached by Liston to letter, Cleary to Liston, 20 December 1924. LIS 16–1, ACDA.
21 Letter, Liston to Director of Education, 1 March 1923. CLE 106–1, ACDA.
22 Paragraph 7 of Cleary's indictment, 1929. LIS 6–6, ACDA.
23 Liston's reply to Paragraph 7. LIS 16–4, ACDA.
24 Paragraph 15, Cleary's indictment. LIS 6–6, ACDA.
25 Liston's reply to paragraph 15. LIS 6–6, ACDA.
26 Ibid.
27 Paragraph 16, Cleary's indictment. LIS 6–6, ACDA.
28 Liston's reply to Paragraph 16. LIS 6–6, ACDA.
29 Liston's reply to Paragraph 16. LIS 16–4, ACDA.
30 Letter, Cleary to Liston, 15 October 1923. LIS 6–6, ACDA.
31 Letter, Cleary to Liston, 18 February 1925. LIS 17, ACDA. Letter, Cleary to Liston, 2 July 1928. LIS 6–6, ACDA.
32 Paragraphs 9, 10, 11, 12, Cleary's indictment. LIS 6–6, ACDA.
33 Liston's reply to Paragraph 9. LIS 16–5, ACDA. The ten parishes listed were Avondale, Thames, Parnell, Paeroa, Pukekohe, Puhoi, Papatoetoe, Papakura, Balmoral and Mt Albert. The parishes which Liston claimed Cleary had burdened with greater debts were Hamilton, Devonport, Whangarei, Te Aroha and Ponsonby (for the building of a church school).
34 Ibid. Also Liston's replies to Paragraphs 10 and 11. LIS 16–4, ACDA.
35 Paragraph 22, Cleary's indictment. LIS 6–6, ACDA.
36 Liston's reply to Paragraph 22. LIS 16–4, ACDA. See also LIS 6–3, ACDA.
37 Letter, Liston to Molloy, 10 January 1922. CLE 119–3, ACDA.
38 Letters, Molloy to Liston, 25 February 1922; Liston to Molloy, 28 February 1922. In a letter to Jeremiah Cahill (8 April 1924), Molloy later ridiculed and made light of Liston's friendly gesture. CLE 119–3, ACDA.
39 Letter, Molloy to Cahill, 8 April 1924. CLE 119–3, ACDA.
40 Letters, Cleary to Molloy, 26 April 1924; Molloy to Cleary, 30 April 1924. CLE 119–3, ACDA.
41 Gallagher, *The Marist Brothers in New Zealand, Fiji and Samoa 1876–1976*, chapter 11.
42 Cleary's letters of 18 and 19 May 1928. LIS 17–4, ACDA.
43 Paragraphs 19 and 20, Cleary's indictment. LIS 6–6, ACDA.
44 Correspondence between Cleary, Edge and McDonald, September 1926. CLE 97–2, ACDA. McDonald was a director of the Phoenix Assurance Company.
45 H.W. Cleary, *The Diocesan Administrative Council*, Auckland, 1929, pp 25 ff (filed in CLE 81–2, ACDA).
46 Letter, Cleary to Marchetti-Salvaggiani, 28 August 1929. CLE 82–5, ACDA.
47 LIS 6–3, ACDA.
48 Paragraphs 5, 8 and 13, Cleary's indictment. LIS 6–6, ACDA.
49 Letter, Cleary to Liston, 24 November 1921. Original of letter in LIS 16–1, ACDA. Typed copy, together with Liston's refutation of these charges, in LIS 16–3 and LIS 17, ACDA.
50 Paragraphs 25 and 26, Cleary's indictment. LIS 6–6, ACDA.
51 Liston's replies to Paragraphs 25 and 26. LIS 16–3 and 16–4, ACDA. The accounts of the orphanage rebuilding fund, 1922–23 (CLE 61–1), are all kept in Liston's handwriting. He himself contributed £500 to a cause he took seriously.
52 Paragraphs 14 and 21, Cleary's indictment. LIS 6–6, ACDA.
53 Editorial, 'Catholics and the Elections', *Month*, 15 September 1922, p. 4.
54 Letters column, *NZH*, 29 June 1928.
55 Editorial, 'Thou Shalt Not Bear False Witness', attacking Canon James, in *New Zealand Worker*, 27 June 1928.
56 'Catholics and Party Politics', *Month*, 21 August 1928, p. 21. '*Month* reprint No.

28 – The State-Religion League. Alleged Catholic Purchase of Labour Party Votes. The League in Politics. The Catholic Church and Party Politics'; and 'Month reprint No. 29 – The Catholic Church and Party Politics – Canon James's Charge of Vote-Jobbing'. Both pamphlets filed in CLE 77, ACDA.

57 Liston's replies to Paragraphs 14 and 21. LIS 16–4, ACDA. For problems with the editor J.C. Gill, see also Nicholas Reid, *The Bishop's Paper*, pp 35–36.

58 Cleary's note setting out the conditions of employment for Gill, which included cataloguing the diocesan library, 6 September 1921. Letter, Cleary to Liston, 18 February 1922, showing his awareness that Gill stole books from the diocesan library to pay for drinks. LIS 16–1, ACDA. Peter McKeefry, who was to edit the *Month* and its successor *Zealandia* for over 20 years, arrived in Auckland from Rome late in 1926. *Tablet*, 1 December 1926, p. 29.

59 Letter, Cleary to Liston, 17 February 1923. LIS 16–1, ACDA.

60 It was Cleary who insisted on a strict interpretation of the Vatican's ban on priests taking part in political activities. Minutes of Bishops' meeting, 4 December 1920. CLE 1–5, ACDA.

61 Letter, Cleary to Liston, 17 February 1923. LIS 16–1, ACDA (Italics added).

62 Letter, Cleary to Liston, 27 February 1923. LIS 16–1, ACDA.

63 Speech reported in *Month*, 15 June 1923, pp 5–11.

64 Letter, Cleary to Cattaneo, 7 July 1928. CLE 82–4, ACDA.

65 See Cleary's friendly exchange of letters on these matters with the Anglican (Anglo-Catholic) Rev Gordon Bell, July 1924. CLE 82–4, ACDA. Also in 1927. CLE 90–2, ACDA.

66 Nicholas Reid, *The Bishop's Paper*, p. 31.

67 Letter, 6 October 1928. Father Eccleton of Tuakau wrote to Cleary a letter of fulsome praise for a special edition of the *Month*, which 'causes every other publication . . . to fade into feeble inanity'. He then proceeded to ask, as a favour, for a meeting with the bishop to discuss parochial matters. CLE 123–2, ACDA.

68 See minutes of 8 December 1927 meeting of the diocesan administrative council, where Cleary proposed selling some of the church's 'Cox's Creek' (Richmond Road) property to underwrite an enlarged format of the *Month*. Minute Book of the Diocesan Administrative Council, CLE 1–3, ACDA.

69 Paragraph 23, Cleary's indictment. LIS 6–6, ACDA.

70 Liston's reply to Paragraph 23, running to 14 pages, exists in different drafts in LIS 6–3, LIS 6–6 and LIS 16–4, ACDA.

71 Sweetman, *Bishop in the Dock*, chapter 14.

72 Letter, Cleary to Liston, 5 April 1922. LIS 16–1, ACDA.

73 Letter, Cleary to Liston, 22 May 1922. LIS 17, ACDA.

74 Letter, Liston to Whyte, 18 July 1922. Whyte Papers, DCDA.

75 Letter, Cleary to Liston, 3 August 1922. LIS 16–1, ACDA. Cleary to Gunson, 3 August 1922. LIS 17, ACDA.

76 Letter, Cleary to Liston, 9 October 1922. LIS 16–1, ACDA.

77 Letter, Cleary to Liston, 21 June 1923. LIS 16–1, ACDA.

78 Letter, Cleary to Liston, 25 August 1922. LIS 17, ACDA.

79 In 1924, the following reports appeared in the *Herald*: 'Missing Schoolgirl' (25 September); 'Missing Girl Appears' (26 September); 'Schoolgirl's Religion' (27 September); 'Schoolgirl's Religion' (29 September); 'Girl Returns Home' (30 September). The following reports appeared in the *Auckland Star*: 'Missing – Where is Margaret Martin?' (25 September); 'Why Girls Leave Home – And When They May Do So' (26 September); 'Schoolgirl's Religion' (29 September).

80 In Australia, Bridget Partridge, a disgruntled ex-nun (the former Sister Liguori), left her convent and later claimed that she had 'escaped'. There was a tussle between members of her Catholic family and the Orange Lodge, which was now sponsoring her, as to where she should live. The Orange Lodge tried, without success, to use her case to have legislation introduced that would allow for regular government inspections of convents. See Kildea, *Tearing the Fabric*, pp 218–226. The case was reported in the *Month*, 15 August 1921, pp 3–4, 7–18.

81 *Month*, 21 October 1924, pp 17–18.

82 It was reprinted in the Melbourne *Advocate*, 30 October 1924, and was also inserted in the (Sydney) *Catholic Press* and the (Dublin) *Freeman's Journal*.

83 H.W. Cleary, *The Martin Case – A Statement*, Auckland, 1924. Copy preserved in CLE 77, ACDA.

84 Paragraph 24, Cleary's indictment. LIS 6–6, ACDA.

85 Liston's reply to Paragraph 24. Different handwritten drafts of this reply exist in LIS 6–6, LIS 16–4 and LIS 17, ACDA. Miss Terry's brother was Fr Francis Henry Terry (1907–78), ordained in Rome in 1928.

86 Liston's allusion is to the report of the drink-driving charges faced by Father Joseph Duffy, which appeared in the *Herald* on the same day as reports of the Eucharistic Congress in Sydney. 'Intoxication Charge – Catholic Priest in Car', *NZH*, 6 September 1928.

87 Documents relating to Liston's financial support for his sister are found in LIS 8–1/3 and 1/4 and LIS 9–1, ACDA. When Liston was in America in 1926, he took an interest in how psychiatric hospitals were run, visiting the Mental Hospital and Home for Incurables of St John of God in Montreal (which catered for both Catholic and Jewish patients). See 1926 diary, LIS 15, ACDA.

88 Letter, Cleary to Liston, 10 April 1929. In a letter mainly about the Knights of the Southern Cross, Cleary remarked, 'Circumstances known to you, and also to me since the end of 1921, made me feel under an obligation to show you special and fraternal consideration, even under those trying circumstances'. LIS 16–3, ACDA.

89 Letter, Cleary to Liston, 30 March 1922. Seeking to recruit priests overseas, Cleary claimed to discover that one Auckland diocesan priest's 'family had insanity in it'. LIS 16–1, ACDA. Letter, Cleary to Liston, 4 March 1929. Cleary turned down a student for the priesthood after Liston queried the student's mentally-unbalanced family background. LIS 17, ACDA.

90 Letter, Cleary to Liston, 4 March 1929. LIS 17, ACDA.

91 Letter, Donne to Liston, 4 June 1929, enclosing letters from the publishers Sheed and Ward dated 8 and 11 February 1929. Liston's thanks are pencilled over Donne's letter. LIS 17, ACDA.

92 Paragraph 18, Cleary's indictment. LIS 6–6, ACDA.

93 Paragraph 28, ibid.

94 Liston's reply to Paragraph 18. LIS 16–4, ACDA.

95 Paragraph 24, Cleary's indictment. LIS 6–6, ACDA.

96 Minute Book of Diocesan Administrative Council, CLE 1–3, ACDA. Cleary's complaint is pencilled between minutes of September 1921 and July 1923, followed by his own excuse for not keeping minutes later. Minutes for meetings of 10 May 1927 and 18 May 1927 have McVeagh receiving correspondence from Liston declining council-related work.

97 Cleary's diary for 1895 is filled with clippings of his letters to the press on these matters. CLE 6–7, ACDA.

98 H.W. Cleary, *The Orange Society*, London, 1899.

99 On 16 June 1922, Liston wrote to Bishop Whyte to check a rumour that the Knights of Columbus had fallen under some sort of papal disfavour. They had not. Whyte Papers, DCDA. In America in 1926, Liston spoke to a number of American bishops about the rules and functioning of the Knights of Columbus. 1926 diary LIS 15, ACDA.

100 Knights of the Southern Cross application form filed in Whyte Papers, DCDA.

101 Boland, *James Duhig*, p. 214.

102 Compare minutes of Australian hierarchy 9–10 October 1924 with minutes of Australasian hierarchy (at which the New Zealand bishops Brodie, O'Shea and Liston were present), 13 September 1937. Box 19, CCDA.

103 Ian F. Thompson, *So Much to Do . . . 75 Years with the Knights of the Southern Cross of New Zealand*, privately published, 2002, chapter 1, pp 23–30 and pp 35 ff.

104 Letter, Brodie to Whyte, 5 January 1923. On 24 September 1922, T.P. Gilfidden of the Auckland Senator's Lodge wrote to Whyte to request permission to set up a branch in Dunedin. Whyte Papers, DCDA.

105 Two extremely long letters (each divided into Parts 'A', 'B' and 'C' from Cleary to Liston, the circular being Part 'D' of the latter letter), 21 March 1929 and 6 April 1929. LIS 16–3, ACDA.

106 Letter, Liston to Cleary, 5 April 1929. LIS 16–3, ACDA. In the same file is Liston's 24-page account of the beginnings of the organisation, claiming it was a lay initiative.

107   Minutes of bishop's meeting, 24 April 1929. CLE 1–5, ACDA.
108   Liston's reply. LIS 6–6, ACDA.
109   July-November 1918 correspondence between Cleary and Dawson and Gray. CLE 89, ACDA.
110   See 'The Licensing Poll', *Month*, March 1919, pp 5–7; 'The Liquor Poll', *Month*, November 1919, pp 13–17; 'The Liquor Problem', *Month*, 20 October 1925, pp 17–18.
111   Newspaper advertisement for the Alliance, dated 3 November 1925, included in CLE 85–2, ACDA.
112   An official publication of the NZ Alliance, Rev J. Cocker and J. Malton Murray (eds), *Temperance and Prohibition in New Zealand*, London, 1930, notes (pp 160–161) Cleary and Todd as the only active Catholic supporters of the cause. Conrad Bollinger, *Grog's Own Country*, Wellington, 1959, p. 56, gives brief notice of Cleary's and Todd's involvement in Prohibition, and of the Prohibitionist lecture tours of Father Hayes. Van der Krogt, 'More a Part than Apart', notes (p. 366) that the Catholic Labour MP Dan Sullivan favoured Prohibition. However, one of the crusading priests was regarded with caution by Cleary. This was the American Father Zurcher, who edited a publication called *Catholics and Prohibition*. On 23 November 1922, Cleary wrote to Liston approving of his circumspect approach to Zurcher. CLE 85–2, ACDA.
113   James Kelly cynically wrote to John Hagan in Rome that Jeremiah Cahill was 'a Prohibitionist with Cleary and otherwise when not with him', 14 January 1920. Hagan Papers, Box 9, ICR.
114   Letter, Redwood to Whyte, 9 September 1922. Whyte Papers, DCDA. Also Redwood's pastorals on the liquor issue, *Tablet*, 28 October 1925, pp 30–31; and 24 October 1928, pp 22–23.
115   Letter, Whyte to Apostolic Delegate, 13 September 1922. Whyte Papers, DCDA.
116   Letter, Whyte to Pesorari, 21 May 1927. Whyte Papers, DCDA.
117   Nicholas Simmons, 'Archbishop Francis Redwood', chapter 6.
118   The brewer Ernest Davis offered Liston, gratis, a plot of land in Whangarei for a new Catholic church. See exchange between Davis and Liston, 18 and 19 September 1922. CLE 124–4, ACDA.
119   Letters, Liston to Whyte, 21 August and 25 September 1922. Whyte Papers, DCDA.
120   Letter, Liston to Whyte, 20 November 1922. Whyte Papers, DCDA. See also Liston's handwritten comments suggesting that the bishops should make a strong joint statement on the danger to altar wine which Prohibition represented, and that they should denounce the Prohibitionist Father Hayes. These comments are written on a letter from Bishop Brodie to Liston, 31 October 1922. CLE 83–2, ACDA.
121   Gustafson, *From the Cradle to the Grave*, p. 103.
122   Liston's 1926 diary. LIS 15, ACDA.
123   See John D. Prince, 'Look Back in Amber: The General Licensing Poll in New Zealand 1919–87', *Political Science*, 48 (1), July 1996.
124   Cleary's handwritten autobiographical notes, LIS 27–1 and CLE 3–2, ACDA. See also his 1924 letter (not otherwise dated) to W.H. Grattan Flood of Enniscorthy. CLE 90–1, ACDA.
125   H.W. Cleary, *An Impeached Nation – Being a Study of Irish Outrages*, Dunedin, 1909.
126   Sweetman, 'New Zealand Catholicism', pp 212–213.
127   Letter, Kelly to John Hagan, 31 December 1918. Hagan Papers, Box 6, ICR.
128   Letter, Cleary to Liston, 26 October 1922. LIS 16–1, ACDA.
129   Letter, Cleary to Liston, 29 September 1922. LIS 16–1, ACDA.
130   Letter, Cleary to Liston, 29 November 1922. LIS 17, ACDA.
131   Letter, Cleary to Killaloe, 2 August 1922. CLE 84–1, ACDA.
132   On Redwood's family background, see Nicholas Simmons, 'Archbishop Francis Redwood', chapters 1 and 2.
133   See minutes of bishops' conference 1920 where Bishop Brodie strongly opposed Cleary's proposal for a 'mutilated' catechism. CLE 1–5, ACDA. See also Van der Krogt, *More A Part than Apart*, p. 351.
134   Letter 'C', Cleary to Liston, 6 April 1929. LIS 16–3, ACDA.
135   See p. 10 of Liston's 24–page handwritten document, 'The Beginnings of the KSC in

New Zealand'. LIS 16–1, ACDA.

136 Liston's response to Paragraph 15 of Cleary's indictment. LIS 16–4, ACDA.
137 Letter, Grennell to Hagan, 14 July 1929. Hagan Papers, Box 27, ICR.
138 See Ernest Simmons, *In Cruce Salus*, pp 229–230.
139 (Unpublished) 'Memoirs of Bishop John Mackey', 2001, p. 19.
140 In 1928–29, there was a major row over the standard of music between the cathedral administrator Leonard Buxton and the cathedral choirmaster Professor Moor-Karoly, which led to Moor-Karoly resigning his conductorship for some years. See correspondence in CLE 103, ACDA.
141 For Father Daniel Silk's 1922 quarrel with Liston over the establishment of a convent in Puhoi, see Silk to Liston, 29 November 1922. CLE 119–2, ACDA. This was the third letter that Silk wrote Liston over the issue. The other two were on 7 and 8 November 1922. For Liston's plans for Puhoi, see his letter to Mother M. Laurence of the Josephites, 15 December 1921. CLE 127–4, ACDA.
142 Letter, Bruning to Superior General, 13 May 1929. Box NZL-3 (1913–34), Mill Hill archives, London.
143 Van Dijk, 'Report on the Maori Mission'.
144 Undated letter Jansen to Superior-General, c. 1924, ibid.
145 In 1921–22, Liston removed Fr Westeinde from Tauranga parish for being continually 'grumpy' to parishioners. On 13 April 1929, Cleary made the Mill Hills Westeinde and Devolder take the pledge to abstain from alcohol. CLE 102–2, ACDA.
146 Letter, Van Dijk to Cardinal Van Rossum, 22 April 1929. CLE 102–2, ACDA.
147 Liston's answer to Cleary's Paragraph 7. LIS 16–5, ACDA.
148 Letter, Cleary to Sisters of Compassion, 6 November 1926, and other correspondence. CLE 125–1 and 125–2, ACDA.
149 March-April 1926 correspondence Cleary-O'Brien. LIS 17, ACDA.
150 Letter, Kelly to Hagan, 7 April 1923. Hagan Papers, Box 15, ICR.
151 Letter, Kelly to Hagan, 8 February 1924. Hagan Papers, Box 16, ICR.
152 Letter, Kelly to Hagan, 31 December 1925. Hagan Papers, Box 21, ICR.
153 Letter, 17 March 1928. Hagan Papers, Box 25, ICR. Further comments by Kelly on the Auckland situation are found in Kelly to Hagan, 30 January 1927 (or 1928 – date uncertain). Hagan Papers, Box 23, ICR. See also Kelly to Hagan, 12 June 1924. Hagan Papers, Box 18, ICR.
154 See letter, Kelly to Hagan, 15 October 1927. Hagan Papers, Box 24, ICR.
155 Letter, Brodie to Liston, 30 May 1929. CLE 83–2, ACDA. See also letter of 8 June 1929, same file.
156 Letter, Whyte to Liston, 12 June 1929. CLE 83–3, ACDA.
157 'Statement by Bishop Brodie', a three-page document. LIS-6, ACDA, and Box 11, CCDA.
158 Letter, Liston to Curran, 25 March 1929. Curran Papers, Box 3, ICR.
159 Letter, Curran to Liston, 30 September 1929. LIS 17–4, ACDA.
160 Undated memorandum from Curran, ibid.
161 Letter, Liston to Curran, 10 November 1930. Curran Papers, Box 4, ICR.
162 Letter, Liston to Mother Helen Lynch, 10 June 1926. A183 Fr John Flanagan Papers, Folder 6, ACDA.
163 Exchange of letters between Cleary and Kelly, 11 July and 15 July 1929. CLE 97–1, ACDA.
164 Letter, Kelly to Hagan, 27 January 1930. Hagan Papers, Box 26, ICR.
165 Letter, Liston to Cattaneo, 19 December 1929. LIS 53 and LIS 27–1, ACDA.
166 Cleary's death was commemorated in a gracious editorial in the *Tablet* (11 December 1929, p. 3) and in a special issue of the *Month* (17 December 1929), both of which gave details of his manner of death but neither of which hinted at any dispute between the bishops. There was a further irony in that the doctor who attended Cleary in his last illness, Dr Edward Burton Gunson, later a Harley Street specialist and Minister of Health in the Northern Territory of Australia, was the brother of the mayor who had urged Liston's prosecution for sedition in 1922. (Information supplied by Dr Hugh Laracy.)
167 Additions to Cleary's (1920) will. LIS 27–1, ACDA.
168 Reports on requiem mass and funeral rites, *Month*, 17 December 1929; and *Tablet*, 18 December 1929.

169 Letter, Kelly to Hagan, 27 January 1930. Hagan Papers, Box 26, ICR.
170 Letter, Apostolic Delegate to Liston, 7 January 1930, informing him that he has received McDonald's complaint about this. LIS 53, ACDA.
171 A handwritten draft of the eulogy is filed in LIS 27–1, ACDA. The eulogy was reported in the *Month*, 21 January 1930, pp 19 and 23–24; and the *Tablet*, 22 January 1930, pp 46–47.
172 *Tablet*, 17 December 1930, p. 50, reports the first of these.
173 *Month*, November 1930, p. 11, has the first of five announcements of the dedication of the memorial chapel. See also [Delaney], *Gracious is the Time*, pp 101–102.
174 See Liston's negotiations with Tole and Massey (Architects), October 1930. LIS 27–1, ACDA. See also *Tablet,* 15 October 1930, p. 48.
175 January 1930 correspondence with John Cleary. LIS 27–1, ACDA.
176 *Zealandia*, 26 September 1935, p. 5.
177 'A Pledge of Loyalty and Affection', *Month*, 18 March 1930, p. 23; also *Tablet*, 12 March 1930.
178 Letter, Cattaneo to Liston, 24 December 1929. LIS 17, ACDA.
179 Letter, Van Rossum to Liston, 10 April 1930. LIS 17, ACDA. The original Latin reads, 'Ex actis vero et probatis clarissime patet nihil grave Tibi esse imputandum; atque accusationes Tibi, non quidem ex malo animo factas, vel errori vel minus aequae interpretationi circa tam agandi rationem tribuendas esse'.
180 Letter, Liston to van Rossum (in Latin), 12 June 1930. LIS 17, ACDA.
181 Letter, Liston to Curran, 20 June 1930. Curran Papers, Box 4, ICR.
182 Propaganda's deliberations on the case are still unavailable to researchers. However, it is notable that in the *Relazione* (Acta de Sac. Cong. de Prop. Fide 291 1920) reporting on the choice of the bishop of Dunedin and the coadjutor of Auckland in 1920, there are frequent marginal scorings in pencil at points where Cleary's words of praise for Liston are recorded. There is the strong possibility that the document was consulted with a critical eye by a Vatican official in 1929, when Cleary's criticisms of Liston were received.

Chapter VI: Bishop Liston 1930–54 – Churchman at Work

1 Figures according to *Zealandia*, 28 January 1954 (issue celebrating Liston's sacerdotal golden jubilee) and the official souvenir programme for the jubilee celebrations. See also Ernest Simmons, *In Cruce Salus*, p. 252 and p. 261. The new parishes, most created in the immediate postwar years, included Wellsford, Raglan, Otorohanga, Fairfield, Waiheke Island, Point Chevalier, Henderson, Balmoral, Three Kings, Papatoetoe, Manurewa, Brown's Bay, Panmure and Owairaka.
2 The negotiations are discussed in a letter, Liston to Hanrahan, 6 November 1930. LIS 157, ACDA.
3 *Month*, April 1931, p. 28.
4 Letter, Liston to Hanrahan, 26 November 1937, reporting the Apostolic Delegate's ruling. LIS 129–1, ACDA. There had been a heated exchange of letters between Liston and the Marist Brother Justin, 17 and 30 March 1931. LIS 128, ACDA. The Marist Brothers lodged a complaint with the Apostolic Delegate and with the Sacred Congregation of Religious, on which Liston kept Hanrahan informed, 1 and 6 May 1936. LIS 157 and LIS 129–1, ACDA. Liston's own exchange with the Apostolic Delegate, in which Liston defends his plans, are dated 6 April and 12 May 1936. LIS53 and LIS 128–1, ACDA.
5 J.C. O'Neill, 'The History of the Work of the Christian Brothers in New Zealand', chapter 9. *Zealandia*, 2 February 1939, p. 15, reports the opening ceremony. Liston hoped the new school would develop as a technical college. See *Tablet*, 14 January 1942, p. 33, and 8 April 1942, p. 28, for his remarks on opening St Peter's new technical block.
6 Gallagher, *Marist Brothers*, chapter 10.
7 Information on plans for new Sacred Heart College, and Liston's donation. LIS 128–2, ACDA.
8 The Apostolic Delegate had blessed the foundation stone in 1950 (*Zealandia*, 16 March 1950, front page), but the stone was laid on the 50th anniversary of the college (*Zealandia*, 11 June 1953, p. 11).

9   *Tablet*, 24 May 1950, p. 42, reports the De La Salle Brothers accepting Liston's invitation.

10   *Zealandia*, 11 June 1953, front page and p. 3. There was, however, a misunderstanding with the Marist priests, who thought that Liston's purchase of land in Whangarei for a primary school in the late 1940s signalled his intention to establish a Marist-run secondary school there. Pompallier College did not come into existence until many years later. See Liston's letter to Apostolic Delegate, 10 November 1944. LIS 53–3, ACDA. And Liston's correspondence with Marist superior Heffernan, February 1947. File AD-1, MAW.

11   Sister A.M. Power, *Sisters of St Joseph*, Auckland, 1997, pp 158–162, pp 245–247.

12   Letter, Gardiner to Liston, 21 June 1953. LIS 88–6, ACDA.

13   Letter, O'Connor to Liston, 27 April 1951. LIS 92–6, ACDA.

14   Letter, Liston to Sister M. Serenus, 13 October 1945, setting up a meeting of religious heads and speaking of the bishops' approval. LIS 188, ACDA.

15   Liston's 1945 correspondence with Sacred Heart Sisters. LIS 139–1, ACDA.

16   See Liston's circular to religious communities explaining the delay caused by the strike, 20 April 1949. LIS 188, ACDA. For reports of the arrival of the Apostolic Delegate and the opening ceremony (on 4 March 1950), see *Tablet*, 8 March and 15 March 1950.

17   Diane Strevens, *In Step With Time*, Auckland, 2001, p. 190.

18   Liston's formal request to the Apostolic Delegate John Panico for permission to make a Dominican foundation, 12 May 1948. LIS 54–1, ACDA. *Zealandia*, 1 July 1948, p. 3, report on Liston's invitation to the Dominican priests.

19   A year after Loreto Hall opened, Archbishop McKeefry praised Liston as 'ahead of the Holy See' in being able to coordinate so many different religious orders in one diocesan enterprise. Letter, McKeefry to Liston, 3 January 1951. LIS 56–2, ACDA.

20   Correspondence June-July 1930, plus Savage to Liston (6 August 1930) and Liston to Stallworthy (September 1930). LIS 200 (Mater Hospital File), ACDA. See also Michael Belgrave, *The Mater – A History of Auckland's Mercy Hospital 1900–2000*, Palmerston North, 2000, pp 51 ff.

21   Belgrave, *Mater*, p. 59.

22   *Zealandia*, 28 July 1938, p. 6; *Tablet*, 3 August 1938, p. 44; *Tablet*, 19 February 1941, p. 32.

23   *Zealandia*, 29 November 1951, p. 11.

24   *Tablet*, 15 September 1937, p. 44; Belgrave, *Mater*, pp 118–120.

25   *Zealandia*, 36 March 1936, pp 2–3; Belgrave, *Mater*, pp 64–65; [Delaney], *Gracious is the Time*, pp 116 ff. Liston had gained permission in 1933 from the Prefect of the Sacred Congregation for the Mercy Sisters to contract a £40,000 debt to build the new wing. See letter, Liston to Prefect of Sacred Congregatio, 22 August 1933. LIS 53, ACDA.

26   *Zealandia*, 20 March 1952, p. 13.

27   *Tablet*, 3 September 1952, p. 34.

28   *St Mary's Gazette*, June 1944, p. 6. Copy filed in LIS 80–1, ACDA.

29   Pastoral dated 15 July 1944. LIS 80–1, ACDA.

30   Letter, Liston to Bleakley, 17 July 1944. LIS 80–1, ACDA.

31   In 1933, clergy commiserated with him when he was briefly admitted to Lewisham Hospital while on a visit to Christchurch. Letter, Fr Silk to Liston, 1 May 1933. LIS 84–6, ACDA. Letter, Bishop Whyte to Liston, 11 May 1933. LIS 59–6, ACDA. Liston's illness was mentioned in passing in *Tablet*, 10 May 1933, p. 37; and 24 May 1933, p. 38. Liston had routine brushes with the 'flu in 1936 and 1939. Letter, Whyte to Liston, 13 August 1936. LIS 59–6, ACDA. Letter, Fr John Higgins to Liston, 13 January 1939. LIS 56–1, ACDA.

32   Letter, O'Neill to Liston, 7 January 1948. LIS 59–6, ACDA.

33   Donnelly, *One Priest's Life*, p. 37.

34   Letter, Buxton to Liston, 17 February 1950. LIS 80–1, ACDA. Letters, 7 Kavanagh to Liston, February 1950, and O'Neill to Liston, 2 March 1950. LIS 59–6. ACDA.

35   Letter, McKeefry to Liston, 3 January 1951. LIS 56–2, ACDA.

36   See Liston's personal notes appended to insurance policy, 29 September 1949. LIS 8–1/3, ACDA.

37   Letter, McKeefry to Liston, 20 June 1948. LIS 56–2, ACDA. Letter, Lyons to Liston,

       22 June 1948. LIS 58–2, ACDA. In the earlier 1940s, Bishop Whyte's letters to Liston routinely made jocular enquiries after 'the loyal Louie' or 'the ancilla Louie'. LIS 59–6, ACDA.

38   *Tablet*, 28 November 1934; *Zealandia*, 3 January 1935, p. 5.

39   *Zealandia*, 9 September 1937, p. 5; 23 September 1937; *Tablet*, 1 September 1937, p. 44; 29 September 1937, p. 43.

40   *Tablet*, 28 April 1948, p. 42; 15 April 1953, p. 34.

41   Letter, Gilroy to Liston, 24 March 1951. LIS 60–1, ACDA.

42   Letter, Liston to Cattaneo, 12 January 1931. LIS 53, ACDA. The provincial of the Mill Hills, Dean van Dijk, put a negative construction on Liston's decision, claiming to his superior, Bishop Biermans in London, that Liston was simply delaying answering awkward questions about the Mill Hill mission in Rome. Letter, van Dijk to Biermans, 28 February 1931. Box NZL3, MHAL.

43   Letter, Liston to Philip Bernardini, 5 January 1935. LIS 53, ACDA. See also press announcements in *Tablet*, 30 January 1935, p. 5; and 6 February 1935, p. 36.

44   *NZH*, 10 March 1935, p. 11; *Tablet*, 27 March 1935, p. 6.

45   *Zealandia*, 11 April 1935, p. 3; *Tablet*, 17 April 1935, p. 31.

46   *Zealandia*, 24 April 1935, p. 5; *Tablet*, 1 May 1935, p. 38.

47   Ormond accompanied Liston to the centennial celebrations in Akaroa in 1940 and to Bishop Brodie's episcopal silver jubilee in Christchurch in 1941.

48   *Tablet*, 29 May 1935, p. 36.

49   Liston called the pope 'gracious and paternal' in a letter to Mother Helen Lynch, 17 May 1935. A183 Fr John Flanagan Papers, Folder 6, ACDA.

50   Liston's letter to *Zealandia* preserved in Obituaries, Historical File, ACDA.

51   *Zealandia*, 4 July 1935, p. 5; and 1 August 1935, p. 5.

52   Letter, Liston to Curran, 26 June 1935. Curran Papers, Box 9, ICR.

53   Liston's remarks in minutes of diocesan council, 10 December 1935. LIS 52, ACDA.

54   Letter, Liston to Curran, 15 July 1935. Curran Papers, Box 9, ICR.

55   Details of Liston's journey in France taken from *Zealandia*, 1 August 1935, p. 5; 15 August 1935, p. 5; and 5 December 1935, p. 5; and *Tablet*, 20 May 1936, p. 36, where Liston recalled for Auckland members of the St Vincent de Paul Society his visit to Frederick Ozanam's tomb. Also letters, Liston to Curran, 4 July 1935 and 15 July 1935. Curran Papers, Box 9, ICR.

56   Liston recalled this visit with McMahon while offering the Archbishop of Dublin condolences on McMahon's death in 1949. Letter, Liston to McQuaid, 4 November 1949. McQuaid Papers, Foreign Bishops, Box 4, DAA.

57   Letter, Liston to Curran, 31 July 1935. Curran Papers, Box 9, ICR. For Liston's return to Clonliffe, see also *Zealandia*, 12 September 1935, p. 4.

58   Including a Benedictine monastery and schools the late bishops had attended. *Zealandia*, 29 August 1935, p. 5.

59   For Irish visits, see *Zealandia*, 26 September 1935, p. 5; 7 November 1935, p. 4; and 5 December 1935, p. 3; also letter, Liston to Curran, 10 September 1935. Curran Papers, Box 9, ICR. The visit to the Irish Sisters of Mercy is mentioned in Delaney, *Gracious is the Time*, p. 30. For Liston's consultation with Frank Duff, see letter, Liston to Duff, 29 November 1935. LIS 212, ACDA.

60   Letter, Liston to Curran, 13 October 1935. Curran Papers, Box 9, ICR.

61   *Zealandia*, 29 August 1935, p. 5.

62   *Zealandia*, 15 August 1935, p. 5.

63   *Tablet*, 4 December 1935, p. 6.

64   For plans for Liston's return, and reports on functions welcoming him back, see *Zealandia*, 21 November 1935, p. 4, and 5 December 1935, pp 3 and 5; and *Tablet*, 20 November 1935, p. 3, and 11 December 1935, p. 7.

65   Letter, McKeefry to (Rector) Donald Herlihy, 6 December 1950, discussing Liston's possible visit to Rome. Herlihy Papers, Box 1, ICR.

66   In 1937, he drafted the hierarchy's pastoral on the forthcoming Catholic centennial and in 1940 he wrote to the Sacred Congregation seeking permission for the hierarchy to set up a junior seminary in Christchurch. See Liston's draft of pastoral, 7 April 1937; Liston's letter to Sacred Congregation, 22 April 1940. LIS 2–2, ACDA.

67   See Liston's memorandum of 16 November 1943 and other materials. LIS 194, ACDA.

68   Letter, Liston to (Rector) Denis McDaid requesting message from Irish College, 16
      January 1950. McDaid Papers, Box 4, ICR. Letter, Kavanagh to Liston, 11 January
      1950. LIS 59–6, ACDA.
69   *Zealandia*, 17 January 1935, p. 3.
70   *Zealandia*, 20 May 1948, p. 3.
71   Letter, Heenan to Liston, 25 May 1952, offering thanks. LIS 60–1, ACDA.
72   Beforehand, McQuaid had written to Liston from Dublin saying, 'When I am
      ordaining at Clonliffe . . . you are looking straight at me from a very good portrait. I
      will be glad to see you in the flesh'. Letter, McQuaid to Liston, 21 March 1953. LIS
      60–1, ACDA. See also *Zealandia*, 28 May 1953, front page.
73   As well as archival resources, the following secondary sources have been used for
      the account of the Bible-in-Schools controversy given here: MacDonald, 'The New
      Zealand Bible in Schools League', chapter 6; I.A. Snook, 'Religion in Schools: A
      Catholic Controversy, 1930–1934', *NZJH*, 6 (6), October 1972; E.O. (Ernest)
      Blamires, *A Christian Core for New Zealand Education*, Auckland, 1960, chapter
      4; Nicholas Simmons, 'Archbishop Francis Redwood', chapter 4; O'Meeghan, *Held
      Firm by Faith*, pp 258–259; O'Meeghan, *Steadfast in Hope*, pp 216–225; Breward,
      Godless Schools, pp 80 ff.
74   See precis prepared by Liston for O'Shea, of 29 April 1930. Education Box 375,
      WCAA.
75   See Liston's memorandum to O'Shea, 29 November 1932. LIS 2–1, ACDA.
76   O'Meeghan, *Steadfast in Hope*, p. 222. O'Meeghan assumes that Liston, in 1930,
      was still smarting over what 'Protestants' had said about him at the time of his trial
      for sedition eight years previously.
77   See Nicholas Simmons, 'Archbishop Francis Redwood', pp 93–95; Snook, 'Religion in
      Schools', p. 171.
78   See Nicholas Simmons, 'Archbishop Francis Redwood', pp 104 ff. O'Meeghan insists
      that Redwood 'remained mentally capable till the end, though with a failing memory',
      Steadfast in Hope, p. 213.
79   See minutes of bishops' meeting, 19 October 1931. LIS 2–1, ACDA.
80   Blamires, *Christian Core*, p. 38.
81   LIS 2–2, ACDA.
82   Ibid.
83   Snook, 'Religion in Schools', p. 173.
84   Letter, O'Shea to Redwood, 8 November 1932. Education Box 375, WCAA.
85   See Suffragan bishops' petition to Apostolic Delegate, 6 February 1933. LIS 2–2,
      ACDA.
86   See O'Shea to Apostolic Delegate, 14 January 1932. Education Box 375, WCAA.
87   Letter, Bernardini to Brodie, 17 March 1934. LIS 188, ACDA.
88   Letter, Brodie to Liston, 9 March 1934. LIS 58–1, ACDA.
89   Nicholas Simmons, 'Archbishop Francis Redwood', p. 108; Snook, 'Religion in
      Schools', p. 177.
90   Nicholas Simmons, 'Archbishop Francis Redwood', p. 93.
91   Snook, 'Religion in Schools', pp 174–175.
92   Letter, O'Shea to Apostolic Delegate, 14 January 1932. Education Box 375, WCAA.
93   Letters, O'Shea to Liston, 17 and 24 June 1937. 56–1, ACDA.
94   See materials in LIS 167, ACDA (file devoted to the Campbell case), and report in
      Month, August 1932, p. 15.
95   Letter, Cleary to Herring, 20 August 1929. LIS 167, ACDA (capitals in the
      original).
96   Letter, Russell, McVeagh to Liston, 21 January 1930. LIS 167, ACDA.
97   See minutes of diocesan council, 19 January 1930 and 21 February 1931. LIS 52,
      ACDA.
98   Letter, Chapman, Tripp, Cooke and Watson to Russell, McVeagh, 2 November 1931.
      LIS 105–1, ACDA.
99   See writ made out against Liston by Leonard Tripp, 15 January 1932. LIS 105–1,
      ACDA.
100   See exchange of letters between Liston and Fr Joseph Giles (secretary to the Apostolic
      Delegate), 25 January 1932 and 2 February 1932, filed in both LIS 53 and LIS 157,
      ACDA.

101 Notes of Evidence in Supreme Court of New Zealand, Wellington District, Wellington Registry, filed in Box 13 GB CCDA and LIS 167, ACDA.

102 *Evening Post*, 1 and 2 June 1932; and *Dominion*, 2 and 3 June 1932.

103 Letter, Liston to Whangarei parishioners, 12 July 1932. LIS 167, ACDA. Liston's diocesan magazine also dissented from the judge's views. *Month*, August 1932, p. 15.

104 Letter, Hampson to O'Shea, 14 June 1932. Box 503, Folder 3, WCAA.

105 Letter, O'Shea to Holbrook, 14 January 1933. Box 503, Folder 3, WCAA.

106 Over 50 years later, an official history of the Marists in New Zealand makes no reference to the case when it mentions Fr Campbell's time in Whangarei. Peter Ewart SM (ed.), *The Society of Mary in New Zealand Since 1838*, Wellington, 1989, pp 49–50.

107 See minutes of the diocesan council, 29 September 1932. LIS 52, ACDA.

108 See minutes of the diocesan council, 9 December 1932. LIS 52, ACDA.

109 See three-way correspondence between Redwood, Brodie and Liston, October-December 1933. Box 13 GB, CCDA.

110 Liston to Redwood, (undated letter) 1933. Box 13 GB, CCDA.

111 Letter, Brodie to Liston, 26 June 1933. LIS 58–1, ACDA.

112 Letter, Liston to Redwood, 22 November 1933. LIS 167, ACDA.

113 *NZH*, 22 December 1933.

114 See Liston's memorandum in Marist Fathers File, 25 March 1935. LIS 126–1, ACDA.

115 See Brodie's letters to Liston describing Whyte's stroke and hospitalisation, 19 December 1941 and 7 January 1942. LIS 58–1, ACDA. On 18 February 1942, Alan Carter, editor of the *Tablet*, asked Liston to write an appreciation of Whyte in the belief that he would soon have to prepare an obituary issue. LIS 59–6, ACDA. See *Zealandia*, 9 January 1958, front page report of Whyte's death.

116 Letter, O'Neill to Denis McDaid (rector of the Irish College), 3 December 1948, in which he discusses his health in detail. McDaid Papers, Box 4, ICR.

117 Letter, McKeefry to Liston, 13 September 1948. LIS 56–2, ACDA. See also Dr Charles Burns and Dr A. McIlroy's reports to Liston on O'Neill's health, 4 December 1948. LIS 59–7, ACDA.

118 See Whyte's pastoral, 2 March 1949. LIS 59–6, ACDA. See also discussion of O'Neill's resignation, minutes of bishops' meeting, 6 March 1949. LIS 2–11, ACDA. And announcement in *Tablet*, 9 March 1949, p. 11.

119 See Vatican's Bull of Appointment of Kavanagh, 14 July 1949. LIS 59–6, ACDA. See also *Tablet*, 24 August 1949, p. 4.

120 Liston was assisted by Archbishop McKeefry and Bishop O'Neill. *Zealandia*, 1 December 1949, front page; *Tablet*, 7 December 1949, pp 1 ff.

121 The hierarchy's 1939 pastoral announcing the eucharistic congress for 1940 is filed in LIS 56–1, ACDA. For the opening mass of the congress, of which Liston was celebrant, see *Tablet*, 7 February 1940, pp 1–2.

122 Letter, Liston to Apostolic Delegate, 1 February 1947. LIS 2–9, ACDA.

123 Letter, Liston to Apostolic Delegate, 4 March 1947. LIS 19–1, ACDA.

124 Editorial, 'The Coadjutor-Archbishop Elect of Wellington', *Zealandia*, 10 July 1947. See also letter, Liston to O'Shea, 20 July 1947, where Liston congratulates the archbishop on having secured such an assistant. LIS 56–2, ACDA.

125 The back page of *Zealandia*, 8 December 1949, has a photograph of Liston with his three former Holy Cross students.

126 Gilroy was assisted by Liston and Lyons. *Tablet*, 15 October 1947, pp 1 ff, and 22 October 1947, pp 1 ff; and *Zealandia*, 23 October 1947.

127 Letter, McKeefry to Liston, 24 October 1948. LIS 56–2, ACDA.

128 See letter of 20 June 1942 to Liston from Brodie's doctors, and other correspondence concerning Brodie's health. LIS 58–1, ACDA.

129 Letters, Fr J. Long to Liston, 15 August 1943; and Mrs M. Darby (Brodie's sister) to Liston, 7 September 1943. LIS 58–1, ACDA.

130 *Zealandia*, 14 October 1943, front page; and *Tablet*, 13 October 1943 and 20 October 1943.

131 *Zealandia*, 27 January 1944, pp 2 and 7.

132 Letter, Fr James Kennedy to Liston, 24 January 1944. LIS 58–1, ACDA.

133 Letter, O'Neill to Liston, 23 January 1944. LIS 59–6, ACDA.

134 *Zealandia*, 3 February 1944, p. 3.

135 File LIS 59–3 is concerned completely with the problem of Ormond's health. It includes the bishops' consultations about the problem (7 March 1944) and Liston's report to the Apostolic Delegate in which he speaks of not being able to reason Ormond out of his severe depression.

136 Ibid., 28 February 1944. Report of Drs J. Cronin and Basil Quin to Liston.

137 To Ormond's first protests that he was not capable of being a bishop, the Apostolic Delegate John Panico had written telling him to dismiss his fears, 3 February 1944. LIS 144–2, ACDA.

138 Letter, J.J. Crashaw (deputy medical superintendent of Kingseat Mental Hospital) to Liston, 31 January 1947. LIS 59–3, ACDA.

139 *Zealandia*, 15 September 1949, p. 3, and 22 September 1949.

140 Announcement of Lyons' nomination and imminent consecration as bishop, *Zealandia*, 29 June 1944, p. 3. See also Apostolic Delegate to Liston, 1 April 1944. LIS 53–3, ACDA.

141 *Zealandia*, 6 July 1944, pp 8–9.

142 On 13 April 1944, Lyons invited Liston to attend his consecration, but Liston was unable to do so. LIS 58–1, ACDA. *Zealandia*, 13 July 1944, pp 8–9, gives an account of Lyons' consecration in Melbourne.

143 *Tablet*, 9 August 1944, pp 3 ff; *Zealandia*, 10 August 1944, pp 1–2, and 17 August 1944, p. 9.

144 Bruce Duncan, *Crusade or Conspiracy?*, Sydney, 2001, p. 169.

145 Letter, Lyons to Liston, 2 August 1946, strongly disagreeing with Liston's proposal. But 5 August 1946, Liston wrote for O'Shea's approval anyway and the exemption was duly granted. LIS 54–1, ACDA.

146 O'Meeghan, *Held Firm by Faith*, pp 264–265, 293–295.

147 Duncan, *Crusade or Conspiracy?* pp 169 ff.

148 *AS*, 9 May 1950, reports Joyce's appointment. *Tablet*, 19 July 1950, pp 2 ff; and *Zealandia*, 20 July 1950, front page and pp 8–9 report Joyce's consecration.

149 Programme of Catholic Centennial Celebration, Christchurch, 15–19 November 1950. LIS 58–2, ACDA.

150 *Tablet*, 5 February 1947, p. 6; *Zealandia*, 13 February 1947, front page. Holy Cross College at Mosgiel no longer took school-age students after the mid-1930s. Norris, *Southernmost Seminary*, pp 50–53. It was Liston who undertook most of the negotiations to get permission for, and staff, the Riccarton establishment.

151 In *One Priest's Life* (pp 15–16), Felix Donnelly retails a story of Liston urging a mother to send her 12–year-old son to Holy Name with the argument, 'Your son is like a tender flower plant, which must be taken and placed in the hothouse and protected and nurtured'. Donnelly does not claim to have been present at this scene.

152 Bernard O'Brien, SJ, *A New Zealand Jesuit – A Personal Narrative*, Christchurch, 1970, pp 74–75; O'Meeghan, *Held Firm by Faith*, p. 265. In 1979, Holy Name amalgamated with Holy Cross. Norris, *Southernmost Seminary*, pp 106–108.

153 *Marist Messenger*, June 1950, p. 22.

154 Caput II of Liston's 1935 *relatio*. LIS 20–2, ACDA.

155 *Zealandia*, 8 November 1945, p. 2; *Tablet*, 16 January 1946, p. 28.

156 Letter, Lyons to Immigration Department, 27 October 1947, seeking to bring two priests into the country, remarks on the assistance in staffing Liston and O'Neill are offering him. LIS 58–2, ACDA.

157 Interview with Fr Purcell, 8 March 2003.

158 Letter, Liston to Apostolic Delegate, 28 October 1937. LIS 53–2, ACDA.

159 Letters, Mgr Bradley, on leave in Europe, to Liston about students for Auckland at All Hallows, Thurles and Carlow, 1 May 1950 and (undated) 1950. LIS 95, ACDA.

160 See Liston's correspondence with Irish colleges. LIS 153–2, ACDA.

161 According to Ernest Simmons, in 1934, of the 227 religious in Auckland diocese, 193 came from overseas. Ernest Simmons, 'The Church in New Zealand 1924 to 1973', *Australasian Catholic Record*, 50 (4), October 1973, p. 326.

162 [Delaney], *Gracious is the Time*, p. 145.

163 Letters, Liston to McQuaid, 28 September 1948 and 5 April 1951. 'Foreign Bishops', McQuaid Papers, Box 4, DAA.

164 *Tablet*, 17 September 1952, p. 34.

165 See correspondence in file on Sisters of St Joseph of Cluny, 1948. LIS 132, ACDA.

166 Letter, Liston to (Rector) Donald Herlihy, 28 February 1951. Herlihy Papers, Box 1, ICR.

167 See 1949 exchange of letters between Liston and Fr Arthur Lenihan of Balmoral parish, who was over-extending the six months leave in Ireland which he had been granted. LIS 69–3, ACDA.

168 See Liston's 1938–40 correspondence with Farragher. LIS 70, ACDA.

169 See Liston's correspondence with Curley, October 1931. LIS 82–7, ACDA. See also diocesan council minutes, 16 October 1931, when Curley's case was discussed and Jeremiah Cahill was delegated to deal with him. LIS 52, ACDA.

170 See correspondence between Liston and O'Hara, January-February 1936. LIS 103–6, ACDA.

171 See correspondence between Liston and Fitzpatrick, 1935–36. LIS 69–7, ACDA.

172 See minutes of the diocesan council, 21 February 1930, 30 May 1930 and 31 March 1936, referring to Taylor, who sent an apologetic letter on 6 May 1931. LIS 52, ACDA. Liston's correspondence with Taylor, including Taylor's explicitly abusive letter of 25 July 1935, is filed in both LIS 143 and LIS 86–7 (Northcote File), ACDA. The quarrel with the Dominican Sisters is filed in LIS 133, ACDA. Taylor did not return to Ireland, but settled in Christchurch, where he said mass privately until his death in 1959.

173 Letter, Brady to Liston, 9 April 1941. LIS 87–4, ACDA.

174 See file on clergy retreats 1930–55. LIS 146–1, ACDA.

175 Liston kept his roll of attendance in the same ledger where he recorded financial returns from parishes. LIS 50–2, ACDA. In order to accommodate all the diocesan clergy, there were four separate retreats each year, three for secular priests and one for the Mill Hills.

176 Interview with Bishop Patrick Dunn, 27 December 2002.

177 Liston's leaflets, and correspondence pertaining to them, filed under 'Catechetical Instructions', LIS 172–3, ACDA.

178 See Liston's handwritten 'Rules for Preachers' included in his notes for clergy conferences, August 1950. After the rules quoted here, Liston then summarised Cardinal Newman's seven rules for good preaching. LIS 13–2, ACDA.

179 Letter, Liston to Terry, 28 May 1940. LIS 143, ACDA.

180 *Tablet*, 29 January 1930, p. 49, gives an account of Liston saying mass with 60 nuns who had been taught Gregorian chant. *Tablet*, 16 May 1934, p. 36, reports Liston consulting the Benedictine choirmaster Dom Moreno. *Tablet*, 24 September 1941, p. 32, reports Liston encouraging members of the Holy Name Society to learn the Latin mass.

181 Letter, Liston to Ryder, 26 February 1948. LIS 197, ACDA.

182 Letter, Liston to Fr McGrath, October 1931. LIS 85–5, ACDA.

183 See April 1946 correspondence between Liston and Downey. LIS 85–4, ACDA.

184 See negotiations between Liston and Heffernan reported in minutes of diocesan council, August-November 1945. LIS 52, ACDA.

185 (Unpublished) 'Memoirs of Bishop John Mackey', pp 18 and 20, ACDA.

186 See 1932 correspondence between Liston and Cambridge parish. LIS 70, ACDA.

187 See exchange of letters between Liston and Bleakley, September-December 1948. LIS 80–1, ACDA.

188 Letter, Lane to Liston, 30 December 1935. LIS 73–6, ACDA.

189 See correspondence between Liston and Higgins, 1939–40. LIS 56–1, ACDA.

190 See diocesan council minutes, 8 January 1940 and 7 August 1941. LIS 52, ACDA.

191 Letter, Higgins to Liston, 7 May 1945. LIS 56–2, ACDA.

192 Most of Liston's correspondence with Eccleston is filed in Tauranga parish file, including Eccleston's 1936 contention over the parish ball and his unflattering (19 March 1939) description of the town. Liston's difference with him over the Legion of Mary was in 1947. LIS 97, ACDA. On 14 September 1941, Sister Ursula of the Cluny Sisters complained to Liston about Eccleston's discussing the sisters' finances publicly. LIS 132, ACDA. Earlier correspondence from Tuakau, including Eccleston's scurrilous letters about other priests, is filed in LIS 103–4, ACDA.

193 See 1938 correspondence filed in LIS 92–6, ACDA.

194 Account of Fr Murphy's funeral and Fr Shore's death included in Te Aroha File, LIS 98–1, ACDA. See also *Zealandia*, 12 April 1951, front page; and 19 April 1951, p. 13.
195 *Zealandia*, 3 July 1952, p. 11.
196 *Zealandia*, 15 August 1971, pp 10–11.
197 Career details from Deceased Priests File, ACDA.
198 Letter, Holbrook to Liston, 30 August 1942. LIS 76–1, ACDA.
199 See Liston's (Latin language) petition, 7 August 1936. Curran Papers, Box 10, ICR.
200 *Zealandia*, 25 June 1942, p. 8.
201 Letters, Liston to McQuaid (concerning Wright), 6 July and 4 August 1953. 'Foreign Bishops', McQuaid Papers, Box 4, DAA.
202 T.J. Ryder, *Following All Your Ways, Lord*, no publisher or date, pp 53–57 and 63.
203 Simmons was at the Irish College in Rome from 1949 to 1953. See Liston's introductory letter, 18 July 1949, McDaid Papers, Box 4, ICR, and also ICR rollbook. In a retrospective article about Liston, Simmons noted that Liston had been a frequent visitor to the Simmons family home when he was a boy, *Zealandia*, 30 January 1964.
204 On 25 August 1944 and 30 September 1944, Peter Fraser wrote to Liston about Flanagan and Snedden. LIS 154–1, ACDA. Their return to New Zealand is reported in *Tablet*, 17 January 1945, p. 28; Snedden's appointment to the editorship of *Zealandia* is noted in *Tablet*, 17 September 1947, p. 42. Other biographical details from Deceased Priests File, ACDA.
205 Letter, Downey to Liston, 1 June 1940. LIS 53, ACDA. Letter, Downey to Liston, 14 March 1943. LIS 142, ACDA.
206 Henry and William Forsman, 'E.A. Forsman – Priest, Padre and Poet 1909–1976', unpublished typescript, 1991, p. 21.
207 S.W. ('Sid') Scott, *Rebel in a Wrong Cause*, Auckland, 1960, p. 53.
208 Letter, Forsman to Liston, 20 March 1938. LIS 84–1, ACDA.
209 Keith Ovenden, *A Fighting Withdrawal*, London, 1996, p. 135.
210 *Tablet*, 8 May 1946, p. 42.
211 The characterisation is from the Deceased Priests File (which was compiled by Ernest Simmons), ACDA.
212 Forsman, 'E.A. Forsman', p. 21.
213 Ibid., p. 30.
214 For information on Sr Dorothea Loughnan, an expert on liturgy who wrote much for the *Catholic Review*, see Sacred Heart Sisters File, LIS 139–1, ACDA.
215 Letter, Liston to Apostolic Delegate explaining his actions over Hilly, 6 February 1934. LIS 53, ACDA.
216 November-December 1933 correspondence concerning Buckley. LIS 53, ACDA.
217 See Buckley's complaints to Apostolic Delegate and Liston's explanations, August 1948. LIS 54–1, ACDA. The 82–year-old Buckley was then an invalid in the Mater.
218 See correspondence regarding Lockwood, 1936–38. Papakura Parish File, LIS 89–1, ACDA.
219 Bishop Dunn interview, 27 December 2002.
220 Letter, Liston to Mrs H.M. Quinn, 12 January 1934. LIS 84–6, ACDA.
221 See minutes of diocesan council, 12 January and 19 February 1943. LIS 52, ACDA.
222 Bishop John Mackey, interview, 19 January 2003.
223 Jocelyn Franklin, interview, 14 April 2003.
224 Father John Edward Lyons, interview, 29 December 2002.
225 Bishop John Mackey, interview, 19 January 2003.
226 Information on Edward Lyons' irremovability in Thames Parish File, LIS 102–8, ACDA.
227 Dean Alink's 1936 report to London. Box NZL5, Mill Hill Archives, London.
228 Liston wrote a preface to *Our Maori Missions*, Auckland, 1933. Much later, he and Bishop Delargey both contributed prefatory words to *Mill Hill's 100 Years – The Story of St. Joseph's Missionary Society 1866–1966. The Years in New Zealand*, Putaruru, 1966.
229 *Tablet*, 6 September 1945, p. 3, reports on Liston's sermon at the funeral of Fr Devolder.
230 *Tablet*, 19 May 1937, p. 43.

231 See words of proposed citation sent by Dutch chargé d'affaires to Liston, 26 February 1948. LIS 107–1, ACDA. The following year, *Zealandia* (3 February 1949, front page) carried a report of the actual presentation of the award by the Dutch ambassador.

232 See complaint made to Bishop Cleary jointly by Fathers van Dijk, Bressers and Langerwerf, February 1929. Mill Hill File, LIS 106–1, ACDA. On 18 April 1929, van Dijk wrote to Bishop Biermans complaining of the precariousness of the mission's finances. Box NZL (1913–34), MHAL. Between June and August 1928, van Dijk had told Cleary that the Mill Hills were not receiving grants from the Fynes Trust when wealthy Pakeha parishes were. This was one of the charges that Cleary brought in his campaign to discredit Liston. Fynes Estate File, LIS 22–2, ACDA.

233 See exchange between Liston and Cattaneo, granting permission to sell the Te Awamutu property, 12 and 13 June 1930. LIS 53, ACDA.

234 See, for example, his advice to McKeefry on the desirability of Maori communities being integrated into general diocesan parishes. Letter, Liston to McKeefry, 16 May 1949. LIS 56–2, ACDA.

235 *Mill Hill's 100 Years*, p. 34. See also Liston to Apostolic Delegate on transfer of parishes, 18 January 1935. LIS 53, ACDA.

236 See Liston reports Mill Hill provincial O'Callaghan's fears of revenue loss in parish transfers, diocesan council minutes, 4 December 1933. LIS 52, ACDA. See also O'Callaghan to Biermans, 25 November 1933. Box NZL (1913–34), MHAL.

237 See Liston's pastoral to Whakatane Maori, 16 April 1934. Whakatane Parish File, LIS 104–5, ACDA.

238 Letter, Liston to van Beek, 15 March 1934. LIS 84–7, ACDA.

239 Six letters between Liston and Alink, May-June 1939, are preserved in both LIS 106–2, ACDA and Box NZL5, MHAL.

240 Patricia Brookes, *By the Name of Mary*, Tauranga, 2000, p. 73. See also Cynthia Piper's chapter on the Mill Hill mission, 'Te Koanga Tuarua – The Second Spring', in Dominic O'Sullivan and Cynthia Piper (eds), *Turanga Ngatahu – Standing Together: The Catholic Diocese of Hamilton 1840–2005*, Wellington, 2005.

241 See (undated) 1930 report from van Dijk. LIS 53, ACDA (capitals in the original).

242 Letter, Liston to Apostolic Delegate, 30 July 1930. LIS 53, ACDA.

243 Minutes of meetings, 8–11 January 1931. LIS 110–2, ACDA.

244 Letter, van Dijk to Biermans, 28 February 1931. Box NZL (1913–34), MHAL.

245 Letter, O'Callaghan to Biermans, 25 November 1933. Box NZL (1913–34), MHAL.

246 Letter, O'Callaghan to Biermans, 19 December 1933. Box NZL (1913–34), MHAL.

247 Letter, Bruning to Liston, 9 March 1936. Waitaruke Parish File, LIS 104–2, ACDA.

248 Letter, Liston to Apostolic Delegate, 1 October 1934. LIS 106–1, ACDA.

249 Letter, O'Callaghan to Biermans, 25 November 1933. Box NZL (1913–34), MHAL.

250 Letter, Alink to Panico, 4 October 1938. Box NZL5, MHAL.

251 See diocesan council minutes, 17 February and 29 March 1932. LIS 52, ACDA. See also Spierings' letter to his Superior-General pleading his ignorance of Maori and desire to be a diocesan priest rather than a missionary, 15 August 1932. Box NZL (1913–34), MHAL.

252 See minutes of bishops' meeting, 12 February 1935. LIS 2–2, ACDA.

253 See Liston's report to Apostolic Delegate, 25 May 1938. LIS 53, ACDA. See also minutes of bishops' meeting where Liston and hierarchy decided one third of the annual missions' appeal would automatically go to the Mill Hills, 4 May 1938. LIS 2–2, ACDA.

254 Apostolic Delegate proposes that Mill Hill provincial be diocesan consultor, February 1938. On 21 April 1938, Alink reported to O'Callaghan (who was now his Superior-General) on Liston's refusal to accept this proposal. On 27 May 1938, Alink expressed to O'Callaghan his reluctant acceptance of the new agreement. Box NZL5, MHAL. Jeremiah Cahill's role is recorded in Fr W. Tuerlings, *Mill Hill – Maori Mission and St Joseph's Foreign Missionary Society*, Mill Hill, London, 2001, p. 44.

255 Letter, Alink to O'Callaghan, 16 February 1943. Box NZL5, MHAL.

256 Letter, Alink to O'Callaghan, 21 April 1944. Box NZL5, MHAL.

257 Letter, Alink to (Superior-General) McLaughlin, 11 June 1948. Box NZL5, MHAL.

258 See correspondence, Kaikohe parish, September-October 1953. LIS 69–4, ACDA.

259 See Liston's memorandum of talks with Bishop Biermans, January 1931. LIS 106–1, ACDA.

260 Letter, Marist provincial Victor Geaney's characterisation of Liston to Fr Rasmussen, 8 December 1939. File A/D1, MAW. Tuerlings' judgement on Liston in *Mill Hill – Maori Mission*, p. 44. The (Auckland diocesan) Mill Hill mission to the Maori, and the (Wellington archdiocesan) Marist mission to the Maori often conferred and consulted with each other, e.g. 12 and 13 November 1948 conference at St Peter's, Northcote, on standardising translations of prayers into Maori. LIS 107–1, ACDA.
261 Fr Peter Ryan, interview, 18 May 2003.
262 All documents relating to Maori Sisters of Mary are filed in LIS 109–1, ACDA. See also *Mill Hill's 100 Years*, pp 30–31. Liston's application to the Apostolic Delegate (11 September 1936) for permission to set up the order, LIS 53, ACDA. Liston's application to the Apostolic Delegate to wind up the order (February-March 1952). LIS 54–2, ACDA. Liston's pastoral explaining the order's demise was printed in *Zealandia*, 29 May 1952, p. 3.
263 See letter van Westeinde to Liston, 27 August 1931, and Liston's pencilled reply. Dargaville File, LIS 73–1, ACDA.
264 *Tablet*, 14 March 1951, p. 42.
265 *Tablet*, 24 June 1953, p. 34, reports Whina Cooper organising Liston's crowning of a Maori carnival queen as a fund-raiser for the hostel.
266 See Michael King, *Whina – A Biography of Whina Cooper*, Auckland, 1991, chapter 8, especially p. 169, for King's negative assessment of Liston.
267 Ibid., p. 161. See also three-way correspondence (Liston, Cooper and Senior Inspector of Native Schools) concerning Cooper's gift, September 1948. LIS 188, ACDA.
268 See entry on Te Awhitu (by Max Mariu), *DNZB*, 5, pp 512–13.
269 *Tablet*, 7 January 1945, p. 27; and *Zealandia*, 11 January 1945, pp 6–7.
270 For background information on St Peter's, see letter Liston to Building Controller, 26 March 1945. Takapuna File, LIS 96–7, ACDA.
271 See Liston's negotiations with Fr Joseph O'Riordan SM, March 1941. Minutes of bishops' meetings, LIS 2–5, ACDA.
272 Liston's appeal for an expanded St Peter's is included in his Maori mission appeal, *Tablet*, 23 May 1945, p. 45. Report of the blessing and opening of the extended college, *Zealandia*, 7 March 1946, p. 13. The bishop's meeting was minuted on this occasion, 1–3 March 1946. LIS 2–8, ACDA.
273 'Future of the Maori', *NZH*, 19 November 1932. Clipping in LIS 53, ACDA.
274 Fr Peter Ryan, interview, 18 May 2003.

Chapter VII: Bishop Liston 1930–54 – The Public Figure

1 Caput X, Liston's 1935 *relatio*. LIS 20–2, ACDA.
2 This is the general thesis of Christopher van der Krogt's, 'More a Part than Apart'. See also van der Krogt, 'Catholic Religious Identity and Social Integration in Interwar New Zealand', *Catholic Historical Review*, 86 (1), January 2000.
3 On 10 July 1934, Fr J.P. Murphy wrote to Liston for instruction on this matter, asking if he should refuse the sacraments to a mother whose son was at the state secondary school. On Murphy's letter, Liston pencilled, 'No law re secondary schools'. LIS 74, ACDA.
4 See exchange of letters between Liston and Fr James McMahon, March 1948. LIS 74, ACDA.
5 *Month*, February 1931, p. 15, gives Liston's outline of such a scheme.
6 From 1930 onwards, however, Liston and other Catholics attended the Anzac Day public function organised at the Auckland cenotaph by the RSA. See van der Krogt, 'More a Part than Apart', pp 147–148.
7 See circular to priests from Fr John Flanagan, 2 October 1953. LIS 173, ACDA.
8 See Liston's circular to Northland priests, 16 February 1937. LIS165–1, ACDA.
9 Liston's 1935 *relatio* reports (Caput XI) that there have been 737 mixed marriages and 1,345 wholly Catholic ones. LIS 20–2, ACDA.
10 See minutes of bishops' meeting, 7 April 1937. LIS 2–2, ACDA.
11 Mgr Paul Cronin, interview, 11 February 2003.
12 Letter, Colgan to Liston, 24 February 1950. On this letter Liston wrote 'No reply'. LIS 101, ACDA.

13   See hierarchy's instruction to clergy, 19 November 1951. Mixed weddings could now be performed before the altar, but other markers were left in place to suggest that this was a second-class form of wedding. LIS 172, ACDA. Only the previous year, Archbishop McKeefry had expressed great surprise that the archdiocese of Sydney was allowing mixed marriages before the altar. Letter, McKeefry to Liston, 19 September 1950. LIS 56/1, ACDA.

14   Caput XI of Liston's *relatio* 1935. LIS 20–2, ACDA.

15   *Tablet*, 8 October 1930, p. 48; *Month*, October 1930, pp 14–15.

16   See minutes of bishops' meeting, 12 February 1935. LIS 2–2, ACDA.

17   *Zealandia*, 22 April 1937, p. 4; *Tablet*, 28 April 1937, p. 6.

18   See three-way correspondence Liston, O'Shea, Higgins, 1938. LIS 56/1, ACDA.

19   Joanna Bourke, 'Catholic Fertility in Australia and New Zealand 1880–1939', MA History thesis, University of Auckland, 1985, especially p. 77. For a similar perspective, see also Barbara Brookes, 'Housewives' Depression – The Debate over Abortion and Birth Control in the 1930s', *NZJH*, 15 (2), 1981.

20   Christopher van der Krogt, 'Pleasure Without Maternity – Catholic and Protestant Attitudes Towards Contraception in Interwar New Zealand', *Colloquium*, 29/1, 1997; and 'Exercising the Utmost Vigilance – The Catholic Campaign Against Contraception in the 1930s', *Journal of Religious Studies*, 22 (3), October 1998. Van der Krogt notes the unhistorical perspectives on the Catholic campaign taken by a chronicler of the Family Planning Association. See also van der Krogt, 'More a Part than Apart', pp 275–277, for Liston's praise for non-Catholic opposition to contraception and abortion, and the favourable review *Zealandia* gave to Gordon and Bennett's anti-abortion polemic, *Gentlemen of the Jury*.

21   *AJHR* (Session 1946), Wellington, 1947, p. 130.

22   Correspondence file, Pat Lawlor Papers, Alexander Turnbull Library.

23   See exchange between Liston and W.T. Quealy, July 1949. LIS 160–1, ACDA.

24   *Zealandia*, 3 August 1944, p. 3; 7 September 1944, p. 10; 12 October 1944, p. 3. *Tablet*, 18 October 1944, p. 36; *HZH*, 3 August 1944. On 2 August 1944, the veteran Protestant campaigner E.O. Blamires wrote to Liston thanking him for his stance. LIS 186, ACDA. Report of the book's condemnation by the Dunedin presbytery in *ODT*, 6 September 1944.

25   On this issue, the power of the Catholic church in America was illustrated by Cardinal Dennis Dougherty of Philadelphia, who was able to threaten film exhibitors in his diocese and make ticket sales plummet when he forbade Catholics to attend the movies. Charles K. Morris, *American Catholic*, New York, 1997, pp 165–167 and 196–209.

26   See Liston's circular, 10 April 1933. LIS 169–1, ACDA.

27   *Tablet*, 9 May 1934, p. 36.

28   On 6 October 1948, Lyons thanked Liston for sending him copies of his condemnation of *Forever Amber*. LIS 52–8, ACDA. See Liston's circular about *Duel in the Sun*, September 1948. LIS 169–1, ACDA. *Tablet*, 29 September 1948, p. 42, reports the University Catholic Society planning a boycott of the film.

29   *Zealandia*, 5 December 1935, p. 5.

30   *Tablet*, 27 May 1936, pp 20–21 and 23.

31   See Ruth Park's note of thanks to Liston, 14 December 1946. LIS 159, ACDA. Park had earlier edited (pseudonymously) the children's pages of *Zealandia*.

32   LIS 214–5, ACDA is a file of Liston's correspondence with Duggan. That he kept her letters, when he destroyed most of his purely personal correspondence, is a measure of how much he valued it.

33   *Tablet*, 18 March 1936, p. 38, report of Liston's speaking at AGM of repertory society.

34   Letter, Liston to Catholic Theatre Conference, 2 May 1938. Catholic Repertory Society File, LIS 213, ACDA.

35   *Zealandia*, 15 February 1951, p. 13; and *New Zealand Law Journal*, 6, March 1951, pp 54–59, both give detailed obituaries of Callan.

36   Sir Ian Barker, interview, 6 April 2003.

37   Sir Maurice Casey, interview, 3 May 2003, and *NZLJ*. The pope had said that Catholic judges should not grant petitions for divorce. Liston was aware that the pope's ruling would be contentious, and in 1949 he wrote to the editor of the *Auckland Star*

thanking him for the very temperate editorial which the newspaper had run on the matter. Letter, Liston to Dumbleton, 16 December 1949. LIS 54–1, ACDA.

38   Reports on Catholic Men's Luncheon Club addresses in *Tablet*, 10 July 1940 (Mr Justice Callan); 25 September 1940 (Mr Justice O'Regan); 12 February 1941 (J.C. Reid); 9 April 1941 (Mgr Buxton); 14 May 1941 (George Joseph); 18 June 1941 (Br Stephen Coll); 30 December 1942 (Liston); 27 December 1944 (Count Wodzicki); 14 August 1946 (M.K. Joseph); 18 December 1946 (Leslie Rumble); 30 March 1949 (John Allum).

39   On 2 January 1945, Bishop O'Neill passed on this joke to Liston after the *Catholic Review* was first publicly mooted. LIS 59–6, ACDA.

40   *Tablet*, 28 December 1938, p. 44.

41   See minutes of study association, 21 November 1938. LIS 216–1, ACDA.

42   Report, Lavelle to Liston, May 1938. LIS 197, ACDA.

43   Letter, Hierarchy to P.F. Giles (Catholic students' national secretary), 20 November 1947. LIS 197, ACDA.

44   *Tablet*, 24 September 1941, p. 32; 7 June 1950, p. 43.

45   Report, 'Catholic Sports Thanksgiving Day – Bishop Liston Honoured at Unique Function', *Tablet*, 28 May 1947, pp 1–3.

46   See correspondence, 1932–33. Boy Scouts Association File, LIS 215–5, ACDA.

47   *Tablet*, 4 November 1936, p. 37.

48   See George Duke Walton's proposals for a 'Credo' League of Catholic Youth, 19 March 1939. On 25 March 1939, Liston approved the general aims but changed the name to the Catholic Youth Movement. LIS 210–1, ACDA.

49   See diocesan council minutes, 8 January 1940 and 14 November 1941. LIS 52, ACDA.

50   *Tablet*, 13 August 1941, pp 31–32.

51   *Tablet*, 5 November 1930.

52   Sweetman, *Faith and Fraternalism*, pp 66 ff.

53   See *Zealandia*, 21 June 1934, editorial, p. 4.

54   See Liston's circular to priests, 12 July 1934. LIS 173, ACDA.

55   Liston's pastoral introducing a New Zealand District HACBS organiser to parishes makes this very clear, 5 August 1936. LIS 214–1, ACDA.

56   *Tablet*, 16 May 1934 and 10 April 1935 record his patronage.

57   See correspondence 1941, 1946 and 1953 in LIS 214–1, ACDA.

58   Sweetman, *Faith and Fraternalism*, p. 99.

59   See, for example, Paul Freedman's negative review of Ian Thompson's history of the Knights of the Southern Cross in New Zealand, *So Much to Do*, in *NZ Catholic*, 13 July 2003, p. 16. Freedman doubts whether secrecy can ever be compatible with claiming to proclaim the message and values of Christ.

60   Sir Ian Barker, interview, 6 April 2003. Barker tells an anecdote of a lawyer friend who attended one meeting but was repelled by the Knights' theatrical rituals 'and he didn't go back'. The organisation's secrecy baffled even some well-informed members of the Catholic laity. When asked about Liston's relationship with the Knights, Sir Maurice Casey's first response was, 'I don't think he allowed them in the diocese, did he?' Sir Maurice Casey, interview, 3 May 2003.

61   Typical reports on the charity ball are found in *Month*, August 1932, p. 33; *Tablet*, 29 June 1932, p. 45; 26 June 1935, p. 6; 20 March 1940, p. 33; 13 June 1945, p. 6.

62   Historical information on the Catholic Women's League drawn from Gillian Frances Puch, 'The Catholic Women's League of New Zealand and the Changing Role of Women – A Sociological Analysis with Emphasis on a CWL Parish Group', MA Sociology thesis, University of Auckland, 1978, chapter 3.

63   See CWL first annual report (1931–32). LIS 205–1, ACDA.

64   See Liston's circular to diocesan priests, 14 July 1931. LIS 173, ACDA. See also Puch, 'Catholic Women's League', p. 61.

65   *Tablet*, 9 September 1931, p. 53; 20 March 1935, p. 38; 13 August 1952, p. 34.

66   *Tablet*, 15 September 1948, p. 42. Mrs Pilling had been elected unopposed as CWL president for her twelfth year in 1944. *Tablet*, 20 September 1944, p. 29.

67   See Fr Victor Geaney's letter to Liston and Liston's reply, 6 March 1947. LIS 82–7, ACDA.

68   Puch, 'Catholic Women's League', pp 72 ff.

69   Liston's address printed as editorial, 'The Catholic Woman in the World', *Zealandia*, 20 October 1949.
70   Puch, 'Catholic Women's League', p. 60.
71   *Zealandia*, 28 September 1939, p. 2; *Tablet*, 15 November 1939, p. 32.
72   See Liston's replies to CWL secretary, 8 March and 11 April 1949. LIS 205–1, ACDA.
73   Sir Maurice Casey, interview, 3 May 2003.
74   *NZH*, 5 March 1937. Liston's notes for this address are included in League of Mother File, LIS 216–5, ACDA. He opened the League of Mothers conference again in 1947.
75   Report of Liston's speech at inaugural Auckland meeting of Homemakers, *Tablet*, 26 October 1949, p. 46.
76   See Bishop Lyons reports to Liston on Homemakers in Christchurch, 8 June 1949. LIS 58–2, ACDA. Liston first promoted Homemakers at the CWL conference. *Tablet*, 14 September 1949, p. 43.
77   Puch, 'Catholic Women's League', pp 70–71.
78   Ryder, *Following All Your Ways, Lord*, pp 68–69. Dame Sister Pauline Engel recalls her mother, a member of the CWL executive in Wellington, being 'very upset by the 'independence' movement' of the Homemakers. [Private communication with Nicholas Reid, September 2003.]
79   See 1954 correspondence. LIS 205–1, ACDA.
80   *Tablet*, 11 December 1935; 22 May 1940, p. 32.
81   Letter, Holbrook to Liston, 15 August 1932. LIS 75–1, ACDA.
82   Letter, Liston to Duff, 29 November 1935. The Legion of Mary was inaugurated in Auckland, 8 September 1938. Details in Legion of Mary File, LIS 212, ACDA. See also *Zealandia*, 12 September 1963, p. 8; and 26 September 1971, p. 8, for retrospective articles on the establishment of the Legion of Mary in New Zealand.
83   These decorations are kept in LIS 5, ACDA, together with correspondence from the Yugoslav consul and from President Albert Lebrun of France, and New Zealand government permission for Liston to wear the decorations on state occasions. See *Zealandia*, 23 April 1936, p. 5; and *Tablet*, 22 April 1936, p. 37, for conferring of the Order of St Sava.
84   On 2 March 1953, Liston wrote to Apostolic Delegate explaining that a papal audience for Queen Salote would be in the interests of the Catholic mission in Tonga. LIS 54–2, ACDA. There is an account of Queen Salote's visit to the Vatican in Elizabeth Wood-Ellem, *Queen Salote of Tonga – The Story of an Era 1900–1965*, Auckland University Press, 1999, pp 246–248. However, Wood-Ellem makes no mention of Liston.
85   *NZH*, 26 May 1948, p. 10; *Zealandia*, 3 June 1948, front page and pp 12–13; *Tablet*, 9 June 1948, p. 47. At this time, de Valera was campaigning for the complete independence of Ireland from the British Commonwealth, to the great annoyance of both Auckland's dailies. See editorials, 'Mr de Valera', *AS*, 25 May 1948, and 'The Commonwealth and Eire', *NZH*, 28 May 1948.
86   *Zealandia*, 3 August 1950, front page; *Tablet*, 9 August 1950, p. 42.
87   LIS 166, ACDA.
88   *Tablet*, 11 November 1931.
89   Letter, Allum to Liston, 14 April 1943. LIS 111–3, ACDA. Letter, Town Clerk to Liston, 20 March 1946. LIS 159, ACDA.
90   On 22 November 1943, Mayor Allum invited Liston to be part of a 'Pro-Palestine Committee' (i.e. a Jewish settlement agency). LIS 159, ACDA. However, *NZH*, 18 October 1945, carries the article, 'Two Disclaimers – Cablegram to Mr Attlee' in which Liston and J.J. North are reported as protesting at the misuse of their names.
91   Boland, *James Duhig*, pp 306–308, records Duhig's misgivings over the bombings, although Duhig did admit their military necessity and dissociated himself from a general cable of protest by the Australian hierarchy. Liston preached a sermon against the proposed bombing of Rome, *Zealandia*, 29 July 1943, p. 2. The controversy over this operation was aired in the Auckland dailies, *AS*, 24 July and 26 July 1943; *NZH*, 26 July and 29 July 1943. On 21 March 1944, the Apostolic Delegate sent a standard letter to Liston, asking him to participate in a formal protest. On 20 April 1944, O'Shea drafted the New Zealand hierarchy's protest. LIS 53–3, ACDA.

92 Like the Vatican, Cardinal Gilroy and the Rector of Manly issued 'prompt and forthright condemnation of the use of the atomic bomb'. K.J. Walsh, *Yesterday's Seminary*, pp 229–230.

93 Liston's sermon reprinted as editorial, 'The Bishop's Statement', *Zealandia*, 16 August 1945, p. 3. In *Peace People* (Christchurch, 1992, p. 155), Elsie Locke claimed that the 'first New Zealander to publish a forthright denunciation of nuclear weapons appears to have been Lincoln Efford'. She apparently wrote in ignorance of Liston's prompt statement.

94 Letter, Liston to Lyons, 4 March 1945, seeking his approval of drafted protest on the Polish situation. Box 12 C, CCDA.

95 On 1 July 1940, the diocesan council discussed the question of placing English Catholic refugee children in Catholic homes in Auckland. LIS 52, ACDA. On 16 and 17 January 1946, the bishops' meeting was setting up accommodation for Polish and Dutch children refugees. LIS 2–8, ACDA. Liston welcomed to Auckland some Polish children refugees who had been at the camp in Pahiatua. See *Tablet*, 20 February 1946, p. 42. In the immediate postwar period, Liston was concerned with setting up an immigration agency for Catholic children. LIS 155–2, ACDA.

96 See exchange on conscription between O'Shea and Liston, 17 July and 26 July 1940. LIS 56–1, ACDA.

97 Early 1940 correspondence Liston to O'Shea, where Liston asks O'Shea to lobby the Minister of Defence to allow a resident chaplain at Papakura. LIS 111–2, ACDA. Also minutes of bishops' conference, 22 April 1940, where Bishop Brodie argued against Liston's proposal and carried the debate. LIS 2–2, ACDA.

98 *Tablet*, 24 April 1940, p. 32.

99 See, for example, the reprint of Liston's consolatory sermon to the bereaved, 'The Hour of Trial', *Zealandia*, 29 May 1941, p. 4.

100 *Tablet*, 14 November 1945, p. 29. At a Sacred Heart College prizegiving in 1942, the principal Br Borgia said 45 old boys of the college had been killed in the war, 32 were missing and a total of 700 were in the armed forces. *Tablet*, 30 December 1942, p. 27.

101 *Zealandia*, 30 April 1942, p. 8; and 16 July 1942, p. 8; *Tablet*, 15 April 1942 and 22 July 1942 (Mayor Allum opens the Catholic Services Club); 2 September 1942 (Liston blesses and opens a special chapel on the premises); and 12 September 1945.

102 *Tablet*, 8 August 1945, p. 6.

103 Letter, Liston to Building Controller asking permission to modify property on the corner of Victoria and Vulcan Streets for this purpose, 10 October 1945. LIS 111–3, ACDA.

104 *Tablet*, 19 February 1947, p. 42.

105 LIS 10–1, ACDA.

106 Letter, McKeefry to 'Dave', 15 December 1953. Folder 2, NZ Bishops' Conference Correspondence 488, WCAA.

107 Liston's address, 'Religion in Education', printed as editorial *Zealandia*, 31 January 1946.

108 'State Aid to Church Schools', Liston's address at the Sacred Heart College prizegiving, *NZH*, 23 November 1948, p. 8. Liston was responding to an article in the Presbyterian *Outlook*. His remarks were reprinted in *Tablet*, 1 December 1948, p. 7.

109 *Tablet*, 30 July 1947, p. 47, Liston corrects Mr Justice Fleming.

110 Letters, McKeefry to Liston and reply, 3 January 1951. LIS 56–2, ACDA.

111 See exchange between Liston and O'Shea, 3 September and 5 September 1941. LIS 56–1, ACDA.

112 'The Call to Arms' report of Liston's speech, *Tablet*, 28 May 1941, p. 29.

113 *Tablet*, 18 April 1936, p. 36.

114 *Tablet*, 23 June 1937, p. 44.

115 See correspondence between Liston and John Totich, October 1934. LIS 165–1, ACDA.

116 For Redwood's friendship with Rabbi von Stavern, see Nicholas Simmons, 'Archbishop Francis Redwood', p. 180.

117 See Astor's message to Liston on the death of Pope Pius XI, whom the rabbi describes as 'a lover of peace, humanity and tolerance', 11 February 1939. LIS 158, ACDA.

118 *NZH*, 9 July 1976, obituary tribute to Liston by D.W. Lochore.

119 *Month*, 2 August 1930, pp 13 and 15 gives an account of requiem masses for Sir Joseph Ward. *Tablet*, 23 July 1930, p. 50, reports Liston recalling his visits to the ailing Ward. *Tablet*, 20 February 1952, p. 39, reports Liston's requiem mass for King George VI.

120 *Month*, May 1932, pp 8–10; *Tablet*, 29 June 1932, p. 45.

121 *Tablet*, 21 February 1934, p. 16.

122 Letter, Liston to French consul M Joubert, 13 August 1937, filed in both LIS 168 and LIS 160–2, ACDA.

123 Letter, de Valera to Liston, 3 February 1938. LIS 168, ACDA.

124 Letter, Liston to MacRory thanking him, 5 April 1938. LIS 168, ACDA.

125 *AS*, 24 February 1938.

126 Account of centennial celebrations taken from special centennial edition of *Zealandia*, 5 March 1938; and *NZH*, 1 March 1938, p. 13. Also from materials relating to centennial, LIS 156–2, ACDA.

127 *Tablet*, 30 March 1938, p. 15.

128 See the final balance sheet, 6 September 1938, signed off by auditor A.W. Christmas, which gives the total costs of the celebrations as £11,979. After all donations were paid in, there was a shortfall of £500. LIS 168, ACDA.

129 Private communication from Professor Russell Stone, June 2003. Stone recalled hearing the sermon as a boy.

130 *NZH*, 1 March 1938, p. 13.

131 *Tablet*, 4 November 1942, p. 28.

132 *Tablet*, 2 December 1942.

133 *Tablet*, 29 August 1945, p. 6.

134 See exchange between Liston and O'Hara, 8 May and 10 October 1943. LIS 111–2, ACDA.

135 On 8 March 1945, Liston sent O'Hara lists of all American servicemen who had contracted marriages in New Zealand. LIS 111–2, ACDA.

136 *Tablet*, 4 March 1931; *Month*, 2 May 1932, p. 16.

137 *Zealandia*, 30 August 1934, front page.

138 *Tablet*, 24 June 1931, p. 44.

139 For comments on the disproportionately working-class nature of the Catholic church in contrast with more middle class and rural Anglican and Presbyterian churches in New Zealand in the 1930s, see Ernest Simmons, 'The Church in New Zealand 1924 to 1973', p. 324; and Kevin Paul Clements, 'The Churches and Social Policy: A Study in the Relationship of Ideology to Action', PhD Sociology thesis, Victoria University of Wellington, 1970, especially pp 6 and 153.

140 New Zealand's only real home-grown approach to Fascism was the small, short-lived and ineffective New Zealand Legion, which had a notably rural base. Much of its membership had earlier been associated with the anti-Catholic Protestant Political Association. See Michael C. Pugh, 'The New Zealand Legion 1932–1935', *NZJH*, 5 (1), April 1977, pp 49–69.

141 Pastoral (dated variously for June 1931) filed in Pastoral Letters Box, DCDA, and LIS 56–1, ACDA. See also *Month*, 1 July 1931; and *Tablet*, 8 July 1931, pp 42–43.

142 Letter, Holbrook to Liston, 21 October 1931. LIS 76–1, ACDA.

143 Letter, Holbrook to Lee, 26 November 1931. Lee Papers, NZMS 828, Series 9, Folder 2 (Auckland Public Library).

144 Pastoral, *Month*, 1 July 1931. See also A.J.S. Reid, 'Church and State in New Zealand 1930–1935', MA History thesis, Victoria University of Wellington, 1961, p. 63; and van der Krogt, 'More a Part than Apart', p. 443.

145 Letter, Liston to Apostolic Delegate, 20 June 1932. LIS 53, ACDA.

146 This is the term used in reference to the construction of St Michael's church by Felix Donnelly in his novel, *Father Forgive Them*, Auckland, 1990, p. 57.

147 According to Mgr Brian Arahill, in the construction of St Michael's church, Fr John Bradley organised for salt-filled sand to be taken from the seashore to make the cement. Later this caused problems in the maintenance of the church. Mgr Arahill, interview, 28 December 2002.

148 See Tony Simpson, *The Slump*, Auckland, 1990, pp 88–89, for details of how the Prudential Insurance Company was able to use relief-work labour in the Depression to build an office block for little more than the cost of materials.

149 *Tablet*, 29 June 1932, p. 45; *Month*, 1 May 1933, pp 18–19.
150 *Month*, 1 March 1932, pp 16.
151 Simpson, *The Slump*, p. 60.
152 A.J.S. Reid, 'Church and State', p. 46; Clements, 'Churches and Social Policy', p. 162.
153 *NZH*, 5 April 1932, p. 11. Other participants in the symposium were Mayor Hutchison, Salvation Army Major Gordon and Anglican city missioner Jasper Calder.
154 A.J.S. Reid, 'Church and State', p. 52.
155 Bishop Brodie commended him for this suggestion, 18 July 1933, Brodie to Liston. LIS 58–1, ACDA.
156 This was how the meeting's agenda was announced, *NZH*, 10 July 1934, p. 12.
157 Report of speech and meeting, *NZH*, 11 July 1934, p. 14; and *Zealandia*, 19 July 1934, front page. See also *Tablet*, 18 July 1934, p. 37.
158 See editorials, all of them entitled 'The Unemployed', *Zealandia*, 27 September 1934, 14 February and 28 February 1935.
159 A.J.S. Reid, 'Church and State', pp 74–75 and 110.
160 See hierarchy's response, 4 May 1938. LIS 2–3, ACDA.
161 On 13 October 1938, Bishop Whyte wrote to Liston expressing his annoyance that one priest in the Dunedin diocese, Mgr Delaney, had apparently blatantly advised parishioners to vote Labour. LIS 59–6, ACDA.
162 Just as, in America, Catholic social scientists came to approve of the 'New Deal'. Morris, *American Catholic*, pp 152 ff, gives an account of Mgr John A. Ryan, theorist for Catholic social justice programmes in America, who seemed to reach the same conclusions about welfare as Roosevelt's administration.
163 Nicholas Simmons, 'Archbishop Francis Redwood', pp 49 ff, gives an account of Redwood's shedding his anti-socialist rhetoric at the time of the Depression. See, too, van der Krogt, 'More a Part than Apart', pp 376 ff.
164 van der Krogt, 'More a Part than Apart', p. 409.
165 Letter, O'Shea to Liston, 24 June 1937. Box 375 (Bible-in-Schools Box), WCAA.
166 Letter, O'Shea to Alan Carter, 28 July 1938. Box 254 (Government and Legislation), WCAA.
167 LIS 154–1, ACDA.
168 *Tablet*, 26 March 1930, pp 48–49.
169 See reports of visits, *Tablet*, 8 January 1936; and *Zealandia*, 16 January 1936, p. 5. (Savage visited the Little Sisters' home in company with the undersecretary for housing, John A. Lee.)
170 Letter, Savage to Liston, 18 May 1932. LIS 155–1, ACDA.
171 Gustafson, *From the Cradle to the Grave*, pp 267–272. See also memo of Liston's requiem mass, LIS 154–1, ACDA; and *Tablet*, 3 April 1940. *Zealandia* ran a special memorial issue on Savage, 4 April 1940, including a front-page photograph of the late prime minister, and editorial (pp 4–5) headed 'A Beloved Leader', and an account (p. 9) of Liston's requiem mass.
172 Letter, Fraser to Liston, 6 April 1940. LIS 154–1, ACDA.
173 Gustafson, *From the Cradle to the Grave*, p. 272. See also *Tablet*, 6 August 1941, p. 33, for account of Savage's casket being moved to the cathedral; and 10 February 1942, Fraser to Liston thanking him for permitting this use of cathedral space. LIS 154–1, ACDA.
174 Letter, 13 August 1930. LIS 2–1, ACDA.
175 Akenson, *Half the World From Home*, p. 183; Sweetman, *A Fair and Just Solution*, pp 29–30. See also minutes of bishops' meeting, 11 April 1945, where it was noted that acting prime minister Walter Nash had given the bishops assurances about the registration of Catholic schools and the provision of bus transport to Catholic pupils. LIS 2–6, ACDA.
176 Letter, Liston to Fraser, 28 October 1938. LIS 187 (Education Correspondence), ACDA.
177 Letters, Fr Daniel Silk to Liston, February 1939, and Fraser to Liston, 19 April 1939. LIS 84–6, ACDA.
178 See Liston's minutes of bishops' meeting with prime minister, 7 September 1944. LIS 2–6, ACDA.

179 *Tablet*, 24 January 1945, p. 6. See also Liston's draft of memorandum after hierarchy's meeting with prime minister after opening of Holy Name seminary, 15 February 1947. Box 12 C, CCDA.

180 *Tablet*, 24 October 1945, p. 30.

181 See minutes of bishops' meeting, 4 April 1948. LIS 2–10, ACDA.

182 Scott, *Rebel in a Wrong Cause*, pp 66 and 92. This was quite unlike the situation in Australia, where by 1930 Communists controlled about 25 per cent of union positions and in 1943 party membership peaked at 23,000. Duncan, *Crusade or Conspiracy?* chapters 1 and 4.

183 Scott, *Rebel in a Wrong Cause*, p. 45.

184 Michael Joseph Savage was annoyed, in 1931, that the Labour Party's decision to expel this group was not being systematically carried out. Gustafson, *From the Cradle to the Grave*, pp 143–144. Bob Semple led the anti-Communist group at the Labour Party conference in 1937, but he had overwhelming support. Keith Sinclair, *Walter Nash*, Auckland, 1976, p. 153. Again, the situation was different from Australia where only in 1949 did the Australian Labor Party ban Communist affiliation. Duncan, *Crusade or Conspiracy?*, chapter 8.

185 *Tablet*, 31 August 1938, p. 4.

186 See circular, 5 May 1948. LIS 159, ACDA. Both Auckland dailies also welcomed Spellman as the 'No. 1 enemy of Communism'. Editorial, 'Cardinal Spellman', *NZH*, 14 May 1948. Front page report on Spellman and Sheen, *AS*, 13 May 1948. A similar anti-Communist talk was given at a civic reception in Auckland by visiting English Bishop John Heenan. See *Tablet*, 6 May 1953, p. 34.

187 Boland, *James Duhig*, p. 262 (Duhig was the chief drafter of the pastoral). *Tablet*, 13 October 1937, reprinted the pastoral.

188 Letters, Liston to Apostolic Delegate, 24 May and 31 May 1937. LIS 53, ACDA. The committee of priests included Fathers Holbrook, Lavelle, Buxton and Higgins.

189 *Zealandia*, 4 November 1937, editorial, 'A Radio Protest' (p. 6) and text of Fr Crowe's talk, 'They Can't Take It! Communism Hates Facts' (p. 7); *Zealandia*, 16 December 1937, editorial, 'A Radio Complaint' (p. 6).

190 *Zealandia*, 10 February 1938, 'Action for Libel', p. 6.

191 *Zealandia*, 30 June 1938, p. 6.

192 Sid Scott claims that Soviet papers of the period were openly pro-Hitler. *Rebel in a Wrong Cause*, p. 113. In her book, *Peace People – A History of Peace Activities in New Zealand*, the former Communist Elsie Locke still finds justifications for Stalin's alliance with Hitler, pp 103 ff.

193 Rachel Barrowman, *A Popular Vision – The Arts and the Left in New Zealand 1930–1950*, Wellington, 1991, chapter 2. See also B.S. Taylor, 'The Expulsion of J.A. Lee and its Effects on the Development of the New Zealand Labour Party', MA thesis, University of Canterbury, 1970, p. 84.

194 Nancy M. Taylor, *The New Zealand People at War – The Home Front*, Wellington, 1986, p. 587.

195 Ibid., pp 590–593.

196 Scott, *Rebel in a Wrong Cause*, pp 140–141.

197 Nancy Taylor, *New Zealand People at War*, pp 599–602. In fact, proportionately more Soviet citizens were collaborators with occupying Nazis than was the case in any other occupied country.

198 Letters, Fr Norbert Berridge to Liston, 22 and 29 November 1941. LIS 111–2, ACDA.

199 Nancy Taylor, *New Zealand People at War*, pp 594–597.

200 van der Krogt, 'More a Part than Apart', p. 419. The Rationalist Association formed a close bond with the Communists at the time of the Hitler-Stalin pact, and were among the sponsors of the Society for Closer Relations with Russia. Bill Cooke, *Heathen in Godzone – Seventy Years of Rationalism in New Zealand*, Auckland, 1998, pp 78 ff and pp 84 ff.

201 Nancy Taylor, *New Zealand People at War*, pp 588–89.

202 Ibid., pp 603–620.

203 Letter, Gordon Dieing (President of the Sacred Heart International Foundation) to Liston suggesting that devotion to Our Lady is 'the best spiritual method to defeat the philosophy of Communism', 5 May 1952. LIS 60–1, ACDA.

204 See programme for reception of statue, 1 May 1949. Cathedral Parish Papers, LIS 62–1, ACDA.
205 *Tablet*, 19 July 1950, pp 6–7.
206 Letters, Liston to Apostolic Delegate, 10 February 1949 and 15 March 1951. LIS 54, ACDA. See also *Zealandia*, 10 February 1949, p. 3, for whole hierarchy's pastoral in support of Cardinal Mindszenty.
207 *NZH*, 15 October 1946, p. 7. Stepinac was sentenced to 16 years' hard labour. See also *Tablet*, 23 October 1946, and *Zealandia*, 24 October 1946 (p. 3), reporting Liston's call for prayers for Stepinac.
208 Caput I, 1935 *relatio*. LIS 20–2, ACDA.
209 Trlin, *Now Respected, Once Despised*, pp 176–178.
210 Letter, Liston to Apostolic Delegate, 21 October 1946. LIS 54–1, ACDA.
211 See correspondence, Forrest-Liston, September 1936. LIS 82–7, ACDA.
212 Letter, Columb to Liston, 27 January 1937. LIS 82–7, ACDA.
213 Letter, Liston to Forrest, 29 January 1937. LIS 82–7, ACDA.
214 *Huntly Press*, 5 February 1937 (clipping filed in LIS 82–7, ACDA).
215 Letter, Liston to chairman of *Catholic Worker*, 11 February 1941. LIS 158, ACDA.
216 Letter, Mannix to New Zealand hierarchy, 22 August 1948. LIS 56–2, ACDA.
217 Mid-1949 correspondence Lyons-Liston. LIS 58–2, ACDA.
218 Regular letters from Santamaria to Liston are filed in LIS 210–2, ACDA.
219 Letter, Fr Norbert Berridge thanks Liston for sending these publications to his men's study group, 20 October 1953. LIS 72–2, ACDA.
220 See Liston's exchange with D.J. Leahy (national organiser of St Vincent de Paul Society), 14 October and 17 October 1949. LIS 207, ACDA.
221 Letter, Liston to Kathleen O'Connor (Dominion president of CWL), 13 April 1950. LIS 205–1, ACDA.
222 Scott, *Rebel in a Wrong Cause*, pp 140–141. Scott's comments on the 'sectarian' Communist nature of the NZ Peace Council are on p. 162.
223 See Flanagan's diocesan report to Apostolic Delegate, 22 May 1950. LIS 54–21, ACDA.
224 Pat Booth notes that even a newspaper as 'generally liberal' as the *Auckland Star* wrote fiery anti-union editorials implying Communist influence at the time of the dispute. Pat Booth, *Deadline – My Story*, Auckland, 1997, pp 40–41. Meanwhile, John A. Lee condemned the watersiders as loafers. Erik Olssen, *John A. Lee*, Dunedin, 1977, p. 204.
225 *Tablet*, 18 April 1951, pp 1–2; and 13 June 1951, p. 11.
226 Letter, Liston to Apostolic Delegate, 27 August 1951. LIS 54–2, ACDA.
227 Nicholas Reid, *The Bishop's Paper*, pp 71 ff. See also Susan Mary Skudder, 'Bringing It Home – New Zealand Responses to the Spanish Civil War 1936–1939', Doctoral thesis, Waikato University, 1986, especially chapter 3 on the 'Anti-Communist Crusade'.
228 'The Swing to the Right in Spain', *Tablet*, 3 January 1934, p. 20.
229 'Tyranny in Spain', *Tablet*, 18 March 1936, p. 3. 'The Spanish Elections – Reign of Terror Begins', editorial page, *Zealandia*, 9 April 1936.
230 Between August 1936 and April 1937, *every* front page of *Zealandia* was dominated by a story on Spain, which remained a frequent front page item for the rest of the war.
231 Cooke, *Heathen in Godzone*, p. 68.
232 Letter, Brodie to Liston, 16 September 1936. LIS 58–1, ACDA. Letter, Whyte to Liston, 15 October 1936. The other bishops also wrote to the daily press about Spain. Whyte wrote to Liston (9 December 1936) praising Bishop Brodie's public statements on the matter. LIS 59–6, ACDA.
233 'Aid for Spain – N.Z. Ambulance Unit – Bishop's Strong Protest', *AS*, 2 September 1936, refers to Bishop Brodie's public denunciation of the scheme.
234 *Tablet*, 16 February 1938, p. 44.
235 Liston preached at the requiem mass which Peter McKeefry said for Dollfuss in St Patrick's Cathedral, *Zealandia*, 2 August 1934, p. 4.
236 Editorial, 'The Roman Trouble', *Tablet*, 15 July 1931, p. 3.
237 *Tablet*, 29 July 1931, p. 45.
238 The Auckland Anglican publication, the *Church Gazette*, spoke of 'Fascism with

which the Roman Catholic church has made an unholy alliance' and declared that 'the policy of the Roman church is Fascist'. *Church Gazette* editorials, 1 December 1937 and 1 April 1938.

239 'Fascism Today Stands Condemned', *Tablet*, 26 May 1937, pp 7–8.

240 *Tablet*, May-June 1939.

241 *Tablet*, 4 December 1935, p. 6.

242 *Zealandia*, 20 June 1940, and editorial, 'The Pope and the World Crisis', p. 4.

243 *AS*, 3 July 1933; *NZH*, 4 July 1933.

244 Nicholas Reid, *The Bishop's Paper*, pp 74–75.

245 *Zealandia*, 15 August 1940, p. 4.

246 Both the *Auckland Star* and the *New Zealand Herald* ran editorials praising the Munich agreement as a triumph of diplomacy. Sir Ernest Davis organised a civic celebration in the Town Hall for Neville Chamberlain's and Edouard Daladier's achievement in averting war. Liston, the Anglican Archbishop Averill and leaders of other churches took part. Laudatory sermons were preached in Catholic, Anglican and Presbyterian churches. One Labour councillor and a small Communist demonstration dissented. See editorial, 'From Despair to Hope', *AS*, 29 September 1938, and editorial, 'A Triumph for Sanity', *NZH*, 1 October 1938. See also news reports, *NZH*, 1, 3 and 4 October 1938. See also Scott, *Rebel in a Wrong Cause*, p. 94; and Locke, *Peace People*, p. 100.

247 The *New Zealand Herald* ran a number of editorials lauding Mussolini's regime in the early 1930s. See editorials, 'Fascism and Democracy', *NZH*, 27 March 1933, and 'Mussolini's New Role', *NZH*, 23 August 1933.

248 *Zealandia*, 10 April 1941, front page.

249 Dennis Sewell, *Catholics – Britain's Largest Minority*, London, 2001, p. 78 and pp 80–81.

250 Cooney, *John Charles McQuaid*, pp 142–44.

251 Boland, *James Duhig*, chapter 13.

252 For a statement of the Catholic opposition to both Communism and Fascism in the 1930s, see the comments by the philosophy professor Fr Arthur Ryan (of Belfast) when he visited Auckland at the time of the Catholic centennial. *NZH*, 3 March 1938, p. 13.

253 See draft of Liston's talk to medical group, November 1952. LIS 13–2, ACDA.

254 Letter, Liston to Lee, 8 December 1922. Lee Papers, NZMS 828, Series 9, Folder 1 (Auckland Public Library).

255 On 23 August 1929, Liston acknowledged books sent by Lee and sent him books in return. Ibid.

256 Letter, Liston to Lee, 29 December 1929. Ibid.

257 Letter, Liston to Lee, 13 July 1931. Ibid.

258 Letter, Lee to Liston, 7 April 1932. LIS 180, ACDA.

259 Letter, Liston to Lee, 2 April 1932. LIS 180, ACDA.

260 Tony Simpson (ed.), *The Scrim-Lee Papers – C.G. Scrimgeour and John A. Lee Remember the Crisis Years 1930–40*, Wellington, 1976, p. 38 (giving Lee's reminiscences of his visit).

261 See Liston's memorandum, 16 April 1932. LIS 180, ACDA.

262 'Golden Jubilee – Celebrations at Mosgiel', *ODT*, 15 November 1937.

263 Letter, Lee to Liston, 28 March 1938. LIS 168, ACDA. In the light of this, and other references to Lee's presence at Catholic functions of the period, it is highly unlikely that Lee was deliberately not invited to the opening of the new wing of the Mater hospital in March 1936, as is implied in Belgrave, *Mater*, p. 65.

264 Lee, 'Myself and the Catholic Church'. Lee Papers, NZMS 828, Series 5, Folder 29 (Auckland Public Library).

265 Ibid.

266 Ibid.

267 Handwritten comments added by Lee (years later) to letters from Liston dated 24 March and 8 December 1922. Lee Papers, NZMS Series 9, Folder 1 (Auckland Public Library).

268 Ibid.

269 See especially chapters 1 and 2 of B.S. Taylor, 'The Expulsion of J. A. Lee', where the mechanics of Lee's expulsion are discussed and there is no evidence of Catholic involvement.

270 See p. 192, ibid.
271 Olssen, *John A. Lee*, pp 81 ff.
272 Lee, 'Myself and the Catholic Church'.
273 Olssen, *John A. Lee*, chapter 13.
274 Ibid., p. 184. See also Moore to Lee, 8 February 1945, and other (undated) correspondence between them. Lee Papers, NZMS 828, Series 5, Folder 29 (Auckland Public Library). See also Cooke, *Heathen in Godzone*, pp 87–88.
275 Ibid., pp 178–180. See also letter from secretary of United Protestant Association of New Zealand, 19 October 1942. Lee Papers, NZMS 828, Series 5, Folder 29 (Auckland Public Library).
276 Cooke, *Heathen in Godzone*, p. 101.
277 John A. Lee, *Simple on a Soapbox*, Auckland, 1963, especially pp 29, 37, 155, 178 and 241–243. There is the added irony that *Simple on a Soapbox* was edited and 'fashioned into something publishable' by a practising Catholic, J.C. Reid, who was then working under contract for the publishers. See Olssen, *John A. Lee*, p. 207. It is possible, but unlikely, that Reid (father of the present writer) suppressed some of Lee's more personal references.
278 For negative comments on Lee's political misjudgements, see Keith Sinclair, 'The Lee-Sutch Syndrome. New Zealand Labour Party Policies and Politics', *NZJH*, October 1974, 8 (2), p. 95; Simpson, *The Slump*, chapter 14, 'The Myth According to John A. Lee', p. 75; a comment on Lee's propensity for fantasising in R.C.J. Stone, 'Sinister Auckland Business Cliques 1840–1940', *NZJH*, April 1987, 21 (2); and on Lee's egotism and alienation of other Labour Party members, B.S. Taylor, 'Expulsion of J.A. Lee', pp 16 and 40, and Olssen, *John A. Lee*, pp 151 and 173.
279 B.S. Taylor, 'Expulsion of J.A. Lee', p. 207.
280 Olssen, *John A. Lee*, p. 204.
281 In 1948, the Sisters of St Joseph of the Sacred Heart ('Brown Joes') bought Davis's Mission Bay residence for a retreat centre, and the Mercy Sisters bought property off him in Kohimarama. See Power, *Sisters of St Joseph of the Sacred Heart*, pp 252–256. Also materials in LIS 134–6, ACDA. Also *Tablet*, 26 April 1950, p. 42, for the purchase by the Mercy sisters.
282 On 1 July 1959, Liston informed cathedral administrator of Davis's donation. LIS 62–1 (Cathedral Parish Papers), ACDA.
283 Bollinger, *Grog's Own Country*, pp 102–03.
284 Lee wrote, 'I was not for sale. Savage washed brewery barrels, Parry was on a stipend. [Davis] was the largest controller of the Trade Slush Fund. This made him the arch corrupter'. Note attached (years later) to letter from Davis to Lee (dated 17 February 1930). Lee Papers, NZMS 828, Series 6, Folder 14 (Auckland Public Library).
285 Stone, 'Sinister Auckland Business Cliques', p. 39.
286 *Zealandia*, 6 February 1941, p. 5.
287 Undated (early 1946) memo, Liston to Forsman. LIS 177–2, ACDA.
288 See diocesan report to Apostolic Delegate, 22 May 1950. LIS 54–2, ACDA.
289 *Zealandia*, 19 February 1970, p. 2, reprinted a speech by Lee on New Zealand youth. *Zealandia*, 14 November 1971, p. 14, ran a tribute by David Ballantyne to Lee on his eightieth birthday. By this stage, Lee's own political views were frequently conservative ones.
290 *Tablet*, 28 December 1938, p. 44.
291 Throughout 1937, Liston received letters from Thomas Stone, a retired engineer, who wanted the pontifical academy to endorse his cure for cancer. LIS 53, ACDA.
292 Article by Brian Healy, 'Sixty Years in the Priesthood', *Zealandia*, 30 January 1964.
293 Liston frequently placed orders with Whitcombe and Tombs for books of a political or philosophical character. LIS 160–1, ACDA.
294 The businessman George Joseph recalled how, when he first arrived in Auckland in 1931, he was suffering from a bad attack of influenza and was surprised to receive a sympathy visit from Liston, whom he hardly knew at that time. Article, 'Archbishop is Foremost a Pastor Among his People', *AS*, 29 January 1967.
295 Private communication (28 August 2001), John Sumich to Nicholas Reid.
296 Sir Ian Barker, interview, 6 April 2003.
297 Sr Margaret Browne, interview, 23 February 2003.

298   Mary Elizabeth Hales, interview, 3 May 2003. (Hales is the daughter of J.M. Simson, a long-time member of the *Zealandia* board.)

299   Sr Judith Leydon, interview, 15 April 2003.

300   D.W. Lochore, 'Tremble? Yes. Falter? No', *NZH*, 9 July 1976, p. 6.

301   *Zealandia*, 4 February 1954, front page; *Tablet*, 10 February 1954, pp 30–31 and 34.

302   Letter, Liston to Fumasoni-Biondi, 19 February 1954. LIS 54–2, ACDA.

303   Programme of sacerdotal golden jubilee celebrations. LIS 14–2, ACDA. See also *Tablet*, 31 March 1954, pp 32–33; and *Zealandia*, 1 April 1954.

Chapter VIII: Before Vatican II – Archbishop Liston 1954–62

1   On 6 February 1954, Liston announced his intended itinerary to the rector of the Irish College in Rome, Donal Herlihy. Herlihy Papers, Box 2, ICR. See also *Tablet*, 10 February 1954, p. 34, for itinerary.

2   Letter, Brown and Nolan to Liston, 15 May 1954. Bishops' Conference Correspondence (489), Folder 1, WCAA.

3   *Zealandia*, 14 October 1954, p. 2. Liston recalls visit to Puteaux in address to Auckland clergy.

4   Letter, Liston to Mother-General of Cluny Sisters arranging visit during his three-day stay in Paris, 19–22 May, 17 March 1954. LIS 132–2, ACDA.

5   Letters, McKeefry to Herlihy, 16 May and 13 June 1954. Herlihy Papers, Box 2, ICR.

6   *Tablet*, 23 June 1954, p. 34.

7   Letter, Fr Daniel Hurley SM to Liston inviting him to preach the English-language panegyric at the Triduum, 26 March 1954. LIS 126–2, ACDA. *Tablet*, 30 June 1954, p. 33, reports Liston's panegyric. On 13 June 1954, McKeefry wrote to Liston congratulating him on the occasion. LIS 57–4, ACDA. For further information on the canonisation of Peter Chanel, see Hugh Laracy, 'Saint-Making – The Case of Pierre Chanel of Futuna', *NZJH*, 34 (1), April 2001, esp. pp 157–58.

8   *Tablet*, 14 July 1954, p. 34.

9   Letter, Liston to McKeefry, 3 June 1954. Bishops' Conference Correspondence (489), Folder 1, WCAA.

10   Letter, McKeefry to Herlihy, asking him to arrange for Liston to collect the pallium, 16 May 1954. Herlihy Papers, Box 2, ICR. See also Letter, McKeefry to Liston, 16 May 1954. LIS 57–4, ACDA.

11   *Zealandia*, 7 October 1954, pp 1–2, Liston's account of his journey.

12   Letter, Liston's letter of thanks to Freyberg, 12 September 1954. LIS 154–5, ACDA.

13   *Zealandia*, 2 September 1954, front page.

14   *Zealandia*, 7 October 1954, p. 2.

15   Letters, Liston to McKeefry, 29 August and 2 September 1954. Bishops' Conference Correspondence (489), Folder 1, WCAA.

16   *Zealandia*, 7 October 1954, pp 1–2.

17   Letter, Liston to McKeefry, 29 August 1954. Bishops' Conference Correspondence (489), Folder 1, WCAA.

18   *Zealandia*, 7 October 1954, pp 1–2.

19   *Zealandia*, 21 October 1954, front page; *Tablet*, 6 October 1954, p. 34.

20   *Zealandia*, 7 October 1954, front page.

21   *Tablet*, 20 October 1954, p. 34; *Zealandia*, 21 October 1954, front page.

22   *Zealandia*, 28 July 1955. See also *Tablet*, 6 July 1955, p. 8.

23   Letter, Bishop Whyte to Liston, 'I hope you are well after your Brisbane visit. Bp Joyce, I understand, thought the sermons too long, except yours. Bravo', 10 December 1955. LIS 58–3, ACDA.

24   Figures according to *Zealandia*, 28 January 1954, p. 11, and 8 December 1960, p. 2; *Tablet*, 23 February 1955, p. 35; and obituary of Liston in Historical File, ACDA.

25   Between 1954 and 1960, Liston opened new churches in Fairfield, Mt Roskill, Tauranga, Manurewa, Mt Albert, Thames, Balmoral, Avondale, Te Kaha, Bayswater, Henderson, Panmure, Howick and Owaraka.

26   Department of Education reports on Auckland diocesan schools filed in LIS 182, ACDA.

27 See exchange of letters between Beeby and Liston, 5 April and 1 May 1957. LIS 183, ACDA.

28 See, for example, report of opening of new classrooms at Te Awamutu, *Zealandia*, 12 July 1956, front page; report of opening of Pompallier School, Kaitaia, *Zealandia*, 27 February 1958, p. 7; report of blessing of Whangarei convent school, *Zealandia*, 16 April 1959, front page; report of opening of St Leo's convent, Devonport, *Zealandia*, 30 July 1959, front page; report of opening St Dominic's convent, Northcote, *Zealandia*, 1 October 1959, p. 9; report of opening Brigidine convent, Meadowbank, *Zealandia*, 3 December 1959, front page.

29 LIS 135–4, ACDA.

30 Letter, Liston to Apostolic Delegate informing him of invitation to Passionists, 12 January 1960. LIS 55–1, ACDA. *Tablet*, 20 January 1960, p. 34, for Liston's invitation to Passionists. *Zealandia*, 23 June 1960, front page, for arrival of Passionists in diocese. Correspondence between Liston and Passionists, LIS 127–2, ACDA.

31 Letter, Liston to Rosminian superior, 18 April 1957; and other material relating to the order's establishment in Auckland. LIS 129–2, ACDA. Letter, Liston to Bishop Kavanagh discussing Rosminians, 15 December 1957. LIS 58–3, ACDA. *Zealandia*, 17 November 1960, front page reports invitation to Rosminians.

32 *Tablet*, 8 February 1961, p. 34, for reports of opening of Black Joes' school and convent. See also Liston's correspondence with Mother M. Adrian, LIS 135–2, ACDA; and Strevens, *In Step With Time*, pp 124 ff and p. 129.

33 For Liston's correspondence with Sisters of the Holy Faith, see LIS 134–4, ACDA.

34 *Tablet*, 24 February 1960, p. 34.

35 *Zealandia*, 1 August 1955, front page.

36 Correspondence between Liston and the city council 1957–58. LIS 62–2, ACDA. See *Tablet*, 20 February 1957, p. 35, for Liston's blessing of the new Catholic library; *Tablet*, 12 November 1958, p. 35, on the demolition of the building for a car-park; and *Tablet*, 27 July 1960, p. 34, for report on how the Catholic library has 'gone into recess' until a new Catholic centre is built around the *Zealandia* offices.

37 Fr Frank (Francis James) Roach, interview, 15 March 2003.

38 Marinovich's 1959 report to Liston says that 40 boys, but only 18 girls, responded with enquiries about entering the religious life after the 1958 vocations campaign. LIS 146–3, ACDA. Even before the Second Vatican Council, girls in Ireland too were becoming less interested in taking the veil. On 23 May 1961, the Mercy Sister Benedict wrote to Liston about her expedition to recruit postulants from Ireland, noting how few recruits she had secured because of the 'general attitude of indifference' among Irish schoolgirls. LIS 137–2, ACDA.

39 *Zealandia*, 26 July 1956, has a front page photograph of Liston ordaining six priests in a ceremony at St Patrick's Cathedral. The following year, a total of 30 priests were ordained nationwide (*Zealandia*, 4 July 1957, front page). This appears to have been a record that was never subsequently equalled.

40 *Zealandia*, 22 September 1960, p. 9.

41 Fr Laurence Sakey, interview, 12 January 2003.

42 Fr James Shannahan, interview, 23 February 2003. See also Liston's pastoral asking for prayers for the new Irish priests who will serve in his diocese, *Zealandia*, 10 July 1958, p. 2.

43 Mgr Vincent Hunt, interview, 4 January 2003.

44 LIS 50–1, ACDA.

45 Fr John Lyons, interview, 29 December 2002.

46 Fr Laurence Sakey, interview, 12 January 2003.

47 See Hunt's request to Liston, 10 November 1958. LIS 80–2, ACDA.

48 Fr James Shannahan, interview, 23 February 2003.

49 Fr Peter Ryan, interview, 18 May 2003.

50 Fr James Shannahan, interview, 23 February 2003.

51 Fr Des Angland, interview, 18 January 2003.

52 Fr James Shannahan, interview, 23 February 2003.

53 Fr Bruce Bolland, interview, 17 April 2003.

54 Fr Peter Ryan, interview, 18 May 2003.

55 *Tablet*, 29 June 1955, p. 34.

56 The front cover of *Tablet*, 3 August 1955, showed Liston with Furlong, preparing

to celebrate Furlong's anniversary. *Tablet*, 11 March 1959, p. 34, also reported celebrations for another long-serving Auckland diocesan priest, Fr Skinner of Puhoi.
57   *Tablet*, 16 July 1958, p. 34.
58   Letter, Liston to McCormack, 31 October 1955. LIS 143, ACDA.
59   Liston's correspondence regarding Bleakley's bequest. Private Will and Bequests File, LIS 28–1, ACDA.
60   Papers relating to Buxton's estate, MAC 67, ACDA.
61   Mgr Vincent Hunt, interview, 4 January 2003.
62   Fr Des Angland, interview, 18 January 2003.
63   Fr Peter Ryan, interview, 18 May 2003.
64   Bishop John Mackey, interview, 19 January 2003.
65   Correspondence between Liston, Derrick and Silk, June 1960. Matamata Parish File, LIS 84–6, ACDA.
66   Letter, Gaines to Liston, 11 December 1956. Epsom Parish File, LIS 73–7, ACDA.
67   On the letter of complaint from Gaines, Liston wrote the memo, 'Rec.15/12/56. No answer. Interview with Fr Dunphy 20/12/56. Fr Gaines appted. to Kaitaia 19/12/56'.
68   Letter, Green to Liston, 25 September 1956. LIS 73–7, ACDA.
69   Mgr Brian Arahill, interview, 28 December 2002.
70   *Tablet*, 8 October 1958, p. 34.
71   *Zealandia*, 25 June 1959 (front page report on Bradley's death) and 2 July 1959 (p. 9 account of requiem for Bradley at Panmure). For far more negative accounts of Bradley, see Donnelly's novel, *Father Forgive Them*, where Bradley is caricatured as 'Monsignor O'Halloran'; and Ryder's memoir, *Following All Your Ways, Lord*, where (p. 73) Bradley is accused of making malicious reports that led to Ryder's being sent to a rural parish.
72   Details on Liston's reasons for changing the system of parish accounts from Fr Bruce Bolland (interview, 17 April 2003) and Fr Des Angland (interview, 18 January 2003).
73   Letter, Liston to Br Edgar, 23 March 1961. LIS 80–2, ACDA.
74   *Zealandia*, 10 February 1955, front page (Liston hears 24 young Mercy sisters make their final vows) and 23 January 1958, p. 9 (Liston presides at the funeral of Mother Gonzaga).
75   Sr Judith Leydon, interview, 15 April 2003.
76   *Tablet*, 22 August and 26 September 1956, p. 34.
77   *Tablet*, 30 March 1960, p. 35.
78   Newsletters of the doctors' guild filed in LIS 209–1, ACDA.
79   *Tablet*, 9 October 1957, p. 34.
80   Liston's address, 'The Morality of the Practice of the Rhythm Method', August 1958. LIS 209–1, ACDA.
81   Letter, Dunn to Liston, 3 January 1961; and correspondence between Liston and Dunn, April-June 1962. LIS 209–1, ACDA.
82   *Tablet*, 14 August 1957, p. 34.
83   Sir Ian Barker, interview, 6 April 2003. The official constitution of the St Thomas More Society was not framed and adopted until 1962–63. LIS 220, ACDA. Members of the legal profession were invited to join, and mass was said during law conferences. *Zealandia*, 24 April 1963, p. 18; and *Tablet*, 17 April 1963, p. 34, report Liston offering mass for lawyers during a conference.
84   Sir Maurice Casey, interview, 3 May 2003.
85   Sir Ian Barker, interview, 6 April 2003. *Tablet*, 17 February 1955, p. 14; and 15 February 1956, p. 34, reports Liston opening student conferences. *Zealandia*, 28 January 1960, p. 7, reports his address to Catholic university students at Orewa.
86   *Zealandia*, 19 March 1959, p. 9; *Tablet*, 1 April 1959, p. 34. At this time, there were 430 Catholic students enrolled at the university. Sir Maurice Casey was part of the team that set up Newman Hall and recalls that Liston 'was anxious to ensure there was a proper Catholic presence in the university' (interview, 3 May 2003).
87   Liston's formal agreement with the Dominicans to run Newman Hall is dated 6 August 1962. LIS 125–2, ACDA.
88   *Zealandia*, 10 May 1962, p. 8.
89   *Zealandia*, 27 July 1961, p. 17, provides an interesting summary of the aims of the Catholic Youth Movement by an early president, Jim Anderton.

90   *Tablet*, 22 July 1959, p. 35.
91   See petition signed by J.C. Reid, M.K. Joseph, Bill Hare, Betty O'Dowd, Max Charlesworth, D.J. Wright and C.A. Wilkins, 21 June 1956; and Liston's reply, 20 July 1956. LIS 196, ACDA.
92   'American Catholicism', *Zealandia*, 23 September 1956.
93   Letter, Lavelle to Liston, 26 September 1956. LIS 81–7, ACDA.
94   *Zealandia*, 18 February 1960, p. 9.
95   *Zealandia*, 15 September 1955, p. 9.
96   See correspondence between Liston and Apostolic Delegate (Romolo Carboni), January-February 1955. LIS 54–2, ACDA.
97   Bishop Robin Leamy, interview, 8 February 2003.
98   Letter, Liston to Marist Provincial, 1 September 1955. File A/D 1 (Provincial's correspondence with Archbishop Liston), MAW.
99   *Zealandia*, 6 August 1959, back page.
100 Fr Neil Darragh, interview, 15 February 2003 (Darragh was ordained in 1966).
101 *Zealandia*, 1 April 1954, front page.
102 See report to Apostolic Delegate, 9 November 1956. LIS 20–5, ACDA. For a dismissive attitude towards Anglican approaches to Catholics over church unity, see Bishop Joyce's letter to Liston, 21 November 1961. LIS 58–3, ACDA.
103 *Tablet*, 21 November 1956, p. 34.
104 *Tablet*, 27 September 1961, p. 35.
105 Jocelyn Franklin, interview, 14 April 2003.
106 Fr Bruce Bolland, interview, 17 April 2003.
107 See draft of broadcast sermon, 27 November 1960. LIS 10, ACDA.
108 See Liston's circular to laity, 16 March 1959. LIS 169–3, ACDA. See also *Zealandia*, 19 March 1959, p. 2.
109 *Zealandia*, 15 December 1955, front page.
110 *AS*, 5 March and 7 March 1956.
111 *Zealandia*, 9 January 1958, p. 2.
112 *Tablet*, 19 March 1958, p. 35.
113 See minutes of bishops' meeting, Auckland, 12–15 February 1962. LIS 57–3, ACDA.
114 Liston's presence at the Charity Ball was reported in *Zealandia* every year, as were his appeals for the Maori Mission and for Peter's Pence, and his presiding at the annual requiem for the clergy at Panmure. See *Zealandia*, 24 March 1960, front page, for Liston's blessing the sick at the Meadowbank shrine; and 2 April 1959, p. 2, for the St Benedict's anniversary.
115 *Zealandia*, 30 April 1959, front page; *Tablet*, 6 May 1959, p. 35.
116 *Tablet*, 15 February 1961, p. 34.
117 *Tablet*, 8 June 1955, p. 35.
118 *Zealandia*, 25 August 1955, p. 2.
119 *Tablet*, 20 March 1957, p. 37.
120 *Zealandia*, 18 November 1954, front page.
121 The progress of the petition is reported in major items in *Zealandia*, 27 September and 4 and 11 October 1956. Its rejection by the parliamentary committee is the main front page item of 1 November 1956.
122 *Zealandia*, 1 October 1959, p. 9; *Tablet*, 7 October 1959, p. 34.
123 *Zealandia*, 27 February and 13 March 1958, front page; *Tablet*, 23 September 1959, pp 10–12.
124 Letter, Liston to hierarchy, 5 June 1958. Box 12C, CCDA.
125 *Tablet*, 16 December 1959, p. 4; and *Zealandia*, 17 December 1959, p. 2.
126 Bruce Duncan estimates that the once-formidable Australian Communist Party was down to 5,000 members nationwide by the late 1950s. Duncan, *Crusade or Conspiracy?*, chapter 20.
127 *Tablet*, 18 May 1955, p. 4.
128 *Zealandia*, 22 November 1956, p. 2; and 20 December 1956, front page.
129 See Liston's circular to priests, 15 November 1956. LIS 170, ACDA.
130 *Zealandia*, 9 April 1959, p. 9.
131 *Zealandia*, 14 May 1959, p. 9.
132 See Nicholas Reid, *Bishop's Paper*, pp 76–77, for comments on *Zealandia*'s editorial policies in the 1950s. *Tablet*, 22 April 1959, pp 30–31, ran an article by Jaime Fouseca

Mora cautiously welcoming the Castro regime ('Cuban Catholics' Guarded Approval of New Castro Regime').

133 They still suspected the motives of Dr William Sutch. See correspondence between Liston and McKeefry, November-December 1956. LIS 218, ACDA.

134 Letter, Colin Morrison to Liston, 30 April 1959. LIS 218, ACDA.

135 Letter, Liston to CORSO, 28 April 1967. LIS 218, ACDA.

136 *Zealandia*, 1 April 1954, front page.

137 (Undated) 1955 circular to priests. LIS 169–3, ACDA.

138 *Zealandia*, 25 September 1958, p. 7, reports the presentation of the portrait to Liston.

139 *Zealandia*, 10 November 1960, front page; *Tablet*, 16 November 1960, p. 35.

140 *Zealandia*, 20 April 1961, front page; Tablet, 3 May 1961, p. 34.

141 See Passionist inscription document, 8 April 1960. LIS 5, ACDA.

142 *AS*, 12 December 1960, news item, 'Clergy Gives Archbishop Liston Car at Jubilee'. *Zealandia*, 8 December 1960, carried a front page editorial on the archbishop's jubilee. Details of celebrations in special issue of *Zealandia*, 15 December 1960; and *Tablet*, 28 December 1960, p. 26.

143 Jocelyn Franklin, interview, 14 April 2003.

144 Sister Judith Leydon, interview, 15 April 2003.

145 On 11 April 1957, Sister Mary Veronica congratulated Liston on returning home so soon after hospitalisation. Mercy Sisters File, LIS 137–2, ACDA.

146 *Tablet*, 1 May 1957, p. 34, simply reported that Liston 'became ill suddenly'.

147 Letter, McKeefry to Joyce, 3 May 1957. New Zealand Bishops' Conference Correspondence (487), Folder 1, WCAA. (489), Folder 2 of the same file contains McKeefry's letter to Kavanagh (27 April 1957), also on Liston's condition.

148 Letter, Liston to Lynch, 24 May 1957. LIS 13–1, ACDA.

149 Letter, Liston to Superioress of St Vincent's Hospital, Fairview, Dublin, 12 August 1957. Also Liston's memorandum to John Flanagan, 5 October 1957. LIS 8–1, ACDA.

150 Donnelly, *One Priest's Life*, p. 75. Donnelly claims that Curran's biographical details were attached to the first official announcement of Delargey's appointment, and deduces from this that Liston had requested Curran as his assistant.

151 Letter, Liston to Cardinal Pietro Fumasoni-Biondi, 8 May 1957. LIS 19, ACDA.

152 Letter, Carboni to Liston, 20 July 1957. Liston's choice is handwritten on this letter. DEL 1, ACDA.

153 See summary of Auckland *terna* voting, 31 March 194. LIS 19, ACDA.

154 See exchange between Marella and Liston, 28 January and 2 February 1950. LIS 19, ACDA.

155 Letters, McKeefry to Delargey, 2 December 1954; Delargey to McKeefry, 21 October 1955. LIS 57–5, ACDA.

156 Exchange between Liston and Apostolic Delegate, March 1957. LIS 55–1, ACDA.

157 On 31 December 1957, the Apostolic Delegate advised Liston of date for announcement of Delargey's appointment. LIS 19, ACDA. *Zealandia*, 16 January 1958, front page; and *Tablet*, 15 January 1958, p. 7, make the announcement.

158 *Zealandia*, 6 March 1958, pp 1–2, 10 and 19. For further accounts of Delargey's consecration, see *Zealandia*, 13 March 1958, p. 8; and *Tablet*, 5 March 1958, pp 36–37.

159 *Tablet*, 15 July 1959, p. 34.

160 Liston's correspondence with apostolic delegate, February-March 1960. LIS 55–1, ACDA.

161 Letter, Liston to Sister Helen Lynch, 15 March 1960. LIS 13–1, ACDA.

162 Letter, Liston to McKeefry (describing Delargey's work in England), 10 May 1960. Bishops' Conference Correspondence (489), Folder 1, WCAA.

163 Letter, Liston to Lynch, 16 June 1959. LIS 13–1, ACDA.

Chapter IX: Archbishop Liston 1962–70 – The Crisis of Authority

1   *Zealandia*, 29 June 1961, p. 2.
2   *Tablet*, 12 April 1961, p. 34.
3   *Zealandia*, 7 June 1962, p. 7.
4   K.J. Walsh, *Yesterday's Seminary*, pp 297 ff. On the unpreparedness of Australian bishops, see also Ian Breward, *A History of the Australian Churches*, Sydney, 1997, pp 163–164; and Patrick O'Farrell, *The Catholic Church and Community in Australia*, Brisbane, 1977, pp 412–419.
5   Letter, McKeefry to Herlihy, 20 February 1962. Herlihy Papers, Box 5, ICR.
6   Letter, Liston to McKeefry, 27 July 1962. NZ Bishops' Conference Correspondence (489), Folder 1, WCAA.
7   Letter, Liston to Apostolic Delegate, 4 August 1962. LIS 55–1, ACDA. See also Liston's letters explaining his condition to Sister Helen Lynch ('as the heart does funny things without pain . . . it would seem good sense to forgo the privilege of attending the Council'), 16 September 1962 and 17 February 1963. LIS 13–1, ACDA. Letter, McKeefry to Herlihy, 26 September 1962, explaining Liston's non-attendance. Herlihy Papers, Box 5, ICR.
8   Letter, McKeefry to Herlihy, 29 January 1963. Herlihy Papers, Box 6, ICR.
9   Letter, Duggan to Liston, (undated). LIS 13–5, ACDA.
10 Letter, Joyce to Liston, 10 November 1962. LIS 58–3, ACDA.
11 Boland, *James Duhig*, chapter 19.
12 Exchange between Liston and Enrici, 6 December and 11 December 1968. LIS 57–3, ACDA.
13 Sir Ian Barker, interview, 6 April 2003.
14 Sir Maurice Casey, interview, 3 May 2003.
15 Sr Margaret Browne, interview, 23 February 2003.
16 Jocelyn Franklin, interview, 14 April 2003.
17 Mgr Kevin Hackett, interview, 22 January 2003.
18 Fr Bernard Dennehy, interview, 1 March 2003.
19 Mgr Vincent Hunt, interview, 4 January 2003. Hunt recalls Liston ordering a priest to remove a garish modernistic crucifix from a church hall, but believes this was for purely aesthetic reasons and had nothing to do with the archbishop's acceptance or non-acceptance of liturgical change.
20 Mgr Paul Cronin, interview, 11 February 2003.
21 Fr John Lyons, interview, 29 December 2002.
22 Joseph Grayland, *It Changed Overnight! Celebrating New Zealand's Liturgical Renewal 1963 to 1970*, Auckland, 2003, p. 24.
23 Ibid., pp 13 and 28–30.
24 *Zealandia*, 14 November 1963, p. 2.
25 *Zealandia*, 19 July 1962, front page.
26 Felix Donnelly, *Big Boys Don't Cry*, Wellington, 1978, p. 14. See also 'Memoirs of Bishop John Mackey' (unpublished), pp 33–34.
27 See Nicholas Reid, *The Bishop's Paper*, pp 109 ff.
28 *Tablet*, 24 March 1965, p. 9, ran a photograph, under the heading 'Mass Facing the People', of Pope Paul VI celebrating mass thus in the Roman Church of All Saints.
29 See Liston's circular to priests, 22 May 1969. DEL 26, ACDA.
30 Letter, McKeefry to Conway, 16 March 1964. Conway Papers, Box 1, ICR.
31 Grayland, *It Changed Overnight!*, pp 46–48.
32 Duggan wrote negative comment on the Jesuit Johannes Hofinger in the *Marist Messenger*. Fr John Kelly wrote from Australia to protest. Liston assured Kelly that he thought Duggan's article was 'silly and offensive', claiming Duggan was known for 'rashness and ignorance'. See exchange between Kelly and Liston, 4 and 9 March 1963. LIS 192, ACDA.
33 Letter, Ardley to Liston, 4 July 1967. LIS 197, ACDA. Liston wrote the words 'Not in favour' over this letter.
34 Minutes of bishops' meeting, 26–28 July 1967. LIS 3–6, ACDA. See also Liston's suggestions for a pastoral affirming the laity, 4 March 1968. DEL 11, ACDA.
35 Letter, McKeefry to Ashby, 30 December. NZ Bishops' Conference Correspondence (487), Folder 1, WCAA. See also Grayland, *It Changed Overnight!*, pp 22–24, on

McKeefry's conservatism.

36 Marginal comments on report from Consilium ad Exsequendam Constitutionem de Sacra Liturgia. LIS 57–3, ACDA.
37 Letter, Liston to hierarchy, 15 February 1969. Box 12 C, CCDA.
38 Letter, Berridge to Liston (with Liston's marginal comments), 8 March 1967. LIS 74–4, ACDA.
39 Letter, Timmerman to Liston, 13 November 1967. LIS 198, ACDA.
40 Letter, Dobbs to Liston, 3 January 1969; and Liston's written comments on this letter. LIS 81–1, ACDA.
41 See Liston's notes *ad multos*, 10 June 1963. LIS 55–2, ACDA.
42 *Zealandia*, 4 March 1956, p. 2; *Tablet*, 3 March 1965, p. 35.
43 See exchange between Liston and Rev D.G. Simmers, 5 May and 8 May 1965. LIS 196, ACDA.
44 Mgr Kevin Hackett, interview, 22 January 2003.
45 Mgr Paul Cronin, interview, 11 February 2003.
46 Correspondence, May 1968. LIS 73–7, ACDA.
47 *Zealandia*, 12 September 1968.
48 *Zealandia*, 14 August 1969, front page (for Liston's hosting of ecumenical meeting). Report on service in Anglican cathedral, 30 October 1969. LIS 223, ACDA. *Zealandia*, 6 November 1969, front page.
49 Correspondence with Anglican leaders. LIS 223, ACDA.
50 Sweetman, *Fair and Just Solution*, p. 39.
51 See Bishop Holland's invitation to the reception for the Archbishop of Canterbury, 19 February 1965 (Mgr Francis Wright was Liston's representative). LIS 80–3, ACDA. Invitation from Rev Kenneth Prebble for Catholic participation in Queen's Birthday liturgy, 22 March 1965. LIS 223, ACDA.
52 Minutes of bishops' meeting, 14–15 March 1968. LIS 3–7, ACDA.
53 See exchange between Liston and Mannix, 22 and 23 August 1966. LIS 105–2, ACDA.
54 *Zealandia*, 16 November 1967, front page, and p. 24. Liston had already protested at the demeaning way the *Auckland Star* reported the Catholic bishops' response to Geering's statements on the Resurrection. McKeefry to all bishops, 12 April 1967. DEL 10, ACDA.
55 *Tablet*, 6 December 1967, p. 7.
56 Invitations and replies, October 1968. LIS 223, ACDA.
57 Exchange of letters between Liston and Holland, April 1967. LIS 80–3, ACDA.
58 Exchange between Montieth and Liston, 6 August and 8 August 1968. LIS 223, ACDA.
59 Report of 1966 government census in *Zealandia*, 8 February 1968, p. 6. It is worth noting that Christchurch diocese then was a third the size of Auckland (63,975 Catholics) and Dunedin diocese a quarter the size of Auckland (41,769 Catholics).
60 Invitation to Franciscan Sisters, 1964, and report on hospital, 1969. LIS 133–4, ACDA.
61 *Zealandia*, 12 February 1970, p. 2, Liston's farewell message to Carmelite priests.
62 Dominican Sisters File, LIS 133–2, ACDA.
63 The Chanel Institute was opened in 1970. Details of its establishment are in LIS 198, ACDA.
64 Fr Grahame Connolly, interview, 5 April 2003.
65 Papers on Bosco House. LIS 179, ACDA.
66 Report from Parnell parish, December 1964. LIS 89–3, ACDA.
67 Meeting of Apostolic Delegate with New Zealand bishops, 16 February 1947. LIS 2–9, ACDA.
68 *Zealandia*, 12 August 1965, front page.
69 Liston's circular, 6 November 1966. LIS 169–4, ACDA.
70 Sir Ian Barker, interview, 6 April 2003.
71 Mgr Paul Cronin, interview, 11 February 2003.
72 Tony Peterson, in Michael Parer and Tony Peterson, *Prophets and Losses in the Priesthood – In Quest of the Future Ministry*, Sydney, 1971, p. 29. Mgr David Price, interview, 17 April 2003.

73   Fr Frank Roach, interview, 15 March 2003; and Mgr Kevin Hackett, interview, 22 January 2003.
74   Bishop John Mackey, interview, 19 January 2003. Also (unpublished), 'Memoirs of Bishop John Mackey', pp 53–54.
75   In Pat Lythe's article on the creation of the Hamilton diocese, there is no mention of plans to divide Auckland diocese before Liston retired. Pat Lythe, 'The New Diocese', pp 155–177, in O'Sullivan and Piper (eds.) *Turanga Ngatahi – Standing Together*.
76   *Zealandia*, 21 May 1964, p. 6.
77   Puch, 'Catholic Women's League of New Zealand', pp 73 ff, for national membership. Report on Liston's remarks to CWL conference, 2 April 1968, in LIS 221, ACDA.
78   Sweetman, *Faith and Fraternalism*, pp 77–78. Letter, D.F. Stewart to Liston, 11 June 1965. LIS 222–3, ACDA.
79   Letter, Fr Philip Purcell to Liston, 1 October 1969. LIS 86–7, ACDA.
80   Minutes of bishops' meeting, 24 June 1967. LIS 3–6, ACDA. On 1 September 1963, one (anonymous) local Knight told Liston that Australian bishops had now advised Knights to publicly declare their membership of the organisation. LIS 222–4, ACDA.
81   Terry Leslie's reports and negotiations for the Orewa property. LIS 220, ACDA. For Anderton's reports on Catholic youth and on indecent literature, see *Zealandia*, 29 November 1962, p. 9; and 24 April 1963, front page.
82   Liston to Apostolic Delegate, 3 March 1964. LIS 55–2, ACDA.
83   *Tablet*, 14 October 1964, p. 35.
84   *Tablet*, 4 November 1964, p. 34.
85   Liston sent to whole hierarchy a memorandum on marriage courses offered at the Oblate Education Centre at Liston House, 9 December 1968. Box 12 C, CCDA.
86   *Tablet*, 13 March 1968, p. 8.
87   See exchanges between Liston and A.J. Wilkinson, 29 September 1963, 5 October 1966 and 17 October 1966. LIS 70, ACDA.
88   Letters, Sherry to Liston, 23 August 1965 and 2 January 1966. LIS 81–7, ACDA.
89   Catholic Education Office report, 11 January 1967. LIS 57–3, ACDA.
90   See exchange between McHardy and Liston, 15 March and 20 March 1970. LIS 105–2, ACDA.
91   Letters, Liston to Ryder, 31 May 1967, and Ryder to Liston, 2 June 1967. LIS 83–5, ACDA. An article on Ryder's 'School of Religion' in a local state primary school had appeared in the *Kawerau Gazette*. See also Parer and Peterson, *Prophets and Losses*, pp 46–48.
92   Liston's memorandum to bishops concerning journal, November 1966; and Liston's letter announcing the discontinuation of the journals, 16 December 1966. Box 12 C, CCDA. See also exchange between Liston and Marist Brother Pastor, where the demise of the journal is linked with Br Stephen Coll's decision to cease editing it, 21 November and 3 December 1966. LIS 128–3, ACDA.
93   *Zealandia*, 19 March 1970, front page.
94   Letter, Broekman to Delargey on Cook Islanders, 18 May 1966. DEL 5, ACDA.
95   *Zealandia*, 15 May 1969, back page.
96   *Zealandia*, 30 December 1965, front page.
97   Letter, Liston to Pio Taofinu'u, 7 March 1968. Also correspondence of 1967–68. LIS 60–2, ACDA.
98   *Mill Hill's 100 Years*, p. 32.
99   *Zealandia*, 7 June 1962, p. 2, gives Liston's appeal for the Maori Missions at the time of Fr Tate's ordination.
100   King, *Whina*, chapter 10.
101   Fr Henare Tate, interview, 29 March 2003. See also Norris, *Southernmost Seminary*, p. 69, for comment on Mosgiel's first Maori student.
102   Editorial, 'A Priest Arises', *Zealandia*, 5 July 1962.
103   Fr Henare Tate, interview, 29 March 2003.
104   *Mill Hill's 100 Years*, pp 43 ff; King, *Whina*, chapter 10.
105   Letter, Liston to McKeefry, 10 August 1964. New Zealand Bishops' Conference Correspondence (489), Folder 1, WCAA.
106   See exchange between Te Heu Heu and Liston, 4 November and 23 November 1965. LIS 103–1, ACDA.

107 Letter, Liston to Shaw (director of St Michael's, Rotorua, credit union), 22 August 1969. LIS 220, ACDA. Letter, Liston to Fr John Mannix concerning the De Surville bicentenary, 12 October 1969. LIS 199, ACDA. Later, however, in honour of the presence of Bishop Martin of Noumea and a contingent from the French navy, Liston made a donation to the Historic Places Trust, and did attend the unveiling of the De Surville monument at Doubtless Bay. Prior to this, he was engaged in much correspondence establishing the identity of the Dominican priest (Fr Villefeix) who accompanied De Surville in 1769. Historical File, 1969, ACDA.
108 Fr Henare Tate, interview, 29 March 2003; and Fr Peter Ryan, interview, 18 May 2003.
109 Letter, Aarts to Liston, 11 April 1967. LIS 108–1, ACDA.
110 Letter, Liston to Aarts, 17 April 1967. LIS 108–1, ACDA. Liston wrote, 'I give permission reluctantly'.
111 See Aarts memorandum to Liston and Liston's comments, 21 January 1968. LIS 108–1, ACDA.
112 Mgr Brian Arahill, interview, 28 December 2002.
113 Liston to Fr Haring, (undated) July 1967. LIS 108–1, ACDA.
114 King, *Whina*, p. 194.
115 Fr Peter Ryan, interview, 18 May 2003.
116 *Zealandia*, 1 May 1969, p. 17.
117 Fr Peter Ryan, interview, 18 May 2003.
118 *Zealandia*, 9 January 1969, p. 3.
119 *Zealandia*, 18 June 1964, p. 3.
120 *Zealandia*, 21 June 1962, back page reports Furlong's sacerdotal diamond jubilee. *Zealandia*, 25 October 1962, p. 2, and 1 November 1962, p. 9, report Furlong's death and requiem.
121 *Zealandia*, 14 May 1964, pp 2–3, report on Buxton's death and editorial. See also McKeefry's letter to [Buxton relative] telling her to trust Liston to administer Buxton's will properly, 2 June 1965. LIS 58–3, ACDA. More letters from Buxton relatives to Liston in LIS 28–1, ACDA.
122 *Zealandia*, 24 July 1969, p. 4.
123 Parer and Peterson, *Prophets and Losses*, p. 3.
124 Compare *Zealandia*, 21 June 1962, pp 10–11, and *Zealandia*, 13 June 1968, p. 5.
125 See exchange of letters between Jordan and Liston, June-July 1965. LIS 142, ACDA.
126 Of the 19 Auckland students enrolled at Mosgiel in 1965, two were never ordained, 12 later left the priesthood and only five continued as priests for a full career. LIS 223, ACDA.
127 Fr Bernard Dennehy, interview, 1 March 2003.
128 Letter, Liston to McKeefry, claiming 'death and sickness' was thinning the ranks of his priests, 10 August 1962. Bishops' Conference Correspondence (489), Folder 1, WCAA.
129 Bishop Robin Leamy, interview, 8 February 2003.
130 Con Kiernan, interview, 12 April 2003.
131 Fr Grahame Connolly, interview, 5 April 2003.
132 Mgr Paul Cronin, interview, 11 February 2003.
133 'Memoirs of Bishop John Mackey', p. 37.
134 Bishops' Conference Correspondence, 14 February 1967. (489), Folder 1, WCAA.
135 Mgr David Price, interview, 17 April 2003.
136 Mgr Paul Cronin, interview, 11 February 2003.
137 Fr Neil Darragh, interview, 15 February 2003.
138 Letter, O'Neill to Liston, 12 March 1963. LIS 81–5, ACDA.
139 Deceased Priests File, ACDA.
140 Correspondence between Wright and Liston, 1956–64. LIS 82–7, ACDA.
141 Mgr Kevin Hackett, interview, 22 January 2003.
142 Fr John Lyons, interview, 29 December 2002.
143 Letter, Liston to Sheerin, 20 April 1967. LIS 103–6, ACDA.
144 There was a struggle to prise Henderson from Lavelle, beginning in 1963, when Liston had to order Lavelle to hand over parish records and accounts to Sherry. Letter, Liston to Lavelle, 11 June 1963. LIS 81–7, ACDA. Only in 1966 was Lavelle installed in Epsom. Here, Lavelle took to defending the reputation of the recently-deceased Fr

Dunphy, whose sermons had caused such strife in the previous decade. Letter, Lavelle to Liston, 9 March 1966. LIS 73–7, ACDA.

145 Letter, Liston to Conway, 6 June 1967. Conway Papers, Box 6, ICR.
146 Letter, Liston to McGinty, 15 November 1965. LIS 148–1, ACDA.
147 Letter, Liston to [seminarian], 14 September 1966. LIS 153, ACDA.
148 Letter, Liston to [deacon], 30 November 1967. LIS 153, ACDA.
149 Norris, *Southernmost Seminary*, p. 47.
150 *Zealandia*, 24 April 1968, p. 10, Liston's commendation at the beginning of the series.
151 See correspondence between Derrick and Liston, October-November 1969. LIS 190, ACDA.
152 *NZH*, 26 August 1968, p. 3, announced the forthcoming march. It is reported in *AS*, 28 August 1968, and *NZH*, 29 August 1968. A brief report appeared in *Zealandia*, 5 September 1968, back page.
153 Fr Bernard Dennehy, interview, 1 March 2003.
154 Ibid. And Con Kiernan, interview, 12 April 2003. Kiernan's banishment to Tauranga is briefly mentioned by Brookes, *By the Name of Mary*, p. 100.
155 Letter, Purcell to Liston, 5 December 1968. LIS 105–2, ACDA. N.B. This was Mgr Philip Bartholomew Purcell (1920–90), *not* Fr Philip Purcell (b. 1939).
156 Letter, Wood to Liston, 4 December 1968. LIS 81–3, ACDA.
157 Mgr Kevin Hackett, interview, 22 January 2003.
158 Con Kiernan, interview, 12 April 2003.
159 Sr Margaret Browne, interview, 23 February 2003.
160 Sr Pauline Engel, interview, 13 February 2003.
161 *Zealandia*, 9 May 1968, p. 15.
162 LIS 124–1, ACDA.
163 Letter, Broadbent to Liston, 31 August 1970. LIS 57–1, ACDA.
164 See *Zealandia*, 10 July 1969, p. 12, for Liston's article on the rite of ordination. Letter, Liston to Murray ordering him to print extracts from letters critical of a humorous article Dorothy Fullerton had written about Catholic schools, because of a complaint he had received from Kevin Pound, 22 January 1969. LIS 175–1, ACDA.
165 See Liston's protest (in bishops' conference) at unauthorised announcement, 9 November 1968. DEL 11, ACDA. Liston expressed to other bishops annoyance at announcements made by *Zealandia*, 11 November 1968. LIS 57–1, ACDA, and Box 12 C, CCDA. Liston wrote 'Ugh!' on letter where Patrick Murray explained himself, 11 November 1968. LIS 175–1, ACDA.
166 Copies of *Insight – A New Zealand Catholic Quarterly* preserved in LIS 197, ACDA.
167 Letters, Liston to Clandillon, 2 May 1967; and King to Liston (upon which Liston has written 'No Answer'), 27 May 1967. LIS 197, ACDA. See also article 'Archbishop Attacks Catholic Youth Periodical' by Michael King in the Wellington student paper, *Salient*, 30 June 1967.
168 Letter, Liston to Gibbons, 14 November 1967. LIS 197, ACDA.
169 'Kennedy and Cuba', *Zealandia*, 1 November 1962, p. 2.
170 Parer and Peterson, *Prophets and Losses*, p. 29.
171 Michael Hogan, *The Sectarian Strand*, Melbourne, 1987, pp 264–65.
172 Letter, Delargey to Liston, 25 February 1968. LIS 162, ACDA. Internal evidence suggests this letter followed a meeting the two bishops had had about the newspaper.
173 'Catholic Papers Must Have Minds of Their Own, Graduates Told', *Tablet*, 21 December 1966, pp 26–27.
174 S.G. (Shaun Gerard) Brosnahan, 'Rugby, Race and Religion: The Catholic Church and Controversy Over Sporting Relations with South Africa 1959–1981', MA thesis, University of Canterbury, 1986, pp 80–81.
175 *Zealandia*, 31 October 1963, p. 2.
176 *Zealandia*, 11 March 1965, front page statement.
177 See bishops' conference minutes, 26–27 July 1967. LIS 3–6, ACDA.
178 Letter, Liston to St Vincent de Paul Society, 25 August 1967. LIS 217, ACDA.
179 *Zealandia*, 26 October 1967, p. 2; and *Tablet*, 1 November 1967, p. 8. See Liston's circular to priests, 29 October 1967. LIS 169–4, ACDA.
180 *Zealandia*, 8 August 1968, p. 2.

181 Ibid., p. 3. Liston's pastoral, 1 August 1968. LIS 169–4, ACDA.

182 *Zealandia*, 22 August 1968, p. 2.

183 Deirdre McMahon, 'John Charles McQuaid, Archbishop of Dublin 1940–72', in Kelly and Keogh (eds), *History of the Catholic Diocese of Dublin*, p. 378. It might be possible to perceive further similarities between Liston and McQuaid in McQuaid's efficient, schoolmasterly relationship with his clergy, his vigilance over sermons and his habit of rusticating priests who did not comply with his instructions. Cooney, *John Charles McQuaid*, pp 320 and 368.

184 Liston's circular to priests, 2 September 1968. LIS 171, ACDA.

185 *NZH*, 7 September 1968, front page.

186 *Tablet*, 11, 18 and 25 September 1968, carried extensive comment and letters on Liston's action. Kennedy's editorial ran on 11 September and June Dunn's letter comparing Liston to Christ on 25 September.

187 Fr Frank Roach, interview, 15 March 2003.

188 Nicholas Reid, *The Bishop's Paper*, pp 110 ff.

189 Petition and McKeefry's correspondence with Mary Hunt, Des Swain, Brian Lythe and others (all dated August 1969) in New Zealand Bishops' Conference Correspondence (489), Folder 1, WCAA.

190 *Tablet*, 6, 13, 20 August 1969.

191 *NZH*, 2 and 4 August 1969, front page; *AS*, 1, 2 and 5 August 1969, front page.

192 Parer and Peterson, *Prophets and Losses*, p. 30.

193 Sir Ian Barker, interview, 6 April 2003.

194 Sister Judith Leydon, interview, 15 April 2003.

195 Bishop Dunn, interview, 27 December 2002.

196 Sir Maurice Casey, interview, 3 May 2003.

197 Liston's circular asking priests to promote *Zealandia* in the face of falling circulation, 10 November 1969. LIS 171, ACDA.

198 'Catholics Search Souls', *Waikato Times*, 25 October 1969 (article provided by Michael King).

199 Fr John Lyons, interview, 29 December 2002.

200 *AS*, 29 January 1964.

201 Profile, 'A Compassionate Hand for Those in Distress', *Weekly News*, 30 October 1963.

202 Anecdote told by Bishop Patrick Dunn at memorial mass in St Patrick's Cathedral for the 25th anniversary of Liston's death, 8 July 2001.

203 *Tablet*, 15 April 1970, pp 5–8.

204 Sir Ian Barker, interview, 6 April 2003.

205 Mgr Paul Cronin, interview, 11 February 2003.

206 Bishop Patrick Dunn, interview, 27 December 2002.

207 *Zealandia*, 21 March 1968, p. 4.

208 Fr David Tonks, interview, 21 December 2002.

209 *NZH*, 31 January 1964, p. 3. Liston received his letter of commendation from Pope Paul VI on 23 December 1963, in time for the diamond jubilee. LIS 5, ACDA.

210 Donnelly, *One Priest's Life*, p. 165.

211 *AS* editorial, 29 January 1964. See also *NZH* editorial, 29 January 1964.

212 *NZH*, 30 January 1964, p. 3; *AS*, 29 and 31 January 1964; *Zealandia*, 23, 30 January and 6 February 1964.

213 *Zealandia*, 13 February 1964, front page, reports a Waikato function for Liston. *Tablet*, 26 February 1964, pp 34 and 38, reports Liston closing his jubilee celebrations by attending functions at St Joseph's cathedral and his *alma mater*, the Christian Brothers' school.

214 Queen's letter conferring award on Liston, 1 January 1968. LIS 5, ACDA. *Zealandia*, 11 January 1968, front page, for Liston's reaction. See also article by 'Pippa' (Eileen Duggan), *Tablet*, 31 January 1968, p .14; and reports on conferring of CMG upon Liston at Government House, *NZH*, 20 April 1968, p.12, and *Zealandia*, 24 April 1968, front page.

215 *Zealandia*, 14 March 1963, front page, and *Tablet*, 13 March 1963, pp 30–31 for Mosgiel chapel-opening; and *Tablet*, 22 May 1968, p. 3, for blessing of new Mosgiel auditorium. *Tablet*, 6 March 1963, p. 35, for Riccarton buildings.

216 *Zealandia*, 26 December 1963, front page.

217 *Zealandia*, 21 April 1966, front page.
218 *Zealandia*, 3 September 1964, p. 9; and 2 April 1970, back page.
219 *Zealandia*, 29 April 1965, editorial (Liston's endorsement of road safety campaign); 31 March 1966 (famine relief); 7 September 1967, p. 12 (commendation for Alcoholism Trust); and 4 April 1968, front page (Liston and Bishop Gowing hosted by Dr Fraser McDonald on visit to Kingseat Psychiatric Hospital).
220 'Archbishop's Tribute to the President', *Zealandia*, 28 November 1963, p. 2.
221 *NZH*, 3, 4 and 5 March 1969. Articles summarised in *Tablet*, 19 March 1969, p. 9.
222 *Zealandia*, 11 September 1969, front page.
223 *NZH*, 15 February 1968 (Liston and Bishop Gowing at service for Supreme Court); 24 June 1969 (Liston accepts invitation to Gisborne celebration). LIS 74–4, ACDA.
224 The induction into the order is dated 26 February 1964. LIS 5, ACDA. See also *Zealandia*, 16 July 1964, p. 6.
225 *Zealandia*, 24 June 1965.
226 Letter, Liston to bishops, 5 December 1966. LIS 57–6, ACDA.
227 *Zealandia*, 12 December 1968, p. 3. Report on Liston's comments at the St Mary's prizegiving.
228 Mgr Brian Arahill, interview, 28 December 2002.
229 Fr Grahame Connolly, interview, 5 April 2003.
230 Letter, McKeefry to Conway, 11 May 1967. Conway Papers, Box 5, ICR.
231 Sr Pauline Engel, interview, 13 February 2003.
232 *Tablet*, 15 June 1966, pp 30–31.
233 Fr Henare Tate, interview, 28 March 2003.
234 Fr Bruce Bolland, interview, 17 April 2003.
235 See Liston's draft of response to offer, 13 March 1962. New Zealand Bishops' Conference Correspondence, (489), Folder 1, WCAA.
236 Bishops' meetings at Bishops' House, Auckland, 13 April and 15 June 1969. DEL 5, ACDA.
237 Minutes of bishops' meeting, 14–15 May 1964. LIS 19, ACDA.
238 Letters, McKeefry to Kavanagh, 22 May 1967; and McKeefry to all bishops commenting on bishops' meetings, 12 July 1967. DEL 10, ACDA.
239 Bishop Patrick Dunn, interview, 27 December 2002.
240 Fr Bruce Bolland, interview, 17 April 2003.
241 Fr Grahame Connolly, interview, 5 April 2003.
242 Fr Neil Darragh, interview, 15 February 2003.
243 Property documents. DEL 13, ACDA.
244 Jocelyn Franklin, interview, 14 April 2003.
245 Sir Ian Barker, interview, 6 April 2003.
246 Fr Bernard Dennehy, interview, 1 March 2003.
247 The pope's acceptance of Liston's petition is dated 4 March 1970. LIS 1–5, ACDA.
248 Minutes of bishops' meeting, 6–11 April 1970. DEL 26, ACDA.
249 Letter, Liston to Ashby, 18 March 1970. Box 12 C, CCDA.
250 Letter, Delargey to McKeefry, 5 June 1970. New Zealand Bishops' Conference Correspondence, (489), Folder 1, WCAA.
251 *Zealandia*, 22 January 1970, front page.
252 Liston's circular publicly announcing his retirement and regretting that it has already been noted in the secular press, 9 April 1970. LIS 169–4, ACDA. He was referring to the report in *NZH*, 8 April 1970. See also *Zealandia*, 9, 16 and 30 April 1970; *Tablet*, 15 April and 6 May 1970.
253 Ibid.
254 The Bull giving Liston titular headship of this see is dated 29 April 1970 (LIS 1–3, ACDA). But it was reported in *Tablet*, 8 April 1970, p. 3.
255 *Zealandia*, 28 May 1970, p. 4.
256 *Tablet*, 22 April 1970, p. 6.
257 'Catholics Still Wait for New Bishop', *AS*, 25 July 1970, p. 5.
258 *Zealandia*, 24 September 1970, front page.
259 *Zealandia*, 12 December 1970, front page; *Tablet*, 16 December 1970, p. 29.
260 *Zealandia*, 3 December 1970, pp 9–12.
261 Letter, Liston to McKeefry, 29 September 1970. New Zealand Bishops' Conference Correspondence, (489), Folder 1, WCAA.

262 His farewell by the pupils of St Mary's College are noted in *Zealandia*, 1 October 1970, front page.
263 Letter, Vice-Chancellor K.J. Maidment to Liston confirming the invitation for his reception of an honorary LLD, 29 May 1970. LIS 162, ACDA. LLD document, 8 July 1970. LIS 5, ACDA.
264 *NZH*, and *AS*, 9 July 1970.
265 *Zealandia*, 16 July 1970, p. 3; and *Tablet*, 29 July 1970, p. 38 (and p. 19 for Eileen Duggan's – 'Pippa's' – tribute, which heavily quotes from Musgrove).
266 Sir Ian Barker, interview, 6 April 2003.

Chapter X: In Retirement 1970–76

1 *NZH*, 14 December 1970; *Zealandia*, 17 December 1970, p. 4; *Tablet*, 6 and 13 January 1971.
2 *Zealandia*, 17 June 1971, front page, and *Tablet*, 23 June 1971, p. 8, both note his ninetieth birthday and his dining with Bishop Delargey at Bishop's House in celebration. *Zealandia*, 17 June 1973, front page, wishes him well for his ninety-second birthday with 'gratitude that God has spared him to remain in our midst, a welcome figure wherever, whenever he appears'.
3 *Zealandia*, 27 January 1974, pp 1–2; *Tablet*, 30 January 1974, p. 5; letter, Delargey to Ashby noting there will be no official celebrations, 12 January 1974. Box 12 C, CCDA.
4 LIS 11, ACDA.
5 *Tablet*, 3 March 1971, pp 14–15.
6 *Tablet*, 6 December 1972, front page.
7 Draft of Liston's short speech for the investiture, 9 March 1975. LIS 10, ACDA. *Zealandia*, 23 March 1975, p. 3.
8 *Zealandia*, 22 June 1975, p. 3.
9 Carolyn Moynihan, *A Stand for Decency – Patricia Bartlett and the Society for the Promotion of Community Standards 1970–1995* (SPCS, 1995) pp 21 ff. Letter, Bartlett to Liston, 6 June 1976. LIS 8–2, ACDA.
10 May 1976 reappointment. LIS 7–4, ACDA.
11 Jocelyn Franklin, interview, 14 April 2003.
12 Mgr Kevin Hackett, interview, 22 January 2003.
13 Liston's correspondence with Sir Bernard Fergusson (Lord Ballantrae) is filed in LIS 7–2, ACDA.
14 *Tablet*, 21 March 1973, p. 6. Liston regularly sent materials on medical ethics to the bishops' conference. See letter, Liston to McKeefry, 28 March 1973. New Zealand Bishops' Conference Correspondence (489), Folder 1, WCAA.
15 Liston's papers promoting the cause of Oliver Plunkett are filed in LIS 7–2, ACDA. Letter, Liston to Rector of Irish College Mgr Eamonn Marron, rejoicing at Plunkett's canonisation, 15 January 1975. Marron Papers 1976 (box not numbered), ICR.
16 *Zealandia*, 27 April 1975, pp 10–11.
17 Exchange between Kennedy and Liston, 10 and 15 January 1973. LIS 7–1, ACDA.
18 Letter, Liston to Snedden, 4 March 1973. New Zealand Bishops' Conference Correspondence (490), WCAA.
19 [The source of this anecdote has asked to remain anonymous.]
20 *Zealandia*, 4 August 1974, front page. This report of the conference refers to Liston as the 'founder' of the CWL.
21 *Tablet*, 3 February 1971, p. 13. Liston declines invitation to parish centenary, 15 February 1971. LIS 11, ACDA.
22 *Zealandia*, 14 March 1976, p. 6.
23 Liston's notes to organisers, 11 May and 17 August 1971. LIS 11, ACDA.
24 *Tablet*, 12 January 1972, p. 29.
25 *Zealandia*, 23 September 1973, p. 3, reports a discussion in which it was decided to leave the diocese undivided.
26 Exchange between Liston and Apostolic Delegate, 17 and 24 May 1971. LIS 11, ACDA.
27 Letter, Liston to Ashby, 6 February 1972. Box 12 C, CCDA.
28 Private communication, Michael King to Nicholas Reid, 31 October 2000.

29   Letter, Donnelly to Liston, 2 November 1970. LIS 11, ACDA.
30   Fr Bruce Bolland, interview, 17 April 2003.
31   Mgr Paul Cronin, interview, 11 February 2003.
32   Fr Neil Darragh, interview, 15 February 2003.
33   Fr Maurice Drumm, interview, 18 March 2003.
34   Sr Margaret Browne, interview, 23 February 2003.
35   Letter, Astor to Liston, 8 April 1970. LIS 12, ACDA.
36   Mgr David Price, interview, 17 April 2003.
37   Fr Bernard Dennehy, interview, 1 March 2003.
38   Bishop Robin Leamy, interview, 8 February 2003; and Mgr Kevin Hackett, interview,
      22 January 2003.
39   *AS*, 31 January 1974.
40   Sr Margaret Browne, interview, 23 February 2003.
41   *Zealandia*, 15 August 1971, pp 10–11.
42   *Zealandia*, 8 October 1972, p. 2.
43   Telegram to Liston, 22 April 1975. LIS 7–2, ACDA.
44   *Zealandia*, 29 April 1973, p. 2, Liston's obituary for McQuaid. In September 1975,
      Liston sent his condolences to the Irish government and attended a requiem mass on
      the death of de Valera. LIS 7–2, ACDA.
45   *Zealandia*, 11 June 1972, p. 3. The requiem was celebrated by Bishop Delargey, who
      had been a classmate of Reid's at Sacred Heart College.
46   *Zealandia*, 25 November and 2 December 1973, front page. *Tablet*, 21 November
      1973 pp 2–3; and 28 November 1973, p. 7.
47   *Zealandia*, 26 May 1974, front page; 2 June 1974, front page; and 14 July 1974, p.
      3, for Delargey's and Mackey's appointments and farewells for Delargey. *Zealandia*,
      18 August 1974, front page, for ceremony in cathedral welcoming Mackey as Bishop
      of Auckland (Liston was in the sanctuary). *Tablet*, 22 May 1974, front page; and 29
      May 1974, p. 2, for Delargey's and Mackey's appointments.
48   *Zealandia*, 17 November 1974, p. 10.
49   *Zealandia*, 26 October 1975, front page.
50   Fr David Tonks, interview, 21 December 2002.
51   Sir Ian Barker, interview, 6 April 2003.
52   *Zealandia*, 22 February 1976, pp 1–2. *Tablet*, 25 February 1976, p. 26. Condolences
      Liston received on the death of Flanagan are filed in LIS 7–4, ACDA.
53   Sr Judith Leydon, interview, 15 April 2003.
54   Henry and William Forsman, *E.A. Forsman – Priest, Padre, Poet 1909–1976* (1991),
      pp 30–31.
55   Letter from lawyer E.J. Wright to matron of St Vincent's, 8 October 1975. LIS 8–1,
      ACDA.
56   *Zealandia*, 23 May 1976, front page.
57   His death certificate gives the cause of death as 'broncho-pneumonia' and heart
      disease, and notes that he had been suffering from a fractured hip. Death certificate
      Ref. 1976/12547 ANZ.
58   Mgr Brian Arahill, interview, 28 December 2002.

NOTE ON SOURCES

The 'core' research materials for this biography were the Liston Papers deposited in the Auckland Catholic Diocesan Archives. These include all documents relating to diocesan and parish administration in the period of Liston's episcopate, Liston's official communications with his fellow bishops, with individual priests and with religious orders, as well as materials relating to lay organisations and to the diocese's finances. The Liston Papers give a very comprehensive overview of both the development of the diocese and of the bishop's priorities in a period of half a century. Official papers of bishops who preceded and followed Liston were also consulted extensively, as were the papers of bishops in other dioceses. Free and unrestricted access was given to all these materials, including permission to quote verbatim as required.

However, there are three matters that necessarily make any archival examination of Liston's life and career incomplete. Firstly, as well as the diocesan archive, which may be made available to researchers, all bishops are required by canon law to maintain a 'secret archive'. This refers essentially to files of confidential correspondence on a wide variety of matters which are still 'live'. At the beginning of his episcopate, a bishop is required to cull his predecessor's 'secret archive', deciding which materials are still sensitive enough to remain in it and which materials may be released to the general archive. In this process, some materials may be destroyed. Partly for this reason, there are very few surviving and available records on such matters as misconduct on the part of clergy. There is further the strong assumption that in really scandalous matters Liston preferred direct interviews with the clergy concerned rather than written correspondence. Secondly, with the best of motives a former diocesan archivist, the late Fr Ernest Simmons, removed and destroyed some materials which he thought would cause distress to individuals. These included welfare reports on boys and girls in custodial care in Catholic institutions such as orphanages. Thirdly, at the time of his retirement, Liston went through his papers and destroyed most of his own personal correspondence. There are thus very few surviving letters to or from Liston's parents, siblings and personal friends.

Fortunately some of Liston's most regular correspondents kept, and eventually deposited in archives, the letters which Liston sent to them. These include the gossipy letters he wrote to Bishop Whyte in Dunedin in the 1920s (now included in the Whyte Papers of the Dunedin Catholic Diocesan Archives), and the regular personal notes he sent to Mother Helen Lynch of the Cenacle Sisters (now included in the Liston Papers, ACDA). Some idea of Liston's private personality can be formed from such sources, and from the memories of individuals which have also been consulted in researching this biography. The record is, however, necessarily incomplete, and some matters, such as the influence of his brother's fate on Liston's decision to foreswear alcohol, must remain matters for informed speculation only.

BIBLIOGRAPHY

A.) Primary Sources

(i.) Periodicals, Newspapers and Magazines

(a.) The Secular Press
Auckland Star (Auckland)
Clare Champion (Ireland)
Dominion (Wellington)
Evening Post (Wellington)
Freeman's Journal (Dublin)
Huntly Press (Huntly)
New Zealand Herald (Auckland)
Otago Daily Times (Dunedin)
Waikato Times (Hamilton)
Weekly News (Auckland)

(b.) Church Publications
Advocate (Catholic – Melbourne)
Catholic Press (Sydney)
Catholic Review (Auckland)
Church Gazette (Anglican – Auckland)
Insight (Catholic quarterly – Auckland)
Marist Messenger
The Month (Catholic – Auckland)
NZ Catholic (Auckland)
New Zealand Tablet (Catholic – Dunedin)
New Zealandia (Catholic – Auckland)
St Mary's Gazette (Catholic – Hamilton)
Zealandia (Catholic – Auckland)

(c.) Other
Craccum (Auckland University students' publication)
New Zealand Books (literary review)
New Zealand Law Journal
New Zealand Worker (New Zealand Labour Party publication)
Saoirse – NZ Irish Post (New Zealand Sinn Fein publication)
Salient (Victoria University of Wellington students' publication)
Sentinel (Protestant Political Association)

(ii.) Archives

Alexander Turnbull Library (Wellington) for Pat Lawlor Papers
Archives New Zealand (ANZ)
> Dunedin Regional Office – for probated wills of James Liston senior, Mary Liston (née Sullivan) and Eileen Liston
> Wellington – for marriage certificate and death certificates of James Liston senior and Mary Liston (née Sullivan) and death certificates of John Patrick Liston and James Michael Liston
Auckland Catholic Diocesan Archives (ACDA)
> **Cleary Papers** (prefix CLE), from the episcopate of Henry William Cleary 1910–29, but also including Cleary's earlier diaries and journalistic research materials.
> **Delargey Papers** (prefix DEL), being official papers from the episcopate of Reginald John Delargey, but also including minutes of bishops' conferences throughout the 1960s.

389

Deceased Priests and **Diocesan Priests Files** (biographical information on Auckland diocesan clergy).

Historical File (vertical file of press clippings on diocesan matters).

Lenihan Papers (prefix LEN) from the episcopate of George Michael Lenihan.

Liston Papers (prefix LIS). Two-hundred-and-twenty-three boxes of official and personal correspondence from the episcopate of James Michael Liston, 1929–70. Includes separate files for correspondence with each diocesan parish, with religious orders, lay societies and diocesan publications, as well as the bishop's circulars and pastorals, notes for homilies, minutes of the bishops' conferences and correspondence with government departments. Officially confined to Liston's own episcopate, but does include material from Liston's years as coadjutor to Bishop Cleary, including two files concerning his trial for sedition in 1922 and three files concerning his strife with Cleary. While there is some personal correspondence, most of Liston's exchanges with members of his family were destroyed by him upon his retirement in 1970. The Liston Papers constitute the 'core' material of this biography.

Luck Papers (prefix LUC) from the episcopate of John Edmund Luck, but includes minutes of Diocesan Council 1883–1930.

Mackey Papers (prefix MAC) from the episcopate of Bishop John Mackey.

Fr John Flanagan Papers (for some correspondence between Liston and Mother Helen Lynch).

Auckland Public Library for **John A. Lee Papers**, especially NZMS 828, Series 5, Folder 29; Series 6, Folder 14 (including the typescript essay 'Myself and the Catholic Church'); and Series 9, Folders 1 and 2.

Christchurch Catholic Diocesan Archives (CCDA) for baptismal certificates of John Patrick Liston and Mary Maud Liston. Also church rating controversies in the 1920s, and papers of Bishop Matthew Brodie (Box 11), correspondence between James Michael Liston and Matthew Brodie (Box 12), materials concerning the Campbell case (Box 13), and minutes of the New Zealand bishops' conference and meetings of the Australasian hierarchy (Box 19).

Collegio Urbano (Rome) for examination results of seminarian James Michael Liston, in 'Laureate ab an.1831 ad an. 1909' and 'Esam. 1901–1903'.

Dublin (Catholic) Archdiocesan Archives (DAA) for Student Accounts, Holy Cross College (Clonliffe) 1899–1901; correspondence with Irish College, Rome; papers of Bishop William Walsh; political papers of Mgr Michael Curran; correspondence with 'foreign' bishops and Australasian bishops of Archbishop John Charles McQuaid, 1940–74.

Dunedin Catholic Diocesan Archives (DCDA) for baptismal certificates of James Michael Liston, Catherine Anne Josephine ('Anne') Liston and the children of John Patrick Liston. Also for Diocesan Reports on Parishes 1902–26; Mgr James Coffey papers; Holy Cross College (Mosgiel) Boxes; Irish Affairs Box; and papers of Bishops Verdon, Whyte and Kavanagh.

Hocken Library (Dunedin) for Christian Brothers' School Register 1885–1934.

Irish College, Rome (ICR) for Irish College Roll Book, and for all correspondence of rectors and staff with Liston and the New Zealand hierarchy and clergy. Papers are filed according to rectors, viz. Kelly and Murphy Papers (1901–1905); O'Riordan Papers (1905–1919); Hagan Papers (1919–1930); Curran Papers (1930–39); McDaid Papers (1939–51); Herlihy Papers (1951–64); Conway and Marron Papers (1965–1980).

Irish National Archives (Dublin) for death certificate of Catherine Anne Josephine ('Anne') Liston.

Marist Archives, Wellington (MAW) for File A/D 1, Marist provincials' correspondence with James Michael Liston.

Missionary Society of St Joseph ('Mill Hills'), Mill Hill, London (MHAL) for Mill Hill correspondence concerning New Zealand during the episcopate of James Michael Liston, Box NZL-3 (1913–34), Box NZL-5 (1935–60) and Box NZL-6 (1960–71).

Propaganda Fide Archives (Rome) (Congregation for the Evangelisation of Peoples)
   Acta.S. Congreg. de Propaganda Fide Anno 1974, p.1 241 (on the selection of Francis Redwood as Bishop of Wellington).
   Prop. Fide 1910 Rubrica 151–162 Vol. 492 (on the selection of Henry William Cleary as Bishop of Auckland).
   Prop. Fide CEP Nuova Serie 1916 160–161 (on the selection of Matthew Brodie as Bishop of Christchurch).

Prop. Fide CEP Nuova Serie 1921 160 707 and Acta S. Congreg. de Propag. Fide Anno 1920 291 (file of unprinted correspondence and printed *Relazione* on selection of James Whyte as Bishop of Dunedin and James Michael Liston as Coadjutor-Bishop of Auckland).

Wellington Catholic Archdiocesan Archives (WCAA) for papers of Lillian Keys (Box 174); personal correspondence of Archbishop Redwood (Box 212); correspondence concerning government and legislation (Box 254); the New Zealand bishops' conference (Boxes 490–497); and correspondence with Auckland and Hamilton dioceses (Box 503).

(iii.) Audiotaped Interviews

In accordance with approved guidelines of the Auckland University Ethics Committee, interviews with the following people were conducted by Nicholas Reid on the dates indicated, and transcribed by him. Tapes and transcripts have been deposited in the Auckland Catholic Diocesan Archives:

Fr Desmond John Angland (18 January 2003)
Mgr Brian Francis Arahill (28 December 2002)
Sir Ian Barker (6 April 2003)
Fr Bruce Bolland (15 April 2003)
Sr Margaret Browne (23 February 2003)
Sir Maurice Casey (3 May 2003)
Fr Grahame Connolly (5 April 2003)
Mgr Paul Cronin (11 February 2003)
Fr Neil Patrick Darragh (15 February 2003)
Fr Bernard Michael Dennehy (1 March 2003)
Bishop Patrick Dunn (27 December 2002)
Dame Sister Pauline Engel (13 February 2003)
Jocelyn Franklin (14 April 2003)
Mgr Kevin Bernard Hackett (22 January 2003)
Mary Elizabeth Hales (3 May 2003)
Mgr Vincent Hunt (4 January 2003).
Con (Joseph Consedine) Kiernan (12 April 2003)
Bishop Robin Leamy (8 February 2003)
Sr Judith Leydon (15 April 2003)
Fr John Edward Lyons (29 December 2002)
Bishop John Mackey (19 January 2003)
Mgr David Desmond Joseph Price (17 April 2003)
Fr Philip Purcell (8 March 2003)
Fr Frank (Francis James) Roach (15 March 2003)
Fr Peter Michael Ryan (18 May 2003)
Fr Laurence Victor Sakey (12 January 2003)
Fr James Cornelius Shannahan (22 February 2003)
Fr Henare Arekatera Tate (29 March 2003)
Fr David John Tonks (21 December 2002).

(iv.) Personal and Other Verbal Communications

Bishop Leonard Boyle (conversation, 28 August 2001)
Fr Pat Crawford (conversation, 27 November 2001)
Fr Maurice Drumm (conversation, 18 March 2003)
Bishop Patrick Dunn (commemorative sermon on the 25th anniversary of the death of Archbishop Liston, preached in St Patrick's Cathedral, Sunday 8 July 2001)
Michael King (letter to Nicholas Reid, 31 October 2000)
Professor Russell Stone (conversation, June 2003)
John S. Sumich (letter to Nicholas Reid, 28 August 2001)

(v.) **Official and Semi-Official Publications**

Appendix to the Journals of the House of Representatives (Session 1946 – Wellington 1947)
Australian Dictionary of Biography
Code of Canon Law (1917)
Dictionary of New Zealand Biography
New Zealand Official Yearbooks

(B.) **Secondary Sources**

(i.) **Books**

Akenson, Donald Harmon, *Half the World From Home – Perspectives on the Irish in New Zealand*, Victoria University Press, Wellington, 1990.
(Anonymous), *Mill Hill's 100 Years – The Story of St Joseph's Missionary Society 1866–1966. The Years in New Zealand* (printed for the Mill Hills), Putaruru, 1966.
Baker, Paul, *King and Country Call – New Zealanders, Conscription and the Great War*, Auckland University Press, Auckland, 1988.
Barrowman, Rachel, *A Popular Vision – The Arts and the Left in New Zealand 1930–1950*, Victoria University Press, Wellington, 1991.
Bassett, Michael, *Coates of Kaipara*, Auckland University Press, Auckland, 1995.
Bassett, Michael, *Sir Joseph Ward – A Political Biography*, Auckland University Press, Auckland, 1993.
Bassett Michael and King, Michael, *Tomorrow Comes the Song – A Life of Peter Fraser*, Penguin, Auckland, 2000.
Belgrave, Michael, *The Mater – A History of Auckland's Mercy Hospital 1900–2000*, Mercy Hospital – Dunmore Press, Palmerston North, 2000.
Belich, James, *Paradise Reforged – A History of the New Zealanders*, Allen Lane/ Penguin, Auckland, 2001.
Blamires, E.O.(Ernest), *A Christian Core for New Zealand Education*, Whitcombe and Tombs, Auckland, 1960.
Boland, T.B., *James Duhig*, University of Queensland Press, Brisbane, 1986.
Bollinger, Conrad, *Grog's Own Country*, Price Milburn, Wellington, 1959.
Booth, Pat, *Deadline – My Story*, Viking/ Penguin, Auckland, 1997.
Bowen, Desmond, *Paul Cardinal Cullen and the Shaping of Modern Irish Catholicism*, Gill and Macmillan, Dublin, 1983.
Breward, Ian, *Godless Schools – A Study of Protestant Reactions to the Education Act of 1877*, Presbyterian Bookroom, Christchurch, 1967.
Breward, Ian, *Grace and Truth – A History of Theological Hall, Knox College, Dunedin 1876–1975*, Presbyterian Church of New Zealand, Dunedin, 1975.
Breward, Ian, *A History of the Australian Churches*, Allen and Unwin, Sydney, 1997.
Brookes, Patricia, *By the Name of Mary – Tauranga Catholic Church 1840–2000*, privately printed, Tauranga, 2000.
Campion, Edmund, *Australian Catholics*, Penguin, Sydney, 1988.
Charlesworth, Max, *Church, State and Conscience*, University of Queensland Press, Brisbane, 1973.
Cleary, Rev H.W. (Henry William), *An Impeached Nation – Being a Study of Irish Outrages*, New Zealand Tablet Printing Company, Dunedin, 1909.
Cleary, Rev H.W. (Henry William), *The Orange Society*, Catholic Truth Society, London, 1899.
Cocker, Rev J. and Murray, J. Malton, *Temperance and Prohibition in New Zealand*, printed for the New Zealand Alliance for the Abolition of the Liquor Traffic, Epworth Press, London, 1930.
Coogan, Tim Pat, *Wherever Green is Worn – The Story of the Irish Diaspora*, Hutchinson, London, 2000.
Cooke, Bill (Charles William Newton), *Heathen in Godzone – Seventy Years of Rationalism in New Zealand*, NZ Association of Rationalists and Humanists Inc., Auckland, 1998.
Cooney, John, *John Charles McQuaid – Ruler of Catholic Ireland*, O'Brien Press, Dublin,

1999.

Davidson, Allan, *Christianity in Aotearoa*, Education for Ministry, Wellington, 1991.

Davidson, Allan and Lineham, Peter (eds), *Christianity Transplanted*, College Communications, Auckland, 1987.

Davis, Richard P., *Irish Issues in New Zealand Politics 1868–1922*, University of Otago Press, Dunedin, 1974.

Delaney, Sister Veronica [published anonymously], *Gracious is the Time – 1850–1950 Centenary of the Sisters of Mercy, Auckland, New Zealand*, printed for Mercy Sisters, Auckland, 1952.

Dickson, Rev J., *Shall Ritualism and Romanism Capture New Zealand? – Their Ramifications in Protestant Churches*, Otago Daily Times and Witness Newspapers Co. Ltd., Dunedin, 1912.

Donnelly, Felix, *Big Boys Don't Cry*, Allen and Unwin/ Port Nicholson Press, Wellington, 1978.

Donnelly, Felix, *Father Forgive Them*, GP Books, Auckland, 1990.

Donnelly, Felix, *One Priest's Life*, Australian and New Zealand Book Company, Auckland, 1982.

Duncan, Bruce, *Crusade or Conspiracy? Catholics and the Anti-Communist Struggle in Australia*, University of New South Wales Press, Sydney, 2001.

Ewart, Peter SM (ed.), *The Society of Mary in New Zealand Since 1838*, printed for the Fathers and Brothers of the Society of Mary, Wellington, 1989.

Farland, Bruce, *Coates' Tale – J.G. Coates*, published by the author, Wellington, 1995.

Fraser, Lyndon (ed.), *A Distant Shore – Irish Migration and New Zealand Settlement*, University of Otago Press, Dunedin, 2000.

Gallagher, Pat, *The Marist Brothers in New Zealand, Fiji and Samoa 1876–1976*, New Zealand Marist Brothers Trust Board, Auckland, 1976.

Goulter, Mary Catherine, *Sons of France – A Forgotten Influence on New Zealand History*, Whitcombe and Tombs, Wellington, 1957.

Grayland, Joseph, *It Changed Overnight! Celebrating New Zealand's Liturgical Renewal 1963–1970*, Good Shepherd/ Te Hapara Pai, Auckland, 2003.

Gustafson, Barry, *From the Cradle to the Grave – A Biography of Michael Joseph Savage*, Reed/ Methuen, Auckland, 1986.

Gustafson, Barry, *Labour's Path to Political Independence – The Origins and Establishment of the New Zealand Labour Party*, Auckland University Press/ Oxford University Press, Auckland, 1980.

Hogan, Michael, *The Sectarian Strand – Religion in Australian History*, Penguin, Melbourne, 1987.

Jackson, H.R. (Hugh), *Churches and People in Australia and New Zealand 1860–1930*, Port Nicholson Press/ Allen and Unwin, Wellington, 1987.

Kennedy, John, *Straight From the Shoulder*, Whitcoulls Publishers, Christchurch, 1981.

Keys, Lillian G., *Philip Viard – Bishop of Wellington*, Pegasus Press, Christchurch, 1968.

Kildea, Jeff, *Tearing the Fabric – Sectarianism in Australia 1910–1925*, Citadel Books, Sydney, 2002.

King, Michael, *God's Farthest Outpost – A History of Catholics in New Zealand*, Penguin, Auckland, 1997.

King, Michael, *The Penguin History of New Zealand*, Penguin, Auckland, 2003.

King, Michael, *Whina – A Biography of Whina Cooper*, Penguin, Auckland, 1991; reprint from 1983.

Lee, John A., *Rhetoric at the Red Dawn*, Collins, Auckland, 1965.

Lee, John A., *Simple on a Soapbox*, Collins, Auckland, 1963.

Lee, J.J., *Ireland 1912–1985, Politics and Society*, Cambridge University Press, Cambridge, 1989.

Locke, Elsie, *Peace People – A History of Peace Activities in New Zealand*, Hazard Press, Christchurch, 1992.

Lovell-Smith, Margaret (with Shannahan, Luisa), *The Enigma of Sister Mary Leo*, Reed, Auckland, 1998.

Macaulay, Ambrose, *William Crolly – Archbishop of Armagh 1835–49*, Four Courts Press, Dublin, 1994.

Mannes, Rev B. (Boniface), *Golden Jubilee – Holy Cross College, Mosgiel, New Zealand 1900–1950*, Whitcombe and Tombs, 1949.

McGill, David, *The Lion and the Wolfhound – The Irish Rebellion in the New Zealand Goldfields*, Grantham House, Wellington, 1990.

McGeorge, Colin and Snook, Ivan, *Church, State and New Zealand Education*, Price Milburn, Wellington, 1981.

McKeefry, Peter [published anonymously], *Fishers of Men*, Whitcombe and Tombs, Auckland, 1938.

Moloney, John N., *The Roman Mould of the Australian Catholic Church*, Melbourne, 1969

Morris, Charles R., *American Catholic – The Saints and Sinners Who Built America's Most Powerful Church*, Times Books/ Random House, New York, 1997.

Moynihan, Carolyn, *A Stand for Decency – Patricia Bartlett and the Society for the Promotion of Community Standards 1970–1995*, SPCS, Auckland, 1995.

Munro, Jessie, *The Story of Suzanne Aubert*, Auckland University Press/ Bridget Williams Books, Auckland, 1996.

Norris, Peter Joseph, *Southernmost Seminary – The Story of Holy Cross College, Mosgiel 1900–97*, Holy Cross Seminary, Auckland, 1999.

O'Brien, Bernard SJ, *A New Zealand Jesuit – A Personal Narrative*, Pegasus Press, Christchurch, 1970.

O'Farrell, Patrick, *The Catholic Church and Community in Australia – A History*, Nelson, Brisbane, 1977.

O'Farrell, Patrick, *England and Ireland Since 1800*, Oxford University Press, Oxford, 1975.

O'Farrell, Patrick, *The Irish in Australia*, New South Wales University Press, Sydney, revised ed., 1993.

O'Farrell, Patrick, *Vanished Kingdoms – Irish in Australia and New Zealand*, New South Wales University Press, Sydney, 1990.

Olssen, Erik, *A History of Otago*, John McIndoe, Dunedin, 1984.

Olssen, Erik, *John A. Lee*, University of Otago Press, Dunedin, 1977.

Olssen, Erik, *The Red Feds – Revolutionary industrial Unionism and the New Zealand Federation of Labour 1908–14*, Oxford University Press, Auckland, 1988.

O'Meeghan, Michael SM, *Held Firm By Faith – A History of the Catholic Diocese of Christchurch*, published for the diocese, Christchurch, 1988.

O'Meeghan, Michael SM, *Steadfast in Hope – The Story of the Catholic Archdiocese of Wellington*, published for the archdiocese, Wellington, 2003.

O'Sullivan, Dominic and Piper, Cynthia (eds), *Turanga Ngatahi – Standing Together: The Catholic Diocese of Hamilton 1840–2005*, Dunmore Press, Wellington, 2005.

Ovenden, Keith, *A Fighting Withdrawal – The Life of Dan Davin, Writer, Soldier, Publisher*, Oxford University Press, London, 1996.

Parer, Michael and Peterson, Tony, *Prophets and Losses in the Priesthood – In Quest of the Future Ministry*, Allela Books, Sydney, 1971.

Power, Sister Anne Marie RSJ, *Sisters of St Joseph of the Sacred Heart – New Zealand Story 1883–1997*, privately printed, Auckland, 1997.

Reid, Nicholas Evan, *The Bishop's Paper – A History of the Catholic Press of the Diocese of Auckland*, Catholic Publications Centre, Auckland, 2000.

Roche, Stanley, *The Red and the Gold – An Informal Account of the Waihi Strike 1912*, Oxford University Press, Auckland, 1982.

Ryder, Fr Thomas J., *Following All Your Ways, Lord* (Recollections transcribed and compiled by Margaret Paton) (no publisher or date given).

Santamaria, B.A., *Daniel Mannix – The Quality of Leadership*, Melbourne University Press, Melbourne, 1984.

Scott, S.W.('Sid'), *Rebel in a Wrong Cause*, Collins, Auckland, 1960.

Sewell, Dennis, *Catholics – Britain's Largest Minority*, Penguin, London, 2001.

Sherry, Richard, *Holy Cross College, Clonliffe, Dublin – College History and Centenary Record 1859–1959*, privately printed, Dublin, 1962.

Simmons, Ernest, *In Cruce Salus – A History of the Diocese of Auckland 1848–1980*, Catholic Publications Centre, Auckland, 1982.

Simmons, Ernest, *Pompallier – Prince of Bishops*, Catholic Publications Centre, Auckland, 1984.

Simpson, Tony (ed.), *The Scrim-Lee Papers – C.G. Scrimgeour and John A. Lee Remember the Crisis Years 1930–40*, AH and AW Reed, Wellington, 1976.

Simpson, Tony, *The Slump – The Thirties Depression: Its Origins and Aftermath*, Penguin, Auckland, 1990.

Sinclair, Keith, *Walter Nash*, Auckland University Press/Oxford University Press, Auckland, 1976.

Strevens, Diane, *In Step with Time – A History of the Sisters of St Joseph of Nazareth, Wanganui, New Zealand*, David Ling Publishers, Auckland, 2001.

Sweetman, Rory, *Bishop in the Dock – The Sedition Trial of James Liston*, Auckland University Press, Auckland, 1997.

Sweetman, Rory, *A Fair and Just Solution – A History of the Integration of Private Schools in New Zealand*, Dunmore Press for the Association of Proprietors of Integrated Schools, Palmerston North, 2002.

Sweetman, Rory, *Faith and Fraternalism – A History of the Hibernian Society of New Zealand 1869–2000*, Hibernian Society, Dunedin, 2002.

Taylor, Nancy M., *The New Zealand People at War – The Home Front*, Historical Publications Branch, Department of Internal Affairs, Wellington, 1986.

Trlin, Andrew D., *Now Respected, Once Despised – Yugoslavs in New Zealand*, Dunmore Press, Palmerston North, 1979.

Thompson, Ian F., *So Much To Do . . . 75 Years With the Knights of the Southern Cross of New Zealand*, privately published, 2003.

Tuerlings, W. MHM, *Mill Hill – Maori Mission and St Joseph's Foreign Missionary Society*, privately printed for the Mill Hills, 2001.

Vaggioli, Felice (John Crockett trans.), *A Deserter's Adventures – The Autobiography of Dom Felice Vaggioli*, University of Otago Press, Dunedin, 2001.

(Various), *The Farthest Jerusalem – Four Lectures on the Origins of Christianity*, Faculty of Theology and Hocken Library, University of Otago, Dunedin, 1993.

Walsh, K.J. (Kevin), *Yesterday's Seminary – A History of St Patrick's, Manly*, Allen and Unwin, Sydney, 1998.

Wood-Ellem, Elizabeth, *Queen Salote of Tonga – The Story of an Era 1900–1955*, Auckland University Press, Auckland, 1999.

(ii.) Pamphlets and Ephemera

Ardley, Gavin, *The Church of St Benedict, Newton, Auckland – A Centennial Narrative* (Parish of St Benedict), Auckland, 1988.

Christian Brothers, *To All Parts of the Kingdom (Christian Brothers in New Zealand 1876–2001)*, no date or publisher given.

Cleary, Bishop H.W., *The Diocesan Administrative Council*, privately printed, Auckland, 1929.

Cleary, Bishop H.W., *The Martin Case – A Statement*, privately printed, Auckland, 1924.

Hanly, John J., *The Irish College, Rome* (No. 64 Irish Heritage Series), Dublin, no date.

Telford, Carl, *'In Their Descendants Remains a Rich Inheritance' – The Centenary of Mt St Mary's, Greenmeadows*, Marist Messenger, Wellington, 1990.

Mill Hill Fathers, *Our Maori Mission*, privately printed, Auckland, 1933.

O'Neill, D.P., *Mosgiel '75*, Tablet Printing Co., Dunedin, 1975.

Official Souvenir Programme for Sacerdotal Golden Jubilee of James Michael Liston, Auckland, 1954.

Pearce, Noreen, *The Catholic Parish of Mosgiel 1900–2000*, privately printed, Mosgiel, 2000.

(iii.) Articles

aan de Weil, Jerome, 'Monsignor O'Riordan, Bishop O'Dwyer and the Shaping of New Relations between Nationalist Ireland and the Vatican during World War One', *Archivium Hibernicum – Irish Historical Records*, 53 (1999), pp 95–117.

Bassett, Judith, 'Colonial Justice: The Treatment of Dalmatians in New Zealand During the First World War', *NZJH*, 33 (2), (October 1999), pp155–179.

Breward, Ian, 'Religion and New Zealand Society', *NZJH*, 13 (2), (October 1979).

Brookes, Barbara, 'A Weakness for Strong Subjects – The Women's Movement and Sexuality', *NZJH*, 27 (2), (October 1993), pp 140–156.

Brookes, Barbara, 'Housewives' Depression – The Debate over Abortion and Birth Control in the 1930s', *NZJH*, 15 (2), (1981).

Callan, Patrick, 'Ambivalence Towards the Saxon Shilling: The Attitudes of the Catholic Church in Ireland Towards Enlistment During the First World War', *Archivium Hibernicum – Irish Historical Records*, 41, (1986), pp 99–111.

Davis, Richard P., 'The New Zealand Labour Party's 'Irish Campaign', 1916–1921', *Political Science*, 19 (2), (December 1967), pp 17–23.

Dunne, Eamonn, 'Action and Reaction: Catholic Lay Organisations in Dublin in the 1920s and 1930s', *Archivium Hibernicum – Irish Historical Records*, 48, (1994), pp 107–118.

Fraser, Lyndon, 'Irish Migration to the West Coast, 1864–1900', *NZJH*, 34 (2), (October 2000), pp 197–223.

Gardner, W.J., 'The Rise of W.F. Massey', *Political Science*, 13 (1), (March 1961), pp 6–23.

Grigg, A.R., 'Prohibition and Women: The Preservation of an Ideal and a Myth', *NZJH*, 17 (2), (October 1983), pp 144–165.

Grigg, A.R., 'Prohibition, the Church and Labour', *NZJH*, 15 (2), (October 1981), pp 135–154.

Jackson, Hugh, 'Churchgoing in Nineteenth-Century New Zealand', *NZJH*, 17 (1), (April 1983), pp 43–59.

'J.A.K.', 'Brother Michael Benignus Hanrahan 1877–1953', *Christian Brothers Educational Record – Necrology*, Dublin (1955), pp 308–341.

Laracy, Hugh, 'Paranoid Popery: Bishop Moran and Catholic Education in New Zealand', *NZJH*, 10 (1), (April 1976), pp 51–62.

Laracy, Hugh, 'Priests, People and Patriotism: New Zealand Catholics and War 1914–1918', *Australasian Catholic Record*, 70 (1), (January 1993), pp 14–26.

Laracy, Hugh, 'Saint-Making: The Case of Pierre Chanel of Futuna', *NZJH*, 34 (1), (April 2000), pp 145–161.

McIntosh, Gillian, 'Acts of 'National Communion': The Centenary Celebrations for Catholic Emancipation, the Forerunner of the Eucharistic Congress', in Joost Augusteijn (ed.), *Ireland in the 1930s*, Four Courts Press, Dublin, 1999, pp 85–93.

McKernon, Michael, 'Catholics, Conscription and Archbishop Mannix', *Historical Studies*, Melbourne, 17 (68), (April 1977), pp 299–314.

McMahon, Deirdre, 'John Charles McQuaid, Archbishop of Dublin, 1940–72', in Kelly and Keogh (eds), *History of the Catholic Diocese of Dublin*, Four Courts Press, Dublin, 2000, pp 349–380.

Mol, Hans, 'Religion and Political Allegiance', *Australian Journal of Politics and History*, Queensland, 16 (3), (December 1970).

Murphy, D.J., 'Religion, Race and Conscription in World War One', *Australian Journal of Politics and History*, Queensland, 20 (2), (August 1974), pp 155–163.

O'Carroll, Ciaran, 'The Pastoral Politics of Paul Cullen', in Kelly and Keogh (eds), *History of the Catholic Diocese of Dublin*, Four Courts Press, Dublin, 2000, pp 294–312.

O'Ceallaigh, Sean T., 'The Late Rt Rev Mgr M.J. Curran, P.P., P.A.', *Reportorium Novum – Dublin Diocesan Historical Record*, 3 (1), (1962), pp 9–15.

O'Connor, P.S. (Peter), 'Sectarian Conflict in New Zealand 1911–1920', *Political Science*, 19 (1), (July 1967), pp 3–16.

O'Connor, P.S. (Peter), 'Some Political Preoccupations of Mr Massey, 1918–1920', *Political Science*, 18 (2), (September 1966), pp 16–38.

O'Connor, P.S. (Peter), 'Storm Over the Clergy – New Zealand 1917', *Journal of Religious History*, 4 (2), (December 1966), pp 129–148.

Olssen, Erik, 'The Impact of John A. Lee's Expulsion upon the Labour Party', *NZJH*, 12 (1), (April 1978), pp 34–50.

Phillips, Walter, 'Religious Profession and Practice in New South Wales 1850–1901: The Statistical Evidence', *Historical Studies*, Melbourne, 15 (5), (October 1972), pp 378–400.

Prince, John D., 'Look Back in Amber: The General Licensing Poll in New Zealand 1919–87', *Political Science*, 48 (1), (July 1996), pp 48–72.

Pugh, Michael C., 'The New Zealand Legion 1932–35', *NZJH*, 5 (1), (April 1971), pp 49–69.

Simmons, Ernest, 'The Church in New Zealand 1924 to 1973', *Australasian Catholic Record*, 50 (4), (October 1973), pp 321–330.

Sinclair, Keith, 'The Lee-Sutch Syndrome. New Zealand Labour Party Policies and Politics', *NZJH*, 8 (2), (October 1974), pp 95–117.

Snook, I.A. (Ivan), 'Religion in Schools: A Catholic Controversy 1930–1934', *NZJH*, 6 (2), (October 1972), pp 169–177.

Stone, R.C.J. (Russell), ' 'Sinister' Auckland Business Cliques, 1840–1940', *NZJH*, 21 (2), (April 1987), pp 29–45.

van der Krogt, Christopher, 'Catholic Religious Identity and Social Integration in Interwar New Zealand', *Catholic Historical Review*, 86 (1), (January 2000), pp 47–65.

van der Krogt, Christopher, ' 'Exercising the Utmost Vigilance' – The Catholic Campaign Against Contraception in New Zealand During the 1930s', *Journal of Religious History*, 22 (3), (October 1998), pp 320–335.

van der Krogt, Christopher, ' 'Pleasure Without Maternity' – Catholic and Protestant Attitudes to Contraception in Interwar New Zealand', *Colloquium*, 29 (1), (1997), pp 3–17.

Watson, James, 'Were Catholics Over-Represented in the Public Service During the Early Twentieth Century?', *Political Science*, 42 (2) (December 1990), pp 20–33.

(iv.) Unpublished Theses, Dissertations and Essays

Allom, B.S. (Barry), 'Bishop Grimes: His Context and Contribution to the Catholic Church in Canterbury', MA History thesis, University of Canterbury, 1968.

Bourke, Joanna, 'Catholic Fertility in Australia and New Zealand 1880–1939', MA History thesis, University of Auckland, 1985.

Brosnahan, S.G. (Shaun Gerard), 'Rugby, Race and Religion: The Catholic Church and Controversy Over Sporting Relations with South Africa 1959–1981', MA History thesis, University of Canterbury, 1986.

Cadogan B.F. (Bernard Francis), 'Lace Curtain Catholics – The Catholic Bourgeoisie of the Diocese of Dunedin 1900–1920', BA Honours History dissertation, University of Otago, 1984.

Clements, Kevin Paul, 'The Churches and Social Policy: A Study in the Relationship of Ideology to Action', PhD Sociology thesis, Victoria University of Wellington, 1970.

Forsman, Henry and William, 'E.A.Forsman – Priest, Padre, Poet 1909–1976', unpublished typescript compiled and bound, 1991.

Kane, Br John Paul FMS, 'The Marist Brothers in New Zealand Education 1917 to 1967', Dip. Ed. dissertation, Massey University, 1972.

Laracy, Hugh, 'The Life and Context of Bishop Patrick Moran', MA History thesis, Victoria University of Wellington, 1964.

Laws, Michael Brian, 'The Sedition Trial of Bishop Liston', dissertation for Postgraduate Diploma in Arts, University of Otago, 1980.

MacDonald, D.V., 'The New Zealand Bible-in-Schools League', MA Education thesis, Victoria University of Wellington, 1964.

Mackey, Bishop John, 'Memoirs of Bishop John Mackey', typescript compiled and bound, 2001.

Martin, Fr Joe, 'Reminiscence of Holy Cross College, Mosgiel', unpublished and ungathered typescripts, provided to Nicholas Reid by Peter Norris.

Moores, H.S., 'The Rise of the Protestant Political Association – Sectarianism in New Zealand Politics During World War 1', MA History thesis, University of Auckland, 1966.

O'Neill, J.C., 'The History of the Work of the Christian Brothers in New Zealand', Dip. Ed. thesis, University of Auckland, 1968.

Puch, Gillian Frances, 'The Catholic Women's League of New Zealand and the Changing Role of Women – A Sociological Analysis with Emphasis on a CWL Parish Group', MA Sociology thesis, University of Auckland, 1978.

Reid, A.J.S. (Anthony John Stanhope), 'Church and State in New Zealand 1930–1935 – A Study of the Social Thought and Influence of the Christian Church in a Period of Economic Crisis', MA History thesis, Victoria University of Wellington, 1961.

Satchell, Max, 'Pulpit Politics – The Protestant Political Association in Dunedin from 1917 to 1922', BA Hons History thesis, University of Otago, 1983.

Simmons, Nicholas Anthony, 'Archbishop Francis Redwood: His Contribution to Catholicism in New Zealand', MA History thesis, Massey University, 1981.

Skudder, Susan Mary, 'Bringing it Home – New Zealand Responses to the Spanish Civil War 1936–1939', PhD History thesis, University of Waikato, 1986.

Sweetman, Rory Matthew, 'New Zealand Catholicism – War, Politics and the Irish Issue, 1912–1922', PhD History thesis, University of Cambridge, 1990.

Taylor, B.S., 'The Expulsion of J.A. Lee and its Effects on the Development of the New Zealand Labour Party', MA History thesis, University of Canterbury, 1970.

van der Krogt, Christopher John, 'More a Part than Apart – the Catholic Community in New Zealand Society 1918–1940', PhD History and Religious Studies thesis, Massey University, 1994.

Vaney, N.P. (Neil) SM, 'The Dual Tradition – Irish Catholics and French Priests in New Zealand: the West Coast Experience, 1865–1910', MA History thesis, University of Canterbury, 1976.

Walsh, Sister Carmel A., 'Michael Verdon 1838–1918, Second Bishop of Dunedin and Founder of Holy Cross Mosgiel New Zealand', MTheol. thesis, Melbourne College of Divinity, 1994.

INDEX

Aarts, Fr, 280–1
Agagianian, Cardinal, 258, 265
Aitken, Dr Casement, 91
Alink, Dean Martin, *185*, 195, 196, 198–9, 201, 281
Allen, James, Minister of Defence, 68, 69, 71
Allum, John, 123
Ambrose, Sister Mary, 253
Anderson, Fr Edwin Arthur, *57*, *58*
Anderton, Jim, 278
Angland, Fr Des, 250, 251
Anglo-Irish Treaty, 110–11, 116, 120; *see also*, Ireland
Apostolic Delegate, 90, *229*, 278, 306; *see also*, Carboni, Romolo; Cattaneo, Cardinal Bartolomeo; Cerretti, Cardinal Bonaventura; de Furstenberg, Maximilian; Enrici, Domenico; Marella, Paul; Panico, John
Arahill, Monsignor Brian, 252, 281, 297, 309
Ardley, Gavin, 270
Ashby, Bishop Brian (of Christchurch), 268, 271, *282*, 298, 299, 306
Astor, Rabbi Alexander, 217, 274, 307
Auckland: Catholic Library, 210, 248; Citizens' Association, 221; Diocesan Building Fund, 248; Diocesan Development Fund, 276–7; diocese of, 15, 17, 20, 30, 31–2, 56, 83, 84–6, 87, 101,135, 152, 153, 162, 172, 177, 183, *184*, 218, 247–9, *273*, 275–7, 283, 291, 292, 298, 299, 306, 316; Town Hall, Catholic use of, 110, 112, 118–19, 142, 159, 168, 218, 226, 242; University of, 254–5, 270, 300; *see also*, Catholic organisations, parishes
Auckland Star, 111, 115, 124, 142, 218, 292, 294
Aunier, Mlle, 299
Australia: 36, 156, 194, 258; and Catholic church in, 20–1, 33, 68, 79, 93, 120–1, 133, 167–8, 230, 266, 268, 278, 289; and Communism, 182, 226, 228, 230, 260; and conscription, 70, 312; and Ireland, 20–1, 25, 26, 27, 120–1; and James Michael Liston (JML), 21; and Knights of the Southern Cross, 146; Catholic press in, 79, 289; clergy in NZ, 49–50, 96, 162, 183, 186, 187, 193, 228; development of Australian nationalism, 120–1; visits of church

hierarchy to NZ, 172, 217, 218, 219; *see also*, JML TRAVELS
Australasian Irish Race Convention, 65
Averill, Archbishop W.W., 138, 217, 221, 235
Avondale Mental Hospital, 90

Barker, Sir Ian, 208, 211, 240, 254, 269, 277, 292, 293, 298, 308
Barrett, Dr, 95
Barrowclough, H.E., 178
Bartlett, Patricia, 304
Baxter, James K., 288
Beeby, Dr C.E., 225, 247
Bell, Dillon, 113, 140, 141
Benedict XV, Pope, 66–7
Benedictines, 88
Bennett, Bishop Frederick, 201
Bennett, Bishop Manu, 274
Bennett, Fr Alfred Ernest, 90, 257
bequests, legacies, philanthropic gifts to the church, 19, 49, 103, 104, 134, 200, 237, 251, 255
Berridge, Fr Norbert, 271
Bible-in-Schools movement: 64, 78, 122–3, 124, 139, 140, 314; bills, 98, 138, 173–7, 179, 180, 223, 314; *see also*, NZ Council for Christian Education
Biermans, Bishop, 196–7
Blamires, E.O. (Ernest), 174
Bleakley, Fr Michael, 106, 153, 166–7, 188, 194, 251, 272
Bloodworth, Tom, 123, 124, 139
Bolland, Fr Bruce, 250, 306
Bollinger, Conrad, 237
Bolt, George, 85
Borromeo, Charles (Saint), 35
Bosco House, Ponsonby, 276
Boyd, Gladstone W., 60
Boylan, Monsignor, 40
Boyle, Bishop Leonard, 61
Boyle, John, 55
Bradley, Monsignor John James, 18, 19, 85, *185*, 191, 213, 252–3, 265, 314
Brady, Fr Cormac Joseph, 187
Brennan, Fr, 113
Bressers, Fr, 198
Brigidine Sisters, 163
Broadbent, Fr John, 288
Brodie, Bishop Matthew (of Christchurch, and later Archbishop): 52, 69, 73, 77, 79, 80, 83, 92, 100, 103, *105*, 106–7, 121, 140, 157, *158*, 161, 173–6, 179,

van Rossum, Cardinal Willem, 160
van Westeinde, Fr, 198
Vatican II, 18, 19, 63, 187, 211, 248, 257, 266–75, 283, 286, 288, 289, 312, 316, 317; pre-Vatican II, 62, 182, 188, 248, 257; post-Vatican II, 147, 183, 286
Verdon, Bishop Michael (of Dunedin): 28, 31, 33, *34*, 35–6, 38–9, 40, 41, 42, 45, 47, 312; and Ireland, 36, 171; Bishop of Dunedin, 31, 33, 38; Council of Vigilance, 63; death of, 35, 72–3, 81; expectations of JML, 39, 44, 47, 50, 54; manner, 33, 35, 62; Memorial Chapel, 258; rector of Holy Cross, 33, 48–51, 56
Viard, Bishop Phillippe Joseph, 31
Vincentians, 49, 80, 187

Waihi, industrial dispute in, 64
Waikato, diocese of, 102–4; *see also*, Hamilton
Waikato Times, 292
Walls, Fr Frederick, 250, 257, 283
Walsh, Archbishop William, 39
Walsh, Canon Michael, 26, 40
Walsh, P.J., 40
Walsh, Vivian, 85, 129
Wanders, Fr Theo, 199–200
Ward, Sir Joseph (PM), 64, 69, 104, 122
Wardle, Fr Joseph, 281
Waters, Fr John, 40
Wellington, diocese of, 16, 31, 82, 84, 258, 275, 277, 283, 288

Whyte, Bishop James: 60, 86, *105*, 106, 107, 114, 146, 147, 149, *158*, 159, 173–4, 175, 176, 182; and Cleary and Liston, 154–5; Bishop of Dunedin, 38, 79–80; correspondence with JML, 87, 106, 114, 118–19, 141, 314; death of, 180, 258; friendship with JML, 81–2
Williams, Joyce, 270
Wood, Fr William, 287
Woods, Fr Henry, 56
Workers' Weekly, 231
Wright, Fr Francis ('Frank'), 191, 243, 285
Wright, Fr George, 149

Yirrell, Francis, 60

Zangerl, Fr, 201
Zanna, Fr Josephus, 96
Zealandia: 11, 15, 61, 104, 106, 218, 226, 238, 239, 255, 263, 277, 289, 300, 305, 308; and Communism, 226, 261, 289; and *NZ Tablet*, 290–1; attacks on John A. Lee, 238; correspondence column, 292; dismissal of editor (Simmons), 17, 289, 291; editorial policy, 288–92; editorials of, 223, 226, 230, 258, 289, 290; editors of, 17, 210, 264, 272, 277, 289, 291, 292; founding of, 61, 208, 210; JML's contributions to, 246, 286, 288, 305; political statements in, 223, 226, 227, 230, 231, 232, 233, 236, 261, 289, 290–1; vetoing by JML, 270, 288, 291–2; *see also*, Month